# NATURE'S STRONGHOLDS

## THE WORLD'S GREAT WILDLIFE RESERVES

# NATURE'S STRONGHOLDS

## THE WORLD'S GREAT WILDLIFE RESERVES

### LAURA AND WILLIAM RILEY

To Joyce + Don —
Warmest wishes from
Laura · Bill

**Princeton University Press**
**Princeton and Oxford**

Distributed by Princeton University Press,
41 William Street, Princeton, New Jersey 08540
In the United Kingdom: Princeton University Press,
3 Market Place, Woodstock, Oxfordshire OX20 1SY

Library of Congress Control Number 2004097392
ISBN 0-691-12219-9

British Library Cataloging-in-Publication Data is available

Maps created by Carte Blanche, Paignton, U.K. using Mountain
High Maps™ Copyright © 1995–2004 Digital Wisdom, Inc.
Revised 2004

Photograph previous page: mountain gorilla

This book has been composed in Melior (main text) and
SkiaCC-Regular (headings and captions)

Printed on acid-free paper. ∞

nathist.princeton.edu

Designed by D & N Publishing, Hungerford, U.K.

Printed in Italy by Eurografica S.P.A.

10  9  8  7  6  5  4  3  2  1

# CONTENTS

# CONTENTS

# CONTENTS

CONTENTS

# CONTENTS

# NORTH AMERICA 427

CONTENTS

# SOUTH PACIFIC ISLANDS 577

# CONTENTS

# INTRODUCTION

MOST OF THE WORLD'S CHARISMATIC AND ENDANGERED
SPECIES OWE THEIR CONTINUED EXISTENCE TO RESERVES SET
ASIDE FOR THEM ON EVERY CONTINENT—BENGAL TIGERS IN
INDIA, BIRDS-OF-PARADISE IN THE WILDS OF NEW GUINEA,
SHAGGY, HUMANLIKE ORANGUTANS THAT SWING THROUGH
FORESTS OF INDONESIA, PENGUINS NESTING BY THE MILLIONS
ON FROZEN BEACHES IN ANTARCTICA.

CHEETAHS, LIONS, AND ELEPHANTS ARE PROTECTED ON
AFRICAN PLAINS. GIANT ANTEATERS FORAGE WITH
ENORMOUS STICKY TONGUES AMONG MAN-SIZED, LUMINES-
CENT TERMITE MOUNDS IN BRAZIL. JAGUARS SKULK THROUGH
PROTECTED JUNGLE RESERVES OF CENTRAL AMERICA.
Gorillas devour thistles in the mountains of Rwanda.
Leopards drape themselves on tree branches in East
and South Africa. Seabirds arrive every spring on
islands off the United Kingdom to nest by the millions.

There are reserves for endangered honeybees in
Russia; for sacred snails in Ghana; and one in Asia
for the legendary Abominable Snowman. There are
reserves for species until recently entirely unknown
to science—like the Vu Quang ox in Vietnam.

These great reserves represent the last places on
earth where the natural world remains largely intact.
Some are as big as European countries and they grow
in numbers and size as people everywhere become
aware of their beauty and importance and learn as
well about the fascinating, precarious lives of their
wild inhabitants.

Some 40 million persons every year undertake jour-
neys around the world to visit nature reserves—at recent
count 15 million of them with the specific purpose of

Osprey, worldwide except Antarctica.

17

observing wildlife, according to figures of the Ecotourism Society. This helps the reserves and the wildlife living in them. Properly managed, with appropriate protection for wild inhabitants, ecotourism is potentially the most powerful single force for preservation of wild creatures and places. Expenditures for guides and lodging increasingly benefit local economies. In Belize and Costa Rica, for example, ecotourism earns more for local economies than any other source. Local communities, in turn, have come to see protection of species and ecosystems as having practical as well as esthetic value, often resulting in incentives for expanded protection and more land set aside.

Here for the first time in one place are the best of these extraordinary places around the world, based on hundreds of on-scene reports, interviews, and personal experiences, with information on how to visit them, what to see, their ecological significance, and often their historical background.

Many of the world's rarest wildlife species, for example, owe their survival today to bygone kings, princes, maharajahs, and other ruling figures who first set aside the land for private hunting preserves. European bison, once one of the most numerous hoofed animals the world has known, roamed forests from the Atlantic Ocean to the China Sea in the tens of millions until hunting and continent-wide deforestation reduced their habitat range to a single large primeval forest owned by royal families in Poland and neighboring Belarus. The last wild European bison was shot during World War I—but a remnant herd, reassembled from scattered individuals given to zoos and private parks, became a renewed breeding entity which was protected during World War II by Hitler's aide Hermann Goering. The species survives now in protected and sustainable numbers in Poland's Bialowieza National Park and a transborder reserve in Belarus.

Hundreds of bird species from thousands of miles around—from painted storks to stately sarus cranes—crowd Bharatpur in India, a lush wetland transformed from a desert by a 19th-century maharajah wishing to return hospitality of British royals who had entertained him at hunting parties in England. He directed thousands of his subjects to divert a river, dig miles of dikes and ditches, and build dams to create ponds and marshes to attract ducks, geese, and other water-oriented birds. Stone monuments record where dukes and princes once shot thousands in a day. Now all are protected in one of the world's great bird sanctuaries.

Great reserves such as America's Yellowstone are well known, but many others are described here in book form for the first time, a unique resource not only for visitors and those who organize trips but for wildlife students and armchair travelers who may never visit these places but enjoy reading about them.

Reserves covered in Africa include not only Tanzania's renowned Serengeti and Kenya's Maasai Mara but Namibia's Skeleton Coast, where lions hunt seals on beaches of the frigid South Atlantic, and its Waterberg Plateau, with endangered species from all over the continent; Botswana's Okavango Delta, where water often is naturally purified to drinking water standard

Jaguar, Central and South America.

by hundreds of square miles of papyrus plants, and where hippos walk on canal bottoms, clearly visible through the limpid water.

Ecuador has not only the world-famous Galapagos Islands with giant tortoises, confidingly tame waved albatrosses and dragon-like marine iguanas that prowl underwater, but five other national parks winding through its mountains and lowlands.

A few miles away from world-renowned luxury resorts at Cancun on Mexico's Yucatan Peninsula are sheltered, little-known lagoons with up to 50,000 brilliant flamingos and, shared with reserves in Belize and Guatemala, one of the world's largest tropical forest preserves sheltering jaguars, yard-long scarlet macaws, ornate hawk-eagles, and much of the wintering population of bright warblers that nest in summer in the U.S. and Canada.

This linking of contiguous or nearby reserves in neighboring countries is a promising development of recent years, creating enormous protected areas where wildlife, requiring no passports, can range freely back and forth. In Africa, some of the continent's main populations of lowland gorillas, forest elephants, and rare, striped, spiral-horned bongo antelopes roam through more than 5,000 square miles (14,000 km²) in a preserve linking Dja Faunal Reserve in Cameroon with Nouabalé-Ndoki National Park in the Congo Republic and Dzanga-Sangha

Reserve in the Central African Republic. In Bhutan, Royal Manas and Black Mountains National Parks adjoin India's Manas Wildlife Preserve creating almost 2,000 square miles (5,000 km²) of uninterrupted habitat with more tigers than any other protected area of south-central Asia. Imperial eagles soar over Ordesa and Monte Perdidi National Parks in Spain, now linked by transborder agreement with Pyrénées Occidentales in France. Conservationists hope the Demilitarized Zone (DMZ) between North and South Korea, with numerous endangered species, will become such a transborder reserve.

Also useful are "debt swaps," as when the World Wide Fund for Nature (WWF) purchased $2 million U.S. in Philippines' external dept, funds than made available for development of St. Paul's National Park on Palawan and El Nido National Marine Park in Benguet. Conservation International paid $650,000 U.S. of Bolivia's foreign debt in exchange for protection of 1,290-square-mile (3,340 km²) Reserva Biosferica del Beni.

Europe is often regarded as denuded of wildlife, but 3,500 scimitar-horned ibexes survive in Italy's mountainous Gran Paradiso National Park. Long-legged greater flamingos turn salt flats rosy in France's Camargue. European lynx make one of their last stands in Spain's Coto Doñana National Park which is essential to the life cycles of more than half of Europe's migratory birds plus an immense variety of permanent residents including red deer, wild boars, otters, and the nearly extinct Spanish lynx.

Reserves set aside for particular species save others as well—whole interdependent ecosystems of rare, interesting, and important insects and plants. The Russian Federation has dozens of these protecting Siberian tigers, Amur leopards, lovely demoiselle cranes and Steller's sea eagles as well as tiny rustic buntings, willow tits, and bird's nest orchids.

Many of these, now set aside as national parks and reserves, began not with governments but with small groups of dedicated individuals who believed them worth saving and worked tirelessly until they convinced others of their importance. Their value can be seen by comparing them with surrounding areas, often laid waste from an ecological view by logging, clearing for agriculture, unchecked construction of roads, dams, resorts, residential housing, and commercial development, and oil and gas exploration.

Reserves in over 80 countries were selected for inclusion, among many thousands around the world, after consultation with major wildlife organizations such as World Wide Fund for Nature and Wildlife Conservation Society. A factor taken into consideration was whether persons with personal or professional interest in wildlife would wish to travel halfway around the world to see them. Along with these principal reserves are others of special interest in the countries covered.

Each entry contains information on the country's gateway city (usually international jet entry point), temperature and rainfall data for each month of the year, best times to visit, and general information about available facilities. In most cases, contact information, such as telephone, fax number, and e-mail address, is included to allow the reader to check for up-to-date information on the country and the principal reserves. A bibliography lists references we found useful.

## Practical Hints

The following additional information will prove helpful to those wishing to travel to see these places for themselves.

Clothing—go equipped to dress in comfortable layers which can be added to or taken off as temperatures dictate. Light cotton long-sleeved shirts and ankle-length pants in fabric that can be washed and dried overnight work best, offering protection from sun and stinging insects, and sleeves and pants can be rolled up as desired. Long underwear in light silk can be useful anywhere. So can a wool sweater, light windbreaker, comfortable walking shoes, and lightweight hiking boots.

ALWAYS take a wide-brimmed hat; sunglasses; sun block and sun lotion; insect repellent; waterproof jacket; flashlight; alarm clock; in cool climates, gloves; an aluminum roll-up bed-covering can be a life-saver; and if photographing

Black-and-white ruffed lemur, Madagascar.

Sambar deer, Asia.

non-digital, plenty of film; if using digital, be sure to check in advance on availability of electrical recharge facilities.

Also useful will be plastic bags (for wet laundry, to protect film and cameras in wet or dusty conditions, and big ones can be a makeshift poncho); binoculars; possibly a spotting telescope; collapsible walking stick (some can double as photographic monopods); and first aid equipment such as aspirins, antihistamines, bandaids, ace bandage, diarrhea controls such as Immodium or Lomotil, antiseptic liquid or lotion, scissors and tweezers (these must be checked in baggage), and perhaps others such as water purification pills and antibiotic medication or lotions, on which your physician can advise. Snacks such as peanuts or nutribars can seem heaven-sent when it's a long time between meals. Some reserves are far off the beaten track where civilization's amenities are few and far between so it never hurts to pack a roll of toilet paper.

Inquire ahead about climate at destination. Three sites which we have found helpful are WorldClimate.com, Weatherbase.com, and BBC World Weather. The temperature and rainfall graphs show data from the gateway cities. Since topography and other local geographic differences can cause microclimates that differ from surrounding areas, it is well also to check local weather in advance with reserve personnel. While checking, inquire also about reserve hours and admission rules—some charge admission, some don't.

Be aware that chances of seeing wildlife are best in early morning and late afternoon, when they are out foraging. Spend time quietly walking, if permitted—many reserves have trails. Wear inconspicuous clothing, no perfume. Stop frequently to let your eyes adjust to the environment. If you are absolutely still, you can better detect wildlife movement and be less detectable yourself.

# INTRODUCTION

Try to background yourself on what you are likely to see by advance reading (*see* Bibliography) or by studying brochures available from many reserves. Bring along material to help identify the wildlife. It's more interesting that way.

A competent guide can make the difference between a good trip and a disappointing one. Choose carefully, well in advance, and with recommendations from others. A good guide is linguistically fluent and experienced in the territory. Go over detailed plans carefully before starting out, making sure he/she understands your special interests and how fast or slowly you want to go.

In many countries, international driving permits are required. Many parks and reserves require permits for entry—best inquire ahead on current rules.

As to diet, it's always safer to drink water from sealed bottles—not because local water is necessarily polluted, but it may contain elements to which your system is not accustomed. Try to use water (for tooth-brushing too!) from bottles that can be recycled, not thrown out with garbage to accumulate in the environment. Eat cooked foods or fruits and vegetables which you can peel. "Boil it, bake it, peel it, or forget it!"

Inquire ahead about and get appropriate immunization for malaria, tetanus, yellow fever, cholera, typhoid, or whatever local maladies might be a problem. The Center for Disease Control (CDC) in Atlanta, Georgia, can advise on medical protection needed and current conditions around the world, with a hotline for international travelers at 1-877-FYI-TRIP (1-877-394-8747), Fax: 1-888-cdc-fax (1-888-232-3299), or via CDC's Website: www.cdc.gov.

Medical insurance companies should be consulted on whether policies apply overseas and cover emergencies such as medical evacuation without purchase of special insurance plans.

A helpful organization is IAMAT, or International Association for Medical Assistance to Travelers. For a nominal voluntary fee, IAMAT will send a handy directory of recommended English-speaking physicians around the world, as well as informative booklets on this subject. Contact them at 417 Center Street, Lewiston, NY 14092, Website: www.iamat.org, E-mail: info@iamat.org.

Avoid traveling on public holidays. Inquire about local holidays that could present a problem—seasonal or religious festivals, for example, when travel can grind to a halt.

Make reservations for lodging and transport well ahead and re-check shortly beforehand. If it's a remote place and you're driving, be sure to take plenty of water and check vehicle for tools, spare tire, emergency fuel.

Spring and fall are usually best for seeing wildlife in temperate zones. (Remember, seasons are reversed in northern and southern hemispheres.) Another determining factor is rainy or dry season. End of dry season can be particularly good, when wildlife are attracted to scarce waterholes. *See* graphs for weather information in text, and also inquire ahead—temperatures and precipitation can vary greatly from year to year.

Take photocopies of such essentials as passports, visas, drivers' licenses, and credit cards, in case of loss or theft. Loss or theft of these should be reported immediately to local police and home embassy or consulate. U.S. citizens may refer to a State Department pamphlet, "A Safe Trip Abroad" and "Medical Information for Americans Traveling Abroad," available by mail from Documents Superintendent, U.S. Government Printing Office, Washington, DC 20402, via Internet at www.access.gpo.gov/su_docs, or via Bureau of Consular Affairs home page at http://travel.state.gov or autoFax: 202/647-3000.

Helpful consular information sheets are available from the U.S. State Department for almost every travel destination. Many other countries have these also.

Travelers should be aware that among credit cards, American Express offers special protection against fraud or other failure in distant places, including expenses for guides, souvenir purchases and all travel expenses—many others do not guarantee this. Read the small print.

Remember, if you like wildlife, be a good wildlife citizen when visiting a reserve. Do not crowd the wildlife or take part in motorized pursuit of animals to take pictures or observe them too closely. This can be as deadly for them as pursuit by weapons, resulting in wildlife injury or death from a variety of causes, including exhaustion, stress, and inability to hunt effectively for food for themselves as well as young families. Don't approach birds' nests closely. Human presence can keep birds away from nests long enough for eggs or young to be fatally chilled or overheated, and human scent can attract predators to a nest site. In marine reserves, don't allow guides to anchor boats in coral formations.

Don't buy or take souvenirs made from animal parts ranging from shells and coral jewelry to skins and feathers, or patronize local restaurants which serve food made with animals taken from wild populations. Do not leave, or allow guides to leave behind, litter and garbage.

Support international wildlife organizations such as World Wildlife Fund (generally called here by the name of its international affiliate—World Wild Fund for Nature), Wildlife Conservation Society and Conservation International—*see* Acknowledgments for web addresses of these and other conservation organizations.

Finally, for us, visiting these great reserves around the world has meant recreation in the most literal sense of that word—our lives have been renewed by the experience; we wish that for you as well.

# AFRICA

CAPE BUFFALO

# BOTSWANA

SUCH IS THE FILTERING EFFECT OF THE MILLIONS
OF PAPYRUS PLANTS IN THE OKAVANGO DELTA THAT
ONE CAN DIP IN AND DRINK FROM THE LIMPID WATERS
IN MOST PLACES IN PERFECT SAFETY. WHILE DOING SO A
VISITOR MAY SUDDENLY HEAR A SOUND LIKE AN EXPRESS TRAIN
ROARING BY—IT IS A HERD OF LECHWE, A MARSH-DWELLING
ANTELOPE, FLEEING WILD DOGS OR OTHER PREDATORS.

WILDLIFE RESERVES MAKE UP NEARLY ONE-SIXTH OF THIS LANDLOCKED COUNTRY ABOUT THE SIZE OF FRANCE IN MID-SOUTH AFRICA. FAMED AMONG THEM IS THE OKAVANGO DELTA, LARGEST INLAND RIVER DELTA IN THE WORLD AND A WILDLIFE PARADISE. Most of the Delta (except for the

Water in the Okavango, world's largest inland river delta, is purified to drinking quality by its waving expanses of head-high gold-green papyrus reeds. It is so clear that hippos can be seen walking along the bottom. Many animals that forage in these vast, nutritious marshes of the "river that never reaches the sea" have special adaptations, such as splayed hooves for better footing.

# BOTSWANA

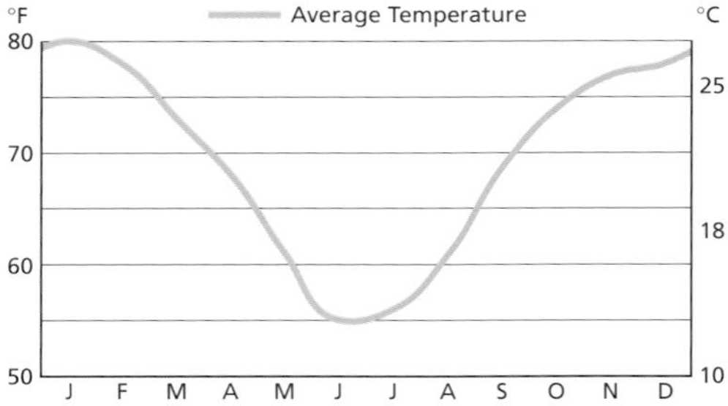
°F
Average Temperature
°C
80
70
60
50
25
18
10
J F M A M J J A S O N D

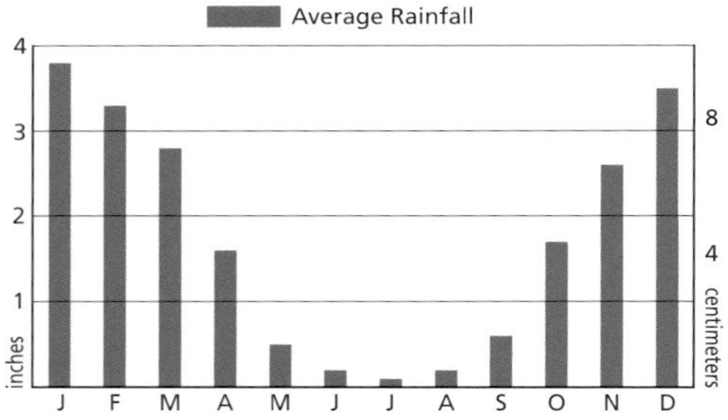
Average Rainfall
4
3
2
1
inches
8
4
centimeters
J F M A M J J A S O N D

Gateway city: Gaborone

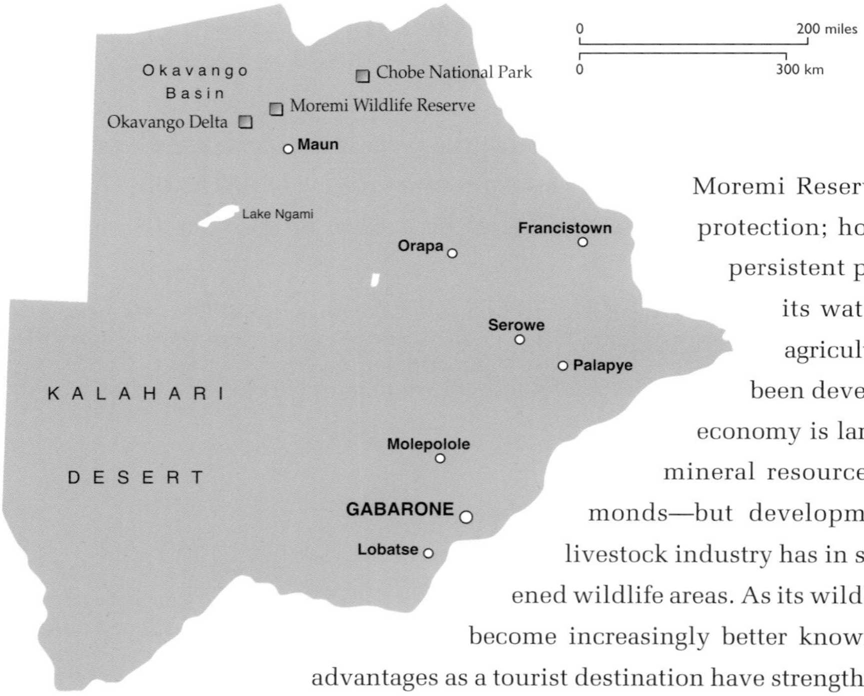
0
200 miles
0
300 km
Okavango
Basin
Chobe National Park
Moremi Wildlife Reserve
Okavango Delta
Maun
Lake Ngami
Francistown
Orapa
Serowe
Palapye
KALAHARI
DESERT
Molepolole
GABARONE
Lobatse

Moremi Reserve) has no formal protection; however, except for persistent proposals to divert its water for mining and agriculture uses, it has not been developed. Botswana's economy is largely supported by mineral resources, especially diamonds—but development of a modern livestock industry has in some places threatened wildlife areas. As its wildlife resources have become increasingly better known, their economic advantages as a tourist destination have strengthened the country's will to protect them.

Botswana's gentle, easy-going people, who have a 70 percent literacy rate, have generally supported wildlife protection, especially where wise policies have given communities an economic stake in it. There remain great pressures on the country—among them one of the world's highest AIDS rates, and neighbors who also covet the water that brings life to Okavango.

MOREMI on the Delta's southeast edge was set aside by tribal landowners concerned about their dwindling wildlife resources as the result of safari hunters. CHOBE NATIONAL PARK, the country's other world-class reserve, partly adjoins Moremi to the east and shares much of its wildlife. Herbivores include large herds of elephants (an estimated 50,000) as well as buffalo, impala, and kudu. Watery areas attract hippos and crocodiles as well as spectacular birds, including rare wattled cranes, African fish eagles, colorful bee-eaters, kingfishers, and others.

The best times to visit are during May–October dry season, but see below for individual variations. May skies are clear and blue, with lush vegetation, and young wildlife families grazing. Later, as vegetation dries, animals are attracted to scarcer water, making for better wildlife viewing (although October can be hot, windy, and dusty). Most rain falls between December–March and in the north can make roads impassable. Winter nights in July–August can be well below freezing (remember, seasons are reversed north and south of the equator).

Small lodges and camping facilities are available in and around many reserves; most visitors use safari operators for guidance.

Driving in the national parks requires 4WD. Fuel, water, and other supply points are few and far between.

---

**FURTHER INFORMATION**

Department of Wildlife and National Parks, P.O. Box 131, Gabarone, Botswana, Tel: (+267) 37-1405.

---

# CHOBE NATIONAL PARK

Chobe National Park is famous for its huge populations of animals—60,000 elephants, 12,000 zebras, and several thousand grazing buffalo, half-ton ungulates whose irritable dispositions can cause them to charge people or sometimes even vehicles.

Zebra migration is a stunning sight that can hardly be imagined without actually seeing it. These vast throngs of striped wild horses, no two patterns alike, cover the landscape. As they move, stripes against stripes, it almost seems as if the ground itself is moving. Sometimes in migration there can be 5,000 in one group.

Elephants along the Chobe River can number 35,000—largest herds in any African national park—with up to 2,000 in a single assemblage, including family members of all ages, from nursing babies to matriarchs. Visitors in off-road vehicles can find themselves surrounded by a sea of these behemoths as far as the eye can see.

These great animals and others trek through Chobe in search of food and water, grazing on Savuti marshlands which green up during the rainy season, and moving to the river during the dry season. Zebras come first, followed by wildebeest, then herds of up to 1,500 tsessebe, also impalas and giraffes, males sometimes wrapping their long necks about one another in an apparently affectionate but actually competitive territorial embrace. Along with them come their predators—lions, wild dogs, hyenas, and more-secretive cheetahs and leopards.

# BOTSWANA

Chobe has three main wildlife-viewing areas depending on where water is found. Savuti, on the Savuti Marsh, left dry when the river channel changed course, now has water only during and immediately after rainy season. The Savuti River has flowed into Savuti Marsh at various times in its history, depending, it is thought, on tectonic plate shifts from the Great Rift Valley. When it is dry, as now, animals depend on artificially pumped water holes, which unfortunately are subject to breakdown.

Linyanti, bordering the upper eastern Chobe River, is a mini-Okavango Delta papyrus swamp. Serondela is on the permanently flowing Chobe River. The Chobe River can get a double dousing of water. Most of the year it flows from west to east, but on meeting the Zambezi in flood, it can back up again.

This 4,100-square-mile (10,698-km²) reserve in Botswana's northeast corner is an area of extreme habitat contrasts, from the near-tropical Linyanti Swamp and the lush Chobe floodplain, to areas almost as dry as the arid Kalahari desert (which covers about 70 percent of the country). One can readily see why any water here acts as a magnet for wildlife.

The diverse habitat attracts a wide variety of birds. Some 450 species have been noted at Serondela—storks, waders, skimmers, and kingfishers around the river; marabou storks and hornbills there and on higher ground; and raptors such as martial and fish eagles. Savuti also has dry land specialties such as kori and Stanley's bustards, exquisite lilac-breasted rollers, and migrant carmine bee-eaters—sometimes dozens swirling around, unmindful of visitors, when a field full of grasshoppers takes flight. During the rainy season there often are thousands of northern migrants as well.

Best times to visit are during the dry season June–October for Linyanti and Serondela, and the end of the rainy season, April into May, for Savuti.

---

**FURTHER INFORMATION**

Chobe National Park Headquarters, Department of Wildlife, National Parks and Tourism, P.O. Box 17, Kasane, Botswana.

---

# MOREMI WILDLIFE RESERVE

Moremi, chief of the Tswana people, alarmed in 1963 at increasing loss of wildlife resources on tribal lands from both native and white safari hunters, convinced his people to set aside the beginnings of the spectacular Moremi Wildlife Reserve—a courageous step requiring many families to move from their traditional lands. It is one of the few instances in Africa or anywhere of a community voluntarily dispossessing itself of its territorial birthright. A debt of

Size is an advantage to three-ton grass-eaters like the hippo whose enormous digestive system can hold food longer to fully extract nutrients. When hippos aren't grazing on land at night they like to forage in rivers where their specific gravity enables them to walk or run on the bottom as easily as on land. They can stay under water up to 30 minutes.

gratitude is owed to them and to the family of the tribal chief whose name it carries, as well as to the vision of conservationists Robert and June Kaye who helped them.

Moremi is one of the most beautiful and rich wildlife reserves on the African continent, covering the eastern corner of the great Okavango Delta along with Chief's Island, a later addition, which is a 62-by-9-mile (100 × 15-km) roadless wilderness of forest and savannah between the Boro and Santantabe rivers. Together, these make up a combined total of 1,160 square miles (3,000 km²), the only officially protected areas of the Delta.

Moremi's varied habitat, ranging from near desert in the east to permanent swamp on the Delta's edge, accommodates an extraordinary variety of species.

Elephants graze in the mopane forests, snapping off branches with loud cracks that announce their presence for long distances. Hippos graze and crocodiles hunt in and alongside its rivers, and sometimes along the bottom of its clear waters. Marsh-dwelling lechwe and rare sitatunga antelopes retire into the reeds. Herds of impala, preferring drier ranges, feed on green grasses and leap lightly between small grassy islands, high-jumping 10 feet (3 m) and broad-jumping 24 feet (7+ m) if necessary.

Lions on the plains find midday shade under isolated tree "islands" (where lionesses sometimes hide newborn cubs) and prey on unwary duikers and other smaller antelopes, as do leopards, which usually hunt alone, often at dusk. Packs of wild dogs go after any likely opportunity that presents itself.

Hundreds of stately sacred and glossy ibis colonize heronries at Xakanasca and Xhobega. So do dozens of such long-legged waders as marabou storks, great white, rufous-bellied and purple herons, and yellow-billed egrets, which gather in cacophonous clusters in tops of fig thickets. Tiny paradise flycatchers with long bronzy tails and neon-blue eye rings weave intricate nests from October to January, and radiantly-plumaged carmine bee-eaters dig shoulder-to-shoulder nest burrows in riverbanks.

Masses of lily pads and arrowhead blooms cover whole sections of lagoons where African jacanas trip lightly and handsome pygmy geese open their own pathways.

"Veterinary" barriers—set up to protect domestic cattle from foot-and-mouth disease (though no one knows whether this is helpful, and it has harmfully disrupted traditional migratory patterns)—wind from north to south on one side of the reserve but otherwise there are no fences, and animals wander freely to and from Chobe National Park to the northeast, which Moremi adjoins. It is estimated that as many as 50,000 elephants roam the Delta and Chobe. Large numbers of these, including family groups of all ages, are commonly seen, especially during dry season, splashing through watery sections of the floodplains. Large herds, sometimes hundreds of buffalo, with graceful impalas, tsessebes, kudus, zebras, and waterbucks, can be seen on open grasslands between wetland and forest fringes.

Most of Botswana's 164 mammal species are here as well as a remarkably diverse array of 540 bird species, 157 reptiles, and 80 fish.

Best times are May–October dry season when creatures seeking water are more visible (October can be hot, dusty, and windy) or, for birders especially interested in seeing migratory species from the north, November–April.

---

**FURTHER INFORMATION**

Senior Warden, Department of Wildlife and National Parks, P.O. Box 11, Maun, Botswana.

# OKAVANGO DELTA

The Okavango Delta was first visited in 1849 by explorer David Livingstone who realized at once—as do most first visitors—that it is one of the great wetlands of the world, teeming with fascinating (though not always conspicuous) wildlife.

Malachite kingfishers like tiny flying jewels flit from reed to reed, peering into waters so crystalline they can see not only their prey but also an occasional hippopotamus walking along the bottom. Crocodiles swirl and take off at alarming speeds when alerted by the approach of a mokoro, the hand-hewn dugout canoe which is the ideal transportation here.

Sitatungas, rare small swamp-dwelling antelopes whose splayed hooves help them keep a footing while foraging, disappear in a sparkle of droplets into gold-green papyrus stretching as far as the eye can see under a clear deep-blue sky. When startled they may submerge almost completely leaving only their nostrils above water.

White-hooded fish eagles glance unconcernedly at quiet visitors and resume their constant search for watery prey which they swoop down and snare in razor-sharp talons.

Diminutive painted reed frogs in myriad patterns of burgundy and white cling to marsh stalks and call like tiny bells in early morning and dusk. Such is the filtering ability of the millions of papyrus and phragmites reeds that one can dip in and drink from the limpid waters in most places in perfect safety; or, pick a water lily, pluck the bloom, drink from the stem, and take back and cook the delicious plant.

Occasionally a sound like an express train roars by. It is a herd of lechwe, the other marsh-dwelling antelopes, being pursued through the shallows by wild dogs or other predators.

The Okavango is like no other place in Africa and perhaps anywhere—the world's largest inland river delta and one of its most beautiful, extending like a great open hand across an area just under half the size of Switzerland over most of northwestern Botswana, with, on its eastern fringe, Moremi Wildlife Reserve. It arises with the Okavango River in central Angola, flows with 24 million cubic yards (18.5 cu. m) of water annually which, on encountering this nearly flat terrain, loses its central course and spreads out into a vast tangled maze of lagoons, channels, and islands ranging in size from Chief's Island to tiny dots of land covered with head-high reeds, in a great marsh which eventually sinks into the thirsty Kalahari desert—"the river that never reaches the sea."

Drawn to it like a magnet are equally thirsty wildlife in some of the largest concentrations in Africa: more than 400 species of birds, including carmine bee-eaters which gather in mass congregations of many hundreds to nest in burrows in nearby fields and riverbanks, and African jacanas stepping delicately along the tops of lily pads. Magnificent Pel's fishing owls standing over two feet (60 cm) tall take fish of more than four pounds (2 kg), spotting them by the moon's reflection on their silvery scales or ripples as they break the surface.

Rare, shy slaty egrets are found only here. Statuesque, stunning wattled cranes, facing extinction elsewhere as farming takes over their habitat, happily feed on floodplain organisms here, as do colorful saddle-billed storks and many others.

On higher ground dozens of species and thousands of individual herbivores graze, including elephants, zebras, buffalo, wildebeest, giraffes, hippos, and kudus, and, finally, some of the larger carnivores such as lions and leopards which prey on them. Some 80 large and varied fish species are here, as well as 1,078 plant species in a density seven times greater than the rest of southern Africa and 50 times greater than that in Europe—all an integral part of this ecosystem.

Best times to visit are May–October dry season when the Delta's water, which comes from far upstream, nevertheless remains abundant.

## ALSO OF INTEREST

**Central Kalahari Game Reserve** with large wildebeest herds, also elands, gemsboks, and springboks as well as predators; however, the area is still inhabited by bushmen, and visitors require special permission.

KALAHARI GEMSBOK NATIONAL PARK—*see* South Africa (p.132).

**Khutse Game Reserve** with many small open pans attracting a variety of mammals, including migratory antelopes and other grazers plus their predators, lions, cheetahs, and smaller species such as bat-eared fox and yellow mongoose. Paucity of surface water limits birds but interesting arid-area species are here such as kori bustards, bronze-winged coursers, and sandgrouse.

**Mabuasehube Game Reserve** with numerous lions and other predators and marvelous birds (but in limited numbers) typical of Kalahari region: kori bustards, pale chanting goshawks, tawny eagles. No visitor facilities, however.

**Makgadikgadi Pans Game Reserve** has two huge salt pans and associated grasslands with grazing species and predators. In infrequent good rain years the pans form shallow lakes, which attract vast numbers of flamingos, avocets, and several duck species. Viewing best January–April.

**Mashatu Game Reserve** is a private reserve with the largest number of elephants on private land; at least 600 may be present. Also grazers and small mammals, and 375 bird species have been recorded.

**Nxai Pan National Park** has large numbers of giraffes throughout the year; otherwise viewing best here in rainy November–April especially for grazers including hartebeest, elands, springboks, and Burchell's zebras. Ostriches are common, also birds of prey and 250 other bird species.

**Stevensford Private Game Reserve** consists of mixed woodland, with kudus, wildebeest, waterbucks, impalas, bushbucks, red hartebeest, warthogs, and spotted hyenas.

# CAMEROON

MANDRILL BABOONS WITH SCARLET-AND-BLUE FACES
FIND HOMES ALONG WITH BULKY WESTERN LOWLAND
GORILLAS AND A DOZEN OTHER PRIMATE SPECIES IN PRIMARY
CONGO RAIN FOREST WHERE TREES TOWER TO A 200-FOOT
(60-M) CANOPY IN DJA FAUNAL RESERVE, A PRIMATES' PARADISE.

CAMEROON IS BLESSED BY NATURE NOT ONLY WITH MINERALS AND AGRICULTURAL RESOURCES—ONE OF FEW AFRICAN COUNTRIES CURRENTLY ABLE TO FEED ITSELF—BUT WITH FORESTS AND WILDLIFE AS ABUNDANT AND DIVERSE AS ANY ON THE CONTINENT.

Lions and giant elands roam the savannah. Bongo antelopes and massive western lowland gorillas survive in still-primeval woodlands with monkeys, baboons, elephants, hippos, and forest

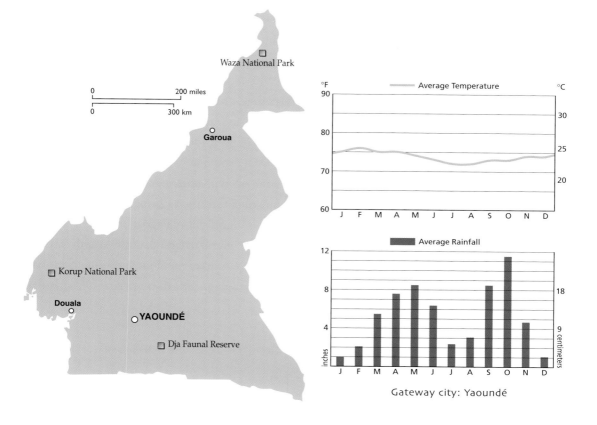

Gateway city: Yaoundé

35

buffalo. There are more than 300 species of mammals, 14 endemic; 850 bird species; 373 species of reptiles and amphibians—including perhaps densest, most diverse frog populations in the world—and an estimated 9,000 plant species, including at least 156 found nowhere else.

Nature reserves cover almost 15 percent of this central African country of 183,521 square miles (475,442 km²), nearly four times the size of England. (An eventual national goal of 20 percent has been set by law.) These include seven national parks, three World Biosphere Reserves, and one U.N. World Heritage Site. Most, unfortunately, are not adequately protected. Some have seriously deteriorated due to lack of funds, mismanagement, poaching, and often official corruption. Forests have been sold off to foreign interests for ecologically unsustainable logging with no benefit to local people while plundering of rare animals through sale of "bush meat" has grown and the crime rate has soared.

The situation may change with increasing awareness of economic benefits of ecotourism dependent on healthy parks and reserves. Organizations such as World Wide Fund for Nature (WWF) and Wildlife Conservation Society (WCS) have helped, but much more help is needed.

## DJA FAUNAL RESERVE

Dja Faunal Reserve is a primates' paradise, a 2,030-square-mile (5,260-km²) U.N. World Heritage Site and Biosphere Reserve almost completely surrounded by the Dja River, in some places by steep cliffs as well, in south-central Cameroon about 152 miles (243 km) southeast of Yaoundé.

At least 14 species, including western lowland gorillas, chimpanzees, and mandrill baboons with bright scarlet-and-blue faces—called the most colorful mammals in the world—populate this magnificent primary Congo rain forest where trees of over 40 species rise to form a canopy in some places 198 feet (60 m) high.

The list includes long-tailed moustached, white-nosed, and crowned guenons, teddy-bear-like pottos, noisy, whooping troops of red-capped, white-cheeked, and agile mangabeys, handsome black-and-white colobus and talapoin monkeys, drills, Demidoff's galagos, chimpanzees, and perhaps others as yet undiscovered in this dense reserve. Water-loving sitatungas splash through streams where they graze near striped bongos, largest of forest antelopes. Forest elephants browse well-traveled woodland paths. Near-sighted armored pangolins snuffle through leaf litter churned up by giant forest hogs. Leopards prey on both.

OPPOSITE: Hyenas' powerful jaws can support their body weight, enabling them to hang from a zebra's or wildebeest's neck after slashing into an artery. Their large teeth can crush bones. Every part of a victim is digested within 24 hours—bones, hooves, horns, even teeth—by acidic stomach fluids. This bony dietary matter makes hyenas' feces white.

Pygmy villagers hunt using ancient ways and weapons.

Dja is one of the largest, densest, most diverse humid forests in Africa, threatened, however, by logging roads up to its boundaries, creating poaching access, and most ominously by proposals for an international road just to the south and a cement quarry inside the reserve to supply it. From these, this ecological treasure's natural barriers of cliffs and river offer little protection.

Visitor facilities at least until recently were nonexistent. Warden's office is in Messamena.

---

**FURTHER INFORMATION**

Coordinateur du Programme Dja, Ministère de l'Environnement et des Forêts, Yaoundé, Cameroon, Tel: (+237) 23-92-32.

---

# KORUP NATIONAL PARK

Korup National Park in an isolated southwestern corner adjoining Nigeria is considered one of the oldest, most beautiful tropical rain forests in the world. Crossed by three major rivers on the inland side of a large coastal plateau, this 486-square-mile (1,259-km²) survivor of ice ages is truly a natural history museum more than 60 million years old. Studies of its teeming pristine ecological diversity have found more than 600 tree species—sometimes within a 1,235-acre (500-ha) plot—including many with important medicinal properties, plus more than 100 mammal species, 435 bird species, 170 species of reptiles and amphibians, and 140 kinds of fish. Many are threatened. Some are entirely new to science.

A tree survey found more than 7,500 standing individuals in a single hectare (2.47 acres). Mammals include elephants, buffalo, antelopes, leopards, chimpanzees, baboons, many kinds of monkeys, and a variety of smaller species. Bird specialties include brilliant blue-headed bee-eaters, long-tailed hawks, Sjostedt's owlets, black guinea fowl, and others.

Visitors check in first at park headquarters at Nguti in the north, or, in the south, at Mundemba (about 93 miles/150 km northwest of Douala) where tours, guides, and camping can be arranged, also boat trips to coastal mangroves. A variety of lodging is available. Visitors should be prepared for 100 percent humidity, biting insects and fording waist-high rivers—but a good look at this special place and its inhabitants can be worth the effort.

Rock pratincoles and several hornbill species usually are on and over the Mana River, crossed by a suspension bridge at the park entrance six miles (10 km) from Mundemba. There are a number of trails, one leading six miles (10 km) to Chimpanzee Camp.

Poaching is a serious problem, also killing fish by poisoning the water, from both the Cameroon and Nigerian side. A planned buffer zone may relieve some of this pressure.

Korup is home to the Bioresources Development and Conservation Plan (BDCPC) established at the Rio Earth Summit of scientists, industrialists, and environmentalists interested in linking human development with rain forest conservation, and supported by a number of governments, including the U.S. and France. Here, that means integration of park development with local people in planning and decision-making, with helpful programs both by WWF and WCS.

---

**FURTHER INFORMATION**

Conservator, Korup National Park, P.O. Box 303 Buea, Cameroon; or P.O. Box 2417, Douala, Tel/Fax: (+237) 343-21-71; Executive Secretary, BDCPC, B.P. 2626 Messa, Yaoundé, Cameroon, Tel: (+237) 31-91-99, Fax: (+237) 31-41-25.

---

# WAZA NATIONAL PARK

Waza National Park and U.N. Biosphere Reserve is one of Cameroon's finest and most accessible—656 square miles (1,700 km²) of acacia forest and open yaéré savannah in the Chad Depression (once covered by Lake Chad), known for enormous numbers of elephants and lions. Ostriches run across the plain at 30 miles per hour (50 kph), reaching 45 miles per hour (70 kph) for short sprints. Arabian bustards stride along at more moderate speeds, flying only if they have to.

Scissor-tailed kites whistle and hover over grasslands, dropping straight down on small rodents. Hippos snooze in waterways. Herons and storks fish at the edges. Exquisite Abyssinian rollers snatch grasshoppers in midair. Hornbills pluck ripe fruit.

Elephants may congregate in the hundreds at Mare aux Éléphants, famous watering hole. Others come for a drink, too—giraffes, hartebeest, tsessebes, lyre-horned kob antelopes, olive baboons, patas and vervet monkeys, warthogs, leopards, cheetahs, even a few shy, burrowing, nocturnal aardvarks, seen mostly by their footprints.

Best times are March–May, hottest but that's when animals are visible coming to water, also masses of waterbirds. Park entrance is on the northwestern edge, not far from village of Waza, where guides (compulsory) are available. Park is open November–June (this changes, check ahead).

Water can be a major problem, especially since construction of the Maga Dam 15.5 miles (25 km) to the south and irrigation dykes along the Logone River, which have reduced grasslands and in some places collapsed fisheries. A Waza Logone Floodplain Restoration Program has been created to address this. There's also poaching, particularly from Nigeria and Chad.

Waza is just off the paved road to Chad, 75 miles (122 km) north of Maroua. A variety of lodging is available and guided trips can be arranged both at Maroua and, nearer the park, the village of Waza, which has camping as well.

## ALSO OF INTEREST

**Bénoué National Park and Biosphere Reserve** in the Guinea savannah belt and **Bouba Ndjida National Park** to the east, are large reserves in the Guinea savannah belt about 93 miles (150 km) north of Ngaondéré with good cross-section of the country's outstanding wildlife, including magnificent giant elands. Also **Faro National Park**, to the west, 1,287 square miles/ (3,300 km²) acres (330,000 ha) with threatened cheetahs, black rhinoceros and elephants, known for its hippo colonies.

**Banyang Mbo Forest Reserve**, 148 square miles (385 km²), east of Ejaghem, coastal Biafran forest with forest elephants, buffalo, red-eared guenons, tusked water chevrotains (tiny, deer-like, most primitive living ruminants) and armored giant pangolins. Rich faunal list includes 325 bird species, 63 reptiles, 71 amphibians (perhaps densest and most diverse frog population in the world), 33 large mammals.

**Lobéké National Park** is newly designated, more than 770 square miles (2,000 km²) bounded on three sides by the Lobéké, Longue, Sangha, and Djombe Rivers, with rich faunal species including high densities of forest elephants, western lowland gorillas, chimpanzees, bongos, but seriously threatened by poaching, unsustainable logging in immediate vicinity by international timber companies. Contiguous with NOUABALÉ-NDOKI NATIONAL PARK in Congo (*see* p.46) and DZANGA-SANGHA FOREST RESERVE, Central African Republic (*see* p.41).

International visitors may fly either to Yaoundé, the capital, or Douala. Local airlines connect the two as well as other larger towns. There's a fairly good modern train and bus network and bush taxis are often available. Rental cars are not always in top condition, however, nor are some of the roads.

Best times generally are dry-season December–March. Lowlands are usually hot and humid, but highlands can be cold at night.

### FURTHER INFORMATION

Département de la Faune et des Parcs Nationaux, c/o Directeur de Forêts, Ministère de l'agriculture, B.P. 194, Yaoundé; Executive Secretary, BDCPC, B.P. 2626 Messa, Yaoundé, Tel: (+237) 31-91-99, Fax: (+237) 31-41-25.

# CENTRAL AFRICAN REPUBLIC

FOREST ELEPHANTS BULLDOZE FOREST TRAILS
FOR RARE SPIRAL-HORNED BONGO ANTELOPES,
GIANT FOREST HOGS, AND UP TO 2,000
MASSIVE LOWLAND GORILLAS—ONE OF THEIR
DENSEST POPULATIONS ANYWHERE—IN
DZANGA-SANGHA DENSE FOREST RESERVE.

SOME OF AFRICA'S GREAT NATURAL AREAS—HUGE, WILD PLACES WITH GREAT HERDS OF ELEPHANTS, LOWLAND GORILLA FAMILIES, LIONS, LEOPARDS, GRAZING ANIMALS, AND STUNNING BIRDS—ARE IN THIS LANDLOCKED COUNTRY ROUGHLY THE SIZE OF FRANCE IN THE CENTER OF THE CONTINENT.

Several adjoin reserves in neighboring countries—a promising development of recent years creating large, trans-border areas of natural protection, the result of innovative work between governments, local communities, and international organizations such as World Wide Fund for Nature (WWF) and Wildlife Conservation Society (WCS).

## DZANGA-SANGHA DENSE FOREST RESERVE

This reserve in the far southwestern corner is one of the newest, with some of the highest population densities anywhere of massive lowland gorillas (an estimated 2,000) and forest elephants (an estimated 3,000) with smaller ears and straighter tusks than their savannah cousins.

Dark crowned eagles, largest and fiercest of Africa's forest eagles with five-foot-plus (1.55-m) wingspreads, perform year-round aerial displays and prey commonly on small forest antelopes as heavy as they are, caching in nearby trees whatever they can't eat or carry away. Blue-breasted kingfishers whistle in forest fringes, more intent on insects than fish. In the underbrush are melodious, orange-breasted, snowy-crowned robin-chats mimicking all the others.

Rare, striped bongo antelopes venture shyly into forest clearings with forest buffalo,

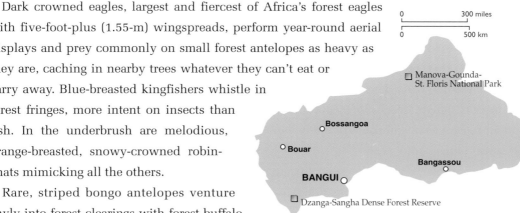

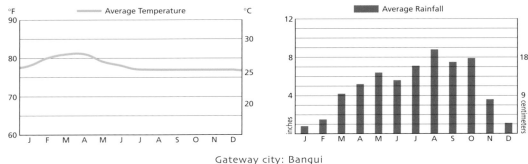

Gateway city: Bangui

warthogs, waterbucks, giant forest hogs, chimpanzees, and DeBrazza's monkeys with piercing eyes and long white goatee-beards. If unwary, all can be prey to stealthy leopards.

Forest elephants, a keystone species, make life easier for everybody by bulldozing forest trails and digging for minerals around tree roots, creating sun-drenched treefall gaps in forest glades that become a tangle of herbaceous vegetation for primates and grazers alike. Everywhere are explosions of colorful butterflies.

Until 1986, anyone could come on this 1,683 square miles (4,359 km²) of wild forest and savannah and shoot anything. Since then, the government working with WWF and others has declared the area a national park and dense forest preserve protecting two core no-hunting areas, Ndoki Park and Dzanga Park, usually referred to together as DZANGA-NDOKI PARK.

## DZANGA-NDOKI PARK

Surrounded and buffered by the DZANGA-SANGHA RESERVE in which limited hunting and other uses are permitted and where Ba'Aka people partner in protected area management while living in traditional ways. Reserve management is shared also with WCS and GTZ, aid organization of the German government.

Visitor facilities have been largely in the planning stage for trails, river trips, lodging, treks to visit western lowland gorillas and forest elephants at salt clearings, so best check ahead for guiding and other arrangements. This can be done with the WWF office in Bangui. Dzanga is 7.4 miles (12 km) from Bayanga, where there is a welcome center located 325 miles (525 km) southwest of Bangui, reachable by minibus, rented 4WD or chartered air. Ndoki, less accessible, is about five miles (8 km) south of Lidjombo.

Dzanga-Sangha adjoins the NOUABALÉ-NDOKI NATIONAL PARK in the Congo Republic (*see* p.46)—to form a protected area altogether of more than 5,000 square miles (some 14,000 km²) where wildlife, unaware of national borders, can cross freely back and forth.

To say poaching is under control would exaggerate, but it has been down significantly. Armed, well-trained rangers patrol, and animals from surrounding areas have moved in (hunting safaris in neighboring areas could, at least until recently, legally shoot a handsome endangered spiral-horned bongo, or, prime trophy, Lord Derby's eland for $30,000 U.S. or so).

## MANOVO-GOUNDA-ST. FLORIS NATIONAL PARK

At the northern corner of the country is Manovo-Gounda-St. Floris National Park and World Heritage Site, a vast wooded savannah and floodplain drained by five major rivers originating in the Massif des Bongo, covering some 8,800 square miles (22,792 km²), including contiguous protected areas. Historically the savannahs have been home to some of Africa's great elephant herds, plus cheetahs, lions, leopards, wild dogs, red-fronted gazelles, hartebeest, topi, giraffes, and

Flightless ostriches are world's largest living birds, six to eight (rarely up to nine) feet tall (2–2.75 m), weighing up to 345 pounds (157 kg), with a lion-like roar. Evolution has weakened their wings but strengthened leg muscles so they can run up to 40 miles an hour (70 kph) and savagely kick any predator that catches up, sometimes delivering a single fatal blow. Males share incubation of up to 80 eggs from various females in one nest (tests show females can recognize their own eggs).

buffalo, with, until recently, black rhinoceros. A list of more than 320 bird species includes rare silvery shoebills or whale-headed storks, ostriches, fish-eating eagles, colorful bee-eaters and rollers, kingfishers, African pygmy-geese, dwarf bitterns, saddle-billed storks, and bateleur and banded snake-eagles.

Unfortunately the vast herds have been reduced drastically along with leopards, rhinos, and others, by poachers thought to be a spillover of civil wars in Chad and Sudan, often with automatic weapons, outnumbering and outgunning park rangers, some of whom have died in the conflict. Proceeds from animal trophies have gone to buy more weapons for warfare. It's been quieter recently, and, as in quiet periods before, the European Development Fund (EDF) has actively helped restore the park. But conditions should be checked before planning a visit, possibly with EDF offices in Bangui. The park is open from December 1 to mid-May, accessed on the south from Bamingui, where chartered flights arrive from Bangui and which has lodging. It's possible to drive the 496 miles (800 km) from Bangui, but roads are rough and fuel stations scarce.

## ALSO OF INTEREST

**Bamingui-Bangoran National Park and Biosphere Reserve** to the west of Manovo-Gounda-St. Floris, 6,488 square miles (16,800 km²), historically with outstanding wildlife populations but recently with some of the same problems as St. Floris, so recent conditions should be checked before a visit.

Continuing threats to all these reserves include foreign timber and mining concessions, poaching for "bush meat," and land-clearing for agriculture. On all these, government instability and resulting unrest have reduced urgently needed protections. This may change, as it has in some other African countries, to a more enlightened view seeing these places as helpful not only to wildlife but to the local economy through ecotourism.

International visitors fly into Bangui, the capital city, with hotels, accommodations, trip information, and (costly) rental vehicles. Streets have not, however, always been safe places for tourists to explore alone, especially at night. Rainy season is May–October in the south, diminishing to June–September in the north—but it can be muggy year-round. Best times to visit are November–April.

---

**FURTHER INFORMATION**

Direction Générale du Centre Nationale pour la Protection et l'Aménagement de la faune
(Le Directeur Général), Ministère des Eaux, Forêts, Chasses, Pêches et Tourisme, B.P. 981, Bangui.

# CONGO
# REPUBLIC

SHELTERED IN NDOKI'S DARK, HUMID TROPICAL
FOREST ARE LEOPARDS, GORILLAS, FIERCE GOLDEN
CATS AND—SOME SAY—CONGO-BASIN
MOKÉLÉ-MBEMBÉS, LEGENDARY HORNED
REPTILES ABLE TO KILL ELEPHANTS.

S O WILD ARE PRIMEVAL FORESTS AND JUNGLES IN THE CONGO THAT ANIMALS ENCOUNTERED THERE BY SCIENTISTS AND RESEARCHERS RECENTLY MAY NEVER HAVE SEEN A HUMAN BEING. Rather than flee, gorillas, chimpanzees, antelopes, and others approached and followed, apparently out of curiosity, to get a better look.

Saving such rare and precious places of untouched wilderness is a modern-day challenge. Slash-and-burn agriculture and unsustainable mechanized logging by international timber companies have destroyed habitat, and road-building connected with them has opened previously remote areas to easy poaching for ivory and "bush meat" both for commercial trade and to feed logging crews.

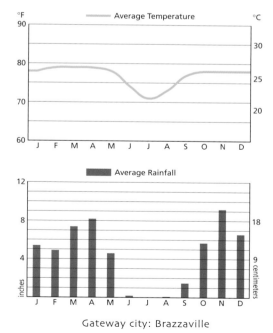

Gateway city: Brazzaville

## CONGO REPUBLIC

WCS-Congo—a partnership between the Congolese government and WCS—is exploring and managing NOUABALÉ-NDOKI and two other reserves—CONKOUATI NATIONAL PARK and LAC TÉLÉ COMMUNITY RESERVE—working toward sustainable management of the region's natural resources.

# NOUABALÉ-NDOKI NATIONAL PARK

One place that holds hope is Nouabalé-Ndoki National Park. In its 1,544 square miles (4,000 km$^2$) of lowland forest in the northern Congo Republic live western lowland gorillas—shorter-haired and with redder heads than eastern gorillas—elephants, chimpanzees, leopards, and over 300 bird species. Established and managed with help from the Wildlife Conservation Society (WCS), U.S. Fish and Wildlife Service, Columbus Zoo, Brevard Zoo, U.S. Agency for International Development (USAID), and others, programs have been started to protect the forest and its inhabitants not only directly but indirectly by educating and informing local people about benefits of ecotourism both to the reserve and to local communities.

Parts of Ndoki's dark, humid, almost inaccessible tropical forest still are not fully explored, but what has been found is extraordinary. One swampy 32-acre (13-ha) clearing alone—Mbeli Bai—is the gathering place of as many as 180 western lowland gorillas along with a number of monkey species—striking black-and-white and red colobus; moustached and crowned guenon monkeys; agile and gray-cheeked mangabeys; and others. Nine monkey species share the forest in densities of up to 50 per square mile.

Forest elephants are here, clearing woodland passageways and openings for others—dwarf forest buffalo, water-loving sitatunga antelopes, shy, striped bongos, stealthy leopards and golden cats, and rare blue duikers. These tiny forest antelopes, horned and weighing 12 pounds tops (5.4 kg), may number up to 100 per square mile. Here perhaps, according to Pygmy legend, is Mokélé-mbembé, legendary long-necked Congo basin reptile said to have a single massive frontal horn used to kill elephants.

Mahogany trees are so shrouded with vines and ferns their tops are invisible. Parrots are mostly heard and briefly glimpsed as they fly through the 150-foot-high (45-m) canopy, along with bats dipping down occasionally for an insect that can make a full meal—a six-inch (15.2-cm) mantis or nine-inch (23-cm) walking-stick.

According to National Geographic Society, Ndoki may have more wildlife per square mile than anyplace else in Africa, a continent renowned for remarkable wildlife assemblages.

In a landmark agreement in 2001 the German logging firm, Congolaise Industrielle des Bois (C.I.B.), voluntarily gave up leases on the adjoining 100-square-mile (259-km$^2$) Goualougo Triangle so it could be added to Nouabalé-Ndoki, and pledged to curb hunting

Leopards compete with larger predators, especially lions, so they like to cache prey in trees where lions don't go. Powerful leg and neck muscles enable them to carry an adult antelope, chimpanzee or even young giraffe up to three times their weight for hundreds of yards to a safe place.

by crews on its other leases. Just to the south, trees exploited for logging average more than 200 years old.

Ndoki is buffered now by underbrush-tangled swamps on the south and further protected by biting, stinging, blood-sucking, illness-carrying insects. It adjoins two smaller reserves in the Central African Republic, DZANGA-NDOKI PARK and DZANGA-SANGHA DENSE FOREST RESERVE (*see* p.41). Still, these obstacles can be no match for determined exploiters with modern-day equipment. Limited visitation is part of future plans, partly to build a local constituency for protecting Ndoki. These could include observation platforms erected for scientific observations near habituated primates at clearings and water holes.

A WCS campsite has been set up just outside Bombassa, about 62 miles (100 km) north of Ouesso. Interested travelers should check recent status with WCS office in Brazzaville, and be aware that visits to these wild places are not easy—perhaps involving motorized canoe, un-motorized canoe, and sometimes just slogging through swamps inhabited by snakes and crocodiles.

## Also of Interest

**Conkouati National Park** is the country's most diverse protected area, 1,947 square miles (5,045 km$^2$) of habitat ranging from a sea turtle reserve off the Atlantic coast through savannah to mountainous zones of the Mayombian forest. Inhabitants include manatees, whales, porpoises, forest elephants, gorillas, chimpanzees, colorful mandrills, and forest buffalo.

**Lac Télé** in the north is the country's only wetlands reserve, permanent or seasonal home to thousands of birds of more than 250 species. Habitat ranging from savannah through semi-deciduous dryland and permanently flooded forest supports western lowland gorillas, chimpanzees, forest elephants, leopards, sitatungas, forest buffalo, otters, crocodiles, and many fish, including several endemic species—plus, guaranteed in its establishment, communities of 22 surrounding villages who live by subsistence hunting and resource extraction in the reserve.

Recent history of this west-central African country about 2.6 times the size of England (132,000 square miles/342,000 km$^2$) has been troubled with civil war, but was stabilized at least temporarily by a relatively calm election in 2002. The U.S. embassy was closed at that time and combined with that in the Democratic Republic of the Congo in neighboring Kinshasa.

International visitors fly to Brazzaville which has hotels and car rentals and is connected by air as well as riverboat to Ouesso, near Nouabalé-Ndoki, also to Pointe-Noire and Libreville. Before planning a trip contact the WCS office in Brazzaville to determine current conditions and availability of logistical support.

Best times are dry-season June–September, also December–January when heavy rains let up a bit—but it's equatorial so all year is hot and humid.

---

**FURTHER INFORMATION**

WCS Congo Country Director, B.P. 14537, Brazzaville, Republic of Congo, Tel: (+242) 81-03-46,
E-mail: wcscongo@yahoo.fr, Website: www.wcs-congo.org; Secretariat General, Direction de la
Conservation de la Faune, Ministère de l'Économie Forestière, B.P. 2153, Brazzaville, Tel: (+242) 81-17-18.

# CÔTE D'IVOIRE

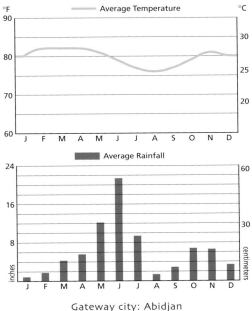

RARE, BEAUTIFUL MONA AND DIANA MONKEYS
WITH FLUFFY WHITE FACE RUFFS SWING THROUGH
THE TREES BY THE HUNDREDS IN THE SMALL, FRIENDLY
VILLAGE OF GBETITAPEA WHERE VILLAGERS WELCOME
AND REVERE THEM AS TOTEM ANIMALS.

THIS STEAMY WEST AFRICAN COUNTRY ON THE GULF OF GUINEA EARNED ITS NAME AS A CENTER OF THE ELEPHANT-TUSK TRADE. A different view has let elephant populations and others gradually rebound after several decades of anti-poaching protection. Lions, leopards, and more than a dozen kinds of primates are at home in these jungles and savannahs, plus striped, spiral-horned bongo antelopes at their northernmost limit. There are more than 690 bird species—dazzling blue-breasted and chocolate-backed kingfishers are among them, also black and blue-headed bee-eaters, red-cheeked wattle-eyes, African finfoots, and spectacularly long-tailed hawks.

A reputation as "the Paris of Africa" has been marred by recent political troubles but Côte D'Ivoire is still beautiful, with friendly people generally supportive of conservation and several wildlife reserves of world renown.

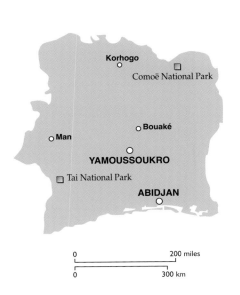

Gateway city: Abidjan

## CÔTE D'IVOIRE

# COMOË NATIONAL PARK

Comoë National Park, a U.N. World Heritage Site and Biosphere Reserve, largest protected area in West Africa, is 4,440 square miles (11,500 km²) tucked in the country's northeast corner. Here the country's largest remaining elephant herds wander freely in forests, grasslands, and savannah of the semidesert Sahel, with buffalo, hippos, waterbucks, bushbucks, kob, and roan antelopes.

Huge Goliath herons build suitably outsized reed platform nests, among more than 400 bird species. Wetlands attract an enormous number and range of ducks, plovers, yellow-billed egrets, black-winged stilts, shining blue and blue-breasted kingfishers, four kinds of storks, Forbes' and striking Egyptian plovers (aka crocodile-birds). Savannah and gallery forest support strident white-throated francolins, Emin's shrikes, spotted creepers, brown-rumped buntings, and hammerkops—and if you don't notice these big, dull, anvil-headed birds, you can't miss their massive stick-and-mud roofed nests in the fork of a tree, often over water.

A remarkable variety of habitat and plant associations ranges through gallery and open forest to savannah woodland and thick rain forest.

Comoë is northerly limit for yellow-backed duikers, diminutive forest antelopes with spotlight-yellow rumps. More than 150 mammal species include such varied carnivores as lions and leopards, little guinea-pig-like rock hyraxes—close relatives, though they don't look it, to elephants—aardvarks and heavily armored giant pangolins with strap-like tongues twice the length of their bodies to probe ant and termite nests.

Anubis or olive baboons troop together in organized clusters of 30 to 150—one of the most social of primates, of which 14 species are here, including white-collared mangabeys, western chimpanzees, black-and-white colobus, and green or vervet, Diana, mona, and white-nosed monkeys. In waterways are hippos and all three African crocodiles, slender-snouted, Nile, and dwarf.

Poaching has been a problem but significantly less so since a 1998 Plan of Action was instituted by the government and local communities with help from the European Union (EU) and World Wide Fund for Nature (WWF) to improve village infrastructure and train management and surveillance staff.

## CÔTE D'IVOIRE

Southern park entrances are a day's drive from Yamoussoukro, and a small airstrip has been under construction. Visitors can stay at a variety of accommodations in Kapin or Ganse at the southern entrances near the Comoë River or in Kafolo or Ouango near the northern entrance on the border with Burkina-Faso. One of the most interesting of 300 miles (500 km) of tracks follows the Comoë River course 143 miles (230 km) southward. The park is open dawn to dusk during dry-season December—May.

**FURTHER INFORMATION**

Directeur de la Cellule d'Aménagement du Parc National de la Comoë, B.P. 104 Bouna, Côte d'Ivoire.

Cape Buffalo graze in large, mixed herds of up to 2,000 on grasses too coarse for other ruminants to process, always within a day's walk of water. Between meals they rest sociably with others of their clan, backs touching, chins supported on a companion's back, often beside or even in water, where they can fall prey to large crocodiles.

## CÔTE D'IVOIRE

# Tai National Park

Tai National Park protects one of the last major undisturbed tracts of vast primary forest that once stretched across present-day Ghana, Côte d'Ivoire, Liberia, and Sierra Leone, and with it a rich store of flora and fauna, many now rare elsewhere. Scientists in the dense moist evergreen forests of this 1,350-square-mile (3,500-km$^2$) U.N. Biosphere Reserve and World Heritage Site are studying tool-use and other behavior among the large chimp population, paralleling pioneering studies of dry-forest chimps by Jane Goodall in East Africa.

Pygmy hippopotami bathe in forest ponds alongside tiny, spotted, rabbit-like water chevrotains or mouse-deer, most primitive living ruminants, virtually unchanged in 30 million years—once worldwide, now only in a few places in Africa and Southeast Asia.

Fruits and flowers are ever-present in this lush setting where temperatures average 80°F (26°C) most of the year and, while December–February is drier, no month is without rain. Food is always available for nectar, fruit and insect-eating butterflies, birds, lizards, and primates including chattering red, green, and black-and-white colobus monkeys, sooty mangabeys, vividly patterned Dianas, and a half-dozen others that swing through the 200-foot (60-m) high canopy. Of 150 species of leguminous trees here, 16 percent are endemic. Massive trunks and huge root buttresses spread through the forest floor, covered with mosses, ferns, and fungi, each in itself an ecosystem for many thousands of other organisms.

Forest elephants keep trails open for bushpigs, giant forest hogs, three kinds of scaly-armored pangolins—giant, long-tailed, and tree—an exceptional number and species of small duiker forest antelopes, including diminutive royal antelopes, along with noisy, clucking, endangered white-breasted guinea fowl. All are vulnerable to ambush from above by leopards and small but fierce golden cats. Alongside flit such moist-forest rarities as Nimba flycatchers, western wattled cuckoo-shrikes, and yellow-throated olive greenbuls, and along streams, chocolate-backed kingfishers, Liberian black flycatchers, and rufous fishing-owls.

Tai is protected by an 80-square-mile (207-km$^2$) buffer zone which has been proposed for park inclusion. December–February tends to be drier but no month is without rain.

---

**FURTHER INFORMATION**

Ministère des Eaux et Forêts, Direction des Parcs Nationaux et Réserves Analogues, B.P. V 178, Abidjan.

---

OPPOSITE: Green (black-faced) vervet monkeys maintain treetop balance and agility aided by long tails and, in effect, four grasping hands—hind feet as well as forelegs equipped with five long toes, with opposable thumbs and index fingers (useful also in rifling tents for interesting items, as many safari travelers know). They are good swimmers, with coarse hair that traps air, functioning as a buoyant, waterproof wet suit. They are widely distributed in Africa south of Ethiopia and Somalia.

## ALSO OF INTEREST

Millions of bats fly in to roost every dusk and out again at dawn in **Ehotilé Islands Park**, a six-island cluster in Aby Lagoon east of Abidjan. Protected recently with help from World Wide Fund for Nature (WWF), it's home also to monkeys, antelopes, waterbirds, manatees.

Monkeys are the totem animal for the small village of **Gbetitapea** near Man, six hours' drive west from Yamoussoukro, and every day hundreds, mostly monas and Dianas—now scarce throughout West Africa—come for their daily handout with a good time had by both monkeys and human visitors. Cascade, a beautiful waterfall in a nearby bamboo forest, attracts large numbers of iridescent dragonflies and butterflies.

**Isle of the Chimpanzees** is an island populated by a small band of chimps in a lagoon about 2½ miles (4 km) from Grand Lahou. Visitors can rent a boat to go out and see them.

Poaching is still a threat to many reserves, as are logging and gold prospecting. In some places promises to help local villages with schools and other infrastructure have not been kept, leading to resentment such as that which caused neighboring hunters and farmers to threaten rangers, destroy park stations, kill animals, and force closure of Abokouamekro reserve near Yamoussoukro.

Most international visitors fly into Abidjan, the country's commercial capital. Yamoussoukro to the north has been the political or administrative capital since 1983. Côte D'Ivoire has one of Africa's best road systems, also (expensive) car-hire, lodging, and food.

Most national parks are difficult of access to visitors without their own vehicles. Local guides may or may not be required but they are useful, usually easily arranged, and help support the reserves.

Local unrest is still possible—check for current conditions.

---

**FURTHER INFORMATION**

La Croix Verte (leading non-governmental conservation organization), B.P. 3770, Abidjan 01 La Croix Verte, 699 Abidjan; and Direction de la Protection de la Nature, B.P. V 178, Abidjan.

# DEMOCRATIC REPUBLIC OF CONGO
## (Formerly ZAÏRE)

THE LAST WILD POPULATION OF NORTHERN
WHITE RHINOS WAS REDUCED TO REMNANT TEENS
BY POACHING WITH AUTOMATIC WEAPONS, HELICOPTERS,
AND EVEN LIGHT CANNONS. NOW WITH PROTECTION AND
RECENTLY ACTIVATED POACHING PATROLS THEIR NUMBERS
HAVE REBOUNDED IN GARAMBA NATIONAL PARK.

WILDLIFE NEAR EXTINCTION ELSEWHERE HAVE FOUND HOMES IN THE VAST TROPICAL LOWLAND RAIN FOREST WHICH COVERS ALMOST HALF THIS THIRD-LARGEST AFRICAN COUNTRY. Through its 400,000 square miles (1,000,000-plus km²), called Africa's Amazonia, the Congo (Zaire) River winds a path longer than the Mississippi with water volume second only to the Amazon. Biodiversity here reflects not only varied habitats but survival through ice ages and built-in protection, at least until recently, by remoteness and inaccessibility.

Here striped-legged, endangered okapis browse with elephants that have evolved adaptations to multiple habitats. Of the country's 1,426-plus bird species, dozens, including the beautiful Congo peacock, exist only here.

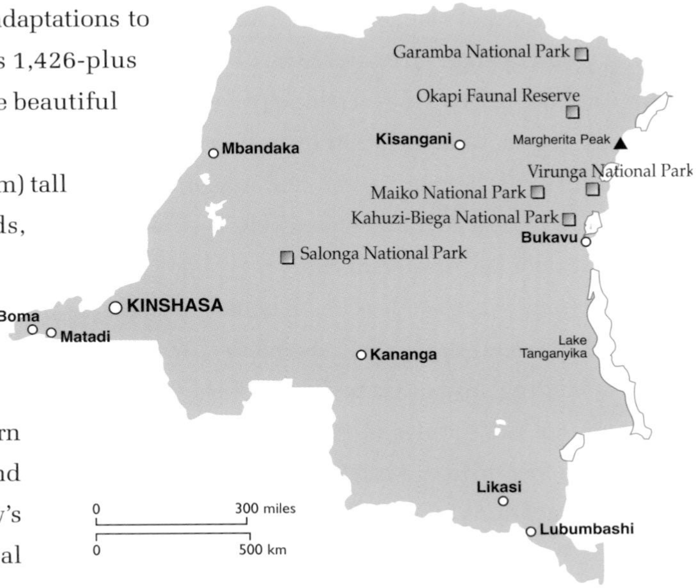

In grasslands standing 17 feet (5 m) tall to the south are giraffes, leopards, and the world's only remaining viable population of northern white rhinoceros. On slopes edging the Great Albertine Rift Valley in the east are eastern lowland gorillas and rare golden and owl-faced monkeys. Of the country's more than 400 larger mammal species, 31 are primates.

Garamba National Park

Okapi Faunal Reserve

Kisangani    Margherita Peak

Mbandaka

Virunga National Park

Maiko National Park
Kahuzi-Biega National Park
Bukavu

Salonga National Park

Boma    KINSHASA
Matadi

Kananga    Lake Tanganyika

0    300 miles
0    500 km

Likasi

Lubumbashi

# DEMOCRATIC REPUBLIC OF CONGO

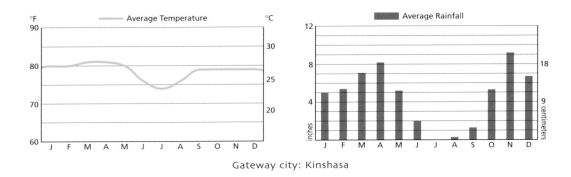

Gateway city: Kinshasa

Among more than 50 amphibians are hairy frogs named for furry hips and flanks which males develop in breeding season. Of more than 10,000 plants, 3,200 grow nowhere else.

Environmental concern in the Democratic Republic of the Congo (aka DRC, formerly Zaire) goes back to creation of Africa's first national park in 1925—Virunga, established to protect mountain gorillas. Now seven percent of the DRC has been set aside in parks and reserves with a stated goal of 12–15 percent.

Future of these natural treasures depends on solution to a host of problems, starting with conflict, population growth, political instability, and corruption (which makes conservation funds disappear). These in turn lead to inadequate attention and control of poaching, slash-and-burn agriculture, illegal logging, and exploitation of DRC's vast mineral wealth and hydroelectric potential (13 percent of the world's). As if that weren't enough, DRC has been overrun in recent years by millions of refugees from Rwanda and Sudan, squatting near or in reserves, clearing, cutting wood, slaughtering wildlife with automatic weapons for "bush meat" and body parts salable at high prices for everything from decoration to folk medicine and aphrodisiacs. Forty-four park guards were killed in related fighting and looting.

If stability can be maintained and a significant start can be made on recovering the parks, then DRC will be a premier ecotourism destination, as it once was.

International jet travelers usually arrive at Kinshasa, which has hotels, car rental and travel agents through which tours can be booked. Roads are poor (at this writing, it is impossible to cross DRC by road) so air travel, scheduled or chartered, using the country's 40 internal airports and 150 landing strips, can be the only way to get around. Also, the Congo (or Zaire) River is navigable for 1,077 miles (1,734 km), and at least a short boat trip through some of Africa's richest rain forest should not be missed.

Accommodations are spotty. Dry (sometimes just drier) seasons are December–February in the north, April–October in the south, wet most of the year at the equator.

## DEMOCRATIC REPUBLIC OF CONGO

**FURTHER INFORMATION**

Département de l'Agriculture, Division de la Conservation de la Nature et Gestion des Ressources Naturelles Renouvelables, B.P. 73, Kinshasa 1, Tel: (+243) 12-32668/33250, Fax: (+243) 12-27547, Tlx: (+243) 12-21112; Ministère de l'Énvironnement, Conservation de la Nature et Tourisme (Le Ministre), 15 Av. Des Cliniques, B.P. 12-348, Kinshasa 1, Tel: (+243) 12-33250/33251.

However, best contacts for visiting the country can be through such international conservation organizations as World Wide Fund for Nature (WWF) and Wildlife Conservation Society (WCS). First-hand reports of conditions are important, given the recent history of insecurity in many areas.

# GARAMBA NATIONAL PARK

In a vast undulating plateau of papyrus marshes, gallery forest, and stream-laced grasslands, some so high only tall Congo giraffes can see over them, is the last wild population of northern white rhinoceros in Garamba National Park and World Heritage Site. Surrounded on three sides of its 1,968 square miles (5,097 km²) by hunting reserves totaling more than 6,250 square miles (10,000 km²), it's an enormous protected area in DRC's northeast corner bordering Sudan, 47 miles (75 km) west of Uganda.

Once Garamba, established in 1938, had thousands of white rhinos, elephants, and others, but poaching by helicopters, automatic weapons, even light cannon, reduced these to remnants. Only 15 rhinos remained in 1984, making it one of the world's most endangered species. Conservation groups around the world, including the Frankfurt Zoological Society (FZS), WWF, and the U.N., joined in efforts to save these magnificent beasts. Poaching patrols gave them needed protection, they began reproducing again and at recent count were 31, with more expected.

Garamba lists 138 species of mammals, including some 3,000 buffalo, 3,000 hippos, 150 Congo giraffes (only known population of *Giraffa camelopardalis congoensis*), lions, hyenas, warthogs, olive baboons, golden cats, wild dogs, otters, roans, kobs, hartebeest, oribi, reedbuck, duikers, leopards, and perhaps 4–8,000 elephants (once 16,000) regarded as a unique subspecies adapted both to forest and savannah. Over 300 bird species include eagles, vultures, storks, white-winged lapwings, rufous-rumped larks, crocodile-birds, vinaceous doves, and blue-spotted wood-doves.

Most visitor facilities here as elsewhere have been damaged by years of neglect and war. Recovery remains in the planning stage. It once was possible to camp in the park or stay in an African-style hut but food supplies recently have been few, and the park has no petrol or diesel to sell to visitors. The park is 207 miles (335 km) northeast of Isiro to the entrance at Nagero, 3 miles (4 km) north of the Dungu–Aba road, or by light aircraft from Bunia or Goma.

African paradise flycatchers weave airy, delicate-looking but durable nests of roots and grasses bound together with spider webs, sometimes adorned with lichens, often over water or a dry streambed. Eggs are cream with red and lilac spots. Males lose long, showy rufous tails after breeding.

# KAHUZI-BIEGA NATIONAL PARK

Eastern lowland gorillas were once widespread under 6,500 feet (2,000 m) elevation at the foot of volcanoes throughout this region. Today they have been driven by land exploitation to find homes farther up. Some 150 of these enormous, gentle apes divided among perhaps 12 families forage now on wild celery and young bamboo in Kahuzi-Biega National Park and World Heritage Site in eastern Kivu province.

Kahuzi-Biega, a 2,316-square-mile (6,000-km²) reserve, takes its name from two extinct volcanoes dominating the physical scene. Its montane habitat ranges from about 2,500 feet (750 m) to 11,000 feet (3,400 m). Here are forest buffalo—smaller than their Cape cousins—forest elephants, forest hogs and in alpine grasslands, antelopes and duikers. An array of primates includes chimpanzees, owl-faced and red and black-and-white colobus monkeys. Among stunning birds are endemic Rockefeller's sunbirds, Shelley's crimsonwings, African green broadbills, Grauer's warblers, and rarely seen yellow-crested helmet-shrikes and Congo peacocks.

Threats have included not only slash-and-burn agriculture, poaching, and gold mining, but aftermath of civil strife in DRC and neighboring Rwanda which brought 1.5 to two million refugees with squatters, deforestation, poaching, occupation of park land, and looting and destruction of facilities.

Plans have been drawn to expand visitor facilities but at least until recently they're limited largely to tourist hut and bare-bones camping at Tshvanga, where there's a warden's office about 31 miles (50 km) west of Bukavu via a road which transects the park east–west. The park staff sometimes leads jungle tours to see habituated families of gorillas. Dry season is June through August.

# MAIKO NATIONAL PARK

Another significant eastern lowland gorilla population is in Maiko National Park, 4,180 square miles (10,835 km²) of dense humid equatorial forest located to the north of the Kisangani–Bukavu road. In this magnificent tract are forest elephants, chimpanzees, leopards, Congo peacocks, okapis, spiral-horned bongos, and other rare species, all at serious risk from poaching and mining. The park has almost no funding or protective staff. Facilities at least until recently have been nonexistent and visitor access not permitted.

---

NOTE: Gorillas are classified into three well-defined races: western lowland gorillas (*Gorilla gorilla gorilla*), in Gabon and Cameroon; eastern lowland gorillas (*Gorilla gorilla graueri*), in DRC between right bank of Congo (Zaire) River and eastern mountains (in Maiko and Kahuzi-Biega reserves); and mountain gorillas (*Gorilla gorilla beringei*) native to Virunga mountain range in DRC, Rwanda, and Uganda.

---

## DEMOCRATIC REPUBLIC OF CONGO

# Okapi Faunal Reserve

The solitary okapi resembles a committee-designed animal if ever one did—reddish-brown-to-black half-horse with striped zebra legs, half-giraffe with a tongue long enough to wash its ears (handy also for stripping leaves). About 5,000 of their world population of 30,000 live in Okapi Faunal Reserve and World Heritage Site, a 5,490-square-mile (14,220-km²) reserve created to protect them, which occupies over a fifth of the vast, rich Ituri forest laced with tributary streams and rivers in the Congo (Zaire) River basin in northeast DRC.

With them are forest elephants, tiny, tusked water chevrotains, bongos, burrowing aardvarks, water-adapted sitatunga antelopes, African golden cats, leopards, armored giant ground pangolins, giant forest or aquatic genets, giant forest hogs, and one of the highest number of little forest duiker antelopes in Africa, including blue, yellow-backed, white-bellied, and black-fronted. Among 13 primate species are owl-faced guenons and crested mangabeys.

Some 329-plus bird species include golden-naped and yellow-legged weavers found only here, lyre-tailed honeyguides, bare-cheeked trogons, sandy scops owls, Congo serpent eagles, joyful greenbuls, and spot-breasted and olive ibises.

This beautiful reserve is one of several impacted by spreading civil conflicts which have brought looting, poaching, and serious damage to facilities. The reserve formerly had good access along the trans-African highway. Based at Epulu are lodging, hiking trails, park staff, and tours of a breeding center set up in 1952 to supply okapis to zoos around the world. Institutional support and technical assistance have been provided to park management by WWF, WCS, and others.

> NOTE: Visitors should be warned of a tourist scam in the Epulu area involving baby chimps, in which visitors are told the baby will be eaten unless they buy it. If tourists do, another baby is stolen (its mother killed) and sold to another tourist. So, hard as it is, don't buy the chimp—just report to authorities.

# Salonga National Park

Wild, remote Salonga National Park and World Heritage Site is one of the world's largest rain forest reserves, 14,400 square miles (37,296 km²) in the heart of the Congo (Zaire) River basin with such rare and endangered species as dwarf or pygmy chimpanzees; beautiful Congo peacocks; three kinds of heavily armored pangolins—tree, giant ground, and long-tailed; and forest elephants.

Leopards drink at streams with small, fierce African golden cats, Congo water civets, and an array of forest browsers and grazers—bongos, bushbucks, rare pygmy Cape buffalo, water chevrotains. Hippos occupy waterways with African slender-snouted or "false" crocodiles. Black and yellow-billed storks pluck small crustacea from stream edges.

# DEMOCRATIC REPUBLIC OF CONGO

It's untamed, untouched Africa, for the most part as it's existed for millenia. But though isolated and accessible only by water, Salonga has had serious problems with poaching, logging, and encroachment. Along with other DRC reserves, it is classified as a U.N. World Heritage Site in Danger, which may bring badly needed UNESCO funds for staff to patrol and protect it.

Salonga, at least until recently, is seldom visited because of transport difficulties and lack of facilities. Park entry is possible only by riverboat. The park is divided midway by a buffer strip, and once inside, movement is difficult. Rudimentary lodging, usually reserved for scientists, is sometimes available at Anga, where the chief conservator is based, and at Monkoto.

Wild dogs are noted for altruism. A pack returned from a kill will stand aside for pups and even infirm adults before eating themselves, as compared with the savage free-for-all frenzy at a lion kill. Adults other than parents often stop to feed regurgitated food to youngsters before proceeding themselves. About the size of German shepherd dogs, they live in tightly bonded social groups, no two with the same patterns of black, tan, and white (Latin name, LYCAON PICTUS, means "painted wolf"). Once common, they are rare now over much of their former range in sub-Saharan Africa as the result of habitat destruction, disease, and persecution for supposed predation of domestic stock.

# VIRUNGA NATIONAL PARK

Africa's oldest national park, set aside in 1925—now a U.N. World Heritage Site—has habitats ranging from marshy deltas to savannahs, lava plains, and snowfields of the Ruwenzori Mountains.

Historically some of the largest wild animal concentrations in Africa have been in this 3,160-square-mile (8,184-km²) reserve—in savannah, African elephants, hippos, buffalo, a range of antelopes including kobs, Defassa's waterbucks, topi, warthogs, lions; in the Semiliki Valley and on slopes of the Virungas, mountain gorillas, chimpanzees, and okapi; in the extreme north, forest hogs and bongos.

Prehistoric-looking shoebill storks, elegant crowned cranes, Goliath herons, and martial eagles are among bird species, as, probably, are rare papyrus yellow warblers.

Virunga is contiguous with Rwanda's PARC NATIONAL DES VOLCANS (*see* p.120) and in Uganda, RUWENZORI MOUNTAINS NATIONAL PARK (*see* p.151) and QUEEN ELIZABETH NATIONAL PARK (*see* p.150) (BWINDI IMPENETRABLE FOREST—*see* p.148—is nearby), altogether an enormous set-aside of wild lands. It has suffered with other reserves in this region from civil strife both here and in neighboring countries which has brought refugees and sometimes armed invasion, with consequent destruction of wildlife and park facilities (timber losses from fuel-wood cutting alone were estimated at 600 metric tons a day at the height of the refugee incursion). Fortunately wildlife if protected and let alone often adapts and survives. Simple conservation measures can help—as distribution of energy-efficient stoves in refugee camps is estimated to have saved at least 16 square miles (40 km²) of forests in two years.

Access to the park is by road from Goma or by light plane. Accommodations have been available at Rwindi and Djomba, and more modestly, at Mabenga and Kanyabayonga. Best times are December–January, when rains let up, and June, start of the dry season (July–September are dry but haze often spoils views). Djomba is the main center for viewing gorillas—best reserve ahead since groups are limited to eight. Rwindi, with the main lodge, is center for much of the rest of the wildlife viewing, both in plains and nearby Lake Edward. Beni is turn-off for the Ruwenzoris and Ishango, with camping and wonderful birding on the north shore of Lake Edward. A sanctuary specifically protecting chimpanzees is at Tongo. Major roads go to all these.

---

**FURTHER INFORMATION**

Parc National des Virunga, Station de la Rwindi, Rwindi, D/S Goma, Kivu, IZCN, B.P. 868, Kinshasa 1; IZCN, Parc National des Virunga-Lulimbi, B.P. 315, Goma; Delegation Regionale au Tourism, P.O. Box 242, Goma (French is preferred language here).

# ETHIOPIA

ROVING BANDS OF HUNDREDS OF PINK-
CHESTED, GOLDEN-MANED GELADA BABOONS,
FEROCIOUS-LOOKING BUT MILD-MANNERED,
WAIL, MOAN, AND CRY OUT TO WARN OF
PREDATORS IN SIMEN NATIONAL PARK.

IBEX HAVE PAID DEARLY FOR THEIR LONG, SCIMITARLIKE HORNS AS WELL AS ALMOST EVERY OTHER BODY PART, COVETED FOR BEAUTY AND SUPPOSED MEDICINAL POWERS AND DRIVING THIS GRACEFUL MOUNTAIN GOAT TO EXTINCTION OVER MUCH OF ITS RANGE. The Walia or Abyssinian ibex survives almost exclusively in Ethiopia's SIMEN NATIONAL PARK and World Heritage Site where it can still be seen, posing as befits the country's national symbol on a rocky crag silhouetted against the sky, its numbers gradually increasing since protection.

Ethiopia has nine national parks plus more than a dozen other nature set-asides. All were greatly affected by the civil war of the late 1980s and early 1990s that led to overthrow of the Marxist regime. Park infrastructures gradually are being restored with limited funds, hampered by the numbers of people living in the parks, which has led to other problems, including poaching, wood and grass cutting.

# ETHIOPIA

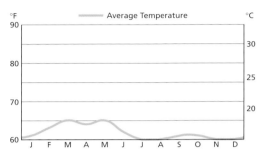

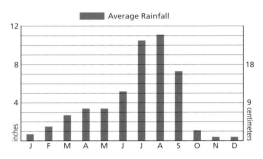

Gateway city: Addis Ababa

Vultures use hooked bills to tear into carcasses which they locate chiefly by sight, soaring high above their territories. These Rüppell's vultures are world's highest flying birds—one hit a jet at an altitude of 37,000 feet (11,000 m). A seething, squabbling feeding group like this can devour an antelope in 20 minutes. Afterward, gorged, they may have difficulty getting airborne again.

# SIMEN NATIONAL PARK

Most promising national park is Simen, although it has over 12,000 persons living in one of its sections, and must make do with an annual budget of around $15,000 U.S. Even so, it belongs among the world's great reserves.

Sharing this spectacular 84-square-mile (219-km²) national park carved out of northern Ethiopia's Simen Mountain Range with ibex are equally-rare Ethiopian wolves, previously known as Simen foxes or Abyssinian jackals, and golden-maned gelada baboons, endemic here. An estimated 20,000 of these striking baboons with pink chest patches—ferocious-looking but mild-tempered—roam the park in bands of up to 400 or so, wailing, moaning, sighing, crying out to alert all in earshot if they spot a predator. They dominate highland grasslands and share the park with gray-furred hamadryas baboons in the dry lowlands. Olive baboons and attractive, mischievous vervet and black-and-white colobus monkeys are found throughout the park, and guereza monkeys in its more wooded sections.

Tiny, agile klipspringers gambol fearlessly on tiptoes on rocks up to 13,000 feet (4,000 m). Striped, spiral-horned Menelik's bushbucks browse on shrubs, bushes, and trees.

Leopards and even more secretive wild and serval cats and caracals prey on smaller grazers, sharing, when they have to, with spotted hyenas and golden jackals.

Powerful lammergeiers or bearded vultures, called "bone-breakers" for their habit of dropping bones from great heights to shatter them and eat the marrow, nest on cliffs where they take off to soar effortlessly on nine-foot (3-m) wingspans on the park's north side. Updrafts along these escarpments attract other raptors as well—Verreaux's eagles, Rüppell's griffons, kestrels, lanner falcons, and augur buzzards.

Simen was occupied for a time by the Tigre People's Liberation Party which led the coalition that overthrew the Marxist regime. Local problems still exist to an extent that Simen has been declared a U.N. World Heritage Site in Danger—consult embassies for up-to-date information.

International visitors fly to Addis Ababa from which Ethiopian Airlines has good service throughout the country including to Gondar, only 60 miles (100 km) from park access at Debark. The park has simple accommodations and campsites, where rangers, guides, and riding and pack animals can be hired for treks of three to 10 days. Best times are November–February (wet seasons are February–March and July–September).

---

**FURTHER INFORMATION**

Chief Park Warden, Simen Mountains National Park, Debark, Ethiopia.

## ALSO OF INTEREST

**Abijatta-Shalla Rift Lakes National Park**, 342 square miles (887 km²) of lakes south of Addis Ababa ranging from shallow Lake Abijatta to 850-foot-deep (260-m) Lake Shalla—important wetlands for over 300 bird species, including lesser flamingos and a large breeding colony of threatened great white pelicans.

**Awash National Park**, 292 square miles (757 km²) in the Great Rift Valley east of Addis Ababa with large ungulate herds including Soemmering's gazelles, Beisa oryx, greater and lesser kudus. Predators include leopards, black-maned Abyssinian lions, cheetahs. Beautiful carmine bee-eaters are numerous, among over 400 bird species.

**Babile Elephant Sanctuary**, 2,656 square miles (6,880 km²) south of Harar, home to a tiny number of a possibly distinct elephant subspecies.

**Bale Mountains National Park** west of Goba, 953 square miles (2,471 km²) of ruggedly beautiful mountains including 14,000-foot (4,317-m) lake-dotted plateaus and the Herenna Forest—second largest moist tropical forest remaining in Ethiopia. It is an important catchment for four major rivers, important refuge for 46 mammals, stronghold for endangered Ethiopian wolves, mountain nyalas, Bohor reedbucks, and klipspringers. Forest-dwelling lions and African wild dogs are here also with 16 endemic birds including Rouget's rails, Abyssinian catbirds, wattled ibises, black-headed siskins, blue-winged geese, black-winged lovebirds, and gorgeous white-cheeked turacos. Even though Simen is better known internationally because of its Endangered World Heritage status, some consider Bale Mountains Ethiopia's finest reserve.

**Gambella National Park** consists of 1,953 square miles (5,061 km²) of lowland plains crossed by two rivers in far south-southeastern Ethiopia, important migration track for large herds of white-eared kobs and marsh-loving Nile lechwes, seriously threatened by agricultural development.

**Mago National Park**, also **Omo National Park** are parts of the Omo–Tama–Mago protected complex covering more than 2,403 square miles (6,226 km²) in the far southeast with large numbers of plains wildlife including buffalo, Beisa oryx, elephants, giraffes, leopards, African wild dogs.

**Nechisar National Park** is 198 square miles (514 km²) of grassy river-crossed plains east of Arba Minch in the south with prolific wildlife, including threatened leopards and Swayne's hartebeest, large herds of Burchell's zebras and Grant's gazelles, and fine birding.

**Yangudi-Rassa National Park** at 1,826 square miles (4,731 km²) is an arid area of flat open grassland and riverine forest northeast of Addis Ababa set aside for Somali wild asses, ancestors of domestic donkeys. The wild ass may or may not have survived recent troubles. Also here are cheetahs and leopards.

Spectacular **Blue Nile Falls** (aka **Tissisat**), 22 miles (35 km) east of Bahar Dar.

# GABON

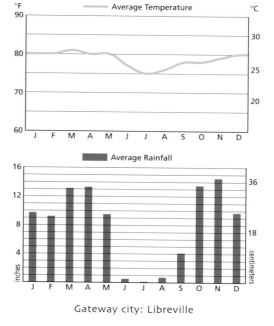

AFRICA

ROSY BEE-EATERS, PURPLE-THROATED
CUCKOO-SHRIKES, AND VIOLET-TAILED SUNBIRDS
SHARE GABON'S WILDLANDS WITH THOUSANDS OF
WESTERN LOWLAND GORILLAS AND FOREST ELEPHANTS.

THE WORLD'S MOST COLORFUL MAMMALS ARE HERE IN THEIR GREATEST NUMBERS ANYWHERE—HEAVY-SET MALE MANDRILLS WITH RED-AND-ELECTRIC-BLUE FACES, BUFF-GOLDEN BEARDS, NAKED SCARLET, PINK-AND-VIOLET RUMPS, AND GRIZZLED, DENSELY FURRED MANES AND BODIES.

Sometimes 1,000 or so gather in a single clearing, foraging on mushrooms or fallen fruit, turning over stones to find insect grubs. They may stay for weeks or months before moving on. No one really knows why they have such bright colors, though it's known that dominant males have the brightest.

Up to 20,000 western lowland gorillas are here as well, along with more than 60,000 forest elephants, an abundance of chimpanzees, forest buffalo, aardvarks, armored giant pangolins, a few rare, shy striped bongo forest antelopes, and some stunning birds, in large part because so much welcoming habitat remains intact or nearly so in this country just twice the size of England. Straddling the equator on Africa's west-central

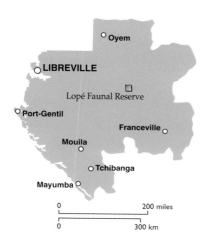

Gateway city: Libreville

67

## GABON

coast, its 103,000 square miles (267,000 km²) are a river-laced patchwork of tidal mangrove swamps, savannah, deep forest, and mountains, part of the Guineo-Congolian region which is the most biologically diverse on the continent. Some 74 percent of its lush rain forest has remained untouched, at least until recently, the largest undisturbed forest block in Africa, its major ecosystems for the most part intact.

Strikingly beautiful birds include black-headed and rosy bee-eaters, purple-throated cuckoo-shrikes, chocolate-backed kingfishers, vermiculated fishing owls, bubbling cisticolas, long-tailed hawks (tails as long as their bodies), violet-tailed sunbirds, brilliant bare-cheeked trogons, among a total of some 670 species.

A dozen reserves have been set aside in various stages of protection and development (not counting forest reserves) covering just over six percent of the country.

# Lopé Faunal Reserve

Of world importance, this 1,900 square miles (4,900 km²) with the highest density of large mammals ever recorded in a tropical rain forest is a reservoir of biological riches essentially undisturbed for the past 10,000 years. Parts of it may never have felt a human footfall. Riverine forests and pockets of savannah are filled with wildlife—mandrills, gorillas, strange, lanky gray-necked rock fowl, rosy bee-eaters, massive forest elephants and forest buffalo, water-loving sitatunga antelopes, bushpigs, chimpanzees, and a variety of monkeys—altogether at least 12 primates including endemic sun-tailed monkeys, only discovered in 1984.

Delicate little blue and yellow-backed duiker antelopes look for fallen fruits along the forest floor, whistling with alarm at the slightest disturbance, which could be anything—70 or so bush pigs snorting as they root along, elephants rumbling low-frequency vibrations that can alert any other elephant within several miles, a troop of mandrills stirring up the underbrush—or a little chameleon rustling along a branch, conical eyes swiveling in all directions like tiny gun turrets to spot insect prey.

Park boundaries were redrawn in 2000 after negotiations between the government, major logging companies, and environmental groups, including Wildlife Conservation Society (WCS) and World Wide Fund for Nature (WWF), opening some places to selective logging but permanently protecting pristine areas. While controversial, most hailed it as a forward-looking agreement by all parties and a victory for African wildlife.

Elephants live in highly organized matriarchal herds of 10 to 50, all related in some way. If separated they can stay in communication over many miles through low frequency sounds below human hearing range. During drought they use tusks to dig to underground water they are thought to locate by smelling the earth above.

Lopé, relatively dry because of its location in the rain shadow of the Chaillu mountain range, is 217 miles (350 km) east of Libreville, seven hours' drive or four hours by express train. Park entrance is near the Lopé railway station, as are several hotels with varying levels of accommodations. There is a well-developed network of paths for observation of large mammals in the savannah and of gorillas at Mikongo.

## ALSO OF INTEREST

**Bateke Plateaux National Park**, in the southern, uninhabited section of the Bateke Plateaux where a program of reintroducing gorilla orphans is under way.

**Crystal Mountains**, situated between Equatorial Guinea and the Ogooué River, said to be Africa's richest reserve in terms of plant diversity.

**Ivindo**, between the Ivindo and Ogooué rivers, with the most important waterfalls of central Africa and large concentrations of easily observed elephants and gorillas.

**Loango**, between the Nkomi and Ndogo lagoons—perhaps the only place in the world where one can see elephants, hippos, gorillas, and leopards on shining white beaches. Offshore is a large variety of whales and dolphins including humpback and killer whales. Tourist camps at Iguela and Sette Cama.

**Mayumba**, a thin strip of sand in far south Gabon, home of the largest concentration of nesting leatherback turtles on earth. Mayumba may become part of a transboundary park linked with CONKOUATI NATIONAL PARK in the Congo Republic (*see* p.48).

**Minkébé**, a large expanse of forest in the extreme northeast of the country, is virtually uninhabited. Ancient trees interwoven with elephant paths are used by bongos and giant forest hogs.

**Mwagné**, between the Lodié and Louayé rivers, adjoining the Congo Republic. Large bais or water-hole clearings with exceptionally large populations of elephants.

**Pongara**, the southern fringe of the Komo estuary, adjacent to Libreville and the Atlantic ocean front. Despite its proximity to Libreville the region still has many larger mammals, including buffalo and elephants.

---

**FURTHER INFORMATION**

Websites: www.gabonnationalparks.com and www.ecotourisme-gabon.com

# GHANA

GIANT SWALLOWTAILS NEARLY EIGHT INCHES
(20 CM) ACROSS ARE AMONG MORE THAN
650 BUTTERFLY SPECIES FLUTTERING AMONG
LEOPARDS, HONEY BADGERS, AND EAGLE-OWLS
IN GHANA'S KAKUM NATIONAL PARK.

S NAILS GLIDE ALONG, ANTENNAE WAVING, PEACEFULLY PROTECTED IN FETISHISTIC FORESTLANDS IN GHANA'S ASHANTI REGION. Nile crocodiles snooze secure in sacred pools at Paga. Chattering mona and black-and-white colobus monkeys frolic freely in consecrated woods in the Brong-Ahafo. Most of surviving southern marginal forest lies in sacred groves—all part of centuries-old totemistic belief here in mystical union between humans and all natural life.

First reserves date back to 1901 under Ghana's Wild Animals Preservation Ordinance. Now there are six national parks and several dozen other kinds of nature reserves in this relatively small West African country of 92,000 square miles (238,000 km²) bordering the Gulf of Guinea between Togo and Côte d'Ivoire.

They protect habitats ranging from virgin rain forest, semideciduous dry forest, and riverine gallery forest to lakes, marsh, and savannah. In them roam dozens of large mammal species including herds of endangered forest elephants, rare chestnut-striped bongos—largest of forest antelopes—and striking Diana monkeys with gray-chestnut bodies and black faces wreathed by white ruffs and beards.

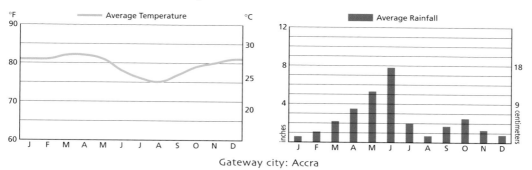

Gateway city: Accra

Shrill, fire-bellied woodpeckers hammer on tall ebony trees. Long-crested hawk-eagles with wind-tousled crests overlook savannah and forest clearings. Barbary shrikes with olive-yellow crowns and scarlet underparts scout for insects, sometimes in brilliant groups. Tall Denham's bustards peer over grasslands, and aptly-named splendid and beautiful long-tailed sunbirds look for nectar-filled blossoms, among more than 700 bird species.

## KAKUM NATIONAL PARK

Kakum National Park, 12 miles (19 km) north of seaside Cape Coast in Ghana's central region, protects—with adjacent Assin Attandaso Reserve—some 135 square miles (350 km²) of tropical moist natural evergreen and semi-deciduous forest. Sheltered in them are forest elephants, rare yellow-backed duiker antelopes, bongos, bushbucks, giant red river hogs, and seven kinds of primates—including handsome long-tailed Diana monkeys—flying squirrels, honey badgers, African civet cats, and a few seldom-seen leopards. More than 650 species of butterflies, many endemic to this place, ranging in size from tiny blues to giant swallowtails just under eight inches (20 cm) across, flutter around flowering vines and moist puddles.

Five kinds of raucous hornbills with outsized beaks sail among fruiting trees. Fraser's eagle-owls roam through the night. Senegal and scarlet-tailed African gray parrots can seem to be everywhere, chattering and screeching, among more than 300 bird species. Best birding spots include Abrafo trails, roads to Antwikwaa, Kruwa logging road.

A spectacular 1,180-foot (360-m) canopy walkway constructed of a series of single wooden planks with rope handrails enables visitors to walk over and through branches 130 feet (40 m) above the forest floor, designed with help from Conservation International. It affords rain forest sights possible in no other way—shining green Verreaux's touracos looping by on red-flashing wings, monkeys swinging through branches, all at eye level. But it can be unnerving for those insecure about heights, especially with a support that tends to sway, despite steel cables and tests meeting world-class safety standards (some say it's a once-in-a-lifetime experience, others say that's what they're afraid of). In any case much of this richly diverse park is best seen from trails below, either self-guided or with a guide usefully pointing out where to look.

A visitor center an hour's drive (20 miles/33 km) north of Cape Coast on the Jukwa Road offers exhibits, helpful staff, and literature, including an excellent *Field Guide to Kakum National Park*. It can be a day trip, or lengthier stay at a nearby rest house.

It's sometimes possible to arrange overnight camping trips with special excursions to watch birds or track elephants. Campers with their own equipment can stay on a tree platform. Or, a few miles south is a "boatel" with lodging on a terrace overlooking a crocodile pool, with excellent birding. Facilities at Kakum as over much of Ghana are not comfort on a world-class scale, but they are improving. At Kakum especially, the government hopes to increase ecotourism with community involvement in permanent sustainable environmental protection. Best times are other than March–June when heaviest rainfall occurs, but humidity averages 90 percent any time.

**FURTHER INFORMATION**

Senior Wildlife Warden, P.O. Box 895, Cape Coast, Ghana, Tel: (+233) 042-23-96 or 22-888, Fax: (+233) 042-28-29; or the Cape Coast Tourist Board, Savoy Hotel, Tel: (+233) 042-29-34.

# MOLE NATIONAL PARK

Mole National Park in the northern region is Ghana's largest—over 1,970 square miles (5,100 km²) of savannah woodland—and, many feel, its premier reserve, with abundant wildlife and numerous trails from which they can be seen, either on foot or from vehicles. Large mammals include about 800 elephants, 1,000 buffalo, and significant populations of hippos, warthogs, antelopes such as Defassa waterbucks, kob, oribi, bushbucks, roan, hartebeest, gray and red-flanked duikers, hyenas, a few (rarely seen) lions and leopards, and five primates, most visibly olive baboons. Two kinds of crocodiles inhabit water holes.

Over 300 bird species include martial eagles—often an easily seen nesting pair—white-headed and saddle-bill storks, white-backed and palmnut vultures, herons and egrets, and, beauties all, Abyssinian rollers, violet plantain-eaters, red, black and yellow Barbary shrikes, and red-throated bee-eaters, which have a nesting colony near a water hole.

To maximize chances, hire a guide and go in a vehicle (best bring your own—the park's aren't always functioning). But to absorb the wild feeling of the place and see smaller creatures, especially birds, guided walking can be best. A network of tracks crisscrosses the park.

Mole is 390 miles (626 km) north of Accra and 85 miles (135 km) west of Tamale. Busses go directly to the park.

Saddle-bills are the largest African storks—up to 57 inches (145 cm) tall—with no voice box muscles, so they communicate by noisily rattling black-banded crimson bills. They feed in shallows on frogs, reptiles, and fish, nipping off spines before tossing them up to swallow them head-first.

Best times are drier November–May when wildlife gather around water holes and it's easier getting around. Visitors can camp at the park or stay at the park's comfortable Mole Hotel—water and power can be unreliable but it's on an escarpment overlooking two busy water holes where elephants trumpet at night. There's also a fairly comfortable rest house at Larabanga, location of reputedly Ghana's oldest and holiest mud-and-thatch mosque and possibly its oldest building.

---

**FURTHER INFORMATION**

Senior Wildlife Warden, Mole National Park, P.O. Box 8, Damongo, Northern Region, Tel: (+233) 071-25-63.

---

## ALSO OF INTEREST

**Bia National Park**, an isolated 120-square-mile (305-km²) virgin rain forest west of Kumasi. More than 80 mammals include forest elephants, bongos, forest buffalo, leopards, giant forest hogs, many duikers, plus more than 235 bird species, 650 kinds of butterflies, 200-foot-tall (60-m) trees.

**Buabeng-Fiema Sanctuary** village north of Nkoranza in Brong Ahafo, where colobus and mona monkey colonies live in a sacred grove symbiotically with human community.

**Digya National Park** on western edge of enormous Lake Volta, with elephants, hippos, waterbucks, others.

**Gbelle Game Reserve**, 10 miles (17 km) south of Tumu, with herds of hippos, elephants, roan antelopes.

**Keta-Angar Lagoon**, important wetland breeding ground for migratory birds.

**Volta River Estuary** has many water-oriented birds, also nest sites for rare hawksbill, leatherback, and green sea turtles.

**Wechiau Community Hippo Sanctuary**, Upper West Region, also nesting red-cheeked cordonbleu birds (usually within a yard of a wasp nest) and possibly threatened crowned cranes.

Most international travelers arrive at Accra's jetport. Many hotels there can advise on rental cars, air travel around the country, taxi-guides, or use of the ubiquitous and generally reliable STC busses, also "tro-tros" (roughly any vehicle other than a bus or car).

---

**FURTHER INFORMATION**

Chief Wildlife Officer, Department of Wildlife, P.O. Box M-239, Accra, Ghana; Ghana Friends of the Earth, P.O. Box 3794, Accra, Tel: (+233) 021-22-59-63, Fax: (+233) 021-22-79-93; Ghana Wildlife Society, P.O. Box 13252, Accra, Tel: (+233) 021-66-35-00, E-mail: wildsoc@ighmail.com, Website: www.ecotour.org.gh

---

# GUINEA

SPECIES THAT SURVIVED THE ICE AGES—
GREEN-TAILED BRISTLEBIRDS, GOLD MALIMBAS,
YELLOW-HEADED PICATHARTES—REMAIN AMONG
DWARF CROCODILES IN DIÉCKÉ AND OTHER
GUINEA FOREST PRESERVES.

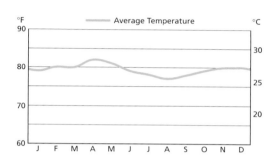

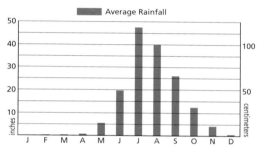

Gateway city: Conakry

## MOUNT NIMBA NATURE RESERVE

The huge species diversity found in Guinea's Mount Nimba Nature Reserve, one of the richest in Africa, is due to the variety of habitats on its eroded quartzite mountain spine, which is known as the "Guinean backbone." This U.N. World Heritage Site and Biosphere Reserve of 66 square miles (171 km²) marks the intersection of Guinea, Côte d'Ivoire, and Liberia. Covered with grasslands, wooded savannah, and stream-laced forests, the range rises abruptly from the plains and rolling hills of the surrounding lowlands, reaching 5,780 feet (1,752 m) at Mont Richard-Molard, a starkly beautiful barrier along the country's northeast–southwest axis. The southern side gathers moisture from the Atlantic, while the rain-shadowed northern side is subject to dry Harmattan winds from the Sahara. Standing in dramatic isolation from its surroundings, it may have served as a refugium for species that endured the last ice ages.

75

Birds of the Guinean Nimba Mountains are likely to be similar at corresponding altitudes to those of the Liberian side where some 380 species have been recorded. Threatened species include green-tailed bristlebills, the very local Sierra Leone prinia, and yellow-headed picathartes (or rock fowl). Some 2,000 vascular plants include more than 100 orchid species, among them at least 35 endemics.

Visits can be arranged for organized groups.

Major threats include slash-and-burn agriculture plus iron-ore mining, which already has damaged the Liberian section by removing soil and poisoning streams with heavy metal runoff, along with collateral damage from mine workers and related logistical activities. As Liberian deposits are exhausted, pressure has mounted on Guinea, which has iron-ore deposits estimated at 300 million metric tonnes as well as diamonds, gold, copper, manganese, uranium, and the world's third-largest deposits of bauxite, used in aluminum. The area is under threat as well from large numbers of Liberian civil war refugees.

---

**FURTHER INFORMATION**

Station Biologique des Monts Nimba, S/C INRDG, B.P. 561, Conakry, Guinea, Tel: (+224) 45-43-06, Fax: (+224) 45-32-17; Guinée-Ecologie, B.P. 3266, Conakry, Tel: (+224) 46-24-96, E-mail: dmsaliou@afribone.net.gm

---

Deforestation has cost Guinea, a country just slightly larger than Britain—95,000 square miles (246,000 km²)—almost 98 percent of its original forest, including much of the mangrove along its 175-mile (280-km) coastline. Environmental consciousness in Guinea has risen in recent years, however, and conservation is becoming a concern.

## ALSO OF INTEREST

Among important protected areas are the following:

**Massif du Ziama**, a 448-square-mile (1,162-km²) World Biosphere Reserve northwest of Mount Nimba (and *c.* 60 miles/100 km northwest of Nzérékoré), with similar ecology. Some 287 bird species have been recorded, including brown-cheeked hornbills, western wattled cuckoo-shrikes, black-capped rufous warblers, and Nimba flycatchers.

OPPOSITE: Baboons are Africa's largest monkeys, their doglike heads unmistakable. They'll eat anything—grass, crocodile eggs, even newborn antelopes. They like to drink every day but can survive for long periods by licking night dew from their fur. Main predators are leopards, but even leopards hesitate to take on a baboon's long, sharp fangs.

**Diécké Forest Reserve**, a 266-square-mile (688-km²) lowland rain forest in the extreme southeast, south of Nzérékoré, close to the Liberian border. Threatened and near-threatened species include chimpanzees, Diana monkeys, sooty mangabeys, four species of forest duikers (Jentinck's, black, yellow-backed, and zebra), bongos, giant forest hogs, and West African dwarf crocodiles. Rare birds include yellow-casqued hornbills, rufous-winged illadopsis, copper-tailed glossy starlings, and gold malimbes, only recently discovered.

**Badiar National Park**, created in 1985, adjacent to Senegal's NIOKOLO-KOBA NATIONAL PARK (*see* p.127), is a mosaic of savannah types and gallery forest, 147 square miles (382 km²) with elephants, roan antelopes, kobs, leopards, spotted hyenas, baboons.

**Haut Niger National Park**, established in 1997, about 2,350 square miles (6,100 km²) protecting one of the last remnants of relatively intact dry woodlands in the West African Guinea savannah belt. A small group of surviving lions has found refuge here. Over 300 bird species have been recorded.

International flights go to the capital, Conakry, with lodging and car rentals. Best time to visit is dry season November–April. Major roads are usually passable year-round, but roads to or in protected areas are often poor, necessitating 4WD. Busses and mini-busses are cheap, but car rental (requiring a driver) is expensive. Some major towns can be reached by air.

---

**FURTHER INFORMATION**

Directeur, Direction des Forêts et Chasse, Ministère de l'Agriculture et des Resources Animales, P.O. Box 624, Conakry, Guinea, Tel: (+224) 44-32-49; Ministère des Resources Naturelles et de l'Environnement (Le Chef de Cabinet), B.P. 295, Conakry; Direction Nationale de l'Environnement, Ministère des Resources Naturelles et de l'Environnement, B.P. 3118, Conakry; Le President, Association des Amis de la Nature et de l'Environnement (Assoane), B.P. 206 bis, Conakry.

# KENYA

SOME OF AFRICA'S RAREST ANIMALS—
SHY, STRIPED BONGOS, MELANISTIC BLACK
SERVAL CATS AND SMALL, FIERCE GOLDEN CATS—
FIND SAFETY IN KENYA'S HIGH, MOUNTAINOUS
ABERDARE NATIONAL PARK.

KENYA'S WILDLIFE IS PROBABLY THE BEST KNOWN OF ANY COUNTRY IN THE WORLD, WITH ITS INSTANTLY RECOGNIZABLE ARRAY OF LIONS, LEOPARDS, ELEPHANTS, GREAT THRONGS OF WILDEBEESTS AND ZEBRAS IN MIGRATION, AS WELL AS MORE THAN 1,000 SPECIES OF COLORFUL BIRDS.

Millions of pink flamingos congregate on alkaline lakes. Giraffes nibble from acacia treetops and rare bongos browse the understory. On mountaintops, alpine plants grow to prodigious heights—heathers can be more than 30 feet (10 m) tall.

In the MAASAI MARA WILDLIFE RESERVE, wildebeests, zebras, and gazelles join in one of the world's great wildlife spectacles every year when they come from SERENGETI NATIONAL PARK in Tanzania (*see* p.145) to forage for fresh grass. AMBOSELI and TSAVO are famous for their elephants. Probably the most familiar picture of Africa is of elephants in Amboseli against a scenic backdrop of snow-capped Mount Kilimanjaro.

One of the world's highest national parks is atop dazzling snowcapped Mount Kenya.

Animals that never (or almost never) need to drink thrive at SAMBURU/ BUFFALO SPRINGS national reserves, which have the only permanent water sources in an other-wise arid, hostile environment.

# KENYA

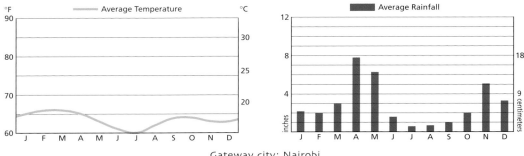

Gateway city: Nairobi

Habitat variety in this East African country of 225,000 square miles (583,000 km²) ranges from Indian Ocean coastal beaches through high plateau country and a chain of volcanic mountains up to 17,058 feet (5,199 m), and finally to the dramatic escarpment of the Great Rift Valley in the west. The equator divides the country roughly in half so its lowlands are hot, and, where well-watered, steamy, and where arid on the northern deserts, searing—but its highlands are cool and pleasant. Rainy seasons are October–December and April–June.

---

**FURTHER INFORMATION**

Kenya Wildlife Service Nairobi Headquarters, P.O. Box 40241, Nairobi, Kenya,

Tel: (+254 2) 602345, 606068, Fax: (+254 2) 505866, 501752, Website: www.kenya-wildlife-service-org

---

## ABERDARE NATIONAL PARK

Some of the rarest animals in Africa—bongos, melanistic black serval cats, and small, fierce golden cats—live in the rarified atmosphere of high mountainous Aberdare National Park.

It is a world apart from the surrounding grasslands and cultivated areas. Much of the Aberdare mountain range is included in this 296-square-mile (767-km²) isolated volcanic massif which forms part of the eastern wall of the Rift Valley. In high moors grow 30-foot (7-m) heathers and lobelias, mutants of alpine plants, and on lower eastern slopes, luxuriant forests where heavy rain falls through most of the year. In rushing trout streams clawless otters compete with giant kingfishers to feed on freshwater crabs. Waterfalls cascade hundreds of feet.

In the forest are red duikers, diminutive suni antelopes, bushbucks, elephants, buffalo, giant forest hogs, and colobus monkeys, and some of the oldest trees in Kenya, gnarled, twisted cedars and hagenias. Cape chestnuts can be covered with delicate pink blossoms.

Black leopards have been recorded, as well as black genets and nearly-black male bushbucks, a melanistic reaction, it's believed, to the sun's burning ultraviolet rays this close to the equator.

Four species of scintillating metallic sunbirds brighten the glades including brilliant violet tacazzes. Crowned monkey-eating eagles are everywhere. Uncommon montane francolins as well as scaly and Jackson's varieties and silvery-cheeked hornbills enliven woods and moors with noisy calls at dusk. African goshawks are here, along with crowned and Ayres' hawk-eagles, mountain buzzards, and rufous-breasted sparrow-hawks, among over 250 bird species.

Aberdare is home to two famous lodges where wild animals come to water holes and saltlicks and can be seen under floodlights through the night: the Ark—most likely place in Kenya to see bongos—and Treetops, where England's Queen Elizabeth was visiting when she learned of her father's death and her accession to the throne. There are also park campsites.

## AMBOSELI NATIONAL PARK

Amboseli National Park is famous for its elephants. However, although the most familiar African picture is of elephants here—trumpeting, in a herd, with families, with babies—against a backdrop of snowcapped Mount Kilimanjaro, that tallest free-standing mountain in the world is not located in Amboseli or even in Kenya. It is in neighboring Tanzania.

But the best view of it is here and its overwhelming presence is a constant. Lions, cheetahs, giraffes, buffalo, impalas, gazelles—most of Amboseli's animals—can be observed in front of this stunning peak which holds one-fifth of Africa's ice, now melting.

Amboseli is affected not only visually but environmentally by Kilimanjaro. Its ancient eruption laid down the light volcanic dust which makes up the mineral-rich topsoil (Amboseli comes from a Maasai word meaning "salty dust"). The moisture which seeps from its higher elevations and makes its way underground to a series of springs here furnishes the only permanent water source in an area which at first glance appears to be an arid dust bowl. The springs are focus for some 95 percent of the region's wildlife. ("How can such enormous numbers of large game live in this extraordinary desert?" the explorer Joseph Thomson asked a century ago.)

When Lake Amboseli, a salt pan, is entirely dry—which is most of the year—spring-fed swamps such as Enkongo Narok in the park's center, bordered by yellow-barked fever trees, are brightly green, providing not only water for drinking and bathing but moistening nearby grass-lands and acacia woodlands as well.

Buffalo luxuriate in its muck. Cattle egrets trail them, snapping up insects flushed by their activities. Hippos grunt in deeper pools.

Zebras and wildebeest wade knee-deep in the Logenya Swamp east of Ol Tukai.

Birds find it welcoming too. Madagascar squacco herons stalk in the reeds, among over 420 bird species recorded here. On floating vegetation are long-toed lapwings with carmine bills,

distinctive plovers with the habits of lily-trotters. Gregarious Taveta golden weavers, rare elsewhere, are locally common.

Bat-eared foxes bask outside dens on the open plains. Black-backed jackals are almost everywhere, as are black-faced vervet monkeys and yellow baboons.

Handsome fringe-eared oryx can subsist in dry parts where most others can't, digesting tough dry forage. Graceful gerenuks almost never drink, getting moisture from tree leaves which they eat while standing erect on their hind legs (their name in Somali means "giraffe-neck").

Elephants may be more conspicuous than anyplace else in Kenya, partly because they have become accustomed to close observation by visitors and scientists, as have lions and giraffes.

## Lake Nakuru National Park

More than a million (at peak, two million) flamingos can turn shores and alkaline waters pink when they gather in stupendous numbers to consume blue-green algae in Lake Nakuru. There are more than 400 other bird species as well—sometimes large gatherings of white pelicans—and among mammals, rare white and black rhinos, leopards, hippos, waterbucks, reedbucks, and klipspringers, and (introduced) Rothschild's giraffes. Flamingo numbers depend on algae which depends on weather and water conditions—but natural life is always abundant and interesting. There are lodges and campsites, 97 miles (157 km) drive from Nairobi.

## Maasai Mara Wildlife Reserve

More than a million grazing animals join in one of the great wildlife spectacles on earth every summer when, following their need for fresh grass, they trek up to Maasai Mara from Serengeti National Park in Tanzania.

Thousands of Thomson's gazelles and a quarter-million zebras join the great throngs of shaggy wildebeests, some marching single-file in long lines, others a dozen abreast. Accompanied by half-grown young ones born in Tanzania, they crowd the landscape as far as the eye can see.

They cross raging rivers, many of them drowning in the attempt, in the drive for renewed sustenance. Sometimes they perish unnecessarily and become food for crocodiles in a river they could easily avoid.

Lions are Africa's largest carnivores and the only cats that live in large family groups—advantageous for their group-ambush hunting style. They're also the most sexually dimorphic—males are significantly larger than females, with long head and neck manes.

Largest lion population in Kenya is here, in family prides of 40 or more individuals. Cheetahs, fastest of big cats, pose regally atop termite mounds, scouting out likely quarry, stalking them through green-gold grass, then streaking after them at top speeds of 70 miles an hour (112 kph).

Stealthy leopards are as visible here as any place in Africa, sometimes with cubs.

Remains of predators' victims or those which die from other causes are cleaned up by smaller carnivores such as jackals and bat-eared foxes, or huge vultures and marabou storks, looking, it is often said, like undertakers. Nothing is wasted. Miniscule scraps go to insects which feed the smallest mammals as well as the abundant and colorful bird population.

# KENYA

Seldom does anything remain which could be food for anybody. That which does becomes fertilizer for the rich variety of plant life that feeds next year's migrants as well as other grazing and browsing animals which are here all year—impalas, Grant's gazelles, kongoni, towering giraffes, massive elephants, Cape buffalo, and a few black rhinoceros, and, uncommon elsewhere, topi and roan antelopes. Huge hippos come up from the waterways to forage at night.

Elephants pull up grass or pull down edible greenery and bark from favorite thickets, consuming up to 300 pounds (136 kg) a day, wearing out their teeth on this harsh provender but growing another set—six sets in a 65-year lifetime.

Pel's fishing owls swoop down along the Mara River while 52 other raptors, including secretary birds, wearing "quill pens" behind their ears, peer for prey about the plains,

which they share with statuesque bustards, the largest birds that can fly. Altogether 65 different species of mammals and more than 400 bird species are here, most of them easily seen on this 700 square miles (1,812 km²) of rolling plains bisected by the Mara River in the Great Rift Valley.

By mid-September wildebeest have exhausted much of the short grass which they prefer (and are best able to eat and digest) and begin to turn south to return to Tanzania where the grasslands have freshened since their departure. There, between late January and mid-March, females will begin to give birth to some 300,000 tiny, reddish-buff, black-faced calves which they conceived eight months earlier, and start the whole cycle again. Fossil evidence suggests they have been doing this here for more than a million years.

Wildebeest give birth to 90 percent of their calves during three weeks early in the rainy season. Young are born looking around and able to run within minutes of their birth—important because herds are constantly on the move, and staying with the group is vital in avoiding predation.

## KENYA

# MOUNT KENYA NATIONAL PARK

Atop dazzling 17,058-foot (5,199-m) Mount Kenya, Kenya's highest mountain, is one of the world's highest and most beautiful national parks—286 square miles (704 km²) of forest, moors, ice, snow, rock, and jewel-like lakes straddling the equator and containing rare and interesting natural life, some found only here.

Heathers grow 30 feet (9 m) high. Lobelias of similar giant proportions offer nectar-filled blossoms to long-tailed scarlet-tufted malachite sunbirds, and their leaves to furry little Mount Kenya rock hyrax.

Black forest hogs up to 500 pounds (225 kg) (tell them from smaller warthogs by skinny tails held down, not up, when they run) root under towering camphor trees 150 feet (46 m) high alongside reclusive bongos, seldom-seen reddish antelopes with bold tiger-like white stripes and thick spiraled horns. Elephants and buffalo are common. Rarely seen elsewhere, but found here, are attractive large-spotted genet cats and greater galagos or bushbabies. Endemic but hard to see are Mount Kenya shrews and mole rats.

Each elevation has its special habitat niche. The lower forest and its clearings have waterbucks, bushbucks, block-fronted duikers, and handsome, acrobatic black-and-white colobus monkeys. Around 11,000 feet (3,350 m) forest ends and moors begin, with less abundant but equally interesting flora and fauna—lumbering ox-like elands, Africa's largest bovids; mountain reedbucks, wild dogs, leopards, and birdlife which includes Mackinder's eagle-owls with wild flame-orange eyes, and confidently tame little mountain chats.

Above 14,500 feet (4,500 m) the mountain becomes a world of rock and ice. Mt. Kenya has seven major glaciers whose gradual melting is the basis for Kenya's most important permanent watershed, providing fertile loams to the country's richest farmlands lower down, and to the 700 square miles (2,000+ km²) of its largest forest reserve.

Its beauty is unsurpassed—"a gleaming snow-white peak" said Joseph Thomson "with sparkling facets which scintillated with the superb beauty of a colossal diamond."

There are four tracks up the mountain. Anyone moderately fit can attempt the ascent of 16,350-foot (4,885-m) Point Lenana, third-highest peak. Be warned, however: it's not the easy walk it is sometimes described and should be taken gradually to avoid acute mountain sickness. More than half the world's cases of sometimes-fatal climbers' pulmonary edema occur here.

Another and fine way to see wildlife is to stay at Mountain Lodge where animals come to saltlicks all day and through the night, visible under lights.

Mt. Kenya is 120 miles (193 km) drive northeast of Nairobi.

# Samburu/Buffalo Springs

Animals that never or seldom need to drink thrive at the twin reserves of Samburu/Buffalo Springs which stretch for miles on both sides of the Ewaso Nyiro River, an oasis amid harsh but stunning scenery (and superb sunsets) in northern Kenya. It is the main Kenyan gathering-place for a wonderfully diverse and interesting array of creatures, some which have adapted to cope with arid, hostile conditions, and others drawn like a magnet to the only permanent water around.

True desert dwellers like the Beisa oryx, gerenuks, and Grant's gazelles are virtually water-independent; others have learned to get by with little. Harlequin-marked oryx can live on moisture from roots and tubers which they dig, and, like the elands here, can endure extreme heat by letting their body temperature rise several degrees in daytime and then cool down at night. Elands also conserve water by halting perspiration.

Gerenuks stand bolt upright on hind legs to stretch for succulent leaves most other browsers can't reach. The gerenuk's high reach is helpful in areas overgrazed by goats, where high-strung little dik-dik antelopes are at a distinct disadvantage—their numbers are declining. Others, such as Grant's gazelles, can make a living beyond the range of water-dependent grazers.

Grevy's zebras in neat pin-striped suits (unlike their broad-striped common cousins) and reticulated giraffes (the most beautiful giraffe with neater geometric markings than the rest) need moisture but not in great amounts.

Along the river, waterbucks feed on riverine grasses. Saddle-billed storks hunt frogs and fish. Crocodiles bask on sandbars.

Elephants come in herds of a hundred or so to drink and bathe making this muddy river even muddier. Huge flocks of helmeted and cobalt-blue-breasted vulturine guinea fowls may quench their thirst here. Thousands of sandgrouse and doves appear at freshwater streams and pools at Buffalo Springs.

Shaggy-maned striped hyenas, uncommon elsewhere, thrive. Lion prides are reclusive, but leopards, for years baited for tourists at lodges, are less shy than elsewhere.

Samburu is about five hours' drive (220 miles/355 km) north of Nairobi, a dramatic descent of almost 6,000 feet (1,830 m) from the flanks of Mt. Kenya to the desert floor. Air temperatures rise as the road descends.

There are several lodges and campsites on the two reserves. Samburu Lodge (which also has an airstrip) has especially good viewing of crocodiles, water-oriented birds and others such as hornbills, weavers, and starlings. Nile monitors, semi-aquatic lizards up to seven feet (2+ m) long, are frequent visitors to the terrace, looking for scraps.

KENYA

# Tsavo National Park

Ruggedly beautiful Tsavo National Park (East and West) is among Africa's largest wildlife reserves—some 8,000 square miles (21,283 km²) where, in Tsavo East, renowned elephant herds sometimes estimated upward of 6,000 are a unique red color different from anyplace else, due to iron-rich lateritic soil in which they take mud or dust baths.

Hippopotami walk on the bottom of clear aqua-blue Mzima Springs, supplied by water which originates on Mt. Kilimanjaro's snowy peak and flows underground until it gushes out here at a peak rate of 110 million gallons (500 million liters) a day.

Habitat ranges from savannah to riverine forest to mountains up to 7,000 feet (2,150 m) and includes huge baobab "upside-down" trees which themselves are habitat to hornbills and dozens of other winged and four-footed creatures.

All the carnivores are here—lions, cheetahs, leopards, and both spotted and striped hyenas—keeping an eye on the grazers and browsers: zebras, giraffes, gazelles, elands, and, in Tsavo East, the only in-situ population of rare hirola or Hunter's hartebeest, the most threatened large antelope in Africa.

Aardwolves are here, but despite their menacing name, these miniature hyenas subsist mainly on harvester termites.

Dainty goat-like klipspringers bound over rocky outcrops on tiny rubbery hooves which cling to the steepest incline, getting what water they need from succulent forage. So do gerenuks, standing on hind legs to get leaves unavailable to others. Fringe-eared oryx, which can regulate their body temperature, are also present.

Lesser kudus with elegant spiraled horns find 118 kinds of nutritious browse plants in the Tsavo East Galana area.

Miniature dik-dik antelopes skitter through busy woodland tracts. Savannah monitors, formidable dragonlike lizards, prowl the plains for small animal prey. Many species and large numbers can be accommodated on these vast parks—more than 70 mammal and more than 1,000 plant species, more than 400 kinds of birds—but they are so spread out the population in any one place may not be dense.

Shrubby woodlands hold an extraordinary array of brightly plumaged birds including yellow-billed hornbills, orange-breasted parrots, metallic-feathered sunbirds on flowering trees, superb and golden-breasted starlings—altogether there are 12 species of starling, including uncommon

OPPOSITE:Giraffes are the world's tallest animals, up to 16 feet (5 m) tall and weighing about a ton. To maintain blood flow up to the brain their blood pressure is about twice that of other mammals; special circulatory valves keep them from fainting when their heads are lowered to forage or drink.

Fischer's—as well as fish eagles, bustards, scops owls, sacred ibis, open-billed storks, and black herons or "umbrella birds" which shade their heads with their wings while hunting.

Migrating palearctic birds sometimes funnel through the gap between the Ngulia and Kichwa mountains in flocks of thousands.

At mid-century there were an estimated 60,000 elephants here, too many for the scrub woodland which their foraging reduced to grasslands. Large-scale poaching in the 1970s and '80s reduced herds by 90 percent. Now, with international ivory trade suspended and intense anti-poaching efforts, numbers have stabilized at around 6,000 and they roam in family herds of up to 100 individuals, from 60-year-old matriarchs to lively newborns. Their distinctive red hue sometimes causes them to be mistaken at a distance for castle-like earthen termite mounds which dot the landscape. The mounds in turn can be mistaken for elephants (except when cheetahs use them as lookout perches).

Tsavo's lions became world-famous when two males began killing workers employed to build the Uganda railroad in the 1890s. The man-eaters were shot and the trait fortunately was not passed on to others (the man-eaters were stuffed and are now on display at the Field Museum in Chicago).

Like many wildlife reserves, Tsavo was set aside for wildlife because it seemed unsuitable for any other purpose—too dry for farming, infested with tsetse flies, now a glorious natural haven.

## ALSO OF INTEREST

Thousands of pink flamingos are attracted to seasonal blue-green algae on alkaline **Lake Bogoria National Reserve**. Uncommon spiral-horned greater kudu live on steep slopes of the lake's eastern and southern shores. Impressive hot springs erupt in boiling geysers on the northern end.

Just 20 miles (32 km) north is **Lake Baringo**, with over 400 species of interesting birds, including Verreaux's eagles, rare bristle-crowned starlings, endemic Jackson's hornbills and the largest nesting colony of Goliath herons in East Africa. It was here that Scottish geologist John Gregory devised his theory of continental drift. The eastern Rift Valley is now named for him. There are lodges and campsites nearby.

**Lake Naivasha** is highest and purest of all the Rift Lakes and many say the most beautiful, with secluded lagoons and channels, fringed by feathery-headed papyrus, ringed by the Aberdare mountain range, renowned for great numbers of birds of more than 400 species. One of the best ways to see these is to take a boat out to the **Crescent Island Wildlife Sanctuary** where there are also zebras, giraffes, antelopes, and a few camels. There are lodges and a camp, just 50 miles (80 km) from Nairobi.

**Nairobi National Park**, in view of Nairobi's skyscrapers, has a large and varied wildlife population, with more bird and mammal species than national parks many times its size.

# LIBERIA

TINY, TUSKED WATER CHEVROTAINS,
HALF-DEER-HALF-PIG, VIRTUALLY UNCHANGED
IN 30 MILLION YEARS OF EVOLUTION, GRAZE
ALONGSIDE STREAMS FREQUENTED BY LEOPARDS,
GIANT FOREST HOGS, AND RIVER OTTERS
IN SAPO NATIONAL PARK.

VIRGIN RAIN FOREST THAT ONCE COVERED MUCH OF HUMID LOWLAND WEST AFRICA REMAINS RELATIVELY UNTOUCHED IN THIS SMALL COASTAL COUNTRY ORIGINALLY SETTLED BY FREED AMERICAN SLAVES. However, civil wars and their fallout have devastated Liberia and its wildlife has not been spared.

What once was the last, best stronghold of fast-disappearing forest elephants was here; now total population is estimated at 100–200 individuals. Pygmy hippopotamus numbers also have been sharply reduced.

Among 125 other large mammal species, almost all affected by years of civil unrest, are bongos with chestnut-and-white striped sides, along with Jentink's duikers, with black heads and necks and white collars, whose Afrikaans name translates as "diver" for their habit of diving into thick cover when startled. Others include leopards, colobus monkeys, chimpanzees, honey badgers, mongeese, African civets.

Some deep forest areas still are uncatalogued, but at least 610 bird species are known to be

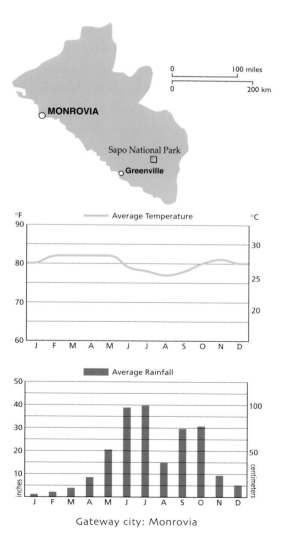

Gateway city: Monrovia

91

here including rufous fishing owls, copper-tailed glossy starlings, yellow-bearded greenbuls, and rare white-breasted guinea fowl. A 1999 survey in one area found a rare black-collared love-bird (a parrot), which had not been seen here in over 100 years.

There are some 74 known reptiles and amphibians, over 2,000 flowering plants, and more than 1,000 described insects.

## SAPO NATIONAL PARK

Sapo National Park is of special significance, 505 square miles (1,308 km²) bounded on the west by the Sinoe River and on the north by the Putu mountains, with all the major wildlife species of the Upper Guinea forests. Mammals include water chevrotains—primitive, tusked, rabbit-sized, looking half-pig-half-deer—golden cats, big, forest-dwelling drill baboons, seven species of monkeys, seven species of duiker antelopes, three kinds of armored pangolins, as well as river otters, giant forest hogs, and African civets. There are hundreds of kinds of butterflies. Birds include African fish eagles, Senegalese kingfishers, great blue turacos, African gray parrots—largest parrot in Africa—bee-eaters, sunbirds, rollers, egrets.

While conditions remain difficult, tourism has been resumed. It remains more than a 10-hour drive along a coastal road to Sapo. The trip itself can be interesting, but for non-Liberians a guide is essential.

Threats include logging, mining, slash-and-burn agriculture, and poaching, all exacerbated by the country's grinding poverty which affects both population and government agencies set up both to help them and protect natural resources.

Six other areas have been proposed as nature preserves, including **Mount Nimba**, with fine birds and wildlife but a center of iron mining.

---

**FURTHER INFORMATION**

Wildlife and National Park Office, Forest Development Authority, P.O. Box 3010, Monrovia, Liberia, Tel: (+218) 271-865/252-250/-251/-252, Tlx: c/o GFM, 44230 AA MONR.LI.

# MADAGASCAR

GOBLIN-LIKE AYE-AYE LEMURS USE
FIVE-INCH (13-CM) LONG MIDDLE CLAWS
TO PROBE TREE CREVICES WHERE KEEN EARS TELL THEM
INSECTS ARE BURIED DEEP IN THE BARK.

MADAGASCAR BROKE AWAY FROM AFRICA ABOUT 165 MILLION YEARS AGO AND WHILE IT DIDN'T GO FAR—ABOUT 280 MILES (450 KM) ACROSS THE MOZAMBIQUE STRAIT—IT WAS FAR ENOUGH FOR PLANTS AND ANIMALS TO EVOLVE INTO LIVING THINGS UNLIKE THOSE ANYPLACE ELSE.

More than 80 percent of all animal species on this world's fourth-largest island are unique to Madagascar—97 percent leaving out those that could fly here, such as birds and bats.

Here are dozens of different species of lemurs with large, round, unblinking eyes that give them one of the most intense, hypnotic gazes of any creature. Known as pro-simians or pre-monkeys because they share characteristics with ancestral primates, they range in size from

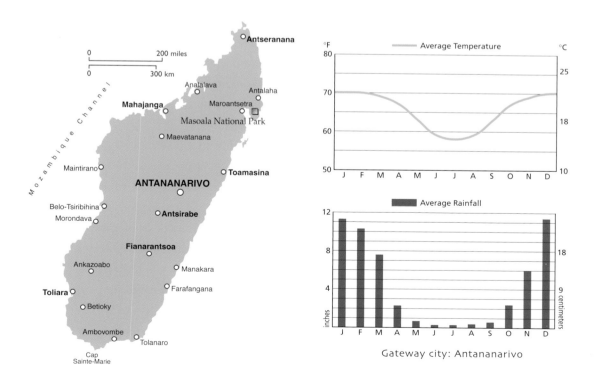

Gateway city: Antananarivo

diminutive pygmy mouse lemurs weighing under nine ounces (25 g) to handsome black-and-white, teddy-bear-like indris at more than 15 pounds (7 kg). Unfortunately, at least 15 other species have become extinct since humans came some 1,500 years ago.

How lemurs got here—evolved from early individuals already present or drifted here on rafts of vegetation—is uncertain. What is certain is that they are nowhere else (except nearby Comoros, probably brought from here) and with their soft, beautifully marked, varicolored fur and startling way of lounging in human-like positions and leaping about in upright posture, they are one of the most appealing creatures on earth.

Two-thirds of the world's chameleon species are here, with conical, multidirectional eyes that swivel independently of each other, and skin color that changes according to circumstance—not so much to match surroundings, it's thought, as to confuse predators and prey and as reflections of their emotional state. All are endemic to Madagascar and highly visible, as are many brilliant geckos. Some of the 87 gecko species here are, however, so inconspicuous they are all but invisible a few inches away, until they move, sometimes to clean their eyes with licks of their long tongues. (Geckos can re-grow lost scales, so that a predator reaching for one of these might find itself with a scaly mouthful while the gecko flees to grow a new set.)

Colorful amphibians of at least 189 species (some estimates run to 300) include aptly named tomato frogs, golden, green-backed, and painted mantella frogs, whose stunning colors warn predators their skins are toxic. Some young hatch from foam nests on the forest floor, either as minuscule frogs ⅒ inch (3 mm) long or as tiny tadpoles that somehow wriggle their way to water.

At least half of some 12,000 plant species are endemic, including ravinalas or "traveler's tree"—the national plant—so-called because its leaf base contains a pure water supply and it's reputed to align its fan-shape on an east-west axis (don't rely on it). There are 1,200 kinds of orchids, many serviced by just one moth species.

Some of the world's most unusual birds have found homes in a dozen or so microclimates among three main climatic zones—in eastern rain forests hung with moss so wet that tadpoles swim in it, in western tropical dry deciduous woods, and in the semi-arid south. Some 260 species include flamboyantly plumaged olive bee-eaters and Madagascar fodys or cardinals, males twittering constantly when on territory; giant and crested couas; Madagascar paradise flycatchers (stunning but sometimes hard to see in dim forest light); cuckoo rollers; and tiny, glistening kingfishers, especially the red-and-white and Madagascar malachites. Three of the world's most endangered raptors are here—the Madagascar red owl, fish eagle, and chameleon-eating serpent eagle.

Mammals include large, handsome, fruit-eating flying fox bats roosting in great noisy throngs, among 28 species of bats; 27 species of small, hedgehog-like insectivorous tenrecs; 20 species of rodents; and nine species of carnivores, including rare reddish fosa (pronounced "foosh"), seldom-seen pumas known as Madagascar's pink panthers, whose chilling nocturnal cries can be heard in wild areas.

Coral reefs offshore are filled with multihued marine life. Huge humpback and right whales migrate to Madagascar waters for breeding. Beyond them swim coelacanths, ancient deep-sea fish long thought extinct, and "flashlight fish" with large light organs under their eyes to help find food and communicate in the murky depths.

Madagascar early became interested in conservation of its unique biodiversity and set aside some 47 protected areas. Some of these, to encourage development of ecotourism, have recently been designated as national parks. Most are small, however, covering altogether not much more than three percent of its 226,657 square miles (587,000 km²). Everywhere protection has been inadequate so that habitat loss threatens many species, including lemurs, with near-term extinction. Madagascar's economy is one of the world's poorest and runaway population growth, with land-clearing for cash crops and cattle ranching, has led to deforestation and disastrous erosion. Less than 20 percent of original forest cover remains, and well over half the land area may be burned every year.

To address this problem, government has developed a National Environmental Action Plan (NEAP) aimed at environmental protection and sustainable development. International groups such as World Wide Fund for Nature, Wildlife Conservation Society, World Bank, CARE International, Peregrine Fund, and others have offered support for these efforts in initiatives to conserve land in ways helpful both to natural systems and local economies. Rural communities are offered training, tools, seeds, schools, and improved water supplies. Efforts are being made to help local people understand how tourism can bring long-term income—but only if environmental degradation stops and visitor facilities, until recently far from adequate, can be set up around the island.

Best times are generally April–October/November, avoiding heaviest rainfall which can make roads impassable January–March. Birds are easiest to spot during breeding season August–December.

## Masoala National Park

Masoala National Park protects Madagascar's largest remaining lowland rain forest, so wild that parts of it still are not fully explored—but what is known presents astonishing diversity of life.

White-fronted brown lemurs with shining orange eyes and snowy ruffs and chests peer from trees towering 100 feet or so (30 m) to the canopy. Goblin-like aye-ayes probe with long, thin, middle claws five inches (13 cm) long into crevices seeking insects which their keen ears detect

# MADAGASCAR

Lemurs' unblinking gaze, said to be the most penetrating and hypnotic of any animal, is the result of a brilliantly reflective retinal tapetum (mirror) plus extra-large corneas that reveal more eye surface than in most other primates. Set side-by-side in a forward-looking facial arrangement, they stimulate a positive response in humans, activating part of our brain cortex that reacts favorably to any facial structure roughly like our own—one reason humans like owls. This is a red-ruffed lemur.

deep under the bark. Handsome red-ruffed and eastern fork-marked lemurs find one of their few homes here.

Among birds are Madagascar serpent eagles and red owls, both once thought extinct, along with helmet vangas with huge light-blue bills, red-breasted couas, scaly and short-legged ground rollers, and their lovely rainbow-hued cousins, pitta-like ground rollers.

Night air can be filled with musical calls of tree frogs, including tomato and beautiful white-and-gold heterixalus, as well as unnerving screams of panther-like reddish fosas.

Boundaries of this 888-square-mile (2,300-km²) reserve across the Masoala Peninsula in northeastern Madagascar were drawn in 1997 to assure protection of these and other rare species. They extend from lush forest filled with rushing rivers and streams to mangroves, bays, white sand beaches where sea turtles haul up to scour out nests, and three marine reserves. Offshore are some of the most pristine, diverse and extensive coral reefs around Madagascar, and near them are areas where large numbers of dolphins and humpback whales gather in recently discovered breeding grounds.

There's no distinct dry season in this wettest place in Madagascar where annual rainfall regularly exceeds 130 inches (350 cm) and occasionally 195 inches (500 cm), but November is likeliest to have a few dry days.

Access, at least until recently, has been by boat, about two hours from Maroantsetra, with no accommodations other than campsites. Several footpaths enter the reserve. Boat trips can be arranged at hotels in Maroantsetra, which lies at the head of the Bay of Antongil, breeding home of the humpback between July–September. Boat trips to see them can be arranged through Parc National Masoala in Maroantsetra.

Transport to the bay's island reserve of **Nosy Mangabe** with aye-ayes, dwarf, mouse, brown, and black-and-white ruffed lemurs is by boat from Maroantsetra. There are trails, campsites, and it is sometimes possible to sleep in the caretaker's hut. Masoala is known for trekking. One of Madagascar's premier treks connects Maroantsetra with Antalaha, 69 miles (111 km) long and about five days, not easy—muddy, steep, with insects and leeches aplenty—but usually enthralling to those who can make it. Several itineraries combine trekking with sea-kayaking along the coast.

## ALSO OF INTEREST

**Parc National d'Andasibe-Mantadia** (aka Perinet), near Andasibe and Antananarivo, with about 60 indri family groups, also aye-ayes and other lemurs, chameleons, over 100 bird species including ground rollers, green sunbirds, rare Madagascar red owls, and over 100 frog species—perhaps world record for frog density—including beautiful golden mantellas. Heavily visited, weekdays best. Hotels nearby and in Moramanga.

**Parc National Andohahela** has a unique range of ecosystems including evergreen forest, transitional and spiny forest, endemic palms, baobabs, and aloes. Many faunal species including sifakas, red-tailed lemurs, and radiated tortoises.

**Parc National Ankarafantsika** and **Reserve Forestière d'Ampijoroa** near Mahajanga are home to seven lemur species, most of them easily seen, including sportive, woolly, gray mouse, fat-tailed dwarf lemurs, and Coquerel's sifakas. Contains the richest avifauna in Madagascar with 117 species, of which 66 are endemic, including Madagascar fish eagles. Over 250 plant species of which 87 percent are endemic.

**Parc National de l'Isalo** near Ranohira, with unique landscape of sandstone rocks cut by deep canyons, unusual vegetation. Among 55 species of birds are rare Benson's rockthrush, with 30 species of orchids and 16 species of lemurs, including ringtail and brown lemurs, Verreux's sifakas.

**Parc National de Mananara-Nord** is a beautiful U.N. biosphere reserve with several lemurs, notably aye-ayes and hairy-eared dwarfs, and a fine marine park.

**Parc National de Montagne d'Ambre**, near Ambohitra (Joffreville), with dramatic scenery, interesting birds, best place to see crowned and Sanford's lemurs. Good trails. Campsite. Hotels in Diego Suarez.

**Parc National de Ranomafana**—large eastern rain forest with thermal sources. Here are diademed sifakas and many lemurs, including easily-seen red-bellied and red-fronted. This is the only known home of golden bamboo and broad-nosed gentle lemurs. Forests abound with birds, geckos, chameleons, beautiful frogs.

**Réserve Privée de Berenty**—private reserve with rare gallery forest, offers unusual close-range wildlife-viewing, especially of ringtail and brown lemurs, sifakas, and nocturnal lemurs.

---

**FURTHER INFORMATION**

ANGAP, or Association Nationale pour la Gestion des Aires Protégées (National Association for the Management of Protected Areas), main office in suburban Ambatobe, B.P. 1424, Antananarivo 101, Tel: (+261) 22-41538, 22-41554, Fax: (+261) 22-41539, E-mail: angap@dts.mg; or in outlying Haute-Ville, adjoining Office Nationale pour l'Environnement, Tel: (+261) 22-25999. Also helpful are WWF, Tel: (+261) 22-34885, Fax: (+261) 22-34888; and CARE Madagascar, E-mail: caremad@bow.dts.mg

# MALAWI

FISH IN EXTRAORDINARY NUMBERS AND VARIETY
POPULATE MILLION-YEAR-OLD LAKE MALAWI—
400 CICHLID SPECIES ALONE, FROM AN INCH
TO TWO FEET LONG, MANY IN DAZZLING HUES.

DEEP, CLEAR, SPARKLING LAKE MALAWI—CALLED BY EXPLORER DAVID LIVINGSTONE "LAKE OF STARS," AFRICA'S THIRD LARGEST, 357 MILES NORTH–SOUTH AND 53 MILES ACROSS (575 × 85 KM)—HAS AN ESTIMATED 500 TO 1,000 FISH SPECIES, MORE THAN ANY OTHER LAKE IN THE WORLD, ABOUT 90 PERCENT OF THEM FOUND NOWHERE ELSE. Notable are cichlids or "mbuna," small spiny tropical fish whose population here represents about a third of all the world's cichlid species. Their importance in the study of evolution has been compared to that of finches on the Galapagos Islands.

Mammals roaming five national parks and four wildlife reserves include rhinoceros, hippos, and large herds of elephants and buffalo, along with nyalas and other antelopes and smaller jackals, warthogs, honey badgers,

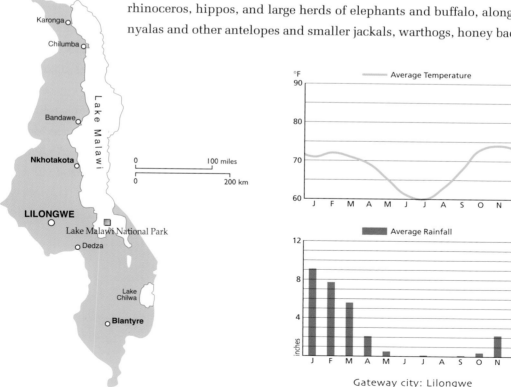

Gateway city: Lilongwe

99

monkeys, and baboons. Among 650 bird species are such spectacular specialties as wattled cranes, collared palm-thrushes, racquet-tailed rollers, Bohm's bee-eaters, and blue swallows.

Almost nine percent of Malawi's 45,733 square miles (118,480 km²) of lakes, mountains, high plateau, and wildlife-rich brachystegia (or miomba) woodlands has been given over to national parks and protected areas and they are among the best-run on the continent, with trails, campgrounds, and lodges. Forest reserves cover another 6.9 percent, with an additional 88 reserves proposed.

# LAKE MALAWI NATIONAL PARK

Notable is 34-square-mile (87-km²) Lake Malawi National Park and World Heritage Site, with million-year-old Lake Malawi and its extraordinary fish population—over 400 species of cichlids alone, ranging from an inch (2.5 cm) to almost two feet (0.5 m) long, many in dazzling tropical colors. Many have evolved into mouth brooders whose young are fertilized, incubated, hatched, and cared for in their mother's mouth. More than 70 percent still are not fully described in their many and changing adaptations and species relationships. Visitors can observe them through snorkel and diving masks along underwater trails.

In shrubby grasslands and stony wooded hills around the lake, leopards stalk impala, gray duiker antelopes, and young spiral-horned greater kudus and bushbucks, occasionally vervet monkeys and young chacma baboons (chacmas are the largest primates in southern Africa). Stocky little klipspringer antelopes skip on tiptoes (or tip-hooves) along rocky outcrops. Hippos gather in pools, grazing on grassy edges.

Fish eagles dive along shorelines where Nile crocodiles bask. Several thousand white-breasted cormorants nest colonially on lake islands. Noted for rich birding are Cape Maclear and the shore and hills around Monkey Bay with Dickinson's kestrels, freckled nightjars, swallow-tailed bee-eaters, trumpeter hornbills, yellow-fronted tinkerbirds, a variety of kingfishers, wading birds, and much more.

The park, 150 miles' drive (250 km) east and south from Lilongwe, has trails for wildlife-viewing, boats for hire, also equipment for diving and snorkeling.

There are hotels, guesthouses, and campsites nearby.

---

**FURTHER INFORMATION**

For more information—Parks and Wildlife Officer, Lake Malawi National Park, P.O. Box 48, Monkey Bay, OR www.malawi tourism.com

# ALSO OF INTEREST

**Nyika National Park**, wild and open, protects the vast, beautiful Nyika Plateau in north Malawi, 1,210 square miles (3,134 km²) of flower-carpeted grassland, marsh, streams, waterfalls, and forested slopes on which grow some 200 orchid species. These lush habitats are home to almost 100 mammal species, including one of the densest leopard populations in Africa, also Burchell's zebras, oribi, elands, blue duikers, roan, klipspringers. Among over 400 bird species are such rarities as wattled cranes, blue swallows, moustached green-tinkerbirds, Malawi batis, Denham's bustards, exquisite scarlet-tufted malachite sunbirds.

There's good park literature, access by air, comfortable accommodations, and many miles of wildlife-viewing tracks for walking, horseback-riding, or driving, including guided night drives, about 62 miles (100 km) west and north of Rumphi. At 385 square miles (1,000 km²), **Vwaza Marsh Wildlife Reserve** just to the south has rare babbling starlings and chestnut-backed sparrow-weavers, also substantial large mammal populations.

---

**FURTHER INFORMATION**

Information for both Nyika and Vwaza Marsh can be obtained from the Nyika Safari Company. They also are involved in funding and development projects. E-mail: info@nyika.com

---

**Kasungu National Park**, about 25 miles (38 km) west of Kasungu, may have on its 894 square miles (2,316 km²) of rolling miombo woodland and open, seasonally flooded flats more large mammal species than anyplace else in Malawi—buffalo, elephants, greater kudus, roans, hippos—and at the other end of the size scale, curious insectivorous four-toed elephant-shrews with noses like tiny trunks. Among birds are giant eagle owls, purple-crested turacos, swallow-tailed bee-eaters, yellow-billed hornbills, red-winged warblers, starred robins, brown-headed parrots, Miombo sunbirds. There's a comfortable lodge overlooking water and a 175-mile (280-km) road network—best viewing toward the end of dry season August–November.

**Lengwe National Park**, 342 square miles (887 km²) in the Shire Valley south of Blantyre, has large nyala herds, suni antelopes, Burchell's zebras, bushbucks, kudus, prolific birdlife including handsome bush-shrikes, barred long-tailed cuckoos, black-and-white flycatchers. Basic accommodations.

**Liwonde National Park**, 224 square miles (580 km²) along the Shire River 40 miles (64 km) north of Zomba, is noted for abundant elephants, one of the densest hippo populations in Africa, crocodiles everywhere along the river, waterbucks, kudus, warthogs, large herds of handsome sable antelopes, yellow (chacma) baboons, black rhinos, and more than 400 bird species including Pel's fishing owls, pygmy-geese, open-billed storks, Lillian's lovebirds. There's a recently renovated lodge with tented camp overlooking river and floodplain, also campsites. Access is by riverboat from Liwonde, a wonderful trip.

**FURTHER INFORMATION**

E-mail: info@wilderness.malawi.net

In the center of the capital is 370-acre (150-ha) **Lilongwe Nature Sanctuary** with over 200 bird species in its thick bush, gallery forest, and bamboo thickets, including white-backed night herons, African finfoots, African and black goshawks, white-faced scops owls, blue-breasted cordon-bleus, magpie mannikins, and amethyst sunbirds. Mammals include bush-bucks, duikers, bushpigs, zebras, serval cats, leopards, hyenas, otters. Unfortunately this

Warthogs' "warts" are fleshy skin-covered projections on each cheek which protect eyes and faces from rivals' tusks in fights. Molars and jaw hinges are modified to grind toughest grasses which they munch while resting on calloused knees. In dry times they root for tubers, aerating the soil, which aids plant growth.

sanctuary has not been adequately maintained in recent years and at this writing, visitors are advised to avoid it, pending improvements.

A number of smaller Malawi reserves are excellent, especially **Elephant Marsh**, a 350-square-mile (910-km²) wetland paradise south of Blantyre, important for hippos, crocodiles, and more than 300 bird species.

Threats to all these include agricultural encroachment, pollution runoff, poaching, logging.

Climate divides into hot-dry September–November, hot-wet November–April, and cool-dry May–August. Best for wildlife-viewing is May–October. The capital, Lilongwe, is served by international air, with local air connections north and south, good bus connections in all directions, rental cars, and a good local road system. Or, take a beautiful lake cruise.

**FURTHER INFORMATION**

Chief Administrator, Department of National Parks, Wildlife and Tourism, P.O. Box 30131, Lilongwe 3, Malawi, Tel: (+265) 72-3505, 72-3566, also 73-0944, Fax: (+265) 72-3089; Wildlife Society of Malawi, P.O. Box 1429, Blantyre, Tel: (+265) 64-3428.

As with all African countries, visitors need to be aware of and check for the possibility of bilharzia, or schistosomiasis, in shallow waters and reedbeds. The cure is a simple tablet, but the disease can be troublesome if not diagnosed.

# MAURITANIA

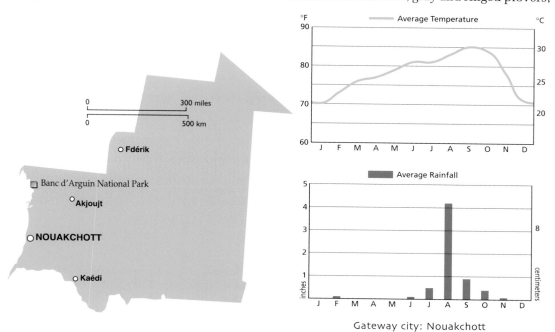

IMRAGUEN TRIBESMEN FISH COOPERATIVELY
WITH WILD DOLPHINS IN CRYSTALLINE WATERS
OFF BANC D'ARGUIN USING TRADITIONAL
SAILBOATS AND AGE-OLD WAYS FIRST
DESCRIBED BY 15TH-CENTURY EXPLORERS.

NO MORE DRAMATIC CONTRAST EXISTS IN THE NATURAL WORLD THAN IN THIS SUB-SAHARAN WEST AFRICAN COUNTRY WITH DESERT SO DRY LITTLE SURVIVES AND SHORELINE SO TEEMING WITH BIRDS AND MARINE LIFE THEY LITERALLY COVER MARSHES, BEACHES, LAGOONS, AND SMALL ISLANDS.

## BANC D'ARGUIN NATIONAL PARK

It can be difficult to see where shoreline ends and sea begins when more than a third of the estimated seven million wading birds that use the Atlantic flyway are at Banc d'Arguin, the world's largest concentration of wintering waders. Records exist of more than two million broad-billed sandpipers alone—and there are hundreds of thousands of black terns, gray and ringed plovers,

Gateway city: Nouakchott

103

knots, dunlins, European spoonbills, bar-tailed godwits, redshanks, greater and lesser flamingos, and others, plus some three million land birds.

Vast shallow tidal flats and sea-grass meadows just offshore offer cover, sustenance, and important breeding and nursery grounds to millions of sea organisms in crystalline waters covering some 300 square miles (800 km²). Nowhere deeper than 16.5 feet (5 m) at low tide, they extend nearly 35 miles (60 km) out from shore for some 100 miles (160 km) along the coast, one of the richest marine areas in the world, sustained by cold, nutrient-filled waters of the Sahelian upwelling.

The enormous aquatic population ranging from fish to microplankton attracts larger sea creatures, including killer whales and five species of dolphins and porpoises. It also feeds one of the world's most diverse breeding colonies of fish-eating birds crowding shoulder-to-shoulder on more than a dozen small islands during twice-yearly nesting seasons—thousands of white pelicans, white-breasted and reed cormorants, gull-billed, Caspian, royal and common terns, and others.

Four species of sea turtles lay eggs on the beaches—loggerheads, green, hawksbill and huge leatherbacks, world's largest, known to reach a shell length up to 6.5 feet (2 m) and weigh close to a ton (800 kg).

Rare monk seals breed at Cap Blanc in their largest known colony—some 150 of these—shy pinnipeds hunted almost to extinction for their fur and by fishermen who blamed them for destroying their nets, now additionally imperilled since collapse of their breeding caves here. (Lone males often hang around the lighthouse.)

This 4,530-square-mile (11,750-km²) U.N. World Heritage Site, designated a Ramsar Wetland of World Importance, is at the migratory limit of both Afrotropical species and palearctics from the northern hemisphere. Half marine, half terrestrial, some 7,440 acres (3,100 ha) is an ancient mangrove swamp dating from a humid past when Banc d'Arguin was a vast estuary draining freshwater rivers flowing from the then-green Sahara.

On the land side are small, stocky, sand cats with ringed tails, jackals, honey badgers or ratels, fennec and sand fox, striped hyenas, possibly relict populations of pale dorcas gazelles, and Imraguen tribesmen who live by subsistence fishing using traditional sailing boats in ways unchanged since first described by 15th-century European explorers. Fishermen act cooperatively with wild dolphins to catch schools of gray mullet.

OPPOSITE: Spoonbills feed by swishing their long, spatulate bills through shallow water until they encounter prey, such as water insects, fry, crustaceans, or small frogs, which they snap up and ingest. In breeding plumage, they develop distinctive "horse-tail" crests. They are voiceless except for grumbling sounds when strangers approach the nest. Found in shallows, reedy marshes, estuaries over southern Russia and central Asia, they winter in East Africa and South Asia.

## MAURITANIA

Park access is possible along a road between Nouadhibou and the capital, Nouakchott, which has an international jetport and where guided tours can be arranged both on land via 4WD and sometimes by water. Both have lodgings and are linked by local airlines. Permission is necessary for entry and can be denied at height of the April–July and October–January breeding seasons—check ahead.

Best times are slightly cooler December–February—but Mauritania is hot most of the time.

Most serious threat is from international factory fishing fleets subsidized by Japan, Russia, Ireland, and the European Economic Community, which in some places have devastated fish populations and turned local fishermen from traditional to more damaging methods such as large-scale netting and dynamite. Funding is needed for patrols, and the government has been urged to negotiate stronger protective agreements with these countries. World Wide Fund for Nature (WWF), the French Ministry of Cooperation, and the Netherlands government all have agreed to help, with marine equipment as well as mounted camel patrols on the land side.

### ALSO OF INTEREST

The new **Diawling National Park**, a saline floodplain with great numbers of waterfowl and wading birds in the lower delta of the Senegal River adjoining Senegal's DJOUDJ NATIONAL PARK (*see* p.129).

Another Ramsar site has been recommended, **Aftout-es-Saheli**, to protect one of the last undisturbed wetlands on the Mauritanian side of the Senegal delta, also **Lakes Aleg** and **Rkiz** to protect inundated forests.

---

**FURTHER INFORMATION**

Parc National Banc d'Arguin, B.P. 124, Nouadhibou; also Ministère de la Pêche et de l'Économie Maritime, B.P. 137, Nouakchott; also Ministère de Direction de la Protection de la Nature, B.P. 170, Nouakchott.

# NAMIBIA

DESERT ELEPHANTS ON THE SKELETON COAST
MAY WALK 30 MILES (48 KM) IN SEARCH OF WATER
DIRECTED, IT'S THOUGHT, BY GENERATIONAL MEMORY,
AND SUMMON OTHERS FROM MILES AWAY BY
INFRASONIC VOCALIZATIONS INAUDIBLE TO HUMANS.

NAMIBIA (FORMERLY SOUTHWEST AFRICA) IS ONE OF THE WORLD'S WILDEST, DRIEST, LEAST POPULATED PLACES. Some one million people live here in a country 50 percent larger than France. Much of it is desert where the sun shines more than 300 days a year, where daytime temperatures can be searing and fall below freezing at night. Terrain ranges from rugged, dramatic canyons approaching the Grand Canyon in size, to flat coastal lands littered with shipwrecks and bones of unlucky sailors. Despite Namibia's rigors, it contains some of the world's premier wildlife reserves.

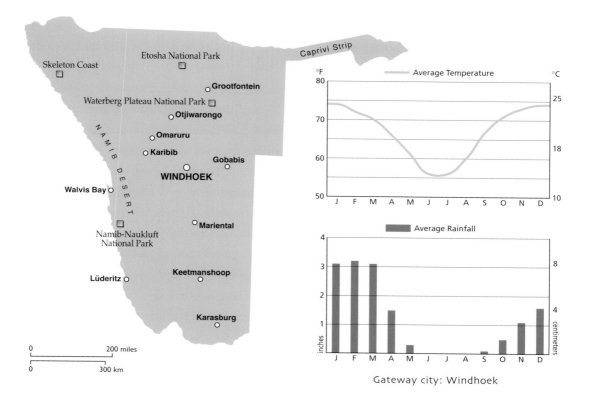

Gateway city: Windhoek

# Etosha National Park

Outstanding among them is Etosha National Park, a formidably arid but beautiful place ("Etosha" means land of dry white water referring to the often-dry lakebed) which may have more spectacular animals to be seen on an intimate basis than any place else on earth.

This is because perennial springs here satisfy their need for water no matter what the weather (it is sunny and rainless 300 days a year) and because this 8,600-square-mile (22,270-km²) national park, larger than the state of Massachusetts, is so remote and protected animals live in a world that belongs almost totally to them.

Thirsty giraffes spread their long legs so their even longer necks—which require a special circulatory system to pump blood up to the brain—can reach down to the water, watchful for predatory lions but little else. Zebras snort and mill about in such numbers that their stripes, each in a different pattern, can create a bewildering (but not to them) kaleidoscopic effect.

There are 114 species of mammals here, 392 kinds of birds—and sometimes large numbers of all these simultaneously in one place. There are curly-horned kudus, prehistoric armored pangolins, 7,000 zebras, 20,000 exuberant springboks (which can go months without drinking) "pronking" in stiff-legged upward leaps, and some 1,500 or so elephants, some solo, others in small bachelor groups, still others in matriarchal herds ranging in age from 50 years to a few hours.

Massive irritable buffalo share nutritious grasses with elands, which at a weight of one ton (900+ kg) are largest antelope in the world, and rare diminutive Damara dik-diks which can tip the scales at less than 10 pounds (5 kg).

Others, seldom seen elsewhere but not uncommon here, are graceful black-faced impalas which can leap 38 feet (12 m) horizontally and 12 feet (3.5 m) high; clown-masked roan antelopes; Hartmann's mountain zebras; and two-ton black rhinoceros—this their last remaining stronghold. Handsome gemsbok, or oryx, frugal water-drinkers, come in great migratory groups.

It is a Namibian version of Tanzania's Serengeti Plain but is relatively undiscovered by outside visitors, in a country where animals greatly outnumber (and are largely undisturbed by) humans.

Focus of this rich reserve is the Etosha Pan, which is more often dry than wet—probably filled historically by the Kunene River, a source cut off by tectonic disturbances 12 million years ago.

Now only in uncommon years of bountiful rainfall does this 2,368-square-mile (6,133-km²) lake bed fill and then it is with highly mineralized water. But usually for a short time each year it fills enough to attract up to a million greater and lesser flamingos which present a marvelous moving mosaic of pink and white as they filter-feed over 180 tons of algae and diatoms daily. There may also be huge flocks of hundreds, perhaps thousands, of chestnut-banded plovers and white pelicans with nine-foot (3-m) wingspreads fanning out to other water holes to drink as well.

Hartebeest are among the swiftest antelopes, capable of 48 miles an hour (80 kph) when fleeing a predator, and, with greater endurance, able to outdistance most of them. They can make do on the toughest grasses, and go without water except when unable to get melons or tubers.

Most of the time, however, the enormous populations of wildlife, resident as well as migratory, depend for potable water on the 40 or so springs and water holes around its edge and throughout the park. These spread along 500 miles (800 km) of graveled park roads where the animals are easily visible, sometimes in huge numbers.

Elephants which drink up to 53 gallons (200 liters) of water every day fill up here and then wallow and cover themselves with mud which dries to a white layer of sun protection. Babies nap in the shadows cast by their ghostly-looking mothers. Male sandgrouse fluff up uniquely adapted breast feathers, filling the interstices with moisture to take back to thirsty nestlings up to 36 miles (60 km) away.

Large numbers of predators are attracted not only by water but by the large number of herbivores, their prey species. Leopards are elusive but the park population is estimated at over 100. They often kill a victim and then drag it up a tree to keep it from hyenas. A leopard's meal might usually be an antelope but they have been known to transport a young giraffe weighing up to 41 pounds (19 kg).

# NAMIBIA

There are cheetahs, jackals, caracals, and lions, which are particularly large and numerous in Etosha—up to 500, largest in proportion to prey in Africa, with black-maned males that can weigh almost 500 pounds (225 kg). Among the smaller predators are African wildcats, jackals, honey badgers, and aardwolves.

Fischer's Pan, often first to hold water and last to dry up, is a good place to find such birds as great crested grebes, Hottentot teals, storks, and sometimes hundreds of curlew sandpipers, little stints, and ruffs. A pair of giant eagle-owls are often at Klein Namutoni.

Orange and black masked weavers chatter in great nesting congregations in wooded belts of leadwood and acacia trees, often joined by pygmy falcons which take up residence in weaver colonies and feed on the residents. Brilliant lilac-breasted rollers scout the savannahs for insects and lizards.

In central and western Etosha, dominated by mopane woodland, are white helmet-shrikes, violet wood hoopoes, gray-backed bleating warblers, and familiar chats, also monotonous larks, white-quilled korhaans, and pale chanting goshawks.

Ostriches, at six feet (2 m) tall the world's largest (though flightless) bird, come to water or graze in wooded grasslands, accelerating to 37 miles an hour (60 kph) and lashing out dangerously with powerful clawed legs if necessary. Males can sound curiously like roaring lions when they "boom."

On searingly hot days, zebras face away from the sun so their stripes, white ones wider in back, will absorb less heat (they turn their sides sunward to absorb heat on cool mornings).

After the rains start, human visitors are fewer; but those who do come see impalas and wildebeest dropping their young, predators following them, and large numbers of birds.

Life can be perilous. The Etosha Pan can dry up before flamingos and pelicans finish raising their young, and adults must leave in order to survive themselves. One year 20,000 parched chicks were captured here and released at still-watered Fischer's Pan. Another year 30,000 young birds, just able to walk, marched 19 miles (30 km) to the nearest water at Poacher's Point, then set out again for Ekuma River Delta, their parents feeding them en route, sometimes making a daily round trip of 60 miles (100 km) until most of the chicks reached safety a month later.

One can see all this by going from water hole to water hole—but it is at least as interesting and often more rewarding to take a lunch and watch the constant parade at one place. Some sites near the camps are floodlit and watchable at all hours.

A curious area is the Haunted Forest not far from Okaukuezo in the southern section, filled with "phantom trees" which give the peculiar appearance of having been planted upside down, their roots pointing skyward.

Best time to visit is in April–October dry season and southern hemisphere winter.

# SKELETON COAST

This searing, rainless, fog-bound, treacherous shoreline with deadly crosscurrents is named for the littered remains of shipwrecks, whales, and human castaways unable to survive these harsh circumstances in a desert that begins right at the water's edge. Annual precipitation averages less than an inch (25 mm) and every year falls in different places. Gale-force winds push up mountainous waves that pound the shore, and on land, create towering sand dunes which march and literally roar when the air pounds their hollows. ("I am proceeding to a river 60 miles north," reads a slate found in the sand in 1860. "Should anyone find this and follow me, God help him.")

Yet these wind-sculpted dunes, desert canyons, and jagged peaks have their own special beauty, and wildlife, both plant and animal, while not abundant are fascinating—in large part because of the adaptations that enable them to be here at all.

Desert elephants can go four days without water, then dig wells just as wide as their trunks in dry riverbeds. If these are too deep for elephant babies to reach, their parents draw up water in their own trunks and pour it into the little ones' mouths. They may walk 30 miles (48 km) in search of promising places to dig, guided, it is thought, by ancient generational memory of these sources. But observations both here and in Etosha indicate they may also communicate with other elephants several miles away by infrasonic vocalizations inaudible to humans. Elephants sometimes come to water holes at a dead run, as if already knowing a water source is there.

Fog-basking tenebrionid beetles drink the only water available to them by standing on their heads in the early morning mist blowing in from the sea, causing drops of condensation to run down their bodies and thence into their mouths.

Lions here have adapted their prey base so that many live on seals captured by the seaside. (Recently some have moved inland for other prey as well.) Jackals subsist largely on what they can scavenge beachcombing. Rhinos, giraffes, kudus, Hartmann's mountain zebras, and a variety of others have adapted to this inhospitable environment.

Rarely, water from rain in mountains far inland breaks through, causing a river that flows briefly toward the sea before it sinks into the sand again, but leaving succulent shrubs that offer respite to grazing wildlife. Other plants offer forage because they can depend for moisture on the thick fog, as do the ganna and more than 100 species of lichens.

More than 203 bird species have been recorded, most of them waders and seabirds that subsist on the rich sea life.

The Skeleton Coast is in two sections. The upper two-thirds, **Skeleton Coast Wilderness Park**, the most interesting from a naturalist's view, extends 373 miles (600 km) between the mouths of the Kunene and Ugab rivers, no wider than 31 miles (50 km) at any point. Visitation is limited to fly-in group safaris by permit. The southern third is the **National West Coast Recreation Area**, a mecca for fishermen, home to 70 percent of the world population of Damara terns, also to the **Cape Cross Seal Reserve** with 80,000 to 100,000 breeding fur seals, open to regular visitation. Two resorts offer accommodations here; campsites available also (reserve ahead).

## NAMIB-NAUKLUFT NATIONAL PARK

Namib-Naukluft is a huge reserve, 19,215 square miles (49,768 km$^2$)—about the size of Switzerland—with the world's oldest desert, tallest sand dunes, and some of the strangest organisms in the world adapted to live here.

An engaging little golden mole has neither ears nor eye sockets—doesn't need them, spending most of its life underground, where it's cooler.

Cheetah cubs stay with mothers 15 months or so, grooming, purring (cheetahs don't roar), and learning how to hunt. Fastest of all animals, they are capable of running up to 70 miles an hour (120 kph) in bounds of 25 feet (7.6 m)—but only for 600 yards (550 m) tops. Then the gazelle gets away.

Translucent geckos have lobed feet that enable them to dance quickly over the burning sand, and long dual-purpose tongues which they use to clean sand sprinkles off their eyes and drink moisture beads that accumulate on them from dawn mists.

The stunted "living fossil" *Welwitschia mirabilis*, among the oldest plants in the world, sends its tap roots down more than 60 feet (20 m), and closes its leaf pores during blistering days. It can live more than 2,000 years, during which it grows only two leaves (they begin to look worn toward the end, their tough, leathery fibers nibbled occasionally by desperate grazers).

Larger animals have learned to survive here too (as they have in the Skeleton Coast to the north)—mountain zebras, springboks, ostriches, gemsbok (whose notable drought accommodations enable them to adjust their blood pressure and perspiration), and their predators, including cheetahs and leopards.

Sand dunes may reach a height of almost 1,000 feet (300 m) and, with varied sunlight and wind direction, assume spectacular shapes and multiple hues, apricot-gold, red and deep maroon, dramatically beautiful in the profiling light of sunrise and sunset.

Dolomite mountains to the east rise in dramatic rock formations to 6,500 feet (2,000 m) and offer suitable habitat for agile klipspringers, black eagles, and Cape eagle-owls, among others. There are hiking trails (some quite arduous). Sandwich Harbor on the western coast is notable for birds, especially September–March when over a half-million birds can be present, including breeding flamingos, pelicans, and various seabirds.

Access to some areas is by permit, on limited schedule, via 4WD vehicles. Accommodations include several comfortable hotels and lodges, as well as campsites (some with limited facilities). Any time of year is interesting, but winter nights can be cold. South of the park is a restricted diamond area where quantities of precious stones have been recovered from sand and gravel. It's important also as a reserve for gemsbok, springbok, and others.

## WATERBERG PLATEAU NATIONAL PARK

Waterberg Plateau National Park was established as a habitat-friendly place to bring rare and endangered species, and it has worked. Rarities introduced or re-introduced in this 156-square-mile (400-km²) park include sable and roan antelope, white and black rhinos, buffalo, steenboks, elands, red hartebeest, blue wildebeest, and impalas. All are thriving. So are wild dogs, cheetahs, tsessebes.

No wonder. Waterberg—the name means "hill of water"—has plentiful rainfall which is stored in the aquifer-like character of its brick-red sandstone. It then flows down to springs at the plateau's base, where frogs as well as plants have evolved independently from the surrounding area. This water is then pumped to the top to fill boreholes and ponds.

This water system with varied soils and elevations makes possible habitat ranges accommodating a great variety of flora and fauna.

The healthy grazing population attracts predators such as leopards—this is one of the best places in Africa to see these elusive spotted cats. There are also black-backed jackals, caracals, and a large and diverse bird population—more than 200 species, including black eagles, pallid flycatchers, hornbills, rockrunners, and short-toed rock thrushes.

Cliffs that rise 500 feet (150 m) above the surrounding bush-savannah are the only known Namibian breeding site for booted eagles. They also support a large population of peregrine falcons, whose main prey is the swifts, primarily Bradfield's and cliff-dwelling alpine swifts but also smaller ones, which ascend in dense flocks each morning.

On the plateau's western side is Namibia's only breeding colony of Cape vultures, which enjoy (or seem to) effortlessly gliding on the early morning air thermals.

Barred owls and freckled nightjars call at night, usually audible from the camp.

Stunning views are all around the plateau, where lush tropical vegetation includes colorful specialties such as silver terminalia trees, flame acacias, yellow-flowered wattles, and purple-blossomed Kalahari apple-leaf.

Best time is May–October dry season. Emphasis is on hiking, with camps and overnight huts for hikers—but there are also good short tracks for casual walkers. Terrain is rough, requiring special heavy-duty vehicles; the Ministry of Environment and Tourism operates tours.

## ALSO OF INTEREST

**Fish River Canyon** claims to be second in size only to the Grand Canyon—in any case it is enormous and spectacular: 100 miles (161 km) long, 17 miles (27 km) wide, in places almost 1,800 feet (550 m) deep. Some rocks are more than 2.6 billion years old. Natural life includes birds around water holes, also (less visibly) klipspringers, mountain zebras, baboons, rock rabbits. Hiking trails can be arduous. Luxury resort accommodations available.

Wildlife populations at **Kaudom Game Reserve** have been called comparable to Etosha, with 64 mammal species, including herds of elephants, buffalo, giraffes, blue wildebeest, red hartebeest, tsessebes, roan antelopes, gemsbok, kudus, and elands, as well as large predators. This 1,480-square-mile (3,800-km²) park in extreme northeast Namibia is one of the country's most recent official reserves, with at present only sandy tracks and minimal visitor facilities.

---

**FURTHER INFORMATION**

Ministry of Wildlife, Conservation and Tourism, Private Bag X13267,
Windhoek 9000, Namibia, Tel: (+264) 061-36975 or 061-33875, Fax: (+264) 61-229936.

---

# NIGER

STURDY ORYX ANTELOPES WITH SHOWY
BLACK-AND-WHITE FACE MASKS AND SCIMITAR
HORNS SURVIVE SEMIDESERT NORTHERN NIGER
WITH BODIES ABLE TO GO FOR WEEKS WITHOUT WATER
AND TO THERMOREGULATE WHEN TEMPERATURES DROP
FROM 122°F (55°C) TO BELOW FREEZING IN WINTER.

## "W" NATIONAL PARK

Lordly elephants in some of Africa's great herds browse among the trees in the Tapoa Valley, which cuts through vast wooded savannahs of a national park and U.N. World Heritage Site called simply "W" after the double-bend of the Niger River where Niger, Benin, and Burkina Faso meet.

With them on freshening grasslands among the scrub move other hoofed grazers in great variety—white-striped bushbucks, sturdy African buffalo, lyre-horned kobs, frisky little red-flanked and common duikers alongside Defassa waterbucks, reedbucks, slender, graceful oribi, roan antelopes, and swift red-fronted gazelles. After them come hartebeest and topi which get along on sparse fodder others leave behind, drinking water only every few days—all these prey for lions, leopards, and cheetahs.

During dry seasons hippos submerge in the river on warm days, only eyes and noses visible, and threatened Nile crocodiles bask on banks of the Mékrou River. Both the Mékrou and the Tapoa Rivers are bordered by riverine forests, with fast-flowing rapids through narrow valleys when rains have been plentiful. Downstream the valleys open to flatter terrain which, together with floodplains of the Niger River, create wetlands noted of world importance by the Ramsar Convention.

More than 80 mammal species include diurnal carnivores once thought locally extinct — spotted hyenas, common jackals, serval cats, fringe-eared caracals,

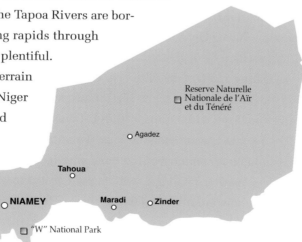

115

# NIGER

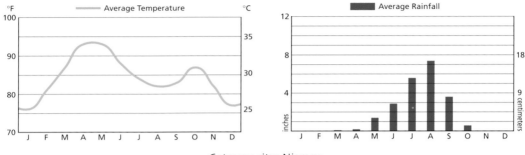

Gateway city: Niamey

and wild dogs—plus aardvarks and crested porcupines which snuffle along forest floors at any hour. Magnets for all these are dozens of water holes, both naturally occurring and scoured out for wildlife benefit.

Birds of more than 350 species find niches everywhere in these habitats covering almost 15,625 square miles (40,500 km$^2$) shared by Niger with neighboring Benin and Burkina Faso in this wilderness virtually without human habitation.

Cackling guinea fowl and clucking francolins move through grasslands. Hornbills sail raucously among fruiting trees. Fish eagles scoop up meals in waterways. Long, fluting musical cries of chanting goshawks float down from tree lookouts in thorny scrub. They compete with baboon troops "yakking" strident warning if a predator appears (harsh growls are reserved for courtship).

Waterfowl share pond edges with long-legged shorebirds and waders—storks, ibises, egrets. Bright chestnut lily-trotters (aka African jacanas), trot nimbly over floating vegetation. Gray pratincoles rest on river sandbanks near where tawny Pel's fishing owls hunt and, between January and June, colonies of brilliant northern carmine bee-eaters nest in burrows, especially along the narrow, steep-banked Mékrou. Migratory species from Europe and Asia are most common during October–April.

Threats include poaching, illegal grazing, and annual cattle migrations, plus uncontrolled bush fires, fishing, cultivation within park borders, and proposals for phosphate mining and damming of rivers (although the Niger Republique says these are unlikely to be approved due to lack of proper environmental impact study). Traditional hunting has little significant effect.

The park is open to visitors December–May, closed during rainy season. Niger (pronounced nee-zhé) is only country of the three sharing "W" where the park can be visited fairly easily, from headquarters at Tapoa, which gives access to 435 miles (700 km) of trails, with comfortable accommodations at the small Tapoa Hotel nearby. Tapoa is 93 miles (150 km) south of Niamey, which has international jet service and hotels where guides and transport can be arranged—best by rental car, via Say and Tamou,with a guide or organized group since public

Nile crocodiles, of a family thought to be the most intelligent reptiles on earth, are Africa's largest, up to 20 feet (6 m) long, and weighing up to 1,600 pounds (726 kg). They can kill whatever comes to water, including wildebeest, pulling them under until they drown—but they can't chew well, so sometimes don't eat until victims start to rot and become more easily digestible. This one guards her nest, which may contain 60 eggs, vulnerable to raids by hyenas, monitor lizards or humans. After 80–90 days' incubation, she may assist hatching by gently cracking eggs and carrying young to water, where they will be protected until they take off on their own.

transport is reliable only part-way. Not all wildlife is easy to see in the bushy landscape of "W", but a good variety can be spotted by a diligent visitor.

## RESERVE NATURELLE NATIONALE DE L'AÏR ET DU TÉNÉRÉ

On the edge of the Sahara in dry mountainous northern Niger, this spectacular—largest protected area in Africa—enormous 29,850-square-mile (77,300-km²) World Heritage Site covers over six percent of the country.

This wilderness oasis said to have the Sahara's most beautiful dunes is a last stronghold of semi-desert Sahelian and Saharan wildlife. Here species of special concern such as scimitar-horned oryx adjust to the desert's extreme temperatures, from 122°F (50°C) in summer to below zero in winter. Handsome addax antelopes conserve water by thermoregulating their bodies and survive on sparse growth that comes after rare, meager rains. Both oryx and addax have been under heavy pressure by poachers.

Long-legged Nubian bustards a yard (m) tall cover ground walking as readily as flying, pluck-ing insects from tall grasses as do Sudan golden sparrows—males with sulphur-yellow heads—in company with a few ostriches, pied cuckoos, sooty, melodious black scrub-robins, spotted and crowned sandgrouse, and noisy, long-tailed, vividly blue Abyssinian rollers. Jackals, hyenas, and cheetahs are here too, adjusting to all habitats and preying on grazers, especially young gazelles.

The starkly beautiful Aïr (pronounced eye-ear) Mountains—a jagged massif of dark volcanic rock the size of Switzerland—are home to slender-horned gazelles and Dorcas gazelles, along with reclusive Barbary sheep with massive horns and long, furry neck-ruffs and pantaloons.

Greatest problems—as in "W"—are overgrazing and overbrowsing of acacias by nomadic live-stock, also poaching and international trade in live animals and their by-products. Tuareg people have invaded the area periodically for the past 2,000 years and still tend camels and goats in small irrigated gardens. Rebel insurgents were a serious threat but not since a 1995 peace agreement.

Agadez and Arlit both have lodging and guides—a good idea since it's easy to get lost here. Mountains start immediately north-northeast of Agadez and the amazing sand desert some 300 miles (500 km) beyond that. Toward Tazolé is a fascinating area 90 miles (150 km) long strewn with fossilized dinosaurs—reminders that the whole Sahara was once fertile and green. There are a number of places with rock paintings of giraffes and other species.

---

**FURTHER INFORMATION**

Direction de la Faune, de la Pêche et Pisciculture, Ministère de l'Environnement, B.P. 721, Niamey, Tel: (+227) 734-069; IUCN Niger Representative, B.P. 10933, Niamey, Tel: (+227) 733-338, Fax: (+227) 732-215.

# RWANDA

SILVERY WHALE-HEADED STORKS AND
670 OTHER BIRD SPECIES SHARE RWANDA
WITH ITS WORLD-FAMOUS POPULATION
OF MOUNTAIN GORILLAS. SO DO THE
WORLD'S BIGGEST EARTHWORMS,
BLUE AND A FOOT (30 CM) LONG.

BULKY, INTELLIGENT MOUNTAIN GORILLAS MADE WORLD-FAMOUS BY THE BOOK AND FILM "GORILLAS IN THE MIST" BUILD LEAFY NESTS AND FORAGE ON SEEMINGLY INEDIBLE STINGING NETTLES IN RWANDA'S HAZE-SHROUDED HEIGHTS, PART OF THE VIRUNGA VOLCANOES WHICH STRETCH ALSO INTO DEMOCRATIC REPUBLIC OF CONGO AND UGANDA.

Black-and-white colobus monkeys with flowing white whiskers and shoulder streamers travel with prodigious leaps through dense tropical forests in troops up to 400-strong—largest arboreal primate groups in Africa. Shimmering golden monkeys found only in these mountains chatter in the bamboo, among a dozen or so primate species in this tiny, beautiful, landlocked central African country astride the eastern Rift.

It has one of the continent's richest and most endangered wildlife populations.

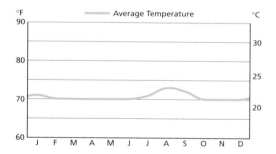

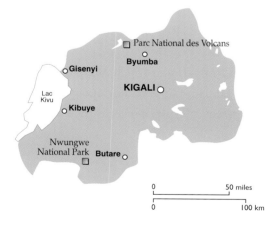

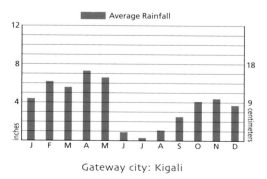

Gateway city: Kigali

Hippos lounge in wild swamps where semi-aquatic sitatunga antelopes splash and graze. Giraffes, elephants, and gazelles forage in savannah and scrub mindful of lions close by.

An amazing 670 bird species include big, silvery whale-headed storks or shoebills—not actually storks but resembling them, with massive heads and large yellow eyes—and multicolored Rwenzori or mountain touracos, unnoticed until they spread crimson wings. Rwanda is a crossroads for migrating raptors—sometimes 550 Eurasian buteos an hour in AKAGERA NATIONAL PARK.

On slopes of six spectacular volcanoes rising over 13,000 feet (4,000 m) are more than 100 kinds of orchids growing in fern and moss-hung hagenia trees. This ecological richness survives precariously in a country devastated by civil war which killed up to one million persons; then by volcanic eruptions which brought great numbers of refugees from neighboring Congo, many into protected wildlife areas where they squatted and now live. Population growth continues unabated—Rwanda has one of the world's highest birth rates. All this exacerbates problems such as habitat destruction and poaching and sets back efforts to encourage tourism on which popular support and effective protection of wild areas depends.

Historically a strong conservation ethic exists. By 1983 this little country a fifth the size of England—10,160 square miles (26,638 km²)—had set aside almost 17 percent of its land (not including forest reserves) in a protected areas system.

## PARC NATIONAL DES VOLCANS (PNV)

Best known is Volcanoes National Park and U.N. Biosphere Reserve—lush forested home of mountain gorillas renowned through George Shaller's and subsequently Dian Fossey's 18-year pioneering work which ended in her brutal murder in 1985. Because of her work and the book and film describing it, thousands of people have come to visit and support protection for these 650 or so of the world's largest primates, which exist only here and in adjoining VIRUNGA NATIONAL PARK in Congo (*see* p.62) and BWINDI IMPENETRABLE FOREST (*see* p.148) and MGAHINGA NATIONAL PARK (*see* p.150) in Uganda.

These enormous gentle beasts, which can be six feet (2 m) tall and weigh 500 pounds (220 kg), survive in a relatively small area—58 square miles (150 km²) in Rwanda, about one-third of that in the Virungas as a whole—hemmed in by agriculture. Despite concerns they would be

OPPOSITE: Mountain gorilla males may stand six feet (2 m) tall, with chests almost that wide, and weigh 500 pounds (220 kg). Known as "silverbacks" for silvery back patches they develop on maturity, they are gentle vegetarians unless provoked. Then they may erupt in fearsome roars, beating cupped hands on barrel chests, sounding like the low-pitched rumble of large drums.

caught up in the bloody civil war, almost all survived, and now have considerable public support, in no small part because they contribute significantly to the country's economy.

Seeing mountain gorillas on their home ground interacting with their families and often showing as much interest in visitors—to whom they have become habituated—as visitors show in them is an unforgettable experience.

Visits can be undertaken by anyone in reasonably fit physical condition. Permission must be obtained from the Rwandan Office for Tourism and National Parks (ORTPN), which is charged with park protection and management and has taken care to ensure safety both for gorillas and visitors.

Rules are strictly enforced. Visitors must stay with park rangers and armed guards and at least 20 feet (6 m) away from gorillas (which sometimes means moving back, as these peaceable creatures may move in for a closer look. Playful youngsters sometimes want to climb into visitors' laps). This is as much to protect gorillas as visitors, out of concern that wild primates could pick up a human virus for which they have no immunity and which could wipe out the whole population.

Pictures may be taken but no flash (fastest-possible settings for these shadowed black subjects). Speak in whispers, make no sudden movements, do not disturb vegetation (a gorilla could be hiding there), turn away and cover your mouth if necessary to cough (chief natural cause of death among mountain gorillas is pneumonia).

Logistics of the trip are, first, go to Kigali, the Rwandan capital which is served by international airlines and has good accommodations, thence by rental car or minibus a 90-minute drive to Ruhengeri, which also has comfortable lodging, or to a lodge just outside park boundaries. From there it's a short distance to park headquarters and a guided one- to four-hour trek through fields and woods to find and observe the gorillas.

Treks are limited to eight persons and visits to one hour. Gorillas are almost always found by the guides, their locations monitored by trackers. In any case, the trip costs $250 U.S. per person, which goes entirely to support the park and its wildlife.

Climate is unpredictable and variable—almost any visit will include both hot and cool weather, rain and sun. Hiking boots are essential, as are hat, gloves to protect against stinging nettles, long sleeves and pants, and light waterproof jacket. Porters are available. Anyone having problems with altitudes above 8,000 feet (2,400 m) should try to come a day or two ahead to acclimate. Best times are dry-season mid-June–September and December–March.

The trek itself can be enthralling (occasionally difficult going if slopes are wet underfoot), winding through giant lobelias and tree-sized St. John's wort covered with delicate yellow bloom. Golden monkeys swing through bamboo, sometimes with dazzling Rwenzori turacos (usually in pairs so if you miss one you might see the other) and underneath, foraging wild buffalo, forest elephants, striped orange bushbucks, and delicate little black-fronted duikers. On the forest floor are some of the world's largest earthworms, blue and a foot long.

But nothing compares with the encounter when—as a primatologist put it—"the human primate views the biggest species in the order", which shares more than 97 percent of our genes. A massive male silverback gorilla reaches out to greet a passing guard he recognizes. Or he stops whatever he is doing—playing with a youngster, munching a celery stalk—to look thoughtfully into a visitor's eyes as if trying to understand him, and the visitor returns the gaze, with feelings described variously as awe, mutual curiosity and an almost mystical sense of connection between two beings that have traveled long, related and finally divergent evolutionary paths.

---

**FURTHER INFORMATION**

ORTPN (Park administrators), P.O. Box 905, Kigali, Tel: (+250) 76514, Fax: (+250) 76512.

---

## ALSO OF INTEREST

**Nwungwe National Park**, largest tract of lower-montane rain forest in East or central Africa—378 square miles (970 km²)—is a rich and ancient center of biodiversity contiguous with Kibira National Park in north Burundi.

Troops of spectacular black-and-white colobus monkeys, sometimes numbering in the hundreds, use branches as trampolines to spring up to 50 feet (15 m) through towering forest openings. Among more than 85 mammal species are 13 primates—25 percent of all Africa's primate species, including rare and beautiful L'Hoest's and owl-faced monkeys and some 500 chimpanzees—plus bushbucks, three kinds of small forest antelopes, Congo clawless otters, leopards, and such smaller predators as golden, wild, and serval cats.

More than 275 bird species include 26 Albertine Rift endemics, among them spectacular crimson-winged Rwenzori or mountain turacos, red-throated alethes, Albertine owlets, handsome francolins, iridescent sunbirds, and the largest world population of Grauer's rush warblers in the crater swamp called "Kamiranzovu—place of the Elephants." Plants include more than 200 tree species plus giant tree ferns and hundreds of flowering plants, among them giant lobelias and dozens of kinds of orchids.

Many endemic flora and fauna descend from species that found refuge here during the last ice age.

Over 12 miles (20 km) of hiking trails wind through towering hardwood stands, alongside gorges and waterfalls and most of the wildlife, including dazzling butterflies.

# RWANDA

The park, which because of elevation is comfortably cool all year, is 85 miles (135 km) southwest of Kigali, transected by the main road between Butare and Cyangugu with a visitor center, comfortable rest house, and campsite along the main road. It can also be visited as a day trip from hotels in Butare and Cyangugu, each about 30 miles (48 km) away. Guides can be arranged for tracking birds and various primate species.

**Akagera National Park** in east Rwanda has been one of the most wildlife-rich reserves in Africa, with zebras, elephants, buffalo, lions, gazelles, baboons, leopards, a dozen kinds of antelopes, and phenomenal birds—over 500 species, including many beautiful and rare endemics—in its acacia savannahs, gallery forests, lakes and huge papyrus swamps. Overrun by rebel forces in 1991, settled afterward by displaced people for whom its total area was reduced from 965 to 347 square miles (2,500–900 km$^2$), its future may depend on its tourism value. It is well worth a visit, not only for wildlife but for its off-the-beaten-track beauty, just a little over two hours' drive from Kigali (4WD best inside the park).

Rwandan accommodations and roads before the civil war were good, as was travel through the country by Air Rwanda, and foreign aid has since repaired much of the damage caused by the civil war. Warnings about insecurity have been discontinued and most of the country is safe, but cautious travelers might still wish to check before visiting.

---

**FURTHER INFORMATION**

Rwanda Office for Tourism and National Parks (ORTPN), P.O. Box 905, Kigali-Rwanda, Tel: (+250) 576514/573396, Fax: (+250) 576512, Tlx: 22542 ORTPN RW; good for park literature, or (for gorillas) (+250) 546645 in Ruhengeri; Projet Environnement et Developement, Ministère du Plan, B.P. 46, Kigali, Tel: (+250) 572235/572237; Division de la Gestion Forestière, Ministère de l'Agriculture, de l'Élévage et des Forêts, B.P. 621, Kigali, Rwanda.

# SENEGAL/ THE GAMBIA

AN ESTIMATED THREE MILLION BIRDS STOP OVER IN MIGRATION AT DJOUDJ NATIONAL PARK, SPREADING SOMETIMES AS FAR AS THE EYE CAN SEE. LORDING IT OVER THE NIOKOLO-KOBA SAVANNAH NEARBY ARE AFRICA'S BIGGEST LIONS— UP TO 10 FEET (3 M) FROM NOSE TO TAIL-TIP— AND LORD DERBY ELANDS, WORLD'S LARGEST ANTELOPES, WEIGHING UP TO A TON.

BIRDS OF EXTRAORDINARY COLOR AND VARIETY FIND HOMES EVERYWHERE IN THESE WESTERNMOST AFRICAN COUNTRIES THAT ARE AN ECOLOGICAL CROSSROADS BETWEEN THE VAST ARID SAHARA AND HUMID EQUATORIAL TROPICS. With them are some of the largest mammals on the continent.

Senegal, about one and one-half times the size of England, touches the southern Sahara on its north, becomes gradually greener as it's crossed by three river systems, and finally is covered with tropical vegetation in the south. It is divided in a slash two-thirds down by tiny Gambia (The Gambia) which has been a separate entity since colonial days when it was a British protectorate surrounded by French territory.

Shorebirds in the millions literally cover coastal marshes in spring and fall—plovers, sandpipers, curlews, whimbrels, godwits—

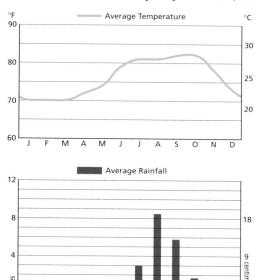

Average Temperature

Average Rainfall

Gateway city: Dakar

probing intertidal mudflats for worms and crustaceans to fuel migration flights between far northern breeding grounds and winter homes to the south.

Long-legged Goliath herons five feet (1.5 m) tall stalk shallow marine estuaries. Jewel-like malachite kingfishers dive for minnows. Delicate rust-colored African jacanas—"Jesus birds"— trip with splayed toes atop floating vegetation. Peach-breasted Egyptian plovers, called crocodile birds for their reported habit of cleaning crocodiles' teeth, look for grasshoppers along pond edges and fields where crowned cranes with golden spray-crests peer over tasseled savannah grasses.

Every possible ecological opportunity is exploited.

Beautiful violet turacos pluck ripe fruit in forest gloom. Enterprising little honeyguides enlist badgers and sometimes humans to break open beehives which they share, feeding on larvae and eggs while their followers get the honey.

At night silent-winged owls take flight—12 species, from diminutive scops owls to Pel's fishing owls and massive eagle-owls over two feet (65 cm) long—preying on everything from small lizards and mice to fish and roosting birds.

In hotel gardens exquisite red-cheeked cordon-bleus flit about shrubbery. Yellow-crowned gonoleks feed on lawns. Red-billed firefinches scrounge seeds at grain stores. Over clearings and roadways graceful scissor-tailed kites—called "white angels"—hover and handsome bateleur eagles teeter as if trying to keep their balance ("bateleur" is French for tightrope walker)—a few of some 660 bird species.

Among more than 80 mammal species are some of the largest lions anywhere—almost 10 feet (2.9 m) long from head to tail-tip—lording it over the savannah, with the world's largest antelopes, giant Lord Derby's elands weighing up to a ton, chestnut with vertical white stripes and massive V-shaped horns.

In rocky outcrops crested (or brush-tailed) porcupines share lairs with 18-inch (45-cm) rock hyrax, undersized relatives of elephants. Desert foxes or fennecs adapt to drier places with rare addax, beautiful white antelopes with great twisted horns. Chimpanzees are here with water-bucks, bushbucks, gazelles, antelopes, spotted and striped hyenas, civets, and a few golden cats and wild dogs, along with elephants, buffalo, leopards—nearly all the great animals typical of African forest, bush and veld.

The first national park was created here in 1925 under French rule. Now Senegal has 11 wildlife reserves including three U.N. Biosphere Reserves, two World Heritage Sites and four Ramsar wetlands classed as of world importance. With forest set-asides they cover over 11 percent of the country. The Gambia has six national parks and reserves covering 3.7 percent, with more planned.

# NIOKOLO-KOBA NATIONAL PARK

In southeast Senegal, this is one of West Africa's finest for large mammals—a beautiful wilderness of Sudanese savannah, lakes, marshes, and Guinea forest, large and varied enough (3,300 square miles/8,500 km$^2$) to support a variety of naturally sustained populations. Here are Africa's largest lions along with elephants, hippos, buffalo, leopards, giant or Derby elands, big, handsome roan antelopes with clown masks and long tasseled ears, baboons, panthers, crocodiles, honey badgers, and a variety of antelopes, among more than 80 mammal species. Green vervet (or grivet) and red colobus monkeys scream and chatter and perform remarkable aerial feats in ancient silk cotton, mahogany, and kapok trees, with troupes of chimpanzees at the northernmost point of their range.

Over 350 bird species recorded here include majestic bateleur eagles, called the world's most beautiful raptor with brilliant rust, white and jet-black markings; long-necked black-bellied bustards striding about grasslands with necks waving back and forth like cobras in a basket; handsome exclamatory paradise whydahs, 4.5 inches (12 cm) long, with tails more than twice that. And there's much more—turkey-sized Abyssinian ground hornbills, violet touracos, dazzling multicolored red-throated bee-eaters, iridescent violet-backed starlings, blue-breasted kingfishers, white-faced tree ducks, Senegalese coucals, saddle-bill storks, and hammerheads, to mention just a few.

In the Gambia River and its tributaries are hippos and all three African crocodiles—the Nile, slender-snouted, and dwarf—plus a variety of water-oriented birds including lovely African pygmy geese with pale lime-green cheeks, orange flanks and black and white faces, pink-backed pelicans, white-faced tree-ducks, curious knob-billed geese with huge combs on their upper bills, great spur-winged geese with pink bills and feet, and green-glossed black wings and mantles.

Main park entrance is at Dar-Salam on the main road between Tambaçounda (park head-quarters) and Kedougou (lodging is available at both), about 300 miles (483 km) southeast of Dakar, where transportation—including two weekly trains—and tours can be arranged. Inside the park at Simenti is an airstrip, visitor center, campsites, and hotel with simple accommodations where morning and evening river trips and guides of varying expertise are available (their use is obligatory, and fees help the park). Walking is allowed only with a park ranger, and vehicles should have 4WD. Many birds (Egyptian plovers, white-headed lapwings, African blue-flycatchers, and oriole warblers) and animals (hippos, elephants, kob, and oribi antelopes) are around the Simenti lodge and nearby. A path from the visitor center leads to an observation hide overlooking a water hole/grazing area—though an even wider range of species is in the eastern sector. More basic accommodations are available in a lovely setting at a bush camp on the Gambia River four miles (6 km) from Simenti, as are several campsites. Best viewing—though it's hot—is in March–May, end of dry season.

## SENEGAL/THE GAMBIA

Threats include plans for an artificial lake and dams on the Gambia, Senegal, and Niokolo-Koba rivers; mining and quarrying; and poaching which has reduced elephant and leopard populations. Contiguous BADIAR NATIONAL PARK in Guinea (*see* p.78) was established to discourage entry by poachers and grazers.

### FURTHER INFORMATION

Parc Conservateur, Parc National de Niokolo-Koba, Tambaçounda, B.P. 37, Tel: (+221) 981-10-97.

Turkey-sized ground hornbills prefer walking on stubby, broad-soled feet to flying. They frequent low-grass steppes and savannahs where they stalk prey that may include snakes, tortoises, squirrels, even small hares. Males' booming calls are audible for miles. One of the world's longest-lived birds, captives have survived more than 40 years.

# Djoudj National Park

One of the most important bird sanctuaries in the world. An estimated three million migrants pass every year through this beautiful 60-square-mile (155-km²) Ramsar and World Heritage Site, part of a vast basin of combined freshwater and saline flats on the Senegal River delta in the country's extreme north. More than 400 bird species have been counted. For many it's their first stop after a long flight over the Sahara. Some go farther, others stay for the winter, still others are resident and nest, including great colonies of pelicans and pink flamingos.

The spectacle of millions of colorful, calling, constantly moving birds spread out in huge variety as far as the eye can see over these channels, creeks, ponds, lakes, marshes, reedbeds, and mudflats is, for most who have seen it, unforgettably moving, and for anyone who has not, almost indescribable. The scene can only be suggested—masses of milling herons, egrets, storks, spoonbills, plovers, sandpipers, ruffs, godwits, swallows, passerines, ducks, tree-ducks, geese, jacanas, rails, moorhens, oystercatchers, curlews, and, periodically sweeping overhead, throwing all into turmoil, raptors such as dark chanting goshawks and Montagu's harriers.

In riverine and semi-desert thickets are arid-savannah specialties—golden nightjars, river prinias, kordofan larks, Sudan bustards.

Mammals and reptiles are here as well—manatees in the water, and in surrounding uplands, warthogs, jackals, hyenas, monkeys, mongeese, and gazelles, and, often resting by the water's edge, an enormous python.

Water, a problem at many reserves, is especially critical here. Dry years such as many recent ones will, if prolonged, be a dangerous threat. A dike and dam system now in place helps ensure against exposure to serious fluctuations. But competition for scarce supplies comes from others such as rice farmers. Djoudj would be safer if it were larger and if hunting reserves were farther away. All this means Djoudj is a fragile ecological treasure which at any point could become perilously endangered.

Accommodations, also campgrounds, are available at park headquarters and main entrance and in St. Louis, 37 miles (60 km) southwest, where tours can be arranged. Keen birders might wish to spend at least several days exploring on their own, getting around by taxi or hired car. It's also possible to hire a boat or canoe (watch out for crocodiles). Observation platforms are at 12 sites. The park is closed periodically for research and maintenance—also some afternoons—check ahead.

---

**FURTHER INFORMATION**

Conservateur, Parc National des Oiseaux de Djoudj, B.P. 80, Saint Louis, Senegal.

## Also of Interest

**Basse Casamance National Park**, 19 square miles (50 km²) of forest and mangroves at Oussouyé in the extreme south, famous for tropical vegetation—rich Guinea forest with kapok trees, oil palms, and imposing parinarias—and wildlife variety, including Derby elands, buffoon cobs, and many monkey species. Reachable by plane or car from Dakar.

**Langue de Barbarie National Park** is a narrow sandy strip between the Senegal River and the Atlantic, refuge for birds and breeding sea turtles. Boat trips from St. Louis.

**Delta du Saloum National Park** has 280 square miles (730 km²) of mangroves, dunes, swamps, and small islands, in the Saloum Delta 50 miles (80 km) east of Kaolack with hundreds of bird species, from Sudan golden sparrows to brown snake-eagles, storks, flamingos.

**L'Ile de la Madeleine National Park**, a 1,200-acre (486-ha) protected marine park 1.7 miles (3 km) offshore from Dakar, with many seabird colonies.

In Gambia, **Abuko Nature Reserve** is noted for bird and monkey populations in protected gallery forest 12 miles (20 km) south of Banjul near the coast. Bird spe-

NOTE: Some birders prefer the Gambia to Senegal. Swallow-tailed bee-eaters and blue-bellied rollers and a few others can be easier to see in the Gambia—but spectacular birds are so abundant over the whole region that comparisons seem irrelevant. Both should be seen and can be, easily, by car, train, bus, and often air.

cialties include white-backed night herons, red-thighed sparrowhawks, white-spotted flufftails, pied-winged swallows—plus various colorful parrots, turacos, paradise flycatchers, glossy-starlings, sunbirds. It's home as well to many sititungas, bushbucks, and acrobatic red colobus, vervet (or green) and patas monkeys. Beautiful forest trails lead to hides overlooking pools. The reserve runs a rehabilitation center for injured and orphaned animals which is an educational center as well for Gambian schoolchildren—but anyone can visit. Chimpanzees are raised here before release on islands upriver.

Most international travelers arrive by air at Dakar—or if going directly to Gambia, at Banjul—both linked by regional airlines to other capital cities in West Africa as well as major in-country centers, also by an extensive rail network and some 2,420 miles (3,900 km) of asphalt roads. A range of accommodations, also campsites, are available. Best times are dry season December–April.

### FURTHER INFORMATION

Service des Parcs Nationaux (Le Directeur des Parcs Nationaux), Ministère de la Protection de la Nature, B.P. 5135, Point E, Dakar Fann, Tel: (+221) 832-23-09; Direction des Eaux, Forêts et Chasses, Ministère de la Protection de la Nature, B.P. 1831, Dakar Fann.

# SOUTH
# AFRICA

KRUGER NATIONAL PARK, SOUTH AFRICA'S
LARGEST, OFFERS HOMES TO MORE MAMMAL
SPECIES THAN ANY OTHER RESERVE ON THE
CONTINENT—HUGE POPULATIONS OF OVER
8,000 ELEPHANTS, 25,000 BUFFALO,
25,000 ZEBRAS—PLUS HIGHEST DENSITY
OF RAPTORS IN THE WORLD.

S OUTH AFRICA HAS ONE OF THE EARTH'S RICHEST WILDLIFE HERITAGES, THE RESULT OF A DIVERSITY OF
CLIMATE, TOPOGRAPHY, ANIMAL AND PLANT LIFE, AND SCENIC BEAUTY WHICH HAS BEEN PROTECTED
IN A GREAT AND COMPREHENSIVE NATIONAL PARK SYSTEM. Some, like KRUGER, help preserve a
variety of ecosystems; some have striking scenic values; some, like BONTEBOK and MOUN-
TAIN ZEBRA reserves, were established for one or a few rare species.

Members of South Africa's National Parks Board have understood the importance of getting
support from the millions of people living near the various park boundaries. To that end they
have undertaken a program to educate leaders and schoolchildren in surrounding communities

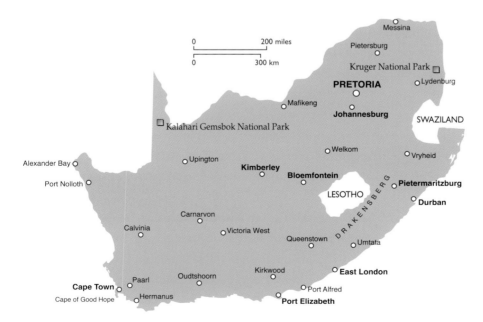

131

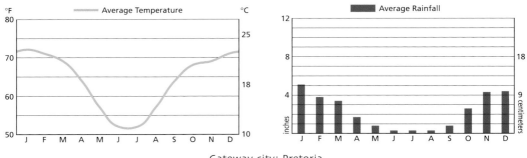

Gateway city: Pretoria

about the benefits to them of preserving wild systems and lands, including economic benefits from employment created to take care of visitors from around the world.

Surplus animals, especially from large herds in Kruger, are transported to other parks or buffer areas around parks. In some of these, limited hunting may be allowed. This also provides financial support and jobs.

South Africa has 17 national parks, each in a unique natural situation, covering more than 7,700 square miles (19,950 km²) and accommodating 1.09 million visitors a year. Premier among these are KALAHARI GEMSBOK and Kruger.

# KALAHARI GEMSBOK NATIONAL PARK

This park is so arid, harsh, and inhospitable that it has survived almost unchanged since ancient times, suitable only for creatures adapted to endure these trying surroundings. It is a place to see plants and animals so adapted, some seen in few other places.

Gemsbok, the antelopes for which the park is named, seem able to exist almost without water, drinking largely to satisfy mineral needs. They don't perspire, thereby conserving valuable moisture. When temperatures rise to 113°F (45°C), their own body temperatures can rise to or above that level for up to eight hours (an internal temperature at which most animals would suffer brain damage) through a special system of blood vessels which cools the blood before it reaches the brain.

Burchell's sandgrouse come to water holes or rivers, sometimes in flocks of hundreds, not only to drink and bathe but to soak breast feathers with water which they carry back in this way to thirsty nestlings.

Many animals are nocturnal, spending the day in burrows, coming out only in cooler evenings to hunt and forage. Perhaps for this reason, the park is rich in owls, notably the scops, white-faced scops, and pearl-spotted owls, and giant eagle-owls. Bat-eared foxes are equipped with huge ears that not only help cool blood vessels but enable them to hear and track down insect prey which survive by spending most of their lives underground.

## SOUTH AFRICA

Kalahari lions seem larger than lions elsewhere because of their heavier manes which may help insulate them from the heat.

Camel-thorn trees along dry riverbeds are supported by extensive root systems which reach deep below the surface. In their branches are sociable weaver birds, well-named, which build huge communal nests looking like haystacks that may have 50 or so nest chambers. Handsome little pygmy falcons take over some of these.

Sheltered underneath are underground colonies of bloodthirsty sand tampans, small ticks that do not attack native antelopes but seek out domestic cattle and humans, which they find with carbon dioxide sensors that are attracted to exhaled breath. Somehow they differentiate.

Important, perhaps indispensable, food plants are tsamma melons and gemsbok cucumbers, both 95 percent moisture. They make subsistence possible for a wide range of insects, birds, rodents, sometimes hyenas and honey badgers. Antelopes unearth and eat succulent cucumber roots.

Supported by all these are the carnivores—lions, leopards, cheetahs, black-backed jackals, and smaller varieties. Among the park's 215 bird species is a population of predators ranging in size from pint-sized pygmy falcons (length 7.5 inches/19.5 cm) to lappet-faced vultures with wingspreads up to 103 inches (2.7 m), known to kill small mammals including hares.

Sometimes herds of thousands of blue wildebeest, red hartebeest, and elands move about in search of water.

Otherwise wildlife is widely spaced and sparse in any one section of this huge semidesert savannah reserve, where temperatures can range from almost 125°F (50°C) on a hot midsummer day to below freezing at night in midwinter. Most wildlife tends to be concentrated in and near the Nissob and Auob riverbeds, though both these are dry except after heavy rains. In dry times animals congregate around boreholes maintained for them.

It is an immense reserve, some 3,700 square miles (9,600 km²), adjoined on the other side of the Nissob River by Botswana's Kalahari Gemsbok National Park, 10,279 square miles (26,600 km²). Their combined area is larger than Belgium and almost twice the size of Kruger National Park. There are no barriers between the two so wildlife can travel freely over the whole area, and recently the two countries entered into an agreement to manage them as one ecological entity, to be called Kgalagadi Transfrontier Park.

Best times are March and April, end of the rainy season, when animals, including large raptor flocks, are concentrated along riverbeds. Afterward they disperse among the red sand dunes.

**FURTHER READING**

*A Story Like the Wind*, a Laurens van der Post novel set partially in the Kalahari.

# KRUGER NATIONAL PARK

The largest national park in South Africa (7,700 square miles/20,000 km², about the size of Wales or Massachusetts) with more mammal species than any other reserve on the continent. It has huge populations of elephants (over 8,000), buffalo (25,000), and Burchell's zebras (25,000), along with a wide variety of other herbivores, including both black and white (wide-lipped) rhinos.

The range of fascinating wild creatures can only be suggested here—49 fish species, 33 amphibians, 114 reptiles, 507 birds, 300 trees, and altogether 147 species of mammals. The mammals include leopards, lions, and cheetahs among the predators, and Kruger also has the highest density of birds of prey in the world, including 15 eagle species.

Impressive statistics aside, it is beautiful, from the mixed vegetation and rolling terrain in the southern section, waving gold or green grassy plains of the south-central district, wooded mopane veld in the north-central, and the sandveld communities and lush riverine forests in the north. Each harbors its own network of species.

Elephants, roan antelopes, tsessebes (a topi subspecies), and elands are mainly in mopane woodland in the north. Burchell's zebras, blue wildebeest, black rhinoceros, giraffes, and impala are mainly in central and southern areas as are lions which prey on the wildebeests and zebras.

Massive buffalo roam throughout the park. Other herbivores include kudus, with spectacular twisted horns, sable antelopes, waterbucks, warthogs, steenboks, duikers, and klipspringers, only antelopes able to live on steep cliffs and kopjes. There they escape less-agile predators by springing from foothold to precarious foothold on the tips of tiny hooves (but their young are vulnerable to eagles and baboons).

Cheetahs, leopards, wild dogs—Africa's rarest, most endangered carnivores, each with their own unique spotted coats—and black-backed jackals may be spotted almost anywhere, though leopards are mainly nocturnal.

Kruger is a stronghold of striking, solitary martial eagles. Goliath herons standing 4.5 feet (1.4 m) tall wade serenely in shallows of all major rivers. Hammerkops may take six months to build huge dome-shaped nests with entrances at the bottom—but when they are through, few predators can disturb them.

Purple-crested loeries or turacos with extraordinary red, green, and glossy purple plumage feed on riverine tree fruits. Kingfishers of varied bright plumage dive for small fish along major rivers, beating their prey against a branch before swallowing it. Five species of exquisitely rainbow-hued rollers snatch insects on the ground to consume on overhead branches.

Masked yellow-and-black male weaver birds weave intricate nests which their mates usually reject on the first try, so they tear them apart and start all over. Usually it takes several tries before they get it right.

## SOUTH AFRICA

Butterflies flutter along riverbanks. Dung beetles, not the most beautiful of insects but arguably the most unusual, make balls of elephant dung in which they lay an egg, then roll along and bury for their offspring to eat later. In this way they also fertilize the soil. They are so highly regarded in the park that drivers are asked to be careful not to run over them on the road.

Kruger was one of the world's first national parks. Paul Kruger, the country's president, set aside land here for wildlife preservation in 1898 and successors have added to it. It is, more than almost any other great world wildlife refuge, a people's park. No place has better facilities for getting around and seeing things. There are hard-surfaced roads throughout, numerous reasonably-priced accommodations ranging from modest to deluxe, and plenty of information available for self-guided tours. There are also guided walking tours on special wilderness trails. Wildlife-lovers on a modest budget can see a great variety of species in large numbers here without the cost of outfitters, private lodges, and Land Rovers. (The downside is that the park is heavily used—700,000 visitors a year. Reservations are a must.)

Lilac-breasted rollers are named for their acrobatic courtship flights, in which loudly calling males climb swiftly and steeply, perhaps 150 feet (50 m), before tipping forward and diving with wings closed almost to the ground, then opening them and rising again. They may repeat this several times before diving at great speed, while rolling to left and right, finally landing near the female, who by then is often calling in response. Calls are less lovely than flights or plumage: a harsh "zaaak" squawk. Common in open scrub and grasslands.

An alternative way to see Kruger's wildlife is through high-priced luxury camps located along the park's western border in private reserves. These offer the same species with much lower visitor density. They also offer open vehicles, off-road vehicles, and night drives, none of which are available in Kruger itself.

Best times are dry season May–September, when wildlife spends more time near remaining water and is more easily seen. But birding is best in the rainy southern hemisphere summer when northern migrants are present and local birds are breeding and nesting.

---

**FURTHER INFORMATION**

Park Warden, Private Bag X402, SKUKUZA 1350, South Africa.

# ALSO OF INTEREST

**Addo Elephant National Park** protects Addo elephants, once nearly exterminated. Now they are seen at water holes, also on night drives along with bushpigs, aardvarks, kudus, rhinoceros, genets, others.

**Augrabies Falls National Park** was founded to conserve wildlife and scenery around these spectacular falls, now a center to preserve highly endangered Cape rhinoceros, a subspecies of black rhinoceros. Klipspringers are here, also springboks, pale-winged starlings, rosy-faced lovebirds, and others.

**Bontebok National Park**—bonteboks are rare, beautifully patterned antelopes, unique to the Cape Floral area, where they were brought back from near-extinction. Here also are clawless otters, Stanley's bustards, numerous blue cranes (South Africa's national bird).

**Karoo National Park** has a great wildlife array amid dramatic scenery—53 mammal species include aardwolves, endangered riverine rabbits; 66 species of reptiles and amphibians; 170 bird species include orange-throated longclaws and black eagles.

**Mountain Zebra National Park**—formerly endangered Cape mountain zebras were brought back from near-extinction here. There are also herds of elands, hartebeest, kudus, black wildebeest, and 200-plus bird species.

**Vaalbos National Park**—breeding populations of black and white rhinoceros are being established here, also gemsboks, giraffes, elands, others. Facilities under development.

**Wilderness National Park** is a key waterbird sanctuary, threatened by development, with 270 bird species including gatherings sometimes of 2,000 ducks of nine species, 100 great crested grebes, others.

**Zuurberg National Park**, with rugged mountainous beauty, visitor facilities being developed, with particularly diverse birdlife—crowned eagles, jackal buzzards, black and martial eagles, orange-breasted and malachite sunbirds.

---

**FURTHER INFORMATION**

South African National Parks, P.O. Box 787, Pretoria 0001, South Africa, Tel: (+27) 12-428-9111, Fax: (+27) 12-426-5500, E-mail: reservations@parks-sa.co.za, Website: www.parks-sa.co.za

# TANZANIA

MORE THAN ONE MILLION MIGRATING
WILDEBEEST TREK ACROSS SERENGETI NATIONAL
PARK YEARLY IN ONE OF THE WILDLIFE SPECTACLES OF
THE WORLD. NOT FAR AWAY IN OLDUVAI GORGE, A GERMAN
ENTOMOLOGIST LOOKING FOR BUTTERFLIES FOUND AN ANCIENT
HORSE BONE WHICH LED TO THE LEAKEYS' DISCOVERY OF LUCY
AND SOME OF THE WORLD'S OLDEST HUMAN REMAINS.

TANZANIA IS A LAND OF SUPERLATIVES. IT IS THE SIZE OF TEXAS AND FRANCE COMBINED. WILDLIFE RESERVES COVER OVER 95,000 SQUARE MILES (250,000 KM²), AND PROTECTED AREAS MAKE UP ABOUT 30 PERCENT OF THE COUNTRY.

They range from the vast SERENGETI in the north, with more than two million grazing animals, to the wild, remote SELOUS in the south, twice the size of Denmark, believed to hold the largest concentration of elephants, crocodiles, hippos, and endangered black rhinoceros anywhere.

## ARUSHA NATIONAL PARK

Sir Julian Huxley called Arusha National Park "a gem amongst parks" for its beauty and remarkable diversity of wildlife and habitat. Elephants, buffalo, warthogs, olive baboons, giraffes, bushbucks, and black-and-white colobus monkeys seem relaxed and comfortable in settings ranging from swamps, rain forest, acacia woodlands to the various elevational life zones on the sides of Mt. Meru, fifth-highest peak in Africa. Huge migrant waterfowl flocks stop by lakes which commonly accommodate flamingos, grebes, African pochards, Egyptian geese, and a

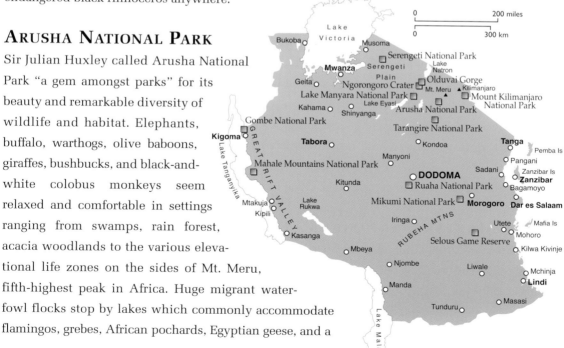

137

# TANZANIA

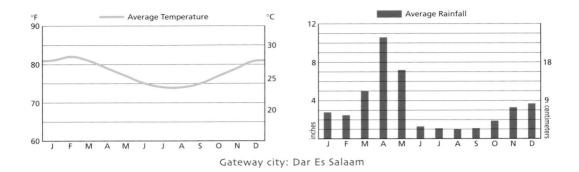

Gateway city: Dar Es Salaam

variety of herons and egrets. Elsewhere are augur buzzards, crowned hawk-eagles, and brilliant white-fronted bee-eaters, among almost 400 bird species in this 53-square-mile (137-km²) sanctuary just 21 miles (34.5 km) from Arusha. Momela Lodge, spectacular set for the movie "Hatari," looks into Meru Crater, called one of the most startling landscapes in Africa. There are other lodges and campsites.

## GOMBE STREAM NATIONAL PARK

Chimpanzees, our next of kin in the animal world, sharing 98 to 99 percent of our genes, use tools, behave in complex social relationships in many ways similar to humans, and show facial expressions of anger, puzzlement, and joy. None of this was known when Dr. Jane Goodall began her pioneering work in 61-square-mile (158-km²) Gombe Stream in 1960. Scientists first doubted, then believed her evidence. Now she and her chimps are renowned, and this small area is a protected national park, where it's possible to stop by and see them all year. It's not easy. Travel to the park is by water only, from Ujiji or Kigoma. Overnight facilities are limited and need to be booked well ahead. A guide is required for walking around the area. It's necessary to be careful. Chimps are strong and unpredictable and while fascinating, can be dangerous, even though Goodall's work has habituated them to humans. Among Goodall's discoveries is that they are capable of murder and cannibalism. Good reading is her *In The Shadow of Man*.

## LAKE MANYARA NATIONAL PARK

Lake Manyara's tree-climbing lions are only the most famous part of what may be the greatest biomass density (weight per area) of mammals in the world, in this relatively small national park which some feel is the most beautiful in Africa.

Massive elephants and buffalo contribute hugely to this mass but there are also 7,000-pound (3,200-kg) hippos, each consuming 132 pounds (60 kg) of sedge daily along the Simba River, impressive wildebeest herds, zebras, giraffes, gazelles, and over 380 bird species including 44 diurnal raptors—and, still, some endangered black rhinoceros.

Thousands, sometimes millions of colorful water-based birds—flamingos, white pelicans, and others—come to feed and rest on the lake that makes up two-thirds of this 125-square-mile (325-km²) park. Immense nesting colonies sometimes can seem to cover tops of lakeshore fever trees.

Behind all this the Great Rift escarpment rises 1,000 feet (300+ m), dissected by deep gorges from which rivers flow constantly into the lake. In a golden afternoon light with the water reflecting intense colors of the evening sky, the vista is unforgettable.

Birdsong rings out early and late in verdant lowland forest. Vervet and blue monkeys swing through the canopy of mahogany and sausage trees. Olive baboons scream to alert all to a leopard's presence. Aardvarks root about for termites, listening for ants' faint rustlings as they cut and carry off dried grass. Scaly armored pangolins hunt for them too, lapping them up with sticky 27.5-inch (40-cm) tongues.

Elephants feeding on fallen figs are followed by troops of banded mongeese which inspect their dung for edible insects.

No one is sure why lions here climb trees. They apparently do it in Ruwenzori to see over the tall grass. Perhaps here they are adapting to get away from the elephants and buffalo, or else to avoid biting flies, of which there are many.

## MAHALE MOUNTAINS NATIONAL PARK

Some of Africa's last wild chimpanzees leap from branch to branch in this remote 623-square-mile (1,613-km²) national park just to the south of Gombe (*see* above), where Dr. Jane Goodall did her pioneering studies. Some 700 to 1,000 of them live in a 40-square-mile (100-km²) forest on the Kungwe Ridge, and about 100 of them have been habituated to human visitors by way of a 20-year study by a team of Japanese scientists. There are also lions and leopards, elephants, bushbucks, brush-tailed porcupines, red-legged sun squirrels, and other primates including black-and-white and red colobus monkeys, and olive baboons. A visit here by surface transport is fascinating but involves a long boat trip. Air charters can be arranged. There are several luxury tented lodges. Best time: May–October dry season.

Both Mahale Mountains and Gombe adjoin **Lake Tanganyika**, the world's longest lake (446 miles/714 km) and second deepest, going down an astonishing 4,700 feet (1,433 m)—one of the richest water habitats in the world. More than 250 fish species live in its clear waters, of which 200 are cichlids, most of them endemic, which have evolved in presence of a subspecies of Nile perch known as lake salmon. Kigoma on Lake Tanganyika is jumping-off place for both

Gombe Stream and Mahale Mountains. (Ujiji, just south, is where Stanley said "Dr. Livingstone, I presume.")

# MIKUMI NATIONAL PARK

This became a national park in 1964 when hunters threatened to destroy herds which gathered on the Mkata River floodplain after road construction gave them easy access. Now its 1,247 square miles (3,230 km²) have stable populations of elephants, buffalo, wildebeest (the handsome Nyasa blue variety with black beards and tan leggings), warthogs, zebras, giraffes, and three antelopes rare in northern reserves—roan, sable, and curly-horned greater kudus. Balancing the ecology are lions, leopards, African hunting dogs, and black-backed jackals. Yellow baboons feed on grass and fruit and occasionally young impalas. Open-billed storks pry apart mollusks at the hippo pool, where hippo regulars are identifiable by individual eye wrinkle patterns.

Pythons up to 20 feet (5.5 m) long here are strong enough to knock down small impalas, which they squeeze and asphyxiate. White-backed night herons, bronze-winged coursers, and spotted-throated woodpeckers are among notable birds. Mikumi, with tented camps and a hotel, is four hours' drive (175 miles, 285 km) from Dar es Salaam (4WD is best inside the park).

# MOUNT KILIMANJARO NATIONAL PARK

Members of London's Geographical Society doubted at first that a snowy peak like Kilimanjaro (the name means "shining mountain") could exist on Africa's steamy equator, though reports first came to the geographer Ptolemy 18 centuries ago. They did not realize its height: 19,340 feet (5,895 m), where temperatures are freezing, tallest freestanding mountain in the world, visible 200 miles (330 km) away, centerpiece of Mount Kilimanjaro National Park.

Climbing Kilimanjaro takes five days for the physically fit and passes through five altitudinal zones, from cultivated lower slopes, through forest, then heath-moor/lower alpine, then high desert/alpine, finally the summit (where a leopard once was found frozen, a puzzle still unresolved).

The forest zone is lushest, with giant 20-foot (6-m) tree ferns and 30-foot (9-m) lobelias, and among fauna, blue monkeys, olive baboons, tree hyrax, bushbucks. On north and west slopes are elephants, elands, giraffes, tiny suni antelopes and, found only in a few mountain forests in northern Tanzania, Abbot's (gray) duikers.

OPPOSITE: This black rhinoceros is having ticks and other parasites removed by a yellow-billed oxpecker, which does the same symbiotic favor for Cape buffalo, zebras, giraffes, wildebeest, warthogs, and a variety of other grazers plagued by these pests.

Best time is drier January–March, August, and October. Contact park office through kinapa@habari.co.tz

# NGORONGORO CRATER NATIONAL PARK

If you could spend one day in Africa, Ngorongoro Crater might be the place to do it. This lush and beautiful caldera, largest unflooded collapsed volcano in the world, is home to a density and variety of wildlife that have made it known as an eighth wonder of the world.

Thomson's are East Africa's commonest gazelle, major prey species for cheetahs, lions, leopards, hunting dogs, and hyenas. Young ones are vulnerable as well to jackals, baboons, eagles, pythons, and smaller cats. Main defenses are keen senses and speed—they can run 40 miles an hour (67 kph), often for longer than a sprinting cheetah can pursue them.

Vista from the rim, a great green bowl 10 miles (16 km) across arrayed with colorful birds, grazing animals, and powerful predators in a tranquil, idyllic setting, is unlike any other in the natural world. Here is Africa's densest known population of lions, lounging about in prides or family groups of unusual size—up to 30 or so, because generally speaking, the living is easy and the prey base can support this many.

Black rhinoceros—possibly the only viable breeding population left in northern Tanzania— look about nearsightedly (and sometimes charge threatening-looking vehicles). Large herds of wildebeest graze.

Animals are free to come and go up and over the 2,000-foot-high (610-m) rim and back again— but most of them don't except in periods of extreme drought. Normally there is enough food and fresh water here for zebras, gazelles, buffalo, elands, hartebeest, warthogs, and all the rest (the crater supports some 25,000 large mammals).

Waterbirds are always around the swamps and streams—spoonbills, jacanas, herons, Egyptian geese. Thousands of lesser flamingos throng Lake Magadi.

Kori bustards, heaviest birds that can fly, weighing up to 41.8 pounds (19 kg), fluff plumage over their backs in elaborate grassland territorial display. Ostriches graze, towering (at six feet/2 m) over the rest. Crowned cranes need not display to look spectacular, and golden-winged sunbirds brighten the highland forest.

Leopards prowl rim woodlands, where blue monkeys and olive baboons swing about and bushbabies call at night, attracting the attention of spotted serval cats. Augur buzzards and Verreaux's eagles glide over the canopy.

Almost all the elephants are males which leave when the courtship urge overtakes them and then return. Females are absent, it's believed, because browse suitable for young families is less abundant here. Giraffes and impalas are missing, partly because they find the angles of climb difficult, and for giraffes, much of the food is lower than their preferred treetop height.

Otherwise, if you picnic, be prepared for almost anything to join you—especially African black kites and vervet monkeys.

## OLDUVAI GORGE

A German entomologist looking for butterflies in Olduvai Gorge in 1911 found fossil bones of a prehistoric horse. Louis Leakey became convinced that Olduvai held more than horses' bones. He and his wife, Mary, started digging in 1931 and found stone tools, many more bones and finally a skull which showed that this dusty 31-mile-long (50-km) gorge has been continuously occupied by humans for almost two million years. Perhaps longer, since Mary Leakey found footprints, identical to modern-day humans', in a 3.5-million-year-old site at Laetoli, not far away. Other discoveries have followed—remains of the famous "Lucy" and more than 150 animal species among which these hominids lived: prototype elephants, hippos, rhinos, antelopes, lions, baboons, warthogs. Some, like black-backed jackals, appear unchanged over the millennia. Research continues. Olduvai, 120 miles (200 km) northwest of Arusha and not far from Lake Manyara, has a museum and guides. Along the route are giraffes and others, some almost certainly descendants of that early now-fossilized wildlife.

## RUAHA NATIONAL PARK

Clawless otters in Ruaha National Park slide into shallows, and king-sized crocodiles bask with open jaws on sandbanks of the Great Ruaha River which forms the southeastern border of this second-largest Tanzanian national park, little changed over the past million years. With Kizigio and Rungwa reserves bordering it on the north, the Ruaha ecosystem represents a protected 9,884 square miles (25,600 km²) as wild and remote today as any in Africa. A wildlife magnet is the river where an 800-foot (240-m) escarpment ecologically divides the valley from western high plateau and miombo forest where sable antelope browse. Most of the elephant population—sizable despite poaching—along with 30,000 buffalo, 20,000 zebras, giraffes, warthogs, spiral-horned kudus, elands, and roan antelopes find their way to its rushing, rocky gorges and acacia-fringed streams, as do leopards, cheetahs, and wild dogs. Among 400 bird species are colorful sunbirds, bee-eaters, kingfishers, and specialties such as Dickinson's kestrels, violet-crested turacos, pale-billed hornbills, racquet-tailed rollers, green wood hoopoes—and, spring and fall, thousands of Eurasian migrants.

Park office at Msembe is 70 miles (112 km) by 4WD from Iringa (there's also an airstrip). Best times are drier July–November. There are two luxury tented camps and a hotel built into a rock kopje along the river.

## SELOUS GAME RESERVE

The largest concentrations of elephants, crocodiles, hippos, and wild dogs in the world are claimed by this wild, remote reserve, at 21,000 square miles (50,000 km²) twice the size of Denmark. Over one million large animals live here. Poaching had reduced their numbers, but recent years have seen a comeback. Elephants, at one time down to 30,000, are now over 55,000 and expected to return to the 1976 level of 110,000.

Among a great species variety are Sharpe's grysbok and Lichtenstein's hartebeest as well as Burchell's zebras, striking Roosevelt's sable antelopes, waterbucks, warthogs, rich birdlife (350 species), and plants (2,000 species so far). Predators include lions, leopards, cheetahs, and wild dogs. Bateleur eagles soar. Selous is an eight-hour drive from any significant settlement but there are airstrips and several tented camps. The rushing Rufiji River bisects the reserve. South of it, sport hunting is permitted. Threats are mainly two proposed dams which would flood large areas.

Cooler, less humid June–October is pleasantest. Many birds visit the Rufiji River including open-billed storks, gorgeous carmine bee-eaters, Goliath herons, fish eagles, along with reed-bucks and spiral-horned greater kudus, and visitors sailing or rafting down the river do not seem to disturb them unduly.

# SERENGETI NATIONAL PARK

One of the stunning spectacles of the natural world takes place in Serengeti National Park every year when the largest group of migratory animals in the world, some 1.5 million wildebeest, trek here in search of fresh grass and water. They line up in columns up to 25 miles (40 km) long, six to 10 abreast, sometimes so close together they seem to cover the ground, leaving only the far horizon in view.

They move westward and then northward to Kenya, then back to the Serengeti again in late winter when rains return bringing water and new grass—a roughly triangular route of almost 500 miles (800 km). Here they give birth to their young. Little wildebeest are all born at almost the same time, thousands on a single morning, tottering to their feet, able to follow their mothers within a few minutes, able by midday to run after them at speeds of 30 miles an hour (50 kph).

They must not lose contact with their mothers. Only their own mothers will accept them, and numerous predators—lions, leopards, and cheetahs—are following closely to prey on orphans, laggards, and weaklings. Around the edges are groups of hyenas and wild dogs. Behind them looking for scraps and pouncing on smaller prey such as rodents, birds' eggs, and squirrel-sized hyrax (closest relatives to the elephants) are jackals, honey badgers, and bat-eared foxes. Keeping an eye on all these are tawny eagles, huge vultures, and marabou storks (looking, as often remarked, like undertakers).

This is but a sampling of the huge ecosystem of which this U.N. World Heritage Site is a part and which includes as well several adjoining conservation areas and game reserves, notably NGOROGORO CONSERVATION AREA (*see* p.142), **Maswa Game Reserve** to the southwest and Kenya's MAASAI MARA (*see* p.82), adjoining on the north.

Other statistics of this most famous and largest African national park, whose name in Maasai means "endless plains," are equally impressive. There are an estimated 250,000 Thomson's gazelles, 200,000 zebras, 1,500 to 3,000 lions, 70,000 impalas, 70,000 topis, 30,000 Grant's gazelles, 20,000 buffalo, 9,000 elands, 8,000 giraffes, and over 350 species of birds. The largest cheetah population in Africa is here. In the water are massive hippos and 18-foot (5.5-m) crocodiles.

It is not without problems, from poaching for elephant tusks, rhino horns, even lion claws (for trophy and medicinal purposes) to population growth around the edges that would usurp land for domestic grazing and agriculture (the country's overall population growth is 3.3 percent a year). A railroad has been proposed that would cut across migration routes. Black rhinos in 1970 numbered 500. Now their extinction here is feared. Elephant numbers are down to a few thousand.

But the spectacle remains overwhelming. Seeing it is to feel something of what the earth may have been before humans were here, with the overwhelming force, power, and beauty of nature operating separately from human plans and machinations.

---

**FURTHER READING**

*Serengeti Shall Not Die* by Bernard Grzimek, Hamish Hamilton, London, 1960.

---

## Tarangire National Park

Tarangire National Park is 1,003 square miles (2,600 km$^2$) of baobab-studded grassland surrounding the Tarangire River, the only reliable dry-season freshwater source for wildlife in a vast stretch of the Rift Valley. As such, it attracts huge migratory gatherings of zebras, wildebeest, elands, oryx, and others.

Elephants herd together in the hundreds. Bird populations are phenomenal—more than 300 species, including hammerkops, ground hornbills, giant kingfishers, Goliath herons, green wood hoopoes, in one of the highest recorded number of breeding species anywhere. Leopards are always here, as are warthogs, giraffes, impalas, and hartebeest. It is the only park where fringe-eared oryx regularly appear as well as, frequently, lesser kudus, gerenuks, and rock pythons. Best time is July–October dry season. All roads are passable then. A good tented camp and campsites overlook the Tarangire River. Get there by driving 71 miles (114 km) south of Arusha, or there is an airstrip.

---

**FURTHER INFORMATION**

Director General, Tanzania National Parks, P.O. Box 3134, Arusha, Tanzania, E-mail: Tanapa@nabari.co.tz, Website: www.Nabari.co.tz/tanapa

---

# UGANDA

VISITORS MAKING EYE CONTACT WITH MOUNTAIN GORILLAS IN BWINDI IMPENETRABLE FOREST FEEL OUR INTEREST IN THEM IS SHARED BY THEIRS IN US. THEY ALSO SHARE 98 PERCENT OF OUR GENES, AND FACIAL EXPRESSIONS OF JOY, SORROW, ANGER, FEAR, AND SURPRISE.

WINSTON CHURCHILL CALLED UGANDA "THE PEARL OF AFRICA." Now, after decades of civil war and tyranny, it is beginning once again to seem the right phrase for it.

More than 1,000 bird species live in this fertile, beautiful country roughly the size of Great Britain, nestled in east-central Africa—almost half of them in QUEEN ELIZABETH NATIONAL PARK. They range from rare silvery whale-headed storks (aka shoebills), spectacular long-crested eagles, and brilliant iridescent sunbirds to great, lumbering, turkey-sized ground hornbills whose diet includes everything from termites to young eaglets and hares.

More primate species than anyplace else in the world live in BWINDI IMPENETRABLE FOREST, richest faunal community in East Africa. Half the world population of mountain gorillas are there, plus chimpanzees, wide-eyed, wooly, little pottos, handsome, flowing-haired black-and-white colobus monkeys, and 120 other mammal species along with 202 kinds of butterflies and 346 kinds of birds.

RUWENZORI MOUNTAINS were called "Mountains of the Moon" by geographer Ptolemy in 150 AD, astonished to learn of snow-covered peaks at the equator. Growing here are extraordinary botanicals—towering

147

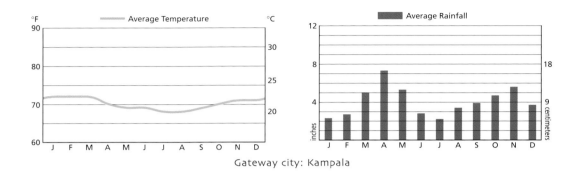

Gateway city: Kampala

versions of usually low-growing heathers, crimson and emerald-green mosses, with alpine flowers that literally dwarf humans.

The greatest concentrations of crocodiles in East Africa patrol banks of the Nile River below MURCHISON FALLS' dramatic 150-foot (45-m) drop into churning rapids.

More mammals than at any other Ugandan park live in KIDEPO VALLEY—28 of them found no place else in the country. Everywhere, wildlife species slaughtered by the murderous dictator Idi Amin are gradually returning.

Best times to visit are dry-season December–February and June–July. Most international travelers fly to Entebbe Airport just south of the capital city, Kampala, where rental cars and accommodations are available and where guides and trips around the country can be arranged.

---

**FURTHER INFORMATION**

Public Relations Officer, Uganda National Parks Headquarters, P.O. Box 3530, Plot 31 Kanjokya Street (Kamwokya), Kampala, Tel: (+256) 530574, 530158, Fax: (+256) 530159.

---

## BWINDI IMPENETRABLE FOREST

Visitors here who make eye contact with mountain gorillas often say they get the impression our interest in them is shared by theirs in us—not inappropriate since, though our ancestors went down separate paths 6.5 million years ago, we share 98 percent of our genes. Gazing across this gulf, long in years, narrow in genealogy, we recognize shared facial expressions of joy, sorrow, anger, fear, and surprise.

Other primates as well—more of this closely-related familial order than anyplace else on earth—find homes in "Omu Bwindi" or place of darkness, and truly almost impenetrable—127 square miles (331 km²) in the Virunga volcanic mountain range on the edge of the western Rift Valley in southwestern Uganda. Chimpanzees grunt and pant-hoot to tell others of a fruiting fig tree—some say altruistically, others suggest they are only trying to attract females. But other species hear and come as well—blue, red-tailed, and L'Hoest's monkeys, baboons and handsome black-and-white and rare red colobus, always on the move since they must eat 33 percent of their weight in leaves every day.

Other primates rule the night—strange little pottos and Demidoff's and needle-clawed galagos, or bushbabies, enlivening the jungle with vocalizations ranging from clicks to spine-chilling wails and screams. Some can hunt in almost pitch darkness with heads that rotate 180 degrees and visual fields 50 degrees wider than ours, able to see 30 yards (27 m) or more when only one percent of starlight reaches the forest floor, and capture swift flying insects and lizards with lightning grabs of sensitive hands.

Bwindi is by IUCN rating the richest and most diverse faunal community in East Africa—202 species of butterflies; some 120 mammal species, including endangered African forest elephants; 346 bird species, including 214 that are forest-specific; and hundreds of plants and trees, many rare and endangered either on a country or worldwide basis.

But it is the mountain gorillas that most visitors come for—about half the world population, around 300, of this rarest subspecies of earth's largest primates, males standing up to six feet (2 m) tall and weighing up to 500 pounds (227 kg). (The other half are in nearby Rwanda and Democratic Republic of the Congo.)

They are not always easy to see—the trek can require hours-long hiking up steep hills through jungle and sometimes swamp-like valleys, with no guarantee the gorillas will feel like being watched on any given day. It is not inexpensive and reservations can be filled months' ahead.

But for those who have sat quietly in the jungle watching—and being watched by—these intelligent beings so closely related to us, it is well worth any difficulty.

Usually the gorillas go about their business, aware of but not disturbed by visitors, which they have become habituated not to fear. Sometimes young gorillas want to take a closer look at visitors than the 25-foot (5-m) distance guards try to maintain, largely to protect the huge primates, vulnerable to human-carried germs.

To minimize disturbance, visitor groups are kept small, usually six to eight, limited to an hour, and no flash photography is allowed—protective measures taken because the government values the gorillas' continued survival as important contributors to the economy. Ecotourism dollars they bring in now far exceed their former value as trophies and souvenirs sold by poachers (everything from baby gorillas to mummified gorillas' hands for ashtrays). Therefore care is taken to maintain and protect gorillas and their refuge and tourist groups as well, which are accompanied these days by armed though usually inconspicuous guards.

Best times are dry-season December–February and June–August. Several comfortable lodges are located in and near the park, reachable by (sometimes rough) road and chartered plane.

# MGAHINGA NATIONAL PARK

Mgahinga National Park, adjoining Rwanda's Volcano and Democratic Republic of Congo's Virunga National Park, also has gorillas. It was closed during Rwanda's civil war and only recently have any of its animals become habituated to visitors. Jumping-off point is Kisoro.

# MURCHISON FALLS NATIONAL PARK

Crocodiles patrol banks of the Nile, giant specimens guarding springtime nests in one of the largest concentrations in East Africa, largely ignoring launches that glide by en route to Murchison Falls. It is a highlight—one of many—of a trip to this largest Ugandan park, 2,400 square miles (3,840 km²) straddling the Nile above and below its dramatic 150-foot (45-m) drop from roaring rapids through a thundering gorge just 20 feet (6 m) wide. Hippos in great herds bare huge tusk-like canines in threat display. Storks of five species fish the shallows, including rare whale-headed or shoebill (best place in Africa to see them). Large flocks of African skimmers, groups of elephants, Defassa waterbucks, and African buffalo wade near Nile perch weighing up to 200 pounds (90 kg). Higher in the woods, chimpanzees forage. Rothschild's giraffes graze in plains alongside hartebeest and Uganda kobs. Leopards can appear any time at waterside.

The launch trip should not be missed, but there are miles of roads and trails where all the mammals and many of the birds can be seen as well. There's a comfortable lodge in the park.

# QUEEN ELIZABETH NATIONAL PARK

At one time or another most of the sizable array of mammals in Queen Elizabeth National Park—elephants, Uganda kobs, hippos, baboons, even leopards—plus over 500 bird species (almost half the number on the African continent) show themselves along the launch trip down the Kasinga Channel connecting Lakes Edward and George.

They drink, forage, and bathe, often oblivious to viewers: warthogs, spotted hyenas, malachite kingfishers, rare prehistoric-looking whale-headed (shoebill) storks, and equally rare black bee-eaters with scarlet throats and cobalt-blue abdomens and rumps. The launch trip is considered one of the great birdwatching trips of the world.

Semi-aquatic sititunga antelopes live in papyrus reeds along Lake George. Defassa waterbucks can carry the finest horns in Africa, up to 30 inches (76 cm).

But there is much to see elsewhere (some less easily accessible) in the remarkable habitat range of this popular park, just south of the famed "Mountains of the Moon," which marks the boundary between east African plains and west and central tropical forests.

Colobus monkeys swing through trees and giant forest hogs root along the road through the Maramagambo Forest. The Kasenyi track, frequented by leopards and hyenas, passes by kobs' mating grounds, scenes sometimes of spectacular territorial battles. The Itasha plains are famous for tree-climbing lions and large buffalo herds.

Flamingos can gather in huge numbers in some crater lakes. Fifty kinds of raptors are on the long bird list.

A comfortable park lodge with spectacular Nile views (with the "cottage" where Queen Elizabeth stayed when the park was dedicated) is reachable by (sometimes rough) road, or chartered air to a strip nearby.

## RUWENZORI MOUNTAINS NATIONAL PARK

The geographer Ptolemy in 150 AD cited the Ruwenzori Mountains as a source of the Nile, calling them "Mountains of the Moon" because it seemed unearthly to have snow-covered peaks on the steamy equator. But there they are, one of earth's great beauties crowning one of its great wild habitats in Ruwenzori Mountains National Park.

Wildlife varies with elevation, blending through mixes of forest elephants, chimpanzees, Ruwenzori hyrax, colobus, blue and L'Hoest's monkeys, black-footed duikers, brilliant-winged Ruwenzori turacos.

But it is the "botanical big game" of this beautiful park on the western Rift Valley which the Swedish scientist Olav Hedberg called "some of the most fantastic…of the planet."

Giant heathers, 18 inches (half-meter) tall elsewhere, grow over 30 feet (10 m) here. Blue lobelias, yellow groundsels, and others are similarly outsized. Primeval trees up to 40 feet (12 m) tall can be covered with crimson, yellow, and emerald-green mosses and clusters of pink orchids. Some of the flowers above the tree line literally dwarf humans.

Kasese, gateway to this World Heritage Site, with hotels and lodges, is 260 miles (437 km) west of Kampala via Mbarara on a main tarmac road. There's also an airport. The park has camping only, but a good trail network and huts for hikers.

The loop trail, for the physically fit, takes six–seven days, or a three-day hike can be arranged. Waterproof bags and clothing are needed (everything is wet here) and sweaters—days can be like summer, nights like winter.

Rabbit-sized rock hyraxes have thickly padded feet with rubbery flaps kept moist by glandular secretions, forming a useful gripping surface for rapid mobility over rocky outcrops where they make homes. Fossil remains show hyraxes once were the size of oxen. Their closest relatives today are elephants.

## ALSO OF INTEREST

**Kibale Forest National Park** northeast of Queen Elizabeth has one of the densest primate populations in the most accessible of Uganda's large forests—most significantly chimpanzees (Chambere Gorge is one of the best places to see them) but at least eight other species also, along with sizable elephant herds, buffalo, bushbucks, duikers, giant forest hogs, and over 300 bird and 144 butterfly species. There's a campsite at Kamyunchi, which is base for chimp-viewing walks, and a guest house in Bigodi, 3.8 miles (6 km) away.

Wild, remote, spectacularly beautiful **Kidepo Valley National Park** with 510 square miles (1,340 km²) of dry savannah in northeast Uganda has more mammal species than any other Uganda national park, 28 of them in no other Ugandan reserve, including cheetahs, caracals, kudu, aardwolves, bat-eared foxes. Most numerous are zebras, elephants, buffalo, Rothschild's giraffes, roan antelopes, and klipspringers. Among 400 bird species are ostriches and many raptors including ten kinds of eagles, three kites, and five kestrels.

It's not easy to visit. The 500-mile (840-km) drive from Kampala is difficult and sometimes dangerous, bandit attacks not unknown. Chartered light aircraft can land at Apoka, where there's a rest camp, but visitors must bring food and water, and 4WD is needed to go from there. But if you make it, you will see a wildlife panorama and scenery unlike any other in Uganda.

Graceful impalas that can high-jump 10–12 feet (3–4 m) and cover 35–40 feet (10+ m) in a single broad-jump find their specialized habitat—gently sloping grasslands with firm footing alongside open woodlands—only in **Lake Mburo** among Uganda reserves. They join hippos, buffalo, zebras, elands, klipspringers, and some lions and leopards plus abundant birdlife in this well-watered (14 lakes) relatively new 200-square-mile (520-km²) national park. Four-wheel-drive is a must; camping only (but hotels nearby). The park offers spectacular vistas; however, large cattle herds roam the grasslands, and it is heavily impacted by grazing. Located just south of the road from Entebbe toward Mbarara and Queen Elizabeth National Park.

**Semuliki National Park** is 75 square miles (220 km) of East Africa's only lowland tropical rain forest, accessible by road 110 miles (180 km) west of Kampala. Over 400 bird species include seldom-seen lyre-tailed honeyguides, often alongside trails. Mona monkeys, forest buffalo, water chevrotains, pygmy hippos, leopards are among more than 60 mammal species. Accommodations in Fort Portal. Campsites planned.

> **FURTHER INFORMATION**
>
> Semuliki National Park, P.O. Box 699, Fort Portal, Uganda.

# ZAMBIA

GLOWING CARMINE BEE-EATERS CAN COVER
RIVERBANKS IN THE LUANGWA VALLEY, WATCHED
FROM BELOW BY MORE NILE CROCODILES THAN
ANYPLACE ELSE (INCLUDING THE NILE).

THIS VAST LANDLOCKED PLATEAU, GREEN AND DOTTED WITH LAKES, CRISSCROSSED BY THE GREAT ZAMBEZI, KAFUE, AND LUANGWA RIVERS WITH THEIR HUNDREDS OF TRIBUTARIES, OXBOWS, AND LAGOONS, HOLDS 45 PERCENT OF ALL THE WATER IN SOUTHERN AFRICA. As a result, Zambia's national parks, some of the largest on the continent, harbor some of the greatest wildlife concentrations in the world.

## LUANGWA NATIONAL PARKS

More than 15,000 elephants live in **South Luangwa National Park** alone, along with up to 15,000 hippopotami, rare Thornicroft's giraffes, and 50 or more other kinds of mammals, with huge colonies of majestic crowned cranes. More than 400 kinds of birds, both migrants and residents,

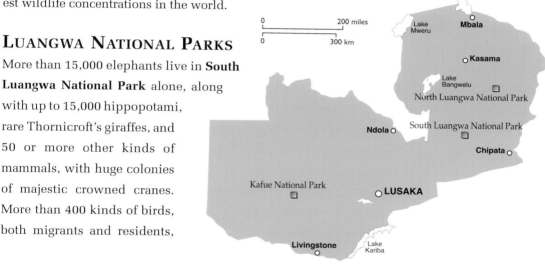

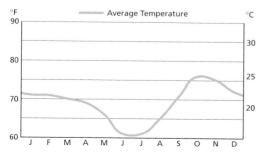

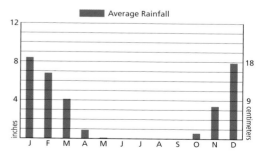

Gateway city: Lusaka

153

crowd along this stretch of the 420-mile-long (700-km) Luangwa valley, southern extension of the Great Rift Valley that cuts a channel down the continent's backbone from northern Africa to the Zambezi river.

Riverbanks can be covered with hundreds of glowing carmine bee-eaters tending their burrow nests. There are as many Nile crocodiles here as there are in any other river (including the Nile). Leopards may be more visible here than anyplace else in the world.

Less well-known and more remote is **North Luangwa National Park**, a mostly wilderness area separated by a narrow corridor to the north with one of the highest lion populations anywhere, and huge herds of buffalo.

## Kafue National Park

Kafue is the largest national park in Africa (8,697 square miles/22,532 km²), with tremendous diversity of habitat and of mammals, some of them exceedingly rare, ranging from elephants, lions, leopards, to red lechwes (unique to Zambia), Cookson's wildebeest, Defassa waterbucks, Lichtenstein's hartebeest, and more kinds of antelopes than any other African park.

Wildlife conservation in Zambia goes back before pre-colonial days when tribal chiefs set aside traditional grazing and hunting grounds for their personal use. The first reserves were formally established in 1925. Now more than 30 percent of Zambia's 290,586 square miles (752,972 km²) are national parks and conservation areas for wildlife and another 10 percent are protected forest reserves. Enlightened programs in which government works with the U.S. Agency for International Development and others in a group called ADMADE (Administrative Management Design for Game Management Areas) gather public support for these by providing benefits such as wildlife activities—jobs and locally beneficial projects for communities. In the program's encouraging first three years, elephant poaching was cut 90 percent and rhino poaching almost to zero.

Zambia's elevation on a 3,000–5,000-foot (915–1,525-m) plateau moderates what would otherwise be a torrid climate, just 10–18 degrees south of the equator. April–August is cool and dry; September–October warm and dry; November–March, warm and wet.

International travelers usually arrive by air in the capital, Lusaka, which has lodging and rental cars (roads around the country often require 4WD).

Some remote parks have little or no access, but the best-known have lodges and visitor facilities ranging from comfortable to luxurious.

OPPOSITE: Melodious carmine bee-eaters are welcomed everywhere (except by bee-keepers). They like to colonize along streambeds where they raise young in burrows they excavate on banks, lining nests with remains of their prey which is 90 percent bees, consumed after they have pounded them violently to de-venom stingers.

## ALSO OF INTEREST

**Bangwelu Wetlands** is an enormous beautiful area surrounding Lake Bangwelu, home to thousands of black lechwe, breeding ground to rare shoebill storks; protected as a game management area.

**Blue Lagoon National Park** comprises a wetland area with huge herds of Kafue lechwe and spectacular numbers and varieties of waterbirds.

**Kasanka National Park** is the world's greatest breeding ground of fruit bats, with a large population of water-loving sitatunga antelopes, also pukus, many hartebeest, sable antelopes, waterbucks, and shoebill storks.

**Lochinvar National Park** is main stronghold of more than 30,000 Kafue lechwe; also 2,000 blue wildebeest, oribi, side-striped jackals, and more than 400 bird species including abundant wattled cranes. Originally a private ranch, it was bought by the Zambian government with support from World Wide Fund for Nature.

**Mosi-Oa-Tunya** (**Victoria Falls National Park**) contains the spectacular Victoria Falls, one of the natural wonders of the world, located along the Zambezi river on the border with Zimbabwe and near to those of Namibia and Botswana—largest sheet of falling water in the world, with both sun and moonlight rainbows on its spray and vapor clouds visible 18 miles (30 km) away. Can be seen via sunset cruise and canoe safari. White-water rafting below can be enjoyed by the most inexperienced visitor—just grab a rain jacket and hang on—keeping an eye out, if possible, for buffalo, elands, elephants, giraffes, and others along the shore.

**Nyika Plateau National Park** has a great variety of orchids and butterflies, also Moloney's monkeys, blue monkeys, leopards, serval cats, and several bird species not seen elsewhere in Zambia.

**Sumbu National Park** borders the huge inland sea of Lake Tanganyika, visited by elephants, lions, elands, pukus, roan antelopes, blue duikers, and Sharpe's grysboks along with hippos, crocodiles, and waterbirds.

---

**FURTHER INFORMATION**

Director, National Parks and Wildlife Service, Private Bag 1, Chilanga, Zambia.

# ZIMBABWE

HUGE THRONGS OF ANIMALS—THOUSANDS
OF ELEPHANTS, BUFFALO, HIPPOS—ARE ATTRACTED
TO MANA POOLS, BEHAVING OFTEN AS IF THEY'VE
NEVER SEEN A HUMAN BEING. AFRICAN GUIDES
CALL IT THEIR GARDEN OF EDEN.

D ENSEST POPULATIONS OF SOME OF THE WORLD'S MOST SPECTACULAR ANIMALS INHABIT THIS BEAU-
TIFUL, LANDLOCKED, MID-SOUTH AFRICAN COUNTRY—ACCORDING TO LEGEND, LAND OF KING
SOLOMON'S MINES—WHICH HAS SET ASIDE MORE THAN 12 PERCENT OF ITS AREA AS NATIONAL PARKS AND
RESERVES. Unfortunately, recent political events have devastated much of the country; if and
when they are resolved the country again will be a premier wildlife destination.

Black rhinos, elsewhere highly endangered, have reached 500 here despite continued pressure
from poachers intent on removing horns for dagger handles, aphrodisiacs, and other folk medicines. Zimbabwe has thousands of elephants, as many as its protected territories can accommodate.

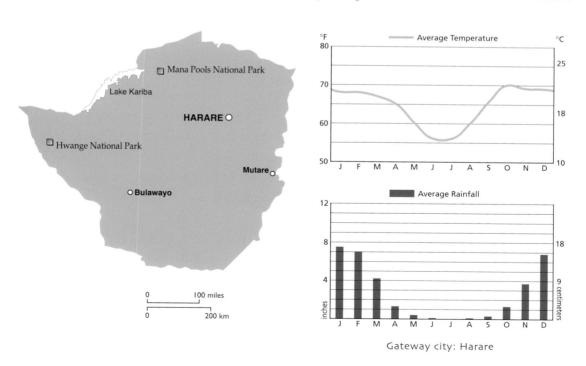

Gateway city: Harare

Bird species range from crowned eagles to tiny, exquisite paradise flycatchers—more than 640 feathered species in all.

There have been, until recently, more ways for a visitor to see all this than anyplace else in Africa—by wildlife drives in open and closed vehicles both by day and night, by walking, and by various water-borne means: houseboat, kayaking, canoeing, white-water rafting, and wildlife drives in guided sightseeing boats.

International flights arrive in Harare and Victoria Falls, with car rental and a variety of lodging. Most roads have been surfaced and are in fair repair.

Farsighted legislation enacted in the 1970s enabled landowners to manage private lands profitably for wildlife, culling excess animals for meat, allowing access by safaris and some limited, controlled hunting, thereby sustaining general environmental support of wildlife by local populations. This plan had been popular and notably successful.

Threats continue. Besides political unrest, mainly these are poaching, mostly for rhino horns and elephant tusks, and a burgeoning population, doubling every 20 years and requiring ever more space in this agricultural and mineral-rich country.

Best times to visit are April–July.

---

**FURTHER INFORMATION**

National Parks Central Bookings Office, Department of National Parks and Wildlife Management, P.O. Box 8151, Causeway, Harare, Zimbabwe, Tel: (+263) 70-6077.

# HWANGE NATIONAL PARK

Once this park was a hunting reserve for Ndebele kings. Then Europeans came and so overhunted prime areas that its rich wildlife populations dwindled. With protection, they rebounded.

Now on a quiet night during a full moon at one of Hwange's water holes, huge numbers of elephants splash about in family groups of all ages. With them may be herds of buffalo, giraffes, 16 species of antelopes including relatively rare sable, roan, and gemsbok, such predators as lions and leopards, hyenas, wild dogs, and numbers of interesting smaller creatures in congregations seldom seen elsewhere.

More than 400 species of birds have been counted. Golden orioles feed on hanging commiphora berries and enliven the acacia and mopane canopy with liquid bubbling notes. So do their black-headed and green-headed cousins, weaving delicate baglike nests of lichens, moss tendrils, and spiderwebs.

Cuckoos of seven species, including the emerald, search for hairy caterpillars in trees or leaf litter on the ground.

Bradfield's hornbills with ponderous-appearing (actually lightweight) bills manipulate not only fruits and nuts but large insects and even small reptiles, sometimes digging in elephant dung around the main camp. Burchell's and double-banded sandgrouse come to the water and soak breast feathers to take droplets back to thirsty nestlings.

Eagles of many species make homes here—bateleur, martial, African hawk, brown snake, and black-breasted snake, joined by large numbers of steppe and lesser spotted eagles after the rains end. Black and yellow-billed kites snatch food from picnickers. Ospreys hover and plunge for fish at Mandavu Dam, and African skimmers scoop up minnows from the water's surface with long lower mandibles.

Hwange, like many wildlife reserves, became a national park almost by default. Its dry soil, with no permanent water source, was unpromising either for agriculture or human habitation. It was set aside in 1929 and its first staff set about to make it attractive to wildlife, drilling boreholes and establishing permanent sources for dozens of water holes and seasonal pans.

This was so successful that more land was added and Hwange became Zimbabwe's largest national park—5,655 square miles (14,651 km$^2$)—in 1949. As a result it has supported an array of inviting habitats ranging from magnificent hardwood forests to large open grassy plains ringed with acacias, scrub mopane bush, and woodland. In them are more than 100 mammal species, 70 kinds of reptiles and amphibians, and a glorious assortment of birds.

Up to 26,000 elephants browse in winter, prying off bark with their tusks, grinding up tough dry grasses, reeds, even branches with their rasplike teeth. During the rains they disperse through the park and consume up to 330 pounds (150 kg) a day of tender grasses and herbs, returning in dry weather to concentrate again at the pans.

White rhinoceros frequently graze near the camp. ("White" is a misnomer; it should be "wide" referring to their wide, square mouths compared to narrow, pointed mouths of the black rhinos.)

Massive buffalo herds of 2,000 or so are not uncommon, and Hwange is an excellent place to see lions—particularly in the northwest section in the morning, where lions most often kill at night, but may remain on a kill for several hours before seeking cover. Leopards also are common but elusive, nocturnal, and not easily seen. Best times are April–June.

# Mana Pools National Park

African guides regard Mana Pools as the Garden of Eden and little wonder. No place else in the world may combine the lush, wilderness character of this 845-square-mile (2,190-km$^2$) national park with stunning vistas that seem to go on forever, where wild animals like lions, elephants, and buffalo roar, trumpet, snort and behave much of the time as if they have never seen a human being or tourist van.

## ZIMBABWE

Some of the highest concentrations of wildlife on the continent are seen in this U.N. World Heritage Site.

Focus of this natural richness is the lower Zambezi River, 1,675 miles (2,700 km) long, which originates in uplands of the Democratic Republic of the Congo (formerly Zaire) near Africa's continental divide. Heading south toward the Indian Ocean, it enters Zimbabwe at Victoria Falls in a spectacular cataract that is one of the wonders of the world, and joins Lake Kariba, one of the great man-made lakes of the world, and then reaches Mana Pools.

"Mana," meaning four, refers to the four largest perennial pools left as the river shifted course over thousands of years, pools which are the main water source around and attract huge numbers of animals. A recent census counted some 6,500 elephants, 16,000 buffalo, 2,000 hippopotami, several hundred endangered black rhinoceros and, among hoofed species, herds of hundreds of zebras, sable antelopes, kudus, elands, and waterbucks, along with thousands of birds of woods, water, and grasslands.

Arrayed among the watercourses on a flat floodplain which goes on for miles, surrounded by terraced banks which seem designed by a park-planner's hand, are graceful impalas in herds of

Female impalas form loose herds of 10 to 50 animals, wandering in and out of male territories, loosely guarded until they come into estrus, when they are tightly guarded by lyre-horned, roaring, grunting, snorting males. Both males and females are prodigious jumpers, easily leaping eight feet (2.5 m) high and spanning 30 feet (9 m) over bushes or even other impalas. The jumps are effortless and sometimes apparently just for their own delight. They are found in southeast African savannah and open woodlands.

200 or so. Large groups of other grazers and browsers include elands, kudus, massive buffalo, endangered black rhinoceros, occasional rare nyalas, and stubby warthogs. Each species has cropped the vegetation at various levels determined by their own dental equipment and stature. As a result acacia, mahogany, and mopane trees and, lower down, shrubs and grasses all are sheared off at perfectly even heights. This gives them a park-like, almost dreamlike appearance over which the strong sun, filtered through the greenery, casts a gold-green light against a backdrop of the river's escarpment which rises suddenly and dramatically 3,300 feet (1,000 m) in places along both sides of the river, both here and across the way in Zambia.

A canoe safari of three to nine days is a wildlife experience unlike any other, moving silently through these waters, getting out and walking from time to time (Mana Pools is one of the few national parks where one is permitted to get out and walk), sleeping in tents along the way and listening to night sounds.

Pods of hippos submerge to keep sensitive skins moist and cool during the day, showing only dozens of round eyes above the surface. One avoids startling them; they can become dangerously enraged at disturbance. At night, these two-ton-or-so (1,800-kg) beasts haul themselves out and forage, their presence evident from plodding footfalls and crunching sounds as they crop the grasses.

Carmine and white-fronted bee-eaters fly up in rosy and azure clouds from colonial nest holes along riverbanks in September.

Elephants in placid family groups bathe, or stand on termite mounds to reach a high acacia branch. Occasionally a mother will flap large ears in warning and make a mock charge. Sometimes they spray water on canoeists. A low reverberation may be an elephant's "tummy rumble" (but it comes from vocal cords) notifying others of the canoe's presence. Unheard may be infrasonic vibrations from forehead nasal passages telling companions several miles away that a canoe has arrived.

Baboon troops of 50 or so swing about, a sudden rasping scream revealing that a predator, perhaps a secretive, nocturnal leopard, has been discovered napping on a tree limb. Leopards are so perfectly concealed by their gorgeous, dappled fur they are seldom noticed unless they move, and not always then. Lions are less retiring and may growl when a canoe appears.

A 10-foot (3-m) crocodile slides into the water. More than 1,000 of these ancient saurians, unchanged in 70 million years, live in Mana Pools and nest on midstream islands.

A dark underwater shape may be a primitive lungfish, member of a group that has survived for more than 400 million years, breathing air with a single lung.

Over 380 bird species are here. Livingstone's flycatchers flirt rufous tail fans as they hawk flying insects in riparian woodlands. Skimmers lay speckled eggs in shallow nest scrapes and ply the waters with bills agape for small fish, whose contact instantly causes these formidable lower mandibles to snap closed. Hundreds of red-winged pratincoles rise in spiral columns, catching warm-air thermals. White-winged pratincoles nest colonially on rock outcrops in Mupata Gorge and emerge in swallowlike swarms at dusk.

Brilliant little Angola pittas, special treat for birders, nest in untidy domes in thorntrees. Lilian's lovebirds chatter in flocks of hundreds in mopane and acacia woodlands. Rare rufous-bellied herons snatch up frogs in Chirundu flood channels.

Curly-horned kudus come to drink and only lift their heads with curious expressions as the canoe glides by.

## ALSO OF INTEREST

**Chizarira National Park** is rugged, remote wilderness with abundant wildlife including elephants, buffalo, elands, Sharpe's grysboks, klipspringers, tsessebes, rich birdlife.

**Gonarezhou National Park** is potentially a great reserve, with prolific populations of hippos, oribi, klipspringers, rich birdlife including such rarities as hooded vultures, blue-spotted doves, Pel's fishing owls, but serious problems with poaching, especially from Mozambique.

**Matobo National Park** is part of the rocky Matobo range with impressive white rhinos, giraffes, zebras, and dense (though seldom seen) leopard population; renowned for birds of prey, especially black eagles.

**Matusadona National Park** comprises a virtually untouched wilderness along the southern shore of beautiful Lake Kariba with an enormous buffalo population, also abundant elephants, kudus, impalas, some black rhinoceros. Leopards are occasionally seen in Santati Gorge. Walking safaris, also wildlife viewing from boats.

**Victoria Falls National Park** and **Zambezi National Parks**—Victoria Falls, a wonder of the world and World Heritage Site, is the largest sheet of falling water in the world—over 150 million gallons (625 million liters) a minute in flood season. Just below the falls, water thrown up by it sustains a magnificent rain forest populated by fascinating plant and animal species, among them African goshawks, African green pigeons, trumpeter hornbills, yellow-bellied bulbuls, collared sunbirds. Rare Taita falcons breed on the cliffs. In gorges below are gray-rumped swallows, African swifts, rock martins, familiar chats, and mocking cliff-chats. Some of the world's most exciting white-water rafting is in the gorges below the falls. Zambezi National Park, adjoining, is known as well for abundance of sable antelopes, elands, buffalo, giraffes.

# ANTARCTICA

GENTOO PENGUINS

# ANTARCTICA

EARLY EXPLORERS THOUGHT PENGUINS WERE FISH,
NOT EXPECTING TO FIND BIRDS FLYING UNDERWATER—
BIRDS, WE NOW KNOW, THAT "FLY" MANY HUNDREDS OF
FEET DEEP, HUNDREDS OF TIMES, UP TO 15 HOURS A DAY,
STAYING DOWN UP TO 20 MINUTES AT A TIME, PROPELLING
THEMSELVES AS FAST UNDERWATER AS OTHERS DO IN THE AIR.

SOME OF THE GREAT WILDLIFE ASSEMBLAGES OF THE WORLD ARE ON AND AROUND THIS SNOW AND ICE-BOUND CONTINENT OF GIGANTIC ICEBERGS AND VAST MOUNTAIN RANGES. It is one of the harshest, most beautiful, most inhospitable places on earth. To survive here wildlife must make extraordinary accommodations.

Penguins here can dive 1,700 feet (518 m) and stay down for 20 minutes. Wandering alba-trosses, with the longest wings of any bird, may circumnavigate the globe in a single feeding trip. Massive elephant seals can hold their breath two hours in underwater hunting trips. Ice fish survive with blood in which red cells have been replaced with anti-freeze glycoproteins. Blue whales can reach 100 feet (30.5 m) in length and weigh an average of 143 tons (130,000 kg), largest animals that ever existed on earth.

Once the climate here was more agreeable. Just 200 million years ago the Antarctic shared one great supercontinent with South America, Africa, India and Australia with flourishing populations of trees and large animals. Now, coldest temperatures ever recorded are here—193.3 degrees F below zero (-89.6°C) at Russia's Vostok station in 1983—and strongest winds, with velocities up to 198.4 miles an hour (320 kph) when dense cold air rushes down off the polar plateau to the coast.

Ninety percent of the world's ice containing 70 percent of the world's fresh water carpets all but four tenths of one percent of this fifth largest, oldest continent in the world (5.5 million square miles, 14.2 million km²), with rocks dating back 3.93 billion years. The Ross ice shelf alone, world's largest, approximates the size of France. Inland is the world's driest desert, which par-adoxically receives more solar radiation than the equator in equivalent periods—but permanent ice cover reflects 80 percent of it back into space, and frigid temperatures rob all water vapor from the air.

Antarctica is 97.6 percent uninhabitable—but on the other 2.4 percent and surrounding islands, glories of the natural world push the edge of survival limits, finding niches in which to live and

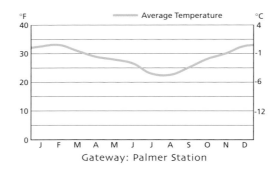

°F | | °C
Average Temperature

Gateway: Palmer Station

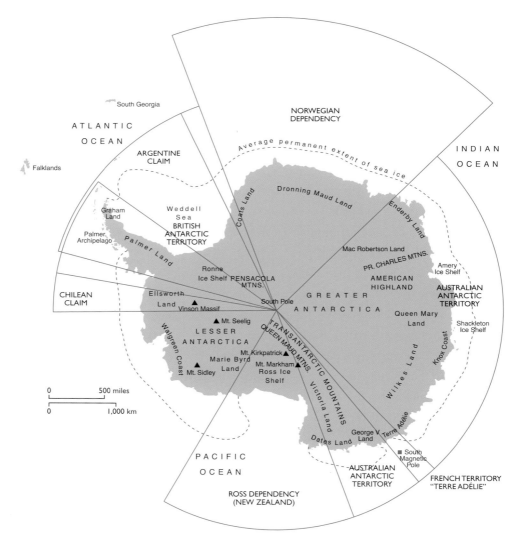

Black-browed albatrosses, like their big cousins, wandering albatrosses, have wings more than twice body length which they can set, face into the wind and then glide literally around the world on a single foraging trip, hardly moving a feather, letting wind do the work. They nest colonially on seaside tussock grass slopes—recently in smaller numbers, impacted by trawlers and long-line fisheries, so they are now classed as an endangered species.

reproduce in brilliant, near-24-hour daylight in the Antarctic summer. They can do this because of the Antarctic Convergence, where cooler, denser Southern Ocean waters meet and churn up warmer, more saline northern seas bringing vast nutrients upwelling to the surface at about 55 degrees latitude. This creates life—a rich plankton soup with trillions of little shrimp-like krill, part of a food chain that supports huge numbers of fish, seabirds, and sea mammals.

At least 45 bird species breed south of the Convergence and some on Antarctica itself—millions of Adelie, emperor, king, and gentoo penguins along with snow and Antarctic petrels and aggressive south polar skuas which make their living in large part at the expense of the others. Snow-free edges furnish avian nesting sites and pupping places for seals. Others of those millions are concentrated on subantarctic islands.

Species number is small compared with lush tropics—but those that *are* here crowd together in some of the world's greatest wildlife concentrations: 7.5 million pairs of chinstrap penguins; 2.5 million pairs of Adelies; up to 1.5 million pairs of kings; 3.7 million pairs of rockhoppers; 11.8 million pairs of macaronis with orange forehead tassels. Almost all must hurry to finish reproductive cycles before another six months' cold and darkness set in, leaving only hardy Weddell seals and emperor penguins to deal with that extreme adversity.

Early explorers thought penguins were fish, not expecting to find birds flying underwater, a niche they've secured to the point where some can fly as fast underwater as others do in the air (gentoo penguins have been timed at 22 miles an hour/36 kph). This is made possible by compact, streamlined bodies of perfect hydrodynamic design that offer no more resistance than a quarter-sized pebble. Deep-keeled breastbones, short, stiff feathers flattened over down layers insulating inches-thick skin and blubber, and paddle-like wings propel them to prodigious depths—many hundreds of feet—repeatedly, up to 15 hours a day. Legs and feet, located well back, are underwater directional controls which on land support erect humanlike posture as they walk slowly and deliberately to avoid overheating. Despite this, they can walk long distances, some species seen hundreds of miles from the nearest sea.

How they survive such dives is imperfectly understood but it is known their diving heart rate slows to perhaps five percent of normal, reducing oxygen needs which underwater are supplied partly from stores in muscles and blood. Deep-diving birds have more blood vessels and blood volume than others, and studies suggest they may be able to turn off temporarily all but essential organs, like heart and brain. Further, they have evolved solid bones, a detriment for most birds which need hollow bones to shed weight for flight, but an advantage for flightless ones that may spend 85 percent of their lives on and in water.

Within these penguin-specific adaptations are species-specific ones allowing each penguin to exploit its own niche in this hostile environment.

World's largest and hardiest penguin is the impressive emperor—only Antarctic bird that has evolved to breed in winter in what has been called the most extreme hardship endured by any warm-blooded animal. Standing well over a yard (or meter) high, with dark heads, dark silvery backs, and orange earpatches, weighing up to 88 pounds (40 kg), emperors lay a single large egg in late summer which is incubated on the feet of the male who stands covering it with a densely feathered flap of furry skin for 66 days, much of the time in total darkness in −80°F (−60°C) temperatures and 100-mile-an-hour (160 kph) winds in some of the fiercest blizzards on the planet.

Males huddle together for warmth sharing the burden of exposure by alternating inside and outside positions, keeping precious eggs 114°F (80°C) warmer than temperatures outside. Meanwhile emperor females, energies depleted by egg production, go off to forage and return at hatching to take over from now-nearly-starved males, which then walk to the nearest sea that now, with additional freezing, may be 100 miles (160 km) away. Emperors have been known to cover 600 miles (970km) on foot in a single round-trip to feed in deeper water than any other bird—their dive record stands at 1,766 feet (535 m) for 22 minutes. For 150 more days parents alternate fishing and returning with full crops to nourish the young before they finally fledge.

About 200,000 emperor pairs breed in colonies in the Weddell Sea and Dronning Maud Land, Enderby and Princess Elizabeth Lands, and the Ross Sea. Because of their breeding schedule, they are less seen by visitors than others—and also more sensitive to disturbance.

Smaller, slenderer look-alikes (with similar looks of impassive solemnity) are king penguins, from which emperors are believed to have evolved. Kings have long breeding cycles that take place in warmer seasons. Parents take turns through the Antarctic summer incubating their single egg on their feet, learning to shuffle along without losing their precious burden—and wooly chicks are reared through the winter, fledging the following summer. King penguins are deep divers, too, recorded over 1,640 feet (500 m) down, staying for 6–7 minutes. They breed colonially on subantarctic islands, sometimes in huge numbers.

Adelies with blue-black heads, white eye-rings and looks of perpetual surprise get the earliest start of the "summer" penguins. Even before inshore ice breaks up they troop sometimes 60 miles or so (100 km) to windswept coastal nest sites all around the Antarctic Continent and Peninsula, marching single-file in a curious rolling gait, one pink foot after another, tobogganing on their chests if conditions favor. Once there they settle by the hundreds of thousands and start noisy courtships, bowing and squabbling over choice pebbles (sometimes ice fragments will do) for nest structures, their collective squawks and groans audible 30 miles (50 km) downwind. After 90-day incubation and finally fledging, downy offspring, as with young of many penguins, herd into large creche groups for safety-in-numbers against predators like skuas and giant petrels. They re-sort themselves at feeding time when parents and young instantly recognize one another and reunite enthusiastically. Finally, adults subside into 20-day moults, having lost in the whole arduous process half their body weight—but in waters teeming with krill, they recover quickly.

Slightly larger gentoos with orange bills and conspicuous white eye patches prefer flatter terrain near water, handy for families which take longer to fledge. Gentoo reproductive seasons stretch out over 120–145 days, hard on parents but good for chicks which start out better able to deal with life's adversities. An estimated 300,000 gentoo pairs gather on subantarctic islands and the Peninsula—colonies of some 100,000 pairs at South Georgia, 70,000 on the Falkland Islands, 30,000 on Iles Kerguelen.

Chinstraps, named for distinctive black neck feathers, often seen standing about on ice floes, like to forage among pack ice. Smaller than either gentoos or Adelies, they pick the highest, rockiest,

PREVIOUS PAGES:
King penguins make no nest. Females lays their one egg on their mate's feet, to be kept warm under a feathered breast flap while she goes off to feed. He moves, if he must, with a careful shuffle to avoid losing the egg. She returns in time to share the 51–57-day incubation while he forages, diving sometimes hundreds of yards deep, able to stay down six to seven minutes, returning with food for the new-hatched chick. Preferred breeding sites are coastal plains in easy reach of the sea, where up to a million may gather. Chicks stay on parents' feet another month or so, then go to enormous crèches of woolly young, surviving the next winter with only occasional feeding, fledging finally the next summer.

most inaccessible nest sites, pulling themselves up flipper by flipper around the Peninsula and on islands south of the Antarctic Polar Front. An estimated five million of them nest on little-visited South Sandwich Islands.

Smaller macaroni, royal, and rockhopper penguins breed in huge summer colonies—5.4 million pairs at South Georgia, 2.2 million at Iles Crozet, 1.8 million at Iles Kergeulen, and two million at Heard and McDonald Islands. One million rockhopper pairs are on the Falkland Islands. Royals are only on Macquarie Island. All three have special hopping and jumping abilities enabling them to breed among tumbled boulders on exposed shores. They pursue lantern fish and small luminescent euphausiid crustaceans for food.

Nine kinds of albatross, widest-ranging seagoing birds, include the celebrated wandering, with the longest wingspan of any bird—up to 12 feet (3.66 m). This construction enables it to spend most of its life airborne, hardly moving a muscle, wings outstretched, alternately facing into the almost continuous winds of the open ocean for lift, then soaring downwind over great distances. A catch-like mechanism sets its wings so it can do this almost effortlessly for days, even months with minimal energy drain, sleeping on the wing, literally flying around the world, covering more than a thousand miles (1,600 km) in a single effortless foraging trip.

Petrels of nine species, including the giant, nest here in the millions—birds named for St. Peter because in hovering over water they can seem to be walking on it (as Scripture says this disciple did with Jesus' help)—along with shearwaters, sheathbills, and large, heavily-built gull-like skuas, which feed on krill but also prey on other birds, including penguins.

Marine mammals include fearsome leopard seals up to 13 feet (4 m) long, which have been known to pursue humans as prey; Weddell seals up to nine feet (3 m) long weighing up to 882 pounds (400 kg), which live farther south than any other mammal, able to dive to 197 feet (60 m) and stay more than an hour; plus such other impressive seals as the Antarctic and subantarctic fur, crab-eater, and bulky southern elephant seals weighing almost a ton (900 kg) which can stay underwater two hours without breathing and have been recorded down to 3,281 feet (1,000 m). Other seals also are deep divers, the Weddell commonly hunting at depths of 1,000 feet (304 m) for an hour or more (one was recorded at 1,969 feet/600 m, where pressure reaches 882 pounds per square inch (62 kg/cm²).

Whales seasonally include Antarctic minkes, humpbacks, southern right, sperm, killer, sei, fin and, rarely, blue whales, largest animals that ever lived. A female landed at South Georgia was 110 ft (33.5 m) long.

This whole wildlife spectrum depends on an ecosystem built around some of the world's smallest creatures, starting with microscopic plankton and ranging up to 2.3-inch (6-cm) Antarctic krill. A blue whale can consume up to 4.5 metric tons of krill a day—but almost all species here are dependent on this little shrimp-like crustacean, which fortunately is difficult to process for human consumption. It can, however, be processed for animal consumption and so has become a target for fisheries. For now, krill fishing quotas have been set by treaty and research begun on its important ecosystem niche—but overfishing is a continuing threat, as is the ozone hole, causing concern that increased ultraviolet exposure could cause gradual breakdown of this vital food-chain link. Global warming, of course, is the biggest threat of all. Proposals to explore and exploit Antarctic mineral resources in this exceptionally vulnerable environment, where almost any human activity has lasting effect and where ordinarily biodegradable waste never disappears, have now been set aside by the Environmental Protocol to the Antarctic Treaty. This bans all mining and oil development for at least the next half-century, and designates Antarctica as a "Natural Reserve, devoted to Peace and Science."

Tourism could be a problem if it continues to grow at the present rapid rate, but most tourists and tourist ships behave well and leave no trace of their presence. Permanent scientific communities may themselves be a threat, since facilities, equipment, and daily human life processes exert constant stress on their environment.

Visitation to and around the Antarctic is by ship, arranged by or in cooperation with ecotourism groups—often museums, universities, and natural history societies—with naturalists aboard to acquaint ecotourists with background information to understand what they are seeing as well as how to see it in a way that minimizes disturbance. Many depart or return through the spectacular Drake Passage roamed by albatrosses and storm petrels sweeping along wavetops which can be relatively smooth or stirred up into 40-foot (12-m) waves with 70 mile-an-hour (115-kph) winds that send passengers looking for seasick pills. It's a preview of the trip, since Antarctic travelers need to be aware that unpredictable weather and pack ice can force last-minute itinerary changes and adjustments at any time.

Best times are summer, starting in late November when pack ice is breaking up and birds are courting and mating. In mid-summer—December into January—eggs are hatching and chicks being fed. In late summer—January into February—chicks begin to fledge, adults are ashore moulting and whale-sighting is best.

No one trip can cover everything of interest in this vast snowy land, but highlights of possible destinations include the following:

## ON AND AROUND THE ANTARCTIC PENINSULA

The **South Shetland Islands**—Livingstone and King George with Nelson Island, just south, with large colonies of chinstrap, gentoo, and Adelie penguins; also Elephant Island, where explorer Ernest Shackleton set out to seek rescue and help for his men in an epic journey to South Georgia; Half Moon Island, where chinstrap penguins tend young along with Antarctic blue-eyed shags, snowy sheathbills and Antarctic fur seals; Deception Island with large mixed colonies, several with more than 50,000 chinstrap pairs alone.

**Palmer Archipelago** where humpback whales congregate and thousands of gentoo penguins crowd icebound shores of Cuverville Island under dramatic cliffs.

**Anvers Island**, especially breathtakingly beautiful Paradise Harbor (aka Paradise Bay) with nesting cape petrels, Antarctic blue-eyed shags, kelp gulls, and Antarctic terns, against dramatic cliffs surrounded by sculpted icebergs and magnificent mountains.

**Paulet Island**, off the tip of the Peninsula, with hundreds of thousands of breeding Adelie pairs, also nearby **Hope Bay** with largest Adelie colony in the world.

## AMONG SUBANTARCTIC ISLANDS

**South Georgia** is vital breeding home to some of the world's greatest wildlife concentrations, including more than two million southern fur seals—95 percent of the world population; 300,000 enormous elephant seals—half that species' world population; five million macaroni penguins and large colonies of king penguins crowding the beach at Salisbury Plain, also at St. Andrews Bay and nearby Bay of Isles; and 250,000 albatrosses, including almost half the world population of wandering albatrosses, which nest here and on nearby Albatross Island. With them are an estimated 10 million other seabirds, especially petrels and prions, in underground burrows. Some 2,000 reindeer of two species are here, introduced by Norwegian whalers in 1909. Bird Island off

the northwest tip is home to 50,000 penguin pairs, 30,000 albatross pairs, 700,000 nocturnal petrels, and 65 breeding fur seals (or one bird or seal for every 1.5 square yards or meters, making this small island one of the world's richest wildlife sites). Sir Ernest Shackleton is buried here, his grave overlooking the sea.

**South Orkney Islands** (including Coronation Island) in the Weddell Sea—seldom visited because of heavy ice packs but with large nesting colonies of emperor penguins, also snow and cape petrels, skuas, prions, chinstrap penguins.

**Iles Crozet** are noted for bird life, including half the world's breeding king penguins and millions of tasseled macaronis and rockhoppers.

**Cape Royds** in the Ross Sea is the world's southernmost penguin colony with 4,000 Adelie pairs.

**Heard** and **McDonald Islands** have more than a million pairs of macaroni penguins. The largest nesting colony of this species is on Heard, with another million on the three small McDonalds, as well as gentoos, kings, rockhoppers. Visits require special permit from the Australian government.

**Macquarie Island** is a U.N. World Heritage Site halfway between Antarctica and Tasmania with huge breeding colonies: 100,000 seals, mostly elephant, and four million penguins, including some 400,000 king penguins and 850,000 royal penguins, which breed nowhere else, plus four albatross species. Visits carefully overseen by Tasmanian Parks and Wildlife Service.

**Shag Rocks** near South Georgia and South Sandwich Islands, with prions, wandering albatrosses and of course, shags (aka cormorants).

Frequently included on trips:

**Falkland Islands**, about 300 miles (500 km) east of South America, which can have high concentrations of seabirds, oystercatchers, and also steamer ducks along rocky shores, one million rockhopper penguin pairs, and black-browed albatrosses nesting on cliffs at West Point.

**Auckland Islands**, off New Zealand, with thousands of wandering albatross pairs, also 50,000 mollymawks (as smaller albatrosses are known, in this case the white-capped). Enderby Island has largest breeding population of rare solitary-nesting yellow-eyed penguins and also one of the world's rarest sea lions, the Hooker's, with about 6,000 present (unfortunately, 70 to 100 are killed annually in squid trawlers' nets).

# ASIA

GIANT PANDA

# BANGLADESH

IN MANGROVES OF SUNDERBANS LIVE RARE
SMOOTH-COATED OTTERS, LEOPARD CATS AND FISHING
CATS, AXIS OR SPOTTED DEER, WHICH WITH WILD BOARS AND
RHESUS MACAQUE MONKEYS ARE PRINCIPAL
PREY SPECIES FOR THE FOREST'S BENGAL TIGERS.

## SUNDERBANS EAST NATIONAL PARK

SUNDERBANS EAST IS PART OF THE WORLD'S LARGEST MANGROVE FOREST, LACED WITH A MAZE OF RIVERS AND INLETS FLOWING INTO THE BAY OF BENGAL, SUBJECT TO SOME OF THE WORLD'S MOST DESTRUCTIVE CYCLONES, FLOODS, EARTHQUAKES, AND TIDAL WAVES. It is famed for its Bengal tigers. Often more than six feet (2 m) long, not counting a three-foot tail, weighing up to 660 pounds (300 kg), with extraordinary strength and agility, the rare, powerful cats in this reserve look, it's been noted, "as if they know they are at the top of the food chain."

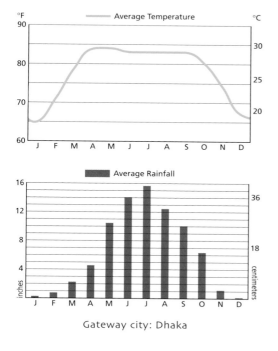

Gateway city: Dhaka

179

# BANGLADESH

Crested serpent eagles' crests rise and fall with their feelings of excitement, over danger, mating, prey possibilities. Otherwise they are almost invisible except for bright yellow eyes, legs and feet, as they perch quietly in the forest, waiting for a snake or lizard to slither along. It's a taste they acquire when young. One nestling only eight inches (20 cm) long was known to swallow a snake three times its length, taking an hour and a half in the process. When not foraging, they can soar for hours over home territories in India, Bangladesh, Pakistan, Sri Lanka, and Myanmar, giving a variety of clear, ringing whistles and screams.

## BANGLADESH

Bangladeshi fishermen, woodcutters, and honey-gatherers enter this forest at their potential peril. It was here that workers discovered tigers are reluctant to attack humans face-to-face, so for a while they were safe wearing face masks on the backs of their heads. But tigers are alert, intelligent animals and many quickly caught on. Electrified human-like decoys may also have helped, but since no systematic tests were made, the effect of both efforts is uncertain. Woodsmen also rely on priests who pray for their safety; even so several die from tiger attacks each year.

The Sunderbans is one of the last great remaining wild areas in the world, a mangrove ecosystem stretching 50 miles (80 km) inland from the coast, covering more than 6,000 square miles (16,000 km²), 60 percent in Bangladesh and the rest in adjoining India. It is part of a vast delta draining the Ganges (Padma in Bangladesh) and Brahmaputra rivers and their tributaries in channels ranging from a few yards wide to three miles (5 km), all of it subject to seasonal and tidal inundation, sometimes in spectacular waves up to 250 feet (75 m) high.

In these mangroves lives a wildlife spectrum—rare smooth-coated otters; leopard cats and fishing cats; beautiful axis or spotted deer which with wild boars and rhesus macaque monkeys are main tiger prey species; estuarine crocodiles basking on riverbanks; Indian pythons; and some 400 fish species. Over 270 kinds of birds include white and gold herons, four kinds of eagles—golden, Pallas' fish-, white-bellied sea, and gray-headed fish-eagle—great flocks of migratory Siberian ducks, 22 kinds of woodpeckers, eight kingfishers including brown-winged, white-collared, and black-capped, rare ruddy swamp francolins, and black-necked and worried-looking mandan-taks or adjutant storks.

Creeks at night come magically alight with glow-worms, fireflies, and millions of bioluminescent microorganisms, food for some 90 fish and 48 crab species which spawn here.

Since 1966 the Bangladesh Sunderbans has been set aside—now as a national park—in three separate reserves with hunting prohibited. Access is not easy. Permits must be obtained from the forestry division office in Khulna, and guides hired (a necessity here). Tigers are not easily seen unless they want to be (often, it is said, too late)—but visitors occasionally tell of one swimming alongside their boat. It's believed that only old or otherwise weakened tigers that have lost their canine fangs attack humans—but local people prudently fear them all. Threats to tigers include poaching both directly and indirectly, through loss of prey animals. Threats to area habitat include illegal logging and shrimp farming—all uncontrolled by an ill-equipped forestry department—as well as pesticide use on surrounding agricultural areas. A proposed fertilizer plant could allow damaging pollutants to enter the water system, and restriction of fresh water from river regulation could threaten mangrove health and regeneration.

Dry season November–mid-March is best for visits.

## BANGLADESH

International jets as well as local airlines fly into the capital city, Dhaka, which has hotels. Here trips to the reserve can be arranged by air, road, or paddle steamer. This can be done also at Khulna, which is closer to the reserve. Guesthouses with more limited facilities but where motor launch trips and guides can also be arranged are at Kotka and Hiron Point, where there are observation towers.

Visitors should realize that wildlife viewing can be chancy in dense jungle—but there's always the possibility of spotting a tiger from a tower with a spotlight, especially on a moonlit night. Be aware also that ground can be muddy and slippery, boatmen often speak little English, and twice-daily tides can come in quickly at 30 miles an hour (50 kph). Drinking water must be carried into the park.

---

**FURTHER INFORMATION**

Permission and Hiron Point reservations can be made through the Mongla Port Authority Chairman in Khulna, Tel: 62331; or at Kotka from the Khulna Divisional Forestry Officer, Circuit House Road, Khulna, Tel: 20654, 20665, 21173; or from the Sunderbans Tourist Complex there, Tel: 21731/2, 23024. Department of Forests, General Administration and Wildlife, Bana Bhaban, Gulshan Road, Mohakhali, Dhaka-12; or in Dhaka, the National Tourist Organization, Parjatan, 233 Airport Road, Tejgaon, Dhaka-12; National Forest Conservator, Bana Bhawan, Gulshan Road, Monakhali, Dhaka-12; General Secretary, Bangladesh Wildlife Society, Zoology Department, Dhaka University, Dhaka-12. *See also* SUNDERBANS U.N. WORLD HERITAGE SITE in India, p.229, which has been subject of less scientific research but can seem more visitor-friendly.

---

## ALSO OF INTEREST

This tropical lowland country, roughly the size of England and Wales combined, has, perhaps because of population pressures for land, relatively few designated parks and reserves. Others worth noting, however, include:

**Madhupur Forest Reserve**, about 80 miles (130 km) northwest of Dhaka (three hours by car)—mixed forest rich in various wildlife species, notably owls—dusky, brown fishing, spotted eagle, and brown wood (unfortunately its area has been cut in half over the past 20 years).

**Lowacherra Forest Preserve** is similar to Madhupur, about five miles (8 km) east of Srimangal.

**Telepara/Satcheri Forest Preserve**, about 37 miles (60 km) southwest of Srimangal, with a sandy basin attracting many birds, also numerous woodland species.

# BHUTAN

TAKINS, STRANGE NATIONAL ANIMALS SEEMING
TO BE PART MOOSE AND PART ANTELOPE, SHARE
HIGH MEADOWS WITH "BLUE SHEEP" AND RARE
BLACK-NECKED CRANES. OVER 600 KINDS OF
ORCHIDS, 50 OF RHODODENDRON PROVIDE
BRILLIANT BLOOM YEAR-ROUND.

THIS SMALL HIMALAYAN KINGDOM SOMETIMES
THOUGHT TO BE THE REAL-LIFE SHANGRI-LA OF
LEGEND HAS AN EXTRAORDINARY 26 PERCENT OF ITS
WILDLIFE-RICH LAND SET ASIDE IN RESERVES, AND A
NATIONAL POLICY PROTECTING ALL NATURAL
LIFE. (The U.S. has 10.5 percent, for
example; France 8.8, Japan 6.5, India 4.2.)

Bhutan's National Assembly has banned
logging and other habitat-destructive activities and vowed to maintain not less than 60
percent of its land under forest cover for all
time. A National Environmental Commission
oversees all environment-related activity,
strongly supported by its hereditary ruler,
King Jigme Singye Wangchuck, in accordance
with Buddhist views respecting all life and
holding that a healthy environment is essential both for material and spiritual happiness.

Rare and threatened species such as clouded
and snow leopards, Asian elephants, greater
one-horned rhinoceros, royal Bengal tigers,
golden langurs, and wild water buffalo are
among some 165 kinds of mammals (perhaps
including legendary "abominable snowmen").

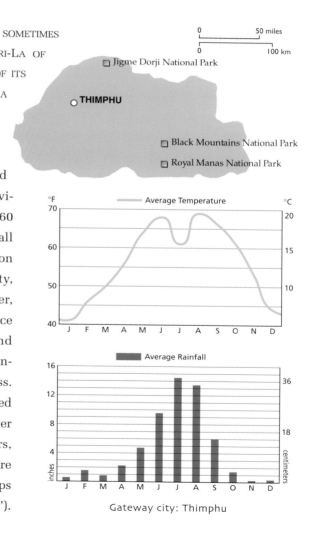

Gateway city: Thimphu

These are at home in sanctuaries rising to almost 25,000 feet (7,625 m) from steamy lowland jungles to white-crowned glacial Himalayas. For some species, these may be among last places offering hope of survival for significant populations.

Takins, strange national animals seeming to be part-moose and part-antelope—also described as oxen with goats' heads—seek out alpine meadows near forest cover, sole members of their scientific family and according to legend the miraculous 15th-century creation of an eccentric Buddhist saint known as "the Divine Madman." Blue sheep (aka bharals)—slate blue, actually sheep-like goats—crop scrubby steep-slope vegetation.

Rare resplendent Blyth's tragopans with lemon-yellow faces and orange-red feathered mantles forage with multihued Sclater's monal pheasants for seeds and insects on the forest floor—among over 700 bird species, at least half of which are found only in the Himalayas.

Endangered black-necked cranes fly from the Tibetan plateau to winter here—arriving always, it's said, on the same late autumn day and then flying three times around a nearby monastery before settling on the marsh, mimicking Buddhist pilgrims' ritual arrival in a sacred place.

Lammergeiers—"bone-breakers" (aka bearded vultures)—drop bones from Himalayan heights to shatter them and get at marrow. Rufous-necked hornbills with bright rufous heads, necks and underparts and enormous yellow bills—rare elsewhere— are common in tropical evergreen forests. Other spectaculars include sapphire flycatchers, blue-fronted robins, fire-tailed sunbirds, slender-billed scimitar-babblers and over 10 species of laughing thrush.

Plants are equally remarkable—over 5,400 species, including more than 600 kinds of orchid, 50 kinds of rhododendron, and 300 valued for medicinal qualities. Because ice-age glaciers had no impact on lower elevations, some plants date back to earth's ancient vegetation.

Something is always in brilliant bloom—yellow Indian laburnums April–June; orange "flame of the forest" February–May; pink Himalayan wild cherries in fall; deep red rhododendrons March–May—all attracting colorful and rare butterflies. Alpine meadows are carpeted with anemones, forget-me-nots, dwarf irises, rhododendrons, delphiniums, and primulas, from snowmelt to early summer and even more with onset of July monsoons.

Climate varies with elevation, dropping to freezing and below in mountains, warm and steamy in lowland jungles. Rains occur any time—but during June–August monsoons, Thimphu, the capital, can get 20 inches (500 mm), and eastern hills many times that. Best times are October–late November with generally clear skies; second-best March–May—cloudier with more rain, but flowers are in glorious bloom and birdlife abundant.

Most of Bhutan's reserves have not been fully investigated or developed for visitors. Plans for future management and protection while permitting gradual development have been under-taken by the Bhutan Trust Fund for Environmental Conservation (BTFEC) in collaboration with the U.N., World Bank, and World Wide Fund for Nature (WWF). The government and WWF also are engaged in planning biological corridors connecting various reserves to allow for dispersal of megafauna such as tigers.

With all Bhutan's environmental consciousness, problems exist with poor land management—overgrazing, clearing for human settlement, and shifting agricultural use (aka slash-and-burn or "swidden" farming)—poaching for illegal trade in live animals and their parts and of rare trees for uses ranging from incense to firewood. Sheepherders eliminate blue sheep, leopards, wolves, and Asiatic wild dogs or dhole, when they feel them competitive with their livelihood.

Bhutan has been open to tourism only since the late 1960s and at least until recently has granted only about 5,000 tourist permits yearly, the government insisting that foreign visitors arrive with pre-planned itineraries arranged through licensed Bhutan tour operators.

The national airline, Druk Air, connects Bhutan with New Delhi, Calcutta, Dhaka, Kathmandu, and Bangkok—but getting around can be hard on roads unsuited to motor traffic.

---

**FURTHER INFORMATION**

National Environment Commission, Post Box 466, Thimphu-Bhutan; Joint Director, Nature Conservation Division, Forest Department, Thimphu; Department of Tourism, Post Box 126, Thimphu, Bhutan; World Wide Fund for Nature, P.O. Box 210, Thimphu.

---

# ROYAL MANAS NATIONAL PARK

Royal Manas National Park is a former royal hunting reserve, now a U.N. World Heritage Site offering sanctuary to more significant faunal species than anyplace else in Bhutan.

Rare, silky, long-tailed golden leaf langur monkeys—a fluffy orange-gold—are found only here, feeding not only on leaves but flowers, buds, shoots, seeds, and salty mineral-rich earth, in rolling forested hill country where, if unwary, they become food themselves for arboreal clouded leopards.

Formidable wild water buffalo with touchy, aggressive dispositions forage on stream-laced savannahs with Indian elephants, the two giving one another wide berths.

Tigers prey on spotted hogs and young sambar deer and, if they can find them, rare hispid hares.

At least 350 bird species include black, Asiatic, and lesser adjutant storks, ibisbills, watercocks, great stone-curlews, mountain hawk-eagles, and Indian rollers, and the park is an important waterfowl staging area for ruddy shelducks and green-winged teal.

Orchids of hundreds of species find support on rare agar trees whose wood is prized for incense and medicine.

# BHUTAN

Abutting Royal Manas' some 395 square miles (1,023 km²) of remote, varied, well-watered habitat are: BLACK MOUNTAINS NATIONAL PARK (*see* below) to the north; on the south, India's MANAS WILDLIFE RESERVE (*see* p.219), with 1,000 square miles (2,600 km²) protecting more endangered species than any other Indian reserve. Together the three represent a huge transborder area covering almost 2,000 square miles (5,000 km²) of immense importance for plants and animals threatened with extinction elsewhere in the Himalayas, including a large tiger population.

The country's first long-range park management has been started by the Forest Services Division (FSD) working with WWF as a hoped-for model for reserves elsewhere, with guard posts, staff quarters, patrol trails, watch tower, water holes, and field equipment including boats and vehicles, with jobs for local residents.

There is a guest house at park headquarters, although at least until recently, it has been unavailable due to Assamese ethnic Bodo tribal insurgency in the area. Additional park access has been only by lengthy detour through India for which Restricted Area Permits are required (*see* Manas Wildlife Reserve, India). Construction has begun on a direct-access road between Gelephu and headquarters. Simple village guesthouses are at Kanamakra, Rabang, and Panbang.

---

**FURTHER INFORMATION**

Warden, Royal Manas National Park, c/o Forest Departrment, P.O. Box 130, Thimphu, Bhutan; World Wide Fund for Nature, P.O. Box 210, Thimphu, Tel: (+975-2) 32-3528, Fax: 32-3518.

---

## BLACK MOUNTAINS NATIONAL PARK
## (JIGME SINGYE WANGCHUCK NATIONAL PARK)

Mountainous 540-square-mile (1,400-km²) Black Mountains National Park (recently renamed Jigme Singye Wangchuck National Park) has many of the same species as Royal Manas, especially—since the whole reserve is at 4,900–16,000 feet (1,500–4,925 m)—those tolerant of higher elevations: serow—shaggy, hardy little goat-antelopes; musk deer—whose glandular secretions used in perfume can bring more by weight than gold, inoffensive-looking except for sharp tusks;

OPPOSITE: Clouded leopards, named for cloud-like spots that provide camouflage in their forest habitat, are (even this young one) arboreal specialists of the cat family. With short, stout legs and low centers of gravity, thick, furry tails the length of their bodies for balance, and flexible back ankle joints that allow hind feet to rotate so they can descend head-first, like squirrels, they can crawl along horizontal branches with backs to the ground, like sloths, or dangle from hind legs only. They often drop on victims from overhead, preying on smaller mammals—deer and wild pigs—as well as birds.

Himalayan black bears; red pandas; wild boars; sambar and Indian muntjac or barking deer; golden leaf langur monkeys; and occasional tigers.

Access and visitor facilities have been minimal, but a small guesthouse is sometimes available.

In the beautiful pristine Phobjikha Valley adjoining Black Mountains' northern boundary is the **Phobjikha Conservation Area**, home from late-October to late-February of rare black-necked cranes getting away from harsh winters on the Tibetan Plateau—home also, since 1613, of the Gantey Monastery, largest Nyingmapa Monastery in Bhutan. A nature study center established with help from WWF is at the valley's southern end at Khebethang. Several small guesthouses are sometimes available.

## JIGME DORJI NATIONAL PARK

Bhutan's largest park—1,679 square miles (4,349 km²)—and biologically one of the richest on the subcontinent. In its eight vegetational habitat zones, from riverine along its many streams to alpine meadows and scrub, in altitudes ranging from 4,600–23,000 feet (1,400–7,000 m) live rare beautiful snow leopards, takins, blue sheep, red pandas, golden leaf langur monkeys. Bird rarities include crimson-breasted blood pheasants, spectacular turquoise, purple, and red Himalayan monals and satyr tragopans, once thought extinct. As with other Bhutan parks, visitor facilities are largely in the planning stage, although trekking is permitted.

## ALSO OF INTEREST

**Sakten Wildlife Sanctuary**, 250 square miles (650 km²)—reputed habitat of migoi, Bhutanese term for yeti or "abominable snowmen," covered except for their faces in fur that can be reddish-brown to black, seldom seen, perhaps because Bhutanese yetis have the power to become invisible, and their backward-facing feet make them hard to track.

**Khaling/Neoli Wildlife Sanctuary**, 105 square miles (273 km²) in southeasternmost Bhutan protects tigers, leopards, Indian elephants, gaur, possibly pygmy hogs, and hispid hares.

**Phipsoo Sanctuary** in southwest, with the only remaining Bhutanese sal forest, protects Bhutan's only chital deer, also axis deer, Asian elephants, gaur, golden langurs, tigers, on 106 square miles (278 km²).

**Thrumshing La National Park**, 296 square miles (768 km²) east of Black Mountains, believed home of red pandas, has over 30 species of rhododendrons in a "park-within-a-park." Remarkably, a tiger recently was sighted at 12,000 feet (3,660 m) in this park.

# CAMBODIA

TONLE SAP, A HUGE LAKE WHICH EXPANDS AND CONTRACTS SEASONALLY FROM 1,150 SQUARE MILES TO 5,000 SQUARE MILES (3,000– 13,000 KM²), CONTAINS ONE OF THE WORLD'S DENSEST POPULATIONS OF FRESHWATER FISH. THOUSANDS OF WADING BIRDS AND WATERFOWL GATHER TO REAP THE HARVEST.

PROBING FEET AND BEAKS OF THOUSANDS OF RARE AND SPECTACULAR WADING BIRDS SWIRL SHALLOW LAKE WATERS OF TONLE SAP EVERY SPRING WHEN THE LAKE SHRINKS TO ONE-FOURTH ITS FLOOD-SWOLLEN MONSOONAL SIZE, LEAVING A MILLING SOUP OF SMALL FISH, FROGS, INSECTS, AND OTHER NUTRITIOUS AQUATIC ORGANISMS.

Painted and milky storks throng lake edges with spot-billed pelicans, waterfowl, and smaller pattering shorebirds.

Tigers and leopards find homes in forests also inhabited by endangered marbled cats, pileated and buff-cheeked gibbons, Eld's deer, and elephants. Banteng and gaur feed in forest openings.

Siamese fireback and Germain's peacock pheasants scratch for seeds and insects on forest floors along with bright blue-rumped and bar-bellied pittas, green peafowl, and giant ibis, among more than 520 bird species in this country one-third the size of France (70,238 square miles/181,916 km²). Orioles, sunbirds, and clouds of butterflies sip nectar from blossoming flame trees, lavender jacarandas, scarlet hibiscus, and fragrant pink and white lotuses, opening mornings and evenings on waterways.

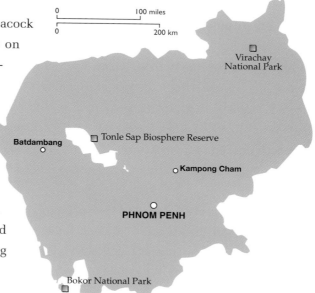

# CAMBODIA

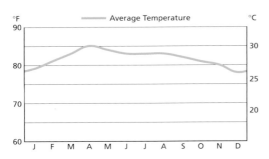

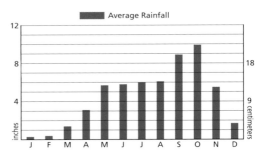

Gateway city: Phnom Penh

Yet Cambodia is not only one of the world's loveliest and most wildlife-rich but also environmentally and war-distressed countries, littered with bomb craters and remnants of some 40 million land mines planted in its tragic civil war in the 1970s and 80s. Its richness is due to the presence of one of the world's most fertile floodplains—the Mekong. Its remarkable situation results from link-up of the Mekong River, 300 miles (486 km) wide in places, rising in Tibet, and the Tonle Sap River which flows seasonally from Tonle Sap Lake and drains rivers north and west.

During June–October monsoon rains, rising Mekong River waters force the Tonle Sap River to reverse its flow and the lake expands from 1,150 to 5,000 square miles (3,000–13,000 km²) and in maximum depth from 7 to 33 feet (2.2–10 m). In ensuing dry months the process reverses and lake waters drain back into the Mekong, leaving Tonle Sap with one of the world's densest populations of freshwater fish in a bounteous aquatic ecosystem that attracts humans as well as wildlife. Grasses grow up to five feet (1.5 m) high in this rich alluvial plain surrounded by thickly forested highlands, some of it with trees 165 feet (50 m) tall.

Cambodia has gone from some 74 percent forest coverage in 1974 to 30–35 percent in 1995. By the end of 1993 more than 26,560 square miles (68,800 km²) had been allocated to timber concessions, amounting to almost all Cambodia's forest outside protected areas—and illegal logging, land clearing, and rampant hunting have made even these not safe. Predictable results have been not only direct habitat loss but problems from overfishing, mangrove-clearing for shrimp farms, and proposed dam projects. (The tragedy is that bootleg logging has meant significant financial loss to this poor country instead of treasury gain possible from controlled timbering.)

Some of the world's last freshwater Irrawaddy dolphins swim in the Mekong River, along with giant catfish more than 16 feet (5 m) long. Both are imperiled by uncontrolled gill-net fishing.

Gradually, however, some of Cambodia's national parks and wildife sanctuaries are opening up with facilities for visitors. As with other threatened wildlife-rich countries, the government may come to see ecotourism benefits justifying an effort to protect priceless natural treasures.

# TONLE SAP BIOSPHERE RESERVE

This is an ornithological wonder when thousands of storks, pelicans, and many others, including waterfowl, gather in huge numbers around receding lake waters in dry December–May, attracted by seasonal concentrations of aquatic life. Visits and boat trips can be arranged in Siem Reap, where there are hotels and guesthouses—the sanctuary director can be contacted there. Day trips with fees going to conservation are run by non-profit Osmose (E-mail: osmose@bigpond.com.kh). Angkor Wat, 9–14th-century architectural wonder, once heart of the Khmer empire, is nearby, its exquisite bas reliefs depicting how the lake affected all walks of Khmer life centuries ago.

Direct daily flights are available from Phnom Penh and Bangkok.

# VIRACHAY NATIONAL PARK

A sprawling 1,330-square-mile (3,445-km²) forest bordering on Laos and Vietnam in northeast Cambodia. During the Vietnam (or "American") war it was a link in the Ho Chi Minh Trail. Like all forest areas in Cambodia, it is heavily hunted for demands of the wildlife trade, but still home to tigers, leopards, Asiatic wild dogs, sun bears, buff-cheeked gibbons, and douc langurs. Facilities are minimal, but friendly, welcoming rangers at park centers in Voen Sai and Siem Pang will try to help visitors see at least park fringes.

# BOKOR (PREAH MONIVONG) NATIONAL PARK

This park, with Asian elephants and significant numbers of birds and other mammals—also a two-tiered waterfall where both wildlife and humans bathe—occupies a 3,280-foot (1,000-m) plateau on the south coast with magnificent views over the forested escarpment to the sea. Roughly 118 miles (190 km) by road south of Phnom Penh, rangers are available as guides (if not away on park duties) and accommodation is available in the Ministry of Environment Park Center at the old French hill station at the summit—also lodging in nearby Kampot, where trips can be arranged.

You can reach Phnom Penh and Siem Reap by international jet, but as of recently Cambodia's road system was arguably Asia's worst, trains and busses slow, crowded, and dangerous, with infrastructure to match. Land mines remain an off-trail threat in some areas after quarter of a century of conflict. With all this, Cambodian people are pleasant and welcoming. Weather is good most of the year—October–March driest. Temperatures through the year average in the 80s°F (25–30°C).

> **FURTHER INFORMATION**
>
> Wildlife Conservation Society, Cambodia Program, P.O. Box 1620, Phnom Penh; Wildlife Protection Office, Department of Forestry and Wildlife, 40 Norodom Boulevard, Phnom Penh, E-mail: wildlifedfw@bigpond.com.kh

# CHINA

GIANT PANDAS AND SIBERIAN CRANES FOUND
HERE SHARE WORLDWIDE CONCERN BECAUSE OF
THEIR RARITY AND BEAUTY, BUT CHINA ALSO HAS A
REMNANT POPULATION OF TIGERS AND ASIAN ELEPHANTS.
STILL UNDER GREAT PRESSURE FROM POPULATION AND
ECONOMIC DEVELOPMENT, THE COUNTRY HAS BEGUN
TO DEVELOP ENVIRONMENTAL RESTORATION PLANS.

B EARLIKE GIANT PANDAS PEER OUT OF BAMBOO GLADES HERE, THEIR BLACK
MASKS AND EXPRESSIONS AT ONCE INNOCENT AND MISCHIEVOUS.
Their endearing appearance has attracted worldwide affection and
concern; they have come to symbolize rare, endangered species
everywhere as they do the beleaguered and wonderful wildlife

Harbin

Changchun

Changbai Shan Nature Reserve
Shenyang

0        300 miles

0        500 km

Karamay

BEIJING

Dalian

Hami

Shizuishan

Shijiazhuang

Qingdao

Aksu

Yumen

Taiyuan

Jinan

Hotan

Lanzhou

Zhengzhou

Mt. K2

K U N L A N   S H A N

Xi'an

Nanjing

Shanghai

Hangzhou

Wuhan

Wenzhou

Yichang

Wolong Nature Reserve    Poyang Lake Nature Reserve

Chengdu

Nanching

Lhasa

Chongqing

Changsha

Fuzhou

Luzhou

Mt. Everest

Hengyang

Zhangzhou

Guiyang

Kunming

Guangzhou

Nanning

Hong Kong

Macau

Xishuangbanna Nature Reserve

Zhanjiang

Hainan

# CHINA

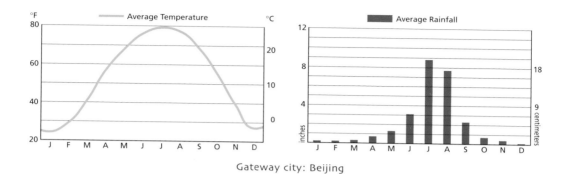

Gateway city: Beijing

of their native land, where much of the landscape has been denuded of natural features by pollution, deforestation, ill-advised land-use projects, and pressures of burgeoning population.

Yet with all its problems, this vast, beautiful country lays claim to some great wildlife diversity. More than 4,400 vertebrate species are here—more than 10 percent of the world's total. They include nearly 500 mammal species, 1,189 birds, more than 210 amphibians, 320 reptiles, and 2,200 fish. Along with snow and clouded leopards are many other rarities—golden monkeys, white-lipped deer, takins (looking like goat-antelopes with long shaggy fur like musk-oxen), Asian elephants, Manchurian tigers, Chinese river dolphins, Chinese alligators.

Flora are equally remarkable—some 32,800 species of higher plants, over 12 percent of the world's total, of which 2,800 are trees—ancient Cathay silver firs, China cypresses, golden larches, towering meta-sequoias 115 feet (35 m) tall. A major 20th-century botanical event was discovery of more than 1,000 meta-sequoias, common worldwide 100 million years ago but thought extinct since ice ages, on the Sichuan–Hubei border. Of the world's 800 azalea varieties, 650 are in Yunnan. Many of the world's rhododendrons, roses, magnolias, and camellias descend from ancestors here.

China's wildlife and habitat suffered severely during the 1966–76 Cultural Revolution. But in reaction, significant efforts have been undertaken to protect remaining natural resources. Laws were passed giving conservation a priority, legalizing citizens' environmental groups, and more than 900 nature reserves have been established covering some 307,956 square miles (800,000 km²), 7.64 percent of this huge country. Habitats range from tropical mangrove swamps and coral reefs to coniferous forests in subarctic permafrost—from the edges of icy 29,087-foot (8,848-m) Mount Everest and high cold deserts of the Tibet Plateau to rivers carving dramatic gorges en route to the world's second-lowest spot, the torrid Turfan depression, 505 feet (154 m) below sea level.

Northeastern mountains support Asiatic sable, moose, and the last Manchurian tigers. Camels, Asiatic asses, wolves, and wild sheep live along the arid Mongolian border.

# CHINA

Red-crowned cranes, one of the rarest of a rare family, depend on breeding and wintering grounds that are themselves precarious—Korea's demilitarized zone and coastal, riverine and freshwater marshes in Russia and northeast China, threatened by dam construction, deforestation, and agricultural expansion. They prefer relatively deep water with standing dead vegetation, signaling location of the right spot with breathtaking courtship dances and unison calls audible for miles.

Red-crowned cranes are making a comeback at Heilongjiang Province's **Zhalong Nature Preserve** on a giant 840-square-mile (2,175-km²) marsh which lies on a migration path extending from the Russian arctic around the Gobi Desert down into Southeast Asia. It's a stopover and nesting area for tens of thousands of storks, swans, herons, harriers, grebes, and others, between April and October.

Southwestern mountains with steep, still-largely-forested river valleys shelter takins, red pandas, and snub-nosed monkeys. The Tibet Plateau is home to wild yaks, snow leopards, Tibetan antelopes, and its lakes and salt marshes are wintering grounds for rare beautiful black-necked cranes, especially on **Caohai Reserve** in northwest Guizhou and **Qinghai Lake** with its Niao Dao (Bird Island) in Qinghai Province.

Huge **Arjin Shan Reserve**, high, flat, remote, uninhabited, a 17,375-square-mile (45,000-km²) wilderness, is one of the last places in Asia where large herds of hoofed animals such as Tibetan wild yaks (some 10,000 of them), wild asses (30,000), Tibetan antelopes (up to 75,000), and gazelles can graze unimpeded over large areas, followed by predators like lynx, wolves, snow leopards, and steppe cats, surrounded by towering peaks which are home to ibexes and blue sheep.

Qomolangma in southernmost Tibet is part of an enormous protected complex contiguous to Nepal's LANGTANG, SAGARMANTHA and MAKALU-BARUN parks (*see* p.246), 16,000 square miles (41,400 km²) altogether protecting much of the Everest ecosystem.

Qomolangma is dedicated to showing how sustainable human development can work with nature preservation. Hunting bans are credited with encouraging recovery of endangered blue sheep, Tibetan wild asses, Tibetan gazelles, and snow leopards.

# CHINA

Alligators bask and Chinese river dolphins frolic in southeastern wetlands near the Chang River mouth. **Lake Poyang** is winter residence of some 80 percent of the world's Siberian cranes. Giant pandas live along the narrow strip dividing this area from mountains to the west. Lakes Bitahai and Napahai in northwest Yunnan are important wintering sites for rare migratory birds.

Fourteen U.N. World Biosphere Reserves are here, some listed as among the world's most important wetlands. Rescue projects have been activated for animals close to extinction—crested ibis, Chinese alligators, Eld's and David's deer. Saiga, with translucent amber horns and grotesquely outsize proboscis, have been extinct in the wild here, but reintroduction projects are under way. China has successfully bred more than 60 different species with the idea of releasing them to restored wild populations.

It's not easy to see all these animals or these places. Many are remote and difficult to access. Few convenient visitor facilities exist as yet. But setting them aside is a start, and there is growing awareness of ecotourism benefits, both in tourism from elsewhere and among increasingly well-off Chinese.

Serious threats continue. They include use of animal parts for medicine—rhino horns, bears' paws and gall bladders, and every part of tigers from eyeballs to sex organs, for epilepsy, paralysis, headaches, skin disease, impotence. Pandas die in snares set for endangered musk deer whose glands are prized in folk medicine. All this has worsened as such customs, ineffective for most medical conditions and disastrous for imperiled species, have been exported around the world.

Sharks' fin soup continues popular while shark populations decline due to practice of taking only fins and releasing sharks to drown if not first eaten alive in the sea.

The pet trade is enormous. Every town has a bird market with a large array for sale—Peking robins, laughing thrushes, shamas, white-eyes, munias, mynas, parakeets, many—especially insectivores—doomed to die quickly in their tiny, exquisitely made cages, which will then be refilled with others. Wholesale export of birds as pets and for feather decorations has caused species to plummet—and so far, educational efforts have helped but little. Tourists should be mindful when dining or souvenir-shopping.

---

NOTE: Severe penalties are making many think twice about poaching pandas since two Sichuan men found with panda skins were publicly executed and another 19 were sentenced to life imprisonment.

---

Spring (March–May) and fall (September–November) are best times to visit (avoid public holidays). Major cities are served by international airlines and there are good internal air, bus, and railroad networks—no car rental without a Chinese driving license, but cars with drivers are readily available.

Accommodations vary throughout the country but quality and service, formerly poor—especially for foreigners—has improved markedly everywhere, though until recently only camping has been feasible in areas far from civilization.

---

**FURTHER INFORMATION**

Division of Nature Conservation (Director), National Environmental Protection Agency, 115 Xizhimennei Nansciaojie, Beijing, Tel: (+86) 1-8992211.

---

# WOLONG (SLEEPY DRAGON) NATURE RESERVE

More giant pandas are in these 800 mountainous wooded square miles (2,070 km²) north of Chengdu than anywhere else. They are endangered by habitat loss but also because they got behind the evolutionary curve—herbivores equipped with carnivores' digestive systems and sharp teeth. One theory has it that their ancestors moved too slowly—as they do today—to be efficient predators and so started eating other things. Today they consume largely bamboo, and of the hundreds of bamboo species, they like only two—the umbrella and arrow—which they digest so inefficiently (17 percent) they must take in up to 45 pounds (20.4 kg) a day.

Their reproductive approach is not much more efficient. Females, fertile only two or three days a year, must attract males quickly in dense woods where these dim-sighted animals usually can't see each other more than a few feet away. Luckily keen senses of smell help them find one another by scent-marking. After mating, a 16-cell embryo floats free in the womb, not implanting for perhaps five months. Young are born not long afterward in a state most non-pouched animals would consider not viable—blind, hairless, fragile, and so tiny compared to their burly mothers that a human infant born in the same size ratio would have a mother weighing around 6,000 pounds (2,724 kg).

Habitat interference is prime cause of their decline. Before that, pandas held their own on earth for millions of years. An estimated 1,000 survive today. China has set aside 32 nature reserves for them, of which best known is Wolong, which had at recent count about 70. About 120 have been brought into captive breeding programs, both in China and in cooperation with zoos elsewhere in the world—in San Diego, New York, Madrid, Mexico—which have helped fund panda conservation, as have organizations such as World Wide Fund for Nature. An encouraging number of captive-born pandas are surviving, and the program is being expanded elsewhere.

Best hope may be a proposal to incorporate 17 connecting bamboo corridors in a government plan to set aside an additional 11,580 square miles (30,000 km²) of panda habitat. Here pandas could move freely between safe areas, with a mixing of now-separated panda populations thereby reducing inbreeding risks.

Pandas, like other endangered species for which land is set aside, become "umbrella" species for others with the same needs so that such places become diverse ecosystems protecting not only these species but others—rare golden snub-nosed monkeys, Asiatic golden cats, red pandas, Sichuan takins, reclusive clouded and snow leopards, Pallas' (steppe) cats. They also protect a great variety of beautiful songbirds as well as Chinese monal partridges, rare stunning Temmink's tragopans with cobalt-blue faces and spotted fiery-red plumage, and five other species of brilliant pheasants.

Because of elevation differences in temperature, warmth-loving species like rhesus monkeys, rare clouded leopards, and sambar deer, live near hardy species of the north, such as Thorald's deer, lynx, bharals or blue sheep—altogether 96 mammals, 300 bird species, 20 kinds of reptiles, and 14 amphibians.

It's not easy to see all these in dense bamboo. Trails exist, but they can be rough going, precipitous, with cloud cover, heavy mist, and drenching rain. May–October is best—winters are numbingly cold. Tours and lodging can be arranged in Chengdu, 87 miles (140 km) and an eight-hour bus trip southeast. No-frills lodging is sometimes available in a former loggers' hotel on the reserve.

Realistically, best chance to see a panda is to visit the giant panda breeding center north of Chengdu, where a dozen or so live, some in relatively confined, some in larger habitat quarters. Best go between 8:30–10 am when they are feeding—they nap in seclusion much of the day.

---

**FURTHER INFORMATION**

Wolong Nature Reserve, Management Office, Wenchuan Country, Sichuan 623006.

---

# CHANGBAI SHAN RESERVE

Whatever number of Manchurian tigers survive are almost certainly in and around Changbai Shan (perhaps mixed with Siberian tigers), at 810 square miles (2,100 km²) one of China's largest and most popular reserves on the North Korean border. But they and other rare, shy creatures tend to stay far from the crowds that get off tour busses to see and photograph Tian Chi—Heaven Pool, a volcanic crater lake surrounded by jagged rock outcrops and 16 mountain peaks—and wildlife-oriented visitors should too. Away from the crowds are leopards, sika deer, otters, sables, colorful butterflies, and more than 200 bird species, including golden-rumped swallows, ornamental red crossbills, rare oriental storks, scaly-sided mergansers, and gorgeous mandarin ducks looking like freshly-painted objets d'art. Wooded areas include some of the few undisturbed large tracts of old-growth forest in China's temperate zone. Much can be seen on the many hiking trails.

Two warnings: weather is routinely changeable. Sunny warm mornings can turn into high winds, rain, and hail by afternoon. Hire a guide or take a good trail map or both. One British visitor strayed unintentionally over the border and spent a month in a North Korean jail. If relations ease, Changbai Shan could be an important trans-frontier reserve comanaged by the two countries. A variety of lodging, also transport, is available in nearby Baihe, reachable by train, bus or hired car from Jilin or Changchun or sightseeing plane from Jilin direct to Tian Chi daily.

# POYANG LAKE NATURE RESERVE

Most of the world's tall, graceful, endangered Siberian cranes—snow-white with scarlet faces, black wing-tips, and ancient lineage going back 40 million years—may spend part or all winter here in central China. Viewing them from bluffs overlooking the lake can be breathtaking as they gather to feed with perhaps a half-million other water-oriented birds on eelgrass and crustaceans in and around China's largest freshwater lake.

Poyang was discovered as the cranes' winter home in 1984 by scientists and ornithologists seeking to trace their hazardous 3,000-mile (4,800-km) migration from summer breeding grounds in wilderness 1,200 miles (1,930 km) north of Siberia's Ob River. The route is hazardous, winding over war-torn Afghanistan and six other countries where the birds are shot for food or feathers or ensnared to serve as winged watchdogs, their clarion calls through trumpetlike windpipes audible for miles. Many former wetland stopovers have been drained for development, and some birds are known to end up in distant KEOLADEO RESERVE in Bharatpur, India (*see* p.207). The reserve was set aside in large part because of untiring efforts of one man, He Xuguang, angered at the senseless shooting of cranes and other beautiful birds seeking safety here.

It now occupies 86 square miles (224 km$^2$) on and around Lake Poyang in the vast Yangtze watershed/floodplain in Jiangxi Province in southeast China, and affords protection to many other species as well. At times more than a quarter-million waterfowl—more than 300 species altogether—may gather in this ideal habitat, especially when dramatic seasonal changes cause lake water levels to shrink from about 1,100 square miles (2,849 km$^2$) in summer to a tenth that, creating a complex of shallow lakes, mudflats, and wet grasslands around the edges. There can be over 2,000 white-naped cranes, threatened Dalmatian pelicans, black-faced spoonbills, mandarin ducks, white and black storks, and perhaps a good part of the world population of swan geese—up to 40,000. In dry grasslands along the shore, hooded cranes, great bustards, grass owls, and Japanese marsh warblers forage observed overhead by white-tailed marsh and hen harriers.

Common in the area are ring-necked pheasants, Kentish plovers, spotted redshanks, oriental skylarks, magpies, and crested mynahs. Goosanders, smews, and pied kingfishers feed at nearby Gan and Xiu rivers.

Threats continue. Changes brought by the huge Three Gorges Dam upriver increasingly will affect the entire watershed and its wildlife, including waters and food plants on which the cranes and others rely. Rapid population growth and economic development have brought industrial waste along with use of pesticides and chemical fertilizers, further damaging bird habitat. International organizations have offered to help, especially with Siberian cranes whose survival is regarded as precarious. Captive breeding programs have been started with assistance from the International Crane Foundation, based in Baraboo, Wisconsin, to back up wild populations. Scientists and conservationists also are working to develop a Waterbird Conservation Plan for the entire Poyang Basin.

Best times are dry season October–March. The reserve is in easy driving distance of Nanching where there is lodging and tour information.

## XISHUANGBANNA

Increasingly rare Asian elephants are prized residents here in the largest stretch of tropical rain forest in China, home as well to more than 100 mammal species including tigers, gaur (world's largest wild oxen, weighing up to a ton/1,000 kg), slow loris, crested (or white-cheeked) and hoolock (or white-browed) gibbons, and golden-haired monkeys. There are 427 kinds of birds including great pied and rufous-necked hornbills, green peafowl, crimson sun-birds, thick-billed flowerpeckers, peacock-pheasants, blossom-headed parakeets, red jungle fowl, as well as Asian barred owls, ospreys, and serpent eagles. The reserve, actually a 926-square-mile (2,400-km²) merger (unfortunately still not fully contiguous) of five reserves in the extreme south of Yunnan Province, is now under threat by population pressures from various directions including shifting agricultural trends, which have replaced forest with rubber and tea plantations, as well as unsustainable forestry harvesting for energy production. These are damaging not only to wildlife but human interests (since 1960, average temperatures here have risen 1.8°F/1°C, and rainfall has dropped 10–20 percent). A joint project by China's South Forestry College with World Wide Fund for Nature attempts to create public awareness and replace unsustainable land use with fast-growing nitrogen-fixing trees. Elephant herds here have increased, helped by payments to compensate farmers for depredations.

Hiking trails afford best viewing, though wildlife is not always easy to see in dense forest. Best times are spring—March–April—and fall—September–October (avoid mid-April water-splashing festivals unless you're prepared to be drenched). Busses and thrice-daily flights connect Kunming to nearby Jinghong which has lodging, good roads, reserve headquarters, and information.

## ALSO OF INTEREST

Other notable reserves include **Caohai Lake Nature Reserve**, one of the most important wintering sites in southwest China, 38-square-mile (96-km²) home to some 100,000 ducks, eagles, egrets, herons, geese, cormorants, and others—more than 185 species, including black-necked cranes. A comeback story, Caohai was drained disastrously during the Great Leap Forward and Cultural Revolution, then dammed, refilled, and declared a reserve in 1982, creating resentment among local landowners and farmers which turned to enthusiastic support through creative interactive aid for and with local groups assisted by the U.S. International Crane Foundation.

**Huanghe (Yellow River) Delta**, major staging area for migrating cranes, swans, and many other waterfowl and wading birds in north China's Shandong Province, of which 196 square miles (507 km²) has become a reserve.

**Yancheng Marshes**, a 180-square-mile (467-km²) coastal Jiangsu reserve important for wetland birds and Chinese parrotbills, adjacent to **Dafeng Reserve** where Père David's deer have been reintroduced.

**Shennongjia**, famous for golden monkeys and mythical "wild men" of Hubei, is 272 square miles (705 km²) in Hubei Province.

**Qinghai Lake**, notable breeding area for bar-headed geese and others, of which a (regrettably) small fraction, 206 square miles (533 km²), is a reserve.

**Tashikuorgan** is important for Marco Polo sheep, snow leopards, other high-altitude species, 5,790 square miles (15,000 km²) adjacent to Afghanistan and Pakistan.

**Chiangtang** is 92,664 square miles (240,000 km²) in northern Tibet preserving cold desert, lake and marsh homes of yaks, snow leopards, and Tibetan gazelles.

**Zhufeng**, contiguous with Nepal's SAGARMANTHA PARK (*see* p.246), located near the peak of Mount Everest.

**Shenzha**, remote breeding ground for black-headed cranes and other waterfowl, is 11,583 square miles (30,000 km²) with marshy steppes in the middle of Tibet.

Purple herons' extra-long toes let them get a good grip on reed stalks where they stand like statues, with long necks retracted in a tight S-curve until prey comes in range. Then cervical vertebrae, constructed so their necks can hardly move laterally, let go and straighten in a flash, thrusting heads forward like a released spring to stab prey or seize it in the beak. Purple herons range through freshwater and tidal mangrove estuaries in Africa and Europe, through temperate Asia as far as eastern Russia and China and in Southeast Asia to Sulawesi and the Philippines.

# INDIA

INDIA RANKS WITH EAST AND SOUTH AFRICA AS
ONE OF THE WORLD'S GREAT WILDLIFE DESTINATIONS.
IT HAS ONE OF THE LARGEST POPULATIONS OF TIGERS,
ONE OF THE WORLD'S MOST SPECTACULAR BIRD RESERVES
AT BHARATPUR, AND HABITAT AND RESERVES THAT RANGE
FROM THE HIGH HIMALAYAS TO THE GANGES DELTA.

THIS TEEMING COUNTRY, SO LARGE AND VARIOUS IT IS KNOWN AS THE ASIAN SUBCONTINENT, HAS RARE ANIMALS EQUAL TO ITS NATURAL BEAUTY, FROM SPLENDID BENGAL TIGERS, DIMINUTIVE MARBLED AND GOLDEN CATS, FEARSOME KING COBRAS, AND DELICATE CHITAL DEER TO CLOUDED LEOPARDS IN HIGH, REMOTE HIMALAYAN RESERVES.

Its national bird is the strutting technicolor-hued peacock, sometimes in flocks of dozens.

Wildlife conservation roots go back to the third century BC. Prime Minister Kautilya then codified the "Arthasashtra" establishing protected areas and advocated creation of the first wildlife sanctuaries or "abhayaranyas." In the next century, Emperor Ashoka issued his Fifth Pillar Edict forbidding slaughter of many animals and burning of forests. The edict also established sanctuaries. This followed an Indian tradition going back even further, when at the dawn of history natural groves were declared sacred and inviolate from human disturbance.

The modern Indian Constitution stipulates, "the State shall endeavor to protect and improve the environment and to safeguard the forests and the wildlife of the country…(this) shall be the duty of every citizen, and to have compassion for living creatures."

Now more than 550 national parks and sanctuaries are reserved for wildlife here.

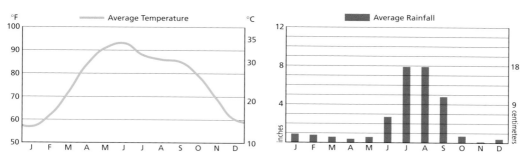

Gateway city: New Delhi

203

# INDIA

Dachigam
National Park □ ○ Srinagar

Corbett National Park

Sariska Tiger Reserve ○ **DELHI**
National Park
**Jodhpur** Dudhwa Namdapha National Park □
○ ○ **Jaipur** □ National Park □
Bharatpur (Keoladeo Ghana) National Park □ **Lucknow** Kaziranga National Park □
Ranthambore National Park ○ □ **Manas Tiger Reserve**
**Kanpur** ○ Gauhati

Varanasi ○
**Ahmadabad** ○ **Patna** **Imphal**
○ ○ **Bhopal** ○
□ Gir National Park Bandhavgarh
○ **Vadodara** National Park

○ **Surat** **Calcutta**
○
□ Sunderbans
□ National Park
○ **Nagpur** □ Kanha National Park
**Mumbai** ○

○ **Pune**

**Hyderabad**
○ ○**Vishakhapatnam**

○ **Dharwad**

0 300 miles
0 500 km

**Bangalore**
○
**Mysore** ○ **Chennai**
○ □ Nagarahole National Park
○**Coimbatore**
□ Eravikulam National Park
Periyar **Madurai**
National □ ○
Park

Andaman Islands

Nicobar Islands

However, needs of a burgeoning population—at recent count, over one billion persons—have conflicted with those of wildlife.

India's great forests are largely gone. Overhunting has driven some animals to extinction, others to the brink of it. Poaching is ever-present and serious, despite efforts like Project Tiger, undertaken by the Indian government at the behest of World Wild Fund for Nature to rescue this magnificent animal whose numbers by 1962 were reduced to several hundred in the wild.

Education as much as protection is necessary. A poor peasant trying to feed a large family can find it hard to understand why a tiger could be worth more alive than dead, when its corpse can bring him many times his annual income—up to $10,000 U.S. in China for its skin, teeth, bones, flesh. Every part of a tiger brings top prices for illegal resale as a trophy or supposed aphrodisiac, or oriental folk medicine cure for a wide array of human ills.

At least as damaging to wildlife is use of lethal pesticides and habitat destruction for agriculture, dam construction, logging, and mining.

There are successes. Many of India's outstanding wildlife reserves and national parks formerly were hunting grounds of maharajahs and India's British rulers. At KEOLADEO GHANA NATIONAL PARK (*see* p.207), popularly known as Bharatpur, thousands of birds used to be killed for sport in a single day. Now hundreds of species live under protection and some fly thousands of miles crossing the high Himalayas to reach this welcoming place.

Massive one-horned rhinoceros, once down to a few dozen on plains they had roamed in the tens of thousands, now are protected and have been brought back to viable populations at a few reserves, especially KAZIRANGA (*see* p.216) in Assam.

These victories have helped others besides target species. Sanctuaries established for the purpose of saving one or more threatened animals have in the same habitat saved a whole ecosystem of insects, birds, fish, lizards, butterflies, trees, and flowering plants.

The value of these places is made clear by contrasting them with immediately surrounding areas. Inside, habitat is lush and full of natural creatures; outside their boundaries the land is often devoid of natural activity, cleared for uses incompatible with the natural environment.

Without these sanctuaries, India's impressive wildlife would be greatly reduced and many species would be gone. Due largely to their existence, India still has over 2,000 species and subspecies of birds, more than 350 species of mammals, more than 700 species of reptiles and amphibians, some 50,000 kinds of insects including large and colorful butterflies, and more than 45,000 plants ranging from those of dry desert scrub to mountain meadows. Over 15,000 of the plants are endemic.

It should be noted that some reserves close during monsoon season—best check ahead.

# Bandhavgarh National Park

The Maharaja of Rewa set aside this area as a wildlife preserve for private hunting parties so his friends could shoot tigers, leopards, deer, wild boars—but tigers particularly. Each maharaja's personal goal was to kill as many tigers as possible. After 1968 and independence Bandhavgarh became a no-hunting sanctuary for these and their impressive companions, including hyenas, jungle cats, jackals, porcupines, elephants, and more than 200 species of birds. This enclave of hilly moist tropical woods and grasslands in north-central Madhya Pradesh now is a relatively small but glorious national park.

More than 20 spring-fed streams either rise in or flow through the reserve. Tigers cool off there in summer, swimming, sometimes almost totally immersing, or they drop by for a drink in all seasons. Their half-moan, half-soft roar can be heard in the early morning mist.

Leopards avoid their larger striped cousins, feeling safer on dry craggy ledges which they negotiate easily and where their spotted coats blend so well with foliage they are seldom seen except when they move.

Main prey here for both these are beautiful little chital spotted deer. Also in the lush grasses are sambar deer, shy chinkara, chousingha, horselike nilgai or blue bulls, and occasionally enormous gaur, world's largest wild cattle, which move down from the hills for fresh grass and water.

Black-faced langur monkeys and sometimes rhesus macaques forage in synchrony with chitals on the ground—chitals following the monkeys' progress through the treetops, watching for them to drop fruit scraps and succulent leaves.

Stork-billed kingfishers and gray-headed fish-eagles monitor streams. Crested hawk-eagles pounce on rufous-tailed hares. Shikra swoop on well-named jungle babblers. Handsome orange-faced white Egyptian or scavenger vultures look for kills, waiting their turn and sometimes rummaging through tiger droppings.

Jungle bush quail chicks appear in November. Young red-wattled lapwings come out in May. Beguiling jungle owlets raise families in sal tree holes. Jungle fowl, colorful ancestors of all barnyard roosters, and gorgeous peacocks noisily alert all to their woodland presence. Yellow-legged green pigeons gather in fruiting trees, especially pipals. Crimson-breasted barbets offer fruit to their mates. Blossom-headed and rose-ringed parakeets prefer ber trees and bamboo seeds.

Multicolored Indian rollers display iridescent wingpatches to impress mates. Purple sunbirds flash plumage of metallic red, yellow, green, blue or purple-black or all these, foraging at bright flowers and nesting in low shrubs. Bright, plump little Indian pittas fill the forest with rich whistles and trilling calls. Nightjars begin evening serenades in February.

Bandhavgarh has good lodges where jeeps and guide-drivers can be hired, also elephants. Accommodations are also available at a former maharaja's residence, and there's a historic fort. Best times January–April. The park is a comfortable drive from Umaria, served by rail, or from Khajuraho, served by commercial airline.

**FURTHER INFORMATION**

Director, Bandhavgarh National Park, P.O. Umaria, Dist. Shahdol, Madhya Pradesh 484661, India.

# BHARATPUR (KEOLADEO GHANA) NATIONAL PARK

A maharaja created this splendid and spectacular wetland bird habitat of Bharatpur (Keoladeo Ghana) National Park in the 1890s because he wanted to entertain British royalty with hunting forays more impressive than those he had experienced with them in England. It was mostly semi-arid scrub then as is much of surrounding Rajasthan. Now it is a world-renowned 11-square-mile (29-km²) sanctuary of shallow lakes and marshes with huge numbers of birds of some 415 species.

Magnificent sarus cranes, year-round residents, perform courtship dances; others, like some of the 22 waterfowl species and rare Siberian cranes, fly thousands of miles, some over high Himalayan peaks, to get here from Tibet, central Asia, and Siberia.

Some 44,000 planted babul trees provide nest sites for herons, egrets, storks, and spoonbills, on islands spotted throughout the wetland. Under them breathtakingly festooned pheasant-tailed jacanas and brilliant purple moorhens raise families on tremulous floating vegetation. Iridescent kingfishers excavate burrow homes in banks and dive for minnows.

The attraction and survival of so many kinds and numbers of birds in a single place is possible because the habitat is a teeming collection of food supplies, the water a veritable soup for various species with different dining adaptations. Foods range from tubers to microorganisms, beetles, toads, frogs, snakes, and fish, from minnows to freshwater sharks and saranas up to 33 pounds (15 kg). Some 50 species of fish have been identified here. Open-billed storks extract snails. Darters swim underwater and harpoon fish. Purple herons spear snakes.

Some 2,000 splashy painted storks raise offspring in an area no larger than a square mile (2.5 km²), their growing families consuming up to six tons of food every day in the 30 to 40 days they are on the nest. Some nesting trees may hold as many as nine species simultaneously during the monsoon breeding season from July through September—spoonbills, ibis, storks, herons, egrets. Raucous red-wattled lapwings and stone plovers try to distract attention from camouflaged eggs on the ground.

In October, waterfowl begin to come—whistling ducks calling musically, greylag and bar-headed geese more stridently. Demoiselle and common cranes float down, and, rarely, Siberian cranes which in India winter only here, and whose appearance here is irregular.

Crested serpent eagles and peregrine falcons are among 40 kinds of birds of prey, including seven kinds of owls—one of the world's largest concentrations of raptors.

Fishing cats peer intently into the water's edge at dusk and scoop out small fish. Otters pursue larger specimens.

Sanctuary habitat follows the original design of the Maharaja of Bharatpur: a network of dikes, sluice-gates, and canals, in and around a number of separate island-dotted lakes and marshes, fed twice yearly from a nearby impoundment of monsoon and river water also used

OPPOSITE: Tigers' apparently conspicuous coloring and markings are perfect camouflage in the brushy undergrowth where they stalk, exploding from cover to bring down prey as large as a young elephant or wild cattle weighing a ton or more in a single 30-foot (9-m) bound. It's not unusual for a tiger to consume 70 pounds (32 kg) a night, covering the carcass and returning to dine on it until it's gone. Only about a third of hunting attempts are successful.

for agriculture. (It was officially named Keoladeo Ghana when it became a national park in 1981, but is usually referred to by its creator's designation.)

Beyond the marsh are semiarid woodlands and grasslands where dryland birds like larks, warblers, chats, and buntings, as well as short-toed eagles and black-winged kites live. Collared pratincoles call raucously at sun-up. Chital deer and elegant blackbucks graze as do sambar and nilgai.

Bharatpur was a huge success as a hunting preserve. Stone tablets record shoots when more than 4,000 birds were killed in a day by Britain's Prince of Wales and other guests. Shooting was banned in 1964, and over the past 40 years this has become one of the world's premier bird reserves.

> **FURTHER INFORMATION**
>
> Deputy Chief Warden, Keoladeo NP, Bharatpur, Rajastan, India.

# CORBETT NATIONAL PARK

In the resplendent Terai belt at the foothills of the western Himalayas, with habitat ranging from riverbank forest to mountaintop, climate from cool to torrid monsoons, are ecological niches for a huge array of flora and fauna and the creatures to fill them—India's oldest national park and one of its finest.

Top among these in the biological scheme as well as worldwide interest is the beautiful and endangered Bengal tiger. Corbett was named after the famous hunter-naturalist who became a leader in the fight to save tigers from extinction. Project Tiger, an Indian initiative with worldwide support to protect tigers from the many threats to their survival and to set aside habitat for them, was started here by Indian conservationists working with the World Wild Fund for Nature. Here tigers are seen frequently but not easily or predictably, being wary, secretive, and well-camouflaged against the dense background of woods, grass, and bamboo thickets they prefer.

Corbett is their ideal habitat: thick jungle (one reason they are hard to see), water—the Ramganga River flows through the reserve—and plentiful prey. These include rufous-tailed hares; porcupines; peafowl; wild boars; armored (but not impregnable) Indian pangolins; ghoral or goat-antelopes; langur and rhesus monkeys which alert the whole jungle with frantic alarm

calls if they spot a tiger or leopard; and four kinds of deer—barking, sambar (largest Asiatic deer), hog, and large herds of chital, considered the most beautiful deer in the world.

Tigers are opportunistic feeders and avail themselves of all these. They also feed on small rodents, fish, crocodiles, turtles, crustaceans, frogs, locusts and, in an emergency, domestic animals. They have even been known to kill much larger animals such as buffalo, and a pair of tigers was once observed bringing down an elephant. (Tigers usually stay to eat whatever they kill, covering an over-large meal with leaves and guarding it for later consumption.) Corbett's enormous boars, up to 220 pounds (100 kg), can give them a tussle, and a large male can kill a tiger.

Leopards are mainly in hilly areas but sometimes venture into the lower jungle. Here also are smaller feline varieties such as jungle, fishing, and leopard cats; sloth bears which dig for termites and ants along the roadsides early and late; jackals; yellow-throated martens; Himalayan civets; Indian gray mongeese; even playful swift otters. Rarely, dholes (wild dogs) and Himalayan black bears are seen.

Elephants, several hundred of them here, are lords of the jungle, and gather in large herds in summer.

Birds are many and varied—more than 580 species including 17 kinds of woodpeckers, more than in all of Europe, crested serpent eagles, handsome black-winged kites, Pallas' fish-eagles, great flocks of blossom-headed parakeets, and familiar-looking red jungle fowl—ancestors of all domestic fowl. Nightjars and owls call at night.

Formidable Indian pythons can kill a chital deer. Rare long-nosed, fish-eating, gharial crocodiles were saved from extinction by captive breeding and release in the Ramganga River here.

Best chances of seeing a tiger are to come late in the dry season—April to mid-June—and go out with mahouts and elephants for several days. (If you see pugmarks, the elongated egg-shaped toes are females', the round, circular ones, males'.)

**FURTHER INFORMATION**

Field Director, Project Tiger, Corbett National Park, P.O. Ramnagar, Nainital District, Uttar Pradesh 24415, Tel: (+91) 05945-85322, Fax: (+91) 05945-85376.

# DACHIGAM NATIONAL PARK

The world's last viable population of Kashmir stags is in Dachigam National Park. Their does produce densely spotted fawns every spring in this sheltered, verdant valley bordered by dramatic mountain crags up to 14,000 feet (4,300 m). They are among a unique range of Himalayan flora and fauna in this scenic national park in far northern India.

Here too are rare serows, goat-like antelopes with bristling chin beards and aggressive dispositions to match, along with leopards, leopard cats, jungle cats, and quick little yellow-throated martens and Himalayan weasels, both peers for the serows in touchy outlook.

Dachigam is divided in two sections, Upper and Lower, with seasonal wildlife populations dictated by their elevations. In winter, upper reaches become inaccessible, clothed in a stunning but forbidding cover of white. Snow partridges bury themselves in it, Himalayan black bears hibernate. Below, multihued plumed monal pheasants eke out a living on seeds in the scrub zone above the timberline. Longtailed blue magpies look for scraps from leopard kills, as do jackals and red foxes. After them come Himalayan griffons and bearded vultures or lammergeiers, which specialize in dropping bones from great heights to get at the marrow (hence their name: "bone-breaker").

Kashmir stags, also called hanguls, descend to survive on valley stubble, accompanied by cinnamon sparrows and black-and-yellow grosbeaks.

In spring, black bears and Himalayan brown bears come out of their holes in the rocks. Small musk deer, hunted for their musk glands (used in perfume and reputedly useful in treating impotence), nibble at new tender grasses. Long-coated gray langur monkeys change their diet from bark to fresh tree shoots. Kashmir stags then head to higher ground. Does wait below until fawns can manage the steep rocky terrain.

Fruiting trees burst into pastel bloom. Golden orioles appear along with pygmy owlets, smartly plumaged Himalayan pied woodpeckers and a throng of bright warblers, babblers, buntings, and laughing thrushes. Orioles start to weave cradle nests. Bears look for early plums and mulberries.

Dachigam was protected first as a pure drinking water catchment for the Kashmir valley. It now covers 55 square miles (140 km²) divided by the Dagwan River, with lodges and rest houses. Hotels and houseboats are in Srinagar, 13 miles (21 km) west. Best times are May–August in Upper Dachigam, September–December in Lower.

Greatest threats have been poaching and grazing, and in recent years, Kashmir's political instability—check before a visit.

---

**FURTHER INFORMATION**

Chief Wildlife Warden, Dachigam National Park, Srinagar, Jammu & Kashmir.
For more details on permits contact Foreign Regional Registration Office, New Delhi 110 001, India.

---

# DUDHWA NATIONAL PARK

This park was established despite opposition from interests that wanted to log its majestic 100-foot-tall (30-m) sal forest, regarded as the best in India, and to shoot its rare Barasingha or swamp deer as well as tigers, leopards, beautiful demoiselle cranes (now gone), and others. Due largely to efforts by the late prime minister Indira Gandhi and famed conservationist Billy Arjan Singh it became a protected sanctuary in 1965 and in 1977 a national park, 190 square miles (490 km²) of forest and grassland watered by perennial streams in northern Uttar Pradesh along the Indo-Nepal border.

Now-rare but once-abundant Indian one-horned rhinoceros were reintroduced in 1985, also due to Mrs. Gandhi's efforts. Snub-nosed crocodiles or muggers bask on riverbanks, given a wide berth by otters, pythons, and huge monitor lizards alike. Feisty Indian ratels, well-nicknamed honey badgers, break open monstrous hanging beehives, insulated from stings by a thick fat layer under their handsome black and light gray fur (protection also when they aggressively compete with animals much larger than they).

Elephants cross over from ROYAL BARDIA NATIONAL PARK in Nepal (*see* p.242). There are sloth bears, civets, fishing cats, jungle cats, leopard cats, jackals, wild pigs, and sambar deer, largest deer in Asia. Spotted deer or chital, considered by many the world's handsomest deer, share grasslands with horse-like nilgai or blue bulls, largest Asiatic antelope, curly-horned blackbucks and smaller, rarer hog deer and muntjac or barking deer.

Rich birdlife includes eight kinds of owls, among them greater Indian horned and forest eagle owls, brown and tawny fish owls, scops owls, and jungle owlets. Eight vulture species include the cinerious. A few rare Bengal and lesser floricans are here.

Imposing scarlet-headed sarus cranes coordinate spectacular courtship leaps with lifetime mates. Eight kinds of storks include painted, open-billed, and black-necked, with a multitude of colorful woodpeckers, orioles, kingfishers, minivets, sunbirds, hornbills, and warblers. Hundreds of migrants, especially waterfowl, come to rest here after flights over Himalayan foothills.

Threats here include poaching, cattle grazing and encroachment by human settlements.

Best times are December–June. Accommodations are forest rest houses and Billy Arjan Singh's farm, famed for successful tiger and leopard re-introductions (write Tiger Haven, P.O. Palia, District Kheri, Uttar Pradesh).

---

**FURTHER INFORMATION**

Field Director, Dudhwa Tiger Reserve, Lakhimpur, Kheri 262001, Uttar Pradesh, India, Tel: (+91) 05872-52106; Deputy Director, Project Tiger, Dudhwa Tiger Reserve, Palia, Dist. Kheri, Tel: (+91) 05871-33485; Principal Chief Conservator of Forests, Uttar Pradesh, 17, Rana Pratap Marg., Lucknow 226001, Tel: (+91) 0522-283902.

# ERAVIKULAM NATIONAL PARK

This park was established to protect nilgiri thar, small, dark endangered grazers of the high slopes, only wild goats south of the Himalayas, their population less vulnerable because of this 37-square-mile (97-km²) national park of rolling grass hills and forests. Protected with them are elephants, occasional tigers, nilgiri langurs, lion-tailed macaques, and giant squirrels. Best time November–April. Rest house.

---

**FURTHER INFORMATION**

Divisional Forest Officer, Munnar Division, P.O. Devikolam, Kerala.

---

# GIR NATIONAL PARK

Lions once roamed over much of Asia and Europe, and flourished in Gir National Park until indiscriminately slaughtered by humans. A disastrous famine further strained their survival prospects until in 1913 all that remained were about 20 individuals that had retreated to the Gir Forest. The last Asian lion in the wild outside Gir had been killed in 1884. Starving, the lions took to man-eating, and might be entirely gone but for the Nawab of Junagadh, whose domain included most of the Gir Forest. He deplored their plight, put their picture on a postage stamp, protected them vigorously, and they began to recover. By 1985, there were 239 and they have continued gradually to increase, to more than 300 by one recent count.

With the lions, a whole wild ecosystem has thrived in this now-protected sanctuary of 545 square miles (1,412 km²) of river-interlaced forest and grassland with a core national park area.

Leopards (sometimes called panthers here) also have been increasing as complementary predators—the lions hunting in family groups able to take on larger prey like the sambar, largest Asian deer, while the agile leopards, usually solo, successfully go after fleet-footed yearlings and hares as well as peafowl, monkeys, and arboreal species unavailable to more earthbound lions. Both go after abundant grazing herds of chital or spotted deer (more than 10,000 in a recent census), young sambar, nilgai, and some four-horned antelopes, and chinkara or Indian gazelles.

Smaller predators like jackals, wild cats, and striped hyenas get the leavings, or like jungle cats or rare desert and rusty spotted cats, go after smaller prey themselves.

More than 2,000 wild boars root about the forest floor. Langur monkeys chatter in spectacular "flame of the forest" trees. Marsh crocodiles bask on lake banks behind Kamaleshwar dam, the largest population of "muggers" anywhere in India.

Gir's rich birdlife—more than 300 species—includes paradise flycatchers, black-headed cuckoo shrikes, pied woodpeckers, crested serpent eagles, painted sandgrouse, white-necked storks.

Diminutive chinkara or Indian gazelles survive in woodlands or desert, going without water for long periods if necessary, eking out moisture from herbage and dewdrops. Standing just 25 inches (65 cm) at the shoulder, they seem constantly on the lookout for danger, nervously flicking their tails, glancing in all directions. Uncommon over much of their range in Iran, Pakistan, and in India in Gir and Ranthambore national parks.

Asiatic lions have thicker coats and darker, slightly smaller manes than their African cousins but like them are highly familial. A small part of their prey base is cattle grazed here by Maldhari herders, a continuing problem along with worry that an epidemic could drastically reduce this isolated, concentrated population. Attempts to start new groups elsewhere have not, at least until recently, been successful.

Best times are December–March.

---

**FURTHER INFORMATION**

Forest Conservator, Sardar Baug, Junagadh, Gujarat 362001, India.

---

# KANHA NATIONAL PARK

Famous as a place to see tigers, Kanha was established to save unique water-dwelling swamp deer or barasingha, slaughtered to the edge of extinction for their long, curving antlers. This graceful large deer, found nowhere else, with a downless coat that sheds water and splayed hooves that find easy support on mucky lake bottoms, was reduced from thousands to 66 individuals in the 1960s. Now a stable population of several hundred graze Kanha's meadows, an Indian conservation success story.

Kanha, one of the first reserves designated under Project Tiger, was the beautiful setting for Kipling's "Jungle Boy" and today is a world of interdependent creatures not too different from those Mowgli found in Kipling's tale. Its 750 square miles (1,945 km$^2$) combine with meadow-like grasslands crossed with rivers and streams, surrounded by the wooded Maikal Hills in a natural amphitheater reminiscent of Africa's Ngorongoro Crater, abutting large forest reserves on the north, west, and south, to protect many of India's most impressive animal and plant species.

Huge gaur or Indian bison weighing a ton or more (1,000+ kg)—world's largest wild cattle— add to the theatrical effect of this great grassland bowl, along with thousands of other grazers: sambar, largest Indian deer; chousingha, world's only four-horned antelope; horselike nilgai or blue bulls (males drop to their knees when fighting, usually avoiding fatal damage); handsome chitals; rare blackbucks with magnificent twisted horns (also a target for trophy collectors); and occasional muntjac or barking deer.

All these are especially vulnerable to an array of predators when calves are born, a tempting meal for leopards, jackals, wild dogs or dhole (also known here as sonha kutta) as well as tigers. Langur monkeys alert all in earshot at approach of predators. Chital and wild boar follow the langurs, gobbling up pieces of fruit and leaves dropped in their untidy treetop foraging.

Shaggy sloth bears, usually unthreatening, are touchier when they have cubs on their backs.

Marsh harriers swoop to flush quails or small rodents in the waving grass, among some 300 avian species. Formidable crested serpent eagles and honey buzzards, black-winged kites, shikra, laggar and black shaheen falcons go for snakes and small mammals and even birds.

Peacocks are everywhere in gorgeous courtship display. Jungle fowl, handsome ancestors of barnyard roosters, proclaim the dawn. Multicolored Indian rollers pursue airborne insects and use aerial skill in hair-raising loop-the-loops to impress prospective mates. Racket-tailed drongos cement woodland nests with cobwebs and drive off intruders with such pugnacity they attract gentler birds as companion nesters in a neighborhood protection group.

Red and yellow-wattled lapwings are a bright presence, with green bee-eaters, black-headed and golden orioles, painted partridges, green pigeons and, around waterways, black ibis, white-necked and lesser adjutant storks, white-breasted and pied kingfishers, and hundreds of herons and egrets. White-backed and scavenger vultures take their turn at luckless corpses. Barn owls, brown fish owls, and nightjars enliven the night.

Best way to see tigers is from the back of an elephant. Both these impressive animals carry such authority that neither seems to alarm the other—but there is no guarantee of seeing tigers, even here. These rare, beautiful cats whose skins, bones, and body parts can bring poachers $10,000 U.S. in oriental markets have learned to be wary. Still, it is worth the effort. No wildlife experience surpasses the increasingly rare sight of a magnificent wild Bengal tiger in its native habitat, especially seen during a forest exploration on the back of a powerful, intelligent elephant.

Best times are March and April. The park is closed during July–October monsoons, and December–January can have severe frosts.

---

**FURTHER INFORMATION**

Director, Kanha National Park, P.O. Mandla, Madhya Pradesh, India; Manager, Madhya Pradesh State Tourism Development Corporation, Log Hug, Kisli, Bhopal, India; Field Director, Project Tiger, Kanha Tiger Reserve, Mandla 481661, India.

---

# KAZIRANGA NATIONAL PARK

Great Indian one-horned rhinoceros graze peacefully along the Brahmaputra River here, wallowing and sometimes swimming in the cool water on hot days. They are unknowingly indebted to a British noblewoman for the beautiful national park where they came back from the edge of extinction.

Lady Curzon learned from tea plantation friends in 1904 that only about a dozen remained of these prehistoric-looking two-ton (almost 2,000-kg) beasts up to 13.3 feet (4 m) long, whose

Indian rollers are often unnoticed perching motionless in open country until a frog, butterfly or large insect is spotted. Then with an explosion of flashing blue wings, purple breast and throat and turquoise crown, lower wings and tail the roller takes out in pursuit. Females get a similar show with different purpose when males perform rolling courtship flights for which they are named, flying steeply upward, then banking and spiraling downward. Pure white eggs are laid in a tree-hole to which the pair may return yearly, anywhere from Iraq and Iran through Pakistan, India, Myanmar, Southeast Asia, Tibet, and parts of China.

deeply folded gray skin makes them look as if they are wearing coats of armor. Once thousands roamed the Indo-Gangetic plains. (Marco Polo thought when he saw them in 1271 he had found the fabled unicorn.) Tea clearing had wiped out many of them; merciless shooting had done the rest. Lady Curzon told her husband something had to be done and in 1905, this inviting riverine forest and grassland was set aside for them; shooting was banned in 1908.

Now Kaziranga National Park is a U.N World Heritage Site, 261 square miles (675 km$^2$) in the Assam district of northeast India, protecting the world's largest population (at recent count 1,129) of these great, lumbering but agile creatures which can trot along at 20–25 miles an hour (35–40 kmh). In the process many other species were saved as well, including more than a dozen of India's most threatened mammals and some near-extinct bird species.

Tigers and leopards find shelter and food, sharing the mixed short and tall grasses and woods along the Brahmaputra River with capped langurs, hoolock gibbons, leopards, and the sambar, swamp, hog, and muntjac or barking deer. If hungry enough, tigers will even take on formidable wild boars or water buffalo (largest herd in India is here). Working as a team, tigers have even brought down enormous gaurs—largest Asian oxen, up to 11 feet (3.3 m) long, 7.2 feet (2.2 m) high at the shoulder—or, rarely, a young Indian elephant.

Gray pelicans have a noisy nesting colony, and more than 300 other bird species find permanent or seasonal homes, some from as far away as Siberia. In moist forests are green imperial pigeons and multihued peacock-pheasants, around the river lesser adjutant and black-necked storks, and overhead, Pallas' and gray-headed fish-eagles. At recent count some 25 Bengal floricans were here.

Insectivorous sloth bears work on termite mounds. Gangetic dolphins streak through river waters where dragon-like, yellow-spotted black monitors up to eight feet (almost 3 m) long are propelled by rudder-like tails at a more stately pace. Playful otter families enliven interconnecting streams and numerous small lakes or "bheels."

King cobras, world's largest venomous snakes up to 18 feet (5+ m) long, make brushy nests, leading secretive woodland lives—luckily, since their bite can kill an elephant in a few hours, a human in 15 minutes.

Kaziranga is flooded every year when the Brahmaputra River overflows during monsoon rains from June to September. Formerly many animals drowned, but islands have been built where they now can safely retreat during rising water. Poachers still kill rhinos every year to satisfy a demand for horns (not true horns but compressed keratin and hair) used in high-status dagger handles or ground up for aphrodisiacs and other Oriental folk medicines to treat ailments from strokes and convulsions to nosebleeds. Rhinos' regular habits, using the same paths every day, make them easy prey for pit traps or ambush shooting. But determined efforts on several fronts (including shoot-to-kill orders to rangers) have been effective. Demand is gradually decreasing, rhino numbers gradually rising.

Many South and Southeast Asian countries have banned trade in rhino products. The World Wide Fund for Nature has funded anti-poaching units. The Rhino Foundation for Northeast India has provided guards' supplies. Kaziranga is now considered the safest homeland for *Rhinoceros unicornis*, and a landmark in India's conservation history.

Another rhino problem poses special difficulty—how to protect these vulnerable, short-sighted vegetarians against an increasing number of encounters with an equally endangered and more dangerous animal, the rhino's arch-enemy in the natural world: tigers.

Best times are November–March, mild and dry, becoming warmer, more humid as May–September monsoons approach. Park is closed May–October.

Best way to move around the park is by elephant, which can be hired at Mihimukhi (book ahead).

---

**FURTHER INFORMATION**

Director, Kaziranga National Park, P.O. Bokakhat, District Jorhat, Assam 785612, Tel: (+91) 3776-5295; OR, Joint Tourism Director, Tel: (+91) 3776-5423.

---

# MANAS WILDLIFE SANCTUARY

Manas Wildlife Sanctuary, with over 1,000 square miles (2,600 km²) of breathtaking scenery and well-watered habitat has more than 40 rare and endangered species, more than anyplace else in India. Tigers are here along with rare golden langur monkeys, marbled and golden cats, and clouded leopards. Stunning birds include rare Bengal floricans, handsomest of the tall grassland bustards with glossy midnight-blue heads and underparts and flashing white wings.

Tiny pygmy hogs—adults no more than 10 inches (25 cm) high at the shoulder—and hispid hares, both once thought extinct, are here, with massive one-horned rhinoceros, swamp deer, and a few Assam roof turtles. For many like the long-horned wild Asiatic buffalo, Manas is probably their last stand.

Reptiles include brilliantly patterned ornate flying snakes, black and yellow with reddish rosettes, which cannot fly but seem to, coiling and straightening out with explosive speed, ribs spread and bellies concave as they sail through the air between treetops. Huge monitor lizards stalk through jungle trails and up trees. King cobras, world's largest venomous snakes, up to 18 feet (5+ m) long, feed mostly on other snakes and small mammals, avoided by all. More than 450 bird species range from great Indian hornbills and stately kalij pheasants to Pallas' fish-eagles and crested serpent eagles. Bright scarlet minivets flit about the canopy.

# INDIA

OPPOSITE: Crested hawk-eagles with short, rounded wings and tails are well-adapted to maneuver skillfully through dense forests of India, Sri Lanka, and continental Asia as well as Indonesia and the Philippines. They are equally at home scouting out open areas and rice fields.

Wet alluvial grasslands and tropical mixed semievergreen and deciduous woodlands supply ecological niches as well for butterflies and others, including millions of invertebrates on which the whole food chain depends.

This U.N. World Heritage Site, one of the first places protected under Project Tiger, is under threat from several sides. Bodo tribal militants have terrorized and killed park rangers as well as many of the rare species which park staffs, with limited facilities and equipment, work to protect. Land use pressure from human settlement, cattle grazing, and agricultural encroachment, jeopardizes habitat. Ill-feeling arises from human/wildlife conflict involving tigers, elephants, buffalo, and others despite compensatory payment. Plans for a dam that would damage both this and protected land in neighboring Bhutan have been shelved but perhaps not permanently.

Manas' northern boundary adjoins lush, undisturbed ROYAL MANAS (*see* p.185) and BLACK MOUNTAINS NATIONAL PARKS in Bhutan (*see* p.186), protecting altogether almost 2,000 square miles (5,000 km²) of contiguous forest habitat. The Bhutan portion is remote, with few visitor facilities, and at least until recently, was accessible from the India side only.

Bodo activity has sometimes closed the park—best check recent situation. Best times are January–March. Accommodations include tourist lodge and forest bungalow at Mothanguri, also rest houses and campsites. The Assam Forest Department arranges river trips and elephant-back tours, also has information on access to adjoining Bhutan reserves. Nearest rail is at Mothangiri, 25 miles (41 km) away; nearest airport at Gawahati (Gauhati), 116 miles (186 km).

| FURTHER INFORMATION |
| --- |

Field Director, Project Tiger, P.O. Barpeta Road, District Barpeta, Assam 781315, India;

Tourist Information Officer, Barpeta Road, Assam, India 781315, Tel: (+91) 3666-32749;

Tourist Information Officer, Station Road, Gawahati, Assam 781007, India, Tel: (+91) 24475.

# Nagarahole National Park

Nagarahole National Park's jungles and savannahs in India's southern peninsula seem unchanged over the centuries, grasses green and golden around herds of grazing animals, high forest canopies buzzing with birds—now as then home to tigers, Indian elephants, and a rich spectrum of wildlife.

# INDIA

With adjoining **Bandipur National Park** and **Wynad** and **Mudamalai sanctuaries**, it is one of the largest and densest ecological continuums in India—some 836 square miles (2,165 km²) welcoming most of the rare and interesting wildlife in this part of the world.

Thickly armored Indian pangolins probe ant nests with sticky tongues so long they are anchored to the pangolins' pelvic bones and supplied from huge salivary reservoirs up to 22 cubic inches (335 cu. cm) in their chests. Toothless, they grind up insect prey in their horny stomachs.

Gaur weighing more than a ton (1000 kg), world's largest oxen, stare green-eyed from grasslands. More than 1,000 wild Indian elephants forage on bark, branches, and low greenery in jungles and bathe in streams. One of the last, best remaining habitats for these colossal beasts is here. Hundreds congregate around water in dry season, especially along the banks of the Kabini Reservoir. Sunset vistas can be breathtaking, with a mile-long stretch of river dotted with elephants, from huge matriarchs to diminutive youngsters taking their first swimming lessons.

Pretty chitals are commonest among four species of deer—shy sambars the largest, up to nine feet (2.7 m) long. Goat-sized muntjac or barking deer are forest sentinels whose calls carry long distances warning of prowling predators. Tiniest are rabbit-sized, nocturnal chevrotain or mouse deer with long canine teeth protruding from their upper jaws. Little four-horned antelopes are the world's only four-horned animal, diurnal but rare and shy, preferring dry hilly terrain but seen in the Karapura area of Nagarahole and Moyar area of Bandipur, flattening themselves in the grass when sensing possible hazard, then dashing off with impressive bounds when discovered.

Shaggy short-sighted sloth bears tote young on their backs while hunting for termite mounds and honey, often in the Karapura area. Wild pigs root around under leaves and black-naped hares nibble on short vegetation. Dhole—wild dogs—hunt in packs and can bring down any of these. Red Malabar giant squirrels travel aerially, covering spaces between trees with 20-foot (6-m) leaps. Sharing the Karapura canopy are langur monkeys and bonnet macaques, all prey for leopards.

All this dense cover and grazing animal prey base have made both Nagarahole and Bandipur strongholds for tigers—perhaps finest habitat for them in south India. Bandipur was one of the reserves where Project Tiger was started—although the dense cover here makes sightings chancy.

Among more than 250 bird species are Malabar trogons, blue-bearded bee-eaters, Alexandrine parakeets, scarlet minivets, fairy bluebirds, paradise flycatchers and, among birds of prey, gray-headed fish-eagles, crested hawk-eagles, serpent eagles, and spectacular king vultures. Large gatherings of cormorants, ducks, teal, and herons, and other waders as well as ospreys are attracted to the Kabini backwaters. Peacocks—the gorgeous national bird—scream wildly and flare some of the world's most flamboyant tail feathers. "Nagarahole" means "cobra river" and other formidable reptiles are here as well—crocodiles, giant monitor lizards, rock pythons, and several kinds of vipers. Best times are October–March. (April–May are hot, June–September, monsoons).

| FURTHER INFORMATION |

Field Director, Project Tiger, Bandipur Tiger Reserve, Mysore 570004; Chief Wildlife Warden, Aranya Bhavan, 18th Cross, Malleswaram, Bangalore 560003, India; Field Director, Nagarahole National Park, Mysore 570004, India.

# NAMDAPHA NATIONAL PARK

Wild and remote, this may be the only place in the world with Bengal tigers and common leopards plus both snow and clouded leopards.

Bewitching red pandas look down from tree perches at higher elevations. Musk deer graze—slaughtered to near-extinction for musk glands used in perfume and treatment of impotence. Asiatic golden cats, so rare that little is known of their habits, have striped faces, are lithe and golden-red, hunt in pairs and are intolerant of human disturbance.

Hoolock gibbons, black, furry, white eyebrowed members of a family once thought to be humans' closest primate relatives, move upright on two legs, and also swing through forests on long arms—primate aerial acrobats.

Big-eyed, nocturnal slow lorises, one of the world's most sluggish animals, are lightning-fast when they want to be, grabbing lizards and large insects which do not realize until too late that this small fuzzy creature can move at all. Strong leg muscles let them sleep motionless through the day, hanging upside-down from tree branches.

Small goat-like ghoral antelopes gallop at breakneck speed along sheer fall-offs, safer than if they went slower because (films show) their hooves have left the loose rocks before the latter begin to roll under their impact. Others among 96 mammal species include Asian elephants, threatened dhole or Asiatic wild dogs, wild Asiatic buffalo, binturongs—small, dark arboreal "bearcats." Also here are shaggy, oxen-like takins.

Rich birdlife includes mountain hawk-eagles, gray peacock-pheasants, imperial pigeons, pin-tailed green pigeons, oriental bay owls, rufous-necked hornbills, red-headed trogons, crimson-winged laughing thrushes, white-hooded shrike babblers, scarlet-backed flowerpeckers. Three major rivers and many lakes attract migratory waterfowl.

This mix of rare Indo-Burmese, Indo-Chinese, and Himalayan wildlife is possible because of the extraordinary habitat diversity of this 698-square-mile (1,607-km²) reserve in easternmost India, ranging from wet evergreen forest at lower elevations to temperate montane forest at 14,800 feet (4,500 m). Major threats are increasingly from slash-and-burn agriculture by surrounding tribal villagers.

Permits are necessary. Access is difficult. Best times are October–March.

**FURTHER INFORMATION**

Divisional Forest Officer, Namdapha National Park, P.O. Box Miao 792 122, District Tirap,
Arunachal Pradesh; Field Director, Project Tiger, P.O. Miao, District Tirap, Arunachal Pradesh, India;
Government of India Tourist Office, Sector C, Naharlagun 791110, India, Tel: (+91) 03781-44328.
To obtain entry permit: Ministry of Home Affairs, Government of India, Lok Nayak Bhawan,
Khan Market, New Delhi 110001, Tel: 619709.

## PERIYAR NATIONAL PARK AND TIGER RESERVE

Nowhere are elephants more visibly familial and vocal than here, where they gather—along with shaggy, near-sighted sloth bears, wild boars and many others—along the shores of Lake Periyar. They regularly hold long elephant conversations—trumpeting, bellowing, softly rumbling in sounds that can be startlingly humanlike—dust bathe, swim, discipline young ones, court, mate, and sling mud at one another.

Here too are endangered lion-tailed macaques with brilliant facial ruffs and tufted tails, troupes of 50 or so leaping through tall virgin forests or paddling across waterways, babies clinging to mothers' backs.

Periyar is 300 square miles (777 km²) of marsh, rolling grasslands, and trees up to 130 feet (40 m) tall in moist forest corridors that are home to "flying" creatures of several species. Ornate "flying" snakes coil like springs and launch flattened bodies to glide long distances between treetops. Indian "flying" dragon lizards, arboreal for most of their lives, sail out on brilliant orange or yellow side-flap "wings." "Flying" frogs "fly" by taking off and extending their toes, connected by wide webbing. "Flying" squirrels leap out on moonlit nights to stay airborne 300 yards (280 m) on furry flaps between front and hind legs.

Tigers retire to wooded thickets, digesting meals and awaiting victims, which might include a wild pig rooting through leaves, an unwary porcupine or more likely, a yearling sambar deer, smaller muntjac or barking deer, or still smaller mouse deer. Less likely prey are huge gaur, world's largest wild cattle weighing a ton or more, or shy, rare, goatlike nilgiri tahrs.

Looking out for agile leopards in the trees are common and threatened nilgiri langur monkeys, bonnet macaques, and handsome Malabar giant squirrels, which like to eat while hanging precariously by their back feet.

Wild dogs, or dhole, signal one another with eerie whistles as they set out on a hunt. Otters and vivid kingfishers fish the shallows, ospreys in deeper places.

Flocks of great Indian hornbills whoosh by with orioles and racket-tailed drongos, to feed in blossoming and fruiting trees.

Perennial water source for all is the 10-square-mile (26-km²) reservoir formed by a dam built a century ago along the Periyar River.

Threats are from illegal timbering, overvisitation, overgrazing by domestic cattle which compete for fodder and can introduce disease, and poachers who sometimes, when unable to kill elephants easily, cruelly cripple them or hang live wires to electrocute them.

Boat is the only motorized transport. A tourist center arranges boat trips, jungle walks, and visits (daily or overnight) to watchtowers. Accommodations are available in forest rest houses and nearby hotels. Best times are drier months, February–April, when water is a special attractant for wildlife.

---

**FURTHER INFORMATION**

Field Director, Project Tiger, Kanjikuzhi, Kottayam, Kerala.

---

# RANTHAMBORE NATIONAL PARK

Ranthambore National Park is a former private hunting reserve of the maharajas of Jaipur. Though relatively small, it is one of the most beautiful wildlife reserves in India. An original Project Tiger site, it held only 14 tigers when it was authorized. Its tiger population has increased, and now has numbers of leopards as well, along with chital and water-loving sambar deer, chinkaras, nilgai or blue bulls, sloth bears, jackals, wild boars, striped hyenas, and others. Leopards catch early sun on ledges. Golden jackals and jungle cats prowl for rodents. Peacocks are everywhere around and in the forests, some of which are remnants of the great virgin jungles which once covered most of central India. Woodland covers much of this well-watered 158-square-mile (410-km²) reserve which also includes a lush system of lakes and streams hemmed in by steep high crags of the Vindhyas and Aravalli Hill ranges in southeast Rajasthan with an additional 40 square miles (104 km²) of adjoining forest sanctuary.

The park is full of old mosques, wells, and other historic relics dating back to the 10th century where tigers appear dramatically from time to time, wandering among and resting atop the structures. Dominating all from atop a high crag is a magnificent fort, former center of a Hindu kingdom, later center of the reign of the Mughal Emperor Akbar. At its feet is India's second largest banyan tree where troupes of langur monkeys spend their days—old ones holding council, young mothers nursing babies.

Among more than 270 bird species are crested serpent eagles, great Indian horned owls, painted partridges, paradise flycatchers, pheasant-tailed jacanas, painted storks, green pigeons and, sighted occasionally, great Indian bustards. Migrant ducks come in winter.

More than 300 tree species are among a rich and diverse flora, including more than 100 of medicinal importance and several used for scent.

Common Indian mongeese, legendary opponents of snakes, have a risky challenge with the reptiles here—huge cobras, common kraits, saw-scaled and Russel's vipers, rock pythons, large monitor lizards, and lovely starred tortoises.

For a while Ranthambore was famous for tigers which became so trustful of humans they appeared in daylight, sometimes hunting, sometimes with cubs, sometimes with mates. Their unwariness sounded their death knell. Poachers killed many, amid charges of official corruption, for the Chinese folk medicine trade, and those that remained have lost their innocence. But they are still here, their population slowly rebuilding.

Best times are October–April. Accommodations available at a number of nearby lodges, the prize being a former maharaja's hunting residence. Get around by 4WD.

---

**FURTHER INFORMATION**

Field Director, Ranthambore National Park, Sawai Madhopur, Rajasthan, India; Project Tiger Office, Sawai Madhopur, Rajasthan, India.

---

## SARISKA TIGER RESERVE NATIONAL PARK

Wild animals (like humans) behave differently when they feel themselves unobserved. They seem to feel that way at water holes in Sariska Tiger Reserve National Park at night—resting, drinking, interacting, nursing and nuzzling young ones, courting, mating, grooming themselves—and others—sometimes killing for a meal or to eliminate a rival.

It is a special world seen from the darkness.

Fruit-drinking bats flutter in for a sip. Fish-eating owls swoop down, their super-keen senses telling them that dinner is there for the taking. An occasional rare, shy, solitary caracal is so quiet it can pass unnoticed. Wild boars snuffle through leaves. Horselike nilgai or blue bulls drop to their knees to settle disputes without undue violence. Touchy porcupines lumber along, seeming to feel invulnerable (without justification; they are widely preyed on, though their needles can make fatal meals).

OPPOSITE: Hanuman or black-faced langurs are the sacred monkey of India, venerated by Hindus as the form taken by the monkey god Hanuman. Their whooping calls are heard in tropical and dry scrublands, alpine and rain forests through Southeast Asia as noisy troops of up to 125 individuals feed on leaves, fruits, buds, and blossoms.

# INDIA

Tigers roar their assertion that they are at the top of the food chain, unchallenged even by the leopards and certainly not by nervous jackals, hyenas, or little jungle cats.

Sariska's 308 square miles (800 km²) of rolling wooded canyons surrounded by starkly dramatic mountain crags, originally shooting preserve of the Alwar ruling family, came under Project Tiger in 1979. It has always been good tiger terrain, having the habitat and prey base these magnificent endangered animals require—chital or spotted deer, sambar, nilgai, chousingha, and other smaller species.

Wildlife, including interesting bird species, can be seen in daytime too along the good road network. There are ninth-century ruins of Shiva temples (one still used by pilgrims) and a Kankwari fort.

Best times are November–March (April–June is interesting but hot). Accommodations include a forest bungalow, rest house and, at the park entrance, a converted royal palace, now a hotel. Rentals are available for blinds or hides for night viewing at water holes (take a sleeping bag and go by early afternoon). Four-wheel-drive vehicles for hire. Threats include mining pressure (sometimes illegal) and overvisitation.

## FURTHER INFORMATION

Field Director, Sariska Tiger Reserve, District Alwar, Rajasthan, India; Rajasthan Tourist Office, Bikaner House, Near India Gate, New Delhi 110003, India.

Nilgai or blue bulls—named for dark bluish sheen of adult males—are largest Asian antelopes, up to 4.9 feet (1.5 m) at the shoulder, weighing more than 440 pounds (200 kg)—so it's a surprise when males in heat of rivalry (perhaps to avoid real damage) drop to their knees before horn-jousting with one another. They are grazers and browsers of lightly wooded grasslands of the Indian peninsula.

# SUNDERBANS NATIONAL PARK

Steamy, untamed Sunderbans National Park is a place of wild superlatives. It is part of what is probably the largest single block of mangroves in the world, covering some 6,120 square miles (16,000 km²) of mangrove forest and water, 40 percent of it in India, the rest in Bangladesh.

It is in the largest tidal delta in the world, almost 50,000 square miles (130,000 km²) of alluvial sediments draining three great rivers, the Ganges, Brahmaputra, and Meghna, in waterways ranging from barge width to a mile (1.6 km) or more across. Tides up to seven feet (2.15 m)—or on coastal islands, 18 feet (5.6 m)—sweep over it twice daily from the Bay of Bengal. Cyclones and enormous tidal waves periodically rearrange its topography and waterways.

At night it comes alive with magical luminescence. Trees glitter with fireflies summoning mates with individual dot-dash light signals. Rivers and channels glow with plankton.

Amidst all this natural chaos tigers hunt for wild boar, spotted deer, and sometimes rhesus macaques—and occasionally, for humans. Especially vulnerable are fishermen and gatherers of honey and wood who eke out a livelihood in the reserve buffer zone (no one is allowed in the core wilderness area). It is the only place where tigers routinely stalk humans, probably because of frequent encounters in secluded situations and past successes. However, so secretive are these stealthy animals that locals say the only time you see a tiger is when it's too late.

This is where woodcutters and honey-gatherers started wearing face masks on the backs of their heads after learning tigers prefer not to attack from the front. Some tigers caught on quickly, and most did eventually.

Tigers' numbers here have increased in recent years due to ample prey base including spotted or chital deer (though poaching is a problem), and dense, remote, albeit watery habitat (tigers are cats that don't mind, even seem to enjoy, swimming).

Aquatic life is lush and abundant. Fishing cats and small-clawed otters make a good living along creeks where some 90 fish species spawn along with 48 species of crabs and a huge variety of mollusks. It is the main shrimp nursery on the Indian east coast.

Three kinds of dolphins frequent tidal waters, including the Gangetic, Irrawaddy, and Indo-Pacific. So do finless porpoises.

A wealth of water-oriented birds are here—several kinds of storks, including the Asian open-bill, black-necked, and greater adjutant; swamp francolins; among kingfishers the black-capped, white-collared, and brown-winged. Birds of prey include formidable Pallas' fish-eagles, white-bellied sea eagles, Oriental hobbies, northern eagle owls, and brown fish owls.

Rare olive ridley sea turtles nest, and Sunderbans is important habitat for huge estuarine crocodiles, Indian pythons, monitor lizards up to nine feet (3 m) long, and 18-foot (5+ m) king cobras, world's largest poisonous snakes.

But water buffalo and Javan rhinoceros are no longer here, nor are swamp deer, muntjac or barking deer, or narrowheaded softshell turtles. Indian gharial crocodiles, once considered holy and protected, recently have been hunted for their skins. Even in this wild, remote place, denominated a U.N. World Heritage Site, they were not invulnerable to threats from poaching and agricultural reclamation, which continue.

Best times are December–mid-March. Monsoons are mid-June to mid-September, when humidity averages over 80 percent and violent storms may occur, sometimes becoming cyclones with huge tidal waves.

The tiger reserve is 998 square miles (2,585 km$^2$) of which 513 square miles (1,330 km$^2$) is a core national park and wilderness area. Only accommodation has been Sundar Cheetal Lodge at Sajnakhali (visitors are not allowed inside the core national park). (Respect signs prohibiting "movement after evening"—tigers sometimes jump fences at night.)

A nearby heronry can be visited by boat, and there are watchtowers. Launches can be hired (warning: tigers have attacked boats in narrow channels). Permit required. Threats include siltation, agricultural reclamation, potential oil spills from passing tankers, and a proposed fertilizer plant that could discharge harmful pollutants.

---

**FURTHER INFORMATION**

Field Director, Sunderbans Tiger Reserve, Government of West Bengal, Directorate of Forests, P.O. Canning Town, District 24-Parganas (South), West Bengal, India.

FOR ENTRY PERMIT: Joint Secretary (Forest), Govt. of West Bengal, 4th Floor, G-Block, Writers' Building, Calcutta 700 001, Tel: (+91) 225-5601, Ext. 411/754.

---

## ALSO OF INTEREST

The tiny island of **Narcondum** was set aside for the Andaman teal and Nicobar pigeon and is sole habitat of Narcondum hornbills.

**Mahuadaur**, 24 square miles (62 km$^2$), was established to protect the once abundant, now rare, gray wolf.

**Pirotanis** a marine national park for corals, along with green sea, leatherbacked, and olive ridley sea turtles.

**Valley of Flowers** is an extraordinary Himalayan locale with huge masses of vivid wild flowers.

International travelers can fly to New Delhi or Bombay (Mumbai), with lodging, rental cars, guides, and connecting internal jet air to most cities.

# KOREA

THE DMZ—SYMBOL TO MOST OF A COUNTRY STILL DIVIDED 50 YEARS AFTER THE KOREAN WAR—HAS BECOME ONE OF THE WORLD'S GREAT WILDLIFE RESERVES. IN THE ABSENCE OF HUMAN POPULATION, WILDLIFE—LEOPARDS, BLACK BEARS, MUSK DEER—HAS FLOURISHED IN SOLITUDE ALONG WITH RARE WHITE-NAPED AND RED-CROWNED CRANES.

A NARROW STRIP OF LAND SET ASIDE TO ENFORCE THE END OF A CIVIL WAR A HALF-CENTURY AGO HAS BROUGHT A NEW KIND OF PEACE TO NATURAL LIFE OF THIS STRIFE-TORN PENINSULA.

Amur leopards, Asiatic black bears, musk deer, and possibly Siberian tigers are among a now-flourishing wildlife population in the approximately 155-mile-long, 2.5-mile-wide (250 × 4-km) Demilitarized Zone, or DMZ, separating North and South Korea. More than 50 kinds of mammals include lynx, red foxes, and at higher elevations, ghorals, hardy, black-horned mountain goats.

Wetlands around five rivers that cross this world's most fortified border have become essential stopovers for flocks of rare, stately white-naped and red-crowned cranes and black-faced spoonbills. More than 20,000 migratory waterfowl include white-fronted geese, spot-billed ducks, and ruddy shelducks. Eagles and harriers prey on fish and smaller mammals.

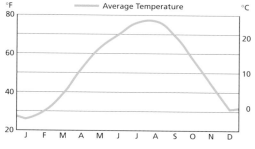

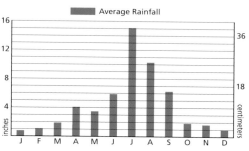

Gateway city: Seoul

231

Great spotted woodpeckers find homes in rugged, forested hills. Shrubby, open areas are habitat of greenfinches, northern shrikes, rustic, yellow-breasted, and Siberian meadow buntings.

Few visitors other than military guards enter this chain-link fenced, mined, razor-wired ribbon of no-man's-land between two countries still officially in a state of war. It is this solitude with lack of human disturbance that has allowed a spectacular rebounding of wild species in this de facto wildlife reserve like no other on earth.

Conservationists worldwide have urged that it become a permanent international peace park patterned after cross-border parks elsewhere. Its future is uncertain, however. As relations between the two countries have thawed from time to time, agreements have been signed to build railroad lines and adjacent highways through the zone, with proposals for commercial development designed without regard for the tract's unique biodiversity and possibilities for economically beneficial ecotourism.

Conservationists say careful planning could accommodate both. Railroads and highways could include wildlife underpasses and overpasses, which have succeeded elsewhere, with ecotourism benefiting all interests.

Until recently, the DMZ has had no visitation without special permits, which are difficult to obtain. But in the past several years, the Korean Bird Protection Association has obtained permits for limited birdwatching tours.

South Korea has more than 20 reserves and national parks. Among those of special wildlife interest, several are reachable by public transport or private vehicle with lodging nearby:

**Odaesan National Park** in the north near the DMZ with bike and hiking trails, high, craggy peaks, lush forests, rushing waterfalls, rivers, beaches, ancient temples, black bears, and deer.

**Junamho Bird Sanctuary**, west of Jinyeong on the main Busan–Masan highway, which often has 80 percent of the world's Baikal teal among 50,000–150,000 birds wintering on its three lakes November–March, also white-naped cranes, spoonbills, whistling swans.

**Eulsukdo Bird Sanctuary** southwest of Pusan, a large, flat sedimentary island reachable by a bridge in the mouth of the Nakdong River, home to over 100,000 migratory birds of over 50 species, including wintering white-naped cranes, spoonbills, white-tailed eagles.

---

**FURTHER INFORMATION**

Korea's official e-mail travel site: www.tour2Korea.com.

# LAOS

DESPITE DECADES OF WAR IN THE LATE
20TH CENTURY, LAOS HAS RETAINED ALMOST 50 PERCENT
OF ITS FOREST COVER. IT HAS MORE ASIAN ELEPHANTS IN
RATIO TO HUMANS THAN ANYWHERE ELSE, INDOCHINESE
TIGERS, LEOPARDS, MARBLED AND GOLDEN CATS, ALONG
WITH SOME OF THE WORLD'S MOST BEAUTIFUL BIRDS.

CLOUDED LEOPARDS AND CREATURES UNKNOWN ANYWHERE ELSE, AS WELL AS SOME 640 SPECIES OF DAZZLING BIRDS, FIND HOMES HERE IN ONE OF SOUTHEAST ASIA'S LEAST DISTURBED ECOSYSTEMS, STILL ALMOST 50 PERCENT FOREST-COVERED.

Foraging under wooded canopies in this small landlocked country of 92,040 square miles (236,000 km²) bordered by China, Myanmar (Burma), Thailand, Cambodia, and Vietnam are Asiatic black bears, Malayan sun bears, and wild Asian elephants. Laos—called in antiquity "Lan Xang" or Land of a Million Elephants—has more of these great beasts in ratio to humans than anywhere else: one for every 7,000 persons, including perhaps 1,100 employed in logging or agriculture.

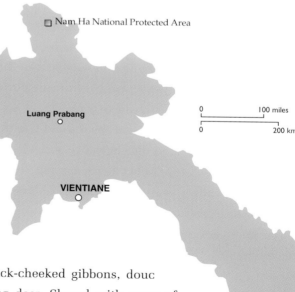

Nam Ha National Protected Area

Luang Prabang

VIENTIANE

| 0 | 100 miles |
| 0 | 200 km |

Only discovered in 1992 was the saola or spindlehorn ox, and in 1996 the Annamite striped rabbit which may be a new genus. Other mammals found only in this region include black-cheeked gibbons, douc langurs, and giant muntjacs or barking deer. Shared with some of its neighbors are such rare species as Indochinese tigers, leopards, Asian golden cats, stump-tailed macaques, Malayan and Chinese pangolins, five kinds of flying squirrels, Javan and crab-eating mongooses.

233

# LAOS

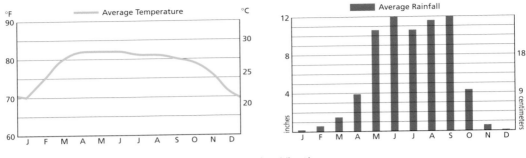

Gateway city: Vientiane

Among remarkable rare birds are flaming Siamese firebacks, lovely sarus cranes, giant ibis, strutting, peacock-like green peafowl, Asian golden weavers, white-winged ducks, red-collared woodpeckers, coral-billed ground cuckoos, and tawny fish owls.

Perhaps rarest of all, frolicsome blue-gray Irrawaddy dolphins cut through waters of the Mekong River, at recent count only about 15 surviving, their long-term outlook bleak unless gill-net fishing can be controlled on the Cambodian side of the border.

Laos, after nearly 20 years of virtual isolation, began in the 1990s to open toward the outside world, and in 1993, working in consultation with the Wildlife Conservation Society, gave legal protection to 20 National Protected Areas (NPAs). These now cover some 12,500 square miles (32,000 km²), more than 12 percent of the country, and WCS has recommended an additional 11 sites. They are not preserves—forests can be selectively logged—and at least until recently, visitor facilities have been minimal-to-nonexistent. But it is a start, and for those determined to see these places, tour agencies and government tourism authority offices in Vientiane, Luang Namtha, and Pakse can help organize trips.

Serious threats remain. Sensitive species and habitats here face less immediate danger than with some of Laos' neighbors due to relative lack of population pressure—Laos has one of Asia's lowest population densities, about 53 persons per square mile (21 per km²), though it is growing at about 2.5 percent per year. However, there is little capacity to enforce existing conservation laws. Subsistence poaching by native people takes a heavy toll, as does smuggling of rare species for the pet trade and as ingredients in folk medicine. Shifting cultivation and illegal logging cause habitat destruction. "Walls of death"—barriers of bamboo, thatch, and small trees—are placed in forests (even in national parks) with small openings where any passing animal is snared by leg or neck to die slowly and painfully. Explosives are used to catch fish, killing all indiscriminately and damaging lakes and streams. Over 20 hydrological projects are planned with potentially disastrous effects. The population generally lacks environmental awareness or concern—and for those offended by animal cruelty, market practices are distasteful, to understate it.

On the other hand, Laotions consume far less of their own natural resources than people of any "developed" country.

Two of the most rewarding NPAs for wilderness travel are NAM HA and PHOU HIN PHOUN.

## NAM HA NATIONAL PROTECTED AREA

Nam Ha—third largest of the National Protected Areas—869 square miles (2,224 km²)—is in the globally important northern Indochina subtropical moist forest along the border with China, Myanmar, and Thailand. It adjoins the Shaing Yong Protected Area in the Xishuangpanna National Nature Reserve of Yunnan, China.

Within its borders are at least 38 large mammal and 288 bird species, notably silver pheasants, Blythe's kingfishers, short-tailed parrot-bills, rufous-throated fulvettas, rufous-necked hornbills, and pied falconets, some globally threatened or vulnerable.

## ALSO OF INTEREST

**Phou Hin Phoun** is a huge wild area, 610 square miles (1,580 km²), with turquoise streams, monsoon forests, striking irregular limestone outcrops and endangered douc and Francois' langurs.

Three other large NPAs with rare and threatened species that are open to tourism are **Phou Xang He** in Savahnakhet province and **Dong Hua Sao** and **Xe Plan**, both in Champasak Province.

Laos has two distinct seasons—wet May–October, dry November–April. Vientiane is connected by air with Bangkok, Hanoi, Phnom Penh, and Kunming in China, and travel and lodging outside the city is readily available. There's reasonably good bus service throughout most of the country. Internal flights can be unsafe. River taxi or long-distance boats are commonly used.

---

**FURTHER INFORMATION**

Wildlife Conservation Society, P.O. Box 6712, Vientiane, Lao PDR, Tel: (+856) 21-21-5400, E-mail: wcslao@laotel.com; International Union for Conservation of Nature (IUCN), 15 Thanon Fa Ngum, Vientiane, Tel: (+856) 21-21-6401; World Wide Fund for Nature, Vientiane, Lao PDR, E-mail: wwflao@laonet.net. Also the NTAL—National Tourism Authority of Laos—set up in the late 1980s and best reachable by Fax: (+856) 21-21-2769 in Vientiane—though it is underfunded, understaffed, and not always responsive. Local tour operators in Vientiane can be helpful.

# MYANMAR
# (BURMA)

WITH VAST, SPLENDID LANDSCAPES STILL
INTACT, MYANMAR IS REGARDED AS ONE
OF THE MOST IMPORTANT INDO-PACIFIC
WILDLIFE RESERVOIRS, PROVIDING HOMES
FOR SUCH ENGAGING MAMMALS AS RED
PANDAS AND OVER **1,000** RESIDENT
AND MIGRATING BIRDS.

MARCO POLO VISITING MYANMAR IN THE 13TH CENTURY
FOUND "VAST JUNGLES TEEMING WITH ELEPHANTS,
UNICORNS AND OTHER WILD BEASTS." Some of that
description remains accurate. Natural forest cover
is estimated at around 43 percent with another 31
percent in secondary forest. Myanmar is rich in
birdlife with an estimated 1,000 resident and
migratory species. Waterways of coastal delta
and inland on the southern peninsula attract
waterfowl from all over Southeast Asia.

Leopards stalk muntjac or barking deer in
lowland jungles where little fishing cats look for
smaller meals in and along streams. Clouded leopards,
whose shorter legs enable them to move swiftly along
tree branches, prey on arboreal species such as monkeys,
squirrels, even birds, at altitudes up to 6,500 feet (2,000 m).

The world's second-smallest deer has been found in
remote mountains, standing just 20 inches (51 cm) high
at the shoulder with antlers just an inch (2.5 cm) long,

OPPOSITE: Sambars are the most widespread deer in the world, ranging over much of the
Asian continent, and also one of the largest, weighing up to 770 pounds (350 kg), standing
up to five feet (1.5 m) at the shoulder, with antlers up to a yard (1 m) long. They're a
favorite tiger prey species, since a large sambar can feed a tiger for several days. Cattle
egrets often accompany them, sometimes as hitch-hikers.

237

# MYANMAR (BURMA)

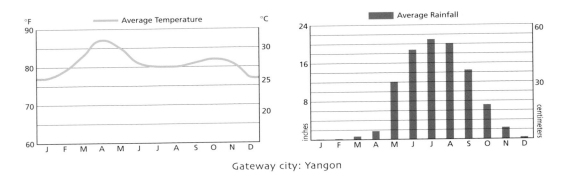

Gateway city: Yangon

and scientists have recently discovered blue sheep, Chinese black barking deer, and stone martens, species previously unknown here.

Engaging red pandas forage in tall trees in northern Myanmar, and serows and ghorals (aka ghorals) skip easily along steep mountain terrain. There are crab-eating mongeese, Asiatic black bears and Malayan sun bears, and thousands of Asian elephants, perhaps a third of those in the world—though most make up the world's largest working elephant herd, employed in logging and agriculture.

With vast splendid landscapes still intact, Myanmar is regarded as one of the most important Indo-Pacific countries for biodiversity conservation. Its species richness is reflected in some 100 kinds of mammals, 300 reptiles, the most diverse bird population in Southeast Asia, and at least 7,000 kinds of plants (over 1,000 varieties of orchid), in habitats ranging from mangrove swamps, tropical rain forests and coral reefs in the south, to temperate forests of conifers, oaks, and rhododendrons in the far north, and snowcapped mountains over 19,000 feet (5,900 m) in the easternmost Himalayas. High mountains form borders with India and Bangladesh on the west, China on the northeast, Laos and Thailand on the east, and are intersected by two great rivers, the Irrawaddy (Ayeyarwady) and Salween.

Tigers have become rare in most places despite Myanmar's having 40 percent of Southeast Asia's best tiger habitat, according to a study by Wildlife Conservation Society. In 1984 at government request the U.N. Food and Agriculture Organization (FAO) assisted a field survey identifying areas suitable for national parks and reserves. But the program largely was not implemented, the government saying its budget was needed for road-building.

Myanmar lists 31 protected area sanctuaries, but little is known about many of them. Their claimed area covers about four percent of the country.

Since shortly after World War II Myanmar has been one of the world's most repressive governments, until recently closed to outside economic contact as well as international travel. Recently the country has opened up somewhat, and visitors will find, despite continuing political difficulties and travel restrictions in some areas, a beautiful country with friendly people. Most wildlife reserves are not easy to see and many are threatened by unsustainable hunting, timber poaching for lumber and charcoal, destructive agricultural practices, mining, dam proposals, and habitat encroachment by high population growth. This may improve if the government comes to respect ecotourism benefits as justifying more reserves with supporting funds for maintenance and protection. Several international organizations are working to help, including Wildlife Conservation Society, Smithsonian, and International Crane Foundation.

Best times are December–February—temperatures rise from March on, and wet season is usually mid-May–mid-October.

Yangon (Rangoon) is served by international airlines, and connecting domestic airlines serve Mandalay and major centers. There's an extensive bus network but few good roads, many requiring 4WD. Foreigners at least until recently have been restricted to designated hotels, which can be basic but costly.

---

**FURTHER INFORMATION**

Forest Department, Wildlife Conservation and Sanctuaries Division, Gyogon, Yangon; Wildlife Conservation Society, Program Director, Building C-3, Aye Yeikomon 1st St. Yadanamon Housing Ave., Hlang Township, Myanmar, Tel: (+95) 1-524-893, Fax: (+95) 1-512-838.

---

# AHLAUNGDAW KATHAPAW NATIONAL PARK

This beautiful designated wildlife reserve has 620 square miles (1,605 km²) of almost undisturbed low and highland forest that provides homes for Asian elephants, leopards, and three rare smaller cats—jungle, fishing, and Asiatic golden—with prey base for all. These include sambar and Indian muntjac or barking deer for the big cats, plus occasionally wild boars (though these are formidable quarry), and for the smaller ones, rodents, hares, and flying squirrels.

Huge gaur weighing up to a ton (1,000 kg) graze in clearings and rest in shady glades, females in small herds of four to eight, older males quiet and solitary except when mating stimulates bellows audible for a mile (1.6 km) or so. Glossy Asiatic or Himalayan black bears with distinctive white V-markings on their throats seek out berries and succulent plant material. Assam and rhesus macaques and capped langurs interrupt chattering to scream with alarm if they glimpse a leopard.

Showy great hornbills up to four feet (122 cm) long with outsize yellow bills and red eyes, rare elsewhere, protect nests in hollow trees with walls of mud, wood pulp, and plant debris, their pairs "singing" duets in loud harsh barks and roars. White-capped redstarts feed along rocky rivers and streams. Common also are red-wattled lapwings, wagtails, sandpipers, and forktails. Raptors and water-oriented birds are fewer, scarcities attributed to pesticide use in surrounding agricultural areas.

May–October is rainy—monsoonal in August–September. There have been, at least until recently, no all-weather roads, and just getting to the reserve can involve travel by plane to Mandalay, then 4WD, then boat across the Irrawaddy River, boat across the Chindwin River, then by tractor, bull-cart, foot, and finally by elephant. Most visitors are pilgrims—some 40,000 come annually to a Buddhist shrine in the park with monks in residence and small rest houses nearby plus one at Magyibin Sakan on the main pilgrimage route. More rest houses are planned at Thabeiksay for official visitors, with other facilities in a long-range plan to encourage ecotourism.

## ALSO OF INTEREST

**Mount Hkakabo-Razi National Park**, Myanmar's largest park—1,472 square miles (3,812 km²)—recently gazetted with help of WCS working with local communities, protecting red pandas, ox-like takins, black muntjac deer previously thought endemic to China, blue sheep, stone martens. Community development programs have been started to educate and enlist local people in park support, also to provide salt after discovery that many animals are poached to provide for this scarce item without which people suffer from sometimes fatal iodine deficiency.

**Kyatthin Reserve**, 104 forested square miles (268 km²) about 100 miles (160 km) northwest of Mandalay with leopards, wild dogs, banteng, hog deer, Indian muntjacs and macaques, possibly also rare white-winged wood ducks.

**Tamanthi Reserve**, Myanmar's second largest wildlife sanctuary, 830 square miles (2,150 km²), 600 air miles (1,000 km) north of Yangon, largely intact evergreen and semievergreen forest with leopards, tigers, wild dogs, hoolock gibbons, green peafowl, and good populations of Asian elephants.

**Hlawga National Park**, one of the country's most accessible, 45 minutes' drive from Yangon, with more than 70 species of herbivorous fauna, 90 species of birds.

**Inle Lake**, 389 square miles (1,010 km²) of shallow waters and marshes in central Myanmar with cranes, lesser spotted eagles, many winter waterfowl migrants, white-tailed stonechats, and rare, local Jerdon's bushchats.

**Lampi Island**, the country's first marine national park.

**Mohingyi Reserve**, with storks, migrant ducks and waders.

**Popa Mountain Park**, also relatively accessible, with monkeys that have become habituated to human visitors.

# NEPAL

BOTH ROYAL BARDIA AND ROYAL CHITWAN
NATIONAL PARKS ORIGINALLY WERE SET ASIDE
AS ROYAL HUNTING GROUNDS WHERE TIGERS,
RHINOCEROS, SLOTH BEARS, AND OTHERS WERE
SLAUGHTERED FOR SPORT. NOW THEY PROTECT
THOSE SPECIES, ALONG WITH LEOPARDS, ELEPHANTS,
AND HUNDREDS OF SPECIES OF BIRDS.

NEPAL IS AN ANCIENT KINGDOM OF BREATHTAKING SCENERY AND CHARISMATIC WILDLIFE, INCLUDING RARE AND ELUSIVE SNOW LEOPARDS, BENGAL TIGERS, ONE-HORNED RHINOCEROS, AND RED PANDAS, AMID SOME OF THE HIGHEST MOUNTAIN PEAKS IN THE WORLD, INCLUDING THE HIGHEST, MOUNT EVEREST.

Once beachfront property with geologic origins 60 million years ago on the Mediterranean Sea, the continental drift which raised the Himalayas left parts of Nepal so isolated they seem untouched by the 20th century.

Life zones of biological diversity range from arctic to tropical within a distance of 100 miles (160 km)—from snow-covered Everest at the top of the world to the Ganges River floodplain a little above sea level and broad, fertile tropical lowlands of the Terai, seasonally drenched with monsoons. (This is where Siddhartha Gautama, later revered as Buddha, was born in 543 BC.)

This diversity includes over 800 bird species, nearly 10 percent of the avian species in the world. Demoiselle cranes fly from Tibet for the winter. There are red-billed blue magpies, great "bone-cracker" lammergeiers, colorful and vocal babblers or laughing thrushes, parakeets, sunbirds, griffons, eight stork species, and six kinds of resplendent multi-hued pheasants, including the Nepalese national bird—the monal or impeyan which dazzles its prospective mate with an incredible blaze of vibrating orange and iridescent blue tail and wing feathers.

# NEPAL

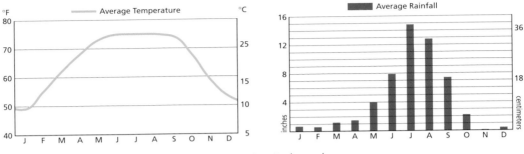

Gateway city: Kathmandu

There are 6,500 known species of trees, shrubs, and wild flowers.

Some of the endangered residents are protected by the remoteness of their habitat but all are threatened to some extent by human population growth and its environmental demands. Many are poached for their physical parts, from hides and bones to internal organs and even urine, some parts regarded as food delicacies, others as trophies, others as valuable folk medicine.

Parks and reserves, including buffer zones, cover over 18 percent of the country.

Of worldwide interest and significance are ROYAL CHITWAN NATIONAL PARK which with contiguous **Parsa Wildlife Reserve** covers more than 859 square miles (2,240 km²) in south-central Nepal, home to Nepal's only significant surviving population of one-horned rhinoceros and such other endangered species as Bengal tigers, Gangetic dolphins, and gharial crocodiles—altogether over 50 mammal species and more than 400 kinds of birds; and in the west, ROYAL BARDIA NATIONAL PARK, also with Bengal tigers as well as blue bulls, a variety of deer, and a small herd of introduced rhinoceros.

## ROYAL BARDIA NATIONAL PARK

This national park in mysterious seldom-visited western Nepal was first set aside, like better-known Chitwan, as a royal hunting preserve where tigers, rhinoceros, sloth bears, and others were slaughtered for sport. Paradoxically this may have contributed to its ultimate salvation since it meant the land was already put aside and available when the government decided in 1976 the time had come for a national park here. Now Bardia's 374 square miles (968 km²) are haven to thousands of rare animals and birds whose survival without it would be doubtful.

Magnificent Bengal tigers are equally at home in its grassland patches and tropical dry deciduous forest dominated by stately sal trees. There they prey on sambar and barking deer and—occasionally and carefully—on fat but prickly porcupines. Shaggy, irritable sloth bears are here also, but the two generally give each other a wide berth. Bears are looking mainly for succulent vegetation and tall termite mounds to raid.

Leopards are here, also civets, monkeys, and such wary predators as hyenas, wild dogs, and jackals, and, trying to escape their notice in the tall grass, hispid hares, believed extinct here until recent sightings. Huge droppings, uprooted trees, and other trees stripped of their bark mean elephants have passed by.

Two of the commonest and most spectacular among Bardia's 350 bird species are peacocks and jungle fowl, the latter strutting predecessors of all barnyard roosters. But there are also bright sunbirds, kingfishers, and migratory waterfowl seasonally in large numbers in the Karnali-Girwa and Babai Rivers, where gray-and-crimson wall creepers dart about gorge cliffs.

In the mosaic of riverine forest and grassland dominated by giant-buttressed simul trees are barasinghas or swamp deer, blackbucks, and ungainly nilgai, the subcontinent's largest antelope. A few one-horned rhinoceros, transplanted from Chitwan in a joint government–World Wide Fund for Nature project, hold their own and spend time in low savannahs.

In the rivers are Gangetic dolphins and otters, and basking on banks, occasional crocodiles. Best times are November–May.

---

**FURTHER INFORMATION**

Park Manager, Royal Bardia National park, National Parks Building, Babar Mahal, P.O. Box 3712, Kathmandu, Nepal.

---

# ROYAL CHITWAN NATIONAL PARK

Royal Chitwan National Park and U.N. World Heritage Site in the subtropical lowlands (Terai) of south-central Nepal was a favorite hunting ground of Nepalese royalty—for good reason. A single famous hunt to entertain the British viceroy left dead 120 tigers, 38 rhinos, 27 leopards, and 15 sloth bears. Mahouts—here called phanits—rode hundreds of elephants (on one occasion 975) to herd animals toward shooters.

But such massacres may not have damaged wildlife as much as massive spraying of the pesticide DDT to eradicate malaria, which caused humans to move in and destroy valley habitat to create farmland. In 10 years more than half the forest was gone and with it the animals that lived there. By 1973, when the park, Nepal's first, was established, only an estimated 20 tigers and 100 rhinos were left in the 859 square miles (2,240 km²) of forested hills, grasslands, oxbow lakes, and three river floodplains that is now Chitwan and its adjoining buffer, **Parsa Wildlife Reserve**.

With protection, wild populations have gradually returned. Chitwan is now renowned for its rich and varied biota which includes a large population of endangered, prehistoric-looking one-horned rhinoceros as well as magnificent Bengal tigers, shaggy sloth bears, and such rare and endangered birds as flashy-winged Bengal floricans, giant hornbills, black storks—altogether more than 450 avian species, more than 50 mammals, more than 45 reptiles and amphibians including green pit vipers and cobras, and 200 kinds of butterflies.

Dense concentrations of two endangered species of crocodiles are in the Narayani River and lakes here, some 70 rare marsh muggers and 150 gharials (muggers are the ones with blunt noses and yellow teeth in the lakes; swift, fish-eating gharials, up to 16 feet (5 m) long with slender noses, usually are in rivers).

Water sources are centers of wildlife activity. Smooth Indian otters fish and play on banks. Indian pythons up to 20 feet (6 m) long wait nearby for hog deer and can consume one weighing up to 45 pounds (20 kg) in a single prolonged gulp. These (understandably) nervous little deer and their cousins, muntjac or barking deer, are favorite prey also for tigers, of which Chitwan has an estimated 100, including about 40 breeding pairs. Dainty spotted chitals, called the world's most beautiful deer, graze the riverine grasslands, along with Asia's largest deer, the sambars. Rhinos spend almost all their time there.

There are also rare armored pangolins, four-horned antelopes, freshwater Gangetic dolphins, striped hyenas, huge monitor lizards, and gaur, world's largest wild oxen standing up to six feet (1.8 m) at the shoulder and weighing up to a ton (1,000 kg). Seldom seen but present are wild dogs, jungle cats, leopard cats, and fishing cats. Also here are a few wild buffalo and irascible sloth bears whose unpredictable temperaments make them reputedly Chitwan's most dangerous animal.

Resplendent peacocks strut and wail and handsome jungle fowl crow to announce dawn. Storks, herons, and egrets feed on aquatic vegetation. Parakeets and green pigeons flock to fruiting trees.

Red-billed blue magpies scavenge at tiger kills. Jungle mynas ride rhinos' backs, flying up for insects disturbed by the clumsy giants' crashing through vegetation. Overhead, crested serpent eagles twist and turn in springtime courtship acrobatics. Jungle owlets rest in forest trees in daytime, hunt at night. Brown hawk-owls call loudly at night, and nightjars and cuckoos fill April dusk with courtship song.

Leopards' favored victims are gray langur monkeys trooping through the sal forest, and rhesus macaques, elsewhere bold hangers-on at temples and rail stations but here, like much of Chitwan's wildlife, shy and elusive.

Recently the Nepalese government, along with World Wide Fund for Nature and several other national and international agencies, have begun developing a project called Terai Arc, aimed at restoring degraded forests outside parks in lowland Terai from Chitwan to Suklaphanta to create habitat for tigers, rhinos, and elephants.

Best times are November–April.

# NEPAL

Painted stork nestlings summon parents with raucous cries which they lose later. Mature storks entirely lack syrinx or voice box muscles—but they make up for it with large multifunctional bills which clatter in rattles to serve all their communications needs, in courting, mating and nesting. In feeding, these bills swing back and forth, snapping shut instantly on touching a small fish or frog in freshwater swamps from the Indian subcontinent through Southeast Asia.

**FURTHER INFORMATION**

Park Manager, Royal Chitwan National Park, National Parks Building, Babar Mahal, P.O. Box 3712, Kathmandu, Nepal, Telex: NP 2203, Cable: NATR.

## ALSO OF INTEREST

**Koshi Tappu Wildlife Reserve**, a 68-square-mile (175-km²) reserve on the beautiful Ganges tributary floodplain of Sapt Kosi in eastern Nepal, home to Nepal's last wild buffalo, also several deer species and 280 kinds of birds.

**Sagarmantha National Park** northeast of Kathmandu along the Tibetan border, a U.N World Heritage Site covering 480 square miles (1,243 km²), all above 9,848 feet (3,000 m) altitude including Mount Everest, with red pandas, musk deer, Himalayan tahr, black bears, wolves, snow leopards, and fascinating birdlife, including impeyan or monal pheasants, Himalayan griffons, choughs, and snow pigeons. Accessible on foot only.

**Makalu-Barun National Park**, inaugurated in 1992, adjacent to Sagarmantha and, in the north, to the newly established 13,500-square-mile (35,000 km²) **Qomolangma Nature Preserve** in Tibet. Ecological zones range from subtropical forest to arctic snows of the Himalayas, and some of the last pristine mountain landscapes in Nepal.

**Annapurna Conservation Area** includes the famous Annapurna peaks. The Annapurna Conservation Area Project, a land trust, has begun exemplary work combining conservation with tourism and human population needs.

**Langtang National Park**, nearest national park to Kathmandu, has red pandas, muntjac, musk deer, black bear, ghorial, and serows (antelopes), snow leopards, and langur and rhesus monkeys.

**Shey Phoksundo National Park** is Nepal's largest park, 1,372 square miles (3,555 km²) billed as "a dangerous 14-day trek from Pokhara", with ghorial, tahr, Tibetan hares, Himalayan weasels, blue sheep, snow leopards.

**Rara National Park** surrounds beautiful Rara Lake, largest in Nepal, important waterbird habitat. A four-day walk from the Jumla airstrip.

**Royal Sukla Phanta Wildlife Reserve** is a last stronghold for endangered swamp deer. Also here: tigers, elephants.

**Kanchenjunga Conservation Area**, named after the third-highest mountain in the world, has good populations of snow leopards, blue sheep, wolves, and red pandas. Kanchenjunga Mountain straddles Nepal, Sikkim, and Tibet.

# OMAN

ARABIAN ORYX, WHOSE WHITE COATS DEFLECT
SUNLIGHT AND TORRID TEMPERATURES IN THEIR
DESERT SURROUNDINGS, RETURNED TO THEIR
WILD HOME IN OMAN IN 1982, 10 YEARS AFTER
THE DEATH OF THE LAST FREE-RANGING SPECIMEN.

THESE HANDSOME HERBIVORES WITH DECORATIVE BLACK MARKINGS, SAID TO BE THE BASIS FOR MYTHO-
LOGICAL UNICORNS, WERE ENDOWED BY NATURE TO SURVIVE DAUNTINGLY HOT, DRY HABITAT. Their
snowy fur reflects heat (and light) efficiently—a built-in cooling mechanism. In ways not yet
understood, they are able to detect rainfall long distances away and move to intercept new, lush
growth for grazing. Their movements may span hundreds of miles—one tracked individual
traveled 46 miles (74 km) in 12 hours. So effectively do their
bodies retain moisture from food and fog-generated dew that
they can go without drinking for almost two years.

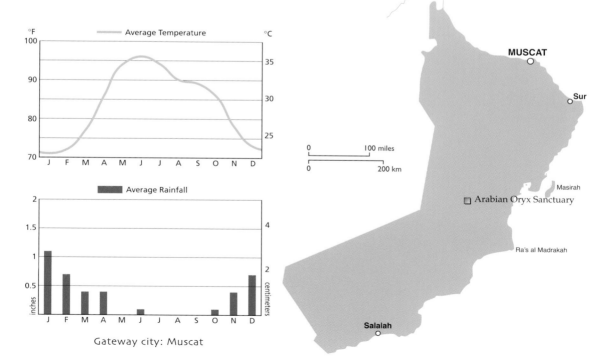

Gateway city: Muscat

OPPOSITE: Powerful, long-eared caracals can kill antelopes twice their weight and, like leopards, carry them up a tree to consume as hunger dictates. Renowned for their ability to leap high on long legs to capture flying birds such as pigeons and guinea fowl, caracals can survive for long periods without water other than metabolic moisture of their prey. They range from central and southern Africa through southern Asia, in dry savannah and woodland, scrubland and semi-desert.

But these superbly adapted creatures fell easy victim to automatic rifles and fast motor vehicles introduced to the Arabian Peninsula during World War II. Fortunately the Sultan of Oman decided an effort should be made to reintroduce them and with help from a consortium of international wildlife organizations, a herd was reassembled from private collections and the Phoenix, Arizona, Zoo. Now several hundred survive in the ARABIAN ORYX SANCTUARY, their numbers gradually increasing.

## ARABIAN ORYX SANCTUARY

This 11,000-square-mile (28,490-km²) U.N. World Heritage Site in Oman's central desert and coastal hills is as well the only wild breeding site on the Arabian peninsula for turkey-like endangered houbara bustards, long-legged striders of barren, open places.

Here too is the largest wild population of Arabian mountain gazelles—some 5,000, with rare dorcas and sand gazelles, goat-like Nubian ibex, sand cats, red and Ruppell's sand foxes, honey badgers, jackals, and a few caracals and Arabian wolves.

Golden eagles nest, as do spotted thick-knees, crested larks, little owls, and coronetted and chestnut-bellied sandgrouse, which fly 40 miles or more (70 km) to fill belly feathers with water droplets which they bring back to nestlings. Coastal beaches and lagoons attract flocks of resident and migrant waders including gulls, terns, flamingos, herons, and several duck species. The reserve is crossed by large numbers of spring migrants, including bright European rollers.

Over 20 reptile species include carnivorous desert monitors and rare Thomas' spiny-tailed lizards. Vegetation, though sparse, includes 11 endemic species. Near Saiwan is evidence of ancient human habitation.

Serious problems in this large reserve, difficult to patrol, are poaching of oryx for meat, hides, and exquisite horns, also overgrazing by domestic herds and lack of regeneration in old woodlands.

The Oryx Introduction Project at Yalooni has limited accommodations for visitors.

Most international visitors fly to Muscat with wide range of accommodations, rental cars, busses with daily service to all main provincial towns, domestic air to several, and comprehensive system of long-distance taxis and microbusses, also many tour operators.

**FURTHER INFORMATION**

Directorate-General of Nature Reserves, Minister of National Heritage and Culture, P.O. Box 668, Muscat, Sultanate of Oman, Tel: (+968) 602285, Fax: 602283.

## ALSO OF INTEREST

**Ra's al Hadd Turtle Preserve** in the Wilayat of Sur, 26 miles (42 km) of coastline where an estimated 20,000 sea turtles come ashore to nest annually—most important green turtle nest site in the Indian Ocean. Visitation possible with permit from Director General of Nature Reserves.

During October/November **Muscat** is said to be raptor capital of the world, with great numbers of migrant steppe eagles, greater spotted eagles, long-legged buzzards, various kestrel species.

In **Salalah** in December/January, waders and waterfowl are attracted to the many khors (inlets) in and around the city—storks, flamingos, herons, gulls, terns—and in May, migrants from Africa, including European rollers, didric cuckoos, gray-headed kingfishers.

**Masirah Island**, with 331-species birdlist—best times September–November; shell-strewn beaches; world's largest loggerhead sea turtle nesting population, with some 30,000 coming ashore to lay about three million eggs every June–August. One small hotel.

Colorful blue-cheeked, European and little green bee-eaters nest along the **Batinah Coast**.

Steppe eagles are members of the AQUILA genus known as true eagles: large and aggressive, with formidable beaks and claws, lancet-shaped head and neck, and feathers that cover the legs. They soar holding wings straight out, with wingtips spread like fingers, preying on small and medium-sized mammals— although when termite populations explode, they can gather in large flocks and each consume up to 2,000 termites a day. Steppe eagles inhabit open country including arid steppe and semidesert; nesting in Africa and southeastern Europe through India and China to Hainan; wintering south to Myanmar and the Malay Peninsula.

# RUSSIAN FEDERATION

HULKING POLAR BEARS, FIERCE SIBERIAN
TIGERS, MAJESTIC STEPPE AND STELLER'S SEA
EAGLES ALONG WITH AMUR LEOPARDS, MASSIVE
BROWN BEARS, AND HUNDREDS OF OTHER
SPECTACULAR AND RARE SPECIES ARE PROTECTED
IN MORE THAN 100 ZAPOVEDNIKS OR NATURE
PRESERVES COVERING SOME 320,380 SQUARE
MILES (830,000 KM²) IN THE RUSSIAN FEDERATION.

THEIR CREATION GOES BACK TO 1916 WHEN THE FEDERATION'S FIRST RESERVES WERE ESTABLISHED, AIMED AT PROTECTING RESIDENT WILDLIFE AND HABITAT WHILE PROVIDING FOR SCIENTIFIC RESEARCH. In recent years they gradually have been opened to wider visitation (and some limited eco-tourism), though in some cases only by permit.

When added to Russia's 33 national parks, they represent virtually every habitat and cover some two percent of this world's largest country—from northern tundra, mountains of the Caucasus, Urals, and Altai, black-earth steppes and taiga to large areas of the Far East and Kolsky Peninsula. They protect virtually all the rare plants and animals listed in the Red Data Book. Without these reserves, continued survival of all these species would be precarious. (As a system, the zapovedniks are more comparable to the U.S. national wildlife refuges than to its national parks, though still much more limited in public access than the U.S. refuges.)

The current government has enlisted international help to maintain these reserves, including that of the World Wide Fund for Nature (WWF), and steps have been taken to work with local communities to gain their support. In addition, reserves, and their supporters, have created a network of small NGOs (non-governmental organizations) much like "Friends" groups elsewhere, to watch over welfare of individual reserves, and EcoCenter Zapovedniks has developed educational programs within the reserves.

Some zapovedniks—still a minority—now have visitor centers with organized trails and visitor programs, but ecotourism for the most part is still in its infancy here, especially as measured by facilities to accommodate visitors from afar. For such visitors, since Russia's southern border is roughly equivalent to that of Canada (45–50 degrees north latitude) best time to visit almost all reserves is in summer—from mid-June to mid-September.

# RUSSIAN FEDERATION

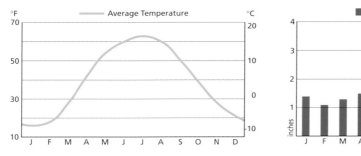

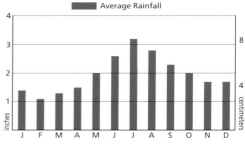

Gateway city: Moscow

Geographic organization of the reserves reflects that of The Center for Russian Nature Conservation and its excellent "Wild Russia" website (www.wild-russia.org). It includes much information provided by Margaret Willliams, Laura Williams, and others, in these fine groups.

**FURTHER INFORMATION**

Center for Russian Nature Conservation, P.O. Box 57277, Washington, D.C. 20037-7277, Tel: (+1) 202-778-9573;

Laura Williams and Igor Shpilenok, Chukhrai, Suzemsky raion, Bryansk oblast, Russia 242181, Tel/fax: (+7-083-52) 2-14-67, E-mail: shpilenok@mail.ru;

EcoCenter "Zapovedniks," Institute of Economics, 15th Floor, Nakhimovsky Pr. 32, Moscow 117218, Russia, E-mail: chipmunk@online.ru;

Federal Forestry Service of Russian Federation (Rosleskhoz), 59/19, Pyatnitskaya St., Moscow 113095, Russia.

# GREAT ARCTIC REGION

## UST-LENSKY ZAPOVEDNIK

Water-oriented birds from every continent flock here in spectacular numbers when brief Arctic summer transforms frozen tundra of the vast Lena River delta into fertile wetlands. Of some 109 bird species in this 9,584-square-mile (24,830-km$^2$) preserve, at least 60 nest on its tens of thousands of islands, lakes, and channels.

Big orange-legged bean geese arrive while snow still covers the 12,352 square-mile (32,000-km$^2$) delta. Then come greater white-fronted geese, black brant and two

Wrangel Island
Zapovednik

*emlya*
*tsa Iosifa*

*Severnaya*
*Zemlya*

*Novosibirskiye*
*Ostrova*

Great   Arctic   Region

K o l y m a

L o w l a n d

Ust-Lensky Zapovednik

O Nordvik

O Dikson

Kronotsky Zapovednik

C E N T R A L

S I B E R I A N

P L A T E A U

*rian*

*land*

O Lensk

Olekminsky Zapovednik

Khabarovsk
O

Kurilsky Zapovednik

Kuznetsky Alatau
Zapovednik

Baikalo-Lensky
Zapovednik

Khingansky
Zapovednik

Vladivostok
O

*sibirsk*

Lake
Baikal

Irkutsk
O

Sikhote-Alinsky Zapovednik

Altaisky Zapovednik

Kedrovaya Pad
Zapovednik

Katunsky Zapovednik

Dalnevostochny-Morskoy
Zapovednik

subspecies of brent (aka brant) geese from Vietnam and Europe. Wild cries of some 7,000 red-throated and 25,000 black-throated loons echo across tundra lakes. Not long after, Sabine's and pink-plumaged Ross' gull colonies settle down noisily with green-winged teals, northern pintails, king and Steller's eiders, and long-tailed and tufted ducks, spotted redshanks, and big, graceful whooper swans. Peregrine falcons swoop from cliffside aeries. Willow warblers with bright blue throats flit through lower vegetation, along with Siberian accentors and Pallas' reed and little buntings.

Pink and purple carnations blanket river terraces. Reindeer come for rich grasses, followed by wolves. Bighorn sheep and black-capped marmots graze high meadows. More than 6,500 river channels and bypasses offer plankton-rich forage for 36 kinds of fish. Belugas and occasionally narwhals swim in outer reaches—once, a herd of 120 belugas in one channel.

By September it's all over. In winter, only such hardy species as polar bears, arctic foxes, musk oxen, mountain hares, snowy owls, and willow and rock ptarmigans remain—and Ust-Lensky once again is frozen to a depth of more than 3,000 feet (1,000 m).

---

**FURTHER INFORMATION**

Director, Ust-Lensky Zapovednik, Russia 678400, E-mail: lena@tiksi.rospac.ru

---

# WRANGEL ISLAND ZAPOVEDNIK

One of the highest densities of denning polar bears and walruses in the world is found on and around Wrangel Island and tiny nearby **Herald Island**, which became reserves to protect these species and their newborns. More than 80,000 Pacific walruses are at home here—huge one-ton males basking in the sun, females swimming 87 miles (140 km) from the mainland to give birth on these secluded shores. Reindeer and wooly musk oxen thrive inland, and tens of thousands of birds—black-legged kittiwakes, pelagic cormorants, and snow geese—come to nest on jagged cliffs and lake shores during the short period they are not covered with ice and snow. Snowy owls raise young in bare depressions on inland ground. In mid-July more than a dozen arctic poppy species create colorful mosaics with pink dryads, pasqueflowers, and exquisite castelleas, blossoming over thin mats of soil overlying deep permafrost on this 3,072-square-mile (7,957-km$^2$) island reserve between the east Siberian and Chukchi Seas.

---

**FURTHER INFORMATION**

Director, Wrangel Island Reserve, Russia 686870, Magadanskaya Oblast, Chukotskaya A.O., Schmidtovsky raion, s. Ushakovskoye.

---

# Northwest Russia and Eastern European Forest Region

## Bryansky Les Zapovednik

Some of the rarest creatures in this part of the world—lynx, northern eagle owls, brown bears (decimated by overhunting, now rebounding), nesting black storks, and more than 16 kinds of orchids—find homes here. This narrow 93-mile-long (150-km) stretch of riverine bogs and conifer and broadleaf forest—one of the last intact in European Russia—is an island of green in a sea of farm fields. It is this isolation with welcoming habitat that attracts one of Russia's richest wildlife populations on one of its smallest nature reserves (83 square miles/214 km$^2$).

Wolf packs pursue moose in winter but otherwise prefer easier prey such as wild boars and roe deer as well as badgers when they can catch them outside their burrows. Rattling cries of all 10 European woodpecker species, including black, middle spotted, three-toed, and Eurasian wrynecks, ring among 300-year-old oak trees. Big male capercaillies—giants of the grouse family—sing and fan turkey-like tails in spectacular communal displays to attract mates in spring. Common and gray herons, corncrakes, and other migrants return. Rare, shy black storks raise young near stream sides where they find crested newts, ground frogs, and small fish for nestlings. Spotted eagles, black kites, and tawny owls are among 16 kinds of raptors and eight owls that prey on small forest rodents.

More than a dozen nature reserves have been established nearby, with plans to develop buffers and connecting corridors. Toward that end, Bryanski in 2001 was made the core of the **Nerusso-Deshiannskoe-Polesie Biosphere Reserve**, with active community involvement programs at its modern visitor center and museum.

---

**FURTHER INFORMATION**

Director, Nerussa Station, Suzemsky raion, Bryanskaya oblast, Russia 242181,
Tel: (+7-083-53) 2-57-74/2-57-75, Fax: 2-25-67, E-mail: nerussa@online.debryansk.ru
(and) zapole@online.debryansk.ru

---

FOLLOWING PAGES: So well insulated are polar bears by fur and thick blubber that a photograph using heat-sensitive film showed nothing but the puff of air, like smoke, from its exhaled breath. Their range is circumpolar, over Canada, Greenland, Norway, Russia. Most have a home territory of a few hundred miles but one satellite-tracked female trekked 3,000 miles (5,000 km) from Alaska's Prudhoe Bay, across the top of the world to Greenland, on to Canada's Ellismere Island, and back to Greenland.

# DARVINSKY ZAPOVEDNIK

Rare golden eagles and one of the largest populations of ospreys and white-tailed sea eagles in Europe nest—sometimes in huge structures in old treetops or cliff ledges—in this 539-square-mile (1,397-km$^2$) largely aquatic reserve, Darvinsky Zapovednik (named for the British naturalist Charles Darwin), on a peninsula in the Rybninskoye Reservoir in northwest Russia. Moose, huge brown bears, and wild boars come to feed along sandy shores with waterfowl and shorebirds which nest or stop in north–south migration. Capercaillie males, largest Old-World grouse, fan out tail feathers and strut in courtship display in clearings among pine stands and birch trees.

Foxes and raccoon dogs prey on rodents, as do badgers and ermine, and from overhead, northern eagle owls, greater spotted eagles, and black kites. Hares forage on summer grasses. Beavers build dens on floating peat islands, inaccessible to most predators, making them attractive nest sites also for common terns and black-headed, herring, and mew gulls.

Some 230 species of migratory and nesting birds include northern hazelhens, northern black grouse, willow ptarmigans, Siberian jays and, on the water, black and white-winged scoters, long-tailed ducks, tufted pochards, bean and greater white-fronted geese. Altogether 15 rare bird species listed in the Russian Red Book are protected in the reserve.

Pollution from Cherepovets Industrial Center, 19 miles (30 km) north is a problem, though the zapovednik's ecosystem cleanses much of it with beneficial effect for the entire region's biodiversity.

---

**FURTHER INFORMATION**

Director, Darvinsky Zapovednik, Russia 162543, Vologodskaya oblast, Cherepovetsky raion, p/o Ploskovo, p. Borok, Tel: (+7-820-2) 66-69-70.

---

# KALUZHSKY ZASEKI ZAPOVEDNIK

Scientists in the mid-1980s rediscovered this long-forgotten tract of old-growth, virtually untouched broadleaf forest, teeming with wildlife, with oak trees dating to Peter the Great, preserved now as Kaluzhsky Zaseki Zapovednik. Deeply hidden within and now buffered by a larger, younger tract, this 79-square-mile (204-km$^2$) dense forest remnant at the edge of the great northern forests, about 155 miles (250 km) southeast of Moscow, once was protected as a natural defense against fierce nomadic horsemen from the steppes. Now it offers safety for wolves, lynx, wild boars, moose, big roe and red deer (cousins of American elks), and endangered European bison (thought was being given to reintroducing them here when a small herd in neighboring Orlovskoe Polesie National Park wandered in on their own).

Beavers, river otters, and muskrats make homes in and around streams. Badgers and foxes prey on voles and other small rodents, food base also for martens, ermines, and mink.

Among some 167 bird species are such endangered (nationally or locally) raptors as greater and lesser spotted eagles, booted and short-toed eagles, peregrine falcons, marsh hawks, marsh harriers, black kites, goshawks, and rough-legged hawks.

Descendants of birds that Ivan Turgenev saw when he wrote, in *A Hunter's Sketches*, "How lovely the forest is in late autumn when the woodcocks return (and) the light air is filled with the perfume of fall, like the scent of wine," may be here today, joined now by their cousins, common and great snipes, and along waterways, white and rare black storks, gray herons, and common cranes.

---

**FURTHER INFORMATION**

Director, Kaluzhsky Zaseki Zapovednik, Russia 249720, Kaluzhskaya oblast, s. Ulyanovo, ul. B., Sovetskaya, 75, Tel: (+7-084-43) 1-19-32.

---

# KANDALAKSHSKY ZAPOVEDNIK

Common eiders, prized for their soft, warm down feathers, were declining when this 272-square-mile (705-km²) zapovednik was established in 1932 to protect them from commercial collectors who not only took the down from nests, mostly for export, but often from the birds themselves, killing them and collecting their eggs as well.

This protected place provides sanctuary to many thousands of eiders and others along the north coast of the Barents Sea and on some 350 islands in the White Sea above the arctic circle—more than 270 species of birds as well as marine mammals and rare plants.

The cacophony can be deafening 24 hours a day when tens of thousands of birds of some 50 species are in concentrated residence during the two months when the sun never dips below the horizon—thin- and thick-billed murres on largest ledges, making no nests but securing their one egg between their feet and covering it with their abdomens. Razorbills do the same but in more protected cliffside niches.

Black-legged kittiwakes, eiders, and Atlantic puffins prefer outskirts of the squabbling colonies. Oystercatchers are among the noisiest—but so are arctic terns, mew gulls, and goldeneyes, among others.

White-tailed sea eagles circle above, along with such uncommon raptors as golden eagles, gyr-falcons, ospreys, and peregrines. Smaller tundra-nesters include Lapland buntings and meadow pipits. In forests inland are capercaillies, black, hazel and willow grouse, and eagle owls with such mammals as blue hares and, among predators, wolves, foxes, wolverines, lynx, bears as well as pine martens, ermines, and weasels, all of which occasionally ford icy waters out to larger islands.

Bearded and ringed seals form breeding colonies as soon as ice starts to melt. Whales visit coastal waters, though only white (aka beluga) whales in significant numbers—often several dozen in Kandalakshsky Bay, several hundred in the Barents Sea.

Greatest threats are oil spills and continuous pollution from oil products in the upper bay.

---

**FURTHER INFORMATION**

Director, Kanlakshsky Zapovednik, 184040 Murmansk oblast,

Kandalaksha, ul. Lineinaya 35, Tel: (+7-815-33) 2-32-50, 2-23-19,

E-mail: Kand_reserve@com.mels.ru (and) ask_kand_reserve@com.mels.ru

---

# KOSTOMUKSHSKY ZAPOVEDNIK

This zapovednik protects a belt of 184 square miles (476 km$^2$) of pristine boreal forest along the border shared by Russia and Finland, with an abundance of wildlife species including reindeer, wolves, brown bears, lynx, wolverines, and golden eagles.

Beaver colonies are on and around most of the 250 lakes and rivers, as are mink and occasionally river otters. Black-throated loons, whooper swans, and bean geese nest on shores and islands and sometimes on beaver dwellings.

Capercaillies and black grouse dance in springtime display for mates in forest clearings alive with songs of small passerines—chaffinches, bramblings, rustic buntings, chiffchaffs, and redstarts. More than 650 species of butterflies and moths sip nectar from flowers of bog bilberries, cowberries, cranberries and cloudberries which later produce bountiful harvests for bears and many birds.

Great gray owls swoop down by day as well as night for voles and lemmings. More than 100 of the 130 bird species nest, including white-tailed sea eagles, ospreys, and peregrine falcons. Long-tailed ducks are abundant in migration and goldeneyes, mallards and teals all summer.

Many are gone by October's first snowfall but some small birds can make it when snowpack is a yard (meter) thick with temperatures of -35°F (-40°C)—among them two-barred, parrot, and common crossbills, diminutive kinglets, and Eurasian dippers which continue to sing and do their thing around (and in) unfrozen rapids of the Kammenaya River.

Kostomukshsky is part of a green belt which in 1990 joined with reserves on the Finnish side of the border to form a trans-boundary area for cooperative conservation and sustainable nature use, a proposed U.N. World Heritage Site. Unfortunately, barbed wire fence now along the border impedes animals' west–east movements and poaching has almost halved reindeer numbers, also moose, and with them, wolves. Other problems include logging on adjacent lands and pollution from the Kostomukshsky iron ore factory.

---

**FURTHER INFORMATION**

Director, 186989 Karelia, Kostomuksha, ul. Priozernaya 2, Tel: (+7-814-59) 9-35-24, E-mail: kost.zap@karelia.ru

---

# NIZHNESVIRSKY ZAPOVEDNIK

For tens of thousands of water-oriented birds, this is a critical rest and refueling stop in long migratory flights between southern winter homes and far northern nesting grounds. It's no less important to thousands of others which stay and nest or make permanent homes here—in all some 261 bird species—along with a flourishing mammal population that includes brown bears, wolves, lynx, and fierce wolverines.

Just 50 miles (80 km) southeast of St. Petersburg, Nizhnesvirsky protects 131 square miles (416 km²) around and in Lake Ladoga, one of the world's largest lakes—136 by 52 miles (219 × 83 km) with average depth of 167 feet (51 m)—and with it a mosaic of muskeg bogs, sphagnum swamps, and taiga forest, the moist subarctic coniferous forest that begins where tundra ends.

Badgers and foxes dig deep nest burrows to raise young. Ermines, European mink, and pine martens thrive on rodents and other small prey. American mink, transplanted here, and furry, short-legged raccoon dogs, brought from eastern Siberia, both are widespread now. Half-ton moose wander through seasonally. Mountain hares nibble on willow shoots all year.

Ubiquitous beavers make more habitat for all, felling trees which then open up space for forage as well as providing hollow trunks for homes, building dams that create ponds which become homes for fish and feeding and nesting grounds for otters and wading birds. Fish species numbered 33 at recent count; with over 350 species of mushrooms in the woods.

But most notable are the enormous numbers of birds, starting in late April with arrival of tens of thousands of waterfowl—barnacle, white-fronted, and bean geese; puddle ducks as mallards, green-winged teal, garganey, northern pintails, northern shovelers; divers as tufted ducks, greater scaups, common and white-winged scoters. Whooper and Bewick's swans enjoy shallow water's edges. Great bitterns nest in reeds. Common cranes, which can forage while marshes are still snow-covered, gather in flocks of 50 or 60 in fall.

Corncrakes and spotted crakes are inconspicuously abundant in wet meadows. In fields are Eurasian curlews, whimbrels, black-tailed godwits, and common snipes, sometimes spotted redshanks, marsh sandpipers, bar-tailed godwits, Eurasian oystercatchers, and red-necked phalaropes. In woodlands are black grouse, white-billed capercaillies, hazel grouse, willow ptarmigans, Eurasian woodcocks.

The birdwatcher's dream-list goes on—among owls, short-eared, common long-eared, eagle, Ural, tawny, great gray, northern hawk, and Eurasian pygmy; among passerines, Lapland buntings, horned larks, red-throated and meadow pipits, whinchats, grasshopper, river, marsh, booted, and reed warblers, reed buntings, and bluethroats.

Rare "Red Book" raptors include white-tailed eagles, ospreys, golden eagles. Rare, shy white-backed woodpeckers find their required undisturbed woodlands here.

---

**FURTHER INFORMATION**

Director, Nizhnesvirsky Zapovednik, Russia, 187710, Leningrad oblast, Lodeinoye Pole, ul. Pravy bereg r. Svir, 1, Tel: (+7-812-64) 2-63-61, E-mail: orlan@orlan.spb.su

---

# RDEISKY AND POLISTOVSKY ZAPOVEDNIKS

More than half the enormous Polistovo-Lovatskoye Swamp—a virtually impassable wetland ecosystem of bogs, marshes, and sphagnum, largest in northwestern Russia—is protected in adjoining Rdeisky and Polistovsky Zapovedniks, together more than 300 square miles (805 km²) of conserved land.

Populating its undisturbed vastness, designated a Ramsar Wetland of International Importance, is the largest nesting assemblage of long-billed Eurasian curlews (aka whaup) in Europe, with greater golden plovers, black-throated (arctic) loons, ospreys, and white-tailed eagles.

Within the wetland are a multitude of large and small lakes with ridges of coniferous and broadleaf woodland communities. These attract northern hazel hens and capercaillies fanning out tails in courtship dances, shy black storks, and moose, badgers, European mink, and Alpine hares. Among protected plants are superb orchids, including moorland spotted, meadow, greater and lesser butterfly, bird's nest, fragrant, Baltic marsh, and common twayblade.

OPPOSITE: The great gray owl's feathery facial discs detect faint sounds which they direct to bony cups surrounding asymmetrical ear openings to triangulate and precisely locate prey, plunging through two feet (60 cm) of snow to grasp in their talons an unsuspecting rodent. Tall, silent, golden-eyed, they range through boreal forests across Russia, Norway, Canada, and Alaska.

Many of these floral and faunal species have all but disappeared elsewhere in the region; but here one still finds golden eagles, great gray shrikes, greater spotted eagles, northern eagle owls, willow ptarmigans.

**FURTHER INFORMATION**

Director, Rdeisky Zapovednik, Russia 175270, Novgorodskaya oblast, Kholm, ul. Chelpanova, 27, Tel: (+7-816-54) 5-14-08, E-mail: rdeysky@mail.ru

# Tsentralno-Lesnoy Zapovednik

Lynx, preying on mountain hares, roam this ancient boreal forest, one of Europe's last stands of virgin spruce woodland. Great brown bears in one of the densest populations anywhere of these half-ton mammals consume fare ranging from small rodents to wild boars, moose, and a bountiful berry harvest in this 272-square-mile (705-km²) reserve halfway between Moscow and St. Petersburg. Located on the Great Russian Divide between the Volga, West Dvina (Daugava), and Dneiper Rivers, its waterways drain into three seas—the Baltic, Black, and Caspian.

Rare golden eagles and black storks make homes in tree hummocks amid swampy muskeg formed by thousands of years of undisturbed isolation, essential habitat for many, including small tree pipits, yellow wagtails, and whinchats. Of more than 200 bird species, 42 are permanent residents and at least 137 nest—in spruce forests, chaffinches, wood warblers, and wrens; in mixed forests, chiffchaffs, goldcrests, willow tits. Open swamps work for common shrikes, northern lapwings, and Eurasian curlews. Willow ptarmigans, common cranes, and great gray shrikes nest on muskeg bogs. Capercaillies dance on 37 courtship leks in nearby sphagnum forests, 25 or more cocks gathering in each to strut and show off their fancy tails, unmindful of greater spotted eagles, merlins, and red-footed and peregrine falcons that scout these same places.

Furry raccoon dogs hunt along rivers and in swampy meadows. Pine martens weave in and out of fallen trees after rodents. Tiny common weasels dart into mouse holes to seize their prey. Tall, lanky wolves pursue moose and wild boars. River otters are everywhere there's water. The dense bear population is due in part to efforts of a dedicated biologist, Dr. Valentin Pazhetnov, who for years has saved cubs orphaned when mothers were killed by hunters and rehabilitated and released them here.

Over 250 butterflies in the reserve include beautiful peacocks and mourning-cloaks.

Primary problems are logging and wetland drainage close to reserve borders, which upsets sensitive hydrology of muskeg bogs, a threat that will remain until the entire muskeg receives (as proposed) protected status.

**FURTHER INFORMATION**

Director, Tsentralno-Lesnoy Zapovednik, Russia 172513, Tverskaya oblast, Nelidovsky raion, p. Zapovednoye, Tel/Fax: (+7-082-66) 2-24-33, 2-24-20, E-mail: c_forest@mail.ru

## ALSO OF INTEREST

In addition to zapovedniks are a number of national parks in northwest Russia. Among them are **Kenozersky**, 537 square miles (1,392 km²) including 81 square miles (234 km²) of lakes with elk, brown bears, wolves, beavers. Also **Yugyd Va**, 7,304 square miles (18,917 km²) on the western side of the Urals with numerous glaciers, spruce and white birch woods. Elk, sable, martens, brown bears, and wolves are common, as are reindeer. Raptors include golden and white-tailed eagles and fish hawks.

# SOUTHWEST RUSSIA—EASTERN EUROPEAN FOREST, STEPPE AND CASPIAN SEMIDESERT

## ASTRAKHANSKY ZAPOVEDNIK

World-renowned bird congregations fill Astrakhansky Zapovednik where the Volga River splits into a fan of hundreds of channels and islands before emptying into the Caspian Sea. More than 250 avian species have been recorded in this 258-square-mile (668-km²) reserve, one of Russia's oldest, where trees, skies, and waters are filled with birds and their songs and wild calls—a U.N. World Biosphere Reserve and designated Ramsar Wetland of World Importance.

White-tailed sea eagles, ospreys, and Saker falcons are among 27 endangered species. Thousands of mute swans, once nearly extinct in the region, nest. Endangered Dalmatian pelicans with curly head-tufts skim water's surfaces for small fish. Great cormorants gather in noisy colonies in riverside willows. Large numbers of diverse wading birds—great white herons, little egrets, glossy ibises, black-crowned night herons, endangered Eurasian spoonbills and pond herons—share colonies.

Gull and tern colonies attract carnivorous catfish hoping to make a meal of chicks fallen or strayed from nests.

More than 25,000 ducks spend a quiet time moulting here in August, many after nesting deep in the reserve's wild interior—mallards, pintails, green-winged teals, garganeys, gadwalls, wigeons, northern shovelers.

Golden orioles weave hanging nest-baskets in willows. Reed buntings, Savi's warblers, and bearded tits nest in thick reeds. Inconspicuous Eurasian cuckoos stealthily lay eggs in other species' nests, especially warblers'; the young are then abandoned to be raised by their hosts.

Wild boars are largest among 30 mammal species. Smallest are tiny harvest mice, nesting on tall plant stems. Major predators are foxes, raccoon dogs, weasels, and mink. Beavers and muskrats are on every water's edge, as are frogs, filling night air from April on with their musical chimes (and croaks), resting on pads of blossoming water lilies and endangered sacred lotuses. Among 61 fish species are important migrants such as endangered herring and, occasionally, sturgeon.

Problems are many. Volga power plants have altered water flow and fish migrations. Poaching and overfishing have brought sturgeon species to the brink of extinction. Deliberate fire-setting has destroyed bird-nesting and fish-spawning grounds, and unregulated tourism has disturbed all wildlife. Conservationists in local communities and fisheries are attempting to help.

### FURTHER INFORMATION

Director, Astrakhansky Zapovednik, Russia 414021, Astrakhan, Naberezhnaya Tsarev 119, Tel; (+7-8512) 30-17-64.

## BOGDINSKO-BASKUNCHAKSKY ZAPOVEDNIK

Elegant demoiselle cranes with snowy head-plumes return every year to perform elaborate courtship rituals with the same mates they have joined for life—only one of the rare, endangered species protected on the plains of this 73-square-mile (189-km²) U.N. Biosphere Reserve.

Thousands of saiga antelopes, with translucent amber horns and outsize noses that can swell to grotesque proportions during rut, travel in migration through this semidesert where broad, dry steppes east of the Volga River enter Russia. Here in the shadow of Mount Bolshoye Bogdo, rising nearly 600 feet (200 m) from surrounding grassland, is 47-square-mile (121-km²) Lake Baskunchak, largest saline lake in Russia, noted for caves and rock formations and, with the region's many freshwater lakes and pools, important habitat for many wildlife species, both migratory and resident.

Engaging little hamsters, gerbils, and jerboas of several species—popular pets around the world, native here—thrive, with ground squirrels and other small rodents, in this arid habitat and attract a large range of species that prey on them. These include red foxes and taller Corsac foxes; golden jackals; reddish-brown Siberian polecats (subject of intense poaching); handsome, endangered marbled polecats and their relatives, ermines and weasels; a few wildcats; and numerous birds of prey.

# RUSSIAN FEDERATION

Endangered steppe and golden eagles and Saker falcons nest, as do rare black-winged stilts, avocets and stone curlews. Fruit-tree groves planted years ago are now wooded areas where long-eared owls and woodpeckers find homes and moose and roe deer browse. Gnome-like long-eared hedgehogs dig for millipedes but gladly take any large insect that comes along.

**FURTHER INFORMATION**

Director, Bogdinsko-Baskunchaksky Zapovednik, Russia 416501, Astrakhanskaya Oblast, Akhtubinsk, Microraion, Melioratorov, 19, #1, Tel: (+7-851-41) 3-14-94, E-mail: bogdozap@achtuba.astranet.ru

## CHERNY ZEMLY ZAPOVEDNIK

Tens of thousands of stocky little saiga antelopes once common through the region, now increasingly rare, raise clouds of dust as they race over miles of this arid zapovednik, once the Caspian Sea bottom, in southwestern Russia.

At speeds up to 60 miles an hour (100 kmh), their bizarre bulbous noses able to filter out dust in this flat, semidesert place, they can outrun packs of lanky wolves for which they are major prey base. But young calves on this major saiga calving and breeding ground are easy victims, and even adult speed cannot outrace motorized poachers' vehicles when the antelopes venture outside reserve borders (sometimes even inside).

Cherny Zemly covers altogether over 470 square miles (1,220 km²) in two sections—desert-like plain to the south, with a smaller northwest section where colonies of wading birds nest on shores and islands of shallow, saline Manych-Gudilo Reservoir. Rare Eurasian spoonbills and eastern white and Dalmatian pelicans raise young along with great and little egrets, great cormorants, whooper and mute swans, and ruddy shelducks, even though some have to fly to freshwater elsewhere in order to get food for chicks.

Exquisite endangered demoiselle cranes, dove-gray with long black chest feathers, red eyes, and streaming white cheek plumes lay large, spotted greenish eggs in bare nest scrapes on arid steppes—among a broad wildlife spectrum making a living on this barren land.

FOLLOWING PAGES: For more than a century scientists puzzled over classification of the saiga, this goatlike, gazelle-like, sheep-like antelope with short, stocky body, spindly legs, mane on the bottom of its neck, bulging eyes that can see almost 360 degrees, and fleshy, humped nose. But all serve a function for this fleet desert wanderer. Large noses filter airborne dust during migration in herds of 100,000 or more over dry steppes of Russia and Kazakhstan, and warm the air before it reaches lungs in icy winters. Poaching for translucent ringed horns for supposed aphrodisiac and medicinal use has reduced once large herds to worrisome remnants. INSET: Newborn saiga.

Handsome endangered marbled polecats are attracted by a range of rodents—hamsters, voles, ground squirrels—as are birds of prey: imperial and steppe eagles, long-legged buzzards, white-tailed sea eagles, Eurasian griffons, and Egyptian and cinereous vultures.

**FURTHER INFORMATION**

Director, Cherny Zemly Zapovednik, Russia 359240, Kalmykia Republic, Chernozemelsky raion, Komsomolsky, Tel: (+7-847-43) 9-12-54.

## ORENBURGSKY ZAPOVEDNIK

Orenburgsky Zapovednik is Russia's only zapovednik protecting every aspect of its last remaining steppe ecosystems. In four separate regions along the Kazakhstan/Orenburg Region border are steppe habitats ranging from woodlands to wetlands alongside more than 20 freshwater springs and flat, semidesert plains at the foot of rolling mountains.

Dwelling here are some 48 mammal species, including beavers, lynx, wolves, and red foxes, and—resident or transitory—some 200 bird species, including vulnerable upland buzzards, imperial and steppe eagles, and lovely demoiselle cranes.

Great bustards, once thought extinct here—one of the world's largest birds, males weighing up to 45 pounds (21 kg)—now nest. Endangered little bustards, pied avocets, and golden plovers are among waves of water-oriented birds which stop by in migration between far northern Russia and Europe and central Asia.

European hares graze grassy hillsides. Badgers den in rocky mountain caves. Roe deer and wild boars shelter in woodland tracts. Beavers build dams along rivers. Weasels, American mink, and ermines prey on ground squirrels and others among a large rodent population, including steppe marmots (aka bobak).

Wild flowers blaze over hillsides and grasslands in spring and early summer—a palette of red, yellow, magenta, and blue tulips, purple pasqueflowers, yellow Siberian pea-trees, pink-blossoming Russian almonds and, later, magenta, red, and purple gladiolus, and military orchids.

All these flora and fauna have returned since protection began in 1989. Chief problems are fires, some human-set, which every year destroy habitat, and separation of the four regions, making oversight difficult.

**FURTHER INFORMATION**

Director, Orenburgsky Zapovednik, Russia 460023, Orenburg Ul. Magistralnaya 9, Tel/Fax: (+7-3532) 56-76-79.

## RUSSIAN FEDERATION

# TSENTRALNO-CHERNOZEMNY ZAPOVEDNIK

Majestic nesting golden, steppe, and white-tailed eagles are among rare and endangered species finding sanctuary in this virgin forest-swamp steppe territory. This 50-square-mile (130-km$^2$) U.N. Biosphere Reserve in the mid-Russian uplands, only six miles (10 km) from Kursk, preserves the world's last intact chernozem, a broad strip of deep rich humus known as "black earth", a yard or more deep.

Mostly converted to agriculture, here it is home to more than 800 species of butterflies, more than 200 bird species, and 46 kinds of mammals, including moose, roe deer, wild boars, red foxes, badgers, Siberian polecats, and blind mole-rats. Living entirely underground, these bizarre creatures with no tails or ear cavities, their eyes closed under a layer of skin, emerge only once in their lives, to burrow a new den.

A succession of brilliant wildflowers burst into bloom from early spring on—purple pasque-flowers, golden-yellow cowslips and pheasant's eyes, blue forget-me-nots, rare, shimmering azure feathergrass and fernleaf peonies, rose daphnes and a succession of wild fruit trees—cherries, apples, pears, blackthorn prunes.

Flutelike songs of European golden orioles float through the canopy in summer, contrasting with screeches of quarrelsome corncrakes. Brilliant Eurasian (European) rollers, aquamarine with bright chestnut backs, nest in hollow trees, as do hoopoes with showy Indian-chief crests. Black kites sometimes re-use nests of other large species such as northern goshawks and common buzzards. Other rare nesters are peregrine and Saker falcons, long-legged buzzards, and Levant sparrowhawks.

Greatest problem is layout of this preserve in six separate tracts vulnerable to encroachment and poaching from surrounding villages. A system for linking corridors is in planning stage.

---

**FURTHER INFORMATION**

Director, Tsentralno-Chernozemny Zapovednik, Russia 307028, Kursk oblast, Kursk raion, pos. Zapovedny, Tel/Fax: (+7-071-2) 57-72-94, E-mail: zapoved@kursknet.ru

---

# ALSO OF INTEREST

In addition to zapovedniks found in Southwest Russia there are a number of important national parks, among them **Nizhnyaya Kama**, 100 square miles (261 km$^2$), particularly good for raptors, including white-tailed, golden, short-toed, and imperial eagles, and Saker and peregrine falcons.

# URAL MOUNTAINS

## SHULGAN-TASH ZAPOVEDNIK

Hulking brown bears, endangered short-tailed snake eagles, and the last wild bees native to central Russia—wildlife from nearly every biogeographic zone in Eurasia—find homes here in the southern Ural Mountains.

This welcoming habitat, bounded by two rivers, intersected by streams, canyons, and ridges, covered with forests and mountain meadows, attracts some 57 mammal species, 198 birds, and 60 types of plant communities made up of 789 species of vascular plants, over 100 of them endangered.

Omnivorous brown bears weighing a half-ton or more (500+ kg) feed in broadleaf forests, on berries when available. So do badgers, which take advantage of the many caves for daytime roosts and hibernation. Enormous Kap Cave, formed by millions of years' erosion by the Shulgan River, is home to thousands of bats and holds wall drawings dating back some 15,000 years, recording presence of mammoths, rhinoceros, and other ancient wildlife.

Russian flying squirrels nest in hollow oak and linden trunks. Mountain hares graze in mountain meadows. Otters frolic and den around stream banks. Moose winter here but in spring swim across the Belaya River to graze in larch forests to the west.

Tawny and great gray owls feed on small rodents. Black storks nest in secluded wetlands. Eurasian dippers plunge into fast-flowing streams and walk on the bottom, feeding on invertebrates.

But perhaps most important species protected in Shulgan-Tash—and a main reason for its existence—is the endangered wild Burzyan honeybee, famed for high production of delicious golden honey, protected and cared for here by rangers descended from beekeepers using centuries-old skills. It is probably the only reserve ever created to protect a bee.

The zapovednik, 87 square miles (225 km²) buffered by adjacent **Bashkirin National Park** on the south and west and **Altin Solok State Nature Sanctuary** on north and east, has environmental education and ecotourism programs, with nature trails, campgrounds, guesthouse, and beekeeping demonstration areas. Greatest threat is proposed construction of a dam on the Belaya River which would flood important habitat.

---

### FURTHER INFORMATION

Director, Shulgan-Tash Zapovednik, Russia 453535, Republic of Bashkortostan, Burzyansky raion, s. Irgizly, Tel: (+7-347-55) 3-22-17, 3-37-21, E-mail: Land13@bausers.bashmail.sovmail.spring.com

# GREAT CAUCASUS

## KAVKAZSKY ZAPOVEDNIK

Sure-footed chamois skitter about high, narrow ledges with gravity-defying agility that enables them and even their newborn kids to escape most predators, including golden eagles, wolves, lynx, and brown bears that share their range in beautiful Kavkazsky Zapovednik. Not far behind them are other agile ungulates, including Eurasian tur, and, grazing at lower elevations in this 1,016-square-mile (2,633-km²) reserve in the Caucasus Mountains of southwestern Russia, rare European bison (a Caucasian subspecies), maral (red) deer, roe deer, and formidably tusked wild boars, among 59 mammal species.

Rare bird populations include, among some 192 species, bearded and griffon vultures, Caucasian blackcocks, and Caucasian snowcocks.

The Caucasus Mountain region, site of this reserve in southwestern Russia, has been called one of the most biologically diverse, beautiful, and endangered in the northern hemisphere.

Some 1,500 species of vascular plants have been recorded—20 of them endemic—including gigantic chestnuts, groves of rare, old-growth yews and box trees, old-growth maples thriving at nearly 9,000 feet (2,745 m), and Nordmann firs almost 200 feet (60 m) tall.

Serious problems which have caused drastic declines in some wildlife numbers in recent years include poaching (here, as elsewhere, sometimes even by officials). Rangers are poorly equipped, without reliable means of transportation and communication. Large-scale commercial timber harvesting along borders threatens valuable tree species. And now, plans have been revived to build a road which would violate environmental laws, cut migration routes, and require felling unique relict forests.

---

### FURTHER INFORMATION

Director, Kavkazsky Zapovednik, Karl Marx Street, 8 Sochi, 354341 Krasnodarski Krai, Russia, Tel/Fax: (+7-862-2) 44-51-36, 44-52-65; Director of Adygeya Unit, Sovetskaya Street, 187 Maikop 352700, Adygeya Republic, Russia, Tel/Fax: (+7-862-2) 69-20-03.

# Central Siberia

## Olekminsky Zapovednik

Olekminsky Zapovednik's 3,270 square miles (8,471 km²) of virgin boreal forest—a U.N. World Heritage Site—offer sanctuary to browsers from enormous moose to tiny musk deer along with their numerous predators. These include wolves, lynx, massive brown bears, red foxes, and fierce wolverines, small but able to take on prey much larger than themselves, including reindeer.

Golden eagles—largest and most majestic of their tribe—nest, as do dusky, rare hooded cranes, among 10 endangered bird species, including ospreys, demoiselle cranes, black storks, peregrine falcons, and little and eastern curlews.

Hawk owls hunt by day but call by night, a bubbling "prullulu" trill, soft accompaniment to great gray owls' booming "hu-hu-hoo." Black woodpeckers 18 inches (45 cm) long announce their presence with manic, high-pitched laughs and long, powerful drum rolls on forest trees. Others among 180 bird species sharing this habitat are red-necked nightingales, Siberian (dark-sided) flycatchers, hazel grouse, capercaillies.

Endemic Siberian sables, hunted to the brink of extinction for their rich brown fur, have come back with protection and number some 2,500 here today. In addition to virgin woodlands which cover 87.9 percent of the reserve are remnant meadows along riverbanks and wetlands that cover 2.1 percent and provide critical habitat for grazers, birds, amphibians, and other aquatic species. The entire zapovednik is covered with permafrost 300–600 feet (100–200 m) thick, topped with 6–12 feet (2–4 m) of soil that thaws in summer, allowing vigorous tundra vegetation to come to life.

Remoteness has made monitoring difficult, given short staffs, which are also charged with researching a neighboring reserve, established with assistance of World Wide Fund for Nature and 1.5 times the size of the zapovednik—an enormous natural treasure-house.

---

**FURTHER INFORMATION**

Director, Russia 678100 Sakha Republic (Yakutia), Olekminsk, ul. Logovaya d. 31, Tel/Fax: (+7-41-138) 2-10-32, E-mail: ecos@sakha.ru

---

OPPOSITE: Gray wolves have the greatest natural range of any land mammals except humans—over northern U.S., Canada, Europe, and temperate-to-polar Russia. Highly social, they form family and hunting packs of two to 12 or more—but only the dominant or "alpha" pair breed, ensuring best survival chance to their pups. They hunt in single file—in snow, stepping in pawprints up to six inches (15 cm) long of preceding animal—and are able to bring down much larger prey, outrunning them in bounds up 16 feet (5 m), crushing their bones with jaws that exert pressures up to 1,500 pounds per square inch (100 kg/cm²).

# SOUTHERN SIBERIA AND BAIKAL

Some of Russia's rarest and most spectacular wildlife roam its Golden Mountains, in deep virgin forests, flowering meadows, rushing streams, rivers, waterfalls, and snowy peaks between central Asia and the vast "Great Belt" of arid, treeless Eurasian steppes.

Endangered snow leopards prey on roe deer in mountain fastness. Massive brown bears fatten on berries but help themselves to Siberian chipmunks and larger mammals when hunger and chance dictate, as do small but ferocious wolverines. Imperial and golden eagles, largest of their tribe, soar on seven-foot (2-m) wingspreads over alpine grasslands, folding their wings and plummeting downward to capture alpine hares before their victims can glimpse their predator.

Three zapovedniks covering 6,848 square miles (17,742 km²) of this varied, welcoming habitat are set aside as strict nature preserves with no human disturbance other than scientific observers and closely supervised tourism.

## ALTAISKY ZAPOVEDNIK (THE GOLDEN MOUNTAINS OF ALTAI)

Wild, woebegone cries of elsewhere rare black-throated loons are heard on more than 1,000 lakes nestled amid mountainous terrain. Thousands of water-oriented birds are attracted to this 3,401-square-mile (8,812-km²) zapovednik and U.N. World Heritage Site to nest and rest on migration—rare black storks, white-tailed eagles, stately whooper swans, horned grebes carrying downy chicks on their backs, great cormorants, common goldeneyes, green-winged teals.

Brown bears follow retreating snowfields in spring, feeding on mice, tubers, and anything else edible, starting around Lake Teletskoye which stretches like a narrow blue ribbon 50 miles (78 km) between mountain ranges and holds some 1,400 billion cubic feet (40 billion cu. m) of crystalline water.

Wild reindeer, Siberian wapiti, and tiny musk deer forage in and around Siberian pine woodlands hundreds of years old which grow everywhere up to the tree line. Above this, rabbit-like alpine pikas share greenery with rare Argali sheep and Siberian ibex, able to graze steepest cliff faces. Wolverines, wolves, and lynx prey on small mammals throughout rocky terrain but leave higher elevations to densely furred snow leopards.

Great spotted and six other woodpecker species rattle woodlands where boreal and northern eagle owls hoot after dark—among more than 300 bird species, 180 of which nest here. On and under trees are 26 orchid species and 35 ferns.

A lamentable pollution source is Baikonur rocket launch site in neighboring Kazakhstan, which drops empty fuel containers and other space debris with every launch, defacing one of earth's most remote, beautiful, and pristine places. Other problems are overgrazing, logging, and agricultural activities on adjoining lands. To ensure protection of Argali sheep, Altai snow-cocks, and endemic plant species, it's been proposed that steppe lands on the right bank of the Chulyshman River be added to the zapovednik.

Nearest cities are Gorno-Altaisk and Barnaul, which has an international airport. Access to Altaisky is by rough dirt road and remote parts only by helicopter, on foot or horseback. Tourism is seen as helpful but at least until recently, except for a lodge at the southern end of Lake Teletskoye, few facilities were available.

**FURTHER INFORMATION**

Director, Altaisky Zapovednik, Russia 659564, Altai Republic, Turachaksky raion, p.Yailyu, Tel: (+7-388-43) 2-64-86, 2-28-35.

# KATUNSKY ZAPOVEDNIK

Endangered snow leopards prey on Alpine pikas and voles high in the tundra, part of a large and varied mammal population in this 579-square-mile (1,501-km²) U.N. World Heritage Site and Biosphere Reserve southwest of Altaisky.

Sleek otters frolic and den along the Katun River for which this reserve is named. Flowing from high in the central Altai Mountains. The river gathers speed and volume as it passes through taiga forests and meadows which are home to brown bears, foxes, wolves, wolverines, lynx, and grazing ungulates such as Siberian deer or marals, moose, roe and tiny musk deer, and at higher levels, rare Siberian ibex and Altai Argali mountain sheep.

Imperial eagles, endangered black storks and lovely demoiselle cranes are among 120 bird species. Of these, 80 nest, including golden eagles and peregrine falcons on cliff niches, and among smaller varieties, European nuthatches, Eurasian nutcrackers, wheatears, ortolan buntings, hazel grouse, and fearless little dippers which dive into swiftest river currents to feed on bottom invertebrates.

Largest glacial system in Siberia runs through Katunsky, with 148 individual glaciers covering nearly 30 square miles (80 km²), source of mountain lakes and streams that eventually feed the great Katun River. Problems include illegal hunting, grazing, fishing, mining. Tourism is considered an important part of this reserve's future, but at least until recently, access and facilities were minimal.

## RUSSIAN FEDERATION

**FURTHER INFORMATION**

Director, Katunsky Zapovednik, 659760 Altai Republic, Ust-Koksinsky raion, s. Ust-Koksa, P.O. Box 24, Tel: (+7-388-48) 2-29-46, E-mail: katunski@zapoved.uks.gorny.ru

# KUZNETSKY ALATAU ZAPOVEDNIK

Kuznetsky Alatau protects high peaks of the Altai-Sayan Mountains of western Siberia, some 2,867 square miles (7,429 km²) of taiga forests, flowering high meadows, and rushing mountain streams that are home to a dense, richly varied wildlife. Among these are reindeer, brown bears, musk and roe deer, wolves, lynx, sables, ermines, golden eagles and 273 other bird species, of which 229 migrate here for the breeding season. Most common at lower elevations are yellowhammers, red crossbills, scarlet rosefinches, great tits, and higher up, Pallas' reed buntings, twites, solitary snipes, and rock ptarmigans.

Beavers colonize rivers. Siberian chipmunks and red and long-tailed ground squirrels along with dozens of kinds of shrews, voles, and other small rodents are prey base for wolverines and badgers as well as larger carnivores.

Among rare "Red Book" bird species are black storks, Bewick's swans, hooded cranes, ospreys, steppe, golden and imperial eagles, Pallas' and white-tailed sea eagles, gyrfalcons, and Saker and peregrine falcons.

Colorful flower communities cover alpine meadows in spring—brilliant orange Asian trollflowers, pink martagon lilies, Pallas' primulas—and in fall, purple columbines, pink persicaria, and Daurian goldenrod, among succulent ripe bilberries sought by birds and mammals alike.

Worst threat is atmospheric pollution, especially acid rain. At least 68 industrial pollution sources are in the plains below the reserve in Kemerovo Oblast. Each year hundreds of tons of harmful chemicals rain down. So far, the reserve's waters are clean, filtered by high-altitude sphagnum swamps. However, since abolishment of the Russian Committee for Protection of the Environment in May 2000, the Natural Resources Ministry has pressured for surveys to search for gold in the reserve. An ecotourism program has been launched to raise conservation funds, and the reserve now offers a variety of trips featuring hiking, trail rides, summer skiing, and more. Guests are housed in a rugged cabin on Fish Lake.

**FURTHER INFORMATION**

Director, Kuznetsky Alatau Zapovednik, Russia 652888, Kemerovo Oblast, Mezhdurechinsk, Prospekt Shakhterov 33/1, Tel/Fax: (+7-384-75) 3-27-28, 3-19-05, E-mail: alatau@rikt.ru

# BAIKALO-LENSKY ZAPOVEDNIK

This zapovednik guards the northwestern rim of Lake Baikal, a U.N. World Heritage Site, deepest lake in the world, holding one-fifth of earth's freshwater. In its 2,548 square miles (6,600 km²) of boreal forests, alpine meadows, steppes, and hundreds of pure lakes and streams scientists have identified 49 mammal species and 240 kinds of birds.

The shoreline is known as "Brown Bear Coast" from the numbers that come down from mountain dens in spring. Barguzin sables, once near extinction for their luxuriant fur, have rebounded and now are the reserve's most numerous predators. Others are lynx, wolves, and wolverines, preying on Siberian chipmunks, mountain hares, northern pikas, and smaller rodents.

Wild reindeer seek out high summer meadows. Siberian wapiti stay through harsh winters as do Siberian roe deer, grazing the coasts year-round in the company of frolicsome river otters.

Baikal seals—world's only freshwater seals—warm themselves on rocks after dives of more than 300 feet (100 m) down into Baikal after fish, their origin here unknown though it's theorized their ancestors swam up the Yenesei River from the Arctic Ocean and became landlocked in the last ice age.

Spotted nutcrackers, Baikal's most conspicuous birds, flit among pine trees gathering pine nuts in throat pouches and hiding them under mosses in coniferous forests. Also here year-round are northern hazel hens, black grouse, and capercaillies. Solitary snipes nest in thickets along with willow and rock ptarmigans. Eurasian dippers run along mountain stream bottoms feeding on invertebrates. Among avian rarities are black storks, golden and white-tailed eagles, Chinese scrub warblers. Steppe species along the Baikal shore include Saker falcons, Siberian meadow and rock buntings, and Isabelline wheatears.

In fall, deciduous trees turn fiery red and gold in dramatic contrast to emerald conifers, and ruby cowberries burst with juice prized by all species. Rare rhododendrons are among unique plant communities clinging to bare cliffs. More than 230 lichen species have been identified, 230 of mosses, 100 of mushrooms. Among 800 higher plant species, 27 are rare or endangered and 36 are endemic.

The great Lena River which flows more than 2,484 miles (4,000 km) north to the Arctic Ocean begins as a mountain trickle here.

Here as elsewhere, remoteness makes reserve management difficult and costly. Zapovednik headquarters are in Irkutsk, more than 185 miles (300 km) south. Parts of the reserve cannot be reached by road; others only by ship in summer; others only by driving over ice in winter. Poaching, pollution, arson, and other encroachments are problems, with little funding to fight them. In an effort to gain support and funding, the reserve offers three ecotourism routes for

adventurous travelers—along the Baikal shore, to the mountains in search of the Lena River source, and rafting down the Lena River.

# SOUTHEASTERN RUSSIA—AMUR SAKHALIN

Rare Amur tigers, Far Eastern leopards, light-footed, high-climbing ghorals and almost half this vast country's avifauna—some 500 species—are in the Russian Far East. Plant life is equally rich—in the Ussuri taiga alone, seven species of maple trees, five of birch, four of elm, three each of lime, alder, and wild cherry, two of oak and ash—with more than 600 species of medicinal plants. It is Russia's most diverse flora and fauna, in habitat ranging from northern taiga—moist subarctic coniferous forest that starts where the tundra ends—to southern subtropics and seashores.

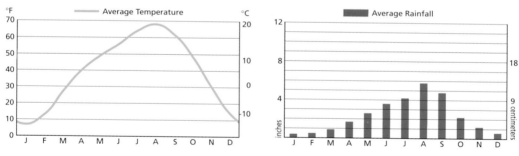

Gateway city: Vladivostok

## DALNEVOSTOCHNY-MORSKOY ZAPOVEDNIK

Safeguarding fragile, spectacular marine ecosystems in translucent blue-green waters of Peter the Great Bay is Dalnevostochny-Morskoy Zapovednik, 248 square miles (643 km²) in and on the Bay of Japan near the North Korean border.

Enormous numbers of birds on nesting islands here are able to nourish hatchlings on rich nutrients in this most biologically productive area in the Sea of Japan, the result of mixing of warm

OPPOSITE: Great snipes depend on vast marshes with sphagnum-covered tussocks and willow scrubs, usually fed by multiple tiny streams, not only for food and nest sites but for elaborate courtship displays. A dozen or so males gather and leap together 5–8 feet (1.5–2.5 m) in the air, breast to breast, bill to bill, tails fluffed, ending with loud drumming wingbeats designed to awe any female within 100–250 yards (93–230 m).

and cold sea currents and air masses within a complex structural relief of shore and ocean floors.

Starfish and sea anemones appear in multicolors from deep red to violet-blue. Giant octopi change colors to match their surroundings and surprise prey—crabs and bottom-dwelling fish—securing them with long suction-cup-fitted arms. Ascidians—sea squirts—filter plankton through red-orange saclike bodies, absorbing vanadium that colors their blood green—among more than 2,000 marine invertebrates.

Giant oysters cling to rocky surfaces as do mussels that can survive 100 years or more if their lives are not cut short by seals, marine birds, and others that prey on them.

Pacific cod, halibut, and other arctic fish dominate winter waters, replaced by over 100 warm-water species in summer—more than 278 fish species in all.

Harbor seals haul out and breed on protected islands where more than 360 bird species alight, many to nest, including ancient murrelets, spectacled guillemots, rare shelducks and Chinese egrets, three kinds of cormorants, arctic and red-throated loons, thin- and thick-billed murres. Largest nest colonies anywhere of black-tailed gulls and Japanese cormorants are here. More than 40,000 birds nest on Furugelm Island alone.

Raccoon dogs and Siberian polecats feed on marine mollusks, rodents, and small fish washed ashore. Sika deer graze and foxes and wild cats patrol coastal territory lined with rare stands of Japanese red pine. Under the forest canopy inland are rare Shlippenbach's rhododendrons, among 900 terrestrial plant species.

---

**FURTHER INFORMATION**

Director, Dalnevostochny-Morskoy Zapovednik, Russia 690041,
Vladivostok, ul. Palchevskogo, 17, Tel: (+7-4232) 31-09-15.

---

# Kedrovaya Pad Zapovednik

This is one of the last homes of the greatly endangered Amur or Far Eastern leopard, of which less than 40 are believed to exist in the wild.

This leopard subspecies (*Pantera pardus orientalis*), distinguished from others by softer, thicker fur, fills its needs—abundant prey base and dense forested habitat—in this 69-square-mile (179-km²) zapovednik nestled in the Black Mountains facing Vladivostok across the Gulf of Amur. Common here though rare elsewhere are its favorite sika deer along with tiny, tusked musk deer, and wild boars.

Smaller predators include foxes, raccoon dogs, badgers, Siberian weasels, and rare Amur wildcats, which prey on an abundant rodent population, including Siberian chipmunks and

# RUSSIAN FEDERATION

Russian flying squirrels, and in winter, Manchurian hares. Playful otters fish in streams and lakesides. Glossy Asiatic black bears with white neck-bibs, here also though largely unseen, follow a vegetarian diet except when fattening for hibernation.

Endangered gray goshawks share the rodents. Rare gray-faced buzzard-eagles take up stands in oak forests where they swoop down on amphibians and reptiles, favorites being oriental tigersnakes and red-backed ratsnakes.

Warblers bring forests alive in spring—Pallas', short-tailed bush, great crowned, and pale-legged willow. Great, columnar Manchurian firs up to 180 feet (55 m) tall and 6.5 feet (2 m) across offer nest sites for Siberian blue robins, brown flycatchers, Tristram's buntings, and a variety of titmice and nuthatches. Mandarin ducks with red bills and orange "beards" and "sails" on their backs demonstrate their striking plumage to females on waterways—among 150 breeding bird species, which also include collared scops and brown hawk owls and rare Chinese sparrowhawks.

Among 57 rare or endangered plants are Schmidt's birches with wood so dense it sinks in water. Among plant beauties are lady's slippers, Dahurian lilies, purple-pink blossoming *Wieglia praecox*, three peony species. There are also 100 kinds of butterflies.

Travel agencies offer one- or two-day trips from Vladivostok.

---

**FURTHER INFORMATION**

Director, Kedrovaya Pad Zapovednik, Russia 692710, Primorsky krai, Khasansky raion, st. Primorskaya.

---

# KHINGANSKY ZAPOVEDNIK

Red-crowned cranes, one of the rarest of their rare family and, many think, the most graceful, leap high in exquisite mating rituals every spring in one of their few remaining homes, 465 lowland square miles (1,205 km²) along the Amur River which forms much of the eastern Russian-Chinese border. Tossing wisps of leaves and grass to their partners with an abandon belying their precarious existence, they unknowingly lay extra eggs which are then incubated by scientists here and raised by surrogate mothers in an effort to increase their population—now estimated at 1,000 to 1,500 worldwide—before starting back south with their "own" families to wintering areas in South Korea and Japan. It's a technique being used as well for similarly beautiful and distressed populations here of white-naped cranes and Oriental white storks. The importance of Khingansky for these and other wild populations has led to its designation as a Ramsar Wetland of International Significance.

The reserve's breeding and reintroduction program, started in 1988, has aided other species as well including golden eagles, greater spotted eagles, and a variety of owls and waterfowl, rescued and healed from injuries in the wild. Notable also among more than 300 bird species are colorful mandarin ducks, and, nesting in scrapes in marshy grasslands, yellowlegged buttonquail, difficult to see but impossible not to hear—cries that start like a low human moan, ending in a piercing howl. Among lovely smaller species are black-naped orioles, ashy minivets, azure-winged magpies, Blyth's blue kingfishers, chestnut-flanked white-eyes.

Commonest among 44 mammal species are roe deer, wild boars, Siberian weasels, rare, brightly-colored Indian martens, and furry raccoon dogs, ancient ancestors of the canine family whose population has been greatly reduced elsewhere through loss of habitat and prey base, both fully protected here.

In smaller numbers in the mountains are Asiatic black bears and brown bears, feeding on acorns and pine nuts.

Major threats include burning of meadow vegetation during dry periods. The reserve has made an effort to enlist local support with outreach education programs including a popular "Crane Festival" to observe crane mating dances. Visitors are welcomed on ecotours to see semi-wild cranes in natural habitat. Lodging is available in homes and reserve guesthouses by prior arrangement.

> **FURTHER INFORMATION**
>
> Director, Khingansky Zapovednik, Russia 676740 Amurskaya oblast, Arkhara, Dorozhny per. 6, Fax: (+7-416-2) 31-82-66, E-mail: hingan@amur.ru

## SIKHOTE-ALINSKY ZAPOVEDNIK

In these remote forested mountains in extreme southeastern Siberia on the Sea of Japan roam endangered, beautiful Amur or Siberian tigers, less than 500 remaining in the wild. Largest cats on earth—significantly larger than their Asian relatives—they differ from them as well with lighter-colored, thicker coats and furry neck ruffs. These top predators, which inspire awe accorded no other creature, require large hunting ranges—up to 350 or so square miles (1,000 km²) for a big male. Even a reserve the size of Sikhote-Alinsky, 1,811 square miles (4,691 km²), which accommodates eight or so of these great beasts and plays the most significant role of any reserve in protecting this species and their natural habitat, should, its supporters say, be larger (it was six times present size before zapovednik closures and shrinkage by Stalin).

But the habitat is ideal—dense well-watered forest untouched by humans, with ample prey base. Here this is primarily Manchurian red deer, wild boars, or smaller, tusked musk deer, which the tigers track along rivers and through deep valleys, springing into attack when 10–30 feet (3–9 m)

# RUSSIAN FEDERATION

Siberian or Amur tigers up to 10 feet (3 m) long, with massive, heavily muscled limbs and shoulders, can leap 10 feet at a single bound. Long, dense, paler coats and furry neck ruffs make them look even bigger than they are. They can consume 75 pounds (95 kg) at a meal. Prey is usually killed by crashing down on the quarry's back and biting the neck, either severing the jugular or crushing the spine—but they've been known to track bears to winter dens to dig out and dispatch a still-sleepy victim. Less than 500 remain in the wild, most in the Siberian Far East.

away, usually crashing down on a victim's back and biting the neck, often severing the jugular and crushing the spine. Prey is then dragged to a secluded place where more than 100 pounds (45 kg) may be consumed in one sitting. The tiger may then climb up a steep slope to find shelter among rocky outcrops or boulder-strewn fields and later seek a victim there among Amur ghorals, agile goat-antelopes of higher elevations. They have been known to take on Ussuri (aka Amur or Asiatic) black bears too, which they track to winter dens, dig out, and dispatch a still-sleepy victim.

The remoteness and density that make this good tiger habitat does the same for others: beautiful, savage little Indian martens with bright yellow throats, black caps, and dark bushy tails; frolicsome otters; graceful Himalayan chamois threading their way over rocks and along narrow crevices; ermines and fierce wolverines; and more than 320 bird species, including Chinese white-eyes, brilliant mandarin ducks, brightly-hued eastern broad-billed rollers, common crossbills, northern three-toed woodpeckers, Hodgsons's hawk-cuckoos, Eurasian and collared scops-owls, and tall, endangered Blakiston's fish owls.

Rich plant life includes 384 mushroom species, 100 mosses, 214 lichens and altogether more than 1,000 species of higher plants, including yellow lady's slippers, Chinese magnolias, pink, white, violet, and red lilies, orchids and irises, three kinds of peonies and two of rhododendrons.

---

**FURTHER INFORMATION**

Director, Sikhote-Alinsky Zapovednik, Russia 692150, Primorsky Krai, Terny, ul. Partisanskaya 46, Tel: (+7-423-74) 9-15-59, 9-13-65, Fax: 9-13-78, E-mail: sixote@vld.global-one.ru

---

# FAR EASTERN RUSSIA— KAMCHATKA PENINSULA AND OKHOTSK SEA

## KRONOTSKY ZAPOVEDNIK

More than 600 brown bears weighing up to 1,500 pounds (700 kg)—largest in Russia—roam vast forests and mountains of Kronotsky Zapovednik on the east coast of Kamchatka Peninsula.

This 4,410-square-mile (11,421-km²) mountain wilderness became a hunting preserve for Kamchatka sables, renowned for their thick, dark, glossy fur, in 1882, then, in 1934, a reserve to protect them from extinction after their dense population was reduced to remnants by hunters who were exporting some 10,000 pelts a year.

Here also are largest known populations of white-tailed eagles and enormous Steller's sea eagles—300–700 of the latter, one of the world's largest raptors, over three feet (1 m) long with eight-foot (2.5-m) wingspans, strikingly brown-black with white shoulders and tail and massive, bright yellow bill, found only on Kamchatka and the east Siberian coast.

Lake Kurilsk is spawning ground for a species of sockeye salmon that does not migrate to the ocean but stays in lakes and rivers here. Populations plummeted in 1953–75 when Japanese commercial fishermen with drift nets caught up to 70–89 percent yearly, but with conservation quickly thrived again. Now, after spawning, their dying bodies furnish a feast for many—brown bears, sables, wolves, arctic foxes, lynx, ermine, ravens, and all other fish-eaters. Lake Kurilsk is a protected part of Kronotsky Zapovednik.

Reindeer (aka caribou) graze on aromatic plants at higher elevations in summer and on mosses and lichens at lower elevations in winter. Here also are bighorn sheep which descend from highlands then and on to the coast for badly needed salt. Steller's sea lions winter in the Sea of Japan but return in spring to Kronotsky's remote rocks, their breeding ground. Here also are ringed seals and sea otters, which like to float on their backs while consuming fish, crabs, and sea urchins. Offshore are nine whale species.

The reserve has volcanoes which spew gas and vapor when not erupting. The tallest, Kronotskaya Sopka, towers 11,575 feet (3,528 m) above the sea. On its slopes and those of other volcanoes are 414 glaciers covering 19 ash-darkened square miles (50 km$^2$). Protected marine areas cover another 580 square miles (1,500 km$^2$)

Enormous flocks of whooper swans winter. Aleutian terns nest on the rocky coast, home as well to noisy guillemot and tufted puffin colonies. World's largest population of Aleutian sea-swallows is here. Snow buntings and buff-breasted pipits shelter on volcanic slopes; cuckoos, woodpeckers, and nightingales are in birch groves—among some 260 bird species.

In five-mile (8-km) Valley of Geysers are 22 large and active geysers and 150 or so smaller ones. The largest, "Vulcan," ejects a jet of boiling water 130 feet (30 m) high in a valley floor strewn with bubbling mud pools, boiling multicolored lakes and pulsing springs. The humid warmth creates a dramatically emerald-green vegetation, with giant herbaceous plants.

Serious threats include domestic reindeer-herding; illegal timber-harvesting; industrial fishing and hunting in reserve coastal waters for rare marine mammals such as sea otters. Scars still remain on this fragile land and its impacted wild populations—notably bears and Siberian capercaillies—from mining and mineral prospecting 30 years ago. Here as elsewhere there is need for regular ranger patrols, creation of a buffer zone, scientific monitoring, and educational outreach with local groups.

Tour groups offer hiking/camping trips.

# RUSSIAN FEDERATION

**FURTHER INFORMATION**

Director, Kronotsky Zapovednik, 684010 Kamchatskaya oblast, g. Elizovo, ulitsa Ryabikova 48, E-mail: zapoved@elrus.kamchatka.ru

# KURILSKY ZAPOVEDNIK

Physical features that have created some of the world's richest fishing grounds around and on the Kuril Island chain from Kamchatka north to Japan have also helped make them among the richest in terrestrial wildlife. Kurilsky Zapovednik is part of this, covering altogether 412 square miles (1,069 km²) of volcanic cones with rocky cliffs where seabirds nest. Rivers teem with millions of spawning salmon where Russia's densest population of massive brown bears reap the bounty. Sable, red foxes, and European mink come for leavings.

Russian Largha seals gather near river mouths for their share, along with endangered Steller's sea lions and harbor seals. Sea otters, a rare subspecies, *kurilensis*, dine on coastal mollusks.

Tufted puffins, rhinoceros auklets, and slaty-backed gulls noisily conduct their affairs in cliff-side colonies, among 260 island bird species, of which 21 are listed as Red Book rarities.

Rare Blakiston's fish owls, one of the world's largest owls, more than two feet (72 cm) tall, glide silently along rivers searching for char, and wade in shallows for crabs or smaller prey.

Forest or large-billed crows with greenish-glittering heads and massive beaks "kroo-kroo" from tall spruces. Babbling trills of gray-capped (aka oriental) greenfinches ring in forests with those of a variety of tits and pipits.

Throngs of waterfowl stop by spring and fall on a major migratory bird route between Alaskan and eastern Pacific nesting grounds and winter quarters in Japan, Australia, and Southeast Asia.

Plant life ranges from arctic barrens to hardwood-conifer forest to tree fern-bamboo rain forest. Springtime brings fields of purple iris, orange daylilies, delicate blue plantain lilies, and in summer, butterfly and feather-leaf orchids, golden Venus' slippers, pink Japanese pogonias.

Reserve lands include half of Kunashir Island, parts of Demina and Oskolki Islands and Maly Kurily Zakaznik, along with six other islands and adjacent rocks, reefs, and Russian territorial waters.

Problems are serious overfishing—uncontrolled plundering of crabs, shrimps, squid, and sea urchins, and ongoing gold mining and mineral explorations.

**FURTHER INFORMATION**

Director, Kurilsky Zapovednik, Russia 694500, Sakhalinskaya oblast, pgt. Yuzhno-Kurilsk, ul. Zarechnaya 9, P.O. Box 42, Tel: (+7-424-55) 2-15-86, E-mail: kurilsky@ostrov.sakhalin.ru

# SRI LANKA

LEOPARDS IN SOME OF SRI LANKA'S GAME
RESERVES ARE SO ACCUSTOMED TO PROTECTION
THAT THEY SOMETIMES COME OUT TO GREET
AND INSPECT VISITORS. AS THE LAST ISLAND STOP
BEFORE ANTARCTICA FOR SOME AVIAN MIGRANTS, SRI
LANKA ATTRACTS HUGE NUMBERS IN WINTER
FROM AS FAR AWAY AS WESTERN EUROPE.

MARCO POLO IN 1290 DESCRIBED THIS TEARDROP IN THE INDIAN OCEAN JUST SOUTH OF INDIA—THEN CALLED CEYLON—AS "THE FINEST ISLAND OF ITS SIZE IN ALL THE WORLD."

Sri Lanka is where legend says Adam, banished from the Garden of Eden, first set foot on earth. If so, it may have been an easy transition to this beautiful place with its treasure of interesting wildlife.

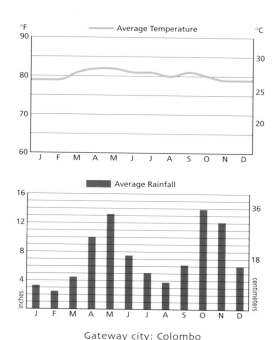

Gateway city: Colombo

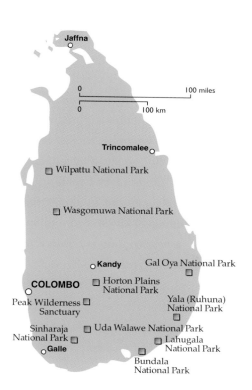

289

# SRI LANKA

Most famous is the elephant, celebrated and decorated in festivals and valued over the centuries for assistance to humans in tasks of war and peace. Many other species live only here, including the world's smallest wild felines, a subspecies of the Indian rusty-spotted cat, little over a foot (30–35 cm) long, and, among 242 butterflies, one of the world's largest—huge Southeast Asia birdwings, 10 inches (25 cm) across, a spectacular chartreuse and blue with black spots.

Wildlife preservation here dates back through earliest known records. The world's first wildlife sanctuary was created by King Devanampiya Tissa in the third century BC. King Nissanka Malla (AD 1187–97) in Polonnaruwa banned all killing of animals within seven gaw (24 miles/39 km) of the city. More than 12 percent of the country now is set aside as wildlife sanctuary, with 11 national parks and more planned.

Leopards, among 86 mammals here, are so accustomed to protection in some places that these usually reticent cats sometimes come out to greet visitors. (It helps that tigers, which prey upon leopards elsewhere, are not present.) Shaggy sloth bears amble about, five deer species graze, porcupines bristle and rattle foot-long spines. Slender loris curl up and nap by day—tiny, big-eyed, nocturnal but easy to detect since they wash hands and feet in urine to mark territory everywhere they go.

Long-tailed gray langur monkeys and toque macaques swing through treetops. Homely one-ton (908-kg) dugongs, gentle marine mammals once incredibly mistaken by sailors for mermaids (after long cruises, it's said), ease along offshore shallows.

Flying fox bats roost in cacophonous forest canopy groups. Over 450 bird species are here, including 26 endemics, with storks, fish-eagles, spoonbills, hornbills, and bright orioles, minivets, and bee-eaters. Since this is the last island stop north of Antarctica, it is seasonal home for huge numbers of migrants from as far away as western Europe and Siberia, here to escape northern winters in and around these 11,200 beautiful lakes or "tanks" (none natural, but most looking so, built by ancient monarchs for irrigation).

Fifty-four kinds of fish include glorious red scissor-tailed barbs and ornate paradise fish (unfortunately coveted by collectors). Two crocodile species frequent freshwater lakes and streams among 40 kinds of amphibians. Some 90 kinds of snakes are benign but six, relatively common, are poisonous—cobras, Russell's and saw-scaled vipers, Indian and Sri Lankan kraits, and the endemic green pit-viper.

Regrettably terrorist activities have made some areas dangerous. Other hazards confronting wildlife include dam construction and habitat loss due to logging and clearing for agriculture and housing. Ironically, elephants tamed to work in timbering have helped reduce their own species' wild habitat. Their numbers, once 19,000, now are down to several thousand and they are listed as endangered.

Best times to visit vary with monsoon seasons—in the southwest, best after September until April; in the northeast, best after March until November.

# BUNDALA NATIONAL PARK

This is the end point for wintering migratory birds from as far away as Europe and Siberia. Many fly thousands of miles over the Himalayas and down through the toe of India to spend September to mid-April on lagoons, estuaries, mudflats, and mangrove swamps of this 24-square-mile (62-km²) national park on Sri Lanka's southernmost landing point, 153 miles (246 km) southeast of Colombo. More than 20,000 shorebirds are here then—golden plovers, black-tailed godwits, green sandpipers, spotted redshanks, Caspian terns—149 species, plus thousands of greater flamingos from Rann of Kutch in India and, in the thorny scrub jungle, elephants, deer, and wild buffalo.

> **FURTHER INFORMATION**
>
> Department of Wildlife Conservation, 18 Gregory's Road, Colombo 07, Sri Lanka,
> Tel: (+94) 1-694241, Fax: (+94) 1-698556.

# GAL OYA NATIONAL PARK

Three rivers flow together into the great scenic Senanayake Samudra reservoir to create a water playground for large numbers of elephants that swim about in family groups of a dozen or so. They paddle among small islands for succulent grasses or bathe onshore, frolicking with young-sters, spraying one another, resting and cooling off on a hot day. When swimming in deep water they seem unconcerned about small boats drifting quietly among them. (Less regularly seen—fortunately since they are less agreeable—are swimming water buffalo, capricious half-ton (500-kg) beasts that can explode in a watery stampede and dump a canoe.)

Leopards, rare small cats, Goliath herons, and a treasure of other wildlife species are here as well.

Magnificent white-bellied sea eagles confront one another in screaming aerial displays, jeal-ously guarding feeding and breeding territories, diving, talons bared (sometimes dropping the fish that caused it all). Pink-splashed painted storks assemble bulky stick nests in noisy congre-gations, 20 or so almost touching one another in a single tree, foraging in shallows, swishing bills back and forth to close on a frog or small fish. Their aquatic food source is shared by spoonbills and ibis, pelicans, bright kingfishers, herons, egrets, cormorants, and elastic-necked snakebirds.

Sambar, Asia's largest deer, come to drink, along with lovely axis or spotted chital deer, wild boars and, toward dusk, shy muntjac or barking deer. Darkness brings lively little palm civets, both black and golden, and sometimes smaller fishing, jungle, and endemic rusty-spotted cats.

Primeval woods are home to vibrant-hued but secretive little scarlet or orange minivets, Layard's parakeets, and bronze strutting jungle fowl. Painted sandgrouse stay on grassy edges.

An ancient treasure of medicinal plants containing specifics for everything from high blood pressure to gallstones and snake bite is believed to have been planted and used by ancient Sinhala monarchs, including King Dutugemunu, to supply his army hospital.

Sloth bears (whose long claws and relatively slow movements resemble sloths) seek out ripe fruits or use formidable nails to tear into termite mounds or dig for grubs, their diet staple.

This 100-square-mile (260-km²) park inland from Sri Lanka's southeast-central coast surrounds the Senanayake Samudra reservoir, formed for irrigation by damming three rivers which flow through the park.

Best times are March–July. Rest house and bungalows (take own provisions) are at Inginiyagala and Eekgal Aru.

The park is a 235-mile (376-km) drive northeast of Colombo. Commercial flights are available intermittently to Amparai. Visitors (accompanied by ranger) can walk or rent boats, sometimes drifting among herds of swimming elephants or birds.

Problems include ongoing civil disturbance—check ahead.

---

**FURTHER INFORMATION**

Department of Wildlife Conservation, 18 Gregory's Road, Colombo 07, Sri Lanka, Tel: (+94) 1-694241, Fax: (+94) 1-698556.

---

# HORTON PLAINS NATIONAL PARK

Horton Plains National Park is noted for elephants, big-eyed, nocturnal slender loris, sambar deer, leopards—some of them black or melanistic—and big, shaggy bear monkeys with purple faces and white beards. (Melanism can occur more frequently at high-altitude light exposure.) Endemic birds include Ceylon white-eyes, dusky blue flycatchers, yellow-eared bulbuls, and powerful mountain hawk-eagles. Scenically the park is famous for stunning World's End precipice dropping startlingly from 7,200 feet (2,200 m) almost straight down for 2,300 feet (700 m).

The altitude variations encourage plants possible only here.

# LAHUGALA NATIONAL PARK

This tiny park (six square miles/15 km²) may be the best place to see elephants, sometimes herds of 150 or more—largest in Sri Lanka—at any time of year but especially around August when other places are dry. No mystery why: it encompasses two former irrigation "tanks," Lahugala

Jacanas are known for long toes and claws that spread their weight so they can trip lightly atop floating lily pads and watery vegetation, thus exploiting a foraging niche unavailable to others. Young are not hatched with those toes, however—they don't fit easily inside eggs—and so must grow them later. This immature bronze-winged jacana is just trying to get the hang of it (but not quite succeeding yet).

(Mahawewa) and Kitulana, both covered in tall succulent jade-green beru grass, an elephant favorite, located in the middle of an elephant corridor connecting Yala and Gal Oya. The park lodge offers superb views of wildlife, including wild boars, deer, occasional leopards, and uncommon butterflies and birds such as blue magpies and red-faced malkohas as well as jacanas, herons, orioles, shikras, Brahminy kites, and white-bellied sea eagles. Lodging at Lahugala and Pottuvil, 195 miles (312 km) east of Colombo.

# PEAK WILDERNESS SANCTUARY

The forest around Adam's Peak in Peak Wilderness Sanctuary is, according to legend, the exact place where Adam set foot after being driven from paradise. Others believe the huge "footprint" at the top was that of Buddha, St. Thomas or Lord Shiva. Whatever—it's a beautiful and fascinating place, with a splendid array of birds, butterflies, and other wildlife, best seen during the pilgrimage season December–April. The peak is a climb of several hours, mostly stairs, to the impressive view from the top (best at dawn).

# SINHARAJA NATIONAL PARK

Sinharaja National Park and U.N. World Heritage Site is one of the oldest national parks in the world, dating to the third century BC. From purple-faced monkeys to the world's largest butterflies—they are all concentrated in this 43-square-mile (112-km²) remainder patch of primeval rain forest that once covered all southwest Sri Lanka (much of it cleared to make plywood, then rice paddies and tea plantations). Densely filled with trees towering to a canopy of 150 feet (45 m) high, crossed with crystalline streams, it dates back to the third century BC when a succession of monarchs set aside "thahanakalle" (forbidden forests). Three-fourths of the trees are unique to this place, representing a gene pool found nowhere else (almost all the plants including thousands of orchids have unique rain forest "drip-tip" leaves enabling them to shed constant moisture). Among 147 bird species are 19 of Sri Lanka's 26 endemics including rare blue magpies, white-headed starlings, green-billed coucals, and ashy-headed babblers as well as red-faced malkohas.

Leopards are here, although rare, along with more than 50 percent of Sri Lanka's endemic mammals, including purple-faced (reddish-purple) leaf langurs and western toque macaques.

Bizarre, rough, sword-nose horned lizards are among 21 endemic reptiles. Rare endemic amphibians include wrinkled frogs, torrent toads, limbless yellow-banded caecilians which live under wet earth, and sharp-nosed tree frogs which lay their eggs in foam on the undersides of cardamom leaves overhanging streams, enabling hatching tadpoles to drop directly into water.

More than half of Sri Lanka's endemic butterflies are here, including rare five-bar swordtails and exquisite, huge chartreuse and blue birdwings.

Threats include illicit logging, gem mining, agriculture, and grazing. Plans (not yet activated) call for buffer zone planting around the park boundary to prevent encroachment.

---

**FURTHER INFORMATION**

Entry has been by permit from the Sri Lanka Forest, 82 Rajamalwatte Road, Battaramulla, Colombo (local address: Range Forest Officer, Range Forest Office, Kudawa, Weddagala).

# UDA WALAWE NATIONAL PARK

Many elephants, their forest homes cleared for farming, voluntarily came to this 119-square-mile (308-km²) national park when it was established around Walawe Reservoir to help compensate for wildlife displacement caused by the Walawe River Development Program. An estimated 350–400 elephants are here now, sometimes in large herds along the Walawe River. Macaques and langurs remain in uncleared jungle in the park's northern section. Grazers—water buffalo and spotted (axis), barking, sambar, and tiny mouse deer—enjoy sprouting greenery available in southern, formerly agricultural land. Fishing, jungle, and civet cats are at home beside waterways, along with crocodiles, six-foot (2-m) water monitors, 50 kinds of butterflies, and many birds including an endemic Sri Lankan subspecies of jungle fowl, spurfowl, gray hornbills, and red-faced malkohas. Brahminy kites circle gracefully. White-bellied sea eagles dive for fish. Painted storks wade for small aquatic prey.

Uda Walawe is 103 miles (165 km) southeast of Colombo. Best times are during or just after May–September monsoons, when fresh grass attracts elephants. A 4WD vehicle is a good idea on dirt roads. Campsites, bungalows available. Civil unrest to the north has not been disruptive, but check ahead.

---

**FURTHER INFORMATION**

Department of Wildlife Conservation, 18 Gregory's Road, Colombo 07, Sri Lanka, Tel: (+94) 1-694241, Fax: (+94) 1-698556.

---

# WASGOMUWA NATIONAL PARK

Wasgomuwa National Park and adjoining protected areas in east-central Sri Lanka (Flood Plains National Park and Somawathiya Chaitiya Sanctuary) provide habitat along the Mahaweli River (Sri Lanka's longest) for a rich variety of wildlife both in its forests and in fields cleared for agriculture. These include leopards, a unique subspecies of elephants, sloth bears, water buffalo, macaques, langurs, four deer species (axis or spotted, sambar, barking, mouse), and among birds, peacocks, jungle fowl, and colorful hornbills and barbets.

# WILPATTU NATIONAL PARK

Magnificent spotted leopards are nowhere more relaxed and at home than here, in a park strewn with sparkling blue lakes and interior sand dunes. They take naps hanging from limbs of umbrella trees. They stroll up to one of the villus or lakes—also sometimes called tanks—to get a drink; when no longer thirsty, they may take a sun or dust bath or go back and rest in the shadows

Large, spotted, reddish-fawn chital (or axis deer) with lyre-shaped antlers, called most beautiful of all deer, and a favorite tiger prey species, graze along shaded streams and grassy forest edges of India and Sri Lanka.

before going hunting again. Sometimes they even court in open view, males jousting, the victor often staying with his mate until offspring are full-grown.

A beautiful series of sand-rimmed freshwater "villus," built for irrigation centuries ago, attracts a broad wildlife spectrum, from water buffalo weighing more than a ton (1,000 kg) to curious, tiny chevrotains or mouse deer no bigger than rabbits, unchanged in 30 million years, males displaying prominent tusk-like upper canines which grow continually.

Jackals come too, along with six-foot (2-m) Bengal and water monitors, sambar and pretty axis or spotted deer, wild boars and jittery mongeese—gray, ruddy, and brown. Sloth bears—sometimes carrying cubs on their shaggy backs—are especially visible when palu and veera trees are fruiting. Timid barking deer or muntjac come after dark.

Elephants might appear any time, as may rare fishing and jungle cats; endemic diminutive rusty-spotted cats, among world's smallest wild felines; also black palm and golden palm civets.

When Wilpattu is open, visitors can stay at park bungalows and campsites (reserve well ahead), or, outside, at Hotel Wilpattu or Wildlife Protection Society lodge, and get around by vehicle on 150 miles (240 km) of roads (4WD can be helpful). Best times are rainless July–September. Park is 115 miles (186 km) north of Colombo on good roads.

> **FURTHER INFORMATION**
>
> Department of Wildlife Conservation, 18 Gregory's Road,
> Colombo 07, Sri Lanka, Tel: (+94) 1-694241, Fax: (+94) 1-698556.

# YALA (RUHUNA) NATIONAL PARK

Yala (Ruhuna) National Park's huge elephants, strutting peacocks, magnificent leopards and others uniquely here have made it known as a premier wildlife reserve of the world.

In an idyllic location on the southeast coast where whales and dolphins sound offshore, endangered dugongs, like seagoing underwater elephants, ease along the shallows, and sea turtles nest on beaches, it offers habitat from high coastal sand dunes and mangrove wetlands to grassy savannahs and dense interior forests.

Armored pangolins snuffle about forest litter. Sambar and spotted (axis or chital) deer drink along the Menik River, along with Sri Lankan jackals and huge water buffalo. All give way to sloth bears which, though primarily vegetarian, are feared for their strength and touchy dispositions, especially when carrying cubs and foraging for palu fruits.

Scurrying small rodents are prey for tiny endemic rusty-spotted cats and golden palm civets, catlike carnivores named for a preference for palm trees. Both often forage at night as do tiny, huge-eyed insect-hunting slender loris whose urine-soaked paws leave territorial scent marks everyplace.

Pretty little toque monkeys vault through tall trees, joined by silver-gray langurs. Both scream alarms when they spot their top predator, a leopard, in the jungle or when these spotted cats lounge atop Vepandeniya or "Leopard Rock," as they often do.

Resplendent peacocks ringingly proclaim territory, danger, courtship—almost anything—fanning out iridescent six-foot (2-m) tails in one of the grandest displays in nature.

Yala's more than 140 bird species include stunning Loten's sunbirds, Brahminy kites, open-billed storks, paradise flycatchers, rose-ringed parakeets, and one of the world's great singers, Sri Lankan shamas. Redshanks, greenshanks, long-toed stints, and long-distance-migrant golden plovers (logging an annual 20,000 miles/32,000 km) winter in wetlands where thousands of spoonbills, Goliath herons, black-necked storks, and others nest.

Yala is famous for its elephants, visible after spring rains start new green growth. Herds of 25 or more bathe and frolic at Palatupana "tank"—mostly peaceful but watch for males with a teary discharge. They are in periodic "musth" which irritates them so they can charge to kill (and run faster than a human).

Some of these were transplanted from a sugarcane plantation built on 16 square miles (41 km²) of cleared forest blocking traditional migration paths and water sources. Seventy-five persons and at least 125 elephants died before hitting on an imaginative solution: coax the elephants 15 miles (24 km) to this 490-square-mile (1,268-km²) reserve where they are now.

Climate is usually hot, dry, with monsoons November–January. Park is closed August–October. In July pilgrims walk across to a festival at Kataragama—interesting to see but dangerous to both humans and wildlife (a famous man-eating leopard once killed a number of pilgrims).

Lodging is usually available in on-park campsites, bungalows, plus nearby hotels, rest houses. Yala is 185 miles (298 km) on good roads from Colombo; 4WD can be good idea inside park (must be accompanied by ranger). Threats include poaching; timbering; cattle grazing; human–elephant agricultural conflicts; also civil unrest (check ahead).

**Yala East** is a 70-square-mile (180-km²) park extension with elephants, bears, leopards, sometimes spectacular birdlife, especially in and near Kumana mangrove swamp in June–July nesting period (watch for red-faced malkohas, blue magpies). Boat rentals available. Access by 16-mile (25-km) 4WD road from Arugam Bay.

---

**FURTHER INFORMATION**

Yala National Park, Department of Wildlife Conservation, 18 Gregory's Road, Colombo 07, Sri Lanka, Tel: (+94) 1-694241, Fax: (+94) 1-698556.

# THAILAND

KHAO YAI NATIONAL PARK IS ONE OF THE
LARGEST REMAINING INTACT TROPICAL RAIN
FORESTS ON MAINLAND ASIA, WITH WILD ASIAN
ELEPHANTS, TIGERS, CLOUDED LEOPARDS, AND RARE
SMALL LEOPARD CATS. THERE ARE 25 MILES (40 KM)
OF TRAILS THAT ORIGINALLY WERE (AND STILL ARE)
ANIMAL TRACKS THROUGH THIS 840 SQUARE MILES
(2,168 KM²) OF FORESTS AND GRASSLANDS.

THAILAND HAS SET ASIDE 102 NATIONAL PARKS AND 55 WILDLIFE SANCTUARIES COVERING 17 PERCENT OF ITS LAND—ONE OF THE WORLD'S HIGHEST RATIOS OF PROTECTED AREAS (THE U.S. HAS 10.5 PERCENT, FOR EXAMPLE). A rich diversity of flora and fauna in them includes tigers, leopards— both common and clouded—wild, trumpeting Asian elephants and more than 940 bird species.

In monsoonal forests in the north and rain forest in the south are over 27,000 flowering plant species, including many varieties of Thailand's national flower, the orchid, and more kinds of bamboo than any country outside China.

Huge wild oxen—gaur and banteng— graze in forest openings. Mouse deer hardly bigger than small rabbits, with ancestry going back 38 million years, forage on fruits and vegetation in deep woods, along with glossy Asiatic black

# THAILAND

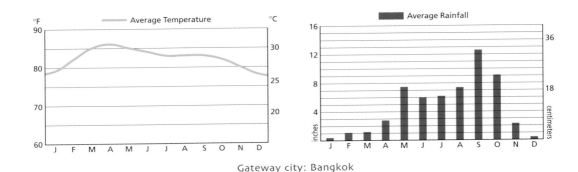

Gateway city: Bangkok

bears and great lumbering tapirs, relatives of rhinoceros. Malayan sun bears climb trees for tender leaves and fruit, sometimes building tree nests of branches and foliage. Armored pangolins shuffle through leaf litter. Rare small jungle cats pounce on rodents. Endangered "chanting" pileated gibbons swing through the canopy.

Four kinds of endangered sea turtles crawl up on white sand beaches and, weeping, lay eggs during full moons—green, hawksbill, olive ridley, and enormous rare leatherbacks, largest turtles in the world, weighing up to 1,500 pounds (680 kg) with shells up to six feet (2 m) across. Offshore, endangered dugongs like giant underwater blimps munch on shallow-growing sea grass alongside the world's smallest fish—little gobies 0.7 inch (20 mm) long—and, farther out, world's largest, whale sharks up to 60 feet (18 m) weighing several tons (3,600 kg).

Slithering among some 327 reptiles are king cobras up to 20 feet (6 m) long and, even more formidable, reticulated pythons growing to almost 50 feet (15 m), whose young emerge from eggs up to 2.5 feet (0.75 m) long. Geckos are everywhere, including inside homes, as are, sometimes, black jungle monitors, searching, fortunately, for insects and small rodents.

Silver pheasants scratch for insects and fallen seeds in broad-leaved evergreen and mixed deciduous woods. Chinese and Javan pond herons forage along stream edges with quiet yellow and cinnamon bitterns. Crested serpent-eagles and mountain hawk-eagles patrol airways. Brown hawk-owls and collared scops owls hunt at night. Heart-spotted woodpeckers batter at tree trunks—and there are seven colorful kinds of pittas, six kinds of broadbills, four forktails, sunbirds, parrotbills and scarlet finches. Coastal and inland waterways are important waterfowl habitats.

Some reserves until recently have been protected more on paper than in practice, but the trend is in the right direction.

Forests once covered 70 percent of Thailand, but by the early 1990s timber demands and pressures from growing population reduced it to less than 30 percent. This and other environmental degradation aroused public support for the government to set aside reserves and pass laws for their protection, setting environmental standards and limiting logging and exploitative coastal tourist facilities. The aim is to increase forest cover to 40–50 percent by mid-21st century, develop reserve management plans with jobs for local populations (most reserves now lack even boundary signs, and some, annual budgets), and provide ecotourism accommodations and facilities, presently limited. But the country must deal with problems including shortage of funds to control timber and wildlife poaching, the latter for purposes ranging from international trade in rare animals and their parts to local restaurant menus featuring endangered species. Of 138 large mammals, 53 are listed as endangered or threatened. Birds are in trouble too, including little swiftlets whose hardened-saliva nests are prized for birds' nest soup. Barn swallows, melodious thrushes, hornbills and their chicks are trapped and sold in markets for food, as pets, and for the illegal wildlife trade.

Poachers are serious. More than 40 ill-equipped, poorly-paid rangers have died in conflicts with them. Once idyllic, wildlife-rich Khao Sam Roi Yot National Park is widely regarded as lost, its habitat destroyed by Thai-Chinese business interests allied with provincial politicians. Despite laws, hill tribes have continued to denude Doi Inthanon, national park site of Thailand's highest mountain and home to some 900 bird species.

Overdevelopment of sensitive coastal areas, including illegal construction of large hotels on the coral-fringed national park island of Phi Phi, is starving coral reefs by blocking freshwater runoff from the interior while smothering them with pollution from large-scale sewage dumping.

But there are environmental victories. Four years of citizen protest blocked dam construction in two major sanctuaries, one in HUAI KHA KHAENG, a U.N. World Heritage Site and one of the largest and best preserved monsoon forests in Southeast Asia. Government pressure has all but eliminated fish industry dynamiting of coral reefs in some sensitive areas.

Ecotourists can help by buying no items derived from either marine or land animals; avoiding restaurants serving "exotic" animals and reporting those that do; insisting boat operators do not lower anchors onto coral formations and that they collect rubbish and dispose of it properly (not at sea or in parks).

Bangkok connects with international airlines, and internally there's a good domestic road and air network as well as frequent, fast busses, reliable, comfortable trains, vehicles for hire and a range of accommodations. Camping is possible in or near most national parks. Most sites are accessible for 2WD.

Best times are November–February in the center and north, April onwards in south Thailand. June–October are wettest months.

**FURTHER INFORMATION**

Forestry Department, Wildlife Conservation Division, Phahok Yothin Road, Bangkhen (north Bangkok), Bangkok 10900; Office of the National Environmental Board, 60/1 Soi Prachasumphan 4, Rama IV Road, Bangkok 10400; Wildlife Fund Thailand, 251/88–90 Phahonyothin Road, Bangkhen, Bangkok 10220, Tel: (+66) 02-521-3435, 02-552-2111/2790, Fax: (+66) 02-552-6083; World Wide Fund for Nature, 104 Outreach Bldg., P.O. Box 2754, Bangkok 10501, Tel: (+66) 02-524-6128.

# KHAO YAI NATIONAL PARK

This is one of the largest remaining intact tropical rain forests on mainland Asia, filled with spectacular birds and mammals—wild Asian elephants, tigers, clouded leopards, rare small leopard cats, dhole, chattering gibbons and macaques, "chanting" baboons, Asian wild pigs, hog badgers, gaur, sambar, and red muntjac. Many are visible from the 25 miles (40 km) of trails that were originated as, and still are, animal tracks through this 840 square miles (2,168 km²) of forested mountains and grasslands laced with rivers and waterfalls just 100 miles (160 km) northeast of Bangkok.

Ferns, air-nourished epiphytes and orchids can cover tree trunks. Wildflowers attract 250 kinds of beautiful butterflies by day, and after these have retired to roost—sometimes hundreds in the same tree—more than 1,000 moth species at night.

Great hornbills four feet (1.2 m) long, with imposing yellow bills and red eyes, swoop down for small lizards around park headquarters. Trail margins are enlivened by scarlet minivets, vernal hanging parrots, ethereal Asian fairy-bluebirds, raucous green magpies, blue-winged leafbirds, bright green-and-blue long-tailed broadbills, along with quietly gorgeous red-headed and orange-breasted trogons, seven kinds of dazzling sunbirds, 12 species of woodpeckers, and hosts of warblers and flowerpeckers. Flights of 1,000 or

Golden jackals have perfected communal living in which no pack member must work harder than another, and all share benefits. Offspring usually stay through the next litter to act as parents' helpers in hunting, feeding of new mother and young, and guarding pups. Their vocabulary of howling calls communicate location, declare territory, finding of food and cementing pair and family bonds. Their intelligence has led to inclusion in Middle East fables in similar roles as Europe's sly fox. They occur in varied habitats of north and east Africa, southeastern Europe and across southern and southeastern Asia to Thailand and Sri Lanka.

more black bazas—raptors with dramatic black crests and rufous-and-white breasts—can be counted on a single day in fall migration.

Silver pheasants, green magpies, white-crowned and slaty-backed forktails, and four kinds of hornbills frequent the short, undemanding Moh Sing Toh Trail, sometimes mixing with Asian elephants, red muntjac, and wild pigs. A trail reservoir is visited by little grebes, red-whiskered bulbuls, and occasionally leopard cats and tigers, and the walk becomes a blossoming avenue of trees in February and March.

Fruiting strangler fig trees along the (also easy) trail opposite Darn Chang attract swarms of birds—sometimes flocks of 12–20 great hornbills and 50 or more thick-billed green pigeons—and mammals as well: palm civets, giant black squirrels, white-handed and pileated gibbons, pig-tailed macaques, bear-like binturongs, hornbills, bats—and since tree fruitings overlap, the parade can go on for months. Farther on, the trail leads to a vast grassland area where large

flocks of wreathed hornbills fly with whistling wings over waving grasses. Deer and sometimes elephants graze, and crested serpent-eagles soar overhead.

Other trails lead to waterfalls and ponds where short-clawed otters swim, salt licks where gaur and elephants get minerals and, rarely, tigers stalk smaller, less challenging prey. Canopy towers offer views of red-whiskered bulbuls, chestnut-headed bee-eaters, and bright-capped cisticolas. Most trails are well-marked, between 1.5 and six miles (2.5–10 km) long, and manageable for the non-expert, though a guide is a good idea for longer, more remote treks.

Trips can be arranged to limestone caves where flights of wrinkled-lipped bats darken the sky at dusk. Night tours with spotting guides are available, and permission is sometimes granted to stay overnight at a tower. Park headquarters has species lists and guides, including a few English-speaking ones.

Accessibility has made Khao Yai Thailand's—and one of the world's—most popular national parks with more than a million visitors a year, a mixed blessing. To reduce crowding the government removed an adjacent golf course and tourist hotel, but more visitors still come than can easily be accommodated without interfering with wildlife, so best avoid weekends and holidays.

Presently the park has dorm-type rooms (bring sleeping bag or bedding) with a few cabins and tenting facilities available by reservation. Limited food is sold near headquarters. More elaborate lodgings are outside the park and on the road to Pak Chong, where tours and English-speaking guides can be arranged.

Problems include human encroachment—the park has become an island in a sea of agriculture—and poaching. A management plan developed with aid from World Wide Fund for Nature and Wildlife Conservation Society includes programs for conservation education as well as park employment for local villagers.

All year is interesting. Heavy rains occur July–October but wildlife is easier to spot then (also more leeches and insects) and rains often last only three–four hours daily.

Convenient air-conditioned busses and trains go to Khao Yai from Bangkok, or a driver-guide can make the trip on good roads in about two hours.

---

**FURTHER INFORMATION**

Khao Yai National Park, 2102–2104 Mitrapap Road, Amphur Muang, Nakorn Rachisma 3000, Tel: (+66) 044-213666-7.

# THUNG YAI-HUAI KHA KHAENG

Spectacular and increasingly rare large mammals such as tigers, Asian elephants, banteng, and enormous gaur, wild oxen weighing a ton (900+ kg) or more, are accommodated in comfortable numbers among the wondrously rich wildlife on this huge, remote U.N. World Heritage Site. Thung Yai-Huai Kha Khaeng is a merging of two national parks covering 2,345 square miles (6,070 km²) along the western border with Myanmar (Burma) in a magnificent protected mountain terrain interspersed with riverine forests, ponds, lakes, and large grassland tracts—one of the most important reserves in Southeast Asia for these and other impressive and diminishing species. Soon it may, with proposed additions, cover almost three million acres (1.2 million ha).

Tapirs lumber through swampy lowland jungles. Rare Fea's muntjak and hog deer graze in forest openings. The largest herd of gaur ever seen in Thailand—50 of these behemoths—was recorded here in 1985. It is last stronghold of only-slightly-smaller banteng. Serows—dark little goat-antelopes with conspicuous manes—graze high shrubby rock outcrops.

Leopards, tolerant of drier conditions than tigers, stalk smaller mammals, avoiding moist jungles dominated by their larger striped relatives. Shorter-legged clouded leopards find tree life more advantageous and leap on victims from overhead.

A half-dozen species of long-tailed catlike civets—considered most primitive of all carnivores—live arboreal lives here, including the largest, bear-like binturongs, one of only two carnivores with completely prehensile tails. Rare Phayre's leaf monkeys are among at least 10 primate species.

Smooth-coated and short-clawed otters fish in waterways frequented by large, brilliant storkbilled kingfishers, shy, rare white-winged wood ducks and, overhead, soaring lesser fish-eagles.

Spectacular green peafowl spread iridescent trains more than six feet (2 m) long. Kalij pheasants nest inconspicuously on scrapes under bamboo clumps. An astonishing 21 kinds of woodpeckers, from white-bellied to the huge great slaty up to 20 inches (51 cm) long, hammer at tree trunks for hidden grubs.

Most of the park's 120 mammal species as well as many of the 400 birds and 96 reptiles visit the numerous natural mineral licks. Visiting entomologists often come up with several new insect species. Lodging, also information about guides, is available in Sangkhlaburi, 21 miles (34 km) north. But this remote reserve is not easy to see, accessible—at least until recently— only by 10–12-hour journey on unsurfaced road from Bangkok via Kanchanaburi or Lan Sak, by permit only from the sanctuary chief or Wildlife Conservation Division in Bangkok.

Problems include logging, agricultural development, poaching, and insufficient funds to train local people for ranger patrol jobs. Plans have been shelved for the Nam Choan dam which would have destroyed lowland habitat for many rare species—everything below 1,200 feet (380 m) elevation—but opponents fear the dam could be revived if environmental opposition dies down. Threatened also are ethnic minority peoples who have lived sustainably here for 200 years but now are considered illegal squatters.

---

**FURTHER INFORMATION**

Kanchanaburi Forest Office, Kanchanaburi, Thailand; ALSO *see* above.

---

# KAENG KRACHAN NATIONAL PARK
This is Thailand's largest park, 1,190 square miles (3,083 km²) of evergreen forest, mountains, waterfalls, and grasslands on the Phetchaburi Peninsula with tigers, Asian elephants, and black bears, leopards, giant squirrels, dusky leaf monkeys, and an abundance of birds and butterflies. More than 300 avian species, some at the southern extreme of their Myanmar and northern Thailand ranges, others at the northern end of their peninsular Thailand and Malayan ranges, include such colorful specialties as laced and bamboo woodpeckers, plain-pouched hornbills, moustached barbets, yellow-vented green pigeons, olive bulbuls, and an isolated population of racquet-tailed treepies. Because this area receives some of Thailand's heaviest rainfall, rain forest is especially lush but also least explored. Best times are November–April. The park (112 miles/180 km by road southwest of Bangkok) has guides (though few speak English) for longer trails; lodging near park headquarters, nearby guesthouses; camping by permit. The park's dirt roads can be explored by 4WD vehicle, and boats can be rented on the Kaeng Krachan Reservoir above the dam. Rafting can be arranged on Phetchaburi River in the park.

# ALSO OF INTEREST
Many Buddhist monasteries throughout the country are, because of Buddhism's reverence for life, de facto sanctuaries. Outstanding among them is **Wat Phai Lom**, home to an extraordinary colony November–May of nesting pairs of Asian open-billed storks and many other species in a 30-acre (12-ha) grove of trees 25 miles (40 km) north of Bangkok.

**Khao Sok National Park** with adjoining protected areas is 477 square miles (1,236 km²) of mostly virgin rain forest with elephants, buffalo, primates, Asiatic wild dogs, clouded leopards, a few tigers and other jungle cats, also rafflesia, world's largest flower, 2.6 feet (80 cm) across. Treehouse-style lodging.

**Thung Salaeng Luang Wildlife Sanctuary** is 487 square miles (1,262 km²) of meadows and dipterocarp forest known for Siamese fireback pheasants.

# VIETNAM

VIETNAM HAS PROVEN FULL OF SURPRISES—
NOT ONLY THE RESILIENCE OF ITS HABITAT, BUT ALSO
NEW MAMMALIAN SPECIES—THE SAOLA OR VU QUANG
OX AND THE GIANT MUNTJAC OR BARKING DEER. VIETNAMESE
NATURALISTS ALSO HAVE REDISCOVERED SPECIES THOUGHT
LOST—THE JAVAN RHINOCEROS AND VIETNAMESE PHEASANT.

NATURE'S RESILIENCE IS NOWHERE BETTER SEEN THAN IN THIS TINY WAR-RAVAGED COUNTRY, POCKED WITH 20 MILLION BOMB CRATERS, SPRAYED WITH DIOXIN AND CHEMICAL DEFOLIANTS THAT DENUDED MILLIONS OF FOREST ACRES—YET STILL HOME TO SPECTACULAR WILDLIFE. Tigers, leopards, Asian elephants, and Malayan sun bears prowl regrown jungles. Dazzling birds—some species known only here—sip at blossoming vines, and discoveries continue of animals previously unknown or long thought extinct.

The saola, originally called Vu Quang ox—first new mammal species reported in the world in 50 years, like a small ox with a deer's graceful manner and daggerlike horns that could fend off a tiger—was discovered in the VU QUANG NATURE RESERVE on the Laotian border in 1992. In 1993 a new kind of barking deer—the giant muntjac—was found nearby, discoveries which led to a logging ban and expansion of that reserve to protect these and perhaps other rare species to science.

Until 1988 Javan rhinoceros were thought to exist only in west Java's UJUNG KULON NATIONAL PARK (*see* p.604); then some were found in woods close to and including NAM CAT TIEN NATIONAL PARK. Another species thought extinct until recently was the lovely

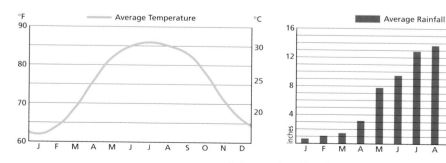

Gateway city: Hanoi

crimson-faced white-crested Vietnamese pheasant. The world's last troupes of golden-headed langurs are on Cat Ba Island's national park. Eastern sarus cranes of the Mekong Delta disappeared during the war; then in 1985 a farmer reported a single bird. Now more than 500 pairs of these world's tallest flying birds with red heads, gray plumage, and reddish legs nest in a reserve set aside for them on these former battlefields in Dong Thap province, and over 200 other species have come as well—among them Chinese pond herons, black-headed cranes, white-throated kingfishers, and buff-throated warblers.

Environmental consciousness has arisen as destructive results became clear not only from wartime devastation but also overfishing, slash-and-burn farming, and unsustainable forest use for charcoal and firewood as well as timber. In 1992 unprocessed timber exports were banned. Government reforestation projects were undertaken and encouraged in schools as well. As a result, the Forest Ministry points out that forest coverage, down to 20 percent in the early 1990s, rose to 28 percent by 1998. In 1993 the country's first law on environmental protection was passed at the behest of Ho Chi Minh City citizens aroused by failure to stop golf course construction in protected Tu Duc National Park.

Plans have been announced to create 100 national parks and reserves covering about five percent of the land area. More than 40 have been officially approved with more, they say, to come. Funds fall short of adequate staffing and protection, but it is a beginning.

It cannot happen too soon for Vietnam's some-273 mammal species along with over 850 kinds of birds, 260 kinds of reptiles and amphibians, and hundreds of fish, along with an estimated

12,000 plants—7,000 so far officially described and 2,300 already known for important uses in food and medicines.

At least 54 mammal and 60 bird species are listed as threatened. Tapirs and Sumatran rhinoceros are believed already extinct, and there are thought to be fewer than 10 koupreys, dark, lyre-horned forest oxen. Other species of special concern still hanging on include remarkable variegated douc langur monkeys, serows—bearded, maned mountain goats—and huge gaur, wild cattle that can weigh a ton (1,000 kg) or more.

Encouragingly, wildlife has returned to restored places. Replanted mangrove swamps again nurture birds, fish, and crustaceans, and areas once devastated by war have become biologically diverse "hot spots."

Much poaching and habitat destruction continues unchecked, however, with little effective restriction on sale of endangered animals' parts such as tiger skins and plundering of dwindling coral reefs for tourist souvenirs. Markets not uncommonly sell monkeys, snakes, turtles, and various bird species—even bears—for collectors or the cooking pot. Coastal mangroves in the Mekong Delta are cleared for commercial shrimp ponds. Even protected areas still suffer from agricultural encroachment and excessive firewood-gathering.

Still, those interested in wild creatures and wild places will find impressive examples of both here.

Major international airlines fly directly to Vietnam, although North American visitors at least until recently have had to connect via Hong Kong, Japan, or Taiwan. In-country travel can be problematic with under-maintained roads and often overbooked local airlines with poor safety records. Accommodations are improving and most national parks have inexpensive basic overnight facilities. Travelers in remote areas should use caution. Best bet can be to hire an experienced driver-guide and consult local authorities on recent conditions.

Best times in the north are less rainy November–April; elsewhere conditions vary.

## FURTHER INFORMATION

World Wide Fund for Nature—IndoChina Programme, 53 Tran Phu Street, Hanoi, Tel: (+84) 04-733-8387, Fax: (+84) 04-733-8388, E-mail: public@wwfvn.org.vn; IUCN—the World Conservation Union—Vietnam, 13A Tran Hung Dao Street, International P.O. Box 60, Hanoi, Vietnam, E-mail: mfk@iucn.org.vn; Fauna and Flora International—Vietnam, 104B Pho Hue, International P.O. Box 78, Hanoi, Vietnam, Tel: (+84) 04-943-2292/3, Fax: (+84) 04-943-2254, E-mail: ffi@fpt.vn; BirdLife International, 293 Tay Son, 11 Lane 167, Dong Ha District, Hanoi, Tel: (+84) 04-851-7217, Fax: (+84) 04-857-3866, E-mail: birdlife@netnam.org.vn; International Crane Foundation, P.O. Box 447, Baraboo, Wisconsin 539913-0447, USA, Tel: 608/356-9462, Fax: 608/356-9465, E-mail: cranes@savingcranes.org

Eurasian kingfishers are a dazzling cobalt-winged blur when bright plumaged males pursue mates with shrill whistles along streambanks where they later nest. Males, able to hold beaksful of fish while still whistling loudly and distinctly, then bring food to tunnels where females incubate round, pinkish-white eggs, sometimes nestled on a litter of fish bones. They are found in Europe, Asia and Africa.

## NAM CAT TIEN NATIONAL PARK

Nam Cat Tien National Park is home to some of the world's rarest, most impressive wildlife in one of the last lowland jungles in Vietnam.

Here live the only surviving Javan rhinos on mainland Asia; tigers; leopards, both common and clouded; rare smaller fishing, leopard, and Asian golden cats; massive gaur and banteng; wild Asian elephants; nearly extinct black-shank douc langurs, nattily attired in varicolored furs of red, brown, gray, black, and white; and hundreds of dazzling birds and butterfly species.

At least 62 mammal species, more than 300 birds and 40 kinds of reptiles have returned to jungles once defoliated and maimed by wartime bombing. Many huge old-growth trees survived and with regrowth, lush orchid-festooned forest now covers 87 percent of this 309-square-mile (800-km²) reserve about 95 miles (150 km) northeast of Ho Chi Minh City (Saigon) off Highway 20, of which almost half is a core "strict protection zone."

Four kinds of storks—painted, woolly-necked, black-necked, and lesser adjutant—forage and nest with quiet yellow and cinnamon bitterns and stately purple and Chinese pond herons around its many lakes and ponds—some, former bomb craters. They and families of lesser whistling ducks and a few rare white-winged wood ducks—discovered here only recently—keep a wary look-out for cruising Siamese crocodiles and, from above, menacing crested serpent eagles and black-shouldered kites.

Forest glades conceal rare shy orange-necked partridges, detected most often by plaintive cuckoo-like "tututututu" calls in series sometimes of 60 or more, and equally scarce Germain's peacock-pheasants cackling noisily. Banded and white-throated kingfishers swoop with rattling cries along streams. Greater flameback, laced, and pale-headed woodpeckers glean tree trunks and brilliant orioles, bee-eaters, and flowerpeckers investigate floral vines with such breathtaking neighbors as Asian emerald and drongo cuckoos, pompadour green pigeons, Asian fairy bluebirds, and stately, iridescent green peafowl.

A joint project by governments of Vietnam and the Netherlands with World Wide Fund for Nature (WWF) works to protect the reserve by raising public awareness of physical and biological values and generating income-producing jobs for local people in park protection, maintenance, and ecotourism. Their efforts have resulted in excellent lists of the reserve's birds, mammals and butterflies, marked trails along rivers and through woods and grasslands. There are guides (limited English-speaking) and simple overnight accommodations. Trips with boats and drivers can be arranged for more remote parts of the park's three sectors, located in three provinces but all managed by the Hanoi Ministry of Agriculture and Rural Development (rhinos are in the Cat Loc sector, slightly separate from Tay Cat Tien and Nam Cat Tien sectors).

Best times are drier November–April, when wildlife can be easier to spot (though wildlife in dense jungle is never easy to spot).

The park can be reached by public transport from Ho Chi Minh, also through government-organized tour groups there—not always effortlessly. Roads can be in poor condition and transport unreliable. This is a wild undeveloped area with the rewards as well as inconveniences that betokens.

---

**FURTHER INFORMATION**

WWF-Cat Tien National Park Conservation Project, 85 Tran Quoc Toan Street, District 3, Ho Chi Minh City, Vietnam, Tel: (+84) 08-932-5995, Fax: (+84) 08-932-5996, E-mail: public@wwfhcmc.vnn.vn; Park office, Tel/Fax: (+84) 06-179-1226 (a radio-phone, not always reliable).

---

# Vu Quang Nature Reserve

Vu Quang became world-famous overnight when the first new mammal species in the world in 50 years—the Vu Quang ox—was reported in 1992 on this remote wooded reserve in high moist Ammanite Mountains on the Laotian border. The next year, not far away, a new deer species now named the giant muntjac was seen. Since then evidence has been found of at least two new fish species, a new rabbit, squirrel, and warbler, possibly another new kind of deer, and Vietnamese warty pigs, last recorded in 1892 and long considered extinct.

The new little ox—known also as saola—and as nyang in the huge adjoining Nakai Nam Theun reserve in Laos, where it has now been seen as well—was initially thought related to Arabian oryx, which it resembles with large eyes, straight sharp horns and patterned spotted head, but it differs genetically. The muntjac has been confirmed as a new, much larger species of barking deer.

Other residents of this biological treasure-house include tigers, leopards, gaur, Asiatic black bears, and rare white-cheeked gibbons. Beautiful Vietnamese pheasants, long thought extinct, were found on nearby **Ke Go Reserve**.

Such astounding species and others perhaps still undiscovered may be protected by enlargement of the reserve—now 234 square miles (607 km²)—with a ban on logging and hunting. A large international reserve has been proposed covering an additional 1,172 square miles (3,036 km²). But such areas are difficult to protect, not only from outside poachers but indigenous people who indiscriminately snare animals for food and have difficulty understanding why they should not.

For now, visitation in this remote, steeply mountainous area is rare-to-nonexistent except for determined scientists with special permission.

## ALSO OF INTEREST

Other splendid reserves here include:

**Cuc Phuong National Park** in north-central Vietnam, a primeval tropical forest preserve, with 1,000-year-old trees, unique species—flying lizards, rare Delacour's langur, marbled cats—fine birdlife including such specialties as white-bellied pigeons, ruddy kingfishers, Malayan night herons, and spot-bellied eagle owls, with an endangered primate center.

**Ba Be National Park** in northeast Vietnam with towering peaks, waterfalls, rain forest, bears, primates, exceptional birdlife.

**Bach Ma-Hai Van National Park** along central Truong Son Mountains, haven for threatened pheasants—especially crested argus—and Siamese firebacks, plus tigers, Asian elephants, Franco's leaf monkeys, rare concolor gibbons, and douc langurs.

**Cat Ba National Park**, largest of 366 islands in the Cat Ba Archipelago, with wild boars, endangered golden-headed langurs, rare plants, spot-billed ducks, white-breasted waterhens, pheasant-tailed jacanas, also Indian cuckoos, orange-breasted pigeons, glorious scarlet minivets, many hornbills.

**Tam Dong Crane Reserve** in the Mekong Delta has a breeding colony of rare sarus cranes, set up by leading Vietnam conservationist Professor Vo Quy with the International Crane Foundation.

**Yok Don National Park**, 225 square miles (582 km²) in wild central highlands, with tigers, hornbills, reintroduced Asian elephants (also poaching problems).

# CARIBBEAN AND CENTRAL AMERICA

OCELOT

# CARIBBEAN

GEORGE WASHINGTON IN 1760
CALLED THEM OUR "ISLES OF PERPETUAL JUNE"
WITHOUT HAVING GLIMPSED SOME OF THEIR GREATEST
MARVELS—IRIDESCENT INSECT-SIZED BEE HUMMINGBIRDS,
HALF-TON NESTING LEATHERBACK SEA TURTLES, PARROTS
REVERED AS REINCARNATED HUMAN ANCESTORS, CARNIVOROUS
PLANTS CLINGING TO CORK PALM SURVIVORS FROM CRETACEOUS
TIMES, BRILLIANT UNDERWATER CORAL-REEF SEA LIFE.

C HRISTOPHER COLUMBUS SAW THE CARIBBEAN'S THOUSANDS OF SMALL ISLANDS AND ISLETS COVERED WITH DENSE FOREST AND FILLED WITH BIRDS. European colonizers destroyed much of these to put in crops—indigo, coffee, sugar, and later bananas—and in the process introduced rats, goats, and mongeese which devastated native flora and fauna. Visitors today come mostly for resort life but increasingly they are interested in ecotourist destinations as well, and environmental groups have become active in saving what is left, including places that deserve ranking with some of the outstanding wildlife reserves of the world.

## BAHAMAS

More than 3,000 islands and islets surrounded by brilliant coral barrier reefs and light-pink sand beaches rise from a 750-mile (1,200-km) underwater platform known as the Bahama Banks, lying 75 miles east of Palm Beach, Florida extending south to 55 miles (89 km) northwest of Cuba. These superbly beautiful low-lying islands, which began to take present form as the Bahamas Archipelago 500,000 years ago, sit atop one of the great limestone masses of the world, a reef-shelf of solid sea fossils 20,000 feet (6,100 m) thick dating back almost 150 million years.

# BAHAMAS

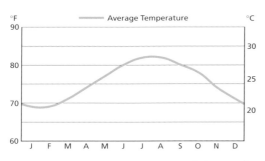

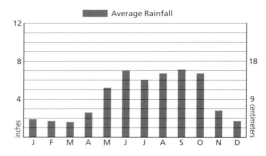

Gateway city: Nassau, Bahamas

Jewel among them is **Exuma Cays Land and Sea Park**, centerpiece of the 365-cay 140-mile (225-km) Exuma chain, a turquoise-jade mosaic covering 175 square miles (460 km²), visible to astronauts in outer space. It is renowned not only for natural beauty and tropical inhabitants but because a far-thinking government set it aside in near-pristine state.

It is a dazzling reservoir for sea life including not only exquisite tropical reef species but huge endangered sea turtles, marine mammals such as dolphins and whales, and conch, lobsters, and groupers overfished elsewhere, along with birds that subsist on and around it. Streamer-tailed tropic birds nest as do Audubon's shearwaters, least terns, and Wilson's plovers, among 97 avian species. All these thrive—and nourish the area around them—because the park sternly enforces a no-take policy banning all hunting, fishing, spearing, and removal of living creatures and natural objects, including shells. As a result, waters teem with tame, beautiful, readily visible marine life in crystalline waters averaging 10 feet (3 m) in depth.

Only way to visit is by boat, in waters acclaimed as best cruising in the western hemisphere. One way to arrange this is to fly from Fort Lauderdale, Florida, to Staniel Cay (three James Bond movies were shot there) where there is lodging and charters can be arranged. Or fly from Miami or New York to Nassau and take a boat tour from there.

Park headquarters is at Warderick Wells Cay, with moorings, visitor center, park ranger, and staff, also bird lists and trail maps. Bahama woodstar hummingbirds come to feeders July–December, and clapper rails, Zenaida doves, yellow warblers, white-cheeked pintails, and graceful wading birds are common. Migrants go through in September and April–May. Land animals include curly-tailed lizards, dragonlike iguanas and on several islands, endangered hutias, cat-sized brown rodents akin to guinea pigs.

Climate is pleasant year-round—George Washington visiting in the 1760s called them the "Isles of Perpetual June"—with rains in May–November coming mostly in short heavy bursts.

Also in the Bahamas is 32-square-mile (83-km²) **Abaco National Park**, breeding and foraging ground of Bahama (aka Abaco) parrots; **Black Sand Cay** off Green Turtle Cay, important wintering waterbird habitat; **Tilloo Cay**, pristine wilderness nest site for streamer-tailed tropic birds; and **Pelican Cays Land and Sea Park**, with abundant reef and terrestrial wildlife.

**Inagua National Park**, 287 square miles (743 km$^2$) on Great Inagua, protects the world's largest West Indian flamingo breeding colony (60,000 birds). **Conception Island Land and Sea Park** is sanctuary for seabirds and endangered green sea turtles. **Andros Barrier Reef** is one of the world's longest, 140 miles (225 km).

---

**FURTHER INFORMATION**

Warden, Exuma Land and Sea Park, c/o Bahamas National Trust, P.O. Box N-4105, Nassau, Bahamas, Tel: (+1 242) 393-1317.

---

# CUBA

Alligator-shaped Cuba, almost as big as all the other Caribbean islands combined (40,533 square miles/105,007 km$^2$) is a country of biological riches with a history of habitat degradation. Reserves have been set aside with few if any measures to protect them. Recent reforestation is a positive step but little has been done about environmentally disastrous practices such as over-fishing for anything edible or decorative, including lobsters and endangered sea turtles; destruction of coral reefs for jewelry; agricultural runoff; industrial pollution; inadequate sewage treatment; and construction of highways, causeways, airports, and tourist facilities in sensitive habitat. Nickel-mining and cement factories have created barren wastelands.

Yet, here if anywhere is the great scarlet-crested black-and-white ivory-billed woodpecker, believed long-extinct in the U.S. after logging of old-growth pinewoods, now feared close to extinction in Cuba as forest habitat disappears.

Among 350 stunning avian species is the shining bee hummingbird, smallest bird in the world, smaller than many grasshoppers (2.25 inches/5.5 cm), males green with iridescent crimson heads and throat plumes, their status threatened by habitat loss.

Uniquely here are other "smallest" species—Cuban pygmy frogs, 0.4 inch (12 mm) long; shrew-like insectivorous almiquis, world's smallest mammals, along with butterfly or moth bats, smallest of their kind; alacras, dwarf scorpions, 0.39 inch (10 mm) long. One tiny orchid's flowers are just 0.07 inch (2 mm) across.

Other beautiful, interesting, uniquely Cuban specialties include Cuban trogons or tocororos, national bird with the colours of the Cuban flag; green Cuban parakeets, wings flashing scarlet in flight; blue-headed quail-doves; nearly-flightless Zapata rails with long red-based green bills,

Resourceful foragers, blue-gray tanagers seem happy flying out to capture insect prey in midair, equally so dining on fruiting and flowering trees or meticulously searching for hidden grubs in branches and leaves. Azulegas, as they're known in Colombia and Panama, build sturdy plant fiber nests that can be found from just above ground to 100 feet (30 m) up in trees through the Caribbean and northern South America.

endangered from repeated wetland burning and introduced predators. Fortunately still fairly common are endemic Cuban pygmy-owls calling plaintively day and night, and endearing Cuban todies, not much bigger than bee hummingbirds, green with red throats, blue throat stripes, pink flanks, and yellow under-tail coverts.

Of over 8,000 plant species, over half are endemic, including hundreds of orchids and the world's only carnivorous epiphyte or air plant. Of 100 kinds of palms, 90 are endemic, including cork palms, regarded as living fossils from Cretaceous times.

Apart from sea creatures, especially manatees—huge gentle saltwater mammals of the shallows—most abundant fauna are reptiles: iguanas, lizards, salamanders, three kinds of crocodiles, and 14 kinds of nonpoisonous snakes, including huge majas. These relatives of South American anacondas can grow to 13 feet (4 m), and kill by suffocation and swallow victims five times the size of their mouths (luckily they avoid humans).

Designated protected areas cover about 30 percent of Cuba, including its marine platform. They include 14 national parks and four U.N. Biosphere Reserves—but designated national parks here include zoos, resorts, and assorted other areas not so categorized in many other countries and few as yet have visitor centers, maps, camping areas, marked trails, and adequate protection.

**Gran Parque Natural Montemar** near Mauanzas, formerly known as **Parque Nacional Cienaga de Zapata**, a vast wetland of mangroves, marshes, and swamps, occupies most of the 1,745-square-mile (4,520-km²) Peninsula de Zapata, home to 160 bird species, including bee hummingbirds, Cuban trogons, endemic Zapata wrens and rails, owls, parrots, flamingos, raptors, plus 31 kinds of reptiles, 12 mammals, countless amphibians, insects, and fish, and primitive alligator gars. Thousands of red land crabs swarm across the swamp's one road every spring night.

**Reserva Peninsula de Guanahacabibes**, U.N. Biosphere Reserve, 392 square miles (1,015 km²) of prime birding area in Pinar del Rio on Cuba's western tip.

**Gran Parque Nacional Sierra Maestra**, in mountains behind Baracoa, in Granma.

**Sierra de Cristal Parque Nacional** (aka **Cuhillas del Toa**), a U.N. Biosphere Reserve, possible home of endangered ivory-billed woodpeckers.

Cuba's pleasant subtropical climate has two seasons: rainy summer May–October and drier winter November–April. An extensive network of tourism promotion offices overseas are good sources of information on travel and accommodations in moderate-priced hotel chains. (The U.S., at least until recently, has not sanctioned travel to Cuba; however, Americans can easily go to Cuba via Canada, Mexico, the Bahamas, or Jamaica. Cuba receives U.S. passport holders under the same terms as any other visitor—but such visitors should know that without U.S. permission, such travel can be prosecuted as illegal back home.)

**FURTHER INFORMATION**

The Centro Nacional de Áreas Protegidas (CNAP) in Havana administers some of Cuba's reserves and parks. Permission to visit restricted areas for scientific purposes is granted by Centro de Inspección y Control Ambiental (CICA), Tel: (+537) 22-5531, ext.430, in the Havana suburb of Kolhy.

# DOMINICA

Dominica in the lush mountainous Lesser Antilles is home to the Caribbean's largest oceanic rain forest, filled with waterfalls, 350 cascading rivers, 50 fumaroles and hot springs, with endangered red-necked and imperial parrots found nowhere else, surrounded by equally magnificent underwater scenery. Named by Christopher Columbus for the day he spotted it—Sunday ("Dominica" in Italian), November 3, 1493—its 160 bird species give it some of the eastern Caribbean's most diverse birdlife. Its reefs, regarded as one of the world's best dive destinations, are home to fish considered rare elsewhere—frogfish, seahorses, batfish, flying gurnards, and spectacular rainbow-hued multi-shaped sponges—and it is one of the best places anywhere for whale- and dolphin-watching.

Notable among several national parks set aside on this small 289-square-mile (112-km²) island: **Morne Trois Pitons National Park**, a 27-square-mile (69-km²) U.N. World Heritage Site in the southern half of the island, covers five ecological zones, from dry to primordial rain forest where 130-foot (40-m) chataignier trees are hung with 79 kinds of orchids, to "elfin" woodlands named for the stunted size of high-elevation cloud forest vegetation such as delicate 20-inch (0.5-m) high kaklin trees. Bright hummingbirds, especially purple-throated caribs, sip from a dazzling array of blossoms. Mournful four-note calls of mountain whistlers fill the canopy along with those of tiny noisy Gounouge tree frogs. Dense vegetation can make bird sightings challenging, but endangered parrots, their populations dangerously reduced by poaching for the pet and collector trade, usually announce their presence. Fauna include small rodent-like agoutis, cave bats, manicous (opossums), mongeese, three-inch (8-cm) Hercules beetles with formidable crablike mandibles, and a few two-yard-long (2-m) green iguanas.

Trails lead through the Valley of Desolation—a ghostly forest destroyed by sulphuric emissions—to Boiling Lake, second largest fumarole in the world, a bubbling mass of 212°F (100°C) mud and water; spectacular 295-foot-high (90-m) Middleham Falls and Emerald Falls and Pool;

Jacamars, such as this rufous-tailed, resemble overgrown hummingbirds with their glittering metallic gold, green, and coppery plumage—an eye-catching display when they zoom after favorite insect prey, often an equally vivid butterfly. After a successful sally they beat their hapless victim against a branch until wings flutter to the ground, and only then consume the body. Jacamars' sharp calls suggest lives of high excitement, and indeed, high-pitched notes of their vocal courtship climaxes ending in long-drawn, clear, soft trills are one of the loveliest sounds of tropical woodlands and streamsides from Mexico to northern Argentina.

98-foot-high (30-m) Trafalgar Falls; and to several mountain lakes and summits, all chances to see much of the island's flora and fauna, though of varying difficulty—best consult as to whether a guide would be advisable.

Lovely **Scotts Head/Soufriere Bay Marine Reserve** may be explored by snorkeling, diving, or kayaking.

**Central and Northern Forest Reserves** protect woodland watersheds and wildlife as does **Cabrits National Park** with dry coastal forests as well as Dominica's largest wetland containing both freshwater marsh and mangroves. New 81-square-mile (210-km²) **Morne Diablotin National Park** protects critical habitat of imperial parrots (the national birds which according to native folklore are reincarnated Carib people) as well as other significant bird, mammal, and butterfly species.

Temperatures average 68–85°F (20–29°C) in January, 72–90°F (22–32°C) in July, with mean relative humidity 65–73 percent, cooler and wetter in mountains. August, wettest month, averages 22 days' measurable rain; April, driest, 10.

Dominica is served by flights from Antigua, Barbados, Guadeloupe, Martinique, Puerto Rico, St. Lucia, and St. Martin.

A variety of lodging is available in locally-run hotels and guesthouses in town, coastal, and mountain retreats, also taxis and car rental (requires international driver's license).

---

**FURTHER INFORMATION**

National Parks Office, Bath Estate, Roseau, Commonwealth of Dominica, West Indies, Tel: (+1 767) 448-2401, or Dominican National Development Corporation, Fax: (+1 767) 448-5840.

---

# HISPANIOLA

Hispaniola's environmental history is an unhappy one, with once-dense forests gone from 90 percent of the Dominican Republic on the island's eastern two-thirds, and Haiti, on the rest, essentially barren, with little environmental consciousness evident in either.

Problems include overfishing, coral reef degradation, urban encroachment, water pollution, and poaching of species supposedly protected (illegally killed sea turtles are common restaurant fare).

Yet even here are beautiful remnants.

## DOMINICAN REPUBLIC

The Dominican Republic has 16 national parks, created to avoid the fate of 98 percent of Haiti, and while funds are woefully inadequate for maintenance and environmental enforcement, it is a start, and a little reforestation work has begun.

## HISPANIOLA

Noteworthy are adjoining **Armando Bermudez** and **Jose del Carmen Ramirez National Parks**, together covering 590 square miles (1,530 km²) in the Cordillera Central which include the Caribbean's highest mountains. These give rise to 14 rushing rivers, important for agriculture and electric power but also including several floral and faunal life zones, from tropical rain forest to alpine, thus home to many of the island's 254 bird species. These include such beautiful rarities as Hispaniola parrots, trogons, woodpeckers and lizard-cuckoos, palm chats (talkative national birds), rufous-throated solitaires, and greater Antillean pewees, plus mongeese and (introduced) wild boars.

Spectacular (but occasionally hazardous) trails with simple cabins (first-come-first-served) attract hikers from around the world (guides are required). Helpful ranger stations are near the start of five major trails—at La Cienaga, Sabaneta, Mata Grande, Las Lagunas, and Constanza (the parks have no roads). Accommodations and information are available in nearby Jarabacoa.

## ALSO OF INTEREST

**Valle Nuevo Scientific Reserve**, montane and oceanic forest with some of the island's best birding (Antillean euphonias, black-crowned palm tanagers, narrow-billed todies, white-winged warblers), reachable by spectacular (4WD) drive from San Jose to Constanza, then on Highway 41 a short way into the forest.

**Isla Cabritos National Park** in saltwater Lake Enriquillo (144 feet/44 m below sea level) has a large American crocodile population plus 62 bird species including green mango hummingbirds, Antillean nighthawks, burrowing owls, and many American flamingos, three hours' drive west of Santo Domingo.

**Sierra de Bahoruco** is a forested highland with 52 percent of Dominican Republic's 300 orchids plus many bird species.

---

**FURTHER INFORMATION**

Dominican Republic National Parks Office (DNP), Avenida Independencia 539 esquina Cervantes, Santo Domingo, Apartado Postal 2487, Tel: (+1 809) 221-5340; Ecotourism office, Tel: (+1 809) 472-3717/4204.

---

# HAITI

Haiti has pockets of amazing biodiversity given the extent of environmental damage and pressures of burgeoning population. Deforestation and resulting erosion have robbed mountains of topsoil which now chokes reefs and marine life, and pervasive poverty among one of the densest populations in the western hemisphere—1,753 per square mile (677 per km²)—cripples land reform.

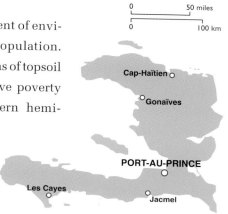

Still, a range of nine life zones, from low desert and mangrove to high cloud forest, supports some 600 fern species, 300 kinds of orchids and most of its neighbor's birds (which don't recognize national boundaries) in Haiti's four national parks that struggle for survival with little money for supervision to prevent poaching by people desperate for food and charcoal.

Virgin cloud forest spectacularly envelops mountains in 19-square-mile (49-km²) **Parc Nacional Macaya** at the west end of Haiti's southern claw, traversed by two roads of varying quality: Route 2 through the length of the claw, and 204 through the mountains to Jacmel, which has lodging and information (in the mayor's office) about park visits. Most of Haiti's wildlife can be seen along trails with fine views both in Macaya and **Parc Nacional Forêt des Pins**, east of Jacmel near the DR border. **Parc La Visite**, northeast of Jacmel, has limestone caves, waterfalls, and cliffs, especially one on the northern park boundary where endangered black-capped petrels nest. **Lake Saumatre**, 90 minutes east of Port-au-Prince, has more than 100 waterfowl species plus flamingos and American crocodiles, best on the north side, reachable through Thomazeau. Rainy seasons are April–May and September–October. June–September can be unbearably hot.

---

**FURTHER INFORMATION**

Secretary of State for Tourism, Rue Legitime, Champs de Mars, Port-au-Prince, Tel: (+509) 223-2143, 223-5631, Fax: (+509) 223-5359.

---

OPPOSITE: Lacy-tailed blue-crowned mot-mots work in pairs to excavate elaborate mudbank tunnel nests without seeming to ruffle a feather of gorgeous plumage. Tunnels up to 14 feet (4.2 m) long with spacious nest chambers 10 × 10 × 14 inches (25 × 25 × 36 cm) are finished in early fall, then abandoned until the pair start spring courtship rituals. Decorative tails are not inborn but plucked out by each bird.

# TRINIDAD AND TOBAGO

In all the lush Caribbean, no place is more exquisite than mountainous, blossoming Trinidad with its neighbor Tobago, with wildlife to match. Dazzling scarlet ibises, iridescent jacamars, streamer-tailed red-billed tropic birds, lacy-tailed mot-mots and 41 kinds of hummingbirds are but a few among more than 430 bird species recorded—more than any other islands in the Caribbean, said to be more per square mile than anyplace else in the world—of which 250 are known to breed. Because the islands are as close as seven miles (11 km) from Venezuela, many are South American.

## TRINIDAD AND TOBAGO

Mammals of 108 species include howler monkeys, anteaters, and armadillos, and there are 55 kinds of reptiles, 25 amphibians—including golden tree frogs—more than 1,600 kinds of butterflies, reefs filled with diverse marine life, and equally diverse and lovely flora. Wild poinsettias are the national flower, with 1,600 other kinds of blossoming plants including spectacular trees such as immortelles, flamboyant pride of India, frangipani, pink and yellow poui, and lavender jacaranda hung with 700 kinds of orchids.

# TRINIDAD

**Asa Wright Nature Center** on Trinidad, which accommodates guests and arranges bird tours, has blue-crowned mot-mots with lacy tail patterns coming to tea from woods ringing with bearded bellbirds' calls. Regular residents along trails from the center—often visible simply

Flamingos feed using a method that is shared only by certain whales, first immersing their bills upside-down in shallow water, then sucking in and expelling water through lammellae or membranes which filter out and retain food organisms of appropriate size. Their bright plumage comes from small crustacea and algae which they ingest in saline lagoons and is lost in captivity unless they're fed similar substances, or even vegetable dyes.

from its front porch—include collared trogons, golden-headed manakins, green, red-legged, and purple honeycreepers, speckled, silver-beaked, and turquoise tanagers. Shining rufous-tailed jacamars nest in stream-bank holes. Raucous parrots sweep through the canopy.

Scarlet ibises stream in flights of hundreds to nightly roosts in **Caroni Swamp**. Oilbirds roost in nearby caves, glowing eyes reflecting visitors' lights.

Red-bellied macaws scream back at hooting red howler monkeys and weeping capuchins in **Nariva Swamp**, a Ramsar Wetland of International Significance with savannah hawks and red-breasted blackbirds. Dawn visits are best, preferably in a silent kayak.

Golden tree frogs peep and orange-billed nightingale-thrushes sing along trails hung with giant bromeliads and orchids in **Northern Range Sanctuary Forest**, among many parts of the two islands designated as parks, reserves, and protected areas by the ministry of agriculture.

## TOBAGO

On Tobago, blue-crowned mot-mots are always on view, among other spectaculars, at **Grafton Wildlife Sanctuary**, which stages impressive evening bird feedings, as do several local inns. Spectacled caymans haul out at **Hillsborough Dam**. Red-billed tropic birds nest on north-facing cliffs of **Little Tobago**, just east. **Tobago Forest Reserve** is oldest protected rain forest in the world, with 123 butterfly species—including spectacular blue emperors—and 210 birds, including seasonal migrants such as plumbeous kites. Giant leatherback turtles, world's largest—up to 7.5 feet (2.3 m) long, weighing 1,200 pounds (540 kg)—nest along the north shore.

Snorkeling and diving (with giant manta rays!) are superb (dive lessons available) but glass-bottomed boats also visit reefs. Sunsets are unsurpassed anywhere. Peak times are January–March—but other times can be equally good and less costly. Sea turtles and seabirds nest in June.

Lectures and field trips are led by the Trinidad and Tobago Naturalist's Club, Box 642, Port of Spain. Helpful trail and other guides are available from Asa Wright Center.

Port of Spain is served by international jet, with connecting flights to Tobago. Both islands

**FURTHER INFORMATION**

Forestry Division, Ministry of Agriculture, Land and Marine Resources, Long Circular Road, St. James, Port of Spain, Trinidad, West Indies, Tel: (+1 868) 622-7476; Trinidad and Tobago Tourism Development Company, 10–14 Philipps Street, Port of Spain, Trinidad and Tobago, West Indies, Tel: (+1 868) 623-1932, Fax: 623-6022, E-mail: tourism-info@tidco.co.tt, reachable toll-free Tel: 888/595-4868 from USA, 0800-960-057 from UK, 0130-81-16-18 from Germany, and 1-678-70272 from Italy.

# BELIZE

IF THAT OCELOT OR PUMA IN COCKSCOMB
BASIN SANCTUARY PURRS, IT'S NOT NECESSARILY
FRIENDLY. IT MAY BE EMOTIONALLY SIZING YOU UP AS
A POSSIBLE ADVERSARY. (IF IT ROARS, IT'S A JAGUAR.)

EMERALD-GREEN MORAY EELS AND JEWEL-LIKE ANGEL FISH, GIANT CORAL HEADS, AND PURPLE SEA FANS MAKE UP ONLY A SMALL PART OF THE ECOSYSTEM THAT IS THE WORLD'S SECOND LONGEST BARRIER REEF, JUST OFFSHORE FROM THIS TINY CENTRAL AMERICAN COUNTRY ONCE KNOWN AS BRITISH HONDURAS.

Jaguars roam free inland in their own COCKSCOMB BASIN JAGUAR SANCTUARY, first and only reserve specifically set aside for these magnificent endangered spotted cats. Protected with them are keel-billed toucans, the impressive national birds, black orchids, the national flower, and the curious national animal, semi-aquatic Baird's tapirs, related to rhinoceros but resembling short-trunked elephants.

Altogether 533 species of birds—from azure and gold-green parrots, scarlet macaws, and lacy-tailed mot-mots to iridescent ocellated turkeys and diminutive hummingbirds—plus 150 kinds of mammals, 140 reptiles and amphibians, and 3,400 species of native flowering plants (including 279 orchid species) are protected in more than 20 reserves, many private. Altogether they cover more than 40 percent of this country about the size of Massachusetts or Wales.

Habitats include more than 1,000 lagoons along mangrove-fringed shore and coastal islands, sheltering one of the world's largest populations of endangered manatees, to savannahs, mountains, and woodlands. Belize is 70 percent forested with more than 40 percent of its primary forest still standing. Independent since 1981, among the first laws passed were a wildlife protection bill and a national parks bill.

## BELIZE BARRIER REEF RESERVE

The barrier reef, 185 miles (290 km) long, second only to Australia's in size and to none in color and brilliance, along with its accompanying cays (pronounced keys) and atolls has attracted world renown among snorkelers and scuba divers as

# BELIZE

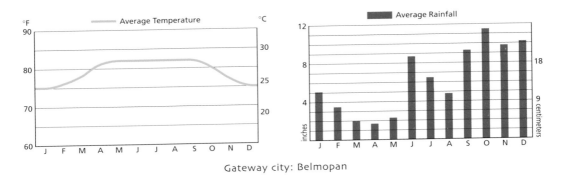

Gateway city: Belmopan

well as marine naturalists. (The Belize government claims it as the world's longest unbroken chain of living coral reef.)

Jewel-like fish and purple sea plumes find homes here along with gentle, friendly, endangered manatees and sea turtles in this largest tropical reef in the western hemisphere.

Biodiversity of this "rain forest of the sea" is as stunning as its beauty. Massive brain corals, branched golden elkhorn, staghorn, and finger corals, small and large stars, and 75 kinds of hard reef-building species coexist with softly waving lavender sea feathers, lacy sea fans, and dozens of others to furnish habitat for a myriad of organisms which are their intimately cooperating neighbors.

Multihued fish of over 500 species interact with sea anemones, octopi, lobsters, shrimps, urchins, sea worms, and almost innumerable others, displaying crimson, yellow, green, and blue scales, fins, and tentacles, which inspire wonder but are also indispensable. They serve as camouflage, identification, warnings, and courtship aids for many thousands of parrotfish, snappers, groupers, bonefish, barracudas, and graceful angelfish, along with harmless rays and nurse sharks.

Reefs and nearby cays are headquarters also for 286 bird species including storks, egrets, herons, pelicans, cormorants, ospreys, roseate terns, spoonbills, black catbirds, and magnificent frigate birds.

Some 4,000 red-footed boobies live on **Half-Moon Cay** on Lighthouse Reef, home also to renowned wish-willy lizards. Flocks of brown noddies come here after a life spent almost entirely at sea to produce families on **Southwest Cay** on **Glover's Reef Marine Reserve**. The cay is an estimated seven million years old, one of the Caribbean's most pristine and scientifically important coral gardens. **Man-O-War Cay** is a significant nesting site for magnificent frigate birds and brown boobies.

Two endangered coastal crocodiles, Morelet's and American saltwater, are here. Loggerhead, green, and hawksbill sea turtles nest on beaches. West Indian manatees—300 to 700, perhaps world's most concentrated population of this endangered sea giant—breed and graze on turtle grass. All these are at risk either from poaching or overfishing (legal seasons still exist for green and loggerhead turtles).

Biggest threats are new population centers with coastal development, sewage, agri-chemical pollution, overfishing, and unregulated boating and diving. But benefits from ecotourism have stirred support for protection of this fragile irreplaceable resource.

## COCKSCOMB BASIN JAGUAR SANCTUARY

Endangered jaguars, largest land predators in Central and South America and the hemisphere's only cat of the *Panthera* genus (in which only the tiger and lion are bigger) are found here. These large, spotted cats—males here are typically around 125 pounds (60 kg)—have responded to safe haven in this 155 square miles (403 km²) of wild forest and mountains. Radiant scarlet macaws are among up to 300 bird species, with 62 other mammals, including four other kinds of wild cats, howler and spider monkeys, anteaters, kinkajous, river otters, "four-eyed" opossums, and 43 bat species.

Secretive, wary jaguars are more often heard than seen. Like other large *Panthera* they have throat cartilage that lets them roar, a startling sound that makes their presence audible for miles. Roars are not in the vocal capability of smaller pumas, spotted ocelets, margays, and dark solitary jaguarundis here which purr like domestic cats. (Purrs may not indicate friendliness; pumas may stand their ground aggressively on encountering humans.) All these cats are efficient predators. They can coexist because each exploits a hunting niche which generally does not overlap others.

The sanctuary, named for the jagged series of Maya Mountain peaks which rise more than 3,000 feet (1,000 m) above lush twin basins, is honeycombed with a maze of creeks and tributaries which merge into the headwaters of two major rivers. Jaguars, good swimmers, vary diets of paca, peccary, and brocket deer to fish here with otters and bright kingfishers. Water-loving Baird's tapirs, largest land mammals in Central America, weighing up to 600 pounds (270 kg), graze on stream vegetation. Red-eyed tree frogs, boa constrictors, and iguanas are equally at home among giant tree ferns, orchids, and huge climbing vines in ancient forests.

Formidable king vultures take precedence over all their kin at kills and soar over treetops with brilliant orange, yellow, and blue wattles notable even in distant flight. Curly-crested, turkey-sized great curassows scratch about forest floors for insects. Keel-billed toucans delicately employ huge (but hollow and lightweight) rainbow-hued bills to flick small berries down their throats with quick head-tosses. Others noted as common on the impressive bird list include laughing and bat falcons, bare-throated tiger-herons, sungrebes, mottled owls, violet sabrewings, fork-tailed emerald and azure-crowned hummingbirds, as well as many wintering northern songbirds, including orioles and hooded, prothonotary, and magnolia warblers.

OPPOSITE: Jaguars, whose native Indian name—yaguara—means "killer that takes its prey in a single bound," tend to stalk prey on the ground, and, empowered by long hindlimbs, spring from ambush, killing with a single crushing bite through temporal skull bones. Pre-Columbian civilizations of Peru and Central America worshipped jaguars as gods, but overhunting for their beautiful spotted fur, as well as habitat destruction, has led to near-extinction over much of their range. They're still found in remote forests and scrublands in Central and South America to Argentina.

The sanctuary is managed by Belize Audubon Society with well-equipped headquarters/visitor center six miles (10 km) west of the village of Maya Center, with self-guided trail literature, picnic area, campgrounds, cabins, tour guides (arranged in advance), and potable water. Accommodations are also available in nearby Dandriga and Hopkins. Swimming in streams and waterfalls is not only permitted but recommended. Dry season is February–May.

---

**FURTHER INFORMATION**

Director, Cockscomb Basin Wildlife Sanctuary, P.O. Box 90, Dandriga, Belize; OR Belize Audubon Society (*see* below).

---

# CHIQUIBUL NATIONAL PARK

Belize's largest national park, 416 square miles (1,080 km²) of south Vaca Plateau and eastern slopes of the Maya Mountains, with forest unbroken since Mayans abandoned it centuries ago. It harbors rare, bright green, long-tailed keel-billed motmots, plus kinkajous, spider monkeys, Baird's tapirs, Belize's largest breeding population of scarlet macaws, and the Chiquibul cavern system, probably largest in Central America. Its full size is unknown but three caverns explored so far total 19 miles (32 km) long, and one chamber is largest ever found in western hemisphere. New insect and crustacean species have been discovered, along with many Mayan ceremonial artifacts. Chiquibul is accessible via the Augustine–Caracol road. There were, at least until recently, no public facilities, but local resorts run trips from area base camps.

# ALSO OF INTEREST

**Crooked Tree Wildlife Sanctuary**, home to vast numbers of native and migrant waterbirds, especially in dry February–May, including jabiru storks with large black bills and 12-foot (4-m) wingspreads, western hemisphere's biggest flying birds. Flocks of hundreds of Everglade kites may be present along with Yucatan woodpeckers, white-collared manakins, northern royal flycatchers, and sungrebes. Some 1,000 limpkins nest.

**Community Baboon Sanctuary** at Bermudian Landing, established by local cooperating landowners, protects a thriving population of black howler monkeys (called baboons here).

# BELIZE

Margays are known for exceptional climbing abilities. Aided by flexible rotating hind feet and, for balance, furry tails up to two-thirds their up-to-31-inch (79-cm) length, they can run straight down trees head-first or somersault to hang from branches or lianas by hind feet alone or, if advantageous, just one hind foot. They're threatened by destruction of forest habitat in central South America.

**Panti Medicine Trail**, named for a Mayan medicine man, has herbal plants reputed to do everything from repel insects to treat dysentery.

**Monkey Bay Sanctuary and Reserve**, west of Belize City along Sibun River, privately owned, protects many indigenous species.

**Rio Bravo Conservation Area**, 323 square miles (840 km²), established by Programme for Belize.

**Shipstern Nature Preserve and Butterfly Breeding Center**, with nearly 200 butterfly species, also tapirs and deer in its savannahs and a shallow lagoon which is major wading bird habitat.

**Belize Zoo**, though not a wildlife reserve, is worth a visit. It was established to care for animals abandoned by a financially strapped nature film company and adopted by a company employee who has made this an admirable center for Central American fauna, all kept in native surroundings. Nearby is a natural lagoon favored by manatees.

Belize also has hundreds of Mayan ruins, including **Caracol**, possibly largest Mayan complex ever found.

---

**FURTHER INFORMATION**

Belize Audubon Society, P.O. Box 1001, 12 Fort Street, Belize City, Belize, Central America, Tel: (+501) 223-5004, Fax: (+501) 223-4985, E-mail: base@btl.net

# COSTA RICA

PECCARIES—WILD SWINE—ARE NOTORIOUSLY NEAR-SIGHTED. A BACKPACKER IN CORCOVADO NATIONAL PARK, SURROUNDED BY A HERD OF 150 OF THEM CLACKING SHARP TEETH, WISELY CLIMBED A TREE TO GIVE THEM TIME TO DECIDE HE WASN'T DANGEROUS.

JAGUARS, THREE-TOED SLOTHS, HARPY EAGLES, AND MORE BIRD SPECIES THAN ARE FOUND IN NORTH AMERICA, AUSTRALIA OR EUROPE ARE PROTECTED IN THIS SMALL COUNTRY WITH THREE-TEN THOUSANDTHS OF THE EARTH'S SURFACE BUT A HIGHER PERCENTAGE SET ASIDE FOR WILDLIFE PROTECTION THAN ANYPLACE ELSE.

Almost a third of Costa Rica is in national parks, wildlife refuges, and biological and forest reserves, including private set-asides. As a result, with its extraordinary natural biodiversity and habitat variety, it supports five percent of all the world's known plant and animal species.

Wildlife threatened with extinction elsewhere thrive here in a dozen distinct tropical life zones. They include dazzling macaws and spotted ocelots in the rain forest and six species of great sea turtles nesting on its beaches, some in huge "arribadas" where thousands may gather simultaneously to scour out egg-laying burrows.

More than 200 mammals include six wild felines—small forest-dwelling tiger cats, powerful pumas, dark jaguarundis, and little leopard-spotted margays. Among notable tropical species are four kinds of monkeys, which include

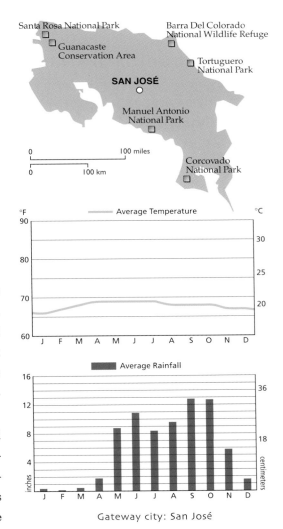

Gateway city: San José

335

eerie-sounding howlers. Herds of collared peccaries root about the forest floor, and two- and three-toed sloths hang motionless from tree limbs or feed on leafy vegetation so slowly they seem all but immobile. From the North American side of this continental land-bridge have come deer, otters, coyotes, foxes.

Some rain forests stand here today as they did a million years ago.

Visitor facilities in some are in various stages of development, including roads, trails, housing, and guided information. Check before planning a trip.

---

**FURTHER INFORMATION**

User Information Office, Tel: (+506) 192-233-4533, Fax: 233-5284.

---

# Barra del Colorado National Wildlife Refuge

The importance of this largest of Costa Rica's wildlife refuges as a wildlife annex to TORTUGUERO NATIONAL PARK (*see* p.343) cannot be overstated. Together they comprise over 470 square miles (1,215 km²) of riverine coastal rain forest, habitat for crocodiles, poison-dart and glass frogs, spider monkeys, sloths, and more than 300 species of colorful birds, as well as miles of precious nesting beach for endangered sea turtles. Other mammal species are jaguars, manatees, white-faced and howler monkeys, tapirs, ocelots, pumas, and among birds, great green macaws, great curassows, great tinamous, keel-billed toucans, and numerous herons.

Barra del Colorado is much like Tortugero but wilder, just south of the Nicaraguan border, with fewer facilities and staff, and not as protected against illegal logging, ranching, colonization, and road construction, especially in the less swampy west. Lodging is available in Barra del Colorado village (a famous sportfishing area); access is by boat from Tortuguero or charter flight from San José. Tours can be arranged.

An interesting natural phenomenon is migration of bull sharks from the saltwater Atlantic Ocean up San Juan River to freshwater Lake Nicaragua. Why these huge relatives of great white sharks do this and how they deal with the salinity change is not known. Fortunately no river attack has ever been recorded. Unfortunately, they are in danger of extinction from unregulated overfishing.

# Corcovado National Park

In Corcovado National Park, a hundred or more scarlet macaws may glide in a single group across the forest canopy, dazzling against a tropical blue sky, each crimson bird almost a yard (84 cm) long with gold and azure wings and trailing tail feathers, noisily seeking fruits and nuts or nightly roosts.

White-lipped and collared peccaries rummage about the forest floor, sometimes several hundred together, soft grunts showing their pig-family connection.

Harpy eagles, largest birds of prey in the world, with powerful feet capable of picking off a sloth or howler monkey, watch and listen. Howler's penetrating wails can be heard miles away, audible over all other jungle sounds except the jaguar.

Corcovado National Park is one of Costa Rica's largest and wildest protected areas, covering a third of the Osa peninsula on the country's southwest Pacific coast. So remote is it that wild creatures often are observed only by other wild inhabitants—although campers and backpackers have returned with lively tales. One was marooned in his tent all night by a trio of roaring, circling, courting jaguars. Another was treed by a herd of 150 nearsighted peccaries clacking sharp teeth menacingly before deciding he was not dangerous.

Corcovado became a national park in 1975 after a squeaker of a conservation success story. Squatters had settled on lands where a North American/Japanese timber firm planned massive logging. Delicate negotiations by the world scientific community and then-President Daniel Oduber Quiros saved the day and won for Sr. Oduber the 1977 Albert Schweitzer award.

Corcovado's wet forests are among the most species-rich in Central America, with 367 kinds of birds, 140 species of mammals, 117 reptiles and amphibians, 40 freshwater fish, and 10,000-plus insects.

Huge trees rise unbranched to the canopy, especially in northern uplands above Punta Llorona—more than 500 species, a quarter of all those found in Costa Rica. A census in one two-acre (1-ha) plot alone found 108 species, the largest 213 feet (65 m) tall and 6.5 feet (2 m) in diameter.

Would-be visitors should be warned: facilities in this remote spot are few. Most trails accommodate foot travel only, with park headquarters at Sirena a day's walk or charter flight away. On a hot day a swim might be tempting, but watch out for crocodiles in freshwater and hammerhead sharks in salt.

With all that, Corcovado is an ecological treasure well worth the trouble to visit. Best time is dry season December–March. Main threats are illegal logging, gold-panning, and poaching.

**FURTHER INFORMATION**

Tel: (+506) 735-5036, Fax: 735-5282 (*see also* Tortuguero, p.343).

# GUANACASTE CONSERVATION AREA

Guanacaste Conservation Area's ocelots, peccaries, white-faced and howler monkeys are among beneficiaries of a bold plan linking Guanacaste National Park with adjoining SANTA ROSA

Living fossils unchanged on earth for some 35 million years, tapirs look like cousins of elephants but are more closely related to rhinoceros and horses. Prehensile-looking upper lips are useful for shoveling food in the mouth and gathering leaves from places their tongues and teeth can't reach. Tapirs are good swimmers and seek out watery, forested swamps in Central and northern South America.

NATIONAL PARK with complementary habitat here of wet and dry forest that continues up and around Orosi and Cacao volcanoes. Together the two create a corridor where wildlife can range safely in traditional migration paths from the coast all the way to the highlands.

Saved as well are magnificent examples of Costa Rica's national tree, for which this park is named—up to 100 feet (30.5 m) tall, supporting under its broad canopy a wildlife community of some of this park's 260 species of brilliant birds, 5,000 kinds of butterflies and moths, 3,000 kinds of orchids and other epiphytic plants (which derive their moisture and nutrients from rain and air), along with hundreds of amphibians, reptiles, and large and small mammals.

Jaguars are at home as are troops of ring-tailed coatimundis which range widely. So do large-billed toucans and sweet-singing bellbirds. Turkey-sized crested guans forage for fallen fruits. Trogons are inconspicuous until they spread their colorful wings and swoop after insects.

A dry-forest specialty rare elsewhere are noisy white-throated magpie jays, long-tailed, sky blue with exotic curly head plumes. They "mob" spectacled owls and any other suspicious-looking visitors, sometimes including humans.

More than a dozen separate biological habitats have been identified here, from salt and fresh-water lakes and swamps through grasslands and wooded savannahs, and dry and cloud forests on volcanic slopes.

In addition, the natural water system in the Palo Verde section adjoining has created an environment capable of supporting one of the largest concentrations of waterfowl and wading birds, both native and migratory (including large numbers of wood storks and roseate spoonbills), in Central America. There are nesting grounds of endangered jabiru storks and the only colony of scarlet macaws in the dry Pacific forest. Crocodiles up to 16 feet (5 m) long patrol the Tempisque River.

Guanacaste, 131 square miles (340 km²), is 174 miles (280 km) northwest of San José on the Inter-American highway, which separates it from Santa Rosa National Park. Best times are January–March dry season; 4WD is a good idea, or taxi service can be arranged in nearby Liberia to the Maritza field station—after that it's mostly trail-hiking. Overnight accommodations (some cold water only) can be arranged in advance at biological field stations. (*See* also Santa Rosa NP headquarters, Tel: (+506) 695-5598.)

## MANUEL ANTONIO NATIONAL PARK

Smallest and most popular Costa Rican national park with pristine white beaches backing up to verdant tropical forests full of wildlife, Manuel Antonio was almost lost to the kind of tourist development that surrounds it. One angry, frustrated developer, in fact, managed to cut down many magnificent trees and pour herbicide into mangrove swamps in an unsuccessful effort to defeat the park proposal.

Now endemic squirrel monkeys chatter in lively troops along trails. Howler monkeys hoot territorially. White-faced monkeys take to the trails after choice leaves and fruit. Anteaters probe insect tunnels with long, sticky tongues. Two-toed sloths hang from tree limbs, languidly turning heads to gaze at passersby.

Some 184 bird species include brown pelicans, brown boobies, tyrant hawk-eagles, gray-headed chachalacas, and brilliant Baird's trogons.

Green iguanas bask on logs as do smaller, grayer counterparts. Green and olive ridley sea turtles nest on beaches.

Twelve offshore island sanctuaries offer nesting habitat for brown boobies and others.

The park—212 maritime square miles (550 km²)—is 4.3 miles (7 km) south of Quepos, reachable by scheduled air from San José or by bus or rental car, a 110-mile (177-km) drive on the Inter-American coastal highway. There are no public roads or campsites, but excellent trails, reachable by a damp estuary crossing. A variety of lodging is in the area. Park visits can be restricted on crowded days.

## SANTA ROSA NATIONAL PARK

Santa Rosa National Park, 148 square miles (385 km²), was set aside to commemorate the historic defeat of a North American mercenary who planned to conquer and rule all of Central America. It's better known now for jaguars, monkeys, parrots, and especially the peaceful nesting of thousands of rare sea turtles which lay eggs in spectacular mass "arribadas" on pristine Pacific beaches just south of Nicaragua.

Formerly these eggs were quickly eaten by hungry animals—and humans. Now they are protected, allowed to hatch, and send new-hatched young members of these endangered species out to sea.

Protection has enabled other wild creatures to flourish as well. In one of the country's last fragments of tropical dry forest—one of the best places in this tiny country to see wildlife—prehensile-trunked Baird's tapirs, peccaries, and others concentrate at water holes during the dry season.

Troops of coatimundis amble along trails. Howler, spider, and capuchin monkeys swing overhead. Turkey-sized great curassows and curly-topped crested guans drink at streams. Five cat species—jaguars, jaguarundis, ocelots, margays, and pumas—lurk warily anywhere.

Orioles weave intricate pouch nests in bull's horn acacias, sharp-thorned trees which also provide nectar and homes to aggressive stinging ants and in return are protected by them from any other creature. Long-nosed armadillos find invertebrates in leafy underbrush. Fishing bats skim estuaries snagging small fish detected by their sensitive sonar.

But the park's major spectacle is the nesting of three sea turtle species, green, huge leatherbacks, and rare, smaller Pacific olive ridleys which come ashore in mass "arribadas" from June to December. During one season alone 288,000 ridleys laid altogether 11.5 million eggs in three "arribadas" lasting three days each. Catching sight of these mass turtle nestings is chance—but at least a few come ashore most evenings through the season. (Caution: watch by moonlight. Artificial lights disorient and can endanger nesting success.) Access is sometimes restricted. There's a fine system of trails, short and long.

Ringtailed coatimundis are a true matriarchal society, females and offspring foraging and grooming in sociable groups up to 30, inviting males to join them when females are in estrus, excluding them when mating is completed. They range through savannahs and forests from southeastern Arizona to Argentina, nosy, busy little creatures, chattering among themselves, holding striped tails erect, leaping into trees with loud clicks and woofs if surprised.

Adjoining Santa Rosa across the Inter-American Highway is **Guanacaste National Park**, which continues up through cloud forest and surrounding volcanoes in an innovative concept (called GCA or Guanacaste Conservation Area) protecting species that migrate seasonally between the two parks.

Down the coast just south of Tamarindo is **Las Baulas Marine National Park** where thousands of leatherbacks, world's largest sea turtles, visit and nest on Playa Grande beach in October–March.

**FURTHER INFORMATION**

Headquarters Tel/Fax: (+506) 695-5598.

# TORTUGUERO NATIONAL PARK

This steamy rain forest, sometimes called Costa Rica's Amazon, interlaced with waterways is home of crocodiles, sloths, river otters, ocelots, pumas, manatees, and raucous green macaws, and one of the most important sea turtle nesting areas in the world.

Every year up to 3,000 female green sea turtles up to four feet (1.2 m) long weighing up to 440 pounds (200 kg) clamber up the tranquil, palm-lined beaches—often the same ones where they were hatched—and scour out sandy depressions. There, weeping, they lay 100 or so rubbery eggs from which two months later tiny replicas tumble out and down toward the moonlit sea.

It is a mystery-filled natural sight like no other, which also occurs in smaller numbers here for three species: hawksbills with beautiful shells plundered for jewelry; loggerheads, named for outsized heads; and great leatherbacks, up to six feet (2 m) long, weighing almost a ton.

That all survive to nest here is due largely to the efforts of one man. Dr. Archie Carr drew attention to their plight and pushed for these reserves when cruel exploitation for food, decoration, and even reputed aphrodisiacs brought them to the brink of extinction. The gentle greens used to be de-shelled alive, edible layers cut from their bodies, the creatures left to die agonizingly on beaches there. First discovered by Dutch explorers in 1539, turtle populations had remained stable until relentless exploitation in the mid 20th century.

Tortuguero is no less important for endangered West Indian manatees, half-ton marine mammals so mild-mannered and slow they are easy victims of hunters and boats' sharp propeller blades. They were thought extinct here until this population was discovered, and their survival is still in question.

Three-toed sloths, even slower, hang from trees, cuddling babies, descending once a month to defecate on the ground.

Spider, white-faced, and howler monkeys swing through trees, sometimes with prehensile-tailed kinkajous which behave almost like kin. Giant anteaters, tapirs, peccaries, and wary jaguars make a living in the understory.

Basilisk "Jesus Christ" lizards resembling yard-long (1 m) dinosaurs dash across water surfaces aided by skin flaps on large rear toes. Thumbnail-sized red and-blue-black "poison arrow" frogs are smallest of 60 amphibians here.

Great habitat variety contributes to wide diversity among the more than 300 bird species—magnificent frigate birds and royal terns among oceanics; plovers and sandpipers among shorebirds; jacanas and green-and-rufous kingfishers along rivers; brilliant hummingbirds and melodious manakins in forests inland. Stately herons, including beautiful uncommon chestnut-bellied and bare-throated tiger-herons, fish along waterways. Colorful macaws almost a yard (79 cm) long congregate around ripe fruit of almendro trees. Chestnut Montezuma oropendulas with blue and pink faces and orange-tipped bills weave long nest pouches in dense treetop colonies. In spring and fall North American migrants come through in large numbers—orioles, warblers, and Swainson's hawks.

Best times to visit are February–March and September. There is no real dry season here, so bring plenty of rain gear and insect repellent. Peak turtle nestings are June–September for greens and hawksbills, March–May for leatherbacks and loggerheads (best go with guide, and never use camera flash or lights which can endanger turtles' nesting success).

Threats include encroachment by loggers, ranchers, resort developers, banana and oil palm plantations, whose pesticides have caused fish kills and which continue to push for road linkage with the rest of the country, a proposal voted down by local residents.

Good related reading includes *The Windward Road* (A.A. Knopf, NY, 1956 and Florida State University Press, Gainesville, 1979), also *So Excellent A Fishe* (Natural History Press, NY, 1967) both by Archie Carr, Jr., who more than anyone else was responsible for parks and movement to save sea turtles from extinction.

---

**FURTHER INFORMATION**

Park ranger station, Tel: (+506) 710-2929, Fax: 710-7673.

---

# ALSO OF INTEREST

**Braulio Carrillo National Park**, 184 square miles (478 km²) of cloud and rain forest, some of it still unexplored, with monkeys, tapirs, jaguars, ocelots, resplendent quetzals (135 mammal species, 500-plus birds), bisected by a major highway just 19 miles (39 km) north of San José.

Common or abundant birds, many rare elsewhere, including tinamous, swallow-tailed kites, crested guans, squirrel cuckoos, swifts, parrots, and the glittering quetzal are here. A foothill corridor and wildlife migration path on the north connects with **La Selva Biological Station** where among other rarities are bare-necked umbrella birds, named for males' umbrella-like crest and scarlet skin patch expanded during courtship. Lodging is nearby and at the station. There are several trails. Adjacent to **Quebada Gonzalez Ranger Station** is a private reserve with an aerial tram through the rain forest canopy, an engineering marvel.

**Cano Negro Wildlife Refuge** is a wilderness in mid-north-central Costa Rica with huge numbers of resident and migratory water-oriented birds—kingfishers, roseate spoonbills, jacanas, jabiru and wood storks, herons, egrets, dizzying crowds of ducks, and the country's largest nesting colony of olivaceous cormorants. They are attracted to seasonally-filled Lake Cano Negro whose remoteness brings mammals in numbers as well—jaguars, tapirs, ocelots, monkeys, sloths, otters, tayras, and others which congregate at water holes in dry seasons. See by boat. Tours arranged at nearby hotels.

**Isla del Coco National Park** is a spectacular island with unique flora and fauna and, by legend, more buried pirates' treasure than anyplace else in the world, 30 square miles (78 km²) some 300 miles (500 km) offshore. Waterfalls plunge into the Pacific where gigantic hammer-head, whale, and white-tipped sharks swim and coral reefs teem with colorful fish. Three of the 97 bird species exist nowhere else. Colonies of nesting seabirds include two species of frigate birds, three of boobies, four of gulls, six kinds of storm petrels, and lovely little "espiritu santo" or holy spirit terns, which hover unafraid a few feet above visitors' heads.

Heavy rainfall—275 inches (700 cm) annually—early attracted sailors to its freshwater supply and coconuts, including the Pirate Benito "Bloody Sword" Bonito. Among his booty was said to be a life-size gold statue of the Virgin Mary and child. Despite searches, only a few doubloons have ever been found. Serious threats are posed by exotic animals and plants (pigs, cats) which upset natural ecosystems, and illegal fishing which disrupts nesting birds' food supplies. Permission is required for entry. There are trails but no lodging; overnight visitors stay on boats. A park station has mainland radio contact.

**Monte Verde Cloud Forest Biological Reserve**, a beautiful cloud forest high on the continental divide is most famous as home of one of the world's most beautiful and endangered birds, the emerald-and-crimson resplendent quetzal. Here as well is the three-wattled bellbird—its "bong" resounding through the canopy—as well as howler monkeys, golden translucent and blue morpho butterflies, Baird's tapirs, ocelots, nine-banded armadillos, and collared peccaries—altogether 100 mammal species, 400 kinds of birds, 490 butterflies, 120 reptiles and amphibians.

Monte Verde was founded by U.S. Quakers, who came after Costa Rica abolished its army in 1948, and was protected subsequently by scientists George and Harriet Powell and a Swedish schoolteacher who marshaled young contributors for the "children's rain forest reserve." The 41-square-mile (105-km²) reserve is 110 miles (180 km) from San José by bus. Driving, 4WD is advisable. So is rain gear. Lodging is nearby. Tours can be arranged. **Santa Elena Reserve** nearby has similar wildlife; both have trails. A private group can arrange visits on forest canopy platforms (not for the height-sensitive).

**FURTHER INFORMATION**

Monteverde Conservation League, Apartado 10165-1000, San José.
Reserve office, Tel: (+506) 645-5112, Fax: 645-5014.

**Palo Verde National Park** in the breathtaking Tempisque River valley northwest is one of the last places on the Pacific coast where scarlet macaws and rare giant jabirus, world's largest storks, still breed. Its 72 square miles (186 km²) augmented just to the north by **Lomas Barbudal Biological Reserve** is a mosaic of diverse moist habitats providing places which attract tens of thousands of herons, egrets, grebes, ducks, and jacanas, both resident and migrant, in some of the largest concentrations in Central America. Crowds of scissortailed flycatchers dive through insect swarms. Great curassows, laughing falcons, gray hawks, and wintering warblers and orioles are in nearby forests—some 300 bird species altogether, plus 177 mammals—howler and white-faced monkeys, jaguarundis, coatimundis, white-tailed deer—and in the river, crocodiles up to 16 feet (5 m) long. "Cracker" butterflies can concentrate in magnificent old trees, snapping their wings aggressively and audibly in territorial display. Best time is dry season December–March before flooding. **Isla de los Pajaros** can be covered with roseate spoonbills and other nesting birds including the country's largest black-crowned night-heron colony, visible either from the trail or by arranging a boat (don't go ashore—it's forbidden, also home to boa constrictors). Camping can be arranged; also lodging at Organization for Tropical Studies research station.

**FURTHER INFORMATION**

Organization for Tropical Studies research station, Tel: (+506) 240-6696, Fax: 240-6783;
Area de Conservación Tempisque office (ACT) in Bagaces, on Inter-American Highway,
Tel: (+506) 671-1290, Fax: 671-1062. Park is 17 miles (28 km) down a turnoff from the ACT office.

**Lomas Barbudal** is famous also for abundance and variety of insects, including a large number of bee species (unfortunately some are the Africanized "killer" variety).

# GUATEMALA

GLITTERING EMERALD-FEATHERED MAGNIFICENT
QUETZALS KEEP AN EYE OUT FOR CRESTED HARPY
EAGLES IN SIERRA DE LAS MINAS, LARGEST CONTIGUOUS
CLOUD FOREST IN CENTRAL AMERICA. BUT HARPIES
WOULD RATHER CARRY OFF A REAL FEAST, A
MONKEY OR SLOW-MOVING SLOTH.

STEALTHY JAGUARS AND OCELOTS ARE PROTECTED HERE ALONG WITH LUMBERING BAIRD'S TAPIRS AND ARBOREAL HOWLER AND SPIDER MONKEYS IN ONE OF THE HIGHEST PERCENTAGES OF CONSERVATION LAND SET SIDE BY ANY LATIN AMERICAN COUNTRY. Reserves include portions of mountains, forest highlands, jungle plains, and much of Central America's largest rain forest.

It is enough undisturbed land—42,000 square miles (109,000 km²), covering 19 different ecosystems—to furnish a reservoir for plants and animals now threatened over most of Central America, as well as for 45 among 1,500 vertebrate species that exist nowhere else.

Some 250-odd kinds of mammals roam free here, including tawny nocturnal kinkajous, related to raccoons but swinging through trees like monkeys. Mexican anteaters slurp up stinging ants (anteaters are conservationists, not destroying ant colonies but only grazing to return another day). Reptiles and amphibians of 200 species include two crocodiles and endangered leatherback, olive ridley, and Tortuga negra sea turtles.

Huge-billed toucans, screaming scarlet macaws, tiny iridescent hummingbirds, and great fierce raptors, including formidable harpy eagles, are among 664 kinds of birds. Streamer-tailed magnificent or resplendent quetzals, birds for which the Guatemalan monetary unit is named, are here. (Ancient Mayan law carried a death penalty for their unauthorized killing.) Gleaming peacock-like ocellated turkeys gobble and strut, and in watered areas, graceful herons, waterfowl, and dozens of migratory species forage for insects and minnows.

0 ——— 100 miles
0 ——— 200 km

☐ Tikal National Park/
Maya Biosphere Reserve

GUATEMALA
CITY
○

☐ Sierra De Las Minas
World Biosphere Reserve

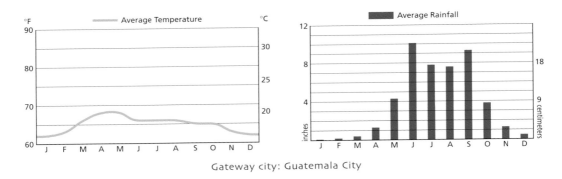

Gateway city: Guatemala City

More than 8,000 plant species are protected—600 kinds of orchid alone, including Guatemala's national flower, the exquisite white nun.

Largest set-aside is 8,125-square-mile (21,050-km²) MAYA BIOSPHERE RESERVE covering the northern third of the Peten region, comprised of seven parks or reserves encircled by a buffer zone where environmentally-compatible human activities are permitted. Among the parks is 222-square-mile (576-km²) TIKAL NATIONAL PARK which has, as well, major Mayan archeological sites. SIERRA DE LAS MINAS BIOSPHERE RESERVE is Central America's most important cloud forest reserve.

Designating such places does not ensure protection. Funds are short to control poaching, squatters, and slash-and-burn farming and logging. This is a problem, as is recurring political unrest. A consular information sheet says no area is "always safe," particularly for private vehicles after dark. Travelers should enquire about recent activities and best ways to visit a destination before setting out.

A promising regional conservation approach would have neighboring countries work in concert to protect large contiguous areas—as in Mexico's CALAKMUL BIOSPHERE RESERVE in southern Yucatan (*see* p.451), adjoining Guatemala's MAYA BIOSPHERE RESERVE and, in next-door Belize, RIO BRAVO CONSERVATION AREA (*see* p.334) and AGUAS TURBIAS NATIONAL PARK. Cooperative ecotourism could help protect this entire region while bringing income to national economies and make natural systems worth more to their people.

## TIKAL NATIONAL PARK/MAYA BIOSPHERE RESERVE

Tikal National Park/Maya Biosphere Reserve, focus centuries ago of a magnificent now-disappeared Mayan civilization, today is 222-square-mile (576-km²) rain forest domain of jaguars, ocelots, spider and howler monkeys, and screaming parrots.

Orange-breasted falcons and lesser swallow-tailed swifts nest in temple and palace ruins where pumas and spotted margays may emerge to hunt when visitors depart.

## GUATEMALA

Mexican anteaters are among 54 mammal species, as are nine-banded armadillos which sense insect caches deep underground and dig them out with manic speed, holding their breath up to six minutes to avoid inhaling flying earth. They consume 40,000 ants at a sitting, curling up afterward in armor-plated balls which few predators can penetrate.

Noisy bright kingfishers fish at lagoons, as do unobtrusive bitterns and graceful herons and egrets, among more than 350 bird species here. Colorful keel-billed toucans and mealy or white-crowned parrots harvest canopy fruits.

Butterflies gather at flowering trees and shrubs along with white-bellied emerald and little hermit hummingbirds and their glittering look-alikes, rufous-tailed jacamars, which are there to feed on butterflies. (Despite appearances, jacamars are related to woodpeckers, not hummingbirds.) Just as colorful but quietly inconspicuous in high tree branches are violaceous, slaty-tailed, and collared trogons, spotted only when they fly out for insects. Aptly-named laughing falcons and sometimes crested eagles keep an eye on them all.

Giant mahogany, cedar, and zapote trees (source of chicle for chewing gum) overshadow remains of more than 3,000 temples, ancient palaces, and ceremonial structures dating from 600 BC to 900 AD, scattered through the forest, many still buried under mounded earth of centuries.

Tikal is Guatemala's oldest national park which, with adjoining CALAKMUL BIOSPHERE RESERVE in Mexico and contiguous conservation areas in Belize, protects an enormous area of Central American mountains, wetlands, and jungle rain forests.

## SIERRA DE LAS MINAS WORLD BIOSPHERE RESERVE

Green-black horned guans—endangered turkey-sized birds with assertive scarlet face-shields and feet—make homes alongside jaguars and tapirs in this 906-square-mile (2,350-km²) reserve in southeast Guatemala. It is the largest contiguous cloud forest in northern Central America and regarded as one of the most important in the world.

Some 70 percent of the country's native species are here, including pumas, deer, and endangered, frilly-crested, great curassows. They find ecological niches in habitat ranging from low, moist tropical to higher coniferous forests, at elevations from 492 feet (150 m) to over 9,840 feet (3,015 m) above sea level.

Glittering emerald-feathered magnificent quetzals breed in higher elevations and move downhill later, so the park hopes to protect their migration areas as well.

The reserve is the only place where huge crested harpy eagles, capable of striking and carrying off monkeys and sloths, have been seen in any numbers lately. Recent studies suggest more endangered species and perhaps others as yet unknown will be found as more thorough inventories proceed.

# GUATEMALA

Sierra de las Minas was being rapidly deforested when The Nature Conservancy included it in its "Parks in Peril" program in the 1980s. It is now managed by a non-governmental conservation group—Defensores de la Naturaleza—with buffer zones of sustainable development surrounding the core cloud forest zone.

It is not easy to visit. At least until recently, permits were required (*see* below). The main cross-Guatemala highway, Route #9, runs through the Motagua Valley with several hotels nearby. But roads into the reserve require 4WD and sometimes long hikes. Visitors sometimes are permitted to stay at rangers' stations. Low-impact tourist programs have been planned—check before coming.

### FURTHER INFORMATION

Unión Internacional para la Conservacion de la Naturaleza, 31 Av. 1-123, Zona 7, Jardines Utatlan I, Ciudad de Guatemala, Tel/Fax: (+502-2) 946-849; Consejo Nacional de Areas Protegidas (CONAP), Edif. Maya 4to. Nivel, Via 5, 4-50 Zona 4, Guatemala City, Guatemala, Tel: (+502) 332-0463, Fax: (+502) 332-0464, E-mail: conap@concyt.gob.gt; Fundacion Defensores de la Naturaleza, 14 Calle 6-49, Zona 9, Guatemala City 01009, Guatemala, Tel: (+502) 334-1885, Fax: (+502) 361-7011, E-mail: defensores@ponet.net.gt

Vocal yellow-crowned parrots have large, muscular feet that are as useful as their wings. Like all their family of blunt-tailed parrots, they use them to pluck fruit and nuts, to hold food items while they are peeling and consuming them, and above all, to climb well, of prime importance in their forest habitat, which ranges from Guatemala south through northern Brazil.

# HONDURAS

GREAT WEEPING SEA TURTLES SCOUR OUT
NESTS AND LAY EGGS ON SANDY BEACHES
IN RÍO PLÁTANO BIOSPHERE RESERVE, WORLD
HERITAGE SITE WITH JAGUARS, PUMAS, TAPIRS,
MANATEES, AND SCARLET MACAWS.

L ANGUID THREE-TOED TREE SLOTHS, PREDATORY COUGARS AND JAGUARS, AND GLITTERING EMERALD
MAGNIFICENT QUETZALS ARE AT HOME IN ORCHID-STREWN CLOUD FORESTS OF THIS MOUNTAINOUS
CENTRAL AMERICAN COUNTRY BORDERING NICARAGUA, GUATEMALA, AND EL SALVADOR. Honduras has
more of these high mist-shrouded habitats, where moisture is so pervasive it is known as "horizontal precipitation," than anyplace else in this part of the hemisphere.

Cloud forests make up about one-third of the country's 100 protected national parks and
wildlife reserves which stretch from Caribbean to Pacific coastlines. Others are in humid
lowland jungles; still others are in thick mangrove and marine parks with beautiful coral reefs
and endangered manatees. In total they cover all the country's eight major life zones, with some
9,600 square miles (25,000 km²) earmarked for eventual protection.

Spotted ocelots, giant anteaters, and howler monkeys are among mammals little-seen elsewhere,
and there are 700 species of birds, including rare harpy eagles capable of seizing and carrying
off monkeys and tree sloths.

A devastating hurricane hit Honduras in 1998, but the country has gradually recovered. Constant
threat, exacerbated by that disaster, is deforestation which at least until recently was proceeding

at a rate of 1,150 square miles (3,000 km²) a
year. Conservation has conflicted also with
cattle ranching, coffee plantations, tourist
development interests, and settlement and
agricultural needs of a growing population,
expressed often in slash-and-burn clearing
that has caused widespread forest fires.
Conservation activist Jeannette Kawas was
murdered in 1995 in the process of declar-
ing Punta Sal a national park.

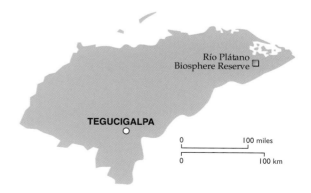

# HONDURAS

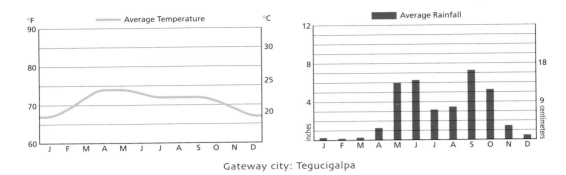

Gateway city: Tegucigalpa

## Río Plátano Biosphere Reserve

This outstanding nature set-aside has superb wildlife—jaguars, pumas, tapirs, manatees, scarlet macaws—also 200 sites of archeological importance covering almost 2,000 square miles (5,250 km²).

Great weeping sea turtles scour out nests on sandy beaches unchanged, like much else here, since Christopher Columbus landed 500 years ago.

Giant anteaters, jaguars, and powerful monkey-eating harpy eagles are at home in virgin tropical rain forest.

Indigenous populations of Amerindian and Afro-Caribbean descent follow native ways with little or no negative impact on natural ecosystems—miniscule compared with more recent human encroachment. (Under the U.N. Biosphere Reserve concept, not only biotic and archeological resources are protected but also indigenous cultures.)

Great flocks of waterfowl feed in lily-choked canals. Raucous parrots, including flocks of scarlet and military macaws, fly over. Small, dark, solitary jaguarundis prey on rodents including, when they can, fat young capybaras. Kingfishers dive from riverside branches. Otters slide down slippery mud banks. Jabiru storks forage in shallows. Spider monkeys chatter and white-faced monkeys scold visitors.

Toucans delicately manipulate colorful outsize bills to pluck small berries, tossing their heads back to send the fruits down their throats. Aplomado falcons hover over forest clearings. Small, swift bat falcons swoop after nocturnal prey in the twilight.

OPPOSITE: Howls of howler monkeys are believed to be the loudest sound of any land animal—achieved by enlarged hyoid throat bones which greatly amplify it—exceeded only by that of blue whales at sea. It's audible three miles (5 km) away in the open, almost two miles (3 km) in dense vegetation. Howlers call on arising in the morning, at intervals through the day, and just before retiring. One howler sets off another, so when a large troop gets going together, it can seem deafening.

## HONDURAS

Over 2,000 vascular plant species have been identified, with more added as scientific inquiry continues. A rich, colorful array of epiphytes, including hundreds of kinds of orchids, clings to cloud forest trees. In concert with mosses and bright green ferns, they sometimes cover gnarled tree trunks to create their own multispecies ecosystems.

Giant manatees graze in mangrove-fringed coastal lagoons protected by coral reefs.

Best times to visit are January–May dry season, but rain gear can be useful anytime (two dominant life zones are described as "humid tropical forest" and "very humid subtropical forest"). International flights available to Tegucigalpa, where lodging, also transport, is available.

Threats include deforestation, poaching, unscrupulous coastal commercial fishing, mineral exploration, lack of management plan, and lack of funding to enforce environmental restraints. (Commercial hunting is sometimes masked as ecotourism.)

## ALSO OF INTEREST

**Cusuco National Park** has cloud forest with large quetzal population.

**Cuero y Salado Wildlife Refuge** is one of the largest protection zones along the Caribbean for endangered manatees.

**Pico Bonito National Park** with six life zones ranging from cloud forest to moist lowland tropical jungle, with many waterfalls and great biodiversity.

**Punta Sal National Park** has tropical rain forest, wetlands, and mangrove forest, with coral reefs protecting manatees and coastal birds plus many migrant stopovers.

**La Tigra National Park** was Honduras' first national park, protecting beautiful cloud forest; also water supply source for Tegucigalpa.

**Cayos Cochinos Marine Reserve** has 13 cays with coral reefs, well-preserved forests, a species of pink boa.

---

**FURTHER INFORMATION**

Instituto Hondureno de Turismo, Edificio Europa, 3er. Nivel, Col. San Carlos, Tegucigalpa, Honduras, C.A., Apdo. Postal 3261, Tel: (+504) 38-3974, Fax: 38-2102; Centro Comercial Central America, Tegucigalpa, Honduras, C.A., Tel: (+504) 32-9018.

---

OPPOSITE: Scarlet macaws are one of the most stunning of the beautiful parrot family, and one of the most dexterous, with zygodactyl feet—two toes in front and two behind—that they use like hands in holding and manipulating objects. Bills are attached to their skulls with special hinges that give them powerful leverage and mobility in performing delicate tasks like preening feathers but also crushing the hardest nuts, and act as third feet in grasping perches so they are excellent climbers as well. These dazzling birds are increasingly endangered by demand for the pet trade through Central and northern South America.

Jaguarundis move like shadows in scrubland and forest they inhabit from Texas south through most of South America, their low, slender bodies slipping through vegetation without a leaf stirring. They're known also as otter cats but more for their appearance—otter-sized, weasel-like, with long, slender bodies and short legs—than for any liking for water, or for their color, which can be gray, reddish brown, or black, sometimes all in the same litter (though they're born spotted).

# PANAMA

MILLIONS OF HAWKS—INCLUDING
BROADWINGS AND SWAINSON'S— SOAR IN
MIGRATION EVERY FALL OVER PANAMA CITY. ON
THE GROUND NEARBY BIRDERS SET WORLD RECORDS
OF HUNDREDS OF SPECIES SEEN IN A SINGLE DAY.

BEAUTIFUL AND INTERESTING WILDLIFE FROM BOTH NORTH AND SOUTH AMERICA—ESPECIALLY BIRDS—WIND UP EITHER PERMANENTLY OR IN TRANSIT ON THIS NARROW MOUNTAINOUS CENTRAL AMERICAN LAND BRIDGE BETWEEN THE TWO CONTINENTS.

Powerful jaguars—New World version of the leopard—are here, along with glittering, emerald, resplendent quetzals, monkey-eating harpy eagles, and endemic golden frogs. Birds of 940 species include scarlet macaws a yard (1 m) long, among largest parrots in the world. Bird counts set world records—more than 350 species in a single day in and around newly created SAN LORENZO NATIONAL PARK at Achiote in the province of Colón; similar numbers in a day on the Pipeline Road at SOBERANIA NATIONAL PARK in Gamboa. Brilliant quetzals are abundant in the highland forests of Chiriquí Province in western Panama, at VOLCAN BARU and LA AMISTAD NATIONAL PARKS.

More than 1,200 kinds of orchids, including Panama's national flower, the ivory holy ghost, cling to towering trees, some with trunks six feet (2 m) across. Hundreds of butterfly species in every conceivable color and pattern cluster around bright nectar-filled blooms.

# PANAMA

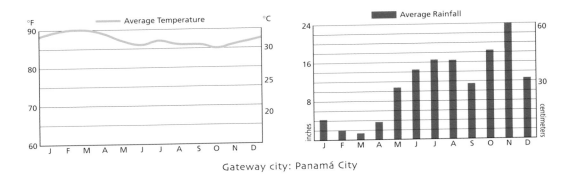

Gateway city: Panamá City

White and black sand beaches are nest sites for endangered green, leatherback, hawksbill, and ridley sea turtles. "Panama" means "place of many fish" and world fishing records have been set for many species along the 477 miles (763 km) of Caribbean and 767 miles (1,227 km) of Pacific coastline. Colorful tropical fish of more than 200 species inhabit offshore coral reefs.

Habitats range from some of the largest mangrove estuaries in the Americas and seasonally dry forests along much of the Pacific coast to rain and cloud forest above 5,000 feet (1,500 m) to stunted and twisted dwarf elfin woodland on the highest peaks. Treeless paramo vegetation is found atop Cerro Echandi in La Amistad National Park and 11,000 foot (3,475 m) Baru Volcano in the rugged Talamanca mountain range of western Panama.

Panama has some of the wildest, diverse, least explored land north of the Amazon. Dense forests, swamps, and mountains of DARIÉN GAP can be crossed only by the most adventurous. Spaniards managed it in 1513 to catch first glimpse of the Pacific by any European and one can understand why, as the poet Keats said, they stood at that moment "silent, [as] on a peak in Darién." While not certain, it is likely that they were not alone—some historians say there may have been as many as a half-million persons living in the Darién then, compared to fewer than 25,000 now.

There are about 500 rivers and 1,600 offshore islands, including Coiba, on the Pacific, now a national park and largest island in the seven-nation Central American isthmus.

National parks and reserves cover more than 29 percent of this country, about the size of West Virginia.

## DARIÉN NATIONAL PARK

Central America's largest tropical rain forest wilderness is found in this outstanding national park, U.N. World Heritage Site and Biosphere Reserve.

This wild, narrow stretch between North and South American continents is refuge for jaguars, ocelots, anteaters, sloths, and wilderness-loving wildlife from both continents.

## PANAMA

White-tailed deer, which prefer open patches, share the park with smaller, forest-loving brocket deer. Capybaras up to 100 pounds (45 kg)—world's largest rodents—swim, looking like small hairy hippopotami. Live oaks and magnolia trees from southern North America compete for sunlight with chiriqui and Darién oaks. American crocodiles share rivers with southern caiman cousins.

For many it is a demarcation line. Coyotes which reach central Panama are replaced in the Darién by smaller bush dogs which range from Panama south through Brazil. Black spider monkeys of Colombia and Venezuela begin to replace red spider monkeys of Mexico in central Panama, and golden-headed quetzals of the Andes—beautiful but lacking the spectacular plumes of resplendent quetzals of Central American cordilleras—begin to appear.

Along with spotted jaguars and ocelots are three other species of felines, among them pumas or mountain lions. Primates include booming howlers and small brown-headed spider monkeys. They are preyed on by monkey-eating harpy eagles, one of the world's most powerful raptors and Panama's national bird. Ponderous 500-pound (225-kg) Baird's tapirs shoulder their way through wet, wooded interior places.

Darién is the only Central American forest with four colorful macaws—red-and-green, blue-and-yellow, great green, and chestnut-fronted.

It is still possible to follow the path of the Spaniards, who, led by Balboa, climbed to get their first glimpse of the Pacific Ocean in 1513—but anyone who has done so recently admires their pluck. Darién Gap is a daunting passage, holding the possibility of impressive wildlife but in sometimes all-but-impenetrable jungle. Trees tower to 125 feet (40 m) and higher with six-foot-diameter (2-m) trunks. Humidity on the forest floor can be 100 percent—30 percent higher than the airy canopy—a dampness which, with continued exposure, induces jungle rot. Painful stinging insects abound, along with swamp parasites and poisonous snakes.

A British Army expeditionary force equipped with Land Rovers, U.S. Army helicopters, and 27 horses took three months to make the 250-mile trek in 1972. Darién is the only break in the Pan-American Highway stretching from Fairbanks, Alaska to Puerto Montt, Chile, an inaccessibility that, as with other intact wilderness, has been its greatest protection.

Mountainous, steep cloud forests are less difficult to negotiate, and still higher are elfin forests stunted by chill and constant winds. This varied forest network has been called by scientists the most diverse ecosystem of Central America, sheltering myriad varieties of colorful songbirds and butterflies fluttering around bright epiphytes and flowering vines.

Fortunately, impressive parts of this 2,345-square-mile (6,070-km$^2$) national park, World Heritage Site and Biosphere Reserve can be experienced without braving hardships. Several birding tour companies offer trips to Cana, which has a remote airstrip deep in the heart of the park.

# Soberania National Park

Soberania National Park in the hydrographic basin of the Panama Canal is a world-renowned birding hot spot in one of the most accessible tropical forest reserves in Central America, 85 square miles (221 km²) encompassing much of the east side of the Panama Canal. It also includes **Summit Botanical Gardens**, where the United States in the first part of the 20th century introduced 15,000 species of ornamental and useful tropical trees and plants, and there is a small well-kept zoo with some of Panama's wilder residents. These include conejo pintados, or pacas, king vultures, peccaries, coatimundis, spider monkeys, and others.

The park's many trails range from short and easy to long and strenuous, many with self-guiding brochures available at park offices. Pipeline Road leads 10 miles (17 km) across the park from Gamboa to Lake Gatun. Warier wildlife in more remote parts include jaguars, tapirs, five monkey species, 57 kinds of amphibians, and 79 reptiles. Bright tropical fish such as blue acaras, "earth-eater" cichlids, tetras, and suckermouth catfish are conspicuous residents of quiet, clear trailside streams.

Soberania is reached by frequent busses from Panamá City. It can be seen in a long day trip or permits obtained for overnight camping. Weekends can be crowded.

# Also of Interest

**La Amistad National Park and Biosphere Reserve** along the Costa Rican border with remarkable flora and fauna in seven wild, steep life zones; access from Cerro Punta (Chiriqui–Las Nubes entrance) and Changuinola (Bocas del Toro entrance).

**Baru Volcano National Park**—with 11,000-foot (3,475-m) Baru Volcano, home to resplendent quetzals and a variety of endemic plants. Access from Cerro Punta and Boquete.

**Bastimentos Island National Marine Park** is an important sea turtle nesting site with more than 200 dazzling fish species in crystalline coral reef waters. Access from Bocas del Toro.

**Cerro Hoya National Park** is home to 30 endemic flora and fauna species including the carato parakeet.

**Sarigua National Park**, along the Pacific coast, hosts pelicans, kingfishers, many butterflies.

OPPOSITE: Even within large sociable flocks of a hundred or so, blue and yellow macaw pairs stay close, flying together with wings almost touching. It is a scene of breathtaking beauty when they fly from daylight feeding in canopies of fruiting forests to evening roosts, sunset light catching their azure backs, then their golden breasts. Unfortunately their beauty and intelligence has made them desirable pets. That and habitat destruction has endangered their survival over much of their range through Central and South America.

**Altos de Compana National Park** is home of famous golden frogs and pacas, woodchuck-sized spotted rodents.

**Metropolitan Natural Park**, an urban rain forest with red-legged honeycreepers, trogons, keel-billed toucans, and marmosets, known locally as "mono titi."

**Camino de Cruces National Park**, an ecological corridor linking forest zones between Metropolitan and Soberania national parks, home to endangered titi monkeys, armadillos, green iguanas, brocket deer, and three-toed sloths. Still visible are vestiges of the trail used by Spanish to transport gold across the isthmus en route to Spain.

**Chagres National Park**, with spider monkeys, toucans, the Chagres River (rafting trips can be arranged), Alajuela Lake, and part of the historic Camino Real.

**Portobelo National Park**, 42 miles (70 km) of coastline, rich coral reefs, a World Heritage Site because of the ruins of a Spanish colonial town where gold was loaded onto ships bound to Spain.

Though not a national park, Panama's **Canopy Tower** (www.canopytower.com) offers one of the world's great birding experiences. A converted radar tower, it has bedrooms at canopy level, home of blue cotingas and green shrike-vireos, among many others.

Another spectacular avian offering is the sight of raptor migrations in October and November, with millions of Swainson's and broad-winged hawks plainly visible from **Ancon Hill**, **Metropolitan Nature Park** and the **Bahai Temple** hill just outside Panamá City.

**San Lorenzo National Park**, on the Caribbean entrance to the Panama Canal, became a protected area in 1999 when the U.S. military handed over to Panama the area formerly used for jungle operations training. It may be the easiest place to see wildlife in Panama, and its Achiote Road bird site ranks with the Pipeline Road as one of the world's best. Access is from Gatun Locks, Colon. *See* website www.sanlorenzo.org.pa.

Also, the **Smithsonian Tropical Research Institute**, **El Cope National Park** in the province of Coclé and the **Taboga and Uraba Wildlife Reserve**, accessible by launch from the port of Balboa, dry forest home to thousand of nesting brown pelicans in March and April.

---

**FURTHER INFORMATION**

Autoridad Nacional del Ambiente (ANAM) Albrook, Panamá City, Website: www.anam.gob.pa; Asociación Nacional para la Conservación de la Naturaleza (ANCON), Panamá City; IPAT (Panama Government Tourist Bureau), Via Israel, Centro Convenciones Atlapa, Zone 5, Panamá, Tel: (+507) 226-7000 or 226-3544, Fax: (+507) 226-6856, Website: www.ipat.gob.pa; OR Panama Audubon Society, Panamá City.

# EUROPE

WHITE STORKS

# BELARUS

LONG-TAILED TAWNY OWLS PEER OUT OF NEST
HOLES IN ANCIENT OAKS IN BELOVEZKSKAYA
PUSHCHA WITH LARGE, DARK EYES THAT GIVE
THEM, IT'S THOUGHT, A KINDLY EXPRESSION.
MORE LIKELY IT'S HUNGER. THEY SPEND
MOST OF THEIR TIME LOOKING FOR VOLES.

## BELOVEZHSKAYA PUSHCHA NATIONAL PARK

Ancient forest with rich wildlife populations such as once covered much of the European continent and Asia now reaches its western limit here and contiguously across the border in Poland, altogether some 350 square miles (900 km²) of towering old-growth trees—oaks 300–700 years old, 450-year-old ash, 220-year-old pines,150-year-old junipers—many more than 160 feet (50 m) tall, largely undisturbed by human activity.

Here live wolves, lynx, otters, red and roe deer, wild boar, and the now-celebrated European bison (aka wisent) or (in Belarus) zubr, largest land mammals on the continent, hunted to near

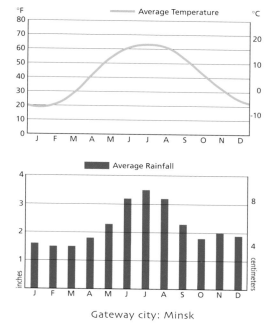

Gateway city: Minsk

365

extinction in the last century. The last wild one was shot in 1923. In a story reminiscent of recovery of American bison, European bison were returned to a viable wild population from a small, reassembled herd of specimens that had been scattered widely to zoos and private collections, and now some 3,200 exist in Belarus, Poland, Lithuania, and Ukraine—protected on lands once hunting preserves for Polish kings and Russian tsars.

Others among some 55 mammal species in the 500 square miles (1,300 km²) on the Belarus side are elk (aka moose), badgers, and along streams, beavers, mink, and otters. Among woodland birds are grouse, woodcock, and partridge, among raptors, peregrine falcons and white-tailed eagles—altogether more than 200 bird species. Of these, 90 nest, including green and three-toed woodpeckers and long-tailed tawny owls whose large, dark eyes give them, it's thought, a kindly expression. Large flocks of waterfowl stop by in migration.

Polish and Belarus authorities have worked together on management issues between the contiguous national parks, including decisions related to a border fence which was a hazardous barrier to wildlife movement between them.

Potential threats are pesticide and fertilizer runoff from farms nearby, canal construction that could disturb the area's hydrological balance, and inadequate logging controls.

Most international travelers fly into Minsk, where rental cars are available with an excellent road to Brest. Five busses a day go from Brest 37 miles (60 km) north to Kamjanjuky, just outside the reserve. To visit in your own vehicle requires—depending on current rules—a permit. The Intourist office in Brest can help with this and other visit arrangements. The park has hotels and guesthouses where visits can be arranged to a local natural history museum and enclosures where animals can be seen in reasonably natural conditions; also walking, driving and horseback trails. Best times are April–May and September—pleasant, cool, not usually rainy.

---

**FURTHER INFORMATION**

Director, Belovezhskaya Pushcha National Park, Settlement Kamenyuki, Kamenets District, Brest Region 225-063, Republic of Belarus, Tel: (+375) (016-31) 56-122, 56-132.

---

## ALSO OF INTEREST

**Berezinsky Biosphere Nature Reserve** 80 miles (130 km) north of Minsk with breeding capercaillies, wolves, fox, bison, elk, and wild boars, among 52 mammal species, and 217 birds. Trails, guided walks, photo safaris, visitor center, comfortable hotel.

**Olmany Mires Zakaznik** is a 364-square-mile (942-km²) Ramsar Wetland of World Importance near Brest, key nest site for threatened spotted eagles.

## BELARUS

**Osveiski**, 87-square-mile (22600-km²) Ramsar complex of lakes, forests, and bogs, 93 miles (150 km) northwest of Vitebsk, breeding ground for thousands of grebes, ducks, cranes, waders, migratory stopover for 20,000 waterbirds.

**Pripiatsky National Park**, 160 miles (260 km) south of Minsk, with European bison, badgers, lynx, beavers, black storks, short-toed and greater spotted eagles. Tours can be arranged via walking, riding, waterways. Hotel.

**Sporovsky Zakaznik**, 75-square-mile (194-km²) Ramsar site near Brest, largest lowland sedge fen mire in Europe, major habitat of endangered aquatic warblers.

**Yelnia**, 90-square-mile (232-km²) Ramsar site near Brest, supports more than 20,000 migratory waterbirds, also many common cranes and bean geese.

**Zvanets**, 61-square-mile (159-km²) Ramsar site near Brest, with threatened spotted eagles, corncrakes, aquatic warblers (3,000–6,000 singing males)—biodiversity hot spot with 664 vascular plant species, 728 arthropods, 168 vertebrates.

Wild boars range over much of the world, in some places having found their own way, in others domesticated, as early as 4900 BC in China and perhaps thousands of years earlier in Thailand, and introduced elsewhere by humans. They are well able to make their own way, and do, with razor-sharp tusks that may grow to nine inches (22 cm), acute senses of hearing and smell (as French truffle-hunters discovered) plus their own high intelligence, omnivorous appetites and adaptability to almost every habitat but deep snow.

# BULGARIA

BIRD MIGRATIONS ALONG BULGARIA'S BLACK
SEA COAST AND MOUNTAIN RIDGES IN FALL
COMMONLY COUNT 6,000 HONEY BUZZARDS,
20,000 COMMON BUZZARDS, 10,000+ LESSER
SPOTTED EAGLES, 20,000+ WHITE PELICANS,
3,000+ BLACK STORKS, AND OVER 130,000
(WITH RECORDS OF 204,000) WHITE STORKS
HEADING FOR WINTER QUARTERS IN AFRICA.

WOODED MOUNTAINS AND QUIET MARSHES OF THIS SMALL COUNTRY ARE BECOMING KNOWN AS A BIRDING PARADISE, AFTER YEARS OF REPRESSION UNDER COMMUNISM.

All the graceful heron species of Europe spend at least part of the year on plains and wetlands of the Danube and Maritza Rivers and Black Sea Coast here, along with spoonbills, glossy ibises, and little bitterns darting long bills after small prey in the shallows. Huge numbers flock to LAKE SREBARNA NATURE RESERVE on a freshwater lake that is a U.N. World Heritage Site and Biosphere Reserve.

A chain of mountain reserves to the southwest attract raptors in great variety and numbers along towering cliffs. They find nest niches and lookout points in rolling green hills of the eastern Rhodopes Mountain—six kinds of eagles (imperial, golden, white-tailed, short-toed,

lesser spotted, booted) plus handsome Egyptian and monk or European black vultures, cinereous vultures, Eurasian griffon vultures, and others. In deep woods, rare three-toed and white-backed woodpeckers hammer on trunks of tall conifers.

Bulgaria is best place in the world to see small, wren-like wallcreepers spreading blood-red wings as they creep over sheer rock faces. It is best place in Europe for golden orioles, rose-colored starlings,

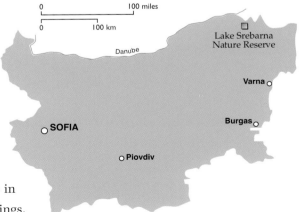

## BULGARIA

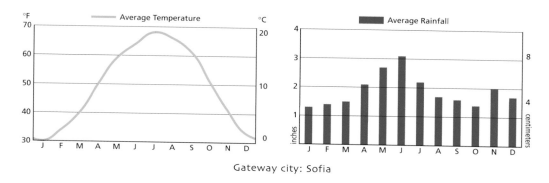

Average Temperature  °F / °C

Average Rainfall — inches / centimeters

Gateway city: Sofia

and eagle-owls. Somber tits, olive-tree and paddyfield warblers, and hoopoes are among 400 avian species.

Otherwise rare European birds can be common here—streamlined pallid swifts which can copulate and sleep on the wing, pudgy little and spotted crakes in soggy marsh vegetation, graceful tern-like collared and black-winged pratincoles nesting colonially on bare-ground scrapes amid wet meadows.

Woodpeckers in great variety occupy almost every treed area—black, green, Syrian, gray-headed, middle-spotted, great spotted, lesser-spotted, and wrynecks.

Spectacular fall raptor migrations along mountain ridges and the Black Sea coast commonly count 6,000 honey buzzards, 20,000 common buzzards, 10,000+ lesser spotted eagles, with sizable numbers as well of booted and short-toed eagles, Levant sparrowhawks and red-footed falcons, 20,000+ (with records of 37,228) white pelicans, 3,000+ black storks, over 130,000 (with records of 204,000) white storks with thousands of smaller species such as wagtails, swallows, pipits, and larks.

Winter brings flocks of white-fronted and dramatically plumaged red-breasted geese, often in great flocks, with good numbers of lesser white-fronted geese and European ducks—along with smew, whooper and Bewick's swans, rough-legged and long-legged buzzards in summer.

Even urban Sofia's well-wooded central park offers fine birds as does **Vitosha Mountain National Park** just minutes' drive to the south (black woodpeckers, Eurasian nutcrackers, rufous-tailed rock thrushes) and dozens of other reserves, some officially protected.

Climate is typically continental, with best times in spring—April–May for migration, late May–early June for breeding, late August–September for peak fall migrants, wintering species January–February.

International jets fly into Sofia from which most places can be reached by rented car, taxi, train, or bus—ski resorts such as Borovets and Pamporovo offering access to the mountains, with many marked trails; Black Sea coastal towns and resorts such as Albena and Burgas for wet lowlands.

## BULGARIA

Problems remain in pollution, overgrazing, and habitat loss—nearly 95 percent of Bulgaria's wetlands have disappeared in the past century—and Italian hunters take a lamentable wildlife toll.

### FURTHER INFORMATION

Ministry of Environment, 67 William Gladstone Str., BG-1000 Sofia, Bulgaria, Tel/Fax: (+359) 52-30-25-36; Institute of Ecology, Academy of Science, Department of Protected Areas, Gagarin 2, 1113 Sofia; Bulgarian Society for the Protection of Birds, P.O. Box 50, BG-1111 Sofia, Bulgaria, Tel/Fax: (+359) 2-72-26-40, also (+359) 2-68-94-13 and (+359) 2-62-08-15, E-mail: bspb.hq@mb.biahg.com; Neophron Limited, c/o BSPB, P.O. Box 492, BG-9000, Varna, Bulgaria, can advise and help book accommodations.

Nothing else looks like a hoopoe with its spectacular pink-cinnamon Indian-chief crest, spread like a fan or laid like a striped spike along its forehead, and butterfly-like flight, dramatically opening and closing boldly-barred black and white wings and tail. Nothing, they say, smells like one, either, when nesting, since they don't remove nestlings' droppings. Hoopoes range over open woodlands, nesting in old tree holes or rocky niches in Eurasia, wintering in Africa and southern Asia.

## LAKE SREBARNA NATURE RESERVE

This 1,482 acres (600 ha) of the Danube River floodplain is breeding home for some 100 bird species, many of them rare or endangered.

Over 200 pairs of Dalmatian pelicans show off red-orange throat sacs to impress nesting partners in spring. Hovering overhead are small red-footed falcons.

Lordly eastern imperial eagles with pale gold nape-shawls pair off. Trees along lake edges support dozens of pygmy cormorant nests each, filling the air with croaks and grunts (though birds are silent away from the colony). It is a nest site for glossy ibis (50–500 pairs), great egrets, and white-tailed eagles.

A few ferruginous ducks nest in reeds, unnoticed until they erupt in flight with showy white bars running full wing-length. Noisy black-headed gulls gather in ear-splitting nest colonies, attracting quieter pairs of terns—black, common, whiskered, white-winged black, and Caspian— it's thought because the gulls' noisy ways divert attention away from terns' breeding sites.

White-fronted and red-breasted geese, ruddy shelducks, and brightly decorated bluethroats are among some 78 wintering species (though numbers drop off in years of severe weather).

Plans to drain marshes along the Danube caused the Bulgarian Interior Department to disconnect Lake Srebarna from the river in 1949, but resulting damage from low water levels caused them to dig a canal to reconnect it and restore fish populations in 1978.

Pollution still is of concern, as are continuing low water levels and siltation with scrub invasion permitting access by predators such as wild boars, foxes, and jackals (which wiped out the Dalmatian pelican colony in 1994, but they have gradually returned).

Visitor facilities include a nature museum, field research station, and nature center from which guided tours are available 11 miles (18 km) west of Silistra, which also has hotel accommodations.

## ALSO OF INTEREST

Also of note is **Pirin (Vikhren) National Park and U.N. World Heritage Site** in high mountains south of Sofia between Sandanski and Bansko—access on foot from secondary roads off route 279—with exceptional flora, including endemics, often in great abundance, plus many species of butterflies and mountain bird species such as wallcreepers, golden and booted eagles, alpine accentors, and alpine choughs in habitat ranging from woodlands to high meadows, lakes, and bogs.

# FRANCE

CRIMSON FLAMINGOS IN THE CAMARGUE
DEMONSTRATE HIGH-STEPPING COURTSHIP
RITUALS THAT BECAME THE STYLISH SPANISH
FLAMENCO DANCE NAMED AFTER THEM—
PERFORMED HERE BY BIRDS COURTING IN
BRINY LAGOONS ORIGINALLY CULTIVATED FOR SALT
EXTRACTION BY ANCIENT GREEKS AND ROMANS.

F RANCE IS ESTEEMED AMONG TRAVELERS FOR CUISINE AND WINES—BUT NATURALISTS FIND ITS SIGNIFICANT
OFFERINGS IN SIX NATIONAL PARKS, 137 NATURAL RESERVES, AND 32 REGIONAL NATURAL PARKS.

## CAMARGUE

The world-renowned Camargue is an enormous wetland and U.N. World Biosphere Reserve covering some 566 square miles (1,467 km²) of the Rhone River delta on the Mediterranean coast.

This unique mix of fresh and salt waters flowing through intricate interwoven habitats in mild Mediterranean climate attracts some 10,000 pairs of high-stepping crimson greater flamingos and millions of other water-oriented birds. Some are permanently at home, others stop seasonally from as far as northern Europe and Siberia.

Hardy white horses of ancient lineage gallop through shallow lagoons, thriving on saline pastures, as do famous black bulls watched over and periodically rounded up by the region's traditional cowboys or *gardians*.

Marsh harriers, black kites and short-toed snake-eagles wheel overhead.

# FRANCE

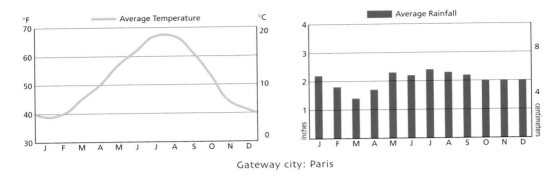

°F / °C — Average Temperature

Average Rainfall — inches / centimeters

Gateway city: Paris

Each species seeks its own niche. Dense marsh reedbeds offer rich foraging grounds and nest supports for bearded reedlings, reed buntings, and purple herons. Great bitterns stand like striped feathered statues, indistinguishable from the reeds. Buffy-brown tern-like collared pratincoles breed on sun-baked mudflats here as gregariously as their rare status permits—they are nowhere else in France. Stone curlews are in open, stony, or short grass areas.

Kentish plovers incubate eggs in nest scrapes on beaches. Tawny pipits and short-toed larks find seeds among waving dune grasses and bright wildflowers. Surrounding higher vegetation attracts spectacled warblers, crested larks, great gray shrikes, and brilliant multihued bee-eaters. In nearby woodlands, melodious warblers and golden orioles appear. Drainage ditches to the north are home to penduline tits and fan-tailed warblers.

Greater flamingos find succulent brine shrimp and perform stylish mating dances (like the Spanish flamenco dance named after them) in heavily saline southern lagoons first cultivated for salt extraction by ancient Greeks and Romans. Less saline ponds to the north are key breeding and nesting sites for elegant, graceful avocets with delicate tip-tilted bills, rare slender-billed gulls, and a variety of terns, including gull-billed, little, and sandwich. Long-legged herons and egrets stalk small prey in lagoons and fly to riverine forests to roost and breed. Ducks rest during the day in *sansouires* (areas of succulent, salt-tolerant vegetation) and move to nearby marshes to feed in early morning and evening.

The wealth of species here is second in Europe only to Spain's **Doñana National Park** (*see* p.416)—over 350 kinds of birds alone.

The region known as the Camargue today is a patchwork of private holdings and public reserves. The 328-square-mile (850-km²) **Parc Naturel Regional de Camargue** includes the **Étang de Vaccares**, 51 square miles (131 km²), state-owned but managed by the private National Society for Nature Protection; **Étang des Imperiaux**, a 6,860-acre (2,777-ha) reserve owned by the community of Les Saintes-Maries-de-la-Mer; and the **Tour du Valat**, a private reserve managed by the public Sansouire Foundation.

**Pont de Gau Ornithological Park** has paths where most bird species found in the Camargue—and mammals such as foxes, wild boars, badgers—can be seen, with a fine visitor center, guides, and explanatory literature. Mention should be made also of the **Petite Camargue** to the west, stony **La Crau** to the east, **Les Baux** to the northeast, and **Pont du Gard** to the north.

Regarded by many as the Camargue's heart, however, is croissant-shaped **Étang de Vaccares**, much of which can be viewed from small roads along west, north, and eastern shores, and from the road between Arles and Saintes-Maries-de-la-Mer.

The region is interesting all year, best starting in April and peaking in September, but it's also an important wintering site for large numbers of ducks, geese, swans, and other waterbirds.

Helpful area maps or *Cartes Touristiques* are published by IGN, also Michelin, available in bookstores and visitor centers. Much can be seen from public highways and dike roads.

International travelers can fly into Paris or, better, directly to Marseille, where rental cars are available. Hotels throughout the region can help arrange guided trips, also individual trips by walking, rental bike, or horseback.

Threats are several, including the Camargue's patchwork nature. Ducks' roosting places are protected but many marshes where they feed are not and hunters shoot them as they move. This has reduced wintering waterfowl here by an estimated 40 percent in recent years, including annual kill of up to 150,000 ducks and poisoning of other aquatic birds which ingest lead shot. Rice farming and enlargement of salt extraction beds reduces habitat and alters wetland water levels.

The Camargue, like many Natural Regional Parks, allows what conservationists feel is excessive consumptive uses, ranging from hunting to thatch-cutting. In some places the semi-wild Camargue horses are tamed by *gardians* and made available for riding, and bulls are sold for bullfights. Local bullfights are often bloodless—challenge for white-clad Camarguaise *razeteurs* is to pluck ribbons from a bull's horns with small hooks held between fingers—but other animals go to Spain and a different fate.

The region's fragility was shown when the Rhône burst its banks and flooded some 47 square miles (121 km²) of the delta in 1993 sending over 4.6 billion cubic feet (129 million cubic m) of fresh water into the saline system. Over 5,000 horses and others were rescued but many birds and mammals died, and concern remains about possible long-term ecosystem damage.

FOLLOWING PAGES: Gannets, large, brilliantly white cigar-shaped seabirds with buff-cream heads nest in great crowded colonies on high cliffs on both sides of the North Atlantic, supplying fuzzy white nestlings with fish gathered in prodigious dives. Flying up to 130 feet (40 m) high, they soar, circle, then plunge headlong in steep diagonals, retracting pointed six-foot (1.8-m) wings just before striking the water's surface, protected from impact by hard skull structure and cellular tissue cushions just under neck and breast skin which automatically fill with air in descent.

**FURTHER INFORMATION (and for Permits to enter certain areas)**

Parc Naturel de Camargue, 13460 Les Saintes-Maries-de-la-Mer, Tel: (+33) (0) 490-97-86-32,
E-mail: Camargue-parc.naturel@wanadoo.fr; Reserve Nationale de Camargue, La Capeliers,
13200 Arles, France, Tel: (+33) (0) 490-97-00-97; Musée Camarguais, Mas du pont de Rousty,
13200 Arles, Tel: (+33) (0) 490-97-10-82.

France has 18 sites designated as Wetlands of International Importance by the Ramsar Convention. A list is available from Ramsar, Rue Mauverny 28, CH-1196, Gland, Switzerland, Tel: (+41) 22-999-0170, Fax: (+41) 22-999-0169, E-mail: ramsar@ramsar.org.

## ALSO OF INTEREST

Several other areas are of special note:

**Grand Briere**, Pays de la Loire, 78 square miles (202 km²) of floodplain, peatland, and vast alluvial marshes, important for otters and numerous wintering and nesting waterbirds.

**La Brenne**, Centre, 540 square miles (1,400 km²) of plateau with 1,500 lakes and ponds, important for passerines, waterbirds, 50 dragonfly and 1,000 floral species.

**Baie de Somme**, Picardy, a vast sandy, mud and grassy area of 66 square miles (170 km²) in the largest estuary in northern France, supports over 120 nesting bird species, many of them rare and threatened. On several important flyways, it is one of the most important European resting and feeding areas for migrating waterbirds—321 species, or over 65 percent of European avifauna have been identified here, also rare plants.

**Étangs de la Champagne Humide**, Champagne-Ardenne, a vast (522 square mile/1,350 km²) lowland complex of rivers, lakes, canals, reedbeds, wet meadows, and alluvial forests, important for wintering and migrant waterbirds, especially ducks, geese, and cranes, also nesters such as purple herons. It is only French wintering site for globally threatened white-tailed sea eagles.

**Étangs du Lindre, forêt du Romersberg et zones voisines**, Lorraine, is a complex of rivers, marshes, and riverine forest and salt grasslands with many rare plant species and an important European wildcat population, also essential breeding, resting, wintering area for many waterbirds.

**Golfe du Morbihan** (89 square miles/230 km²) of almost enclosed estuarine embayment and salt marsh complex with vast, rich mudflats at the mouths of three rivers, with up to 130,000 wintering waterbirds as well as many nesters and migratory visitors.

**Pyrénées National Park** (177 square miles/460 km²) with 77 of 107 mammals to be found in France, including highly endangered bears, recovering isard or Pyrenean chamois, desman, and pine martens. Birds are equally notable, including black woodpeckers, capercaillies, ptarmigan, and lammergeiers (aka bone-breakers), along with nesting Egyptian vultures.

# HUNGARY

DOMESTICATED GRAZERS OF ANCIENT ORIGIN—
SPIRAL-HORNED, LONG-HAIRED RACKA SHEEP,
HUNGARIAN GRAY LONGHORN CATTLE, MANGOLICA
PIGS, AND NONIUS HORSES SHARE HORTOBAGY'S
OPEN GRASSLANDS WITH SOME OF EUROPE'S LARGEST
AND MOST-VARIED RAPTOR POPULATIONS.

## HORTOBAGY NATIONAL PARK

Trumpeting common cranes fill the skies in fall as in bygone days over steppe-grassland "puszta" of Hortobagy National Park, 312-square-mile (810-km$^2$) U.N. World Heritage Site on the Great Hungarian Plain, which has come to be regarded as a premier birding spot of Europe. Up to 72,000 of these tall, stately birds swoop over Hortobagy's vast waving marsh grasses, rising and falling in great waves of 20,000 or so with a rushing sound like the wind en route to feeding grounds or nightly roosts.

Rarities in numbers seldom seen elsewhere are here, either in migration or as permanent residents. Over 1,000 long-legged, endangered great bustards, one of the world's largest birds—largest that can also fly—known as the "Hungarian ostrich," peer over tall grasses, males up to a yard (1 m) tall, weighing almost 50 pounds (22 kg). Drab and hard to see in everyday plumage, males are spectacular in courtship display when they throw their heads back, with tails forward and wings almost inside-out to all but cover themselves with vibrating snowy feathers.

Over 1,200 pairs of elegant white-winged black terns dip gracefully for insects and tiny fish on the water's surface. Over 600 pairs of sweet-singing aquatic warblers claim foxtail meadow territories. Over 100 pairs of swift saker falcons patrol airways—fearless hunters that readily rival imperial eagles and go after prey as large as geese and hares—distinguishable from peregrines, also here, by slimmer body, longer tail, and wider, blunter wings.

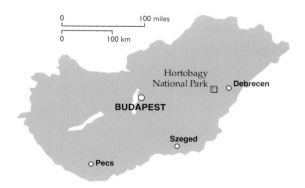

# HUNGARY

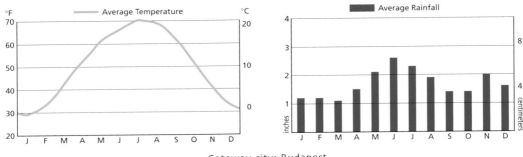

Gateway city: Budapest

Sociable, noisy crow-like rooks and protected, rare spoonbills, glossy ibises and purple and black-crowned night herons nest colonially in lowland copses, also home to nesting kestrels, long-eared owls, red-footed falcons, and in recent years to imperial eagles and long-legged buzzards. Reedbeds shelter families of bitterns, threatened corncrakes, pygmy cormorants, great reed warblers, and bluethroats with brilliant azure bibs. Water lilies hide floating nests of red-necked and black-necked grebes. Collared pratincoles and Kentish plovers are content with nest scrapes on bare ground. Altogether almost 350 bird species are here.

In late summer to early fall red-footed falcons hunt in loose flocks, sometimes 100 or so. Ferruginous ducks, handsome pochards, and red-breasted, greater, and lesser white-fronted geese are on ponds. Grasshopper hordes attract flocks of white storks, rose-colored starlings, and Eurasian dotterels to the flat "puszta" plain.

Shorebirds forage on mudflats around some 24 square miles (60 km²) of fish ponds originally dug for economic purposes, now ideal habitat for broad-billed sandpipers, red-necked phalaropes, Temmink's stints, and rare slender-billed curlews.

Up to 28 white-tailed eagles can be around in winter along with great gray shrikes, bearded tits, and little owls.

Sharing open grasslands are now-rare descendants of domestic agricultural grazers of ancient origin which made Hortobagy (pronounced Horto-baj) possible, the result of more than 2,000 years of mutually helpful coexistence with humans. After herdsmen cleared woodlands, grazers kept the wet sodic plain, formed by centuries of saline flooding from the Tisza River, fertile and open, attracting and permitting survival of the remarkable collection of species here today—spiral-horned long-haired racka sheep, Hungarian gray longhorn cattle (and their some-time-companions, short-toed larks), Mangalica pigs, Nonius horses and their herdsmen's puli and komondor sheepdogs.

The park has trails, 20–30 lookout towers, and offers a two-hour bus tour April–October. Some of the more interesting parts require a guide, going by horse, carriage, or afoot.

Great bustards, more than a yard tall (100 cm) weighing 45 pounds (20 kg) or more, largest birds that can fly, are drab until they go into courtship frenzy. In a visual display aimed at attracting females from thousands of yards away in their flat puszta habitat, males throw heads back and inflate feather-covered neck sacs to soccer-ball-size. Heads entirely disappear, wings turn inside out and tails raise over their backs until what remains is a towering pile of quivering white feathers, which then deflates and re-inflates repeatedly until females are sufficiently impressed to mate. They're increasingly rare in Hungary and eastern Europe, Turkey, Ukraine, China. Britain has started a restoration program in grasslands around Stonehenge.

Threats include disastrous cyanide pollution from a gold mine spill into the Tisza River, long-term region-wide effects still not known.

---

**FURTHER INFORMATION**

Hortobagyi Nemzeti National Park Directorate, 4024 Debrecen, Sumen u.z., Boszomenyi ut 138, Hungary, Tel: (+36) 52-349-9122—excellent literature, also visitation permits; Hungarian Ornithological and Nature Conservation Society (MME), 1121 Budapest, Kolto utca 21, Hungary, Tel: (+36) 1-395-2605; Ministry for the Environment and Regional Policy, 1011 Budapest I., Fo u. 44-50; Levelcim, 1394 Budapest Pf 351, Tel: (+36) 1-56-2133, Fax: 1-74-7457, Tlx: 226115.

---

Most international visitors arrive by air in Budapest, three hours' drive (124 miles/200 km) west of Hortobagy. Best way to get around Hungary (though costly) is by rental car since bus and rail transport is limited. A wide range of good accommodations, including campsites, can be found in most places (as in Debrecen 25 miles/39 km east of Hortobagy).

Much of the year is pleasant, though temperatures can range from above 85°F (29°C) in summer to below freezing in winter. Best times are late April to mid–late May for migrations; May for breeding, including great bustards displaying; September–October for common cranes, also flocks of great bustards and lesser white-fronted geese.

## ALSO OF INTEREST

**Kiskunsag National Park**, a short distance southwest of Hortobagy and almost as impressive, with similar birds.

**Koros-Maros National Park**, near Szvaras, with great bustards, otters, little egrets, protected snail-forest (12 snail species), trails, cycle paths, visitor center.

**Lake Ferto-Hansag National Park** in Hungary's far northwest section of the Neusiedlersee, with woods and marshes, wading birds, red-crested pochards, little crakes, penduline tits, warblers uncommon elsewhere.

**Zemplen Forest Reserve** northeast of Miskolc, one of a number of (mainly broadleaved) forested hill ranges across Hungary's north with black storks, collared and red-breasted flycatchers, eight woodpeckers including black, spotted, green, and Syrian, great raptors including Ural and eagle owls, imperial, golden, booted, and lesser spotted eagles.

White storks nest throughout the country on chimneys and over 1,500 pylon supports erected for them by the Hungarian Ornithological Society.

# ICELAND, GREENLAND, AND THE FAROE ISLANDS

NESTING BIRD POPULATIONS HERE MAY BE
DENSEST IN THE WORLD. FEW DOUBT IT WHO
HAVE SEEN THE VESTMANNA BIRD CLIFFS IN THE FAROES
LITERALLY COVERED WITH FULMARS, KITTIWAKES,
RAZORBILLS, PUFFINS, AND GUILLEMOTS, AND INLAND,
ENORMOUS COLONIES OF GOLDEN PLOVERS, SNIPES,
OYSTERCATCHERS, EIDERS, AND OTHERS.

## ICELAND

Birds of the northern climes, many seldom seen elsewhere, spend the summer and breed in enormous numbers on Iceland and its surrounding cliffs and islets.

Gyrfalcons and rare white-tailed eagles, each Europe's largest of its kind, have strongholds here. Three monumental cliffs rising sheer nearly 1,650 feet (500 m) from the sea can be covered in summer with guillemots, Brunnich's guillemots, razorbills, fulmars, and kittiwakes. One of them,

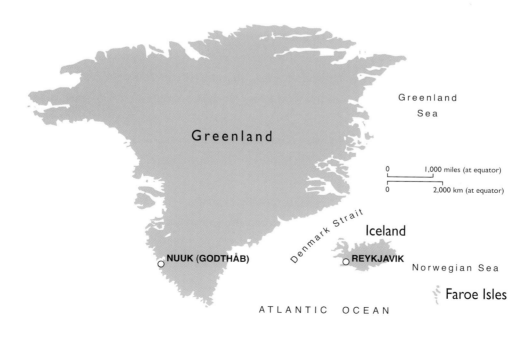

Greenland

Greenland
Sea

0 — 1,000 miles (at equator)
0 — 2,000 km (at equator)

Denmark Strait

Iceland

NUUK (GODTHÅB)

REYKJAVIK

Norwegian Sea

Faroe Isles

ATLANTIC OCEAN

# ICELAND, GREENLAND, And The FAROE ISLANDS

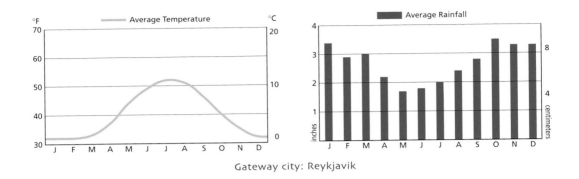

Gateway city: Reykjavik

**Látrabjarg** (1,467 feet/441 m) holds probably Europe's largest seabird colony with a million or more auks, including confiding little Atlantic puffins, which seem almost to enjoy photographers, and the world's largest razorbill colony (400,000 pairs, a third of the world population).

**Mývatim**—translated: "Lake of Midges" which this 14-square-mile (37-km²) combination of shallow water, lava formations, and sulphur pools definitely is—is Europe's greatest duck breeding center. Some 50,000 pairs of 15 species nest on dozens of islands and islets and along its deeply indented shores, including Barrow's goldeneyes, long-tailed, tufted, and harlequin ducks, goosanders, scoters, plus Slavonian grebes, whimbrels, red-necked phalaropes, golden plovers, wheatears, snow buntings, merlins, ptarmigans, and others.

Large, graceful whooper swans raise cygnets in southern lowlands at the **Ölfus river estuary** and marshes of the **Flói Wildfowl Reserve**, with large colonies of black-tailed godwits and dunlins, as well as graceful red-throated and great northern divers.

The **Vestmann Islands** off the southwest coast have some of the world's most spectacular cliff colonies with huge numbers of puffins and other auks, including Brunnich's guillemots, great crowds of gannets, Manx shearwaters, and the world's largest Leach's petrel colony (hard to see because of their nocturnal habits).

Auks in enormous numbers breed on **Grimsey Island** off the northeast—Brunnich's guillemots, razorbills, puffins, also a large fulmar colony. Little auks are no longer here, perhaps driven away by warmer climate.

Even the center of Reykjavik has breeding birds on **Lake Tjörnin**—graylags, gadwalls, scaup, eiders, and arctic terns, and the city boasts an excellent salmon river, the Ellioaár, on its eastern outskirts.

White-tailed eagles and gyrfalcons are strictly protected from disturbance while breeding, as are high-density waterfowl areas during hatching. Otherwise most places are accessible by road or ferry.

# ICELAND, GREENLAND, And The FAROE ISLANDS

Clownish little puffins with outsize multihued bills nest at the end of tunnels up to 16 feet (5 m) long in rock crevices or on cliffs at the edge of the sea, where they lay one egg—then raise their chick in total darkness. After it hatches, they feed it silvery small fish, bringing as many as 30 at once in bills ridged so when they catch one, they can tuck it back and catch another until they reach capacity. Adults drop these at the burrow, feeding the chick up to its weight in fish daily, finally stopping, at which point the youngster totters out and off the cliff-edge into the sea, where it must fend for itself. Four years later, if all goes well, it will return, find a lifelong mate and nest here itself. Atlantic puffins nest on both sides of the North Atlantic, with huge colonies on Iceland and the Faroes and Scottish islands.

## ICELAND, GREENLAND, And The FAROE ISLANDS

Guillemots spend most of their lives at sea, coming to land only to nest—but when they do, they come in tens of thousands, crowding together on rocky islands and sea cliffs on both sides of the North Atlantic—60,000 on Scotland's St. Kilda alone. Each pair lays a single egg which is pointed or pyriform in shape so it won't roll off narrow cliff edges, since they use no nesting material. They are—like other members of the auk family—sometimes known as penguins of the northern hemisphere, black and white with bolt-upright posture, rear-end legs that make them awkward on land but swiftly graceful at sea, where they literally "fly underwater."

Chief environmental threats include a proposed Kárahnjúkar hydroelectric power plant which is likely to put at risk thousands of pairs of pink-footed geese, of which Iceland has 90 percent of the world summer population. It would turn their main breeding grounds near Mount Snæfell into a hydroelectric power reservoir. There has been fierce debate also over plans to dredge its muddy bottom, on which the wildlife depends, for diatomaceous material. Overgrazing by sheep remains a contributor to serious erosion problems.

Surprisingly, though Iceland has more than 80 nature reserves, many of the main bird areas have no formal protected status.

Keflavík airport near the capital, Reykjavík, has daily flights to many east coast U.S. cities as well as London and Scandinavia. Lodging, also vehicle and motorbike rental are available throughout the country (it's also possible to get around in some places on the engaging little Icelandic horses, still a pure breed, which probably came here with ninth-century Vikings).

FURTHER INFORMATION

Náttúruvernd Ríkisins (Nature Conservation Council), Skulagata 21, IS-101 Reykjavik,
Tel: (+354) 570-7400, Fax: (+354) 570-7401, E-mail: natturuvernd@natturuvernd.is

# GREENLAND

**Northeast Greenland National Park** is the world's largest, a 375,000-square-mile (972,000-km²) U.N. Biosphere Reserve covering the northeastern quarter of this North Atlantic island wilderness. Beyond its towering cliffs meeting the sea in walls of glacial ice and ancient rock—some of the oldest on earth—live musk oxen, polar bears, caribou, arctic wolves, foxes, hares, and delicate flora. Whales, seals, and walruses shelter in fjords. Long closed to all but scientific teams, it's now open to private groups, though with limited facilities and difficult access. The short visitor season is early July–September. Permit applications must be in by December of the year prior to a visit.

FURTHER INFORMATION

Dansk Polarcenter, Tel: (+45) 32-88-01-00, Fax: (+45) 32-88-01-01, E-mail: dpc@dpc.dk;
OR Greenland Tourism, E-mail: greenland.tourism@greennet.gl

# FAROE ISLANDS

Bird populations of the Faroe Islands some 250 miles (400 km) northwest of Scotland's Shetland Islands may be densest in the world—no one seems sure. But few will doubt it who have taken the unforgettable boat trip through caves and narrow sounds of the **Vestmanna Bird Cliffs** when they are literally covered with fulmars, kittiwakes, razorbills, Atlantic puffins, and guillemots. Inland are large colonies of golden plovers, snipes, oystercatchers, eiders, and others.

Most visitors arrive at the international airport on Vagar. After that, the road and ferry system are excellent and bed and breakfast accommodations are widely available. Inter-island helicopter is available, as are car and motorbike rental. As in Iceland and Greenland, best times are late April through August. Visitors should be braced—islanders still net and eat the comical, trusting little puffins, as they have for centuries.

FURTHER INFORMATION

Faroe Islands Tourist Board, P.O. Box 118, FO 110 Tórshavn,
Tel: (+298) 316055, Fax: (+298) 310858, E-mail: tourist@tourist.fo

# ITALY

NIMBLE IBEXES WITH DECORATIVE
BACKSWEPT HORNS GRAZE FEARLESSLY IN
HIGH MOUNTAIN MEADOWS OF GRAN PARADISO
NATIONAL PARK, SET ASIDE TO SAVE THEM BY KING
VITTORIO EMANUELE II IN 1856. ONCE ENDANGERED
BY DEMAND FOR BODY PARTS SUPPOSED TO HAVE
THERAPEUTIC PROPERTIES AS WELL AS FOR TROPHY
HORNS, WITH PROTECTION THEY HAVE THRIVED.

WITH ALL ITS DRAMATIC BEAUTY, ITALY SEEMS AS LITTLE CONCERNED WITH WILDLIFE AND THE ENVIRONMENT AS ANY COUNTRY ON EARTH. Pollution from industrial and urban waste, carbon monoxide and lead emissions, and rubbish dumping everywhere leave the general populace untroubled. Hunters have decimated wild populations, almost wiping out magnificent golden eagles. Colorful small birds are more readily seen in the relative safety of city parks than in their countryside habitats.

Italy is part of the Central Mediterranean Corridor for birds of prey flying between European nest sites and African wintering areas. In spring some 27,500 raptors of 16 species move through—some 11,400 honey buzzards alone crossing over the Straits of Messina. But despite local groups' energetic protests, thousands are shot there and at other crossings every year.

Still, interest is growing in environmental organizations and in setting aside wildlife parks and reserves, especially in remote and

## ITALY

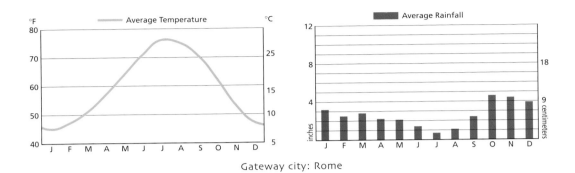

Gateway city: Rome

mountainous areas where habitat remains. A Ministry for the Environment, created in 1986, has been activated, partly as a result of European Union directives. A Lista Rossa (Red List) by World Wide Fund for Nature (WWF) reported 60 percent of Italian vertebrates are threatened—but many are legally protected now, and some, like brown bear and lynx, are slowly recovering after reintroduction in remote places where they had disappeared.

There are now 17 national parks and reserves covering almost 4,700 square miles (12,150 km²), just over 4 percent of the country—not always well maintained and protected, but designated—with the prospect of more since passage of a 1991 law permitting creation of 14 new ones.

# GRAN PARADISO NATIONAL PARK

Of the national parks, oldest and best known is Gran Paradiso, set aside to save the ibex—mountain goat-antelopes with spectacular backswept horns almost a yard (85 cm) long. Now this reserve, like many others, saves a number of other species as well.

King Vittorio Emanuele II first declared Gran Paradiso to be a Royal Hunting Reserve in 1856 after populations of ibex (aka steinbock) had decreased alarmingly due to intensive hunting pressure for body parts supposed to have therapeutic properties (a cross-shaped chest bone was thought to have magical powers). He formed a protective guard force and laid out paths still used today for that purpose, part of the present 450 miles (724 km) of marked trails and mule tracks. In 1920 his grandson, King Vittorio Emanuele III, donated the original 5,187 acres (2,100 ha) to create Italy's first national park.

Even inside the park and despite superb mountaineering skills, ibex were poached until in 1945 only 419 remained. Now, with greater protection, there are almost 4,000 of these stocky, fearless, remarkably trusting grazers in lush mountain pastures in summer, descending to lower elevations in winter, only glancing up in mild surprise when quiet visitors approach within a few yards.

Alpine chamois with distinctive backward-hooked horns have thrived as well, their elastic-based hooves enabling them to leap nimbly among crags. Males clash in spring, ramming each other violently, marking tree trunks with smelly glandular secretions from the base of their distinctive horns (which females wear also).

Alpine marmots lumber along like small furry bears, foraging on plants around the snow line and whistling loudly at the slightest disturbance from any source—an ermine darting after a mouse, a thickset Eurasian badger padding through low vegetation with swaying gait, even an inoffensive mountain hare—but especially the first sign of a red (or silver) fox.

Golden eagles soar overhead and nest on rocky ledges, sometimes in trees—among more than 100 bird species, including fierce eagle owls, rock ptarmigans, sociable little alpine accentors, and choughs. On steep cliffs are wallcreepers (clinging so tightly they are almost invisible despite red wings) and in the woodlands, big, handsome red-crested black woodpeckers and speckled nutcrackers, which hide nuts at harvest time and memorize locations so accurately they can find them again in deepest snows.

Gran Paradiso is 270 square miles (some 700 km²) of beautiful alpine terrain shaped by torrents and glaciers where snow-covered peaks—including the mountain for which it was named—rise from lush green valleys, wooded bottomlands, and some 60 ponds and lakes fed by mountain streams with dramatic waterfalls. High meadows can be covered with wildflowers—wild pansies, brilliant deep-blue gentians, rare handsome martagon lilies and alpenroses—that attract clouds of butterflies: apollos, peak whites, southern white admirals, and others, peaking in June and July. Some 1,500 plant species can be seen at **Paradisia Botanical Garden** near Cogne inside the park.

Together with France's **Vanoise National Park** which adjoins, it forms the largest protected area in western Europe, with, according to park claims, as much wildlife for its size as any reserve in the world outside Africa.

It has become so popular with summer visitors that litter has become a problem, also noise pollution, damage to trails and fragile habitats, and controversial proposed developments both in and just outside the park.

Italy's high-speed autostradas linked to France and Switzerland by mountain tunnels afford easy park access. Hotels and restaurants are not far from any park border.

Good starting point for park exploration is Aosta, 9.3 miles (15 km) north, reachable by commuter air from Torino (Turin) and Geneva international airports, both about an hour away by car or bus. Busses from Aosta's Piazza Narbonne connect with most villages inside the park.

Best times are April–October. Families and casual visitors like the northern part of the park for its higher mountains, more spectacular views, and abundant hotels and picnic areas. Serious hikers like quieter, wilder southern valleys. The Gran Piano di Noasca is a good place to see grazing ibex and chamois, also the excursion from Valnontey to the refuge "Vittorio Sella," especially in evening and early morning. Campgrounds, refuges, and mountain huts are available for overnight stays, both in summer and for cross-country skiers in winter.

The Noasca Visitor Center, Valle Orco, is open all year, with displays, publications, information, including advice on how to arrange for guided trips—Tel: (+39) 0124-901070; others open seasonally are Ronco Canavese, Val Soana; Ceresole Reale, Valle Orco; Rhemes Notre Dame, Valle di Rhemes, Tel: (+39) 0165-936193; Degioz, Valsavarenche; and Giardino Botanico Alpino Paradisia, Valnontey-Cogne. The Aosta tourist office, Piaza Chanoux 8, Tel: (+39) 0165-35655 has accommodation guides, maps, and a list of refuges.

---

**FURTHER INFORMATION**

Manager, Ente Parco Nazionale Gran Paradiso, Via della Rocca, 47-10123 Torino, Tel: (+39) 011-8606211 or 871187, Fax: 011/8121305, E-mail: segreteria@pngp.it; Ministerio dell' Ambiente, Servizio Conservazione della Natura (Director General), Piazza Venezia 11, 00187 Rome, Tel: (+39) 6-679-7124; Commissione per la Conservazione della Natura, e delle Rich Richerche, 7 Piazzela delle Scienze, 00158 Rome.

---

## ALSO OF INTEREST

**Abruzzo National Park**, 154 square miles (400 km²), two hours east of Rome, with some of Italy's wildest and most scenic country. High in the Apennines, it still contains Marsicano brown bears, lynx, and Apennine wolves, along with chamois, roe deer, golden eagles, goshawks. Abruzzo also has superb flowers, including many endemics. Offices in Viale delle Medaglie d'oro 141, 00136 Roma, Tel: (+39) 06-349-6993. Campgrounds, refuges, also hotels nearby.

**Circeo National Park**, 33 square miles (85 km²) with wild boar, fallow deer, mouflon, 240 bird species including black and white storks, flamingos, glossy ibises. Offices in Via Carlol Alberto 107, 04016 Sabaudia (LT), Tel: (+39) 07-735-7251.

**Stelvio National Park**, 528 square miles (1,370 km²) with 30 mammal species including ibex, chamois, roe deer, marmots; 131 bird species including golden eagles, capercaillies, heathcock—and an extraordinary variety of plant species in some of the loveliest valleys in the Central Alps. Offices in Via Monte Braulio 56, 23032 Bormio (So.), Tel: (+39) 03-429-01582.

**Calabria National Park**, 49 square miles (127 km²) split in three parts with Apennine wolves, wild cats, black woodpeckers, goshawks, Bonelli's eagles. Offices in Viale della Republica 26, 87100 Cosenza, Tel: (+39) 09-842-6544.

# NORWAY

LUMBERING BULL WALRUSES WEIGHING WELL
OVER A TON WAIT TO MATE IN MIDWINTER.
TUSKS ALMOST TWO FEET (0.6 M) LONG MAY
BE USED TO PRY MOLLUSCS OFF SEABEDS BUT SEEM
PRIMARILY SOCIAL RATHER THAN PRACTICAL IN FUNCTION.
THEY LOCATE FOOD IN PITCH-BLACK DEPTHS USING
SENSITIVE NASAL SKIN AND WHISKERS AND DISLODGE
CRUSTACEANS BY SQUIRTING LARGE JETS OF WATER UNDER
HIGH PRESSURE FROM THEIR MOUTHS, AN
ABILITY FAMILIAR TO ZOOKEEPERS.

Environmental legislation dates back almost a century in this narrow mountainous country with one of the world's most irregular coastlines, just over 1,000 air miles (1,609 km) long but more than 12 times that counting indentations plus more than 53,000 small coastal islands.

By the end of 1990 this western half of the Scandinavian peninsula had nature reserves covering 5.6 percent of the country including 17 national parks, with more planned.

Despite this and a relatively benign environmental stance by European standards—Norwegians strongly favor clean air and water—habitat loss from logging, wetland drainage, hydroelectric dams,

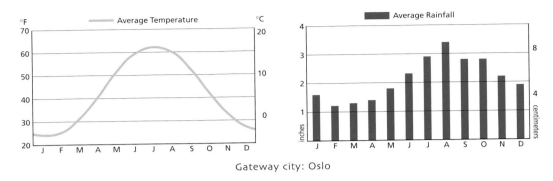

Gateway city: Oslo

and acid rain has placed 898 plant and animal species on the endangered or threatened list. Overfishing has caused drastic decline in once-bountiful fish stocks, nearly wiping out herring and greatly depleting cod and others. Aquaculture escapes have damaged wild populations, and environmentalists worldwide have protested Norway's stance on resumption of sealing and whaling.

Still, places of great beauty and wildlife interest remain both in and out of protected land. Among them:

**Dovrefjell National Park**, Romsdal, southeast, known for musk oxen.

**Hardangervidda National Park**, vast 1,320-square-mile (3,422-km²) upland alpine plateau dominating south-central Norway, home to Europe's largest wild reindeer herd.

**Jan Mayen Island**, 147 square miles (382 km²), out in the Arctic Ocean 620 miles (1,000 km) west of Norway, 310 miles (500 km) east of Greenland and 373 miles (600 km) north-northeast of Iceland, with Norway's only active volcano and highly important breeding seabird populations, without protected areas but deserving of some.

**Ovre Dividal National Park**, lovely wild 287 square miles (743 km²) lying at the heart of a network of trekking routes in northern Norway, Sweden, and Finland, home—still—to some of Norway's rare predators: brown bears, wolverines, wolves, lynx.

**Ovre Pasvik National Park** is only 26 square miles (67 km²), tucked between Finland and Russia, boreal forest, large muskeg areas, a few rare brown bears, many migratory birds in summer.

### FURTHER INFORMATION

Ministry of Environment (Miljoverndepartementet), Nature Conservation Division, Myntgata 2, P.O. Box 8013, N-0030 Oslo, Tel: (+47) 22-24-90-90; Fax: (+47) 22-24-95-00, Tlx: 21480 env-n, OR Ministry Information Center, Tel: 22-24-57-87, Fax: 22-24-27-56; Directorate for Nature Management (Director), Tungasletta 2, N-7004 Trondheim, Tel: (+47) 73-58-05-00, Fax: (+47) 73-91-54-33; Norger Naturvernforbund (Norwegian Society for the Conservation of Nature), Postboks, Hammersborg, Oslo 1.

# SVALBARD

One-ton walruses laze in the sun, reindeer graze, and more than a million seabirds nest in summer on Svalbard, northernmost point of Europe's northernmost country—nine small islands in the Arctic Ocean, just south of permanent pack ice.

Polar bears den here in large numbers. Arctic foxes with fur that offers better insulation from cold than any other animal—smoky-gray in summer, white in winter— follow them around, even out on drifting ice floes, hoping for seal meat scraps.

Diminutive little auks, which spend the rest of their lives entirely at sea, raise downy chicks on stony slopes and cliffs all over the archipelago, their nestlings' shrieks audible as a steady summertime buzz all over the Longyear Valley.

Their breeding activities trigger an essential connection in the arctic land–sea ecosystem. When birds bring organic material from sea to cliffs to feed themselves and their young, food bits fall to terrain below along with feathers, carcasses of dead birds and fish, and their own droppings (guano), which fertilize growth of lush vegetation important for herbivores such as barnacle and pink-footed geese and reindeer. Meanwhile predators such as arctic foxes, glaucous gulls, and great and arctic skuas feed on both eggs and young birds to build up energy reserves for winter.

With the auks are thousands of individuals of other species—Brunnich's guillemots, fulmars, kittiwakes, purple sandpipers, ivory gulls, red-throated loons (or divers), long-tailed ducks (or oldsquaws), red (also gray) phalaropes.

Arctic terns—world's longest-distance migrants, wintering a hemisphere away—dive fiercely on interlopers near their nest scrapes. The only songbirds among 30 bird species are hardy little snow buntings in bright black-and-white breeding plumage, sweetly trilling after a 700-mile (1,126-km) flight across the Barents Sea, smallest bird to make that often stormy crossing.

Stout, short-legged Svalbard reindeer—smallest of the world's reindeer, sometimes called Svalbard caribou—graze hungrily on moss and lichens, having dropped a third of their weight when winter darkness and cold made greenery scarce.

Like all the islands' mammals, both land and marine (polar bears are classed as marine mammals), they were hunted to near-extinction in the last century, but after years of protection all (except for whales offshore) are once again common. Polar bears up to eight feet (2.5 m) long, weighing almost a ton, cover great distances with their fluid loping gait, and can be anywhere on the archipelago. They are so powerful, irascible, and unpredictably aggressive that all other creatures—including humans—keep a constant lookout for them.

Huge bull walruses with tusks up to two feet (0.6 m) long, temporary bachelors, await females' return from summer sojourns farther north. They mate in midwinter—some think in the dark freezing water. Their enormous tusks seem, like deer antlers, to have social rather than practical function—food is located largely by touch, using highly sensitive nasal skin and whiskers to find crustaceans in pitch-black water, unearthing them on beaches in summer using tough upper nose skin or by shooting high-pressure jets of water from their mouths (an ability well-known among zookeepers).

By late summer all residents that can fly away are gone except for Svalbard ptarmigans which (like arctic foxes) molt from dark to pure white so that against snow only their dark eyes and bills are visible as they pick around scrubby growth for dwarf birch buds and willow catkins, even conifer needles if hungry enough.

Once Svalbard was lush tropical jungle, roamed by Iguanodon dinosaurs whose footprints are still visible in hardened sands near Barentsburg. Some of the oldest rocks on earth—fragments up to 3 billion years old—came to rest on this now-desert island group before it drifted north 60–300 million years ago carrying layers of organic material which became rich coal seams that now drive Svalbard's economy.

Now 60 percent of Svalbard is covered with sheets and rivers of ice outlining mountains and glaciers in dramatic landscapes of breathtaking beauty. Over them upper atmosphere electrons create spectacular multicolored aurora borealis displays when they collide with charged sun particles in midwinter skies.

Air this cool with no moisture burden is so clear it changes distance and depth perception. Barry Lopez in his book *Arctic Dreams* reports a Swedish explorer had all but completed a written description of "a craggy headland with two unusually symmetrical valley glaciers, the whole of it part of a large island" when he discovered what he was looking at was a walrus.

Best times are spring and summer. Mean annual temperature is 25°F (−4°C), in July 43°F (6°C), though it can soar a dozen degrees over that, warmed by the Gulf Stream which reaches Svalbard's western side. Midnight sun is from April 20–August 20, deep polar night October 28–February 14, the rest something in between. Svalbard's small population marks the sun's return on March 8 with annual parades and celebration.

Serious threat to the wildlife reserves that cover more than half of Svalbard (and 72 percent of waters around it) is human-produced pollutants transported, it's believed, from distant sources by wind and ocean currents. Scientists have found PCB levels in polar bears so high they fear it could lead to reduced reproduction and higher mortality.

Svalbard is reachable by scheduled air daily in clear weather—and by ship in summer—from Tromsø to Longyearbyen, which has lodging, restaurants, and tour facilities. A ferry with cabins makes weekly summertime cruises around northern Spitsbergen. Tromso has direct air connection with international jetports at Oslo and Bergen.

Whimbrels' long down-curved bills enable them to make use of a comprehensive diet including worms and mollusks they can find only by probing deep into mudflats, leading to their nickname "elephant bird" in Southeast Asia. Circumpolar, their far-carrying "pe-pe-pe-pe-pe" whistle is heard over breeding grounds in subarctic and Arctic from Iceland across Eurasia, Alaska, and Canada.

Visiting Svalbard is not always easy. Local transport can be a problem, permission is required to visit parks, sensitive nesting areas are off-limits, and independent tourism not encouraged. Dangers are such from polar bears, drift ice, weather, and terrain, that rescue insurance can be required for visits to remote areas. Bears cannot legally be shot except in extreme danger and only if all other means of self-defense have been exhausted.

Most visitors opt for group tours, which are organized in Spitsbergen and Longyearbyen.

### FURTHER INFORMATION

Svalbard Wildlife Service, Tel: (+47) 7902-1035, Fax: 7902-1201, E-mail: wildlife@mail.link.no, Website: www.svalbard.com/wildlife

Highlights of Svalbard's wildlife reserves include:

**Forlandet National Park**—King and common eider nesting, world's northernmost harbor seals.

**The Island of Hopen** in the Barents Sea. Hopen is protected as a nature reserve, and is a denning area for polar bears. Hopen is also listed among Birdlife International's important bird areas in Europe, due to the large colonies of seabirds such as Brunnich's guillemots and kittiwakes. The waters surrounding Hopen are also a winter habitat for walruses, and there is a haul-out site on the southern part of the island.

**Moffen Nature Reserve** is a walrus haul-out area, also nesting birds.

**Nordenskold Land National Park**, south of Longyearbyen, which includes some of Svalbard's richest areas of lowland tundra, including wetlands in Reindalen. The park is an important area for Svalbard reindeer. The western part of the park includes seabird colonies and habitats for species such as eiders and barnacle geese.

**Nordre Isfjorden National Park** includes areas of rich tundra vegetation on the coastal plains north of Isfjorden and includes wetlands and complexes of small lakes and ponds that are habitats for waders and waterbirds such as eiders, barnacle and pink-footed geese. The fjords here are also habitats for ringed seals.

**Northeast Svalbard Reserve** has bear denning, strictly protected from all traffic including aerial overviews.

**Northwest Spitsbergen National Park** with large seabird colonies, reindeer, fox, walrus haul-outs, historic sites including remnants of failed schemes to reach the North Pole in hydrogen-gas balloons.

**Sassen-Bunsow-land National Park** in the inner part of Isfjorden includes areas of lowland tundra which are also habitats for reindeer. It also includes areas for waders and waterbirds, including a Ramsar site at the islets of Gasøyane (nesting site for barnacle geese). The fjords harbor ringed seals.

**Southeast Svalbard Reserve** has a large reindeer population, and many polar bears.

**South-Spitsbergen National Park** has nesting eiders, barnacle geese, large seabird colonies.

There are also 15 special bird reserves for nesting eiders, and barnacle geese and others, mostly on small islands along Spitsbergen's west coast, strictly protected, plus two plant protection areas.

Svalbard is among hundreds of Norwegian nature set-asides.

# POLAND

POLISH KINGS, RUSSIAN TSARS, AND EARLY
DUKES OF RUTHENIA APPROPRIATED THE BEST
WILDLIFE HABITAT OF POLAND FOR THEIR PRIVATE HUNTING
RESERVES. THEIR SUCCESSORS—POLISH NATIONAL PARKS SUCH
AS BIELOWIECZA—PRESERVE NOT ONLY RARE ANIMALS SUCH
AS THE EUROPEAN BISON BUT TOWERING OLD-GROWTH
FOREST WITH TREES UP TO 600 YEARS OLD.

MASSIVE EUROPEAN BISON BROUGHT BACK FROM NEAR-EXTINCTION ROAM FREE IN POLISH NATIONAL PARKS, ALONG WITH EUROPEAN WILDCATS, BROWN BEARS, WILD BOARS, WOLVES, OTTERS, AND MORE THAN 400 KINDS OF BIRDS.

Few European countries have such varied landscape and large tracts of wildlife-rich parkland preserving marsh, coastal dunes, lakes, streams, mountains, and ancient forests.

More than 400 plant associations are here of which 20 are endemic. Added to native floral and faunal types are those of Atlantic and Mediterranean origin, steppe species, and north-northeastern species with post-glacial roots.

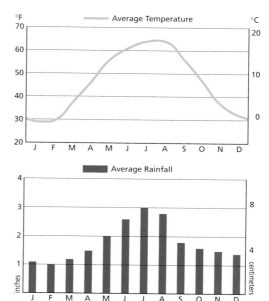

Gateway city: Warsaw

Beaver, lynx, and Polish elk (similar to North American moose) have been successfully reintroduced.

Birds include powerful white-tailed eagles—Poland's national symbol and Europe's largest raptor—along with Ural owls, alpine accentors, corncrakes, red-crested flycatchers, water-loving bitterns, and colorful warblers and bee-eaters.

White storks breed throughout the country on haystacks, chimneys, roof corners, and supports erected for their benefit, in huge nests in the sides of which sparrows and other small birds often excavate their own nest holes.

Poland's national parks have an 80-year official history but like many of the world's great wildlife reserves, some go back to nobility and monarchs—early dukes of Ruthenia, Polish kings, and Russian tsars—who set aside land as their private hunting preserves.

Now the reserves protect some 90 mammal species and hundreds of kinds of birds, insects, reptiles, amphibians, and fish in 23 national parks and altogether almost 1,200 natural set-asides of various kinds in this 120,000-square-mile (312,000-km²) country on the Baltic Sea.

Reserves range in size from 259-square-mile (670-km²) BIEBRZANSKI NATIONAL PARK to little 3,800-acre (1,592-ha) OJCOWSKI with rare plants, foxes, martens, owls, black woodpeckers, masses of butterflies. Six of them—BABIOGORSKI, BIALOWIEZA, BIESZCZADY, KARKONOSKI, SLOWINSKI, and TATRZANSKI—have been designated by the U.N. as World Biosphere Reserves. Most have trails, nearby lodging, and guides—all in a country with some of the most environmentally degraded areas in Europe, forests dying of acid rain, streams polluted with chemical discharges while "developing the forest industry" in a country already heavily logged. But environmental interests are gaining support in efforts to improve conditions.

## BIALOWIEZA NATIONAL PARK

Bialowieza (pronounced Bee-o-VEE-zha), part of a forest complex reserve of 578 square miles (1,500 km²) located on both sides of the border between Poland and Belarus, is renowned as the place where European bison were saved from extinction. It's one of the world's great conservation stories, not dissimilar from that of American bison—most numerous hoofed animals ever known, brought near extinction in a few decades by relentless, pointless slaughter.

These two massive animals half a world apart are physically similar. European bison—also called wisents—slightly bulkier at 2,200 pounds (1,000 kg), forage in and around forests rather than on the grassland plains of American bison. Despite their size (nearly six feet/2 m at the shoulder) they can easily jump over a six-foot (2-m) fence and charge at 30 miles an hour (50 kmh). Once they ranged through ancient woodlands from the Atlantic Coast to China Seas and were depicted in ice-age paintings. Forest clearing across Europe forced them back to this dense glade where they were culled by royal hunting parties until early 20th-century wars and revolutions. Huge additional forest areas were cleared then and World War I saw decimation of all wildlife.

The last wild bison was shot by a poacher in the Caucasus in 1923. Luckily, enough had been given to zoos and private collections to re-form a viable European breeding nucleus which then was saved by an unlikely protector during World War II—Hitler's chief deputy, Herman Goering, who, aping past royalty, wanted them for his private hunting preserve. A small herd reared by Polish scientists was released back into the wild in 1952. It has thrived and now a stable herd of 300 is here (500 altogether counting those on Bialowieza and its Belarus equivalent) with animals beyond the land's carrying capacity being reintroduced elsewhere.

Birdlife prospers too in this protected tract which has been called the most valuable natural area in the European lowlands—altogether some 251 (177 breeding) species. Woodland types thrive in the ancient 460-square-mile (1,200-km$^2$) primeval oak, hornbeam, and pine palearctic forest of Belovezhskaya Pushka, dating back to 8,000 BC, shared across the border with Belarus (formerly Byelorussia of the USSR). For moisture-oriented species, its location in the watershed of the Baltic and Black Seas encompasses one of Europe's prime inland wetlands.

Nine kinds of woodpeckers including white-backed, gray-headed, black, and three-toed, hammer on tree trunks towering hundreds of feet high, some of them several hundred years old. Eagles, including lesser spotted and booted, prey on smaller birds and mammals as do goshawks, pygmy, Tengmalm's, and eagle owls, black kites, honey buzzards, and white-tailed eagles, which will prey on even large geese. Every habitat possibility is used. Great overturned tree roots are nest sites for robins, blackbirds, dunnocks, song thrush, and mice.

Marshes can be alive with clouds of white-winged and black terns, booming bitterns, trumpeting common cranes, secretive corncrakes, and marsh warblers, which have no song of their own but good memories, carrying on 45 minutes straight mimicking those of 70 other species. Red-breasted and collared flycatchers feast on some of 8,000 species of insects attracted to glades, swamps, and river meadows, with more than 1,200 kinds of plants, including more than 500 flowering species.

Lanky Polish elk graze on lush tangles of water foliage. Wild boar families led by bulky patriarchs rip up black soil to get at underground roots. Gray wolves and lynx slip between trees usually unseen except briefly by their victims, though small but quick and fierce martens, ermines, and badgers often elude them. River otters pursue two dozen varieties of fish. European beavers, once extinct here, now fell saplings for dams and lodges, having reintroduced themselves over the Belarus border to the other 60-some mammal species. (Shy park mammals can be difficult to spot, however, in deep woodlands.)

# POLAND

Hulking European bison, once one of the most numerous hoofed animals the world has known, roamed ancient forests from the Atlantic coast to China Seas. Clearing and over-hunting brought them to the brink of extinction. They were saved in a conservation story similar to that of their U.S. plains' cousins, American bison, their recovering numbers conserved during World War II by an unlikely protector: a Nazi aide of Adolf Hitler. Now they graze peacefully in Poland's Bialowieza forest and elsewhere.

Climate is temperate-cool, with an average 92 days' yearly snow cover between December and mid-March. Best times are spring and golden autumn (summer's insect clouds and density of forest glades can make wildlife-viewing difficult). Administrative and tourist facilities are in Bialowieza Village on the park boundary, where guides can be arranged, also horse-drawn carriages. Park headquarters has excellent bilingual booklets. Special permits for entry to core areas are available from the national park office for serious researchers—but hundreds of miles (km) of surrounding forest are generally available for riding and hiking through permits available from the nearby forest service.

The Bialowieza Glade, where a palace was built for the tsar in the 19th century, now is the area's tourism center with wildlife exhibits, museum, hotels, and restaurants, also access to trails and campsites. Threats include air pollution, tourism impact from traffic, trampling of rare plants, also disturbance from land reclamation in contiguous Belarus forests to create a river reservoir.

---

**FURTHER INFORMATION**

Bialowieski Park Naroodwy, 17-230 Bialowieza, Poland,
Tel: (+48) 835-12306, (+48) 835-12350, Fax: (+48) 835-12323;
General Board of National Parks, 00-922 Warsaw, ul.
Wawelska 52/54. *See also* Belovezhskaya Pushcha National
Park in Belarus (p.365).

## ALSO OF INTEREST

Among other notable Polish reserves are:

**Babiogorski National Park** on the Babia Gora continental divide, with lynx, badgers, foxes, wild boars, wolves, occasional brown bears, and 120 bird species including wood grouse, hazelhens, and nesting great eagle owls.

**Biebrzanski** (aka **Biebrza River**) **National Park** (pronounced Bee-EB-zha) in northeast Poland's Biebrza Valley, huge wetland stopover or home to 270 bird species, including battalion ruffs, great curlews, spotted eagles, aquatic warblers, black grouse, great snipes, whooper swans, marsh owls, Montagu's harriers, jack snipe, ferruginous ducks, white-winged terns, black storks, many others, including great numbers of common cranes. Its importance, noted by the Ramsar Convention, cannot be overstated—it's estimated that its loss (threatened by woodland encroachment) would mean loss of 40 percent or more for some of these species, which can fill the skies and marshes in spring migration late March to mid-May (perhaps 2–3,000 ruffs and 100 black-tailed godwits in a single flock) and only a little less so in fall, peaking in October. It's home as well to large numbers of roe deer, beavers, otters, wolves, and Polish elk which close their nostrils to feed on underwater marsh marigolds. Park offices have maps, bilingual literature, and information on trails and lookout towers.

**Bieszczady National Park** in the eastern Carpathian Mountains, a U.N. World Biosphere Reserve with some 200 rare and spectacular floral and faunal species—marsh helleborine, gentians, sundews, splendid brown bears, European bison, lynx, European wildcats, wolves, roe deer, endemic Hucule ponies (descendants of primitive mountain horses), golden and lesser spotted eagles, Ural owls, alpine accentors, and hedge-sparrows, many others. Some 84 miles (135 km) of well-marked, accessible trails. Closest tourism center is Ustrzyki Gorne.

**Gorczanski National Park** with parts of the Carpathian primeval forest with Carpathian stags, roe deer, red foxes, wildcats, nesting eagle owls, Ural owls, black grouse, black storks, ring ouzels.

**Kampinos National Park** bordering Warsaw in central Poland, with peat bogs, also dunes covered with primeval pine forest, where beavers, lynx and Polish elks were successfully reintroduced. On a bird migration route, it also has black and white storks, nesting spotted eagles, honey buzzards, goshawks, and rare plants (martagon lilies, pasque-flowers).

**Karkonoski National Park** in the Karkonosze mountains protects 89 Polish Red Book rare species including mountain sheep, black grouse, alpine accentors.

**Magurski National Park** with brown bears, wolves, lynx, roe deer, rare golden eagles, hazel grouse, interesting reptiles and amphibians (spotted salamanders, mountain newts, fire-bellied toads).

# POLAND

**Narwianski National Park**, between Bialowieza and Biebrza National Parks, protecting ecosystems of the winding Narew River—"the Polish Amazon"—with 33 mammal species and 150 breeding birds, many rare elsewhere in Europe.

**Ojcowski National Park** with deep canyons, white limestone cliffs, varied flora and fauna (numerous bats in cliff caves), plus 600 butterfly species. Park headquarters is Pieskowa Skala, a Renaissance castle.

**Pieninski National Park** with Dunajec River Gorge, one of Europe's most beautiful, with lynx, wild cats, wolves, 14 bat species, great Parnassian Apollo butterflies (white wings decorated with black lines, red spots), river rafting.

**Poleski National Park** protecting swamps and peat bogs, ermine, otters, elk, beavers, wolves, 146 bird species including Montagu's and hen harriers, aquatic warblers, redshanks, great snipes.

**Slowinski National Park**, 20 miles (33 km) along the Baltic coast with forest, lakes, bogs, beaches, shifting sand dunes up to 185 feet (56 m) high with unique desert ecosystem—255 bird species, some in large numbers (great crested grebes, mute swans, 20,000 pairs of black-headed gulls).

**Tatrzanski National Park** in Tatra Mountains with high-elevation flora and fauna including chamois, marmots, brown bears, lynx, eagles.

**Wielkopolski National Park**, nine miles (15 km) south of Poznan with beautiful forested lakes and uplands, home to red and roe deer, wild boars, nearly 200 species of nesting and migratory birds, 50 miles (80 km) of hiking trails.

**Wigierski National Park** in the northeast with more than 40 lakes, six rivers, 200-year-old woods, home to wolves, lynx, roe deer, elk, wild boars, black storks, white-tailed eagles with six-foot (2-m) wingspans.

**Wolinski National Park** on a coastal island with spectacular cliffs, some 300 bird species including shelducks, swans, terns, grebes, kites, sparrowhawks, goshawks, nesting white-tailed eagles, spectacular stag beetles (Europe's largest), and a small bison reserve.

# ROMANIA

THOUSANDS OF WHITE PELICANS FLY UP TO
FILL SUNSET SKIES WITH A PINKISH GLOW—AN
UNFORGETTABLE SIGHT, AS ARE LAKES COVERED WITH
BLACK-WHISKERED TERNS NESTING ON WHITE-BLOSSOMING
LILY PADS. THEY ARE AMONG MILLIONS OF BIRDS OF OVER
300 SPECIES THAT FIND HOMES IN THE 3,000+-SQUARE-MILE
(5,000-KM²) DANUBE DELTA, LARGEST WETLAND IN EUROPE
AND ONE OF THE MOST IMPORTANT IN THE WORLD.

THIS SMALL, MOUNTAINOUS COUNTRY IN EASTERNMOST EUROPE, ALTHOUGH RULED FOR MOST OF ITS RECENT HISTORY BY A REPRESSIVE REGIME THAT OUTLAWED CONSERVATION ORGANIZATIONS, HAS SOME OF THE MOST GLORIOUS WILDLIFE AREAS IN EUROPE.

Rare bird populations in their millions congregate where the Danube River ends a journey of 1,788 miles (2,850 km) through 10 European countries and spreads out in an enormous Black Sea delta covering more than 2,200 square miles (almost 5,800 km²). Birds come from Africa and Asia to nest in summer; others fly from northern Europe to winter among these channels, dunes, and floating islands in the world's most extensive wetland reedbeds.

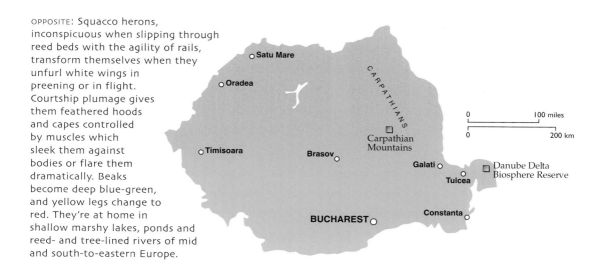

OPPOSITE: Squacco herons, inconspicuous when slipping through reed beds with the agility of rails, transform themselves when they unfurl white wings in preening or in flight. Courtship plumage gives them feathered hoods and capes controlled by muscles which sleek them against bodies or flare them dramatically. Beaks become deep blue-green, and yellow legs change to red. They're at home in shallow marshy lakes, ponds and reed- and tree-lined rivers of mid and south-to-eastern Europe.

## ROMANIA

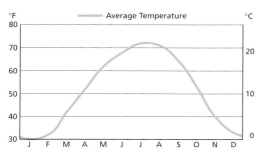

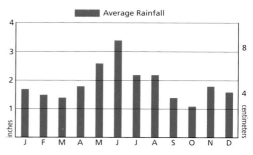

Gateway city: Bucharest

In the Carpathian Mountains, a stone's throw from the Transylvanian castle of Count Dracula (fictional villain based on Romania's real-life prince Vlad Tepes), live Europe's largest populations of lynx, wolves, and brown bears, roaming in ancient beech, spruce, and oak forests.

Both delta and mountains are major spring and fall migration corridors for north European and west Asian raptors.

When dictator Nicolae Ceaucescu was overthrown in 1989, conservation-minded Romanians formed the Societatea Ornitologica Romana (SOR) and began a vigorous public-awareness campaign. It was the first of several nongovernmental organizations aimed at effective support and protection for nature reserves and national parks, either proposed or designated, and led to a new national Department of the Environment set up in the mid-1990s.

Now this 92,500-square-mile (237,500-km²) country—1.8 times larger than England—has 586 protected natural areas including 13 national parks, 18 protected landscapes, and 46 scientific reserves, and the DANUBE DELTA is protected additionally as a U.N. World Biosphere Reserve and World Heritage Site.

Serious threats remain, exacerbated by Romania's poverty. They include industrial and agricultural pollution, soil erosion on 30 percent of arable land, deforestation, acid rain, and tourism lacking appropriate restrictions to protect sensitive natural areas. In January 2000, a gold mine tailings dam broke letting 100,000 cubic yards of cyanide-contaminated water into the Danube and Tisa Rivers killing thousands of fish and birds in Romania, Hungary, and Yugoslavia. Two months later a lead and zinc plant let 20,000 tons of metal waste into the Tisa—and dozens of other mines hold similar threats.

Few protected areas, at least until recently, have organized public access, but many can be visited on one's own. Local guides often are available, and efforts are being made to encourage ecotourism.

Visitors can fly to Bucharest International Airport. From there it is a few hours by road to Tulcea, good starting point for visits to the Danube Delta or in another direction to the Carpathian Mountains. Once there, in either case, visitors may find it best to hire a vehicle, perhaps with a guide, to get around (though some places have cheap public transport). A wide range of accommodations is available, also campsites, especially in beach or ski resorts.

Climate is continental with seasonal extremes of heat and cold. Birding can be good from April to mid-December.

---

**FURTHER INFORMATION**

Department of the Environment, Ministry of Water Management, Forests and the Environment, R-Bucharest-Artera Noua N-S, Tronson 5-6, Sector 5, Bucharest, Tel: (+40) 316044, Fax: 316199, Tlx: 10455/10435.

---

# DANUBE DELTA

Millions of birds—over 300 species—find temporary or permanent homes where the Danube River, longest in Europe, winds up a journey from Germany's Black Forest to the Black Sea and broadens into the 56-mile-wide (90-km) Danube Delta, largest wetland in Europe and one of the most important in the world.

At least 176 species nest among this labyrinth of floating islands of vegetation (plaur), wooded dunes and embankments, lily-covered lakes and channels, and an expanse of reedbeds covering some 603 square miles (1,563 km²)—largest contiguous reedbed in the world. Many others come to spend the fall and winter.

The visual impact of some of these is unforgettable—as when thousands of white pelicans with nine-foot (3-m) wingspreads cover the waterways or fly up to fill the air with a pinkish glow, the combination of a setting sun and carotene from their oil-preening glands.

The astonishing figures include 5,500 pairs of cormorants, among them 2,500 pairs of threatened pygmy cormorants—61 percent of the world population; 2,100 night heron pairs; 2,000 pairs of buffy-gold and white Squacco herons; 1,500 pairs of glossy ibises; 2,500 pairs of white pelicans—50 percent of the palearctic breeding population; 25–150 pairs of threatened Dalmatian pelicans, to mention just a few.

Terns include 20,000 breeding pairs of whiskered, twittering over nests on acres of white-blossoming lily pads; 20,000 pairs of common; 10–20,000 black; among raptors, more than 300 marsh harrier pairs, eight white-tailed eagle pairs, and 150 pairs of red-footed falcons; plus thousands of little bitterns, iridescent multicolored bee-eaters, violet rollers, bearded and penduline tits, and Savi's warblers.

Fall and wintering concentrations are equally impressive: records of 45,000 dramatically plumaged and globally threatened red-breasted geese—almost 95 percent of the world population (weather conditions can move them into neighboring Bulgaria in midwinter)—150,000

# ROMANIA

Sociable white pelicans nest together, fly together and even feed cooperatively together, flying low over water in tight V-formation until they find a school of fish close to the surface. Then they flap their 10-foot (3-m) wingspans and dip bills in water, driving fish to shallows where they scoop up as many as they can in expandable bills which can hold over three gallons (11 liters) of food and water. They then strain out the water and consume the rest whole. Since their daily requirement is only two to four fish, they're usually through by mid-morning and can spend the rest of the day basking and preening.

teal, 200,000 mallards, 14,000 pintails, 40,000 shovelers, 32,000 red-crested pochards, 970,000 pochards, 13,000 threatened ferruginous ducks, a half-million white-fronted geese, and 30–40 white-tailed eagles.

Among mammals on floating reed islands and wooded dunes are wildcats, otters, raccoon dogs, steppe polecats, wild boar, foxes, wolves, and European mink in one of their last European refuges—plus rare reptiles (Aesculapian snakes, Orsi's vipers, and Eremias lizards) and amphibians, butterflies and dragonflies.

The **Danube Delta Biosphere Reserve**, so designated in 1992, covers a total transfrontier area of 2,417 square miles (6,264 km$^2$) with more than 25 types of natural ecosystems—20 percent of it across the border in Ukraine—and, with millions of tons of riverborne silt, its boundary growing every year by about 100 feet (30 m).

The delta ecosystem, usually described as "intact," unfortunately has been degraded both by activities within and land use outside it. Agriculture and irrigation projects pour pesticides, herbicides, and fertilizers into a Danube already heavily laden with chlorine, nitrogen, and potassium, all made worse with drainage and removal of upstream reedbeds that formerly filtered it. Overflows from upstream mines have poisoned fish with cyanide and other heavy metal sludge. Overfishing, introduction of exotic species, and creation of breeding ponds, have adversely affected 160 native fish species, along with anadromous varieties such as sturgeon that swim upstream to spawn. Some of these may improve as this natural treasure comes into worldwide focus.

Tulcea, ancient city settled by Dacians and Romans from the 7th to 1st centuries BC, is a good starting point for visitors, who can stay in hotels and arrange for channel cruises and overnight stays on comfortable boat "floatels" between there and equally ancient Sulina, 45 miles (71 km) away. Other waterside villages, such as Maliuc and Crisan, offer a panoramic view of the delta; or take smaller boats into channels for a quieter, more intimate view. Another useful stop is Murighiol on the delta's southern edge, where boats can be hired to enter the channel and nearby lakes. Sinoe and Razelm, two large lakes south of the main delta, can be alive with birds, both reachable by dirt road near Istria. Cars can be rented in Mamaia, beach resort just north of Constanta, which has an international airport.

Many areas can be difficult or impossible to reach due to variable water levels and constantly changing positions of dense floating reedbeds. All visitors to the reserve need permits, available at travel agencies and hotels in Tulcea, Crisan, Sulina, and Murighiol—but special permission is required to enter more rigorously protected areas, especially during nesting time.

| FURTHER INFORMATION |
| --- |
| Governor, Danube Delta Biosphere Authority, Department of the Environment, Ministry of Environment, R-Bucharest, Artera Nova N-5, Tronson 5-6, Sector 5; Danube Delta Biosphere Reserve, Str, Portului 34A, CP 32, OP 3,8800 Tulcea, Romania, E-mail: gbaboianu@ddbra.ro/arbdd@ddbra.ro; Societatea Ornitologica Romana (SOR), Str Republicii 48, RO-3400 Cluj, Romania or SOR Tulcea, Romania, E-mail: petrescu_alcedo@yahoo.com |

In **Ukraine**, numerous hotels, campsites, chalets, and private homes offer rooms at Yalta, with further information available at the West Ukrainian Avifaunistic Commission, L'viv State University, Zoological Department, Grushevsky str. 4, L'viv 290005, Ukraine.

In **Slovakia**, contact the Slovenia Ornithologicka Spolocnost (SOS/The Slovakian Society for the Protection of Birds), Zapadoslovenske muzeum Trnava, Muzejne namestic 3, 91809 Trnava, Slovakia.

# CARPATHIAN MOUNTAINS

Most of Romania's protected areas are in the Carpathian Mountains which curve down 930 miles (1,500 km) from Slovakia and northern Poland through western Ukraine, covering some 81,000 square miles (213,000 km²) in seven European countries. In this U.N. World Biosphere Reserve is a remarkable wildlife population—largest concentration of carnivores anywhere in Europe, including over 9,000 huge brown bears, 4,000 gray wolves, 3,000 lynx, along with stags, wild boars, deer, and foxes, and at rocky, higher elevations, a thriving chamois population.

In remnants of the primeval forest that once covered most of Europe are golden eagles, eagle owls, Ural owls, green, black, and three-toed woodpeckers, mountain cocks, capercaillies, golden pheasants, and one-third of Europe's plant species.

It is a vital corridor for dispersal of plant and animal species through the continent. Wolves are actively repopulating southern Europe through the Carpathians, which also furnish freshwater for the region's major rivers. It's believed that without rainfall originating from the Carpathians, more than 80 percent of Romania's water supply and 40 percent of Ukraine's would dry up.

Over half of the chain—55 percent—is in Romania; 17 percent in Slovakia; 11 percent in the Ukraine; 10 percent in Poland; four percent in Hungary; three percent in the Czech Republic; and less than one percent in Austria. About one-sixth of it is under some form of protection. Threats are from pollution, population pressures, excessive logging, and poaching. Wolves especially suffer from centuries of baseless fears that they attack humans, although their defenders point out that while dozens of persons are accidentally shot by hunters, there is only one record of a wolf attack in the past 50 years, and this in self-defense. As a designated endangered species, they are fully protected in Poland, Hungary, and the Czech Republic, though not at all in Ukraine.

Reserves have not always been well managed, but recent help from both the World Bank and European Union holds promise of better in the future, not only to implement park regulation and facilities but to support important biodiversity projects.

Romania's Carpathian Large Carnivore Project (CLCP), an example, combines pioneering field studies with an innovative ecotourism program based in Bucegi Nature Reserve head-quartered in Prejmer, near Brasov.

Major Carpathian reserves in Romania include:

**Bucegi Nature Preserve** protects the entire spectacular 116-square-mile (300-km$^2$) Bucegi mountain range, with miles of well-marked trails—for more information, Nature Protection Society (Asociatia Pentru Protectia Naturii) in Brasov, Str Maior 44, Tel: (+40) 068-419-210; also CLCP Project, Wildlife Research Department, Soseaua Stefanesti 128 sect 2, Bucharest RO-729904, Website: www.clcp.ro.

**Retezat National Park** was Romania's first national park, 210 square miles (544 km$^2$), with one of the largest tracts of pristine mixed forest in Europe, more than 80 glacial lakes, good numbers of brown bears, gray or timber wolves, lynx, wildcats, wild boars, roe and red deer, mountain goats, badgers, otters, chamois, and among birds, lesser spotted and a few golden eagles, capercaillie, pygmy, Ural, and eagle owls, wrynecks, and red-breasted flycatchers.

**Rodna National Park and Biosphere Reserve**, 219 square miles (567 km$^2$) in the eastern Carpathians, with brown bears, lynx, gray wolves, black grouse, capercaillies, eagles.

**Piatra Craiului National Park**, with mountain goats, mountain cocks, gray wolves, stags, unusual hazel-colored bears.

**Apuseni Mountains**—with wild boars, deer, stags, bears, designated as future national park but at risk with uncontrolled hunting.

The city of Brasov is a good orientation point with hotels and information for Carpathian travel. From there, best access to Bucegi is from the resorts of Busteni and Sinaia. Approach Retezat from the east at Petrosani, from the north at Ulpia Traiana-Sarmizegetusa or Nucsoara. Main entrance to the Rodna Mountains is from the Complex Turistic Borsa, just east of the town of Borsa. Best access to Piatra Craiului is from Zarnesti, southwest of Brasov.

---

**FURTHER INFORMATION ON OTHER CARPATHIAN RESERVES**

In **Slovakia**: Ministry of the Environment, Administrator, National Park Poloniny, P.O. Box 47, Partizanska 1057, 069-001-Snina, Slovakia; Tel: (+421-932) 7685-615/7624-424, Fax: (+421-932) 7685-615, E-mail: poloniny@ke.telecom.sk, Website www.fns.uniba.sk/zp/biosfera/brmabvku.htm

In **Ukraine**: Director, National Nature Park "Uzhans'ki", Shevchenka St.54, 295050 Velykij Bereznyj, Transcarpathian region, Ukraine, Tel/Fax: (+380) 8-10-03135-21037, E-mail: park@uzhansky.karpaty.uzhgorod.ua; ALSO at Carpathian Biosphere Reserve, 77 Krasne Pleso Street, Rakhiv 90600 Ukraine, Tel/Fax: (+380) 3132-22193, Website: http://cbr.nature.org.ua

In **Poland**: Director, East Carpathians Biosphere Reserve, Bieszczady National Park, Ustrzyki Gorne 38-714, Poland, Tel: (+48-13) 461-0650/0610, Fax: (+48-13) 461-0650/0166, E-mail: janowski@poczta.onet.pl (*see* also under Poland).

# SPANISH

More than half of Europe's avian species spend some of their time in Doñana National Park, some in huge numbers—20,000 bar-tailed godwits, 10,000 slender, graceful avocets, flocks of 70,000 graylag geese, 126,000 common teals, 100,000 wigeon, 40,000 northern pintails.

W ILDLIFE IN THIS PENINSULAR COUNTRY WHERE ENVIRONMENTALISM GOES BACK 2,000 YEARS IS AMONG THE MOST VARIED AND ABUNDANT IN EUROPE—PERHAPS BECAUSE PREDATORS AND HUGE WETLAND BIRD FLOCKS THAT HAVE DISAPPEARED ELSEWHERE CAN STILL FIND WILD LAND.

Brown bears survive in the Cordillera Cantabrica and a few in the Pyrenees. Small populations of wolves remain in the mountains of Galicia and northwestern Castilla y Leon. Iberian or Pardel lynx, down to fewer than 200 individuals but now stringently protected, prowl southern and western woodlands.

415

# SPAIN

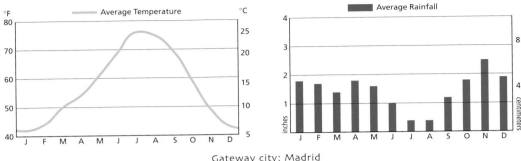

Gateway city: Madrid

Spanish imperial eagles, almost killed off by hunting, use of poisoned baits, and decline in rabbit populations, are still in Doñana, Monfrague, and the country's mid-south—about 170 pairs recently. Lammergeiers soar, dropping victims' bones from on high to crack them and get at the marrow (enacting their name, "bone-breaker").

Millions of water-oriented birds are attracted to some of the most important and extensive protected wetlands in Europe, once (and still periodically) under threat—a legacy of ancient Roman set-asides of important wildlife areas with programs for tree-planting and forest management.

## DOÑANA NATIONAL PARK

Most famous is Doñana National Park, U.N. World Heritage Site and Biosphere Reserve on the Guadalquivir River delta on the Mediterranean coast in southern Andalucia. This 200 square miles (550 km²) of marsh, fresh and saltwater lagoons, stable and moving sand dunes, woodlands, and scrub is permanent or winter home or essential migratory stopover for an estimated six million birds.

More than half of Europe's avian species are recorded here, some in huge numbers. About 80 percent of western Europe's wild ducks fly in to winter here when fall rains fill the marismas (marshes)—flocks of up to 70,000 graylag geese, 126,000 common teals, 100,000 wigeon, 40,000 northern pintails, and among smaller wading birds, some 20,000 bar-tailed godwits and 10,000 slender, graceful avocets with uptilted bills. Many stay to nest. Breeding species include over 1,000 pairs of black-winged stilts, 350 pairs of Eurasian spoonbills, hundreds of pairs of little egrets and purple herons.

As waters recede in spring, almost 10,000 pink greater flamingos begin prancing courtship dances like the Spanish flamenco dance named after them. Spoonbills, white storks, hoopoes with wildly erect buffy crests, and black-winged stilts arrive, and many nest. Multicolored bee-eaters hover and glide swiftly after flying insects. Great crested grebes dance on the water in pairs, shaking head plumes, later swim about with downy young riding on their backs. Spectacled

416

warblers nest in dry scrub. Flocks of noisy, stunning azure-winged magpies scold anything that moves.

Doñana's emblem is the brilliant purple gallinule—found mainly in the reeds here, along with such other rarities as marbled teal, white-headed ducks, and red-crested pochards.

Beaches where Columbus and Magellan set sail can be full of sanderlings and oystercatchers, with seasonal influxes of whimbrels. Peregrines nest in former wartime defense lookout towers.

In midsummer, fish are trapped in drying pools and thousands of white storks, red and black kites gather with otters and others to feast on them.

Some 50 square miles (144 km²) of Doñana is scrub and woodland, stone pine and cork oak forests, home to red and fallow deer, wild boars, fierce, catlike small-spotted genets, wild horses, rare Egyptian mongeese and Spanish or Iberian lynx—among 29 mammal species.

Butterflies (Spain has many endemics) flutter over wild blooms, and dragonflies and bright damselflies zoom like small fighter planes over wet areas.

Europe's greatest concentration of raptors is here—short-toed, booted, and Spanish imperial (aka Adalbert's or simply imperial) eagles with 82-inch (210-cm) wingspans, lanner falcons, honey buzzards, hobbies—both residents and migrants between Europe and Africa. For these powerful birds of prey whose migratory flight pattern requires heated thermals rising from land, Doñana, with its abundant prey species, is a vital rest stop before the short pass over Gibraltar Strait to Africa.

Spur-thighed tortoises, Lataste's vipers, spiny-footed and ocellated lizards are among numbers of reptilian rarities here.

For over 700 years Doñana was a royal hunting preserve (its familiar name, "Coto Doñana" means "Doñana game preserve"). Owned by the Duke of Alba, who named it after his wife, Doná Ana, Doñana formed part of the backdrop for her famous "Maja" portraits, clothed and unclothed, by Francisco Goya, painted in the ducal palace which still exists (not open to the public).

All year is of interest, but midsummer can be blisteringly hot—and best avoid the seventh weekend after Easter when Pentecostal pilgrims come from all over Spain for a riotous celebration.

International jets fly into Seville, about 30 miles (50 km) northeast of the park. Rental cars are available, and busses go on good roads to Matalascañas at the park's southwestern corner via El Rocio at the northwestern corner. Busses also stop outside the Las Rocinas and El Acebuche visitor centers. Lodging and tourist information are at El Rocio and Matalascañas, also Mazagon, 17 miles (28 km) northwest. Three campgrounds are available by permit.

Park access is carefully controlled. Trips are offered in 26-person all-terrain vehicles from El Acebuche, often booked far ahead (sometimes not available July–August). Occasional trips to the interior are offered in eight-seat Jeeps—ask. (Unless you speak Spanish, ask or arrange for a translator-guide.) Otherwise there is a well-developed system of guides, tours, visitor centers,

## SPAIN

Black storks—more than three feet tall (100cm) with red beaks, legs and feet and wingspans up to 81 inches (205cm)—nest deep in old forests, so silent and retiring they are seldom seen, despite enormous nests. Built by both pair members, often near a marshy forest clearing, nests can measure five feet (1.5 m) across and a yard (1 m) deep. Spain's population has been resident and stable, isolated while elsewhere in Europe, the largely migratory species was driven near extinction by habitat destruction and pollution. Its comeback through protection recently has been an encouraging success story.

observation points, blinds or hides, and marked trails. Marsh viewing is especially good at Cerrado Garido, the El Rocio bridge, also a path a short distance behind Las Rocinas—ask directions at visitor centers.

Four-hour guided park boat trips leave from Bajo de Guia going upriver with stops at salt lagoons with good birdlife.

Threats go back before the park's formation in 1969 when environmentalists, alarmed that spreading rice-growing, roads, and tourism would damage wetlands, raised funds internationally and with World Wildlife Fund arranged its purchase. Battles have continued since over projects that would degrade park fringes and water supply. In 1986 an estimated 30,000 birds died of poisoning from massive agricultural pesticide runoff. Tens of thousands of chicks and eggs were accidentally destroyed in the same years by crayfish hunters. In 1998 a zinc mine's dam broke, flooding the Rio Guadalquivir with 6.5 million cubic yards (5 million cubic m) of sludge loaded with acids and heavy metals, damage which still causes concern. Luckily environmental awareness has grown. Spain now has more than 200 voluntary conservation groups which monitor threats to Spain's wilderness.

Helpful books include *A Birdwatchers Guide to Southern Spain and Gibraltar*, by Clive Finlayson, Prion, 1993.

---

**FURTHER INFORMATION**

Park headquarters, "El Acebuche," Route El Rocio-Matalascañas, 21760 Matalascañas, Fax: (+34) 959-448-576; Doñana Biological Station of C.S.I.C. (Council of Scientific Research), Avda. Maria Luisa, s/n. Pabellon de Peru, 41071 Sevilla; Central Administration, Instituto Nacional para la Conservacion de la Naturaleza (ICONA), National Parks Department, Gran Via de San Francisco, 28005 Madrid, Tel: (+34) 91-347-6159/6189, Fax: (+34) 91-265-8379, Tlx: 47591-aeico-e; Sociedad Espanola de Ornitologia (Spanish Ornithological Society), Facultad de Biologia, Pl.9, 28040 Madrid, Tel: (+34) 91-449-3554, with information center and observation post in El Rocio, Tel: (+34) 50-506-093.

---

Altogether some 15,000 square miles (40,000 km²) of this ecologically important country is in some kind of protection, nearly all at least partly open to visitation, many reserves with walking trails and lodging nearby. Their importance can hardly be overstated for a wide spectrum of species. Whales and dolphins are among 27 marine mammals offshore—**Cabo de Peñas** near Gijon on the Bay of Biscay is a noted gathering place. Dolphin-spotting trips are popular at **Gibraltar**, whose Barbary macaques are Europe's only wild monkeys.

## ALSO OF INTEREST

Notable national parks include:

**Montaña de Covadonga**, 66 square miles (170 km²) on the western peak of the Picos de Europa mountain range, with imperial eagles, capercailles, and other threatened species.

**Ordesa**, 63 square miles (160 km²), with alpine choughs, alpine accentors, the world's only herd of Pyrenees mountain goats, many raptors—imperial, short-toed, and booted eagles, griffon and bearded vultures, lammergeiers—on the Spanish side of France's **Pyrénées National Park** (*see* p.378).

**Maritimo-Terrestre** of the Cabrera Archipelago, 4,500 acres (1,835 ha) on the largest unpopulated Mediterranean island, with seabird flocks, abundant Eleanora's falcons.

# UNITED
# KINGDOM

MILLIONS OF SEABIRDS SEEM TO FILL EVERY
CLIFF-SIDE NICHE ON ST. KILDA AND THE SHETLAND
ISLANDS—PUFFINS, GANNETS, FULMARS, AND OTHERS—DRAWN
BY PROTECTED NEST SITES AND RICH SURROUNDING WATERS
WHICH PROVIDE BOUNTEOUS FOOD FOR NESTLINGS.

T HE UNITED KINGDOM IS RELATIVELY SMALL IN AREA, MUCH OF IT DENSELY POPULATED. MOST OF ITS RESERVES REFLECT THIS—FOR WHILE THEY ARE NUMEROUS AND INTERESTING, ONLY A FEW ARE OF WORLD SCALE. These are the extraordinary bird reserves that lie off Scotland and harbor staggeringly large numbers of seabirds in some of earth's most dramatic sea and landscapes.

Notable among these are ST. KILDA and the SHETLAND ISLANDS. Millions of seabirds that otherwise spend their entire lives on waters far from land return to Scotland's northernmost shores and cliffs every summer to cover the cliff-sides with nests. Adults and downy offspring cling to rock ledges inches wide, barely wing-lengths from one another—squawking, flapping, parents planing out and returning from fishing trips with silvery meals for demanding young-sters, obeying an urgent need to reproduce and start a new generation during the short northern season.

It is one of nature's wildlife spectaculars, best known of hundreds of places set aside for birds and other wildlife in the United Kingdom of Great Britain and Ireland, where lands and coasts are dotted with protected areas, large and small—perhaps more per capita than any other country in the world.

Some are official parks and reserves, others set aside and protected by private groups. Others exist simply because special habitat has attracted wild

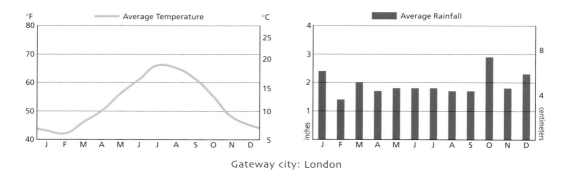

°F / Average Temperature / °C

°C / Average Rainfall

Gateway city: London

creatures and local people have taken an interest in their continued well-being—no place has more enthusiastic and numerous protectors of the natural world than here.

Premier among them are the world-famous islands of St. Kilda, 50 miles (80 km) out in the Atlantic Ocean off the northwest tip of Scotland, and the Shetlands, directly to the north of the Scottish mainland just six degrees south of the Arctic Circle.

The boisterous throngs there include clown-like little Atlantic puffins with rainbow-hued bills colored especially for breeding; ivory-plumaged gannets with buff-golden heads and six-foot (2-m) wingspreads; murres with pyriform eggs pointed at one end so they don't roll off the cliff but stay in a small tight circle safely within the nest area; gentle, pigeon-like fulmars with built-in nasal wind-velocity sensors enabling them to exploit varying wind speeds and avoid slamming into cliff-sides. Great rarities also find their way—especially to the Shetlands—sometimes in large numbers, ocean-going migrants blown off-course, finding safe landing and resting places on these remote islands.

## St. Kilda

Europe's most important seabird colony and one of the major breeding stations in the North Atlantic is tiny St. Kilda archipelago, a U.N. World Heritage Site and Biosphere Reserve of four inhospitable rocky islands and some sea stacks, 3.6-square-mile (9-km²) remnant of an ancient volcano.

Over a million birds are here in the short breeding season. They include the world's largest colony of gannets—over 60,000 pairs; largest colony of fulmars in the British Isles—some 65,000 pairs; 500,000 Atlantic puffins; 60,000 guillemots; 16,000 kittiwakes; and many others. It is one of the few known breeding sites for Leach's petrels.

Superlatives abound. Marine reserve status is being considered for its crystal-clear waters populated by jewel-like anemones with vivid yellow, pink, red, blue, and green tentacles and a kelp forest 150 feet (45 m) deep. It has been designated a National Scenic Area for its beauty, with the highest sea cliffs in Britain rising a sheer 1,410 feet (430 m) and towering sea stacks regarded as most majestic in the world. It also is designated a Site of Special Scientific Interest for unique plant and animal species, including a feral flock of primitive black-faced Soay sheep.

Hardy humans are believed to have lived on St. Kilda for 4,000 years—primarily on Hirta, which has its only conceivable harbor—supported mainly by oil, feathers, and meat of seabirds which they gathered by scaling precipitous cliff-sides barefoot (legend says in so doing they gradually evolved unusually long toes). A 17th-century traveler said most St. Kilda men died before they could grow old by drowning or breaking their necks. The population dwindled for various reasons—smallpox was accidentally introduced, it's believed in clothes sent by mail, and for a period 80 percent of newborns died because of a mistaken idea that umbilical cords should be anointed with fulmar oil. The last 36 residents were voluntarily evacuated in 1930. It was bequeathed in 1957 by the fifth Marquess of Bute to the of the National Trust for Scotland which leased it to the Nature Conservancy Council, now the Scottish Natural Heritage.

Visiting St. Kilda is not for the faint-hearted. Only conceivable landing from sea is on south-facing Hirta Island. Occasionally it is possible to hitch a ride on a helicopter serving the small Army missile-tracking station. Otherwise visitors must come by sea, and, with permission of the National Trust for Scotland, anchor in the harbor, sleep aboard, and visit during the day. Permits occasionally are given to camp on land. Even with permission, weather and ocean swells can prevent harbor entry.

Best chances for good weather and seeing birds are in late May–early July. Charter boats usually leave from Oban (beware of trips that mention St. Kilda as one of several destinations which they may fulfill—they often don't). Main reserve threat would be an oil spill polluting seabird feeding areas.

---

**FURTHER INFORMATION**

Secretary, National Trust for Scotland, 5 Charlotte Square, Edinburgh EH2 4DU; ALSO Warden, Scottish Natural Heritage, 135 Stilligarry, South Uist, H58 5RS, Tel: (+44) 01870 620238, Fax: (+44) 01870 620350.

---

## SHETLAND ISLANDS

Cliff-sides in the Shetlands abound with summer populations of gannets, kittiwakes, fulmars, puffins, and others, often in vast squawking throngs that number in the many tens of thousands, each clustered with others of its kind in inaccessible niches that overlap little if at all with others.

Sturdy gannets occupy wider ledges than little kittiwakes. Special adaptations to rich fishing grounds can determine location too—kittiwakes with onomatopoetic calls ("Kitt-e-wake! Kitt-e-wake!") dip to or just below the surface, gannets dive as deep as 100 feet (30 m).

# UNITED KINGDOM

Fulmars, most abundant species, look out mildly from precariously balanced grassy overhangs—six feet (2 m) is diving limit of these plump little birds.

Atlantic puffins raise young in deep nest burrows on grassy cliff edges, often in burrows excavated and occasionally still inhabited by rabbits. They come with bills full of sand-eels and disappear into pink-flowering thrift that can all but cover nest holes, delivering up to 60 tiny fish at a time.

Seemingly uninhabitable boulder beaches are home to black guillemots.

It's a birds'—and naturalists'—feast, inland as well, where rolling moorlands are claimed by arctic and great skuas (known as bonxies), so fiercely defensive near nest territories that prudent visitors carry stout sticks to fend them off. Lower-profile grassland breeders include Europe's smallest falcons—swift-flying merlins—along with whimbrels, dunlins, greenshanks, and golden plovers in gorgeous breeding plumage.

Arctic terns which fly up to a 22,000-mile (35,000-km) round-trip yearly between nesting and wintering grounds as far south as Antarctica—world's longest-distance migrants—hover with supreme aerial grace over downy nestlings on short grassy peninsulas and holms, along with ringed plovers and scarlet-billed oystercatchers. (Some of these flashy crustacean-crackers are familiar lawn birds at local inns where they've found insect-probing produces an easier meal.)

Smaller lochs attract red-throated divers; larger ones, ducks such as teal, mallards, and red-breasted mergansers; damp margins and peat bogs, snipe, redshanks, and lapwings.

Even tiny European storm petrels, usually hard to see since they come ashore to visit burrows only at night, are easily spotted by visitors with flashlights on the island of Mousa where they nest not only in great numbers but often in above-ground cavities in ancient stone dikes and towers.

OPPOSITE PAGE:

MAIN PIC: Gentle, pigeon-like white fulmars use built-in nasal wind-velocity sensors common to shearwater family that enable them to fly out and return safely from fishing trips bringing food for chicks, avoiding sudden gusts that could slam them dangerously into rocky cliff-sides. Magnificent fliers and gliders, they've been clocked up to 50 miles an hour (80 kph) by fishing boats. Both adults and chicks defend nests by spitting foul-smelling stomach oil at predators such as eagles, with fatal consequences for some of their targets, unable to fly with oil-soaked plumage. Fulmars breed on coastal ledges and grassy slopes around Iceland, Norway, Spitsbergen, Britain, and Russia.

INSET: Famous longest-distance migrants, arctic terns can travel more than 22,000 miles (35,000 km) in a round-trip yearly between far northern nesting grounds in summer and northern winters as far south as Antarctica, probably seeing more daylight than any other living creature. Circumpolar, they nest through northern Europe, Britain, the Netherlands, Denmark, Sweden, Iceland, Russia, Greenland, and across Canada to Alaska and Siberia. Long, 33-inch (84 cm) swallow-like wings are, appropriately, their striking physical feature, almost twice as long as their bodies, with legs so short they can walk only with a mouse-like glide, and when standing, they appear to be crouching.

Birds here are spectacular as well in spring and autumn—sometimes huge fall-outs of migrants and always a parade of rarities, peaking mid-May–mid-June and mid-July–early November. Winter can be bitterly cold and windy but exciting as well with arctic breeders such as whooper swans, goldeneyes, occasionally king eiders, gyrfalcons, ivory gulls.

Most remote and famous of the more than 100 Shetland islands—partly because of its beautiful sweaters—is **Fair Isle**. Much of Fair Isle is in Special Protection Area status both because of its nesting seabirds, of which nine species breed here in nationally or internationally important numbers May through July, and for the rarities which show up regularly. All these are closely monitored by the Fair Isle Bird Observatory, where lodging is available for a limited number of visitors who fly in from Sumburgh on the South Shetland mainland. There also is a ferry.

Other easily visited islands are the Mainland, West, North and South; Yell; Unst; and Fetlar, all connected by bridge or ferry.

Each has its special natural spectaculars as well as accommodations where lodging and guides can be arranged. International visitors can fly to London, connect to Aberdeen, thence by air to Sumburgh or by overnight ferry to Lerwick, both on the South Shetland mainland, where cars can be rented to drive around the islands.

---

**FURTHER INFORMATION**

Superb informational leaflets are available with maps, lodging, species descriptions, and much more from the Scottish National Heritage, Stewart Building, Alexandra Wharf, Lerwick, Scotland, Tel: (+44) 01595-693345, Fax: 01595-692565; Fair Isle Observatory, 21 Regent Terrace, Edinburgh EH7 5BT, Scotland, Tel: (+44) 031-556-6042, Website: http://www.fairislebirdobs.co.uk, OR Bird Observatory, Fair Isle, Shetland ZE2 9JU, Tel/Fax: (+44) 01595-760258, E-mail: fairisle.birdobs@zetnet.co.uk; Shetland Bird Club, Website: www.wildlife.shetland.co.uk

---

## ALSO OF INTEREST

**Hebrides** and **Orkney Islands**—contact the Scottish Ornithologists Club, 21 Regent Terrace, Edinburgh EH7 5BT; or for a list of over 150 nature reserves of the Royal Society for the Preservation of Birds, The Lodge, Sandy, Bedfordshire SG19 2DL, Tel: (+44) 01767-680551, Website: www.rspb.org.uk/wildlife.

Informational handbooks are available as well from any of these organizations.

# NORTH AMERICA

MOUNTAIN GOATS

# CANADA

BEST WAY TO SEE EVERYTHING IN A WILDLIFE
RESERVE CAN BE JUST TO SIT QUIETLY AND OBSERVE.
ONE WOMAN, WATCHING MOTIONLESS IN THE
CANADIAN ROCKIES NATURAL AREA, HAD
A BEAVER COME CURL UP IN HER LAP.

CANADA'S HUGE ANIMALS—SHAGGY MUSK OXEN, HALF-TON POLAR BEARS AND ENORMOUS BROWN BEARS—NEED TO BE BIG. Animals with more body mass in proportion to skin surface retain heat better in this place of long winters, where temperatures fall dozens of degrees below zero and ice and snow remain much of the year.

Other adaptations help too. Wolverines are not large but their fur sheds ice crystals. Arctic foxes' special blood-vessel mechanism keeps foot pads warm so they seldom need to seek

429

# CANADA

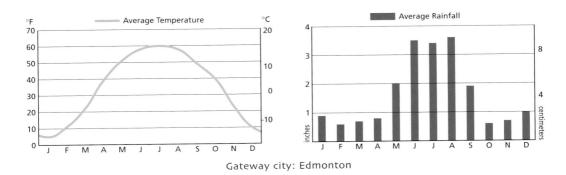

Gateway city: Edmonton

shelter but can sleep in the open, maintaining constant body warmth even when temperatures fall to −112°F (−82°C).

Caribou and polar bear fur is not only dense but hollow for extra insulation. Fish here can lower blood hemoglobin, slowing metabolism.

Snowshoe hares' furry paws skim over snowdrifts; willow ptarmigans plunge into them head-first, seasonally-white feathers making them invisible to predators. Other birds have blood circulatory mechanisms similar to foxes, controlling blood flow into legs, dilating and constricting the vessels as appropriate.

But most birds don't stay through the dark, bitterly cold months unless they have special survival adaptations. They go south, and come later in spring and summer by the millions to court and nest, finding plenty of food then to raise families on both abundant water organisms and swarming insect hatches. All life then rushes to reproduce and raise young as quickly as possible.

Even plants adapt. They grow close to the ground, minimizing exposure, then appear all at once in dazzling spring carpets of bloom on the sides of some of North America's highest mountains, amid some of the world's most extensive glaciers and ice fields—some a half-mile (1 km) thick. Visitors come from around the world to view these breathtaking phenomena.

Canada claims the oldest continuous national parks service in the world, with 38 units covering over 75,000 square miles (194,250 km²) of mountain ranges, grassy plains, great rivers, and frozen tundra. The plan is to include every ecosystem represented in this vast subpolar region covering more than half the North American continent.

Best known is the spectacular cluster covering over 7,800 square miles (20,000 km²) in the CANADIAN ROCKIES, of which most famous is Banff, formed originally as a tourist spa around hot springs the government felt "promise to be of great sanitary advantage to the public." Now millions of visitors come every year to see not only the fabled snowcapped mountains but the wildlife—grizzly bears, elk, mountain goats, wolves, moose, and eagles soaring over peaks known to aboriginal peoples as "the shining mountains."

# CANADA

The Canadian Rockies are one of the world's largest protected mountain landscapes. The designated natural region extends over some 69,480 square miles (180,000 km²), with the core U.N. World Heritage Site including BANFF, JASPER, KOOTENAY, and YOHO national parks and three provincial parks.

Jasper, just north of Banff, is larger and wilder. Shy, striking harlequin ducks nest on riverine islands. Grizzlies forage along highways in spring. Bighorn sheep rest alongside and sometimes on the sun-warmed Icefields Parkway.

Kootenay, just west, swept by fire in 1968, is recovering and cleared areas offer tender grazing for moose and elk. Yoho, just north of Kootenay, has similar fire-cleared grazing meadows, also Canada's highest waterfall and a renowned quarry with fossil remains of 120 marine creatures resident here 500 million years ago.

Beautiful **Glacier** and **Revelstoke** are just down the road.

Other reserves elsewhere are equally spectacular with entirely different ecosystems.

A million or more of the world's most interesting and rare birds nest in the rugged mountains and deep fiords of GWAII HAANAS' islands in a national park reserve with the west coast's largest breeding colony of Steller's sea lions. Multihued sea stars light up low tides. Six kinds of whales feed offshore.

KLUANE National Park is a vast joint U.N. World Heritage Site with U.S. Wrangell-St. Elias National Park and Preserve in Alaska, together the largest subpolar ice field outside Greenland, surrounded by habitat where black and brown or grizzly bears roam among timber wolves, moose, small fierce wolverines, and nesting songbirds, all surrounded in summer by multicolored alpine wildflowers.

CHURCHILL is known as polar bear capital of the world, with the largest concentration of them anywhere, waiting for the ice to freeze in fall so they can go out and hunt seals. But Churchill also has great numbers of birds that come in spring from over the western hemisphere, some to nest, some en route north, all in dapper breeding plumage. Up to 3,000 pearl-white beluga whales visit the Churchill River in June, and just southeast is new WAPUSK NATIONAL PARK, with one of the world's largest polar bear denning sites.

WOOD BUFFALO NATIONAL PARK, largest in Canada and one of the largest in the world, is home to lynx, wolves, bears, and in summer, in a tract of wild muskeg larger than Denmark, to rare and magnificent whooping cranes.

The last two free-roaming herds of plains bison still on their original range graze in Wood Buffalo and PRINCE ALBERT National Parks. Prince Albert is home as well to 10,000 nesting white pelicans and 235 other bird species. Fishers, three-toed woodpeckers, and others increasingly scarce elsewhere are still numerous in this wilderness.

GROS MORNE on coastal Newfoundland is known for its geologic record of tectonic events 1.5 billion years ago—but wildlife have found it hospitable, most swimming or trekking over winter pack ice: caribou, lynx, black bears, foxes—along with 235 bird species which fly in.

And, a splendid recent addition, the **Muskwa-Kechika** wilderness, part of more than 15,600 square miles (40,000 km²) of almost untouched high mountain ranges, deep rivers and valleys, with dense caribou, grizzly bears, and wolverine populations now to be safeguarded in the northeastern corner of British Columbia.

---

**FURTHER INFORMATION**

Parks Canada, Department of Canadian Heritage, 25 Eddy Street, Hull, Quebec K1A 0M5, Canada, Tel: (+1) 819-997-0055 (*see* also individual entries).

---

# CANADIAN ROCKIES

The Canadian Rockies were "the shining mountains" to aboriginal people astonished at glistening glaciers and rocky snowcapped peaks which arose from sea-bottom sediment 1.5 billion years ago. But it is the grizzly bears, elk, mountain goats, wolves, moose, and eagles that have made this dramatically beautiful place world-renowned.

This U.N. World Heritage Site is one of the world's largest protected mountain landscapes—a designated Natural Region extending over some 69,480 square miles (180,000 km²) and a dozen or so protected wilderness areas, including **Waterton Lakes** adjoining U.S. GLACIER NATIONAL PARK (*see* p.479). The core site covers some 8,000 square miles (23,010 km²) including Banff, Jasper, Kootenay, and Yoho Canadian National Parks, and three British Columbia provincial parks.

Hundreds of jewel-like blue-green ponds and lakes owe brilliant hues to eroded silt from milky streams fed by glaciers constantly grinding away at the 11,000-foot (3,355-m) continental divide. Largest of ice concentrations descending from this ancient spine is the great Columbia Icefield, covering 130 square miles (325 km²) and estimated to be more than 1,000 feet (305 m) thick, source of rivers flowing to three oceans.

OPPOSITE: Many animals hibernate but few as totally as American black bears, which can go for 100 days without eating, drinking, urinating, defecating, or exercising. Heartbeats in midwinter can fall to eight an hour. This works out well for birth of young, since mating occurs in summer but fertilized eggs are not implanted to start growing until hibernation begins. This way they are born in midwinter, naked and blind, weighing 7–16 ounces (200–450 g) each, smallest birth weight relative to adult size of any placental mammal—but by the time they emerge from dens, they're ready to follow mothers around. Black bears range throughout North America, from frozen tundra to Florida Everglades.

## CANADA

Coyotes, black bears, bighorn and Dall sheep, rare woodland caribou, and others—69 mammal species—wander about as if they own the place, which in a sense they do. Bighorn sheep rest alongside Highway 16 east of Jasper, seemingly unencumbered by spiraled horns which grow to 45.3 inches (115 cm) and weigh 33 pounds (15 kg). Their white-pelted cousins, Dall sheep, lounge alongside the Alcan highway near Summit Lake.

Mountain goats lick salty rocks near trails below Mount Wardle in Kootenay National Park. Elk in the Canadian Rockies were almost hunted to extinction early in the 20th century, but have thrived since reintroduction in 1917 and now nibble grassy lawns and shrubbery in and around the park.

Predators tend to be more retiring; they include lynx, red foxes, and small but fierce wolverines, solitary, stealthy stalkers of snowshoe or varying hares but capable of bringing down a deer. Their fur sheds ice crystals—handy up here. Prickly prey for all are slow-moving porcupines, protected by climbing agility and some 30,000 quills which are soft at birth but harden to dangerous spines within an hour.

Western jumping mice, yellow-pine chipmunks, meadow voles, and other small rodents are prey for glossy-brown martens, mink, and short-tailed weasels which become snowy ermines in winter. (Weasels don't easily catch an alert jumping mouse, which can leap up to 10 feet/3 m in a single bound.)

Bald eagles cruise ridge lines. Northern harriers patrol meadows for ground squirrels. Ospreys dive for cutthroat trout. River otters streak after them underwater. Loons call eerily. Up to 8,000 golden eagles move north overhead from March to May, joined by smaller numbers of other raptors, and pine siskins, bohemian waxwings, and ruby-crowned kinglets begin to move in.

The Canadian Rockies are renowned for alpine-zone species: gray-crowned rosy finches, golden-crowned sparrows, pipits, approachable willow and white-tailed ptarmigans, whose plumage changes to white every fall.

Dapper western grebes pair up for graceful springtime courtship ballets. Barrow's goldeneyes lay blue-green eggs in hollow tree stumps. Belted kingfishers' rattling cries are heard along streams. American dippers, our only aquatic songbirds, dive into fast-flowing streams and literally fly underwater to catch tiny fish, able to do this in current too swift and water too deep for humans to stand.

Black-billed magpies socialize raucously. Colorful varied thrushes are almost as common but secretive. More easily spotted are red and white-winged crossbills and many bright warblers—yellow, yellowthroat, Wilson's, Macgillivray's, Townsend's, Tennessee.

Great horned owls announce nightfall, echoed by little boreal owls' winnowing snipe-like "hoo-hoo-hoos."

The Rockies have 277 bird species—but only one kind of turtle, two toads, four snakes, and six frogs, one of which clings to life above the tree line, freezing solid every winter. Built-in antifreeze enables it to thaw undamaged every spring.

Ninety kinds of butterflies rush urgently through brief summer life cycles among dazzling valleys of blue harebells, orange arctic poppies, pink alpine moss-campions. In the fall, valleys are filled with ripening blueberries, black bears' favorites. September hillsides shimmer with golden larches.

Best way to see everything can be simply to stop and sit quietly and observe. Moose come out to nibble willow shoots at the bog's edge. A curious weasel might sniff your shoes, a mountain chick-adee land on your head. One woman, watching motionless, had a beaver come curl up in her lap.

The value of saving these matchless lands can be seen by comparing them with surrounding areas which, unprotected, have been threatened or laid waste by logging, oil and gas exploration, dam and road construction, deleterious ranching and agricultural practices, and unchecked resort or residential housing and commercial development. But some of the greatest wildlife hazards are inside the parks, where careless motorists kill hundreds of animals every year.

Best times are late June–mid-September, but many prefer late September–early October, with fewer visitors, though some facilities close then. Weather is cool but still pleasant. Variable temperatures can require jackets even in summer. Fall colors are stunning. Most parks are open all year for wildlife-viewing.

---

**FURTHER INFORMATION**

Parks Canada, Information Services, Box 2989, Station M, Calgary AB T2P 3AH, Canada, Tel: (+1) 403-292-4401, Website:www.pc.gc.ca

---

# BANFF NATIONAL PARK

Banff is best-known of Canadian Rockies' reserves and Canada's oldest, most cherished national park—a mixed blessing in midsummer when it can be overrun by more than four million annual visitors. They arrive on Canada's main transcontinental railroad and transcontinental highway, both routed through Banff's main valley. There are three ski resorts and the town of Banff, with 7,600 residents, fully equipped—some say too fully—with shops, restaurants, and visitor facilities. There have been declines in large predator populations.

Historically hunted, wolves were poisoned and at one time exterminated in the park. Now scientists seek to protect and identify critical habitat and study their behavior (they learned recently wolf packs may feed and care for old, crippled members no longer able to hunt for themselves).

Elk males yearly grow ponderous antlers weighing up to 40 pounds (18 kg) used to attract and vigorously defend harems during mating. Zeal to protect harems can so distract them, however, that they inadvertently allow young bulls to sneak in and mate with some females on the side. Called wapiti in Canada—Shawnee Indian word for "white rump"—they are Holarctic, distributed over northern parts of both Old and New Worlds. In Eurasia, North American elk are known as red deer (whereas, confusingly, the species known in North America as moose—also Holarctic are known in Eurasia as elk).

Elk have adapted almost too well to human presence. They forage on residential landscaping, and visitors don't always realize a mother elk with calf and bull with five-foot (1.5-m) antlers may not be as friendly as they look. Wildlife watchers should keep at least 100 ft (30 m) away from large animals.

But there are also 800 miles (1,287 km) of quiet trails to explore, where most of the wildlife visit at one time or another, as well as stunning Lake Louise below Victoria Glacier and beautiful Moraine Lake in the Valley of Ten Peaks. It should be remembered that Banff, now 2,564 square miles (6,640 km²), was originally established in 1885 not as a nature preserve but as a tourist attraction and spa.

---

**FURTHER INFORMATION**

Superintendent, Banff National Park, Box 900, Banff AB T1L 1K2, Canada, Tel: (+1) 403-762-1550, Website: www.pc.gc.ca/pn-np/ab/banff

---

# JASPER NATIONAL PARK

Wildlife at Jasper, just to the north, is more numerous and visible, understandably since Jasper is more than twice as big as Banff—4,200 square miles (10,878 km²)—with less than half the visitors.

Shy, striking harlequin ducks nest amid low vegetation, especially on riverine islands, and feed on mayfly, blackfly, and caddisfly larvae in the Maligne and Athabasca Rivers near Jasper townsite. Elk roam through meadows grazing all along the Athabasca valley. So do mule deer (named for their sensitive, outsize ears), coyotes and, in berry season, black bears. Endangered woodland caribou are often in the Maligne valley. Grizzlies summer in alpine areas but are often along highways in May and June (tell black bears from grizzlies by humps on the latters' backs. Both can be brown or cinnamon-colored).

Black swifts swirl around a nest colony along the walls of Maligne Canyon.

Mountain goats come to naturally-occurring Mount Kerkeslin goat lick at Disaster Point, bleating when young ones wander too far off, their white coats shedding great furry clumps in summer. Bighorn sheep with massive 360-degree horn curls watch passing traffic along Icefields Parkway, most often where rock cliffs are at the road's edge, and sometimes rest on the sun-warmed parkway itself.

Wolves are fairly common—50 to 60 in the park—sometimes seen at Pyramid Lake. They have no natural predators but they do have sworn enemies—grizzly bears kill wolf pups when they can, perhaps because wolves (looking to the future?) kill bear cubs when they can.

Beavers busy themselves at Cottonwood Slough and in the Valley of the Five Lakes, particularly at dusk. These are prime areas too for birds—common snipe, barred owls, and flame-crested foot-long pileated woodpeckers, also migrant and breeding ring-necked ducks, Barrow's goldeneyes, green-winged teal, and buffleheads fanning out showy white facial discs.

Moose favor grassy water's edges at Maligne Lake, along Yellowhead Pass and at Pocahontas Ponds along the Miette River, a wetland flooded much of the summer by overflow from glacially-fed Athabasca River. More than 60 water-oriented species nest here, and it is an important seasonal staging area for whistling swans and other waterbirds.

---

**FURTHER INFORMATION**

Superintendent, Jasper National Park, Box 10, Jasper, AB T0E 1E0, Canada,
Tel: (+1) 780-852-6176, Website: www.pc.gc.ca/pn-np/ab/jasper

---

# KOOTENAY NATIONAL PARK

Kootenay National Park, adjoining Banff on the west, was devastated by a 1968 wildfire, but this resulted in cleared, sunny areas where wildflowers have flourished, also short, tender regrowth, attractive browse for moose, elk, and deer. Storm Mountain can be covered with brilliant fireweed and yellow columbine.

Mount Wardle is home to many mountain goats which spend most of their time on high slopes but in spring and early summer bring young ones down to lick at naturally-occurring minerals in road banks. Bighorn sheep are attracted to iron-rich cliffs in Sinclair Canyon.

To get there take the spectacular Banff–Windermere Highway (Route 93s) west off Route 1A at Castle Junction in Banff. The full scenic drive to Radium Hot Springs, bisecting the park, is 65 miles (105 km), with few services.

---

**FURTHER INFORMATION**

Superintendent, Kootenay National Park, Box 220, Dept. K, Radium Hot Springs, BC V0A 1M0, Canada,
Tel: (+1) 250-347-9615, Website: www.pc.gc.ca/pn-np/bc/kootenay

---

# YOHO NATIONAL PARK

Yoho National Park, adjacent and north of Kootenay, is reachable by taking Route 1 west from Banff toward Lake Louise. One of Canada's highest waterfalls is here, 1,248-foot (381-m) Takakkaw. Wildlife includes black and grizzly bears, elk, moose, coyotes, wolves, snowshoe hares. Bald and golden eagles soar over owls, migratory birds, and a Columbian ground squirrel colony at Waptka Lake Viewpoint. Yoho shows some of the same fire effects as Kootenay.

Fossil remains of more than 120 marine animal species have been found in Burgess Shale at Walcott's Quarry—some, though soft-bodied, so well preserved that scientists know what they were eating when they died 500 million years ago. Yoho has campgrounds, also accommodations at Field village.

---

**FURTHER INFORMATION**

Superintendent, Yoho National Park, P.O. Box 99, Dept. K, Field, BC V0A 1G0, Canada, Tel: (+1) 250-343-6783, Website: www.pc.gc.ca/pn-np/bc/yoho

---

**Mount Robson Provincial Park**, adjoining Jasper on the west, has the Canadian Rockies' highest peak—12,972-foot (3,956-m) Mount Robson; also mountain goats on rock slides at Yellowhead Lake, moose at Moose Lake, mule deer and black bears throughout the park, and in August–September enormous scarlet chinook salmon fighting upstream past rapids and waterfalls in the Fraser River to lay eggs after a 600-mile (1,000-km) journey from the sea.

# MANITOBA

## CHURCHILL NATIONAL PARK

People esteem wildlife in the little town of Churchill on the northernmost edge of Hudson Bay in Manitoba, which is fortunate, since wildlife often outnumber people. Churchill's 1,100 residents can be outnumbered by visiting polar bears in fall.

Beluga whales and tens of thousands of nesting birds from half a world away arrive in May and June.

Some 1,200 polar bears converge every autumn on this part of the cape to wait hungrily for Hudson Bay to freeze hard enough to hold their weight so they can go out to catch seals. This is usually around Halloween, so parents keep a close guard on their youngsters in "trick-or-treat" costumes. So do police and natural resource officers on "bear patrols" which tranquilize and transport out of town any bears that seem threatening.

Churchill, known as polar bear capital of the world, has the largest concentration anywhere of these largest land carnivores, which can weigh a half-ton, with paws a foot (25 cm) long, capable of killing a 600-pound (270-kg) bearded seal with a single blow.

# CANADA

Arctic fox fur has the highest insulation value of any mammal, useful in treeless arctic tundras where they live in Eurasia, North America, Iceland, and Greenland. Soles of their feet are covered entirely with fur—hence their scientific name, Lagopus or "rabbit foot." Small, rounded ears restrict heat loss. Long, thick, bushy tails reach around them like fur stoles when they curl up to sleep, able to endure temperatures of −70°F (−60°C). No other canid species lives so far north.

After freeze-up the land is left to hardy arctic foxes, snowshoe and arctic hares, and willow ptarmigans which molt from off-white and brown summer plumage to snowy winter feathers. Then night can last nearly 24 hours, illumined by some of the brightest northern lights in the world. Only in Norway and Russia does the swirling blue, green, and white aurora borealis get this close, only 25 miles (40 km) from earth.

Equally overwhelming are the great numbers of rare and interesting birds that arrive in spring from all over the western hemisphere, many in striking breeding plumage not seen elsewhere. Over 200 species come, plus more "accidentals." Some nest here, some continue farther north. Flocks of thousands of Lapland longspurs accompany a flood of waterfowl, shorebirds, Pacific and red-throated loons, golden plovers, Hudsonian godwits, a dozen kind of warblers, hoary redpolls, sometimes rare pink-breasted Ross' gulls, snowy owls, merlins, and arctic terns, whose migrations can cover 26,000 miles (42,000 km) a year.

By June, up to 3,000 pearly-white beluga whales crowd into the Churchill River estuary to stay for two months in the warmer, fresher water, mating, giving birth, rolling over on sandbars to scratch off old skin. Once they were heavily hunted—now they hang around small boats "whooshing" through blowholes and chirping friendly greetings that sound, through under-water microphones, something like canaries.

Wildflowers carpet the summer tundra—purple rhododendrons, pink alpine azaleas, yellow, pink, and white saxifrage, 14 orchid species, and later, bright blankets of multihued mosses, orange lichens, deep purple bearberries, and dwarf birch, spruce and cranberry.

Churchill is reachable by air or rail, with views from the Winnipeg train of sharp-tailed and spruce grouse, great gray and northern hawk owls, waterfowl, willow ptarmigans, and caribou. Churchill has modern, comfortable motels, also vehicle rentals, tour guides, and outfitters (reserve ahead). High waterproof boots, warm clothing, and rain gear can be useful any time, insect repellent a must in summer.

Much can be seen in the town's environs, but now just southeast there is also new **Wapusk National Park**, 4,429 square miles (11,470 km²) of wetland covered by bogs, lakes, and the most extensive mantle of peat in North America, with, inland, one of the world's largest known polar bear denning sites where females give birth in snow and earthen dens to white cubs every November and December. It is, as well, critical staging habitat for hundreds of thousands of waterfowl and shorebirds and a breeding colony of some 90,000 lesser snow geese. Also there are Ross' gulls, swans, loons and, among mammals, arctic foxes, lynx, timber wolves, wolverines, black bears, and 3,000 caribou.

---

**FURTHER INFORMATION**

Wapusk National Park, c/o Parks Canada, Box 127, Churchill, MB R0B 0E0, Canada, Tel: (+1) 204-675-8863, E-mail: wpusk-np@pch.gc.ca

---

# ISLANDS

## NEWFOUNDLAND—GROS MORNE NATIONAL PARK

Boulders of 1.25-billion-years-old granite at Gros Morne National Park tell of violent geological events when tectonic plates under continents heaved and collided, destroying the ancient North American rim and leaving the ocean floor atop it.

# CANADA

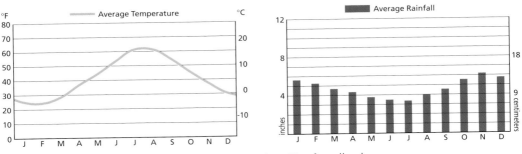

Gateway city: St. Johns, Newfoundland

So dramatically clear is the rocky historical record that this insular 697-square-mile (1,805-km²) U.N. World Heritage Site on Newfoundland's west coast is important to scientists everywhere.

It is equally important to woodland caribou, lynx, arctic hares, red foxes (here multicolored), black bears, moose, mink, and others. All were brought here or came under their own steam—swimming, flying, or walking on winter ice or snowpack in the 15,000 years since the last ice age.

Habitat ranges from coastal lowland with dune formations up to 100 feet (30 m) high, to alpine plateaus, waterfalls, deep fiord valleys, and glacial lakes.

Wild newcomers keep arriving. Coyotes showed up in 1987. And there are snowshoe hares, ermines, an occasional drop-in polar bear, and some 235 arctic, boreal, and pelagic bird species with strays from both sides of the ocean. It is an important migratory shorebird stop, and significant breeding site for rare, beautiful harlequin ducks as well as blackpoll warblers, arctic and common terns, rock ptarmigans, American tree sparrows, and bald eagles.

Harbor seals colonize the coast. Pilot, minke, and finback whales swim by. Atlantic salmon and arctic char spawn here after a life at sea while other species, including brook trout, fill the streams.

Alpine bearberries and azaleas coexist with purple-fringed orchids and carnivorous sundews in wet meadows among a remarkable 1,000-species array of plants (700 vascular, 300 mosses), some exceedingly rare and delicate (the park urges visitors to stay on established trails).

Some plants have developed into distinct island forms, different from those of mainland cousins from which insular lives have separated them.

Black bears tend to be bigger here. Red foxes can be black, silver-tipped, yellowish, or a patchy-calico mixture. (Some have lost fear of humans, perhaps from illegal feeding, which is dangerous if they come to resent a human without food. Some such animals must be destroyed—thus the park warning: "A fed fox can be a dead fox.")

Weather can be cool but pleasant through October, though always unpredictable. Hypothermia can occur in any season.

# CANADA

Nowhere in nature are predator-prey destinies more intertwined than furry lynx and snowshoe hares, which closely resemble one another in dense pelage and broad, spreading hairy paws, able to support both species in snow. When hare numbers rise, lynx females ovulate more, mate more often, more successfully, and have larger litters of which more survive. When hare numbers plummet, lynx decline and so do their offspring, even when alternate prey is available. Lynx live deep in coniferous forests and mountains of Canada and the northern United States.

A ferry goes to Newfoundland from the mainland. Air Canada flies to nearby Deer Lake, where rental cars are available for the 50 miles (80 km) to park headquarters. There are miles of paved roads and hiking trails, and campsites and motels in nearby towns. Snowmobiles, popular in this snowy, beautiful place, are permitted in winter, but may conflict with wildlife on trails.

---

**FURTHER INFORMATION**

Superintendent, Gros Morne National Park, P.O. Box 130, Rocky Harbour, Newfoundland A0K 4N0, Canada, Tel: (+1) 709-458-2417, E-mail: GrosMorne-info@pch.gc.ca

---

# BRITISH COLUMBIA

## GWAII HAANAS NATIONAL PARK RESERVE

More than a million interesting and rare birds nest along the shoreline and spectacular deep fiords of Gwaii Haanas National Park Reserve, 138 rugged "islands of wonder and beauty" (their Haida name) off Canada's northwest coast. They are attracted by undisturbed breeding habitat and abundance of food both in off- and inshore waters, including huge numbers of spawning salmon.

Marine mammals are attracted as well—17 whale species, some resident, some transient: humpback, sei, finback, minke, gray, and handsome small orcas—as well as up to 10,000 harbor seals and a large breeding colony of Steller's sea lions. Multihued sea stars illuminate low-tide zones.

Small plump marbled murrelets, a seriously threatened species, lay single eggs in depressions on mossy limbs (unfortunately on trees favored by the logging industry).

Eagles nest along the coast along with peregrine falcons, common murres, and cormorants.

Rhinoceros auklets, bearing a rhino-like bill tuft, raise young in burrows. So do ancient murrelets, tufted puffins, Cassin's auklets, and Leach's and fork-tailed storm petrels.

Black bears and pine martens—both larger than mainland cousins, due in part to rich seafood diets—live in one of the finest old-growth forests on the Pacific coast.

Access to Gwaii Haanas is by air or sea. There are no campsites, trails, and few visitor services, though licensed tour guides and lodging are nearby.

---

**FURTHER INFORMATION**

Superintendent, Natural British Columbia, Tel: 1-800-663-6000 for Canada and U.S. and 1-250-387-1642 for other countries; or Gwaii Haanas National Park, Reserve and Haida Heritage Site, P.O. Box 37, Queen Charlotte, BC V0T 1S0, Canada, Tel: (+1) 250-559-8818, Fax: (+1) 250-559-8366, E-mail: gwaii.haanas@pc.gc.ca

---

# YUKON TERRITORY

The last ice age retreated 15,000 years ago to Canada's Yukon Territory where it remains in beauty and grandeur amid Canada's highest mountain range (including its tallest peak, 19,524-foot/5,959-m Mount Logan).

## KLUANE NATIONAL PARK

Of Kluane National Park's 8,500 square miles (14,760 km²), 5,700 (9,900 km²) are encased up to a half-mile deep in the largest subpolar ice field outside Greenland, surrounded by more than 2,000 glaciers. The longest of these have an active flow over 45 miles (65 km). Sometimes a surge shatters one into a giant ice pincushion, or forms a dam that breaks up later in a spectacular wall of water. One historic dam-break gushed for two days at a rate comparable to that of the Amazon River.

Varied habitats in the rest of the park—brooding spruce forests, braided river valleys, mountain-circled lakes, and alpine meadows—harbor a hundred or so black bears and twice that many grizzlies. Packs of timber wolves stalk huge moose—a larger-than-normal subspecies—that nibble on young willow growth. And there are lynx, coyotes, red foxes, a few cougars, small but ferocious wolverines, and thousands of small rodent prey species.

White Dall sheep and mountain goats leap over crags where bald and golden eagles soar. There are 106 bird species, from falcons to tiny water pipits, rosy finches, and warblers, though only a few, like spruce grouse and willow ptarmigans, stay year-round (temperatures drop from summer highs of 91°F/33°C to −58°F/−50°C in midwinter).

Life adapts. Multihued alpine flowers hug the earth, minimizing exposure. Pollinating butterflies are dark, absorbing maximum solar energy. Small pikas foraging among rocks are stocky with short ears and limbs, lessening heat loss. During cyclical snowshoe hare declines, predators, both animal and bird, may prey on one another to avoid starvation.

Kluane (pronounced Kloo-wahn-ee), Tuchone word for "lake with many fish," has 150 miles (240 km) of backcountry trails and old mining roads. There are visitor centers in Sheep Mountain and Haines City with campgrounds 35 miles (56 km) south of Haines Junction.

### FURTHER INFORMATION

Kluane National Park, P.O. Box 5495, Haines Junction (Yukon), Y0B 1L0 Canada, Tel: (+1) 867-634-7250.

NOTE: Kluane is a joint U.N. World Heritage Site with the vast U.S. Wrangell-St. Elias National Park and Preserve, adjoining across the border in Alaska, with similar impressive wildlife and physical features.

OPPOSITE: Massive American bison or buffalo once formed the largest mass of animals ever to roam the earth—an estimated 60 million of them, bearded bulls with high humped shoulders and short, sharp upcurved horns standing six feet (2 m) at the shoulder, weighing more than a ton, running 30 miles an hour (48 kph). Within a few decades wild populations were almost gone, many lost to drive-by "sport" shooting by railroad car passengers, their bodies left to rot on the prairie. Luckily a remnant herd was saved and a reserve set aside for them, and they thrive now in Prince Albert National Park and elsewhere.

# SASKATCHEWAN

## PRINCE ALBERT NATIONAL PARK

One of the last free-roaming herds of great wild plains bison grazes over its original range in Prince Albert National Park, wilderness home as well to 10,000 white pelicans, endangered woodland caribou, wolves, lynx, black bears, and 235 bird species. Established to preserve diminishing southern prairie adjoining northern coniferous boreal woods in central Canada, it is a diverse habitat mosaic of spruce bogs, sedge meadows, aspen uplands, fescue grasslands, and more than 1,500 lakes in one of the few North American parks with an intact balance of predators, herbivores, and furbearers.

Fishers, three-toed woodpeckers, and great gray owls increasingly rare elsewhere are still comfortably numerous here along with elk, badgers, barred owls, spruce and sharp-tailed grouse, bald eagles.

Moose browse on red osier. Ospreys fish for brook trout. Wolves howl at Rendezvous Ridge. Bay-breasted and Blackburnian warblers nest high in intricate bowls of fine grass and spider silk.

Prince Albert was final home and resting place of famed writer/conservationist/adopted Ojibway Indian Gray Owl, whose cabin incorporating a beaver lodge remains part of the natural world where he found and urged on others "enrichment other than material prosperity."

# NORTHWEST TERRITORIES

## WOOD BUFFALO NATIONAL PARK

In 1954 a pilot fighting a forest fire in the Northwest Territories looked down and discovered one of the natural world's most significant and hitherto secret places—the nesting site of the rare majestic whooping crane. It was deep inside a tract of wild impenetrable muskeg larger than Denmark in Wood Buffalo National Park.

# CANADA

Whooping cranes are America's most beloved endangered species, partly for their majestic, snow-white beauty and ringing call, that of "no mere bird," said naturalist Aldo Leopold, but "symbol of our untamable past"—and partly their peril-fraught lives. Twice yearly these tallest North American birds, standing five feet (1.5 m) with eight-foot (2.6 m) wingspans, fly 2,500 hazardous miles (4,300 km) between remote nesting grounds in Canada's Wood Buffalo National Park, threatened by industrial development, and winter quarters in Aransas National Wildlife Refuge in Texas, vulnerable to passing tankers' oil spills. In between they are still occasionally shot or die colliding with power lines. Still, their numbers, once down to 15, at recent count showed 422.

He instantly recognized the glistening scarlet-crowned pair of snow-white birds and their chick. Once seen, they are unforgettable—five feet (1.6 m) high, North America's tallest bird, with wingspreads up to eight feet (2.6 m)—unchanged since they evolved with the saber-toothed cat. Their bugling cry from yard-long (1 m) windpipes can be heard for miles. Formerly they nested across the continent. A number of factors, some natural, some human-caused, reduced their numbers to 15 in 1941 and scientists predicted their imminent extinction. But with protection here and elsewhere, on their Texas gulf coast wintering grounds and along their peril-fraught 2,500-mile (4,300-km) migration route, there are now more than 400 including 40 breeding pairs, and the outlook is more encouraging.

Wood Buffalo, largest park in Canada and one of the largest in the world (17,295 square miles/44,807 km²), was created in 1922 to protect one of the world's last free-roaming herds of wood bison which now numbers some 2,500. Its subarctic wilderness of boreal forest, sand dunes, shallow lakes, marshes, and meandering tree-lined streams contains the largest undisturbed grass and sedge meadows in North America.

# MEXICO

MORE THAN SEVEN MILLION BIRDS OF PREY OF
MORE THAN 20 SPECIES—EAGLES, FALCONS, HARRIERS,
HAWKS—SOAR THROUGH THE AIR EVERY FALL OVER RIO DE
RAPACES—RIVER OF RAPTORS—ON THE MEXICAN COASTAL
PLAIN. THAT'S MORE THAN ANYPLACE ELSE IN THE WORLD.

MEXICO HAS OVER 1,000 BIRD SPECIES—MORE THAN SOME WHOLE CONTINENTS. JAGUARS PROWL THE JUNGLES, ALONG WITH SPOTTED OCELOTS AND MARGAYS, PUMAS, AND DARK, SECRETIVE PANTHER-LIKE JAGUARUNDIS. Primitive tapirs, close relatives to rhinoceros but looking more like elephants, teach striped babies to swim. Howler monkeys howl, proclaiming forest territories.

Glittering resplendent quetzals, emerald and crimson, called most beautiful birds in the world, preen feathery tails as long as their bodies in MONTES AZULES BIOSPHERE RESERVE. Fierce harpy eagles, world's most powerful birds of prey, peer out from under angry-looking crests, talons ready to seize and carry off a spider monkey.

# MEXICO

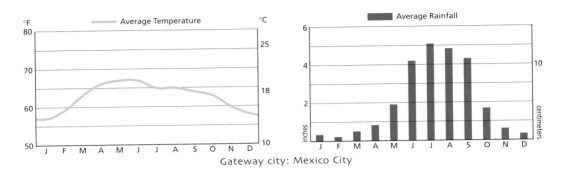

Gateway city: Mexico City

Tens of thousands of bright flamingos feed and nest along the Yucatan Peninsula with storks, anhingas, frigate birds, masked boobies, and thousands of seabirds. Endangered sea turtles lay eggs on beaches.

Endangered manatees graze in shallows protected by 70 miles (113 km) of the world's second longest coral reef in SIAN KA'AN. CALAKMUL, together with adjoining reserves in Belize and Guatemala, is the second-largest mixed tropical forest in the western hemisphere, surpassed only by the Amazon.

Millions of birds of prey fly over Veracruz in an autumn "RIVER OF RAPTORS" unequalled anywhere else.

Up to 100 million orange-and-black monarch butterflies winter on wooded mountain slopes at EL ROSARIO MONARCH BUTTERFLY SANCTUARY west of Mexico City, in a natural marvel still unexplained.

Great gray whales wind up the longest migration of any mammal, 6,000 miles (9,600 km) from summering grounds off Alaska, to give birth to 20-foot-plus (6+ m) calves in saline coastal lagoons at EL VIZCAINO on Baja Peninsula, mothers and young buoyed by highly saline waters.

Yucatan may hold a secret of dinosaurs' extinction. Dinosaurs died out, one theory now holds, because of a natural event 65 million years ago when an enormous comet or asteroid hit here. Dust resulting from the collision may have obscured the sun, causing plants to die and cutting off dinosaurs' sustenance. Satellite pictures show a huge perfect semicircle, the crater's edges, outlined by cenotes (or sinkholes) over the region.

Mexico has 45 national parks and 230 biosphere reserves. Smaller ones are called "Special Biosphere Reserves," a U.N. designation protecting pristine ecosystems having species that are endemic, endangered, or at risk of extinction but with buffer "cooperation" zones that can include use in research, tourism, and by local communities to cull natural resources that do not endanger ecosystems.

**FURTHER INFORMATION**

Coordinator of Protected Natural Areas, Instituto Nacional De Ecologia, Unidad Coordinadora De Areas Naturales Protegidas, Av. Revolucion No. 1425, Nivel 25, Col. Tlacopac, San Angel, C.P. 01040, Mexico, D.F., Tel: (+52) 5-624-3329, Fax: (+52) 5-624-3589.

# CALAKMUL BIOSPHERE RESERVE

This vast jungle with prowling jaguars, ocelots, scarlet macaws, screaming eagles, and howler monkeys—2,660 square miles (6,883 km²) in the southern Yucatan peninsula—adjoins 5,160 similar square miles (13,360 km²) in Guatemala and Belize. Together these three reserves make up the second-largest tropical forest in the western hemisphere—second only to the Amazon— a habitat with some of the greatest diversity of life on the planet.

Counts of fauna and flora, still incomplete, include among 94 kinds of mammals more wild felines than any other North American reserve—five, including jaguarundis, margays, and pumas—as well as 329 kinds of birds and 1,500 kinds of plants, many endemic or endangered.

Long-tailed spider monkeys scream shrilly in treetops. Endangered water-loving tapirs wade in alongside endangered Morelet's crocodiles. Tamandua or collared anteaters climb trees after choice insects. Ocellated turkeys vibrate multihued iridescent plumage. Curly-crested turkey-sized great curassows boom resoundingly for mates. King vultures shake orange wattles. Colorful toucans and raucous parrots seek out ripe fruit.

Almost a third of the avian species are increasingly rare migratory neotropical songbirds. Threatened hawk-eagles are among 30 raptors. Spectacular orchids of 40 species cling to tree trunks. Many plants furnish traditional Mayan medicines as yet unstudied.

The Mayan city of Calakmul thrived here in 500 AD leaving massive pyramids, fascinating relics such as a large renowned jade mask and more Mayan stelae than anywhere else.

Threats, especially in Guatemala, include poaching both of animals and lumber, along with slash-and-burn farming. Environmental groups are working with citizen groups to educate and start programs of local benefit that will avoid exhausting natural resources.

Lodging is available at nearby Xpujil. Roads are unpaved—travel should be attempted only during the dry season October–June.

**FURTHER INFORMATION**

Pronatura Peninsula de Yucatán, A.C., Calle 1-D #254-A x 36 y 38, 97120 Merida, Yucatán, Mexico, Tel: (+52) 99-44-22-90; Fax: (+52) 99-44-35-60; Coordination de Tourismo, Calle 12 #153, Campeche, Mexico, Tel: (+52) 59-816-6068; E-mail: 1mavalos@etzna.uacam.mx

# Celestun and Rio Lagartos National Parks

A visual sea of up to 100,000 coral-pink flamingos (their Spanish name means "flaming") feeding in a lagoon at Celestun National Park and Biosphere Reserve on the Yucatan coast, or nesting at Rio Lagartos (also a National Park and Biosphere Reserve) to the east, is a never-to-be-forgotten spectacle. Standing five feet (1.5 m) tall on slender 30-inch (76-cm) legs, their long necks are raised and lowered in a rhythmic, dance-like motion as they first hold heads upside down to allow sieve-like bills to gather and strain out insect larvae, algae, and tiny crustaceans stirred up by high-stepping webbed feet, then straighten up to swallow. Those ready to mate spread five-foot (1.5-m) wings and do a circling prance. Then they fly off, many to Rio Lagartos, to construct dome-like mud nests where they will raise a single chick, hatched with white down but fed a red carotene-rich "milk" from a parent's esophagus which may help develop their brilliant plumage. Best time at Celestun is June to late March, before birds begin nesting. Best at Lagartos is April–June.

Both reserves have hundreds of other interesting bird species—herons and egrets, pelicans, magnificent frigate birds, wintering northern songbirds such as scarlet tanagers and rose-breasted grosbeaks. But flamingos are the stars. Boat tours can be arranged. Visitors who stay overnight nearby have the sublime sight of these glorious birds waking en masse at dawn.

# El Vizcaino Biosphere Reserve

Huge, friendly, barnacle-laden gray whales come here in the thousands every winter to peaceful, salty lagoons on the Baja Peninsula to court, mate, socialize, and give birth, after a journey of 6,000 miles (9,600 km) from arctic feeding grounds—longest migration of any mammal.

These dramatic natural phenomena take place in sheltered bays along Baja's irregular west coast, especially in two lagoons—**San Ignacio** and **Scammon's** (or **Ojo de Liebre**), ironically named after the whaling captain who discovered them in 1850 and then slaughtered them almost to extinction.

The population, now protected, has rebounded almost to pre-whaling numbers, around 20,000, and whale-watching has become popular, making these marine mammals more valuable alive than dead—important for continued recovery.

They are so comfortable now in the 55,555-square-mile (143,600-km$^2$) reserve that frolicsome ones flip 10-foot-wide (3-m) tails and play dangerously close to visitors' small boats, peering at them with myopic four-inch (10-cm) eyes. Any visitors' unease vanishes when a trusting 40-foot-plus (12-m) mother and calf half her size hang around to be patted.

Vizcaino is the largest protected area in Latin America. Within it the Mexican government has set aside 16 core areas for special protection. These include islands with hundreds of elephant seals, herds of sea lions, nesting petrels and other seabirds, and 10,000-foot (3,050-m) mountains with bighorn sheep. There are caves with paintings recording prehistoric wildlife, and a desert tract where endangered pronghorn antelopes whizz along at 70 miles an hour (113 kph)—the western hemisphere's fastest mammal—leaping 20 feet (6 m) at a bound. They adapt to the desert by erecting their fur to admit cool breezes, warming up on cold nights by flattening fur over dense guard hairs.

Vizcaino's varied altitudes, climates, and habitat in relative isolation over millions of years have given it (and Baja overall) interesting, often unique biota—imperial eagles, black and peregrine falcons, magnificent frigate birds, brown and white pelicans, giant Mexican cereus cactus, bobcats, mountain lions. Of 38 mammals, 15 are endemic. Dense zooplankton riding the California coastal current attracts a broad seagoing wildlife spectrum including four endangered sea turtles and 60 kinds of seabirds.

Three other whale species are here—killers; highly endangered humpbacks, still killed illegally when their friendly approach to boats makes it easy for poachers; and blues, up to 100 feet (30.5 m) long with average weight of 143 tons (130,000 kg), probably largest animal that ever lived, only a few thousand believed surviving worldwide.

Best times are February–March. San Diego, served by international airlines, is a starting point for boats taking visitors to Baja, with visitors staying aboard overnight. So is Ensenada just south (where Robert Louis Stevenson wrote *Treasure Island*). Guerrero Negro, a village named for another whaling captain and closer to the lagoons, has a restaurant and motel where tours can be arranged, or whales can be watched less intimately from shore.

Visitors should be sure to take sun lotion, sweaters, and waterproof slickers.

The whole 800-mile (1,300-km) Baja peninsula, longest in the world, separated from mainland Mexico by the Sea of Cortez (or Gulf of California), is largely undeveloped and fascinating, with fin, minke, sperm, and pilot whales, three kinds of dolphins (sometimes pods of 1,500 or so) in the sea, and red-billed tropicbirds, blue-footed boobies, elephant trees, elephant cacti ashore. Fifty-three islands are a special U.N. World Biosphere Reserve, sanctuary for both land and marine birds. **1857 Constitution National Park**, 45 miles (72 km) east of Ensenada, and **San Pedro Martir National Park**, 150 miles (240 km) south, are extraordinarily beautiful mountain and forest reserves with bobcats, gray foxes, mountain lions, mule deer, raptors, acorn woodpeckers, pinyon jays.

# EL ROSARIO MONARCH BUTTERFLY SANCTUARY

Twenty million monarch butterflies taking flight sounds like a gentle whispering wind. It looks like a shimmering blizzard of dancing orange-gold motes. It is a natural phenomenon that takes place on south-facing Sierra Madre mountain slopes west of Mexico City every winter and spring.

OPPOSITE: Tens of millions of monarch butterflies set out every August on a six-week 3,000-mile (5,000-km) journey from Canada and the northern U.S. to a destination they have never seen in Mexico. There they gather for the winter in El Rosario Sanctuary, covering trees, sometimes flying up from winter naps in a softly-whispering blizzard of black and orange insects. In spring they will reawaken, mate, and their descendants will return to the same places their ancestors came from—exactly how, no one knows—but the next generation will make the same miraculous-seeming journey the following year.

Perhaps 100 million monarchs from Canada and the U.S. east of the Rocky Mountains spend winters here. They disperse among several sites where ideal conditions of food, temperature, and moisture exist for them in dense oyamel fir woods (monarchs west of the Rockies go to California).

When they cluster at night and on cool days, they can almost cover branches and trunks of trees. When sun warms the air, they fly up and gather to drink at streams and sip nectar from flowers.

The life story of these dazzling, fragile creatures is one of the most remarkable in the natural world. What they do has been known only since 1975. How they do it is still unknown.

Butterflies arriving to winter here have flown up to 3,100 miles (5,000 km), obeying an instinctive directional pull handed down by ancestors which preceded them by five generations. Once here, they become semi-dormant, gradually awakening as northern spring beckons. In March, they mate. Females then fly to Texas to lay eggs, and, five short-lived generations later, their descendants will be in Canada, Montana, Maine—wherever their ancestors came from. That generation will delay sexual development and start fluttering southwest in fall across the U.S. and Canada at average speeds up to 20 miles an hour (33 kph) covering up to 120 miles (200 km) a day, to start the cycle over again.

Scientists have taken Maine and Montana monarchs and exchanged them. All have ended up together here on a Mexican slope they have never seen but whose existence and location they sense unerringly.

Threats to this natural marvel are multiple—logging and habitat loss in Mexico among poor residents who value income from a logged tree more than a butterfly (one of the five protected areas is already seriously damaged); and all along summer and migration paths from loss of milkweed, their only larval food plant, often considered an undesirable weed. Conservation groups such as non-profit Monarca and World Wide Fund for Nature are working to enable Mexicans to benefit from ecotourism, and elsewhere to encourage milkweed-planting.

## MARIPOSA MONARCA AT EL ROSARIO RESERVE

The Mariposa Monarca at El Rosario Reserve is near El Rosario, also Angangueo, a pretty former mining town 80 miles (135 km) west of Mexico City, which has a small inn. Lodging is also available at San Jose Purua and Zitacuaro. Visitors can drive to the sanctuary over unpaved road or arrange guided trips. It's a steep climb—but worth it. Best times are February–March, drier then and butterflies are awakening.

---

**FURTHER INFORMATION**

Monarca AC, Constituyentes 345, Eighth Floor, 11830 Mexico, Tel: (+52) 5-592-8137 or 5-703-1544, Fax: (+52) 5-703-0391.

---

# MONTES AZULES BIOSPHERE RESERVE

Emerald and crimson resplendent quetzals, called most spectacular bird in the New World, drape extraordinary fringed tail feathers from high limbs in Montes Azules Biosphere Reserve, largest expanse of pure tropical rain forest in Mexico and North America.

Fierce harpy eagles, world's strongest raptors, rise to yard-long height (1 m) to peer from huge crested heads, powerful talons ready to seize and carry off a spider monkey. Keel-billed toucans delicately pluck ripe fruit with enormous, colorful (but feather-weight) bills.

Diversity in just 2.47 acres (1 ha) of this 1,278 square miles (3,311 km²) in the state of Chiapas includes on average 30 different tree species, 50 kinds of orchids, 40 kinds of birds, 20 mammals, 300 butterflies, and more than 5,000 insects.

The reserve is home to spotted jaguars, ocelots, tree-climbing tamandua ant-eaters, noisy howler monkeys, and handsome little grisons (weasels) with black and white masks, among some 167 mammal species which find jungle homes, often amid Mayan ceremonial ruins. Crocodiles are among hundreds of aquatic types in 1,000-foot-deep (305-m) Laguna Miramar.

Many species are endemic, including the strange *Lacandonia schismatica*, only higher plant possessing a single male reproductive organ surrounded by female ones.

Montes Azules feeds and protects the Usumacinta River which carries 20 percent of the water in Mexico. It is threatened by illegal logging and destructive slash-and-burn agriculture, as well as political unrest. Imaginative projects would channel funds for local use from sustainable forest programs such as handicrafts and butterfly ranching.

---

**FURTHER INFORMATION**

Desarrollo Sestentable Montes Azules, S.A. de C.V. Camino a San Pablo #5860, Col. La Noria C.P. 16029, E-mail: bly@ma.com.mx

---

# RIVER OF RAPTORS

More than seven million birds of prey of more than 20 species fill the air over the Mexican coastal plain at Veracruz, Mexico, every fall between late September and early October—more than any-place else in the world.

A recent sampling between August 20 and October 23 counted 2.5 million broad-winged and 1.2 million Swainson's hawks alone, along with such non-raptors as pelicans, storks, ibises, and thousands of songbirds. In a single day there can be 435,000 birds rising on thermal air patterns and funneling down from Texas onto this narrow coastal corridor area.

This Rio de Rapaces, or River of Raptors, is protected by a private group, Pronatura Veracruz, working with Hawk Mountain Sanctuary in the U.S. Lodging is available in Veracruz.

---

**FURTHER INFORMATION**

Pronatura Veracruz, Apartado Postal 399, Xalapa, Veracruz Mexico 91000,
Tel: (+52) 28-12-88-44, Fax: (+52) 28-12-94-15, E-mail: verpronatura@laneta.apc.org

---

# SIAN KA'AN BIOSPHERE RESERVE

Spotted jaguars, ocelots, margays, and stealthy panther-like jaguarundis steal warily through rain forests ruled 1,000 years ago by Mayan civilizations. Mayans looking out then over this seamless vista of sea and sky called it Sian Ka'an, "where the sky is born" or "gateway to heaven."

Now 2,040-square-mile (5,282-km²) Sian Ka'an Biosphere Reserve, U.N. World Heritage Site on the Yucatan Peninsula, bounded on one side by pristine beaches, coastal lagoons and 70 miles (113 km) of the world's second longest coral reef and on the other by marshes and dense tropical rain forest, has treasures from both worlds. Pyramids, canals, temples, and entire Mayan cities rise from the jungle at dozens of significant archeological sites.

Manatees, once mistaken by long-at-sea sailors for plump mermaids, loaf in shallows protected by reef homes of spiny lobsters, changeably-hued octopi and dozens of species of bright tropical fish. Endangered green, hawksbill, leatherback, and loggerhead sea turtles lay eggs on white sand beaches. Primitive tapirs, close kin of rhinoceros but looking more like elephants, browse, swim, and forage on aquatic vegetation with their tiny white-striped babies.

Howler monkeys expand furry black throat pouches emitting other-worldly howls.

Prehensile-tailed kinkajous and tribes of 70 or so black-handed spider monkeys compete for the same fruits, screaming shrilly on spotting a puma (or mountain lion) or one of the spotted felines, well concealed by their beautifully patterned fur.

Collared anteaters and peccaries snuffle through understories. Tiny red brocket deer, 14 inches (35 cm) high, forage on savannah grasses. Tayras, alert little South American martens, are omnivorous. So are handsome small pacas—red-and-white patterned beaver-like rodents— among 103 mammal species, the smaller ones prey for ornate hawk eagles.

Flame-feathered flamingos and toucans holding up colorful ponderous-looking bills (actually almost weightless) are among some 350 spectacular bird species, including orioles, tanagers, and other wintering northern songbirds. Iridescent turquoise-browed motmots pluck lacy patterns in tail feathers. Red-crested woodpeckers hammer tree trunks. Pygmy-owls whistle at night.

Thousands of wading birds nest, some on offshore keys, including roseate spoonbills, wood storks, magnificent frigate birds, broad-billed herons, and rare jabiru storks. Great curassows and brilliantly-plumaged ocellated turkeys pick through forest litter.

Sian Ka'an, funded in part by World Wide Fund for Nature, is 85 miles (136 km) south of Cancun. A range of lodging is available nearby.

Threats include plans that have been discussed for an international airport near Tulum, just 10 miles (16 km) from important nesting areas.

---

**FURTHER INFORMATION**

Amigos de Sian Ka'an, Av. Coba #5 (Plaza America Loc 48 y 50, Apartado Postal 770, Cancun 77500, Quintana Roo, Mexico, Tel: (+52) 98-84-95-83, Fax: (+52) 98-87-30-80, E-mail: sian@cancun.com.mx

## ALSO OF INTEREST

Also of interest on the Yucatan Peninsula is **Contoy Island**, a 440-acre (178-ha) Biosphere Reserve off Isla Mujeres, near Cancun, where thousands of migratory birds stop off every year and thousands more nest. The bird list includes masked and brown boobies, sooty and bridled terns, frigate birds, storks, gray and black hawks, yellow-headed vultures, pelicans, pauraques, clapper rails, white-crowned pigeons, and cinnamon and green-breasted mango hummingbirds.

All Yucatan reserves are in easy driving distance from Cancun, served by international airlines. Lodging is available at Cancun, and of a simpler variety, out in the countryside, near (and on) the reserves. Guided trips can be arranged in Cancun, or directions, if driving yourself.

---

**FURTHER INFORMATION**

Pronatura Yucatán, Calle 1-D No. 254-A x 36, Col. Campestre, 97120 Merida, Yucatan, Tel: (+52) 99-44-22-90 and 99-44-35-80, E-mail: ppy@pibil.finred.com.mx

# UNITED
# STATES

MILLIONS OF BIRDS FROM SIX CONTINENTS—
SONGBIRDS, SHOREBIRDS, WATERFOWL—FIND THEIR
WAY EVERY SPRING TO YUKON DELTA, DECKED OUT
IN COURTSHIP PLUMAGE AND FOCUSSED ON A SINGLE
OBJECTIVE: STARTING A NEW GENERATION.

WILDLIFE RESERVES OF THE UNITED STATES EXCEED THOSE OF ANY OTHER COUNTRY IN THE GEO-GRAPHIC SPAN THEY COVER, THE DIVERSITY OF HABITAT THEY PROVIDE, AND THE VARIETY AND NUMBERS OF WILDLIFE THEY PROTECT. Reserves range from the east coast of Maine almost to Siberia, from above the Arctic circle to below the tropic of Cancer in habitats ranging from Alaskan tundra to tropical rain forests and coral reefs.

Alaska is home of the world's two largest land carnivores, where polar bears hunt seals off ice floes and great Kodiak brown bears fatten for winter at streams brimming with millions of spawning salmon.

Monstrous alligators bellow in Florida's EVERGLADES swamps and majestic bald eagles soar over sawgrass expanses where otters play and panthers scream.

Rare, graceful whooping cranes dance on Texas' ARANSAS REFUGE. Elk, timber wolves, and grizzlies coexist in YELLOWSTONE, world's oldest national park. Millions of migratory birds—geese, ducks, and bright small songbirds—move in spring and fall along both coasts and on flyways through the country's midsection.

Despite these reserves, up to a third of these species are at risk from human and environmental pressures—so places such as these are essential.

# ALASKA

## ARCTIC NATIONAL WILDLIFE REFUGE

Alaska's Arctic National Wildlife Refuge is sometimes called "America's Serengeti," northern version. It is one of the world's biggest and northernmost reserves with one of the most spectacular assemblages of arctic plants, animals, and landforms anywhere.

The polar ice pack is always off the coast, even in summer. Permafrost is seldom more than a yard or meter underfoot, and in some places extends some 2,000 feet (610 m) down. Daylight lasts around the clock from May to August. Then it begins to decline to near 24-hour darkness. Winter has a few hours of twilight around noon, otherwise is illuminated only by stars and the northern lights.

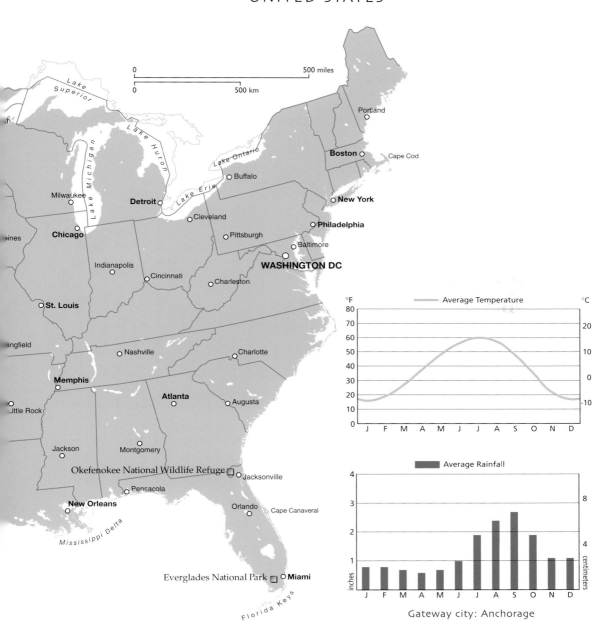

Gateway city: Anchorage

The growing season is so short that many willow trees are only a few feet tall, and most other plants form a carpet a few inches high. But what a carpet!—a mosaic of scarlet bearberries and orange and gold lichens and mosses in fall, of wildflowers (arctic poppies and lupines, pink plumes and lousewort) in spring and summer. Permafrost makes this possible by blocking moisture loss so the ground is soft and spongy, despite low annual precipitation.

Alaskan brown bears, same species as grizzly bears found through Canada and parts of the northern U.S. and Eurasia, reach their largest size in Alaska—world's largest land carnivores, up to 10 feet (3+ m) long, weighing more than a half-ton, with 10x16-inch (25x40 cm) hind pawprints. This is attributed partly to their rich seafood diet there, especially on spawning salmon which swim upstream by the millions as bears are emerging lean and hungry from hibernation. They may consume 35 pounds (16 kg) or more a day, taking advantage of this nourishing fare during its brief abundance.

So harsh yet fragile is this unsparing environment that lichen trodden underfoot may not regrow for a century.

Yet it seems ideal for some. Great flocks of migratory birds—waterfowl, shorebirds, birds of prey from four countries and the South Pacific—come to breed in splendid isolation of the north slope tundra, finding plenty of food for growing young families.

The great Porcupine caribou herd—in a good year 180,000 of them—complete a 2,000-mile (3,300-km) round-trip migration, crossing the river for which they are named to give birth to calves on the northern coastal plain. The young can stand and nurse almost immediately and in 24 hours run after their mothers—important because predators such as bears, wolves, and sometimes golden eagles are watching.

Later they form huge post-calving groups—sometimes tens of thousands grazing on nutritious cotton grass, many by late summer moving south and east to Canada. (Some of the steep inclines they cover suggest it's no wonder their ankle bones click, but the cause is not known.)

Stocky musk oxen, whose survival was once imperiled by their defense tactic of forming outward-facing circles against predators—effective against wolves but not repeating rifles—are doing well after reintroduction a few years ago, their shaggy coats cozy protection against deeply subzero windchills.

Northernmost herds of Dall sheep—whiter than bighorn mountain sheep with thinner horns—leap gracefully about the snowclad Brooks Range, their remarkable eyesight, equivalent to eight-power binoculars, able to spot predators miles away. Where the south slope of the range tapers off to spruce forest, black bears find cover. Moose forage on willow shoots along rivers.

Polar bears stay near sea ice, living off ringed seals, digging dens in snow to give birth to cubs during winter hibernation. Beluga and bowhead whales migrate along the coast. In river deltas and lagoons are 12 species of anadromous fish which spend their lives partly in fresh, partly in salt water.

Grizzly bears and wolves roam almost everywhere on these nearly 31,250 square miles (81,000 km²) of tundra, mountains, forests, marsh, and lakes, bounded by the Arctic Ocean on the north and Canada on the east, which was set aside originally at the urging of a broad spectrum of national and Alaska-based conservation organizations, including a Fairbanks garden club. Favorite spots for the big bears are the lovely Sheenjek and Ignek valleys.

Diminutive, quick arctic foxes are as active in winter as summer but change summer coats of gray-brown or occasionally blue to snow-white. Thickly-furred lynx have large padded feet which support them like snowshoes—as do their prey, snowshoe hares. Fierce wolverines, built like small bears, are as much scavenger as predator, but will take on caribou, moose, and even bears many times their size. They totally consume killed prey with powerful jaws that can crunch even thick bones.

There are 36 species of land mammals here. It is not easy living but with berries and roots and plenty of mice, voles, and arctic ground squirrels for the carnivores, it's possible.

Birds are everywhere during the arctic summer—some 180 species: longspurs, wheatears and gray-crowned rosy finches in alpine tundra; white-winged crossbills on the south slope; and yellow wagtails, hoary redpolls, and arctic warblers in riparian thickets.

Arctic and red-throated loons breed on small lakes. Dippers (aka water ouzels) dive for grayling fry in rocky streams. Formerly endangered peregrine falcons, rough-legged hawks, and golden eagles in their northernmost breeding populations build aeries on cliffs.

# UNITED STATES

OPPOSITE: Dense feathers cover all but sharp, curved claws of snowy owls, maintaining body heat of 100°F (38–40°C) when temperatures plummet in their circumpolar tundra habitat to –60°F (–52°C). Standing 20–27 inches (50–68 cm) with wingspans more than twice that, they locate prey by hearing—stiff feather discs direct faintest sounds to ear openings—plus overlapping binocular vision with light-gathering properties many times that of humans', and flexible necks that swivel for a 270-degree view. Prey varies widely but they rely most on lemmings, especially when nesting, so when these crash every few years, owls temporarily move south.

But probably the most important bird habitat is the lacework strip of marsh, braided streams, and coastal lagoons along the northern coastal plain where 10 major rivers drain into the Arctic Ocean.

Tundra swans, snowy owls, red and northern phalaropes (species whose males do nest duty), and thousands of golden plovers and pectoral and semipalmated sandpipers nest here. Later 40,000 or so oldsquaws molt here, amid a diversity of other migrants—common, king, and spectacled eiders, snow geese, pintails, wigeons, buffleheads, and others.

The Arctic Refuge is one of the largest, northernmost, and most scenically spectacular reserves in the world. Its magnificent vastness can hardly be conveyed—from snowclad 9,000-foot (2,745-m) peaks of the Brooks Range sloping off to spruce forest on one side and treeless tundra on the other, through which 10 major rivers drain into the Arctic Ocean. But it is also fragile and destructible, which is why environmentalists have fought to prevent exploration for oil, which could damage forever an irreplaceable natural heritage.

Best times are mid-June through early August for best weather and best water levels for river-rafting, but July is the top mosquito month, sometimes not bearable without mesh screens. (Snow lasts nearly eight months here, ice is on coastal lagoons until July.)

There are no roads, trails, or lodges. Access is primarily by air. Commercial service is available from Fairbanks to Fort Yukon, Arctic Village, Deadhorse, and Kaktovik, from there by charter for float trips or tenting. Guides and outfitters can be arranged. Refuge staff can be helpful with advice, contacts, and trip-planning information. Plan as far ahead as possible.

Take lots of insect repellent. Boil or treat drinking water. Use the land lightly to avoid permanently marking delicate habitat.

---

**FURTHER INFORMATION**

Refuge Manager, Arctic National Wildlife Refuge, Room 236, Federal Building and Courthouse, 101 Twelfth Avenue, Fairbanks, Alaska 99701, Tel: (+1) 907-456-0250, Fax: (+1) 907-456-0428, E-mail: r7anwr@.fws.gov

# DENALI NATIONAL PARK

Denali National Park in Alaska was created as a sanctuary to protect graceful little Dall mountain sheep from overhunting. It has become world-renowned home for what may be North America's most diverse and highly visible subarctic ecosystem, recognized as a U.N. World Biosphere Reserve.

Caribou, grizzly bears, wolves, golden eagles, and others coexist in this huge, largely undisturbed wilderness at the foot of snowy Mount McKinley, or "Denali" as the native Athabascan Indians call it—"the high one"—highest mountain on the North American continent.

So vast are uninterrupted viewing distances and so clear the fresh northern air that under ideal conditions a dozen or more species and many individuals may appear in one sweeping vista— a scene of unsurpassed natural beauty and drama within hours from Anchorage and Fairbanks.

Caribou, visible a half-mile (0.8 km) away on the permafrost-underlaid tundra, ramble along with ankle bones clicking. They feed on nutritious mosses and lichens, matlike plants designed to survive harsh northern winters. Males and females both grow showy antlers.

Tall scarlet-crowned sandhill cranes stop en route to and from farther north nesting grounds, dancing in anticipation of mating in spring with high bugling cries heard for miles, conversing with new families in lower mutterings in fall.

Golden eagles soar on seven-foot (2+ m) wings over mountain ridgelines striped with well-worn wildlife trails, chittering to one another when bringing food to nestlings with bright chirps more suggestive of small

The power and strength of grizzly or brown bears—the names are interchangeable—are legendary around the world. A first-hand account tells of one "running full-tilt down a mountainside with a 300-pound bighorn sheep in its jaws, the sheep's legs flapping like a man's tie in the wind." Another tells of one killing a large black bear in Yellowstone National Park with a single blow that knocked its victim against a tree five yards away. As if showing the confidence engendered by such power, this mother grizzly lies vulnerably on her side to nurse her cubs.

songbirds than our mightiest avian predators. But arctic ground squirrels know the difference and stop munching grass seeds to tear for cover at the first sign of eagles overhead.

Largest known breeding population of golden eagles in Alaska is here, handy for gyrfalcons which often use old eagle nests rather than build their own. Both they and peregrines are here— no soaring for them, just a breathtaking "what was that?" as they streak across the sky with speed only falcons command.

Nesting sandpipers are invisible among tiny alpine azaleas, Lapland rosebays, and bog rosemarys until, startled, they jump up and run about with anxious musical cheeps. But brightly-patterned harlequin ducks are never unnoticed, bouncing in stream riffles probing for small edible organisms caught there.

Loons summon one another with haunting calls day and night. Boreal and northern hawk-owls whistle in the dark until northern nights grow short or disappear entirely, when they may whistle and hunt any time (the hawk-owl's long slender tail gives it a falcon-like appearance, especially when it hovers).

Dall sheep, the only wild white sheep, snowy cousins to similar Rocky Mountain bighorn sheep, come to drink at brooks but feel more secure on higher slopes. There they nimbly negotiate places less accessible to their predators (but not inaccessible to long-range rifles; their creamy fur and handsome curled horns made them a popular trophy before park establishment).

Shy, half-ton moose, world's largest deer, nibble on alders and pondside willow shoots, wading neck-deep when mosquitoes are fierce, which is at least until mid-July. (Caribou may lose a quart of blood a week to these biting pests.)

Grizzlies nose around for blueberries and bearberries and dig for roots or for an arctic ground squirrel if they can find its hole. A favorite spot for the big bears is Sable Pass.

Beaver dams create ponds where waterfowl gather—though divers like mergansers prefer deep Wonder Lake. White-crowned sparrows sing "Three Blind Mice" and red foxes and occasional tri-colored cross foxes appear anywhere on this national park, bigger than the state of Massachusetts, just 200 miles (320 km) south of the Arctic circle.

Towering over all is majestic Mount McKinley, at 20,320 feet (6,194 m) crown of the 600-mile (965-km) Alaska Range which divides south-central Alaska from the interior plateau. Named after U.S. President William McKinley, it is a mountain so large it creates its own weather systems with storm winds that can gust up to 150 mph (240 kph). Temperatures down to −95°F (−70.5°C) have been recorded, and that not on the summit. Permanent snowfields cover more than half of the mountain and feed still-moving glaciers up to 40 miles (64 km) long at its base.

By one measurement McKinley is the highest mountain in the world: its vertical relief of 18,000 feet (6,200 m) is greater even than Mount Everest.

Best times are June–mid-September. June and post-Labor Day visits avoid bulk of 340,000 yearly visitors. There's comfortable lodging at Denali Park Hotel, just outside park entrance; also lodges at Kantishna, 95 miles (153 km) inside park; seven campgrounds. Reserve ahead. Limited backcountry camping by permit. Other accommodations available just outside park.

Commercial airlines go to Anchorage and Fairbanks. Thence by car the park is 240 miles (386 km) north of Anchorage, 120 miles (193 km) south of Fairbanks, both on Alaska Highway 3. Regular busses, trains go in summer, weekend trains only in winter—or air charter to park airstrip. In the park, shuttle-busses and guided tour busses travel the 87-mile (140 km) park road, mostly closed to private vehicles except briefly after Labor Day. Mountain-climbers need permits.

Problems include merlin nest failures from thinning eggshells and tests showing pesticide residues believed from Latin American wintering grounds. Still controversial are recreational snowmobiling, hunting and trapping rights granted to non-natives, both with/without snow-mobiles; active mining claims and recreational gold panning.

---

**FURTHER INFORMATION**

Denali National Park and Preserve, P.O. Box 9, Denali Park, Alaska 99755, Tel: (+1) 907-683-2294.

---

# KATMAI NATIONAL PARK

Great, powerful Alaskan brown bears gather sometimes in the thousands in Katmai National Park on the Alaskan Peninsula to breed, hibernate, and in summer and fall to feed and fatten on salmon spawning by the millions in rushing streams of this stunning pristine wilderness.

It is the largest protected population anywhere of these titans among terrestrial carnivores. They are larger here—many well over a half-ton (500 kg)—because of rich seafood diets, not only salmon but clams, crabs and occasional whale carcasses along the rugged 480-mile (775-km) Katmai coast.

At home as well against this dazzling backdrop of snowy mountains, green glacial-hewn valleys, and deep blue lakes are beaver, moose, caribou, wolves, lynx, snowshoe rabbits and, among birds, tundra swans, black-billed magpies, ravens, seasonally great flocks of ducks and shorebirds, and majestic bald eagles. Five species of salmon breed as do supersized rainbow and lake trout, arctic char, grayling.

Katmai's more than 6,250 square miles (16,000+ km²) was set aside originally to preserve the famed 40-square-mile (103-km²) Valley of 10,000 Smokes, fumaroles left after ash was deposited 100 to 700 feet deep (30–210 m) in the June 6–9, 1912 eruption of Novarupta, called the most explosive event of the 20th century. At least 14 volcanoes remain active though none currently in eruption beyond an occasional steam plume.

Archeologists in the interior of the park have found remains of North America's highest concentration of prehistoric human dwellings, nomadic hunters' camps 9,000 years old.

The park is open all year but Brooks Camp, most popular destination, only June 1–September 17. Park office is in King Salmon, 290 spectacular air miles (467 km) southwest of Anchorage (there is no road access). From there transport to Brooks, also two other park lodges, can be arranged by air or boat. Weather can be extremely changeable, cool even in summer. There's one campsite; hiking trails; bear-viewing platforms; fishing with strict catch-and-release and bag limits; backpacking by permit.

In all activities visitors are cautioned: Katmai is prime bear habitat.

**FURTHER INFORMATION**

Katmai National Park, P.O. Box 7, King Salmon, Alaska 99613, Tel: (+1) 907-246-3305.

# KODIAK ISLAND NATIONAL WILDLIFE REFUGE

The world's densest population of one of the world's largest land carnivores is on ruggedly beautiful Kodiak Island National Wildlife Refuge, called Alaska's Emerald Isle, said to be as green as anyplace on earth. Along with huge Kodiak bears—largest subspecies of the brown or grizzly—are hundreds of majestic bald eagles flourishing in a northern ecosystem rivaling in splendor and abundance that of the tropics. Reindeer graze with Sitka black-tailed deer, snowshoe hares, mountain goats, beavers, and more than 200 kinds of birds, land-based as well as oceanic.

Pacific salmon of five species—pink, sockeye, coho, king, chum—return in waves of hundreds of thousands to spawn in lakes and streams brimming from June to October, furnishing rich diets to present and future generations.

Dozens of the 2,700 bears on the refuge may gather along a few miles of streambed during peak runs, upright males standing nine feet (3 m) tall and weighing 1,400 pounds (635 kg). More than 200 pairs of majestic bald eagles nest here and bring the fall population up to 1,000 or so.

Playful otters and weasels den under refuge cabins. Foxes often are the handsome silver and multihued "cross" color phases of the red.

Whales, porpoises, sea otters, seals, and Steller's sea lions feed in estuaries with (and sometimes on) tens of thousands of seabirds which return in spring to nest on shores and cliffs of nearby islands—sooty and short-tailed shearwaters, pelagic and red-faced cormorants, black-legged kittiwakes, murres, pigeon guillemots, and horned and tufted puffins.

Tundra swans and goshawks nest. So, commonly, do black oystercatchers, surfbirds, glaucous-winged gulls, marbled murrelets, lapland longspurs, snow buntings, and willow and rock ptarmigans. Some of these are year-round residents.

Hardier species leave to nest farther north—many in YUKON DELTA (*see* p.472)—and return for the winter, well over a million birds including debonair oldsquaws, Steller's eiders, white-winged and surf scoters, and emperor geese.

Wildflowers are abundant in this mild, moist climate where temperatures seldom fall to 0°F (−17°C) in winter and only rarely rise to 80°F (27°C) in summer—orchids, irises, fields of fireweed, shooting stars, Indian paintbrush, with thousands of fruiting salmonberries, elderberries, blueberries, against a backdrop of 4,000-foot (1,220-m) mountains, hundreds of lakes and 800

Graceful, frolicsome river otters spend a third of their time in water, muscular, torpedo-shaped bodies protected by coarse guard hairs over dense undercoats that keep them snug and waterproof in all seasons. Small ears and nostrils automatically close and pulse slows to a tenth of normal 170 beats a minute to conserve oxygen so they can stay under more than four minutes at depths of 60 feet (18 m) or more. Britain's King James I kept a pack of tame otters to catch fish for his table. However, studies show they catch mainly non-game fish, thereby strengthening game fish stocks. Found in well-watered habitat north of Mexico.

miles (1,290 km) of dramatic fiordlike inlets. Afognak Island on the northwest corner has dense stands of virgin Sitka spruce forest.

To get there, fly to Kodiak from Anchorage or take a ferry from Seward or Homer. Visitor center is on the airport road to the town of Kodiak where there are motels, rental cars, charter planes, and boats for hire. Cabins can be reserved (plan well ahead) on refuge and in nearby **Fort Abercrombie State Park**. There are bear-viewing platforms.

CAUTION: Hiking is not easy nor facilities plush. Take raingear and hipboots. Kodiak is wet, wonderful and much of it as wild as when Russian explorer Vitus Bering sailed by in 1741 without noticing it in the fog.

**FURTHER INFORMATION**

Kodiak National Wildlife Refuge, 1390 Buskin River Road, Kodiak, Alaska 99615, Tel: (+1) 907-487-2600, Fax: (+1) 907-487-2144, E-mail: r7kodwr@fws.gov

# YUKON DELTA NATIONAL WILDLIFE REFUGE

Millions of birds from six continents find their way to Alaska's Yukon Delta National Wildlife Refuge every spring. They come to this vast coastal plain to raise families on these 40,625 square miles (105,250 km²) of lakes, ponds, and streams—one of the wildest, largest, most isolated wildlife reserves in the world.

It is an extraordinary sight, the air literally filled with flying, calling birds—waterfowl, shore-birds, and passerines—all in handsome breeding plumage for courtship, mating, and family duties in the safety of this ecosystem teeming with fish and insectivorous food for nestlings. All this must be accomplished during the short arctic summer between June ice-breakup and early fall, August or September at the latest.

Golden plovers, bar-tailed godwits, and rare bristle-thighed curlews arrive after non-stop flights of 2,000 miles (3,225 km) or more over open ocean from islands throughout the South Pacific, some from Australia. Whimbrels, black-bellied plovers, surfbirds, black turnstones, dunlins, and rock, least, and western sandpipers travel along the Pacific Coast; solitary, pectoral, and semi-palmated sandpipers take inland routes from as far south as Cape Horn or Tierra del Fuego.

Eighty percent of the world's emperor geese are here, and most of the tundra swans of both Pacific and Atlantic flyways. Arctic terns fly up to 22,000 miles (35,400 km) round-trip—longest migratory journey of any creature.

No other area of similar size may be so critically important to survival of so many kinds of water-oriented birds.

Small birds find their own places—redpolls, snow buntings, Lapland longspurs, savannah, tree, and fox sparrows, gray-cheeked thrushes with Asian visitors such as arctic warblers, northern wheatears, and yellow wagtails. Fierce raptors include golden eagles, rough-legged hawks, and gyrfalcons. There are long-tailed and parasitic jaegers, Pacific and red-throated loons—altogether 145 breeding bird species.

Huge numbers of fish as well—from fingerlings to enormous Dolly Vardens, grayling, burbot, whitefish, northern pike—inhabit every body of water. Millions of salmon swim up the Yukon and Kuskokwim rivers to spawn—chinook (king), coho, sockeye, chum, and pink—and beluga whales and occasional walruses come up rivers in early spring.

Mountains on the east side of the refuge rise to 2,000 feet (615 m). Almost all Alaska's land mammals are there—black and brown bears, moose, caribou, red and arctic foxes, timber and arctic wolves, wolverines, otters, mink, muskrat, tundra hares.

But birds own this refuge, its fragile habitat uniquely suited to their needs.

Visits are not easy to arrange. Trips should be planned well in advance and checked with refuge headquarters in Bethel, reachable by commercial air from Anchorage. Bethel has lodging

Gray foxes are only member of the canid or dog family that can climb trees. Strong hooked claws and short powerful legs enable them to scramble up trees and leap agilely from limb to limb, catching squirrels, raiding birds' nests, dining on ripe fruit—they are omnivorous—sometimes dropping on small animal prey from above, if necessary pursuing them at speeds up to 28 miles an hour (45 kph). They range over broadleaf woodlands and rocky or brushy areas from southern Canada to northern South America. Cubs are born in underground dens or rock crevices, sometimes in trees, and are able to hunt on their own at four months.

and it's possible to charter flights over the refuge, arrange to be put down for a week's camping and picked up later—restricted tent camping sometimes permitted—or ride with a scheduled mail plane to an Inuit village where guides may be available.

Best time is June but weather can be rainy, overcast, and windy, anytime. Warm clothing is always prudent; hip boots useful almost everyplace.

Nunivak Island, 1,719-square-mile (4,450-km²) unit of Yukon Delta 20 miles (32 km) located west of the Alaskan coast in the Bering Sea, is main home today of great, shaggy Alaskan musk-oxen which once roamed over much of Asia and North America. Musk-oxens' historic defense—forming a circle with massive horns pointed outward—was effective against wolves but no match for repeating rifles and, by 1920, indiscriminate slaughter had decimated their numbers. Protection here has stabilized them and some have been taken to restart nucleus herds elsewhere.

These bulky animals are not easy to see even here though they stand four feet (1.2 m) high at the shoulder with long fur draped almost to their feet, since they can space themselves widely over this large tract. But Nunivak is a fascinating island in any case, with a large reindeer herd and some of the world's largest seabird nesting colonies for kittiwakes, murres, pelagic cormorants, horned and tufted puffins, parakeet and crested auklets, and pigeon guillemots as well as songbirds, including rare McKay's buntings, winter visitors which nest only on Bering Sea islands.

Restricted tent camping is permitted and it is sometimes possible to stay with local families. Best way is to fly to Mekoryuk, Nunivak's only village, and hike out from there or arrange to go by boat (a somewhat hazardous trip) in summer or by snowmobile in winter (it's cold then but often bright and beautiful). In any case, visits should be planned as far ahead as possible in consultation with refuge staff.

### FURTHER INFORMATION

Yukon Delta, NWR P.O. Box 346, Bethel, Alaska 99559, Tel: (+1) 907-543-3151, Fax: (+1) 907-543-4413, E-mail: r7ydnwr@fws.gov

Minks' high-energy, nervous dispositions are such they appear always on the verge either of departing at top speed or pouncing on some luckless victim. Voracious killers, they eat everything they kill and kill almost anything up to and including (sometimes exceeding) hares—fish, frogs, clams, snakes, rats, squirrels, muskrats, birds—all go to nourish a rich brown fur world-renowned for its beauty. North American mink range along watercourses across the continent. European mink, slightly smaller, usually with white patches on upper lip, historically ranged through Europe east into Russia. However, naturalized American mink, fur farm escapees, in some places have supplanted European mink.

# WESTERN STATES

Gateway city: Denver

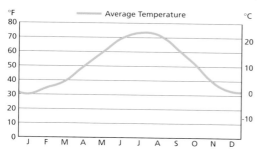

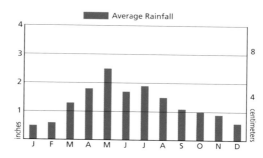

## ARANSAS NATIONAL WILDLIFE REFUGE (TEXAS)

Whooping cranes, regal, scarlet-crowned, one of the world's most beautiful and endangered birds, came back from the brink of extinction at Aransas National Wildlife Refuge on the Texas Gulf Coast, where they make winter homes. Tallest North American birds, standing five feet (1.5 m) tall with snowy black-tipped seven-foot (2-m) wingspans, their population was down to 15 in 1941. With discovery in 1954 of their nest site in Canada's WOOD BUFFALO NATIONAL PARK (*see* p.447) and publicity and protection along their hazardous 2,600-mile (4,300-km) migration route, their numbers have gradually risen to around 190 birds in the Aransas/Wood Buffalo flock.

Hazards continue, including the ever-present possibility of a disastrous oil or chemical spill from barges plying waters just off marshes where the birds feed from October to May, as well as increasing demand by upstream users for freshwater vital to the bay ecosystem surrounding the refuge.

Much else is at stake as well at this 180-square-mile (466-km²) barrier island and coastal wetland 85 miles (142 km) from Corpus Christi, including more than 394 bird species—second-most of any U.S. National Wildlife Refuge. These include dazzling roseate spoonbills, scissor-tailed flycatchers, wood storks, pelicans, 10 heron and egret species, white-tailed hawks and 15 other raptors, avocets, long-billed curlews, waterfowl, bright painted and indigo buntings, 25 or so warbler species—sometimes in great numbers—and, among mammals, graceful white-tailed deer, mountain lions, peccaries, armadillos, alligators, coyotes, and bobcats.

For birders, Aransas is part of a spectrum of outstanding birding places along the Texas Gulf Coast, for which literature is available.

**FURTHER INFORMATION**

Aransas National Wildlife, P.O. Box 100, Austwell, Texas 77950, Tel: (+1) 512-286-3559, Fax: (+1) 512-286-3722, E-mail: 2rw_ar@mail.fws.gov

# BEAR RIVER NATIONAL WILDLIFE REFUGE (UTAH)

The explorer Captain Howard Stansbury said in 1849 of the place where Bear River National Wildlife Refuge now is, "I have seen large flocks of birds before—but never did I behold anything like the immense numbers here congregated together…as far as the eye could see."

In the mid 1980s neighboring Great Salt Lake rose after record snowmelt and flooded this 116-square-mile (300-km²) Utah refuge of upland, shallow marsh and mudflats with salty water that destroyed much of its habitat. Clean-up efforts and replanting are beginning to pay off. Large numbers of birds are beginning to return.

Sometimes in spring and fall migration, millions of birds of more than 200 species have been here—thousands of golden-tufted eared grebes, a half-million swallows in a great windborne cloud, hundreds of marbled godwits and long-billed dowitchers. There can be 20,000 tundra swans, largest concentrations anywhere, and a half-million or more ducks flying up against the snowy Wasatch Range and blue Promontory Mountains.

In spring the dikes can be alive with killdeer doing "broken-wing" acts to distract attention from nests, and thousands of black-necked stilts and russet-hooded avocets with young families. White pelicans commute to nesting islands in the Great Salt Lake. Young western grebes ride atop their parents' backs.

Visitor facilities are in process of reconstruction but a 12-mile (19-km) auto tour route is open mid-March through December.

> **FURTHER INFORMATION**
>
> Bear River Migratory Bird Refuge, 58 South 950 West, Brigham City, Utah 84302,
> Tel: (+1) 435-723-5887, Fax: (+1) 435-723-8873, E-mail: r6rw_brr@mail.fws.gov

# BOSQUE DEL APACHE NATIONAL WILDLIFE REFUGE (NEW MEXICO)

Bosque Del Apache—"Woods of the Apache," named for Indians who once camped in the shade of cottonwoods along the Rio Grande in New Mexico—has been called the most spectacularly situated wildlife refuge in the lower 48 states. One can see why on a fall or winter day here with some 100,000 birds in the air at once—stately sandhill cranes with seven-foot (2.1-m) wingspreads, snow geese, and waterfowl of a dozen other species—calling to one another overhead, flying out to feed in a rosy dawn and back to nightly roosts against a dramatic backdrop of scenic mountains silhouetted by a crimson sunset.

A few rare whooping cranes may be with them. In summer nighthawks swirl around for insects. On the ground are roadrunners, strutting wild turkeys, and cackling white-winged pheasants.

Porcupines doze in tree forks. Beavers nibble saplings. Mule deer browse. Coyotes look for unwary geese but may settle for field mice. Less conspicuous among 75 resident mammals are badgers, bobcats, and mountain lions.

Birders usually see new species: lark sparrows, blue and black-headed grosbeaks, Chihuahuan ravens, neotropic cormorants, black-chinned hummingbirds or other uncommon varieties among the 325+ species on this 89-square-mile (232-km²) refuge of flooded marsh, desert, mountains, woods, and grassland along the Rio Grande 93 miles (150 km) south of Albuquerque, New Mexico. Late fall to winter is the best time but all year is interesting, especially in spring when thousands of colorful songbirds "fall out" to rest and feed on their trip north.

---

**FURTHER INFORMATION**

Bosque del Apache National Wildlife Refuge, P.O. Box 1246, Socorro, New Mexico 87801, Tel: (+1) 505-835-12828, Fax: (+1) 505-835-0314, E-mail: r2rw_bda@mail.fws.gov

---

# GLACIER-WATERTON LAKES INTERNATIONAL PEACE PARK (MONTANA)

Two magnificent reserves on the western U.S.–Canadian border combine to make up Glacier-Waterton Lakes International Peace Park with stunning wildlife and scenery in near-total wilderness. It is one of the continent's largest most intact ecosystems, much of it undisturbed by almost two million visitors annually.

Hulking grizzly bears survive unmolested here. Once 10,000 roamed over the western U.S. and Canada. They were largely exterminated along with gray wolves because their presence seemed incompatible with humans, but with protection, populations gradually rebounded. Discussion arose in the early 1980s on the wisdom of reintroducing wolves, which had been completely wiped out—more than 80,000 shot, trapped and poisoned between 1883 and 1918—to restore a full, healthy Glacier ecosystem. Wolves settled the question by reintroducing themselves, walking over the international border in 1985. They are readily at home in these northern climes—wolves can sleep comfortably in the open at –40°F (–40°C).

Wildlife now moves freely between the two parks which were established in 1932 as the world's first International Peace Park, joining Glacier National Park in the U.S. and Waterton Lakes in Canada. A joint U.N. World Heritage Site, they share aims and an ecosystem and are administered separately but cooperatively.

Mountain goats, bighorn sheep, bears, coyotes, and mountain lions are at home in both, along with black bears, badgers, snowshoe hares, mink, martens—even a few lynx, wolverines, and fishers—and 250 kinds of birds, including both bald and golden eagles.

Bighorn sheep are known for dramatic head-to-head clashes between males in which rams equipped with curled horns weighing 30 pounds or more (14 kg) crash into rivals at speeds up to 20 miles an hour (32 kph) for 24 hours or more, ending when one ram concedes. To protect themselves in these duels males have evolved double-layered skulls supported by bony struts plus massive tendons linking skulls to spines to help heads pivot and recoil from blows. Shock-absorbing elastic pads enable them to leap 20 feet (6 m) or so along rocky ledges just two inches (5 cm) wide. Once numerous in the American west, they are now endangered victims of human activities such as overhunting, trophy collection, and depletion of water holes.

Elk with antlers spreading five feet or more (1.5+ m) graze the meadows, along with more delicate mule and white-tailed deer. Shy half-ton moose prefer marshes and edges of hundreds of jewel-like lakes.

The highway through Glacier has been called the most spectacular 50-mile drive in the world, and most visitors travel it more than once, seeing different wildlife and vistas every time. Much of the rest of the combined Glacier-Waterton Lakes 1,802 square miles (4,667 km²) remains a wilderness solitude for animals, the more than 900 miles (1,500 km) of trails traversed by relatively few hikers and backpackers. They can find the splendid solitude that moved naturalist John Muir a century ago to say that time spent in Glacier "will not be taken from the sum of your life. It will indefinitely lengthen it, making you in that way truly immortal."

Glacier National Park is the third largest U.S. national park, 1,600 square miles (4,144 km²) in northwestern Montana, with stunning Rocky Mountain scenery. Grandeur of 10,466-foot (3,220-m) glacier-scoured Mount Cleveland descends to deep woods, cascading waterfalls and wildflower-strewn valley meadows, with elk, moose, grizzly and black bears, and smaller golden-mantled ground squirrels, pine martens, badgers, and coyotes. Higher elevations are home to mountain goats and bighorn sheep, wolverines, lynx, mountain lions and, rarely, gray wolves—altogether some 60 mammal species. Bald and golden eagles—altogether more than 250 bird species—soar overhead. In woods are pine siskins, flickers, red-naped sapsuckers, Clark's nutcrackers, and Steller's jays which join picnics. Water ouzels (aka dippers) forage on stream bottoms. More than 400 glaciers cling to high mountain cirques.

Best times are mid-May–September—best weather, most visible wildlife, most park facilities available. Temperatures range from hot in low valleys in midsummer to windy and bitterly cold with snow anytime at high elevations—a foot (30 cm) fell in August, 1992. Five lodges and hotels include two historic chalets (recently under reconstruction) with many campgrounds in the park. Glacier is open all year but only limited facilities are available off-season.

To get there, drive to park entrances on U.S. Highway 2 from east or west—or Amtrak trains stop at East Glacier and Belton (West Glacier). In the park drive the Going-to-the-Sun road (size limits on large vehicles). Glacier also has bus tours, boat transport to glaciers and trails, 900 miles (1,500 km) of foot trails, backpacking; river-rafting. Snowshoeing in winter.

Nearest airports are in Kalispell and Great Falls, Montana, also Glacier International Airport, halfway between, 30 miles (48 km) southwest. Car rentals are available.

---

**FURTHER INFORMATION**

Superintendent, Glacier National Park, National Park Service,
P.O. Box 128, West Glacier, Montana 59936, Tel: (+1) 406-888-7800.

OPPOSITE: Few animals have survived more human persecution than coyotes—everything from flame-throwers to strychnine—because of real or imagined encroachment on human activities. Such is the adaptability and resourcefulness of these keen-sensed "little wolves," that they can run almost 40 miles an hour (64 kph), eat anything from small mammals, insects, reptiles, to fruits, berries and carrion, and breed with both domestic dogs and wolves. They not only have survived persecution, but extended their range over much of North America from eastern Alaska and New England, south through Mexico and Panama.

**Waterton Lakes International Peace Park**, 200 square miles (525 km²) adjoining Glacier north of the U.S.–Canadian border, has nine inns/lodges/hotels in or close by, including magnificent but aging Prince of Wales Hotel; also three campgrounds.

Nearest airport is at Lethbridge, 90 miles (128 km) northeast, about 1.5-hour drive to park, approachable from the east by Provincial Road 6; from U.S. by US 89 to State/Provincial Road 17, known as Chief Mountain International Highway, linking the two parks (visitors may need a visa, passport, or driver's license to enter from U.S.). See the park by horseback, boat, hiking trails, or driving tours on Chief Mountain Highway, Red Rock and Alkamine Parkways. More than 114 miles (183 km) of backcountry trails.

---

**FURTHER INFORMATION**

Superintendent, Waterton Lakes International Peace Park, AB T0K 2M0, Canada, Tel: (+1) 403-859-2224.

---

# GRAND TETON NATIONAL PARK (WYOMING)

Grand Teton National Park in Wyoming may be the most scenically spectacular national park in the lower U.S.—a magnificent 40-mile (64-km) stretch of snowy glacier-strewn peaks rising abruptly to 7,500 feet (2,287 m) off the valley floor. Much of the same wildlife as in neighboring Yellowstone find welcoming habitat here ranging from lush marsh to desert to alpine peaks. Wildflowers display in brilliant sweeps at all levels and in most seasons—sagebrush buttercups, scarlet skyrocket gilia, Engelmann asters, alpine sunflowers and forget-me-nots, purple larkspur, lupines, fireweed, Indian paintbrush.

Elk and mule deer graze. Eagles scream and sometimes dive on ospreys to steal their fish. Trumpeter swans, world's largest waterfowl, carry young cygnets on their backs. River otters scoop trout from rushing eddies along the Snake River.

Mountain bluebirds pluck insects from grassy fields also favored by sage grouse and stately sandhill cranes. Dippers, America's only aquatic songbirds, dive to clear-stream bottoms, wings propelling them to underwater prey.

# UNITED STATES

But it is the visual power of the jagged, dramatic Teton Range (many peaks more than 12,000 feet/3,650 m high) seen from almost every part of this 485 square miles (1,256 km²) in north-western Wyoming that is forever memorable.

It almost failed to become a national park. Local ranchers opposed it as a government takeover. John D. Rockefeller, Jr. quietly bought private tracts, assembling some 52 square miles (134 km²) which he planned to give to the National Park Service. Local resentment to "outside interests" prevented its acceptance until President Franklin D. Roosevelt declared parts of Jackson Hole a national monument in 1943. Resulting tourist dollars quickly melted opposition.

Now more than 300 kinds of animals and 700 plant types find homes here, sharing water-ways with eared grebes, Barrow's goldeneyes, buffleheads, redhead and ring-necked ducks, green-winged and blue-winged teals. Canada geese swap young—some pairs, more parentally-inclined, take over others' broods and may care for 35 goslings in one family.

Bright songbirds include western tanagers, pine grosbeaks, warbling vireos, Steller's jays, raucous black-billed magpies, redpolls, MacGillivray's warblers, and sociable Clark's nutcrackers.

Bighorn sheep spring lightly about upper slopes where tiny pikas gather grass for winter food supplies. Swift pronghorns watch for danger on Antelope Flat with wide-placed eyes covering 360 degrees at a glance. Beaver dens on rivers create willow marshes for moose. Coyotes accommodate themselves to all habitats except extreme high elevations—and occasionally are found even there.

Elk, which summer in surrounding high country, come down to spend winters in National Elk Refuge just north of Jackson.

All year is interesting. July–August can be crowded, less so in cooler September–October. Winter is spectacular but can be cold, stormy, some roads closed (Moose Visitor Center open all year, also main road US 26/89/191). The park has comfortable lodges, cabins, campgrounds (some close seasonally Oct. 1; reserve well ahead); also some nearby outside the park.

Scheduled air goes to Jackson Hole; from there take US 89/191/26 to south entrance; from Yellowstone take the scenic highway through John D. Rockefeller, Jr. Memorial Parkway to the north boundary. East entrance is on US 287/26. Good roads; also 200+ miles (320+ km) of trails in park (permits needed for overnight). Hikers are warned of treacherous ice and snow, even in summer. Most trails start at 6,800 feet (2,074 m)—high enough for shortness of breath.

Compromises had to be made in park establishment, resulting in many inholdings, contin-ued grazing, water draw-downs of Jackson Hole for irrigation. This is the only U.S. national park permitting hunting, also with a commercial airport.

| FURTHER INFORMATION |
| --- |

Grand Teton National Park, P.O. Drawer 170, Moose, Wyoming 83012, Tel: (+1) 307-739-3300.

Several other refuges are nearby:

**National Elk Wildlife Refuge**, adjacent southeast of Grand Teton; established to replace historic elk wintering grounds displaced by ranches and residential development. The world's largest wintering elk herd—up to 10,000—come down from high country to spend cold months here.

**Red Rock Lakes National Wildlife Refuge**, 50 miles (80 km) west of Yellowstone, with trumpeter swans, nesting bald and golden eagles, sandhill cranes, moose, elk, stunning scenery.

# OLYMPIC NATIONAL PARK (WASHINGTON)

Olympic National Park and its surrounding buffer zones make up most of the extraordinarily diverse Olympic Peninsula in Washington, almost one million acres (400,000 ha) in the northwest U.S. corner just south of Canada. It is one of the most varied ecosystems in the lower U.S., a largely pristine U.N. World Heritage Site and Biosphere Reserve where up to 200 inches (510 cm) of rain every year drenches North America's only temperate rain forest. Mostly remote and roadless, almost everything the eye falls on is bright green—gigantic virgin Sitka spruce and western hemlocks 300 feet (100 m) tall and 25 feet (8 m) around, draped with mosses, ferns, lichens, and epiphytes, under a canopy so thick that winter's snow never reaches the ground.

The park includes snow-capped mountains, glaciers, and fragile alpine meadows dotted with wildflowers and over 60 miles (100 km) of primitive Pacific seacoast, rugged, surf-torn, often fog-shrouded, marked with majestic arches and sea stacks, myriad-hued sands strewn with driftwood and tidal pools teeming with marine life, patrolled by black oystercatchers and bald eagles.

Olympic has 12 major rivers, 200 streams, and a lake over 600 feet (200 m) deep. Thick vegetation along 600 miles (1,000 km) of hiking trails makes most wildlife except black-tailed deer difficult to see. Yet black bears, bobcats, mountain lions, river otters, brilliant harlequin ducks, and the large Roosevelt elk for which Olympic was set aside, all are here. Altogether there are 70 mammal species, 300 kinds of birds, and over 1,200 higher plants, some of which exist only on the Olympic Peninsula. Best times are summer through early October.

---

**FURTHER INFORMATION**

Olympic National Park, 600 East Park Avenue, Port Angeles, WA 98362, Tel: (+1) 360-452-0330.

---

# C. M. RUSSELL NATIONAL WILDLIFE REFUGE (MONTANA)

The sweep of America's west along the Missouri River "breaks" with their abundant wildlife is the site of C. M. Russell National Wildlife Refuge, some of which appears today almost as when first viewed by the explorers Lewis and Clark in 1805.

Prairie dogs may have most sophisticated of all animal languages, recent studies suggest, able, for example, to communicate warning calls specifically identifying at least eight different predators. These intelligent ground squirrels—unrelated to dogs—construct complicated burrows extending 100 feet (30 m) or more. Their colonies or "towns" historically spread over much of the western U.S. One, in Texas, covered 25,000 square miles (65,000 km²) and housed some 400 million "dogs." They have been widely eradicated due to claims—unjustified by some views—that they destroy grazing range, and are being considered for threatened status.

## UNITED STATES

A cow elk grazes with her calf on river-bottom grasses. White-tailed deer forage on skunkbrush sumac. A mule deer finds shade under a juniper. Fluffy Canada goslings toddle after stately parents.

Bull elk "bugle" and challenge one another with antlers spreading five feet (1.5 m) and more.

Sage and sharp-tailed grouse inflate gold and lavender throat sacs and stamp the ground at dawn on traditional spring courtship dancing "leks."

Sturdy pronghorn antelopes hurtle across grasslands at speeds clocked up to 70 miles an hour (117 kph), fastest and keenest-sighted North American mammal, with protruding eyes that see both forward and backward and discern small moving objects four miles (6+ km) away. Bighorn sheep clamber up rocks.

Prairie dog "towns" cover thousands of acres, a whole interlocking ecosystem shared with burrowing owls, desert cottontail rabbits, rattlesnakes, and now black-footed ferrets, highly endangered but successfully reintroduced here. Mountain plovers use the gravelly substrate around the burrows as nest sites.

Preying on the frolicsome little "dogs" along with the ferrets are coyotes, badgers, bobcats, and a whole range of raptors including golden eagles and ferruginous hawks. One golden eagle family grew up in a cottonwood tree a quarter mile (0.4 km) from a "dog-town" where an eagle parent went daily for dinner as to a neighborhood supermarket.

Some 45 species of mammals share these 1,720 square miles (4,453 km$^2$) in north-central Montana with 240 bird species as well as reptiles, plants, and fossil remains of *Tyrannosaurus Rex* dinosaurs which once lived here.

Raptors are attracted to this wild area—swift prairie falcons, merlins, kestrels, red-tailed and rough-legged hawks, and five kinds of owls. Short-eared owls hunt the grasslands on fall afternoons. Snowy owls can be seen in winter.

White pelicans and 20 waterfowl species stop in migration and some stay to nest along with great blue herons, ospreys, endangered piping plovers and least terns, and attractive mountain and western bluebirds, lark buntings, horned larks, and Bohemian waxwings.

Paddlefish, strange ancient creatures with no true bones, grow to around 140 pounds and more (63+ kg).

This wild western refuge, named after the revered cowboy artist who, uninstructed, magnificently painted life here in the last century, still is not fully explored. Visitors today can take the winding 20-mile (37-km) auto-tour route or hike less-traveled trails, camping by the same streams Lewis and Clark did in a wilderness so vast and rugged that Clark said "I do not think it will ever be settled," a prediction that fortunately proved correct.

Best times to visit are late spring and fall. Motels are in nearby Jordan, Fort Peck, Glasgow, Malta, Lewiston. Camping is permitted everywhere.

**FURTHER INFORMATION**

Charles M. Russell National Wildlife Refuge, P.O. Box 110, Lewiston, Montana 59457,
Tel: (+1) 406-538-8706, Fax: (+1) 406-538-7521, E-mail: r6rw_cmr@fws.gov

# YELLOWSTONE NATIONAL PARK (WYOMING)

Yellowstone National Park, named for brilliantly mineralized cliffs along the Yellowstone River, is the world's oldest national park and many feel its most splendid.

Buffalo roam here and deer and antelope play as in America's old west, against extraordinary scenery, amid more boiling-hot springs and spectacular geysers than are in all the rest of the world combined.

About 300 huge, lumbering endangered grizzly bears (dangerous themselves if crossed) forage for berries and nuts and dig winter dens on these 3,472 square miles (8,987 km²) of forest, grassland, meadows, lakes, streams, and the extraordinary "Grand Canyon" of the Yellowstone River, located in adjoining portions of three western states of Wyoming, Montana, and Idaho.

Thousands of elk grow five-foot (1.5-m) antlers every fall and "bugle" for mates through yard-long windpipes, resounding for miles. This is one of the places where bison—now 2,000 here—were brought back after indiscriminate killing reduced them from an estimated 60 million, most numerous hoofed animal the world has known, to a scattered few.

There are mountain lions; shy, half-ton (up to 450 kg) moose standing seven feet (2+ m) high at the shoulder; swift pronghorn antelopes—fastest animal in North America, clocked at up to 70 miles an hour (113 kph)—as well as black bears, bighorn sheep, big-eared blacktail or mule deer, and now, in a conservation success, gray wolves, reintroduced after ill-conceived management practices exterminated them, and so far doing well (mistaken sometimes for coyote look-alikes pouncing on rodents around Mammoth Hot Springs).

Trumpeter swans, world's largest waterfowl, once thought to be extinct—snowy white, up to 34 pounds (15.5 kg)—float serenely along the Madison River, honking occasionally, sounding, some say, like a French taxi horn. Flocks of white pelicans soar in summer on nine-foot (2.7-m)

OPPOSITE: Mule deer are named for their remarkable ears, nearly a foot long and half-foot wide (30 × 15 cm) which move constantly and independently, working like dish antennae, gathering even faint sounds, helping them detect predators at great distances. They may then perform a stiff-legged bound called "stotting," bringing all four feet off the air simultaneously in a pogo stick-like leap up to eight feet (2.4m) high for an elevated view of terrain. They can turn bodies completely around in mid-air and start off "stotting" in the opposite direction in great bounds up to 28 feet (9 m) long reaching speeds of 45 miles an hour (72 kph). Mule deer are found throughout the western United States.

wingspreads over Yellowstone Lake where they nest. The bird list of 290 species includes dippers, small songbirds that forage underwater in mountain streams, warbling vireos, pine grosbeaks, Barrow's goldeneye ducks, and both bald and golden eagles. Gray jays and Clark's nutcrackers try to panhandle picnickers, though feeding them or any other wildlife is prohibited.

When early explorers and fur trappers sent back stories of huge numbers of animals, spectacular scenery, and boiling cauldrons here, no one believed them. "Jim Bridger's lies," they said. Finally a government-appointed group went out and found it was all true—and still is.

Porcupines cannot throw their 30,000 quills, as sometimes said, but it can seem they do, so easily do these needle-sharp modified hairs detach at a predator's touch. Loosely attached to a layer of voluntary muscles, they drive forcefully into an adversary's skin, where body heat causes microscopic barbs to expand and become embedded. Wounds may fester and cause death or blindness in a vital place or starvation if driven into the mouth. But their fatty flesh makes them a tempting quarry, and some, especially fishers, have learned to flip them over to get at unprotected undersides. But even fishers can suffer fatal injury. Found in wooded or scrubby areas through Canada and northern U.S., south in the west to Mexico.

Besides finding what is still the continent's largest and most varied large mammal population and a glorious birdlife, they found 10,000 thermal features, including fumaroles, mudpots, and geysers spewing hot water hundreds of feet skyward. There are fossil forests, waterfalls plunging hundreds of feet down, rushing rivers in a volcanic crater 47 miles (76 km) across, and a deep canyon 20 miles (32 km) long, 800–1,200 feet (245–370 m) deep, and as much as 4,000 feet (1,230 m) across. The Yellowstone still is the longest undammed river in the lower U.S.

It became a national park by act of Congress and signature of President U.S. Grant in 1872, setting the pattern for similar significant set-asides the world over. Exploiters still wanted to develop it for financial gain, so the U.S. Army was given the mission of protecting it, serving as model for today's national park rangers.

Two locales particularly frequented by wildlife are Mammoth Hot Springs in the north, with moose, elk, deer, coyotes, and others; and on the western side, Norris Junction to Madison Junction, Madison west to the river crossing, and Madison south to Old Faithful geyser, at all of which are numerous elk, bison, coyotes, trumpeter swans and, frequently, moose.

Smaller four-footed residents (more than 60 mammal species in all) that can be encountered at any time include bobcats, badgers, river otters, foxes, golden-mantled and flying squirrels, beavers, snowshoe hares, porcupines, pocket gophers, and a few wolverines.

About 45 percent of the park was burned in a huge forest fire in 1988 and evidences of it remain, but wildlife populations, while changed somewhat in composition, do not appear to have been adversely affected; long-term studies continue.

Best times are September–October, though any month can be grand. July–August are popular but often jammed with most of the annual 3-million-plus visitors. Antlered animals are at their best in fall, and bison and bighorn sheep come nearer then. Winter is bitterly cold but gorgeously snow-covered. Geysers erupt in steamy mists. Spring can be anytime from April to June, and brings young animals and wildflowers en masse.

Dozens of lodges and campsites are in the park and nearby, some open year-round (reserve well ahead). Check out historic, elegant Lake Yellowstone Hotel, also Old Faithful Inn, even if you don't stay there (both close seasonally in October).

Best and closest air connections are through Jackson Hole, Wyoming, and Bozeman, Montana. There are five park entrances, accessible from Gardiner, Cooke City, and West Yellowstone, Montana, and from Jackson and Cody, of which only the north entrance from Gardiner stays open in winter.

More time-consuming and sometimes hair-raising over switchbacks—but worth it if it's possible—are driving the Beartooth Scenic Byway or Chief Joseph Scenic Byway to the northeast entrance (best plan all this ahead). The park has 370 miles (595 km) of paved roads (not all maintained all year), 1,200 miles (1,930 km) of trails and in winter, snowcoach transportation. Yellowstone is known as best place in the lower 48 states to photograph wildlife, though it should be remembered, park rules, enforced, require visitors to stay 25 yards (23 m) way from most wildlife and 100 yards (93 m) away from bears.

Incompatible activities, some inside park perimeters, include various kinds of development, including mining and oil and gas extraction, which threaten wildlife. Some animals which wander outside park boundaries are shot. What is needed is an overall ecosystemwide protection plan. For these reasons, the park has been listed as an endangered U.N. World Heritage Site.

The park has a wealth of literature on everything from park geothermal activity to trip-planning and where to see and photograph bighorn sheep, available from park service, bookstores, Internet sources.

Places of interest nearby include GRAND TETON NATIONAL PARK (*see* p.480), just south, NATIONAL ELK and RED ROCK LAKES NATIONAL WILDLIFE REFUGES (*see* p.483).

**FURTHER INFORMATION**

Yellowstone National Park, P.O. Box 168, Yellowstone National Park, Wyoming 82190-0168, Tel: (+1) 307-344-7381, TDD: (+1) 307-344-2386, Website: www.nps.org. Yellowstone Institute Website: www.yellowstoneinstitute.org

# SOUTHEASTERN STATES

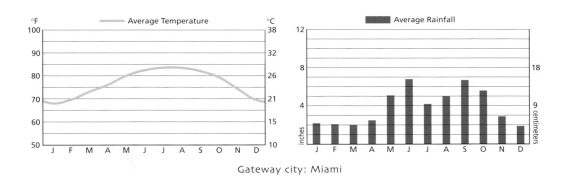

Gateway city: Miami

## THE EVERGLADES (FLORIDA)

The Everglades is a wildlife-rich wetland ecosystem unique in the world—literally a "river of grass" protecting a delicate web of life with more threatened and endangered species than anyplace else in the U.S.

This 2,344 square-mile (6,070-km²) area, much of which is now protected as a National Park, World Biosphere Reserve and U.N. World Heritage Site, is the world's largest freshwater marsh. Its origins are 250 miles (402 km) north of the Florida toe in the headwaters of the ancient, formerly meandering Kissimmee River. From there historically water entered and spilled over the banks of Lake Okeechobee, seeping along in a gradual southward path 50 miles wide and 100 miles long (80 × 160 km), until it finally reached Florida Bay and the gulf. Along the way its mixture of slow-moving water, sunlit vegetation, and teeming microorganisms provided homes and nourishment for a prodigious wildlife community.

Last stand of southern bald eagles was in the Greater Everglades ecosystem after DDT pollution thinned eggshells and for a time brought hatching populations of this magnificent national symbol close to extinction.

Florida panthers, only a few dozen left in the wild, are stealthily at home here. It is a major nesting place for rare wood storks and sunset-hued roseate spoonbills, whose odd-shaped mandibles swish about in the shallows to exploit a special food-gathering niche. There are wailing limpkins and fierce-looking Everglade kites, both of whose numbers crashed when their sole food source, apple snails, lost habitat.

Alligators boom mating calls through the night and stand guard over warming vegetation nests, gently nudging their eggs to check incubation progress. Finally, with careful razor-toothed jaws, they pick up their young and carry them to water.

# UNITED STATES

OPPOSITE: Bald eagles can see fish swimming in water from several hundred feet up (100+ m) and dive on them at speeds over 100 miles an hour (160 kph). If necessary they can swim a butterfly-stroke until they get enough lift to take off again. They return to the same nest yearly, adding to it until it becomes huge—one on record was nine feet (3 m) across and weighed two tons. "Bald" comes not from lack of feathers but an Old English word, balde, meaning white. Once endangered from pesticide use and habitat loss, their status with improved conditions has been raised to threatened over much of their North American range.

Formidable survivors of the age of dinosaurs, alligators can weigh up to a record half-ton. Powerful jaws come equipped with 74–80 teeth and enough replacements so one 'gator can go through up to 3,000 teeth in a lifetime. Yet females are gentle, aggressively vigilant mothers until hatchlings are fully 18 months old. Once endangered, populations have rebounded with protection so they can be found now in freshwater lakes, ponds, rivers, and wetlands over much of their former range in the southern U.S.

American crocodiles can seem sleepily unaware but they are fearsome hunters that run on land up to 11 miles an hour (17.6 kph), swim up to 20 miles an hour (32 kph), stay underwater up to an hour and cruise about seeing both above and under water. They differ from alligators in being shyer and more reclusive, preferring salt or brackish to freshwater, with pointed, not rounded, noses, and teeth visible even when jaws are closed. They need warmer climates, hence their range from southern Florida and the Caribbean through Mexico and along the Central American coast to Venezuela.

Great egrets, glossy and white ibises, snowy egrets, tri-colored herons, great blue and great white herons, yellow-crowned and black-crowned night herons, as well as green-backed and little blue herons all are here. Exquisite courtship plumes threatened their survival when demand for them to decorate ladies' hats raised their world price per pound over that of gold. Plume-hunters defeathered birds alive and left both adults and helpless young to perish on their nests. An Audubon warden engaged to protect them was murdered. Public outrage forced a halt to the cruel slaughter.

# UNITED STATES

The Everglades has kaleidoscopic-hued birds like purple gallinules and painted buntings; frigate or man-o-war birds inflating scarlet throat balloons; brown and white pelicans with up to nine-foot (2.7-m) wingspreads. Anhingas—whip-necked "snake birds"—stand like statues so the sun can dry their feathers after a swim. Golden warblers of a dozen species stop over in the thousands in migration.

Black skimmers ply waters with lower mandibles dropped, snapping shut to trap small organisms for their dinner. Swallow-tailed kites soar overhead in spring and stay to nest. Scarlet-crested pileated woodpeckers hammer pine trees with blows that resound over the marsh.

Rare short-tailed hawks are here with similarly uncommon Cape Sable seaside sparrows and white-crowned pigeons, mangrove cuckoos, and black-whiskered vireos.

Snowy, carmine-crowned whooping cranes, one of the world's loveliest and most endangered birds, range over upland sections of the Kissimmee in a newly-established flock associating with stately sandhill cranes. Watching from bare branches are caracaras, uncommon colorful raptors.

The list is too long to enumerate here. Altogether there are more than 400 bird species.

Below them in the waters are river otters and endangered crocodiles (tell them from alligators by their underslung jaws) and, in drier sections, bobcats, white-tailed deer, and black bears—altogether over 40 mammal species among some 600 kinds of animals (not counting 40 species of mosquitoes!).

Five endangered species of ponderous sea turtles crawl up the beaches in summer to lay eggs.

There are more than 1,000 seed-bearing plants and 24 epiphytic orchids.

This incomparable area has come under serious threat in recent decades from two directions: encroaching population—Florida's warm climate attracts 900 new occupants every day—and agricultural activities which have added pesticides and fertilizer to water sent into the Everglades. Agricultural demands also have interrupted water timing with disastrous effects on natural reproductive cycles (shorting water supplies as well for metropolitan areas like Miami which draw from the same aquifer).

Wading bird populations once estimated at two million (250,000 white ibises alone) recently have been down as much as 90 percent. Some species no longer may have viable self-sustaining nesting populations.

OPPOSITE: Anhingas control air bladders in their bodies so they can ride high in water or low with only waving heads and necks showing, looking like "snakebirds", which is what they are often called. Hinge-like neck vertebrae help them strike instantly to spear watery prey, which they toss up to swallow head-first. In courtship, feathers flare so their small heads seem to double in size around electric blue-turquoise eye rings as they croak, rattle and sometimes entwine necks with mates' in wetlands from Everglades National Park south, occasionally as far as Argentina.

Remedial measures are beginning to help. Congress has directed The U.S. Army Corps of Engineers to implement a restoration plan that includes land purchases to hold water for timely release coordinated with the Everglades' natural cycle and clean-up of damaging agricultural runoff in a federal-state partnership. It will be the largest ecosystem restoration ever undertaken. Where a start has been made, the situation has improved and wildlife has responded. The Kissimmee River, channelized in an ill-conceived engineering project, is being re-dug in a natural, meandering path, which already has attracted renewed life of all kinds.

Centerpiece among tracts set aside to protect sections of the Greater Everglades ecosystem is world-renowned **Everglades National Park**. Others include **Big Cypress National Preserve**; **Lake Okeechobee** and **Lake Kissimmee**; **Corkscrew Swamp Audubon Sanctuary**; **Florida Bay**; **Fakahatchee Strand State Preserve**; and three national wildlife refuges—**Loxahatchee**, **Ten Thousand Islands**, and **Florida Panther**.

Best times to go are October–May. Summers are hot, humid, buggy.

International airlines fly to Miami, where car rentals are available to drive to three national park access points:

To main park headquarters and entrance, take Florida Turnpike south to Florida City, then FL Route 9336 to park entrance and headquarters.

Shark Valley entrance is at northern boundary, 35 miles (56 km) west from Miami on US 41.

Everglades City, on the park's western edge, borders the watery Ten Thousand Islands area, 4.8 miles (8 km) south on FL Route 29 from Tamiami Trail intersection to visitor center.

---

**FURTHER INFORMATION**

Everglades National Park, 40001 Road 9336, Homestead, Florida 33034-6733, Tel: (+1) 305-242-7700.

---

## ALSO OF INTEREST

**Big Cypress National Preserve** contains 1,138 square miles (2,946 km²) of spreading prairies dotted with cypresses, deep pools, and sloughs, with wading birds, including some storks, also panthers, a few endangered red-cockaded woodpeckers. Limited access; best seen from the (sometimes rough) Loop Road and Turner Road. Compromises in its set-aside permit mineral exploration and hunting—so best avoid hunting season, mid-November–December. Visitor information at Oasis Ranger Station on Route 41, halfway between Naples and Miami, or Tel: (+1) 239-695-4111.

**Corkscrew Swamp Sanctuary**, a National Audubon Society sanctuary, has largest U.S. nesting colony of wood storks and world's largest remaining subtropical old-growth bald cypress forest—also wading birds, barred owls, limpkins, otters and, in spring, warblers and painted buntings, with an excellent two-mile (3.2-km) boardwalk. Fifteen miles (25 km) east of I-75 Exit 17; or from Naples (nearest good lodging) drive nine miles (15 km) north to U.S. 41, 21 miles (35 km) east on FL Route 846; left at sanctuary sign. Tel: (+1) 239-687-3771.

**Fakahatchee Strand State Preserve**—97 square miles (250 km²) of forested swamp, seven miles (11 km) west of Route 29 on Route 41—shelters Florida panthers, black bears, Everglades mink, wood storks, North America's last stand of native royal palm trees, and largest concentration and variety of (protected!) native orchids.

Take Big Cypress Bend boardwalk off US 41 or a day hike on a logging tram road—maps available at ranger station on Route 29 north of Everglades City. Tel: (+1) 239-695-4593.

**Lake Okeechobee** can have huge numbers of water-oriented birds, along its edges wild turkeys, sandhill cranes, burrowing owls, alligators.

Gentle-looking painted buntings will battle to the death over territories. Courtship displays combine elaborate feather-fluffing and moth-like flights with deep shuddering quivers—all this seldom seen except by mates due to the bird's preference for dense understory along streams and forest edges. They summer in southeastern U.S. and Texas, winter as far south as Panama and Central America, where sweet songs and colorful plumage have led to their widespread capture and sale as caged birds. This has led to population declines so they are listed now in some locales as a species of special concern.

OPPOSITE: Mountain lions, known also as Florida panthers, cougars, pumas—same species—have the largest range of any New World cat, from southern Argentina to southeastern Alaska. Powerful rear leg muscles with proportionately the longest legs of any cat give them extraordinary jumping abilities. Running broad jumps can be over 45 feet (14 m) and vertical leaps up to 15 feet (5 m). This makes them efficient predators on animals as large as moose, exploding from a hidden crouch to seize prey in two or three bounds, usually breaking a victim's neck with a single powerful bite at the base of the skull.

Take boardwalk off intersection of US 441 and FL 78 at Parrot Avenue Wayside Park, or 40-mile (67-km) auto tour of lake's northwest rim, or explore by boat.

**Loxahatchee National Wildlife Refuge** preserves 228 square miles (590 km²) of northern Everglades marsh with wading birds, alligators, snail kites, wintering waterfowl, limpkins, ospreys. Boardwalk, dike and canoe trails. Visitor center is 20 miles west and south of West Palm Beach on US 441. Tel: (+1) 561-734-8303.

**Florida Panther National Wildlife Refuge**, with 41 square miles (106 km²) adjoining Big Cypress National Preserve, protects endangered Florida panthers, also black bears, bobcats, otters, alligators, wood storks, varied birdlife. Some sections closed to public use. Also administered from this office is **Ten Thousand Islands National Wildlife Refuge**, 31 square miles (81 km²) of coastal estuaries just north of Everglades National Park—a last remaining stretch of undeveloped Florida coastline, protecting breeding and feeding grounds for fish, endangered manatees, sea turtles, bald eagles. Tel: (+1) 239-353-8442.

Not part of the Everglades but with similar birdlife and well worth side trips are **Ding Darling National Wildlife Refuge** at Sanibel Island off Fort Myers on the Florida west coast; **Merritt Island National Wildlife Refuge**, off Titusville further north on the east coast; and for snorkelers and scuba divers, dazzling **Biscayne National Park**, with the northernmost U.S. coral reef, offshore southeast of Miami; and farther south, off Key Largo, **John Pennekamp Coral Reef State Park**.

# OKEFENOKEE NATIONAL WILDLIFE REFUGE (FLORIDA–GEORGIA)

One of the great primitive wildernesses of the world—a dark, brooding cypress swamp with wet prairie openings, its only sounds those of natural communications: musical frogs' chorusing, owls twittering, minnows splashing, wildcats' screams, wind blowing through rain-spattered trees, herons squawking. Alligators bellow for mates, and wild turkeys gobble for theirs.

One of the largest alligator populations anywhere is here—10,000 or so of these primitive reptiles, once close to extinction, that grow up to 13 feet (4+ m) long, and whose offsprings' sex is determined by their temperature as incubating eggs in the nest.

# UNITED STATES

OPPOSITE: No other bird is mistaken for the flame-crested pileated woodpecker—larger than any other in North America—with flashing black-and-white wingpatches and ringing, cackling call. Their rolling tattoo followed by heavy, deliberate drumming reverberates like a giant hammer through tall, old forest trees of their preferred habitat. Favored foods are carpenter ants and wood-boring beetles chiseled out deep in wood by their powerful bills. New nest cavities are excavated yearly, usually with recognizably angular holes, in wooded tracts across Canada, south through eastern U.S.

Graceful, long-legged wading birds gather in the hundreds—herons, egrets, ibises, endangered storks—roosting and nesting in colonies covering many acres.

Flame-crested pileated woodpeckers a foot long (30+ cm) hammer for grubs on moss-hung cypresses. Endangered red-cockaded woodpeckers search out tall pines so old their centers have turned to soft "red-hearts" ideal for nest hollows. As they drill holes for them, sap runs down the trunks, deterring predation by hungry snakes.

This is one of the last southern U.S. strongholds for lumbering 400-pound (180-kg) black bears. These adaptable intelligent mammals have disappeared from much of their former territories, replaced by land development, driven off by persecution.

Here too are handsome, gentle indigo snakes, a threatened, non-poisonous New World snake—and some of its poisonous relatives, cottonmouths, coral snakes, and three kinds of rattlers.

Bobcats, white-tailed deer and, possibly, endangered Florida panthers prowl quietly along forest paths which, it is hoped, will one day link Okefenokee with **Pinhook Swamp and Osceola National Forest** in a wildland corridor offering more protection for larger mammals.

Families of river otters, swift enough to catch any fish, porpoise through waterways, sliding down banks in playful games. Gorgeous wood ducks, called the world's most beautiful waterfowl, nest in tree cavities from which downy ducklings emerge and drop safely 40 feet (12 m) immediately after hatching. Migratory ducks of a dozen species—teal, shovelers, gadwalls, redheads, ring-necks—come for the winter.

A variety of orchids bloom in remote areas, where crimson-lipped carnivorous sundews and pitcher plants set sticky traps for insects.

Golden prothonotary warblers find nest sites in tree cavities low over the water. Parulas higher up weave snug cups of Spanish moss, not bothered by omnipresent brown-headed nuthatches, yellow-billed cuckoos, wood pewees, and Carolina wrens, but warily watchful for Cooper's and red-shouldered hawks. Chuck-will's-widows tirelessly announce and re-announce their names and territorial rights throughout spring nights.

Moist open prairies are abloom with golden club and sunflowers. Crimson-crowned Florida sandhill cranes leap high in spectacular courtship dances, proclaiming their mating union with one of the wildest cries in the animal kingdom.

# UNITED STATES

White ibises fly up by the hundreds from marshes that stretch golden in the sun as far as the eye can see. (Bitterns are here, but less easily seen, stretching motionless in a disappearing act against reeds.)

Altogether some 235 bird species, 50 mammals, 64 reptiles, 37 amphibians, and thousands of plants make their homes on these 619 square miles (1,600 km²) covering adjoining parts of the southeastern states of Florida and Georgia, and named for the Seminole word meaning "Land of Trembling Earth." The name denotes what happens when 15-foot-deep (5-m) peat beds explode continually from a vast bog of ancient geologic origin—once part of the ocean floor—sending to the water's surface new islands which quake at a footfall even after they are firm enough to support tall trees.

The Okefenokee is headwater of two major rivers—the famed Suwannee which empties 270 miles (450 km) west in the Gulf of Mexico, and the St. Mary's which flows 50 miles (83 km) east to the Atlantic Ocean.

The wonder of this multifaceted ecosystem is in the sum of intricately combined workings of thousands of separate natural components each with its necessary niche. Tiny colorful spiders watch over delicately balanced webs hung with jewellike crystalline droplets. Massive mossy cypress trees stand as they have for centuries against crimson sunsets while waves of birds fly to nightly roosts past alligators' eyes glowing red in day's last light.

Perhaps the greatest wonder is continued existence at all of this 619 square miles (1,600 km²) of freshwater marsh, pine uplands, islands, lakes, and dense forest swamps set aside in Florida and Georgia after efforts of more than half a century to drain its wetlands and destroy its primeval forests and their wondrous inhabitants forever.

Best times are February–May and October–December (but it's always interesting). Motels are nearby at Folkston, Waycross, and Fargo in Georgia. Campgrounds are near Folkston, also in nearby state and county parks; also, by prior arrangement well in advance, along refuge canoe trails—more than 80 miles (135 km) of them.

To get there from Jacksonville, Florida, international airport take I-95 north to Kingsland exit, then Route 40 to Folkston, Georgia. Main entrance and visitor center is 11 miles (18 km) southwest of Folkston off Route 121/23. There are walking and biking trails, boardwalks, observation towers, and guided boat, canoe, and night tours.

---

**FURTHER INFORMATION**

Okefenokee National Wildlife Refuge, Route 2, Box 3330, Folkston, Georgia 31537, Tel: (+1) 912-496-7366, Fax: (+1) 912-496-3332, E-mail: r4rw_ga.okf@mail.fws.gov

# OFFSHORE ISLANDS

WANDERING ALBATROSSES

# GOUGH ISLAND
## (UNITED KINGDOM)

TRISTAN ALBATROSSES SOAR FOR WEEKS,
MUSCLES LOCKED IN PLACE ON 12-FOOT (3.9 M)
WINGSPANS, BEFORE COMING DOWN TO NEST ON
THIS TINY ISLAND SPECK HALFWAY BETWEEN SOUTH
AMERICA AND AFRICA—THEIR ONLY HOME—ALONG
WITH NINE MILLION SHEARWATERS, 300,000
ROCKHOPPER PENGUINS, WANDERING, SOOTY,
AND YELLOW-NOSED ALBATROSSES, AND OTHERS.

GOUGH ISLAND IS ONE OF THE MOST IMPORTANT SEABIRD NESTING COLONIES IN THE WORLD. UP TO SIX MILLION WAVE-SKIMMING GREATER SHEARWATERS RETURN YEARLY FROM A STORM-TOSSED LIFE TO RAISE NOISY YOUNG IN BURROWS AMONG COASTAL TUSSOCKS ON THIS LUSH, GREEN, U.N. WORLD HERITAGE SITE. It is one of the most remote islands in the world—a 25-square-mile (65-km²) speck in the South Atlantic Ocean roughly halfway between South America and Africa.

More than 300,000 jaunty little northern rockhopper penguins—almost half the world population—with bushy yellow eyebrows, red eyes, and bright pink feet make stony nests on beaches and cliffsides above spectacular cataracts that plunge 1,500 feet (450 m) to the sea.

Tristan albatrosses that can soar for weeks with muscles locked in place on 12-foot (3.9-m) wingspans—one of the longest of any seabird—come down to nest nowhere else but here, up to 2,000 pairs of them. So do almost all the world's surviving Atlantic petrels. Gough, with its surrounding islets, sea stacks, and rocks, is an essential breeding site as well for little shearwaters, several million pairs on the two islands. With them are the largest nesting population of sooty albatross and large numbers of Atlantic yellow-nosed albatross.

Some 6,000 endemic Gough moorhens (aka flightless rails) forage in thick fern and heath vegetation edging moist peat bogs. Up to 4,000 Gough Island buntings feed in seed-bearing tussock grasslands.

Subantarctic fur seals—at recent count 350,000 and increasing—breed on rocky beaches

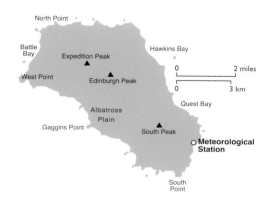

# GOUGH ISLAND
## (UNITED KINGDOM)

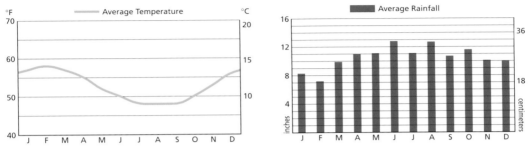

Gateway: Gough Island

all around the island. About 100 southern elephant seals mate and breed on the sheltered east coast. Swimming offshore are southern right and Shepherd's beaked whales and dusky dolphins.

Gough Island has been largely unpopulated throughout its history. Two centuries ago sealers stopped here, periodically living off birds, fish, eggs, wild plants, and cultivated potatoes, but nothing remains of their presence, other than a few weedy potatoes and a thriving population of introduced house mice. These have evolved to large size and may offer a threat to the island's seabirds. Only structures now are a meteorological station and helicopter landing site, with no visitor facilities. Access is prohibited except with prior written permit from the Administrator, the Residency, Tristan da Cunha, South Atlantic.

# SEYCHELLES

MORE THAN 150,000 GIANT LAND TORTOISES
THAT CAN LIVE MORE THAN 100 YEARS, WEIGH UP
TO 700 POUNDS (320 KG), AND HAVE WHAT'S BELIEVED
TO BE THE LOUDEST MATING CALL IN THE REPTILE KINGDOM,
LIVE ON ALDABRA ISLAND ALONG WITH ENDANGERED NESTING
SEA TURTLES AND OTHERS. COUSIN ISLAND HAS THE
DENSEST LIZARD POPULATION ON EARTH.

THE SEYCHELLES BROKE AWAY FROM THE SUPERCONTINENT THAT BECAME AUSTRALIA, AFRICA, ASIA, AND THE AMERICAS ABOUT 70 MILLION YEARS AGO AND DRIFTED 1,000 MILES (1,609 KM) INTO THE ISOLATION THAT HAS RESULTED IN THEIR RICH AND UNIQUE ANIMAL AND PLANT LIFE TODAY.

Bird populations on this tiny island group in the Indian Ocean can exceed seven million individuals of some 65 breeding species.

Reptiles, here in greater concentration than anyplace else on earth, include more than 150,000 Aldabra giant land tortoises—behemoths that can live more than 100 years, weigh up to 1,100 pounds (500 kg), and have mating calls believed to be

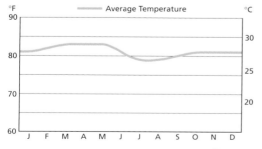

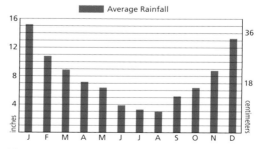

Gateway city: Victoria

507

loudest sound in the reptile kingdom. Islanders once gave every newborn girl a baby tortoise which was raised until her wedding day, then slaughtered for the nuptial feast. Now these rare creatures have full protection, as do hawksbill and green sea turtles which nest on beaches here from August to April. It is the only place in the world where hawksbill turtles nest during the day, easy for visitors to spot.

Amphibians, absent from most oceanic islands, have 12 species here including the beautiful Seychelles tree frogs, croaking carrycot frogs that carry tadpoles about on their backs, and minuscule pygmy piper frogs, almost impossible to spot but vocal, sometimes dominating all other sounds in higher hills.

At least 250 of some 2,000 plant species are indigenous—here before humans settled in the 1770s—and 80 are endemic, evolved into species found nowhere else. Most famous among them are coco de mer palms whose seeds are largest in the world, weighing up to 44 pounds (20 kg) and famous for being shaped roughly like female sexual apparatus, while their enormous catkins are like males'.

Because the Seychelles drifted off before mammals evolved, both birds and reptiles have thrived—at least before humans arrived—in near-total absence of mammalian predators such as rats and cats. Only mammals occurring naturally are those that flew here—large Seychelles fruit bats (aka flying foxes), squabbling noisily in trees at night, along with Seychelles sheath-tailed bats, thought to be the rarest bat species in the world. Others such as rats and hedgehog-like tenrecs were brought by humans, sometimes with unfortunate results for other species.

Some birds are present all year here, others migrate from northern climes thousands of miles away. Eighteen species are seabirds, feeding on the surface and up to 65 feet (20 m) down in surrounding waters on fish which they regurgitate to feed nestlings.

None is lovelier than little snow-white fairy or white terns, hovering with exquisite grace, laying a single egg precariously on a bare tree branch, taking turns standing carefully over it rather than risk its breaking or tumbling off by sitting on it.

World's largest colony of frigate or man-of-war birds is here on Aldabra atoll, males soaring like giant black cut-outs against the sky, gular sacs expanded for breeding display into outsize scarlet throat balloons, swooping on other birds to make them regurgitate their catch. Their thievery is at the expense of brown and masked or blue-faced boobies, black and brown noddy terns, and some-times beautiful long-tailed tropic birds, both white-tailed and the much rarer red-tailed.

Among land birds are enchanting Seychelles black paradise flycatchers hawking after insects on La Digue Island, long streamer tails rippling. In shrubbery on three small islands, Seychelles warblers, once one of the world's rarest birds—whose confiding ways put them at risk among humans—have been restored to healthy populations, and similar programs are being undertaken for Seychelles magpie-robins and others by the Ministry of Environment and Nature Seychelles, a private organization.

All are protected on reserves that cover some 163 square miles (420 km²) or 42 percent of these 155 small islands spread out across 154,000 square miles (400,000 km²) of ocean, 987 miles (1,590 km) east of the African mainland and 1,740 miles (2,800 km) west of the Indian subcontinent. Forty-two of these are granitic fragments of the original Gondwanaland; the rest are coral and sand surrounded by reefs with brilliant marine ecosystems, explored by visitors in glass-bottomed boats, snorkeling around shallow rocks, and scuba-diving expeditions by day or night. Major potential threats are habitat destruction through development and urbanization, and continuing introduction of alien species. While the Seychelles are considered a model of conservation, they continue to need international assistance to maintain protection.

Of special note are two U.N. World Heritage Sites—ALDABRA ATOLL and VALLÉE DE MAI.

## ALDABRA

Aldabra, largest coral atoll in the world and among the most ancient, is a 125,000-year-old crown-shaped group of 13 islands and islets around a huge 60-square-mile (155-km²) tidal lagoon, dominated by more than 150,000 giant tortoises lumbering about almost everywhere. There are, as well, 14 notable land bird species, including flightless white-throated rails along with endemic Aldabra drongos and prolific seabirds. Some 7,000 pairs of frigate or man-of-war birds nest, along with red-footed and masked boobies, red-tailed and white-tailed tropic birds, rare Aldabra sacred ibises, terns, herons, and flamingos.

Hundreds of hawksbill and green sea turtles haul out to lay eggs on beaches.

Giant orange-and-rust-colored coconut crabs skitter about, climbing palms, picking fruits and nuts which they open with one clip of pliers-like claws.

Flowering plants and ferns of some 275 species include at least 40 endemics, among them beautiful Aldabra lilies.

In crystalline turquoise waters is a brilliant, almost untouched marine ecosystem of astonishing diversity—a recent study identified 185 fish species in just over one square mile (3 km²) of reef (including sea goldies that change sexes as appropriate for their situation).

Aldabra sees few visitors apart from occasional charter boats from Mahé. A small resident population consists of Seychelles Island Foundation (S.I.F.) employees and a maximum of 15 visiting scientists. When their quarters are not filled, others can use them with permission from the Foundation. Wet season is November–April, drier May–November.

Threats include poaching and introduction of goats, cats, rats, and mealy bugs, which have damaged native vegetation. Patrols and eradication programs have not yet brought these under

Aldabra giant tortoises are among the largest of their kind in the world: males up to 700 pounds (320 kg), and noisiest as well, with rumbling, muffled mating grunts believed loudest in the usually mute reptile kingdom. They may live more than 100 years, filling the ecological niche of elephants in Africa and Asia, using elephantine hind legs to knock over trees to get at foliage, clearing forest paths for others. More than 150,000 of them live on Aldabra, largest raised coral atoll in the world and among the most ancient, in the Seychelles Islands in the Indian Ocean.

control, and financial support for these is dependent on grants from the Seychelles government and from voluntary donations to the S.I.F.

> **FURTHER INFORMATION**
>
> Chairman, Seychelles Island Foundation (*see* below).

## Vallée de Mai

Vallée De Mai is one of the smallest natural U.N. World Heritage Sites and one of the most beautiful, a 43-acre (20-ha) community of unique plants and animals in a lush forested valley within

**Praslin Island National Park**. Its six kinds of palms include at least 4,000 famed coco de mers, some more than 300 years old, found in the wild now only here and on nearby Curieuse Island. The extraordinary tree has spawned many legends. One, by General Charles Gordon in Victorian times, said this valley was the original Garden of Eden, since the shape of the huge seed and flower suggested Adam and Eve's sexual organs; and that this was the original Biblical Tree of Knowledge whose fruit they were forbidden to eat lest they gain knowledge of Good and Evil. Before the palm's origin was known—when the seeds were mysteriously washed up on distant shores, or, some say, brought by ancient navigators—they were named "cocos de mer" as perhaps coming from trees growing underwater and thought to have mystical powers. Rare seeds were given great value and mounted in gold and silver as objets d'art. They remain subject to poaching, which could endanger their future.

Fauna include rare, noisy but—in the thick canopy's dim light—successfully secretive black parrots, also yellow bitterns, Seychelles bulbuls, and glorious Seychelles blue pigeons. Seychelles tiger chameleons and multicolored geckos, lizards, and insects live among the luxuriant lichens, mosses, and air plants that can cover tree branches along a stream which tumbles through the valley, home to indigenous prawns and shrimps.

Access is by marked foot trails from the road dividing the national park. Praslin, three hours by boat or 15 minutes by air from Mahé, has a number of top-grade hotels and guesthouses where guided tours can be arranged.

## ALSO OF INTEREST

Other Seychelles highlights (visits to many of these are possible only on specific days of the week—inquire):

**Cousin Island**, only 70 acres (28.3 ha) but with permanent land- and seabird population of some 500,000 plus up to 300,000 others that come to nest in April–May. Species include Seychelles warblers, Seychelles magpie-robins, plus white-tailed tropic birds, fairy terns, noddies, wedge-tailed and Audubon's shearwaters, and bridled terns, many amazingly tame. World's densest population of lizards, with highest biomass of fish in the granite islands, and most important nesting site for hawksbill turtles in the western Indian Ocean. Strictly protected.

**Curieuse Island**, with a glorious marine national park. Giant tortoises, introduced from Aldabra, are easily photographed in the wild. Also natural home of the coco de mer. Restored colonial house turned into education center. Contact Ministry of Environment.

**Aride Island** is one of the lushest seabird sanctuaries in the Indian Ocean, with unique ecosystem interrelationships, including six tern species—fairy, sooty, roseate and bridled, lesser (black) and common (brown) noddies, both white-tailed and red-tailed tropic birds, roosting frigate birds.

# SEYCHELLES

Only place where fragrant magenta-spotted Wright's gardenias grow in the wild. Home to recently introduced magpie-robins and Seychelles fody, a joint project of Royal Society for Nature Conservation and Nature Seychelles. Strictly protected.

**Bird Island** is breeding home to about one-and-one-half million sooty terns—one of the world's densest bird populations—April–October. Privately owned, this island has successfully implemented conservation policies for many years. Hawksbill sea turtles lay eggs in daytime October–February. Private, with a fine lodge run by local people and managed for ecotourism. Accessible by inter-island plane.

**Frégate**'s rich fauna includes nesting sea turtles, skies overhead constantly filled with birds including 40 percent of the population of Seychelles magpie-robins. Habitat restoration by Nature Seychelles and the island's ecology department has resulted in thriving indigenous forest and an increase in bird populations. Luxury resort catering to celebrities and the super-rich.

**La Digue**, accessible by ferry or helicopter, stunning four-square-mile (10-km²) island, exclusive home of Seychelles black paradise flycatchers, also Chinese bitterns, Seychelles cave swiftlets, with Anse Source d'Argent at L'Union Estate—said to be most photographed beach in the world. The Estate also has a working ox-driven coconut oil mill, a magnificent example of a colonial dwelling and captive giant tortoises. The Ministry of Environment recently has purchased a large tract of land to extend habitat for the rare flycatcher. Excellent lodging, restaurants.

To get there, international airlines and Air Seychelles fly from Europe, Africa, Asia, and Mauritius to Mahé Island, with the Seychelles' capital, Victoria, having good hotels where arrangements can be made for inter-island travel. Mahé itself has **Morne Seychellois National Park**, miles of unspoiled, protected countryside, and a network of footpaths where much can be seen.

Best times are March–May, though temperatures are pleasant all year.

---

**FURTHER INFORMATION**

Ministry of Environment, P.O. Box 445, Victoria, Mahé, Seychelles Islands, Tel: (+248) 22-46-44, Fax: (+248) 22-45-00, E-mail: doe@Seychelles.net; Seychelles Island Foundation, P.O. Box 853, Victoria, Mahé, Seychelles, E-mail: sif@seychelles.net; Nature Seychelles, P.O. Box 1310, Mahé, Seychelles, E-mail: stma@pureasitgets.com, Website: www.aspureasitgets.com

# SOUTH AMERICA

GALAPAGOS LAND IGUANA

# ARGENTINA

TRUSTING, FURRY GUANACOS AND VICUÑAS
GRAZE HERE TODAY, LOOKING JUST AS THESE COUSINS
OF CAMELS ARE DEPICTED IN CAVE PAINTINGS ALONG
THE PINTURAS RIVER DRAWN THOUSANDS OF YEARS AGO.
HERE TOO ARE GIANT ANTEATERS WITH STICKY TONGUES
MORE THAN A FOOT (30 CM) LONG, SHY, UPSIDE-DOWN
TREE SLOTHS, AND RARE MANED WOLVES.

ARGENTINA'S HABITAT RANGE IS ENORMOUS, PERHAPS MORE THAN ANY OTHER COUNTRY IN THE WORLD. Its north–south distance exceeds that from London to Moscow. It descends from the Americas' highest point—22,800-foot (6,900-m) Mount Aconcagua—to one of the world's lowest, the Valdez Peninsula salt flats, at 180 feet (55 m) below sea level. And it is thinly settled—most of Argentina's 33 million people live in and around Buenos Aires.

This is reflected in its wildlife. With relatively few persons on 1.1 million square miles (2.5 million km²) of Pampas grasslands, snow-capped Andes volcanoes, cloud and subtropical forest, Chaco woodlands, and arid windblown Patagonia—which itself is a half-million square miles (1.3 million km²) fronting on 2,000 miles (3,200 km) of coastline—there's room for huge numbers and diversity of wildlife in the country's 18 national parks and numerous private and provincial reserves.

Furry guanacos and vicuñas, cousins of camels, are here, grazing as shown in earliest cave paintings on the Pinturas River. So are giant anteaters with tongues

515

# ARGENTINA

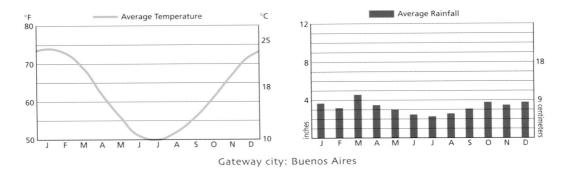

Gateway city: Buenos Aires

more than a foot (30 cm) long; great flightless rheas, New World ostriches; shy, nocturnal upside-down tree sloths; rare maned wolves; pumas; jaguars; monkeys; hundreds of rare, colorful birds from green-backed firecrown hummingbirds to tall, red-legged maguari storks; monstrous four-ton, 20-foot-long (6+-m) elephant seals; right whales up to 40 feet (12+ m) long weighing more than 30 tons; and a million Magellanic penguins.

Some of the greatest variety and abundance of birds and marine mammals in the world occurs where cold, nutrient-rich Falkland currents sweep against the arid steppe country of Patagonia. Outstanding among reserves is a 60-mile-long (100-km) headland surrounded by sea, connected to the mainland by the narrowest of necks—VALDEZ PENINSULA—and nearby PUNTA TOMBO.

## PUNTA TOMBO

Punta Tombo, 66 miles (107 km) down the coast from Trelew, is the world's largest nesting colony for Magellanic penguins—in fact, largest penguin colony of any kind outside Antarctica—500,000, or in a good year a million pairs of them. They start porpoising ashore on this promontory in September and soon are marching to burrows in long columns, bowing, getting acquainted with new mates or re-acquainted with long-time ones, contesting for territories on the moonscape-like colony, fearless with visitors, a loud, hoarsely braying crowd audibly living up to their other name—jackass penguin. (They received their better-known name from their first sighting by one of Portuguese explorer Magellan's sailors in 1520.)

Egg-laying begins after usually-non-lethal territorial squabbling and ceremonious courtship in October, often at a pair's previous burrow. Young hatch in November and both parents forage at sea, returning with up to two pounds (1 kg) of food in their stomachs for chicks. With such nurturing chicks thrive and start fledging in January (but may stay until March) and head out to sea on their own, not to return until they themselves nest a year later.

In 1981 a Japanese company asked Argentina for permission to harvest 40,000 penguins a year, increasing to 400,000 a year, for food, oil, and glove leather. Public outcry led to a law banning their killing and establishment of this 500-acre (200-ha) reserve by the provincial government working with the Wildlife Conservation Society.

Protected here as well are guanacos, rheas, sea lions, and a variety of seabirds including king and rock cormorants, giant petrels, black oystercatchers, and striking scarlet-legged-and-billed dolphin gulls. Rare pampas cats occasionally nap in unused penguin burrows.

Get to the reserve by tour bus from Trelew or hire a guide, taxi, or rent a car (which permits you to tarry as long as you wish). Another reserve 165 miles (275 km) south of Trelew, **Cabo Dos Bahias**, also has a sizable penguin colony, is quieter and more remote, with lodging and campgrounds.

# VALDEZ PENINSULA

Wildlife spectaculars go on all year at Valdez Peninsula, a privately owned U.N. World Heritage Site run cooperatively with the government.

Some 7,000 southern sea lions, permanent residents, wake from beachside snoozes from January to March, females to give birth and nurture young and males to shake their manes and battle bloodily amid deafening bedlam for mates to start the next generation. Handsome, formidable orca or killer whales with exquisite timing arrive in March to feed on sea lion youngsters taking their first sea plunge.

In June, southern right whales once exploited for meat and oil—called "right" by whalers because they conveniently stayed afloat when killed, making them the "right" quarry—arrive peacefully to breed and give birth in quiet gulfs and inlets.

Some 30,000 southern elephant seals, here all year, gather to bellow and breed (undeterred by partners' foul breath) September through mid-October, males with hugely enlarged proboscises which suggest their name and are resonance boxes for harsh roars of their threat displays.

Southern fur seals give birth in crowded colonies. Sea otters splash up on wave-exposed rocky coasts. Five species of cormorants duck under for silvery fish. American, austral, and blackish oystercatchers patrol shores of multihued pebbles. Four kinds of steamer ducks—flightless, Falkland, flying, and chubut—frantically flail their wings when startled and paddle away like small steamboats. From October to March, penguins strut around territorial burrows (their major breeding area is on nearby Punta Tombo).

Dolphins of several species swim among diving terns while onshore a half-dozen kinds of gulls and plovers feed, all watched hungrily by southern giant petrels and predatory skuas.

Haughty, rust-colored guanacos graze. So do rheas, mostly on greenery, berries, and seeds, females abandoning parental duties as soon as they lay eggs, males incubating them while looking for another female to repeat the process. Zealous males gather huge flocks of chicks—whatever they can round up, sometimes 100 or more of varying ages.

Elegant crested-tinamous, like miniature rheas with similar foraging and polygynous habits, appear in family groups from August to January.

Maras, related to domestic guinea pigs but looking like faintly bewildered short-eared rabbits— also called Patagonian hares or cavies—thrive or dwindle depending on food supply, predation, and cyclical ailments. When numerous they socialize by the dozens around burrows, unafraid of visitors.

Hairy armadillos covered with bony shell-plates (their hair is sparse) burrow and climb trees, larger animals mostly nocturnal, smaller ones, called pichis, diurnal but shy.

Get there by international jet to Buenos Aires, thence by domestic air or bus to Trelew, which has good accommodations, as does nearby Puerto Madryn. Car rental or guided tours available at both (car rental best for leisurely exploring). Lodging and camping are available as well on Valdez at Puerto Piramides. Good viewing points are Punta Norte for sea lions, elephant seals, fur seals, and orcas, February–March; Caleta Valdez for year-round elephant seals; Isla de los Pajaros for breeding birds—kelp gulls, neotropic cormorants, many others (telescope available)—flamingos on tidal flats; whales in clear, warm Golfo Nuevo, Golfo San Jose, and Caleta Valdez, June–December (August best). Whale-watching trips can be arranged at Puerto Piramides. Visitors' information center is at the reserve entrance. Weather is pleasant October through April.

Threats include ever-growing fishing which drowns wildlife in nets and has diminished wildlife food sources (the South Atlantic fishery is the world's fastest-growing); pollution from a huge aluminum smelter in Puerto Madryn; and oil slicks from tanker spills and ballast-cleaning which kill penguins, cormorants, seals, fish—all marine-oriented wildlife, along with their food supply. El Niño occurrences can bring torrential rains which upset nesting.

---

**FURTHER INFORMATION**

Administración de Parques Nacionales, Av. Santa Fe 690, cp 1059 Capital Federal, Buenos Aires, Tel: (+54) 1-312-0257, Fax: (+54) 1-315-8412.

---

## Also of Interest

**El Rey National Park**, Argentina's southernmost and most biologically diverse, 170 square miles (441 km²) of humid forest studded with clear lakes and streams between two hilly ranges, with river otters, tapirs, foxes, monkeys, wary jaguars and Geoffrey's cats, and among 152 bird species—fasciated tiger-herons, roseate spoonbills, orange-breasted falcons, spectacled owls, blue-crowned trogons, glittering-bellied emerald and red-tailed comet hummingbirds, toco toucans, storks, condors, hawk-eagles, with a good check-list. Check for recent data on trails,

Sunset-plumaged roseate spoonbills are named for uniquely spatulate bills that they swing back and forth to snap up fish, crustaceans and large insects in mangrove marshes and lagoons. They're equally useful for males seeking to attract mates by clapping these bills resoundingly to show off ability to gather useful nesting material. Once endangered by popularity of their feathers in ladies' fans, they're now protected over much of their range in coastal South America, the Caribbean and southern United States, threatened mainly by habitat destruction for tourist development.

519

Great dusky swifts astonishingly fly headlong through plunging cataracts of Iguazú waterfalls (Iguaçu in Brazil)—but these little birds are aerodynamic wonders. Swifts are fastest birds in the world, with long, narrow, pointed wings, feeding on aerial insects, able even to mate, sleep and spend nights on the wing. They cut through the falls at such great speeds, turning on their sides momentarily to present almost no water resistance, that they are unaffected by the torrent. On the other side they cling to vertical cliffs with curved, sharp toenails supported by tarsal calluses and rigid tails and build cuplike nests glued together with spittle from extra-large salivary glands, safe from predators, for no one else can do what they do.

camping, accommodations, access, tours, at helpful office in Salta, Espana 366, 3rd Floor. Best times May–October.

**Iguazú National Park** protects one of the world's most spectacular waterfalls, some 9,000 feet (2,700 m) around its J-shaped length with hundreds of cascades dropping up to 269 feet (80+ m), and with it 255 square miles (660 km²) of subtropical forest and a prodigious list of flora and fauna. Both are shared across an international border with Brazil. Flora include 60 kinds of orchids; among 68 mammal species, little and red brocket deer, white-eared opossums, and (warier) jaguars, ocelots, pumas, margays, bush dogs, 422 bird species including five kinds of toucans, black-and-white hawk-eagles, and thousands of great dusky swifts darting in and out of the falls; and an astounding butterfly and moth array. Both countries have trails and good views (*see* also p.530 under BRAZIL). The border is easily crossed with a passport. Puerto Iguazú, with hotels, taxis, car rentals, is a two-hour drive from Buenos Aires, or fly to Iguazú International Airport. (Driving here is not for the faint-hearted.) Threats include regional population growth; tourist-laden helicopters roaring overhead; logging to replace forests with grazing, cash crops, and paper pulp plantings. Best views are mornings and afternoons November–March.

---

**FURTHER INFORMATION**

Intendencia Parque Nacional Iguazú, Avda. Victoria Aguirre 66, cp 3370, Puerto Iguazú, Misiones, Tel: (+54) 757-20722, Fax: (+54) 757-20382.

---

**Los Glaciares National Park** in the southern Argentinian Andes has some 250 glaciers, the largest—Upsala—230 square miles (595 km²), largest ice mantle outside Antarctica. Guanacos graze, gray foxes prey on rodents. Some 100 bird species include torrent ducks, Patagonian tinamous, Magellanic woodpeckers, and nesting Andean condors. Visitation is mostly November–March and it's not easy then, from Rio Gallegos, a five-hour rocky drive to El Calafate, with limited lodging, thence by bus or taxi to the glaciers. Views are magnificent.

# BOLIVIA

MORE THAN 1,000 BIRD SPECIES HAVE BEEN
RECORDED IN BOLIVIA'S NEW, HUGE MADIDI NATIONAL
PARK. THAT'S MORE THAN 50 PERCENT OF ALL NEOTROPICAL
BIRD SPECIES, 11 PERCENT OF ALL BIRD SPECIES ON EARTH—
PLUS SOME 44 PERCENT OF ALL NEOTROPICAL MAMMALS
ON SOME 4.7 MILLION ACRES (1.9 MILLION HA) OF
LARGELY UNTOUCHED HABITAT RANGING FROM CLOUD
FOREST AND GLACIERS ALMOST TO SEA LEVEL.

SPOTTED JAGUARS, OWLISH-LOOKING SPECTACLED BEARS, BRIGHT PINK RIVER DOLPHINS, AND GIANT ANTEATERS WITH PREDATORY TWO-FOOT (60-CM) TONGUES FIND HOMES IN THIS PEACEFUL COUNTRY OF GREAT NATURAL BEAUTY AND CULTURAL WEALTH WHICH HAS BEEN CALLED THE TIBET OF THE AMERICAS.

Landlocked, more than eight times the size of England, lying dramatically astride the widest stretch of the snow-capped Andes—highest and most isolated of Latin American republics—it spills over into textured hills and green valleys, wild temperate and subtropical forests, and finally into savannahs, lowland swamps, and steamy jungles of the Amazon and Plata river basins.

This enormous range of climate and geography in at least 13 separate "life zones" combined with relatively low population density—about 20 persons per square mile (7 per km²)— makes possible a remarkable range of wildlife on some extraordinary reserves.

Fuzzy vicuñas, with meltingly soft fur that nearly brought them to extinction, graze highland plains and valleys. Great lumbering tapirs, looking like elephant cousins but actually New World relatives of rhinoceros, crash through moist jungles.

# BOLIVIA

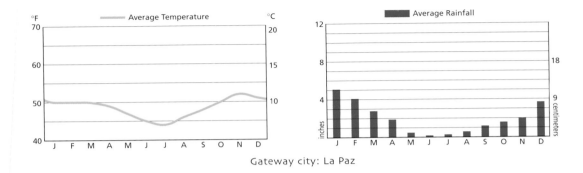

Gateway city: La Paz

Monkeys of 15 species howl, groan, and chatter in forest canopies. Among them are emperor tamarins with imposing white moustaches as wide as their heads, draping down to their chests—named after Emperor Wilhelm II of Germany—that belie their small size. Just 9–10 inches long (23–25cm), they can venture out to feed on farthermost tender shoots of trees and shrubs.

Andean condors wheel overhead on 10-foot (3+-m) wingspans, able to drag a 45-pound (20-kg) carcass. The broadest range of non-marine birds on the continent is here—almost 1,400 species, including 18 endemics—from brilliant yard-long (1-m) parrots and bizarre umbrella birds to scintillating sunbirds and hummingbirds along with hundreds of kinds of moths and butterflies.

Best times are March, end of the southern summer, and September, when dazzling spring flowers emerge at winter's end (rainy season is November–April). Altitude changes bring wide temperature swings anytime—in a single day, from damp, misty mornings to scorching midday sunshine to low nighttime temperatures.

Scheduled flights are available to La Paz, Santa Cruz, and Cochabamba. After that, only about five percent of Bolivia's few roads are paved, making 4WD often essential. But modern busses run regularly, railways cross the altiplano south of La Paz, there's an extensive internal air network, and riverboats are often available for good wildlife-viewing along the Mamore, Ichilo and, to a lesser extent, Beni River in Bolivia's portion of the Amazon basin, as well as Lake Titicaca with its famed totora reed boats, at 12,500 feet (3,810 m) the world's highest navigable lake. (Travelers should check with embassies about potential risk of travel to interior coca-growing districts.)

Insects are formidable, not only mosquitoes but leaf-cutter ants, some of which relish tent materials and have been known to devour one entirely, also bee "cities" where up to 10,000 can gather. Wildfires start easily. Campers should use fire only with great care

Threats are human encroachment and short-sighted exploitation with irreparable damage to natural resources from dams, mining, logging, and burning to huge forest tracts cleared for agriculture and cattle-ranching. In Bolivia alone this has meant loss of 780 square miles (2,025 km²) annually.

# BOLIVIA

**FURTHER INFORMATION**

Fundación Amigos de la Naturaleza (FAN), Casilla 2241, Santa Cruz, Tel: (+591) 3-52-4921,
Fax: (+591) 3-53-3389; Conservación Internacional, Calle Pinilla #291,
Esq. Av 6 de Agolsta, La Paz, Tel/Fax: (+591) 2-243-4058, 2-243-5225, 2-243-1184; Asociación
Boliviana para la Proteccion de las Aves (ABPA), Casilla 3257, Cochabamba, Bolivia;
Armonia/BirdLife International, 400 Avenida Lomas de Arena, Casilla 3566,
Santa Cruz de la Sierra, Bolivia, Tel/Fax: (+591) 3-356-8808, E-mail: armonia@scbbs-bo.com;
WWF Bolivia, Calle Los Pitones 2070, Santa Cruz de la Sierra, Bolivia, Tel: (+591) 3-343-0609;
Wildlife Conservation Society, San Miguel Calle 21 #11, Dpto 102, Calacoto, La Paz,
Tel: (+591) 2-211-7969, Fax: (+591) 2-277-2455.

# AMBORÓ NATIONAL PARK

Amboró National Park, said to be the wilderness home of more floral and faunal species per acre than anywhere else on earth, is the unique, imperiled, near-pristine convergence of vast areas of Amazon River basin and Andes foothills on more than 1,560 square miles (4,050 km$^2$) just three hours' drive west of Santa Cruz between two of Bolivia's most heavily traveled roads.

Rare spectacled bears with white or buff eyeglass-markings forage at all elevations but prefer humid fruiting trees. Three kinds of spotted jungle cats are here—jaguars, ocelots, and margays— along with most mammals native to the Amazon region: capybaras, collared and white-lipped peccaries, tapirs, howler and capuchin monkeys, orange-brown agoutis, red and gray brocket deer.

More than 700 bird species exploit every avian niche, notably cock-of-the-rocks and nearly extinct blue-horned curassows, along with harpy and crested eagles, heavy-billed cuvier toucans, and chestnut-fronted macaws flashing brilliant scarlet underwings in flight, among a breathtaking variety of bromeliads and orchids in lush jungles of giant ferns and bamboo.

This wilderness gem in central Bolivia is threatened by a wide range of human activity, from poaching and slash-and-burn agriculture to squatting pressure which already has caused both de facto and official shrinking of park borders.

Access is just off the main highway at Samaipata, three hours' west of Santa Cruz, where buses, taxis, and 4WD rental are available. Guided hiking, driving, and motor tours, also camping, can be arranged there and at Buena Vista just outside the park. Lodging is available at both.

**FURTHER INFORMATION**

Contact park offices in Santa Cruz: Barrio Urbarí, Calle Baracea # 210,
Santa Cruz de la Sierra, Bolivia. Tel: (+591) 3-355-5003.

# BENI BIOSPHERE RESERVE

Beni, a U.N. Biosphere Reserve in the northern lowlands, was established in a debt-for-nature swap to protect 1,290 square miles (3,340 km²) of this area's fast-disappearing scrub and forest habitat which is home to 53 percent of the country's birds and 50 percent of its mammals, including monkeys, jaguars, otters, foxes, anteaters, deer, and bats. Conservation International was able also to set aside the adjoining 4,440-square-mile (11,500-km²) **Chimane Forest Reserve** for limited sustainable development by local indigenous populations. At least 500 tropical bird species and 100 mammals are here, readily visible in this largely flat terrain. Entry station is on the main La Paz–Trinidad Road at Porvenir, where guides, horses, and camping trips can be arranged to pristine northern forests (best times June–July). A popular two-hour walk is Laguna Normandia with hundreds of rare black caimans, survivors of a bankrupt leather business and airlifted here. Trips also can be arranged through Academia Nacional de Ciencias de Bolivia, Av. 16 de Julio 1732, Casilla 5829, La Paz, Tel/Fax: (+591) 2-350612, E-mail: cmiranda@ebb.rds.org.bo.

# MADIDI NATIONAL PARK

Madidi National Park is one of the newest and most spectacular of the world's reserves—enormous, encompassing some 7,345 square miles (19,000 km²) of largely untouched forest bordering Bolivia's western frontier with Peru.

Still not fully counted, more than 1,000 bird species have been recorded—more than 50 percent of all neotropical bird species, 11 percent of all bird species on earth. Some 44 percent of all neotropical mammal species are here and 38 percent of all neotropical amphibians, in habitat rising through cloud forest and glaciers close to 20,000 feet (6,000 m) and dropping to just 820 feet (250 m) above sea level.

Spectacular macaws—some of the world's largest parrots, more than a yard (1 m) long, both scarlet and scarlet-and-green—gather in raucous flocks to ingest mineralized clay in riverbanks. Mammal species only sparsely present elsewhere have been observed in numbers here—abundant populations of tapirs and spider monkeys—along with such extreme rarities as short-eared dogs, in forests likely to be as species-rich as any on the continent. Grasslands are equally rich, with heartening populations of avian species declining precipitously elsewhere, such as cock-tailed tyrants and black-masked finches.

Final counts for all biota on this huge largely unstudied tract can only be estimated. With adjacent **Tambopata-Candamo Reserve** and nearby MANU NATIONAL PARK to the west in Peru (*see* p.567), down to adjoining **Apolobomba Reserve** on the Bolivian altiplano to the southwest, which has the largest vicuña and condor populations in Bolivia and huge numbers of flamingos and other waterfowl, this may be the most biodiverse terrestrial site on the globe.

Efforts to establish the park, joint project of Conservation International, Wildlife Conservation Society, and local peoples aided by several ecotourist agencies, began after logging and mineral exploration and drilling became a serious threat. Now Conservation International in partnership with Quechua-Tacana Amerindians are working out plans for community-based tourism, with sustainable harvest of plant products, handicraft production, and a tourist lodge with posted trails and guiding facilities on remote Lake Chalalan, two to five hours by boat from the nearest airstrip near Rurrenabaque, a stopover point from La Paz with lodging (also with interesting side trips available to wildlife lagoons at Reyes and Santa Rosa). Trips can be arranged through tour guides in La Paz. White-water rafting trips through cloud, tropical dry, and primary rain forest, camping on riverine beaches—best for the physically fit—can be arranged through tour guides in Cuzco, Peru.

## NOEL KEMPFF MERCADO NATIONAL PARK

Noel Kempff Mercado National Park, named for the distinguished Bolivian biologist murdered by drug renegades, is a huge (nearly 6,250 square miles/10,650 km²), remote, pristine wilderness with an astonishing array of habitat and wild inhabitants.

Jaguars silently tread forest floors; maned wolves bound through grasslands after rodents and the occasional small armadillo; delicate pampas deer graze meadows; spider and howler monkeys swing through tall trees; habitat ranges from dry virgin gallery forest to dripping rain forest, savannah, and marsh, amid some of the continent's most spectacular scenery.

Here the 2,000-square-mile (5,000-km²) Precambrian Caparu Plateau, crisscrossed by rivers and streams, rises 1,900 feet (600 m) from the surrounding plain, sending waterfalls plunging dramatically off steep escarpments to join the Itenez-Guapore River which forms the Bolivian border with Brazil.

Some 139 kinds of mammals are here; 650 birds—about one-fourth of all those in the neotropics; 250 fish; 74 reptiles; 62 amphibians; and over 4,000 kinds of vascular plants. At least 75 invertebrates are listed as rare, threatened, or endangered.

Near-sighted tapirs nibble on low woodland shrubs and aquatic vegetation, sniffing for signs of jaguars, which sometimes prey on their babies. Giant anteaters shuffle through leaf litter. Giant river otters fish along with piranhas and pink river dolphins (also known as bufeos). Capybaras, world's largest rodents, forage in shallows along with jabiru and maguari storks. Black and spectacled caimans submerge, only their eyeballs showing.

Harpy eagles, world's fiercest raptors, carry off sloths and monkeys. Primeval turkey-sized hoatzins nest low over water, their blue-eyed young able under threat either to swim or climb trees to safety. Over 20 parrot species chatter raucously, including the world's largest and most brilliant, the macaws—yard-long (1-m) blue-and-yellow, scarlet, golden-collared, and chestnut-fronted. Umbrella birds roar through inflated gular sacs to impress mates, flaring glistening metallic crests the length of their heads and shaking fluffy throat wattles as long as their bodies.

This park's remoteness has protected it to a great extent from human-caused problems such as agricultural encroachment and poaching, although illegal mahogany logging and drug-running have been problems. Overland access is possible though not easy via 125 miles (200 km) of mostly unpaved road from San Ignacio to Florida, which has basic accommodations in a former ranger station, also guide services; from there it's 15 miles (25 km) to the park entrance at Los Fierros, which has information on hiking trails and camping. Many visitors rent vehicles or come by chartered air from Santa Cruz, starting guided tours on the western river border. FAN (see above) which runs the park with SERNAP (with financial and technical support from The Nature Conservancy and the Dutch government) has a comfortable lodge at Flor de Oro, where there are rare zigzag herons and flame-crested manakins, and can arrange boat trips.

> **FURTHER INFORMATION**
>
> Contact FAN and/or Armonia/BirdLife International (see above).

## ALSO OF INTEREST

**Gran Chaco Kaa-Iya National Park**, newly set aside, at 13,280 square miles (34,400 km²) Bolivia's largest park—second largest on the continent, and the only one administered by indigenous people—protecting unique dry forest habitat. Bird species include greater rheas, endemic black-legged seriemas, king vultures, Andean condors, three eagles (crested, black-and-white, and hawk), and 10 parrots.

There are 70 mammal species, including a species of peccary that was only recently discovered for science, some 30 species of bats, giant anteaters, and giant armadillos plus seven other armadillo species.

**Reserva de Vida Silvestre Rios Blanco y Negro**, 5,470 square miles (14,170 km²), the country's fourth largest park, created in 1990 to protect rare floral and faunal species, including capuchin and squirrel monkeys as well as jaguars, tapirs, wild dogs. Few facilities, accessible only by air.

**Sajama National Park**, adjoining Chile's magnificent LAUCA NATIONAL PARK (see p.541; minimal facilities on Bolivian side).

# BRAZIL

AMAZON RAIN FOREST SOIL ISN'T RICH BUT
NATURE HAS ADAPTED SO FUNGI AND INSECTS
SPEED DECOMPOSITION FOR IMMEDIATE USE BY LIVING
PLANTS AND ANIMALS. SO WELL AND QUICKLY DO FOREST
PLANTS ABSORB NUTRIENTS THAT 98 PERCENT OF ALL
PHOSPHATE DISSOLVED IN RAIN IS USED BEFORE IT
REACHES THE FOREST FLOOR.

B RAZIL IS FIFTH LARGEST COUNTRY IN THE WORLD, LARGER THAN ALL OF WESTERN EUROPE—ALMOST HALF THE SOUTH AMERICAN CONTINENT—ITS HABITAT SOME OF THE MOST WILDLIFE-HOSPITABLE AND ENDANGERED ON EARTH.

The Amazon River basin, world's largest rain forest, interlaced and drained by the world's greatest river, occupies more than a third of the country. Southeast lie Brazilian highlands covered with dry rolling grasslands known as "campo," and scrubby "cerrado" woodlands; just southwest of the central plateau is the world's largest seasonally flooded freshwater wetland, the Pantanal. Here live some of the continent's greatest wildlife concentrations—world's biggest jaguars, rare maned wolves, crab-eating foxes, and huge colonies of wading birds.

On the southwest border with Argentina lies IGUAÇU, surrounded by subtropical forest harboring ocelots and tapirs. Here one of the world's most spectacular waterfalls thunders down on thousands of tiny intrepid nest-building swifts. To the far south, in Rio Grande do Sul, are vast pampas grasslands, and along southeast coasts the narrow isolated Serro do Mar mountain range, its highest peak rising to 9,508 feet (2,898 m). Slopes once covered by cloud and subtropical

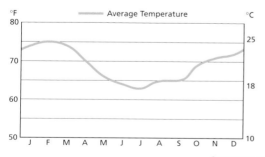

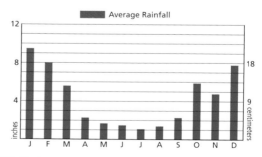

Gateway city: São Paulo

# BRAZIL

Atlantic rain forest are now mostly cut, and its birds, including 160 that are endemic there, survive only in a few reserves protecting the remnants.

Brazil's 350 national and state parks and ecological stations officially protect about five percent of the country—over 115,800 square miles (300,000 km²). Regrettably, so far more than two-thirds of them exist only on paper. The underfunded and understaffed Brazilian Institute for Environmental Protection—IBAMA—has been unable to oversee them adequately, and visitors may find it hard to get information. More enlightened government policies may yet halt continuing destruction of Amazon rain forest and the remaining five-to-seven percent of original Atlantic forest, whose rich habitats and wild inhabitants are among the most imperiled anywhere. However, despite many problems, spectacular places remain.

The Amazon, world's largest river, discharges a quarter of all the free-flowing freshwater on earth in its 200-mile-wide (330-km) mouth—in flood season 50 million gallons (200 million liters) per second—depositing a load of sediment visible 120 miles (300 km) from shore. Its

1,100 tributaries, many themselves among the world's largest rivers, originate in Peru, Bolivia, Colombia, Venezuela, and Brazil and drain over half of South America, over 4.7 million square miles (12 million km²)—an area almost the size of Australia.

Named for fierce female warriors reported by Spanish explorers, the Amazon for almost half its 4,007-mile (6,448-km) length flows through the world's greatest rain forest covering an area larger than all of western Europe. Rain forest soil is not rich but nature has adapted so fungi and insects help dead leaves and other vegetation decompose rapidly here, releasing minerals and nutrients for immediate use by the living. So well do forest plants absorb nutrients that 98 percent of the phosphate dissolved in rain is incorporated before it reaches the forest floor.

During flood season the river rises the height of a eight-story building, with fish evolved to feed on tree fruit dropped in the water in surrounding forest. During new and full moons a tidal bore or wave front up to 16 feet (3 m) high sweeps in from the ocean at speeds more than 40 miles an hour (65 kph), its ultimate effects reaching some 400 miles (640 km) upstream.

The Amazon ecosystem is so vast that though much has been despoiled by shortsighted and irreversible exploitation, large areas remain wild and unexplored, home to earth's greatest diversity of birds, insects and plants.

Over 2,000 kinds of birds are here—almost a quarter of the world's total—and over 2,000 freshwater fish species, half of all those known in the world, including species that have evolved armored protection against 30 kinds of rapacious piranhas.

There are more than 300 mammals and at least one million insect species, including 1,800 kinds of butterflies; a Goliath bird-eating spider; 80,000 woody plants alone including Victoria water lilies two yards (2 m) across; among reptiles and amphibians, 10-yard-long (10-m) anacondas and exquisitely colored "poison arrow" frogs; and scientists believe many more in all of these categories remain to be discovered and identified.

Sun is directly overhead all year so days are always about 12 hours' long. Temperatures are warm but not torrid, ranging generally from 74 to 86°F (24–30°C) over 24 hours with rains in short heavy downpours several times weekly, so humidity can be oppressive, 80 percent or higher. Best times generally are drier July–November.

Despite environmental threats from logging, mining, pollution, hydroelectric projects, illegal human settlement, and poaching for everything from skins of rare spotted cats to endangered turtles and rare ornamental fish, several outstanding reserves are here.

Of consummate importance is recent link-up of three huge reserves: the new **Amañã Sustainable Development Reserve** (SDR), 9,180 square miles (23,780 km²)—an area the size of Belgium in the central Amazon Basin between the Negro and Japurá Rivers, two main Amazon tributaries 250 miles (400 km) west of Manaus—with **Jaú National Park** to its east and **Mamirauá**

**SDR** to its west. It creates a 400-mile-long (640-km) rain forest corridor, the largest protected forest area in the world, some 22,250 square miles (57,660 km²), part of an ambitious corridor protection program of state government with World Wide Fund for Nature (WWF) and Sociedade Civil Mamirauá to be managed under a conservation category allowing indigenous peoples to remain and become active participants in protecting resources on which their livelihoods depend.

Concentrations of endangered Amazonian manatees, pink river dolphins, black caimans, jaguars, harpy eagles, parrots, toucans, brilliant macaws, great lumbering tapirs, and more are here; much of the region is still unexplored and uncatalogued. Scientists beginning research in Jaú already have found a woodcreeper long thought extinct; a beetle the size of a human palm; and one of the world's largest, rarest moths, an imperial with six-inch (15-cm) wingspan, as well as 150 new fish species.

Also, **Amazon National Park**, almost 3,900 square miles (10,120 km²) near Itaituba (with hotels) south of Santarém, is a good way to sample the basin and its wildlife, with cabins (no restaurants) and campsites near the entrance in Urua.

Although roads are being built, rivers remain the easiest way to get around the Amazon basin, both for local people and ecotourists. Brazilian Amazon's two gateway cities are Manaus and Belém, both reachable by major scheduled air, with hotels and tour companies where arrangements can be made for guides, boat travel (most interesting trips are upriver from Manaus, not down), and jungle lodges. Internal Brazilian air-taxis are relatively efficient and inexpensive for touching down in several places.

## IGUAÇU FALLS

Thousands of tiny dusky swifts dart where no other creature ventures, wheeling through a curtain of water plunging up to 229,000 cubic feet (6,500 cubic m) per second over a 230-foot (70-m) cliff in a great J-shaped cataract that is one of the wonders of the world.

Visitors throng to see this spectacle—at 2,950 yards (3 km), wider than North America's Niagara—where ground and air reverberate for miles with the force of more than 250 separate plunges and 180-degree rainbows are omnipresent (sometimes on moonlit nights).

But a few miles back from the crowds Iguaçu belongs to the animals. (Brazilians call it Iguaçu, Argentinians Iguazú, Paraguayans Iguassu.)

With abundant sunshine and 90 percent humidity, trees of great variety grow well over 100 feet (30 m), adorned with gardens of epiphytes—bromeliads, mosses, lichens, philodendrons, and stunning orchids. Virtually every tree supports orchids in a variety of forms, sizes, and stages of development. Flowers on more than 2,000 kinds of vascular plants can fill the air with fragrance.

Dense foliage can make fauna next to invisible—but 700-pound (320-kg) tapirs, largest jungle

# BRAZIL

animals in South America, nose through moist vegetation with long proboscises, giving away their presence as they crash loudly through the forest. Behind them they leave big three-toed tracks.

Monkeys swing along on lianas. Capuchins with black skullcaps and long prehensile tails converse in high-pitched chittering mistakable for birds. Smaller groups of howlers communicate in eerie roars audible for miles, terrifying unless one knows the source.

White-lipped peccaries forage in bands, fiercely attacking if they feel threatened, formidable because of long sharp tusks and group size. Collared peccaries roam in smaller, less irritable groups, along with raccoon-like coatimundis. Pumas, jaguars, and smaller ocelot and margay cousins prowl largely unseen.

Fluttering electric-blue morpho butterflies seem to flash like flickering lights in jungle gloom, along with more than 700 other dazzling lepidoptera, often clustering at pools where moisture releases dietary minerals from soil and rocks. Tegu lizards, a yard (1 m) long, are called "chicken wolves" by farmers.

Birds in astonishing diversity fill every possible niche.

Toucans and toucanets with technicolor bills as long as they are swoop about fruiting trees with pileated parrots and maroon-bellied parakeets. Emerald trogons perch unseen until they dart after flying insects in an explosion of purple, crimson, and metallic gold feathers.

Helmeted woodpeckers call maniacally. Hummingbirds hover and zip away like bright bullets.

Caciques with scarlet rumps and backs weave dangling nests suspended from palm fronds. Short-tailed nighthawks wheel about dusk skies awakening rusty-barred owls.

Iguaçu is a stronghold of predatory birds such as elsewhere-threatened harpy and crested eagles.

Brazil shares Iguaçu with Argentina, the countries joined by a bridge over which busses run frequently to Foz do Iguaçu (Brazil) and Puerto Iguazú (Argentina). Most visitors like to see both sides of the falls. Brazil's view is more spectacular, especially at sunset, with spray-swept observation tower and close-up walkway surrounded by roaring foam from Garganta do Diablo. Argentina is better for stunning panorama and better park literature (*see* p.520). Both have hotels and extensive trails. Ask Brazil's park office for permission to walk a six-mile (10-km) track to upper Rio Iguaçu section with fine birds and wildlife.

Most comfortable weather is June–August; most spectacular views in high-water February–March.

Brazil's park gateway city, Foz do Iguaçu, is reachable by air or comfortable bus from all major cities, car rental possible for the steel-nerved.

Threats here as in Argentina include population pressures; agrochemicals from soybean plantations which surround the park; logging; siltation from hydroelectric development; poaching (including destruction of trees for palm-hearts); roaring helicopters which disturb wildlife.

**FURTHER INFORMATION**

Administrator, Iguaçu National Park, Rodovia BR-469, km11, 851-970 Foz do Iguaçu, Paranã, Tel: (+55) 45-574-1697.

Woolly spider monkeys, or muriquis, are largest New World primates and one of the world's rarest and most endangered. Opposable thumbs are almost absent but long, muscular tails, up to 32 inches (80 cm), almost one-and-a-half times their body length, serve almost as fifth hands. They hang by them, climb with them, grasp and hold food and other objects with them. Because of their extreme rarity, their habits are little known—but one characteristic repeatedly observed is their gentleness and lack of aggression, reinforced by constant hugging, between the same and opposite sexes as well as all infants in their social group. Their range is restricted to Atlantic coastal mountain forests of Brazil, habitat greatly reduced by deforestation and clearing.

# MATA ATLANTICA BIOSPHERE RESERVE

Mata Atlantica Biosphere Reserve is an awesome complex amalgamating almost 300 protected areas covering 112,500 square miles (291,450 km²) of critically endangered Atlantic coastal rain forest—forest which thrived 20 million years before the Amazon started flowing but now, through shortsighted cutting, 93 percent gone. Scattered remnant patches are ranked the world's second most critical tropical forest ecosystem (after Madagascar). Of 202 threatened Brazilian species, 171 are here, including tiny gorgeous golden lion tamarins, several near-extinct forest cats as well as some 1,000 orchid species.

One of these remnants is **Caraça National Park**, a spectacular Atlantic forest ecosystem in mountains east of Belo Horizonte, with three primates, maned wolves, and rare, endemic birds such as hyacinth visor-bearers, long-trained and scissor-tailed nightjars, Brazilian ruby hummingbirds, swallow-tailed cotingas, and gilt-edged, brassy-breasted, green-headed, and cinnamon tanagers.

Another is **Caratinga Biological Station**, a private reserve which takes visitors by arrangement and has one of the world's most endangered primates—also the largest primate in the Americas, the leaf-eating muriqui or wooly spider monkey—along with three other primates and over 200 rare birds including rufous-capped motmots, blue-winged macaws, flame-crested and black-goggled tanagers, streamer-tailed tyrants, crescent-chested puffbirds, and tawny-browed owls.

Third is Brazil's oldest national park, **Itatiaia**, on a dramatically beautiful forested slope extending into 9,000-foot (3,000-m) cloud forests, last stronghold for such avian endemics as spot-billed and saffron toucanets, variegated antpittas, mantled hawks, Surucua trogons, blond-crested woodpeckers, and many others including a superb hummingbird array.

### FURTHER INFORMATION

Parque Nacional Itatiaia, Estrada do Parque Nacional, km 8.5, Itatiaia-RJ CEP 27580-000, Tel: (+55) 24-3521-1461.

# PANTANAL

The Pantanal is known in Brazil as "O Grande Pantanal" or sometimes as South America's Wild West, home to some of the greatest concentrations of fauna in the New World—giant anteaters, yellow anacondas 13 feet (4 m) long, rare maned wolves, pumas, crowned eagles, and powerful 300-pound (135-kg) jaguars. Half the size of France, it is the world's largest wetland and one of its outstanding reserves, some 140,000 square miles (363,000 km²) of which 38,600 square miles (100,000 km²) spill over into neighboring Bolivia and Paraguay.

Giant river otters' metabolism—20 per cent higher than most similarly sized animals—keeps them alert for location of prey, predators, family, and everything else in their world, with quick reactions to match. It makes it possible—also necessary because of high-energy demands—to dart with webbed feet after swift-swimming fish or, for extra boost, folding feet and legs to become speeding torpedoes, propelled by ridged, flattened tails almost half their sinuous, up-to-six foot (1.8m) length. Once wide-ranging in the Amazon basin, they remain rare due to poaching for velvety chocolate-brown fur, habitat disturbance, and pollution.

Black howler monkeys (the male is black, the female gold) fill the night with unearthly cries. Long-legged maned wolves bark to summon dark-furred young to dens in tall grass thickets. Basking jacarés, toothy jaws agape, crowd sandbanks.

Bands of engaging little capybaras, world's largest rodents, graze both on land and in water. Spotted ocelots pounce on rodents, and oversized jaguars leave paw prints five inches (18 cm) across in moist earth of this vast alluvial plain which 65 million years ago was an inland sea.

But it is the remarkable abundance of birds that leaves visitors awestruck, not only resident species but tens of thousands that wind up here at the southern end of their migratory routes. Brilliant, resident, yard-long (1-m) hyacinth and golden-collared macaws fly over in gabbling flocks. Flightless ostrich-like rheas stalk about grassy areas like overage ballerinas. Gilded hummingbirds probe bright blossoms.

Crested caracaras take up high tree lookouts, their penetrating two-note calls like wood planks rubbing together (as in their scientific name, *Polyborus plancus*). Stately jabiru, maguari, and wood storks stalk fishy fare, as do fierce-looking rufescent tiger-herons, sunset-hued roseate spoonbills, elegant scarlet-and-yellow-billed wattled jacanas tiptoeing on lily pads, southern screamers, whistling ducks, and others.

It is one of the largest gatherings anywhere of graceful wading birds—storks, herons, egrets, ibises—literally filling the sky as they fly back to nightly roosts. Birders often see 100 or more avian species in a single day just on the 93-mile (150-km) Transpantaneira road.

# BRAZIL

The reason for this abundance is moisture—the Pantanal, just 300 to 700 feet (100–200 m) above sea level, receives surrounding highlands' runoff in seven rivers which annually flood the area before joining to form the Rio Paraguai and eventually draining into the Atlantic Ocean.

In rainy October–March this overflow covers much of the Pantanal leaving patches of dry upland where animals of all kinds cluster—caimans, snakes, capybaras, giant anteaters, wading birds, ocelots, deer. Waters reaching 10 feet (3 m) or more provide ecological niches for thousands of species from microorganisms to over 400 kinds of fish, many foraging on fruit dropped in the water by flooded trees, and all that feed on these, from giant river otters to stealthy, dark jaguarundis, eagles, and wading birds.

Tea-colored floodwaters recede gradually over the slight altitudinal variation starting in March, concentrating organisms in pools—a lush food supply for nestlings, leaving surrounding nutrient-replenished soil a rich green savannah for grazers like graceful Pantanal deer.

Rainfall and drainage differences make the southern Pantanal shallow earlier so wading birds feed there then. This is reversed after April and birds fly north to nest, peaking from July on in crowded noisy colonies that can spread over several square miles—a flooding pattern which has limited human incursion by making year-round farming impossible.

There are two main national park areas. One is a band on each side of the **Transpantaneira**, an elevated 93-mile (150 km) roadway with splendid wildlife-viewing of predators and prey in a wide variety of both winged and four-footed types, itself well worth a day trip. The other is **Parque Nacional do Pantanal Matogrossense**, 84 square miles (219 km²) of land and water accessible only by air or river, as by cargo boat from either Caceres or Cuiabá to Corumbá. This park is mainly for biological research but camping permits can be obtained from IBAMA in Cuiabá. (Most of the Pantanal is privately owned by ranching families with little apparent cattle-wildlife conflict.)

The Pantanal has two main approach routes: from the south, Corumbá, reachable by road from Campo Grande; and the north, Cuiabá, with an airstrip. From Cuiabá, three gateways are Cáceres, Barão de Melgaço and Poconé, all leading to Porto Jofre on the Transpantaneira.

Best time to go is drier April–October. Bring clothing for hot days, cool nights, lotion for sun and mosquitoes. Accommodations range from fazendas (ranch-style hotels, some with boats and horses), pousadas (simple to standard lodging), pisqueiros (catering to fishermen), and "boatels" (floating boat-lodges, often costly but luxurious), many located in and around Corumbá, Cuiabá, Porto Jofre, or along the Transpantaneira. (The Pantanal and Amazonia both have remarkable wildlife but, being more open, the Pantanal's is more easily visible.)

Threats include poaching and pollution, especially from agrichemicals and mercury washed down from the neighboring altiplano.

**FURTHER INFORMATION (AND FISHING PERMITS)**

IBAMA offices in Cuiabá, R Rubens de Mendonça, CEP 78008-000, Tel: (+55) 65-644-1511/1581; AND Campo Grande, Tel: (+55) 67-382-1802.

## ALSO OF INTEREST

A remote little-known wildlife paradise is **Das Emas** (the Rheas) **National Park** deep in Brazil's southern highlands. Perhaps because it is so undisturbed, rare maned wolves, rheas, and pampas deer roam freely in this 513-square-mile (1,330-km²) undulating grassland savannah with cerrado woodland and gallery forest on one side and vast marshes on the other.

Yard-long (1-m) blue-and-yellow macaws in dazzling aerial flotillas turn azure and gold as they turn this way and that against the sky, here in their largest concentration outside the Amazon. Blue-winged, red-shouldered, and red-bellied macaws stream across with colorful toco toucans, squawking parrots and parakeets, buff-necked ibises, and predatory raptors.

Tall, gangly, blue-eyed, red-legged seriemas stride along better than their short wings can fly, looking for grassland insects, mice, and frogs, among a kaleidoscopic avian array including red-winged tinamous, curl-crested jays, white-winged nightjars, dot-eared coquettes, pale-crested woodpeckers, white-vented violet-ears, and dozens of others.

Peccaries and coatimundis snuffle through leaf litter. Armadillos named for their armor plating—three, six, nine-banded, and giant (up to five feet/3.5 m long)—dig for grubs.

But Emas' visual drama is its stunning, otherworldly landscape—brick-colored vari-shaped termite mounds as tall as a man as far as the eye can see, and wandering among them, great bushy-tailed giant anteaters with claws that tear open rock-hard mounds, probe deepest recesses with sticky tongues up to two feet (60 cm) long to consume up to 30,000 termites a day. Periodically these hundreds of square miles of mounds glow greenish-blue at night with luminescent larvae of coresident beetles which prey on millions of emerging flying termites attracted to their eerie light during the first September–October rains—a ghostly, unearthly sight.

Emas is 300 miles (483 km) south of Brasilia over nearly deserted roads; park service permits are required; and though crossed by dirt roads and tracks with marvelous wildlife-viewing, there is no convenient lodging. Ranch families sometimes take in visitors, and park offices near the entrance (dirt airstrip nearby) have guesthouses where visitors sometimes stay. Best times for weather and wildlife are June–August.

**FURTHER INFORMATION (AND FISHING PERMITS)**

Parque Nacional das Emas, IBAMA, Rua 10, quadra 1, lote 13, Setor Nossa Senhora de Fátima, Mineiros-GO CEP 75830-000, Tel: (+55) 62-661-4186.

# CHILE

MOUNTAIN LIONS (OR PUMAS) PROWL
TORRES DEL PAINE IN CHILE'S SOUTHERNMOST
TIP IN THEIR DENSEST POPULATIONS ANYPLACE.
THEY'RE BIGGER THAN ANYPLACE ELSE, TOO, IN PART
BECAUSE OF ABUNDANT PREY BASE, ESPECIALLY FURRY
GUANACOS WHEN YOUNG ARE BEING BORN.

THIS NARROW RIBBON OF LAND, LONGER THAN SOME CONTINENTS, 2,666 MILES (4,300 KM) ALONG THE WEST COAST OF SOUTHERN SOUTH AMERICA—FARTHER, COUNTING CHILE'S ANTARCTIC CLAIMS— EMBRACES A DAZZLING ARRAY OF WILDLIFE HABITAT. From its rocky spine of Andes peaks and snow-capped volcanoes topping 19,680 feet (6,000+ m) where condors soar, it drops through icy deep blue glaciers and fjords, steep canyons and broad river valleys dotted with turquoise lakes to the world's driest desert and finally to sandy sea-level beaches.

It is more underwater than terrestrial in some places, its land at narrowest less than 124 miles (200 km) wide, but with territorial claims extending 200 miles (320 km) offshore where the cold Peruvian or Humboldt coastal current, richest, most productive anywhere, brings nutrients and moisture-laden fog and cloud cover for rich sea and shore life.

Contentious seals and sea lions, looping dolphins, high-diving pelicans, and wave-dancing storm-petrels come for this bounty with cormorants, albatrosses, penguins and, cruising by the southern Magellanic Strait, a few streamlined blue whales 68–90 feet (20–30 m) long, weighing more than 100 tons, largest animals that ever lived. Once hunted close to extinction, now protected but still perilously few in number, a sighting is always cause for celebration.

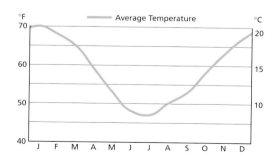
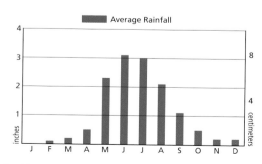

Gateway city: Santiago

# CHILE

Onshore wildlife is equally various, from extraordinary diademed sandpiper-plovers, called world's rarest, most beautiful shorebirds—Chile is the best place to see them—to dainty pudu, world's smallest deer standing just over a foot (35 cm) high at the shoulder, and their stately cousin, the regal and endangered huemul which gazes out of the Chilean coat of arms.

Four camel relatives thrive in the harsh altiplano: llamas and alpacas, wild guanacos and vicuñas, gentle bearers of some of the world's softest fur whose only defense—spitting, to temporarily blind a nearby aggressor—proved ineffective against guns and ruthless demand for pelts. Survivors for 10 million years after ancestors crossed the Siberian land bridge, merciless shooting quickly brought them near extinction.

Solitary mountain lions or pumas are here along with smaller predators—Culpeo fox, sometimes called "Andean wolf", and rare Geoffrey's and colo colo or mountain cats. Recovering remnant populations of another once-numerous and softest of animals, tiny silvery-gray chinchillas, brought close to extinction by years when 350,000 skins were exported annually, forage on mosses and roots in desert terrain and rocky mountainsides.

In farther southern forests are small, rare Darwin's or Chilote foxes, coypu or nutria, Magellanic woodpeckers, and green-backed firecrown hummingbirds sipping at wild fuschias. Shallow lakes on the southern altiplano brim with bright flamingos.

Chile's island territories—famed Rapa Nui (aka Easter Islands) and Juan Fernandez Islands, sometimes called the southern Galapagos—nurture species which in isolation have formed their own unique gene pools.

Best times vary with geography and altitude—December–March for the Lake District and far south; spring (September–November) or fall (March–April) for the Santiago–Central Valley area. North can be extremely hot and dry—June–September will be cooler there. Avoid January–February in the altiplano, when "Bolivian winter" rains can be unpleasant. Hats and sun lotion protect against strong ultraviolet rays at high altitudes, and an extra jacket can be handy.

International flights enter Chile at Santiago; from there, travel is good via road, rail (to the south), or domestic air, with comfortable accommodations through much of this friendly country (higher elevation can give visitors

Arica

Antofagasta

SANTIAGO

ARCHIPELAGO DE
LOS CHONOS

□ Torres Del Paine National Park

ARCHIPELAGO
REINA ADELAIDE

Punta Arenas

Tierra del Fuego

Cape Horn

0                    500 miles

0          500 km

"soroche" for which mate de coca can be an effective and legal remedy). In Santiago, the city zoo offers a survey look at creatures difficult to observe elsewhere. Good birding relatively nearby includes **El Yeso Reservoir** southeast in the Andes for diademed sandpiper-plovers and others; crag chilia and moustached turca at **Farellones** on the northeast; and at **Laguna El Peral** on the coast near Las Cruces.

Much can be seen as well from waterways. Over 20 rivers between Santiago and Tierra del Fuego have excellent rafting (some white-water) through spectacular mountain scenery and lush temperate rain forest—outstandingly **Rio Petrohue**.

---

**FURTHER INFORMATION**

CONAF (Corporación Nacional Forestal), Avenida Presidente Bulnes 259, oficina 206 (main office at No. 285), Santiago, Tel: (+56) 696-0783/699-2833 or 02-671-1850, which has maps and also publishes booklets about the national park system; CODEFF (Comité Nacional Pro Defensa de la Fauna y Flora), Sazie 1885, Tel: (+56) 2-696-1268.

---

Chile has 30 national parks and 36 forest reserves managed by CONAF comprising more than 26,000 square miles (70,000 km²), over 10 percent of Chile's land surface, and they are some of the best-run in South America.

## Torres del Paine National Park

Torres del Paine (pronounced pie-nee) at the continent's southernmost tip is one of the world's loveliest reserves, with abundant wildlife—cameloids, pumas, condors—free from human harassment for years and thus relatively unfearful of visitors.

The dramatic vista which is the memorable centerpiece of this 935-square-mile (2,425-km²) national park and wildlife treasure is almost as familiar worldwide as the Taj Mahal but uncrowded with visitors—three 6,500-foot (1,950-m) pillars of Pleistocene granite which rise dramatically from the flat steppe, reddish, purple, and gold in different lights. Around them icy-blue glaciers boom and crash as they calve through summer months on snowcapped mountains often topped with spectacular snow-plume displays, descending through waterfalls, undulating plateaus of sepias and reds, rivers and sparkling lakes of white, turquoise, and ocher, dark forests. Hillsides are splashed with flowering spring blankets of orange and purple. Chilean Nobel poet Gabriela Mistral attributed her inspiration to times spent in contemplation here.

Powerful mountain lions or pumas with the widest range of any western hemisphere land mammal—from subalpine forests to sea-level swamps and desert, from the Canadian Yukon to the Strait of Magellan—hunt here in the densest populations anywhere. They also are larger here than anywhere else. The prey base which makes this possible is an abundant population of other mammals, prime among these being furry rust-colored guanacos, particularly when young are being born. These tallest of South American cameloids seem to know they are protected from

Magellan's sailors first saw these penguins in 1520 and named them after their captain. We know them now for hoarse, braying calls which make a breeding colony of hundreds of thousands of jackass (aka Magellanic) penguins sound almost deafening in enormous colonies ranging from north of Punto Tombo in Argentina, south to Tierra del Fuego, then north up the Pacific coast of Chile to Algarrobo near Valparaíso.

hunting and merely eye visitors with curiosity—this is the only place where sizable herds are still a common sight. There are occasional glimpses also of stately huemules or Andean deer, once thought to be part-ibex-part-deer for their preference for high altitudes and habit of rearing back on hind legs.

Several dozen Andean condors may be seen at one time, wheeling against blue sky, sometimes swooping almost to ground level. Swift aplomado and peregrine falcons cleave the air. Bright coral Chilean flamingos in flocks of up to several thousand course overhead, long legs and necks extended, calling to one another in soft, frog-like gurgles. Black-necked swans with pure white bodies dabble elegantly on aquatic plants, alerting young with high-pitched whistles. Great and silvery grebes build floating reed nests.

Diminutive Patagonian or gray foxes and their larger cousins, Culpeo foxes, pounce on rodents and large insects, as do rare, shyer Geoffrey's cats. European hares introduced in the 1880s are a predator's staple as are nandus or Darwin's rheas, New World ostriches reared by males, sometimes in huge families. Males induce females—often several females—to mate and lay eggs which males then incubate and lead about in broods of 70 or so—a startling spectacle when all run off across the steppe at speeds up to 25 miles an hour (40 kph).

Over 155 miles (250 km) of some of the world's most spectacular walking trails wind through the park, from an easy afternoon's hike to a more ambitious 7-to-10-day round-the-park circuit with camping. (For safety, solo trekkers are not permitted.) But much can be seen by road—bus or rental car—in day trips operating from nearby Puerto Natales, where lodging is available. First-class accommodations also are available in the park in a converted estancia and on Lago (Lake) Pehoe. Park visitors from Santiago can fly to Punta Arenas stopping over in Puerto Montt, thence by bus or boat to Puerto Natales.

Best times are snow-free November–April—but it's spectacularly beautiful in southern hemisphere winter when persistent winds die down in May–September and most visitors are gone. Weather is unpredictable and quickly changeable at any season.

> **FURTHER INFORMATION**
>
> CONAF (*see* above); or local park administration center, Tel: (+56) 61-691-931.

## ALSO OF INTEREST

**Lauca National Park**, 532 square miles (138,000 ha) in the far northeastern Chilean corner is home to more than 17,000 rare vicuñas—up from a precarious 1,000 in 1970—along with mountain vizcacha that look like rabbits but leap like kangaroos, pumas, alpacas, and 150 bird species. Birds gather in huge wetland assemblages at one of the world's highest lakes, emerald Lago Chungara, against a theatrical backdrop of snowy volcanic peaks towering to 20,000 feet (6,000 m). Diademed sandpiper-plovers are here (and around the whole area), also three species of flamingos, giant coots, Andean avocets, white-throated sierra-finches. Vicuñas often call on visitors soaking in the hot thermal baths or at the Las Cuevas park entrance, 50 miles (80 km) east of Arica (surrounded by northern reaches of high Atacama dunes and the sea) where day trips—also accommodations, at least until recently of an informal nature—can be arranged. Accommodations are also available outside the park entrance in Putre.

Adjacent to Lauca but more difficult to access are **Reserva Nacional Las Vicuñas** and **Monumento Natural Salar de Surire**, a Ramsar site of world-important wetlands with a steady population of 10,000+ birds, three nesting flamingo species including the rare James, and flocks of rheas, as well as pumas, Culpeo foxes, and a few extremely rare Andean cats.

**Salar de Atacama**, world's third largest salt flat, part of which forms 285-square-mile (740-km²) **Reserva Nacional de los Flamencos**, (administered by CONAF out of San Pedro), lakes filled with flamingos of three species, also hot springs, eerie desert forms, and spectacular night vistas when a full moon reflects off salt crystals.

**Tierra del Fuego**, visually stunning 680,000-acre (275,000 ha) tract, protects old grown beech forest, alpine meadows, snow-capped mountains, unique grasslands, and globally important wetlands, with Magellanic woodpeckers, firecrown hummingbirds, culpeo fox, and guanacos. This recent gift of Goldman Sachs charitable trust to the Wildlife Conservation Society will be managed partnering with Chilean conservationists, scientists and government leaders, with ecotourism to benefit local communities.

**Parque Nacional Archipelago de Juan Fernandez** is three islands several hundred miles west of Valparaiso, an ecological treasure with spectacular scenery, great variety of endemic plants, exile site of Scottish mariner Alexander Selkirk, immortalized in Daniel Defoe's novel *Robinson Crusoe.*

**Monumento Natural Los Pinguinos** is two small Magellanic Strait islands honeycombed with burrowing Magellanic penguins and other seabirds. Easily accessible from Punta Arenas.

**Parque Nacional Pan de Azucar** is 170 square miles (44,000 ha) of starkly beautiful coastal desert at Chañaral south of Antofagasta with pelicans, penguins, marine otters, and sea lions.

**Reserva Nacional Pinguino de Humboldt** is several offshore islands with breeding Humboldt penguins; access difficult.

**Pumalín Park**, 1,250 square miles (3,240 km²), one of the world's largest private parks, with fine birds, wildlife, trails, accommodations, 80 miles (130 km) south of Puerto Montt, where further information is available—Tel: (+56) 65-250-079, Fax: (+56) 65-225-145.

# COLOMBIA

FROM ANDEAN CONDORS SOARING ON
10-FOOT (3-M) WINGSPANS TO OVER 140 SPECIES
OF TINY FLASHING HUMMINGBIRDS, COLOMBIA HAS MORE
THAN 1,700 BIRD SPECIES, MORE THAN ANY OTHER COUNTRY
IN THE WORLD AND ALL OF EUROPE AND NORTH AMERICA
COMBINED. PLANTS INCLUDE 3,000 SPECIES OF ORCHIDS,
PLUS, AMONG MAMMALS, JAGUARS, OCELOTS, SPECTACLED
BEARS, GIANT ARMADILLOS, A DOZEN KINDS OF MONKEY,
AND MORE THAN 550 KINDS OF AMPHIBIANS.

THE GREATEST ABUNDANCE, VARIETY, AND DENSITY OF PLANT AND ANIMAL SPECIES IN THE WORLD IS CLAIMED BY THIS NORTHWEST SOUTH AMERICAN COUNTRY ON THE PANAMANIAN BORDER BETWEEN VENEZUELA AND ECUADOR, ROUGHLY EQUAL TO THE COMBINED AREA OF FRANCE, SPAIN, AND PORTUGAL.

Wildlife here has been evolving uninterrupted since before the ice ages, many in isolated biological islands which developed entirely independently while ice eliminated life elsewhere in North America and Eurasia. Unique species and adaptations found nowhere else are here in remote places still not fully explored and catalogued.

Such rich, diverse natural life is possible because literally hundreds of climatic and microclimatic zones are supported in equatorial topography ranging from sea-level marshes to snowcapped Andes, from arid desert to some of the wettest places on earth in drenched coastal rain forests.

543

## COLOMBIA

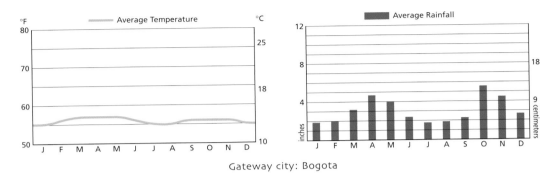

Gateway city: Bogota

An impressive and growing network of reserves has been set aside to protect this natural wealth—49 national parks plus hundreds of smaller sanctuaries covering altogether almost 10 percent of the country's 440,762 square miles (1,141,573 km²).

The bad news is that almost all of these are seriously underfunded and understaffed, a situation exacerbated by years of political instability, guerrilla warfare, and widespread uncontrolled lawlessness, much of it drug-involved.

Threats also include illegal capture and export of wildlife, especially birds, for pet trade (among them rare macaws, which ironically are easily raised in captivity and often die in transit); proposed roads cutting through national park areas; deforestation at the rate of 1,170–3,125 square miles (3,040–8,100 km²) yearly, which has destroyed over 30 percent of the native forest; and even plans for industrial port complexes within park boundaries.

Habitat destruction is rife both outside and inside reserves, with endemic species increasingly limited to remote forest remnants. More enlightened, productive policies are desperately needed, since no country anywhere has more important natural treasures to protect and preserve.

More than 1,700 bird species have been recorded here, exceeding those of any other country in the world, more than all of Europe and North America combined—from Andean condors soaring on broad 10-foot (3-m) wingspans to over 140 species of tiny hummingbirds flashing like opals around trees of brilliant blooms. There are dazzling scarlet and blue-and-yellow macaws, coral-hued flamingos, toucans with giant rainbow-hued bills, long-wattled umbrella birds, northern screamers, golden-chested and multicolored tanagers, orange-breasted fruiteaters, to mention but a few.

Flora includes 3,000 species of orchids among over 40,000 to 50,000 plants, including *Victoria amazonica* water lilies with leaves two yards (2 m) across, strong enough to support a child.

Big, shy, water-loving Brazilian, mountain, and Baird's tapirs with zebra-striped babies, jaguars, ocelots, spectacled bears, giant armadillos, red and gray brocket deer, and a dozen kinds of monkeys inhabit the forests, plus over 550 amphibians—more than any other country in the world—and lists of flora and fauna grow as remote sites are investigated.

## COLOMBIA

Colombian habitat divides roughly into several sections, the western half mostly mountainous with extensions of the Andes running parallel to the Pacific coast and, rising independently on the Caribbean coast, snow-capped Sierra Nevada de Santa Marta. The east is divided between Los Llanos in the north—vast open plains and savannah covering some 96,500 square miles (250,000 km²) in the Orinoco River basin—and the Amazon basin overspreading some 154,400 square miles (400,000 km²) in the south, with anomalies like the Serrania de la Macarena rising in lofty isolation from the eastern plains, La Guajira desert in the northeast tip, and sodden jungles on the Pacific coast.

Equatorial temperatures vary mostly by elevation, falling about 10.8°F (6°C) with every 3,281-foot (1,000-m) rise in altitude, with dry/wet seasons governed by complex geographic and altitudinal relationships—but the main dry season is December–March with a shorter, less dry, July–August. These are reversed in the Andean region. Los Llanos has one dry season December–March; the Amazon moderately dry only in July.

Park system management was taken over from INDERENA in the Department of Agriculture by the fairly new (1994) Ministry of the Environment (Ministerio del Medio Ambiente) through its department for Unidad Administrativa Especial del Sistema de Parques Nacionales (UAESPNN), located mostly in old INDERENA offices in Bogota and branch offices at or near various parks. Most parks offer some visitor facilities, and some have excellent visitor accommodations. Several offer camping. Some are or have been, at least until recently, virtually inaccessible, and many are impacted by guerilla activity.

Most air travel goes through Bogota, with a well-developed internal air and bus network and car rentals (not for the fainthearted) and widely distributed simple-to-spartan overnight accommodations. Travel can be difficult late-December–mid-January when many Colombians take holidays.

---

**FURTHER INFORMATION**

Unidad Administrativa Especial del Sistema de Parques Nacionales, or the Ministerio del Medio Ambiente (Environment Ministry or MA) at Carrera 10, No. 20-30, 8th floor, Bogota, Tel: (+57) 1-283-0964, Fax: (+57) 1-341-5331; or at Carrera 13 No. 93-40, Oficina 401, Bogota, Tel: (+57) 1-623-3474, 1-623-3075, Fax: (+57) 1-623-3016.

FOR INFORMATION ON NUMEROUS PRIVATE NATURE RESERVES—Red de Reservas Naturales, Calle 21 No.8N-18, in Cali, Tel: (+57) 2-653-4538/39, E-mail: Resnatur@resnatur.org.co, Website: www.resnatur.org.co

# SANTA MARTA NATIONAL PARK

Santa Marta National Park (Parque Nacional Natural Sierra Nevada de Santa Marta) covers in 10 miles (18 km) as the crow flies habitat ranging from coastal mangrove-lined lagoons, freshwater marshes, and arid woodland, to temperate and subtropical forests on slopes rising dramatically just inland to snowcapped peaks.

Forested mountain slopes support 14 of Colombia's 66 endemic species of birds, including chestnut-winged chachalacas, bright blossom-crowns, Santa Marta parakeets and woodstars, white-tailed starfrontlets, white-tipped quetzals and warblers along a road up to the TV towers on San Lorenzo Ridge.

Guerrilla activity is reported from time to time (check) but otherwise excellent wildlife-viewing, especially for birds.

Red-footed boobies can be seen from the Santa Marta seafront. Rare northern black-necked screamers, Everglade kites, and endemic sapphire-bellied hummingbirds, among others, are along the 59-mile (95-km) road passing by marshes and woodlands west from Santa Marta to Barranquilla, and around the huge Cienaga Grande (first Ramsar Wetland site in Colombia) with mangroves and marshes opposite the Los Cocos entrance to **Salamanca National Park**, which has a visitors' center and boardwalks over several lagoons, also beaches and estuaries with large concentrations of waterbirds and shorebirds, many northern migrants, and the only known population of bronze-brown cowbirds.

---

**FURTHER INFORMATION**

MA office in Santa Marta, Calle ww #2A-33, Santa Marta, Tel: (+57) 75-423-0752.

---

**Tayrona National Park**, 45 square miles (116 km²) about 130 miles (211 km) east of Santa Marta, offers paved drives through tropical deciduous forests often alive with birds—over 300 species including military macaws, lance-tailed manakins, crimson-backed tanagers, king vultures, ferruginous pygmy-owls (whose calls can be mimicked easily to attract others)—also sandy beaches which are a significant sea turtle breeding area.

OPPOSITE: Cock-of-the-rock males, heads enveloped in scarlet-orange plumage covering all but their eyes, give a show for females on a communal courtship lek where a dozen or more gather in deep mountainous forest and serially perform. One dances, tossing his head, calling, spreading wings and tail, hopping on one foot, then another, posing dramatically for moments at a time, and finally retiring to let another take his turn. A grayish female shows herself, and all males as if signaled drop to the ground and wait until she flutters down and pecks one on his rump. He hesitates as if stunned by his good fortune, then hops on her back for a quick mating. Then she's off, to handle the rest herself.

# SERRANIA DE LA MACARENA NATIONAL PARK

Serrania de La Macarena National Park is about 2,385 square miles (6,175 km²), still largely unexplored but believed from initial studies to be one of the richest biological reserves in the world, with numbers of species found nowhere else. The Serrania itself, laced with spectacular waterfalls, rises in stunning scenic beauty, a huge outcrop of Ordovician–Cambrian sandstone 350–400 million years old, predating the Andes and covering 2,026 square miles (5,250 km²) of a transition zone between Andean, Orinoco, and Amazonia habitats. Its isolated height, over 8,200 feet (2,500 m), has created its own microclimates, with rich primate diversity, unique floral ecosystems, and over 450 bird species. A park entry is 12.5 miles (20 km) south of Vista Hermosa, with information on access and guides—also directions to adjacent **Tinigua** and **Cordillera de Los Picachos National Parks**—but check with Bogota office on safety before going. Simple lodging and food are available at nearby Mesetas and San Juan de Arama on the park's northern end, both reachable by bus from Bogota—but getting around the park is for hardy hikers and campers.

# ALSO OF INTEREST

**Los Llanos**, much of it privately owned, is made up of vast open savannahs punctuated with small islands of woodlands and large numbers of wildlife. The llanos are divided between Venezuela (67 percent) and Colombia (33 percent)—similar in both countries, much more easily visited in Venezuela (*see* p.576).

Humid forests of the Pacific slopes are known as the "tanager coast" for their large mixed flocks of these multicolored birds—but in addition, especially at **La Planada Nature Reserve** between Pasto and Tumaco, are many other species, among one of the continent's highest concentrations of native birds, plus, in the forest preserve, huge diversity and numbers of orchids. A visitor center has trail maps, simple cabin accommodations—Tel: La Planada, Apartado Aéreo 1562, (+57) (27) 7533-95/96/97; Pasto, Tel: (+57) (27) 723-0761.

Other notable reserves include spectacular **Chiribiquete**, largest park in Colombia, with 5,000 square miles (13,000 km²), accessible mainly by helicopter; **Puinawai**, several days by boat; and **Farallones de Cali** and **Orquideas**, presently within guerilla-controlled areas. All these may some day open to ecotourism, and they are among the most spectacular in the world.

# ECUADOR

FAMOUS FOR GALAPAGOS ISLANDS, ECUADOR IS HOME AS WELL TO NATIONAL PARKS WITH JAGUARS, SPECTACLED BEARS, THREE-TOED SLOTHS, ELECTRIC-BLUE BUTTERFLIES WITH 10-INCH (25-CM) WINGSPANS AND MORE THAN TWICE AS MANY BIRD SPECIES AS IN ALL OF NORTH AMERICA—ANDEAN CONDORS, MONKEY-EATING HARPY EAGLES, 120 KINDS OF HUMMINGBIRDS, 25 PARROT SPECIES, AND MUCH MORE.

TWENTY-TWO-YEAR-OLD CHARLES DARWIN, A "YOUNG MAN OF ENLARGED CURIOSITY" ABOARD THE SAILING SHIP *BEAGLE*, STOPPED BY THE GALAPAGOS ISLANDS IN 1835 AND OBSERVED CREATURES IN SITUATIONS THAT LED TO HIS SEMINAL *ORIGIN OF SPECIES* AND THEORY OF EVOLUTION. Today this string of islands 672 miles (1,120 km) out in the Pacific Ocean makes up Ecuador's most famous national park, a mecca for eco-travelers and world scientists.

It is not, however, the only significant natural feature of this relatively small country which has 26 of the world's 32 major life zones in habitats ranging from cold, high Andes to lowland rain forests and sandy coast and is regarded by ecologists as a "megadiversity hotspot," one of the most species-rich nations on the globe.

More than 300 mammal species here include rare spectacled bears, wary jaguars, tapirs, ocelots, llamas, and two-and three-toed sloths with algae-green-tinged fur, hanging from trees. They are accompanied by the wail of howler monkeys, engaging little tamarins and marmosets, and a half-dozen other primate species.

More than twice as many bird species as in all of North America—over 1,600—include 120 kinds of iridescent hummingbirds, 45 parrot species, harpy eagles which can carry off large monkeys, dozens of

549

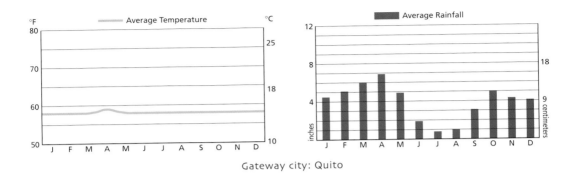

Gateway city: Quito

bright tropical tanagers and cotingas, and the world's largest flying birds, 22-pound (10-kg) Andean condors sailing on nine-foot (3-m) wingspans.

Dazzling butterflies include electric-blue morphos with up to 10-inch (25-cm) wingspans. Some 400 kinds of amphibians include frogs that spend their whole lives in trees, laying eggs in water caught in bromeliad cups; poison-arrow frogs with colorful toxic skins; marsupials that carry, fertilize, and hatch eggs in pouches under their skins. More than 400 snake varieties include poisonous fer-de-lance and 30-foot (6-m) anacondas; 1,000 kinds of fish include piranhas and electric eels that carry a 600-volt charge.

More than 20,000 kinds of vascular plants support unique ecosystems. Each rain forest tree species can harbor 400 individual animal varieties in complex interrelationships, many still being discovered, making rapid destruction of these forests particularly distressing.

National parks and reserves cover about 18 percent of Ecuador's 99,000 square miles (256,000 km²). For the most part, however, they lack tourist infrastructure, staff to protect them adequately, and some are so remote they are difficult to visit. All are under threat from varied sources—poaching for skins and the pet trade, oil drilling, logging, mining, ranching, illegal fishing, shrimp farming which permits mangrove destruction, and colonization. Nevertheless in almost all of them are nongovernmental organizations (like Fundación Natura) that work with communities developing activities focused on sustainable management.

Ecuador's capital, Quito, and Guyaquil on the coast are served by international jets, internal airlines link major cities, busses connect all but the most remote villages, and car hire is available at Quito airport.

The Galapagos and coastal areas are always hot but especially so January–April with periodic torrential downpours. Drier times can be foggy and misty. Dry season in the highlands is June–September and briefly around Christmas.

Flightless cormorants of the Galapagos Islands have lost much of the breastbone keel that supports flight muscles in other birds. They make up for it with heavier, stronger legs and feet that propel them through water with powerful kicks to capture squid, octopus, eels and bottom-living fish in rich upwellings of cold Cromwell and Humboldt currents off Fernandina and Isabela islands, their only homes. After fishing, they hang their skimpy vestigial wings out to dry as do other cormorants, obeying ancestral orders that no longer apply to their situation.

Some 250,000 giant tortoises up to six feet long (1.8 m), weighing up to 550 pounds (250 kg) lived on the Galapagos when Spanish sailors arrived in 1535 and named the islands after them. In the years following, Spaniards, whalers and other seamen greatly reduced their numbers by taking them aboard for food while also introducing feral rats, cats, goats, pigs and other animals that preyed on tortoises and their eggs or competed with them for grazing. Today they are protected in a national park where efforts are made to restore populations, including subspecies adapted to different feeding conditions on different islands (those with saddleback shells, for example, evolved as a modification to reach up and browse on taller vegetation).

**FURTHER INFORMATION**

Parks are administered by the Environment Ministry through the Biodiversity and Protected Areas Direction, Av. Eloy Alfaro y Av. Amazaonas, Quito, Ecuador. The most influential nongovernmental organization is Fundación Natura, Av. Republica 481 y Diego de Almagro, Tel: (+593 2) 250-33-85, E-mail: natura@fnatura.org.ec. International agencies which have provided help include World Wide Fund for Nature, Conservation International, The Nature Conservancy, and Natural Resources Defense Council.

## GALAPAGOS NATIONAL PARK

The Galapagos archipelago, made up of 13 major islands, six minor ones and 42 named islets plus scores of unnamed smaller rocks and islets, is Ecuador's preeminent national park and indeed one of the preeminent in the world, not only because of Darwin's famous observations but for the creatures that inspired them.

Here are giant tortoises weighing up to 550 pounds (250 kg), living 150 years or more, such as once roamed most of the world's continents, including Europe and the North American midlands. Now giant tortoises exist only on the small Indian Ocean atoll of Aldabra in the Seychelles and here, where their inter-island differences, noted by Darwin, show adaptations that enabled them to survive in varied environments—higher shells and longer necks and limbs on islands where they had to stretch for food, modifications discarded where food was easily reachable on the ground.

Here are the famous finches which, as Darwin observed, have at least 13 different bill adaptations to deal with different foods, from soft insects to hard seeds, and some have evolved tool-using techniques enabling them to pry edibles from hidden crannies with sticks.

# ECUADOR

Here are flightless cormorants with wings shriveled through eons of disuse so they are functionless in the air, though the birds still stand "hanging them out to dry" after fishing forays just as normally-equipped cormorants do.

Some Galapagos iguanas live terrestrial lives, great golden dragons clumping about, looking dangerous but subsisting on flowers.

A marine variety has returned to the sea, dark, prehistoric-looking, up to a yard (1 m) long with spines from head to tail, carrying young on their backs and grazing on watery vegetation as much as 35 feet (11 m) below the ocean surface, world's only seagoing lizards.

Here are the world's farthest-north penguins, along with three kinds of boobies—blue-faced, red- and blue-footed—along with waved albatross, swallow-tailed gulls (which feed nocturnally by sonar using red eye-rings), red-billed tropicbirds, flamingos, magnificent frigate birds with scarlet throat pouches inflated for courtship, and endemic Galapagos hawks and doves. Two-thirds of resident birds are endemic—found nowhere else—including four mockingbird species.

In and around the sea are sea lions, fur seals, and engaging little scarlet Sally Lightfoot crabs.

Because they have not been harassed by humans—except indirectly by introduced now-feral goats and pigs—all the wildlife are enchantingly fearless of visitors.

Each of these islands, once known as the Encantadas or Enchanted Isles, is different.

**Santa Cruz** has the highest human population, also facilities where visitors can arrange overland or boat tours, stay at hotels, and see the Charles Darwin Research Station which has park information and readily visible giant tortoises. Except for the Tortoise Reserve, a day trip, most are in or within walking distance of Puerto Ayora. Most visitors arrive by air at Baltra Airport and transfer from there to Santa Cruz or to prearranged tours.

Among most-visited islands:

**Santa Fe**, one of the best places to see land iguanas and giant cacti over 10 yards (10 m) tall.

**Bartolomé** has Galapagos penguins; sea turtles nest on beaches January–March.

**Seymour**, outstanding seabird nesting grounds, especially blue-footed boobies in elaborate courtship.

OPPOSITE: Courting male blue-footed boobies put their best foot forward, goose-stepping back and forth, lifting bright blue feet as high as possible. Responsive females mimic this and soon the pair are goose-stepping together, ritualistically picking up twigs for an imaginary nest. They actually lay eggs on bare ground, warming them with webbed feet, swiveling during the day to shield them from direct sun, defecating as they do, thereby forming a round guano nest boundary within which young must stay. Some 10,000 blue-footed boobies live on the Galapagos Islands.

**San Salvador** (aka **Santiago** or **James**), marine iguanas sun themselves on black volcanic rocks and fur seals swim in crystalline pools, often with snorkelers.

**Rabida** (aka **Jervis**), hundreds of sea lions and their babies play on dark red sand, and bright flamingos feed on a marshy lake.

**Genovesa** (aka **Tower**), main red-footed booby colony (140,000 pairs), also masked boobies and three types of Darwin finch.

**Espanola** (aka **Hood**), southernmost of the islands, famous for seabirds—masked and blue-footed boobies and especially waved albatross, some 12,000 nesting pairs active in various stages January–April, almost the whole world population.

**Fernandina**, most westerly, with impressive lava flows, penguins (nesting in September–October), flightless cormorants, hordes of marine iguanas.

**Isabela** (aka **Albemarle**), largest of the islands (1,803 square miles, 4,670 km$^2$), with volcanoes, especially Volcan Alcedo where

Frigatebirds are unmistakable among seabirds, great black cut-outs soaring against the sky— equally distinctive later when males attract mates by inflating throat pouches into spectacular crimson balloons which they keep expanded through much of the breeding cycle. Frigatebirds come to land only to nest, often on coastal and remote islands such as the Galapagos, Ascension and Aldabra, raising a single chick with the same feisty disposition as its parents, able early to protect itself while they're out foraging—which they notoriously do by pirating other birds' catches. But there's a reason: frigates have smaller oil glands, so dropping into water would run risk of saturating plumage and becoming un-airworthy.

hundreds of tortoises live amid steaming fumaroles (it's a steep climb up and down to see them), also lagoons with flamingos and migrant birds.

Best times to visit generally are May–June and November–December.

---

**FURTHER INFORMATION**

Superintendente, Servicio Parque Nacional Galapagos, Puerto Ayora, Isla Santa Cruz, Galapagos; Charles Darwin Foundation for the Galapagos, Av. 6 de diciembre 4757 Pasaje California, Aparto Postal 17-01-3891, Quito, Ecuador, Fax: (+593) 2-443-935; Charles Darwin Research Station, Puerto Ayora, Galapagos, Tel: (+593) 5-526-146/7, Fax: (+593) 4-564-636, Website: www.darwinfoundation.org

---

## ALSO OF INTEREST

**Antisana Ecological Reserve**—463 square miles (1,200 km²) in Napo Province with prodigious wildlife, especially birds, not fully censused because of steep, difficult terrain in the Cordillera de Huacamayos, covered by lower montane and montane cloud forest with dense bamboo-dominated understory and almost constant rain or cloud cover. Inhabitants include black-and-chestnut and solitary eagles, lyre-tailed nightjars, orange-breasted falcons, greater scythebills, flame-faced, paradise, and vermilion tanagers, greenish pufflegs, scarlet-breasted fruiteaters, and many, many more. At Lago Micacocha are silvery grebes, black-faced ibises, and carunculated caracaras. Mammals include spectacled bears, pumas, mountain tapirs, Culpeo foxes, and Brazilian rabbits. Lower elevations are more easily reachable from Tena, where accommodations are better; they're simpler in Baeza, but roads are better. Either way, a good guide is important.

In early 1999 President Jamil Mahuad issued a decree blocking future oil exploration, mining, logging, and colonization in the **Cuyabeno-Imuya** and **Yasuni National Parks** which together protect some 4,219 square miles (10,930 km²) of old-growth rain forest. Part of the lush and biologically rich Amazon basin, they contain a vast river and lake system, thousands of plant and animal species—considered one of the most biologically diverse in the world—as well as indigenous peoples unchanged there for thousands of years. It is a great victory, though challenging to make it stick. Both areas have been (and still are) under threat from various causes, especially poaching of rare birds and animals, of which most of Ecuador's most spectacular species are represented here.

Yasuni's western border is 190 miles (306 km) from Quito, reachable only by motorized canoe. Several good lodges are on or near the park's border, however, with trails, boardwalks, and guides; trips can be arranged in Quito.

# GUYANA

IN IWOKRAMA'S 1,250 SQUARE MILES
(3,250 KM²) OF NEWLY PROTECTED RAIN
FOREST ARE RARE GRAY-BILLED GOSHAWKS, HARPY AND
CRESTED EAGLES, OCELOTS, AND ONE OF THE WORLD'S
LARGEST FRESHWATER FISH—ARAPAIMA, UP TO FIVE YARDS
LONG (4.5 M), WEIGHING UP TO 900 POUNDS (400 KG).

GUYANA HAS ONLY ONE NATIONAL PARK BUT IT'S A WONDER, NAMED FOR **KAIETEUR FALLS**, A STUNNING
DROP 820 FEET (250 M) DOWN AND NEARLY 400 FEET (122 M) WIDE DURING WET SEASONS, WITH FAS-
CINATING WILDLIFE. Tiny intrepid Kaieteur swifts dart through the sparkling torrent to roost and nest
on drenched but protected cliffs surrounded by pristine tropical forest with silver foxes, tapirs,
ocelots, scarlet Andean cocks-of-the-rock, armor-plated armadillos, anteaters, and monkeys.

On the northern edge of Guyana's Rupununi savannah to the southwest is **Iwokrama**, 1,250
square miles (3,250 km²) of newly protected primary rain forest, a reserve for research into

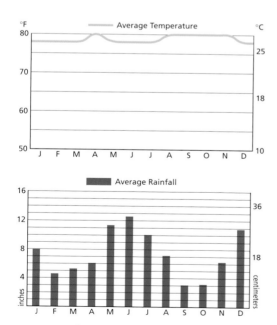

Gateway city: Georgetown

# GUYANA

Flamingos feed anywhere their long legs can take them, bending over until box-like "upside-down" bills touch the water's bottom and built-in filtering mechanisms go to work. Tongues pump water back and forth through membranes sifting out a constant flow of watery organisms that supply not only nutrition but ingredients that help maintain their brilliant plumage, feeding over northern South America up through the West Indies.

sustainable forestry and home to rich birdlife—rare gray-billed goshawks, yellow-knobbed curassows, harpy and crested eagles, along with scarlet macaws, six species of iridescent jacamars, spangled and pompadour cotingas, also ocelots, black spider monkeys, brown and weeper capuchins, tapirs, two-toed sloths, giant anteaters, gray foxes.

Also in **Rupununi** are arapaima, one of the world's largest freshwater fish, up to five yards (4.5 m) long, weighing up to 900 pounds (400 kg), now rare from overharvesting.

Neither reserve is easy to reach. Planes can be chartered and cars rented (but roads are poor) in the capital, Georgetown ("garden city of the Caribbean" fronting on the Atlantic Ocean), where there are accommodations and tours can be arranged. Best avoid January–February and August–September, the main wet seasons (when, however, the falls are most spectacular). Threats include inadequate government protection of natural areas and destructive logging by multinationals.

**FURTHER INFORMATION**

Ministry of Home Affairs, National Parks Commission, 6 Brickdam, Georgetown, Tel: (+592) 225-9142.

# PARAGUAY

RARE MANED WOLVES HAVE BEEN CALLED
CALLED "FOXES ON STILTS", WITH SHARP FOX-LIKE FACES,
LONG LEGS SO THEY CAN SEE OVER TALL PAMPAS GRASS,
AND BACK HAIRS THAT ERECT INTO A MANE WHEN THEY
WANT TO BE CONSPICUOUS, AS IN SEXUAL RIVALRY. PERSECUTED
BECAUSE OF SUPPOSED PREDATION OF DOMESTIC STOCK, THEY
FIND HOMES WITH OTHER RARITIES—SMALL GEOFFROY'S CATS
AND CHACO PECCARIES, UNTIL RECENTLY THOUGHT EXTINCT—
IN DEFENSORES DEL CHACO IN THE GRAND CHACO, ONE
OF SOUTH AMERICA'S GREAT WILDERNESSES.

LANDLOCKED PARAGUAY DIVIDES INTO LUSH, WELL-WATERED ROLLING GRASSLANDS WITH MOST OF THE COUNTRY'S HUMAN AGRARIAN POPULATION TO THE EAST OF THE RIO PARAGUAY AND, ON THE

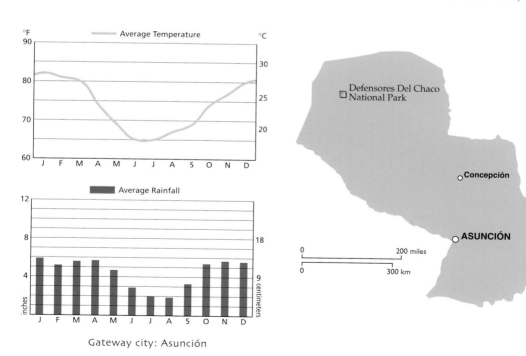

Gateway city: Asunción

# PARAGUAY

WESTERN 60 PERCENT, THE VAST, ARID, INHOSPITABLE GRAN CHACO WHICH HAS BEEN CALLED ONE OF SOUTH AMERICA'S GREAT WILDERNESSES. In the Chaco are most of Paraguay's wildlife, including rare hyacinth macaws, caimans, and giant anacondas. There are three large national parks, outstandingly the **Defensores del Chaco**.

Defensores' dense thorn forest and wooded alluvial plains protect Paraguay's most endangered animals—big cats such as jaguars, pumas, and ocelots; smaller, rare Geoffroy's cats; Chacoan peccaries once thought extinct; giant anteaters; maned wolves; Brazilian tapirs; among birds, jabiru and wood storks, spectacular parrots, and bright tropical songbirds.

Defensores is 515 miles (830 km) northwest of Asunción over roads often impassable to all but 4WD vehicles. Trips sometimes can be arranged with park rangers. Fundación Moisés Bertoni (FMB), a private group, has set up a number of Private Nature Reserves (PNRs) with sympathetic ranchers, with whom visits sometimes can be arranged. Best times are September–November, the austral spring.

Another reserve of great interest is the **Natural Forest Reserve Mbaracayu**, which harbors jaguars and tapirs as well as a splendid variety of birdlife.

---

**FURTHER INFORMATION**

Secretary of the Environment (SEAM), Avda. Madame Lynch Nnro.3.500-Campo Grande-Asunción, Tel: (+595) 21-615-806, Fax: (+595) 21-615-807; Fundación Moisés Bertoni, Procer Carlos Arguello Nro. 288 casi Mcal Lopez, Asunción, Tel: (+595) 21-600-855; Fundación Des Chaco, E-mail: fdschaco@2telesurf.com.py

---

Wood storks may forage up to 25 miles (40 km) from their nests, spreading broad wings and gliding on thermals with little energy expenditure. They walk up to belly-deep in freshwater ponds, marshes and sloughs groping with down-curved opened bills which snap shut on frogs, tadpoles, snakes, young alligators, even large insects. These they carry back and regurgitate, partly digested, to nestlings which can consume some 50 pounds (23 kg) of food each before fledging from dense tree colonies from the southern U.S. south to Buenos Aires.

# PERU

DAZZLING SCARLET MACAWS WHEEL AND
SQUABBLE WITH MULTIHUED PARROTS OF 28 SPECIES,
SOMETIMES HUNDREDS TOGETHER, SHOULDERING
ONE OTHER ASIDE FOR PLACES TO SNATCH MINERAL-RICH
BILLSFUL OF CLAY FROM CLIFFS ALONG THE MEANDERING
MADRE DE DIOS RIVER IN MANU NATIONAL PARK.

PERU RANKS WITH COLOMBIA IN HAVING AS GREAT DIVERSITY AND CONCENTRATION OF WILDLIFE—INCLUD-ING SPECTACULAR BIRDS—AS ANY OTHER COUNTRY ON EARTH, IN ALMOST INNUMERABLE HABITAT NICHES.

From Pacific coastal desert, one of the driest places in the world, to jagged heights of the Andes, dropping to deep, almost sea-level Amazon jungle swamps live powerful jaguars, rare spectacled bears, and shaggy maned wolves, among hundreds of other mammal species including tapirs, tree sloths, 32 species of monkeys, and 152 kinds of bats.

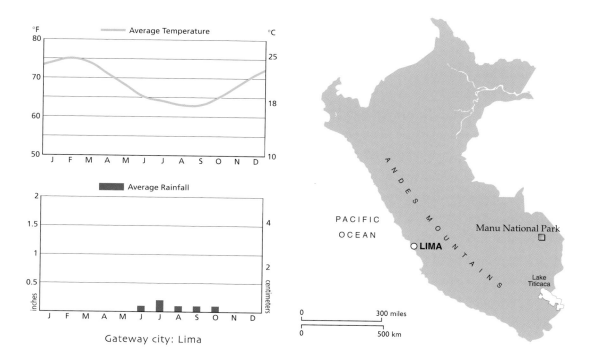

Gateway city: Lima

# PERU

Velvet-coated cameloids—guanacos and vicuñas with perhaps the softest, most valued pelts of any animals—graze mountain meadows, and there are some 1,800 bird species, almost twice as many as in all of North America.

Giant Andean condors with silvery-white wingpatches soar over peaks on 10-foot-plus (3-m) wingspreads, fingerlike primary feathers spread to catch every thermal nuance. Brilliant scarlet macaws and rainbow-hued parrots crowd jungle stream banks, hundreds at a time, for valuable dietary minerals. Bejeweled hummingbirds of 100 species described by names such as sapphire-spangled emerald, festive coquette, and black-eared fairies, sip nectar at all elevations. And there are remarkable Amazonian umbrella birds, orange-crimson Andean cocks-of-the-rock, marvelous spatule-tails, melodious nightingale wrens, great potoos, and long-whiskered owlets.

Tremendous biodiversity results from continuous overlap of almost innumerable microhabitats created by variable combinations of elevation, latitude, and moisture in Peru's three main natural regions. In lowlands unaffected by ice ages, species have evolved without hindrance for eons. Over most of history the remote, forbidding character of Peru's wild areas has discouraged exploitation (not all, as during the Spanish Conquest) and to a great extent it still does, though logging for valuable timber is a constant threat, as are mining, oil and gas exploration, cattle-raising, and other aspects of encroaching civilization.

Frisky dolphins, sea lions, and sea otters compete with huge swarms of seabirds—gulls, terns, pelicans, boobies, cormorants, and Humboldt penguins—for bounty from the Humboldt current running offshore most of Peru's length. This strong current churns up cold water and nutrients from the deep Pacific. This creates coastal desert by holding moisture in the ocean—but its nutrients sustain a rich plankton community which supports vast fish numbers, prey base in turn for others.

Seabirds gather in the many thousands to feed over fish schools in a frenzied oceanic carpet of flapping, diving feathers. Islands such as the Ballestas off Paracas Peninsula support teeming colonies of water-oriented birds of dozens of species. One, the Guanay cormorant, is an economic treasure, its mountains of droppings harvested as guano, a potent natural fertilizer.

Life ashore is drier and sparser but notable. Plover-like Peruvian thick-knees wail plaintively. Small desert foxes sound like car tires screeching as they bark through the night (and sometimes day). Vermilion-headed Peruvian flycatchers flit over oases where rivers tumble from high mountains. Long-legged herons, egrets, and coral-pink flamingos forage in shallows, joined spring and fall by flocks of migrants.

Land rises precipitously from the desert, pushed up by tectonic plates to more than 18,000 feet (6,000 m) just 60 miles (100 km) inland. Pumas hunt in low riparian valleys but also venture up through stunted elfin woods and cloud forest homes of small, graceful Andean deer, velvet-furred chinchillas (Peruvian chipmunks), and shy little pampas and Andean cats, whose tracks have been seen at 16,000 feet (5,000 m). Diademed sandpiper-plovers pipe their calls. Patches of shrubby colorful polylepis cling to life at the highest elevation of any tree.

These eastern Andean slopes, among the least accessible and least known on the planet, are secure haunts of seldom-seen spectacled bears and mountain tapirs.

Other habitat variations occur as land descends again, more gradually, to the Amazon rain forest basin, which originates in Peru and makes up half the country—oldest continuous terrestrial habitat on earth. This is domain of giant river otters, bubble-gum-pink river dolphins, and slow-moving tree sloths.

In this fragile but rich environment, over 6,000 plant species have been found in just one 250-acre (115-ha) plot. (Tropical rain forests cover less than four percent of earth's surface but support over 50 percent of all its species, an estimated half of which have yet to be identified.) There are crocodilians in rivers, musky-smelling peccaries, bulky water-loving cabybaras—world's largest rodents—and at least 1,000 bird species. These include prehistoric-looking hoatzins, whose young come equipped with claws enabling them to climb from watery riverside nests into overhanging trees where they clamber about until they learn to fly.

Over 12 percent of Peru's 496,222 square miles (1,285,000 km²) is set aside in 56 protected areas within SINANPI—the Peruvian state protected area system.

They include:

MANU NATIONAL PARK AND BIOSPHERE RESERVE—a vast and stunning jungle of 6,600 square miles (17,100 km²), bigger than the state of Connecticut—with adjoining **Alto Purus Reserved Zone**, covers 10,000 square miles (25,900 km²), a huge protected area which scientists think may contain the richest flora and fauna of any place on the planet.

**National Reserve of Pacaya-Samiria** is Peru's largest defined protected area, some 7,150 square miles (18,520 km²) of tropical forest at the heart of the upper Amazon in northern Peru, undeveloped at least until recently for tourism, but guides can be arranged in Iquitos or Lagunas.

**Huascaran National Park**, 1,170 square miles (3,030 km²), with high Andes species, a popular hiking/climbing area.

**National Reserve of Pampa Galeras**, 25 square miles (65 km²) near Nasca, set aside for rare vicuñas, smallest, most beautiful of South American cameloids brought near extinction for their precious soft fur.

**Paracas National Reserve**, an 1,295-square-mile (3,350-km²) coastal peninsula with stunning birdlife both onshore and just offshore at the Ballestas Islands, with huge nest colonies of penguins, pelicans, terns, boobies, cormorants, waved albatross, along with seals, sea lions.

These are immense, largely pristine areas designated by the National System for Conservation Units where nature is not controlled or organized. Many have minimal if any visitor facilities. In 1992 the Peruvian National Trust Fund was established, managed by the private sector, to provide funding to protect the country's main reserves with help from the government and national and international nongovernmental groups such as World Wide Fund for Nature, The Nature Conservancy, the World Bank facility, and U.N. Environment Program.

There is also **Colca Canyon**, said to be the world's deepest terrestrial chasm—twice as deep as the Grand Canyon—where it is sometimes possible at the rim to view soaring condors at eye level. Snows across the canyon at Mismi peak—elevation 18,200 feet (5,600 m)—are birthplace of the mighty Amazon River.

Best time here is the May–September dry season; otherwise travel can be difficult with roads sometimes impassable, flights cancelled, and landslides blocking train and bus routes (also, clouds can obscure spectacular scenic views).

Threats include mining, oil and gas exploration, grazing, poaching, and illegal logging, particularly of high value mahogany trees.

---

**FURTHER INFORMATION**

Asociación Peruana para la Conservación de la Naturaleza (APECO), Parque Jose Acosta 187, p 2, Magdalena del Mark, Tel: (+51) 616316; Fundación Peruana para la Conservación de la Naturaleza (FPCN), Av de los Rosales 255, San Isidro, Lima, Tel: (+51) 14-426706/-426616, Fax: (+51) 14-446-9178; Rumbo El Dorado Ecotourism Venture, promoting ecologically compatible tourism that benefits local communities, E-mail: greenlife@pacaya-samiria.com, Website: www.Pacaya-samiria.com

# MANU NATIONAL PARK

Manu National Park with adjacent areas has the largest, most diverse concentration of birds and other wildlife of any park on earth, and some of the rarest and most interesting. Here as in few

---

OPPOSITE: Crow-sized hoatzins appear prehistoric—with bare, bright-blue faces, red eyes and wild, bristly red-and-black mohawk crests. Indeed, their nestlings carry claws on their wings like those of ARCHAEOPTERYX, the oldest bird ancestor from 150 million years ago. They use these along with the ability to swim when danger approaches, plunging from the nest (usually over water), and swimming away, using their claws to climb back up after danger has passed. Both these skills are lost in adulthood. The birds are the modern-day counterparts of hoatzin fossils found from Oligocene times, and they have yet another unique aspect: a cow-like vegetarian digestive system based on fermentation, that gives them permanent bad breath.

other places are monkey-eating harpy eagles, rainbow-hued macaws, spectacled bears, giant armadillos, mountain tapirs, and formidable 31-foot (9.6-m) aquatic anacondas, occasionally prey themselves for formidable giant river otters.

To suggest its extraordinarily rich biodiversity—15 percent of the world's bird species can be found here. Census of a single 2.2-acre (1-ha) forest tract turned up 41,000 invertebrate species including 12,000 kinds of beetle. A single tree had 43 types of ant belonging to 26 different genera.

The Amazon River basin originates in Peru and much of it is made up of a rain forest which comprises half the country. It is the largest tropical forest in the world, covering 2.7 million square miles (7 million km²), the oldest continuous land environment on earth, and Manu National Park protects 5,920 square miles (15,350 km²) of it. With adjoining protected tracts, it is as close to pristine wilderness as exists anywhere. Small, nomadic, indigenous tribes live here as they have for eons, subsistence users of the forest, hunting with arrows, many all but unaware of its few visitors.

The U.N. Biosphere Reserve of which it is a major part touches eastern slopes of the cool high Andes and drops to a steamy few hundred feet above sea level. Along the way it offers uncounted small and large interrelated wildlife habitats that accommodate some 1,000 bird species, more than 200 mammals, and 15,000 plants. A half-million arthropods—insects and spiders—have been found, including more than 1,200 butterflies, and more of all these are being identified continuously as scientists explore and classify all that is here.

In the Andes, great Andean condors, black with flashing white patches on wings spreading 10 feet plus (3 m), soar high over hook-billed flower-piercer and thistletail birds in high grasslands and stunted elfin forest.

Descending to 7,500–10,200 feet (2,500–3,400 m), gray-breasted mountain toucans with blue eye-rings and outsized orange-spattered bills share tree bounty with barred fruit-eaters. Swallow-tailed nightjars, bills agape, scoop up insect swarms among huge tree-ferns and 15-foot-tall (5-m) bamboo stands in humid temperate forest which is based in sedimentary and metamorphic rocks more than 440 million years old.

Below in subtropical forest dwells of one of the world's most spectacular birds, Andean cocks-of-the-rock, orange-scarlet with black wings, and permanently erect helmet-like crimson crests nearly covering their bills. These foot-long (32-cm) birds are quiet except on courtship leks where males gather to work themselves up to a fluttering frenzy, one of the world's avian marvels, for often seemingly indifferent females.

Mixed bird flocks at this altitude may include dozens of species and hundreds of individuals—cerulean-capped manakins, versicolored barbets, paradise tanagers, orange-fronted plushcrowns, and others. Some forage in the forest canopy, others at mid-level, others in the understory, associating harmoniously because most employ species-specific foraging techniques. This reduces competition, while flocking together offers safety-in-numbers protection against forest falcons and other predators.

Below, humid tropical forest drops to 500 feet (150 m) in the Amazon basin proper where the Manu and Madre de Dios rivers slowly meander, offering ecological niche-opportunities for almost innumerable wild creatures. White sand beaches exposed in dry June–October are crowded with nesting large-billed and yellow-billed terns, pied lapwings, sand-colored night-jars. Statuesque jabiru and American wood storks and roseate spoonbills feed in the shallows, and thousands of migrating shorebirds touch down. On recently formed islands are willow-loving orange-headed tanagers and river tyrannulets. In the forest, rarities like fruit-loving black-faced cotingas and, on the floor, rufus-fronted ant-thrushes can be seen with certainty only here. The air is melodic with songs of drab but tuneful nightingale wrens and musician birds.

On high riverbanks, hundreds of screaming scarlet macaws three feet (1 m) long converge with multihued parrot relatives of 28 species. Wheeling and squabbling, each looks for a place to snatch up clay (packed with important dietary minerals) with their bills.

Hunting quietly around oxbow lake edges are fasciated tiger-herons, wattled "walking-on-water" jacanas, silvered antbirds, sungrebes, sunbitterns, and wild-looking, primitive hoatzins, which scientists once speculated incorrectly might be a link with dinosaurs. Two feet (61 cm) long with bright blue faces, red eyes and long, frizzled, "bad-hair-day" crests, they are almost entirely vegetarian, a heavy fibrous diet that makes flight and balance clumsy and difficult. Young hatch in waterside nests where they hiss and pitch into the water if disturbed, diving and swimming, equipped with wing-claws that enable them to clamber up and around trees in safety—adaptations lost in adulthood.

Shy, dark, tousled spectacled bears with markings like white eye-glasses follow their primarily vegetarian diet in mountain woodlands. They are the only native South American bear and sole surviving "short-faced" bear—a group that once inhabited North and South America.

Jaguars, western hemisphere's largest cat species, prowl lower forests, as do powerful pumas and smaller spotted ocelots, wary but frequently sighted in this protected tract, sometimes while drinking along rivers. Here rare, deceptively slow-looking black lizard-caimans up to 15 feet (almost 5 m) long bask, and playful groups of giant otters over 6.5 feet (2 m) long fish for everything from piranhas to electric eels. These insatiably curious, seemingly fearless mammals, endangered from overhunting for their sleek, luxurious fur, have been known to take on giant anacondas, world's longest snakes. Up to 30 feet (9.6 m) long, these formidable water serpents lurk in shallows to capture unwary drinkers.

At least 13 kinds of monkeys chatter and swing about lowland forests, preyed on by monkey-eating harpy eagles with seven-foot (2+ m) wingspreads and talons seven inches (18 cm) long, the

# PERU

Amazon's most powerful birds. Among primates are roaring red howlers, diminutive, restless, emperor tamarins decorated with superb imperial white mustaches, also woolly, spider, and the world's smallest monkeys—tiny pygmy marmosets, each weighing barely four ounces (120 g).

Butterflies of dozens of species and every imaginable color and pattern gather at moist places (sometimes on moist passersby) not only to drink but for minerals released by the moisture (and on humans, perspiration). In the forest, iridescent blue morpho butterflies opening and closing their wings can shine like flickering spotlights in the gloom as far away as 60 feet (18 m).

Daylong—and nightlong—sounds range from interesting to borderline-deafening when eagles, kingfishers, songbirds, thunderous howler monkeys, jaguars, owls, giant crickets, and thousands of others sound off. Best times here are the (relatively) dry season May–October.

Threats include discovery of an enormous natural gas deposit believed to extend under the park's northeast. Exploration already has damaged wildlife, polluted rivers, and driven out indigenous groups. Also proposed is a power station with road and gas pipeline passing through the reserve. Also poaching—spotted fur rugs still can be obtained!

## FURTHER INFORMATION

Manu National Park Administration, Holders 157, Of. 34, Apartado 1057, Cuzco, Peru; Manu National Park Office, of 1, Av El Sol, Edificio San Jorge, Pasaje Grace, Cuzco, Tel: (+51) 084-224-683, Fax: (+51) 084-221-020 (*See* also under PERU); Peruvian Conservation Association for the Southern Rainforests (ACSS), Avenida Sol 627-B, oficina 305, Cuzco, non-profit, dedicated to forest protection.

# VENEZUELA

FAT OILBIRDS LIVE DEEP IN CAVES, NEVER
SEEING DAYLIGHT BUT FLYING LIKE BATS WITH
ECHOLOCATION, AVOIDING COLLISIONS BY REACTING
TO ECHOES OF SOUND PULSES THEY EMIT AT 7,000
CYCLES PER SECOND AT INTERVALS OF 2.3 MILLISECONDS.
ONCE SOUGHT FOR OIL RENDERED AND USED IN LAMPS
AND COOKING, THEY'RE PROTECTED NOW IN CUEVO
DEL GUACHAROS—CAVE OF THE OILBIRDS.

RARE, OWLISH, SPECTACLED BEARS AMBLE ALONG IN HIGH MOIST CLOUD FORESTS IN FAR NORTHERN EXTENSIONS OF THE SNOW-CAPPED ANDES WHILE JAGUARS AND TAPIRS MAKE THEIR WAY IN LOWLAND SAVANNAHS AND FORESTED JUNGLES ON FRINGES OF THE AMAZON BASIN.

In between stretch vast plains known as Los Llanos, with ocelots, giant anteaters, and some of the continent's densest, most varied bird populations, covering a third of the country and extending south into Colombia and east to the 1,335-mile-long (2,150-km) Orinoco River and its great delta crisscrossed by mazes of channels. In the southeast, flat open savannah is dotted with steep-sided 3–6,000-foot-tall (1–3,000-m) mesas or tepuis, each mesa so isolated from others they have evolved separate ecologies over millions of years, in eerily dramatic scenery made famous in A. Conan Doyle's science-fiction novel *Lost World*.

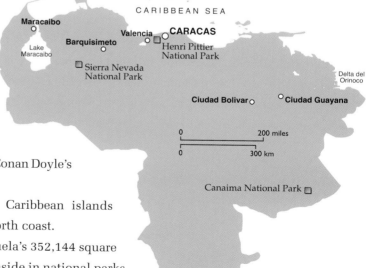

Dazzling marine life inhabits Caribbean islands and brilliant coral reefs off the north coast.

More than 15 percent of Venezuela's 352,144 square miles (912,052 km²) has been set aside in national parks and monuments protecting some 250 mammal species

571

# VENEZUELA

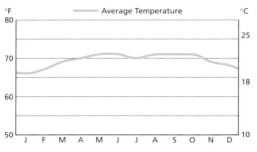

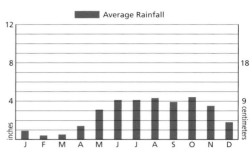

Gateway city: Caracas

including pumas, ocelots, chattering monkeys, and prehensile-tailed porcupines, plus, among reptiles, formidable anacondas up to 30 feet (10 m) long, weighing up to 500 pounds (225 kg), and five kinds of crocodiles, including huge caimans del Orinoco 16 feet (5 m) or more long.

Venezuela has more bird species than in all of Europe and North America combined—some 1,360 including brilliant hummingbirds beating their wings 80 times a second, high-stepping coral-hued flamingos, yard-long (1-m) scarlet macaws, and fat, cave-dwelling oilbirds that never see daylight and fly by echolocation—plus a breathtaking butterfly array.

Temperatures vary mainly by elevation, dropping about 10°F (6°C) for every 3,000-foot (1,000-m) going up. Dry season is usually December–April.

International jets touch down at Caracas. From there serviceable roads go almost everywhere, and there's an excellent internal air network, though travel arrangements can be unreliable during Easter, Christmas, and Carnival celebrations.

Environmental threats are many and serious—indiscriminate deforestation for lumbering, pastureland, farming, construction, and industry, leading to widespread erosion; ill-advised hydrological schemes; oil drilling; mining using mercury which has poisoned rivers and endangered not only wildlife but human health; poaching. Almost universal lack of environmental awareness means some of the best environmental laws in South America are not enforced, swamped in a sea of bureaucracy, corruption, and a weak judicial system.

---

**FURTHER INFORMATION**

Instituto Nacional de Parques (INPARQUESO, Museu de Transporte, Edif Sur, Av Rómulo Gallegos, Parque del Este, Tel: (+582) 284-1956, Caracas; Ministerio del Ambiente y de los Recursos Naturales (MARNR), Centro Simon Bolivar, Torre Sul, p 19, Caracas 1010, Tel: (+582) 483-3164/1071; FUDENA (Fundación para la Defensa de la Naturaleza), Apartado 70376, Caracas 1071-A, Venezuela, Tel: (+582) (12) 238-29-30/238-17-61/238-17-93, Fax: (+582) (12) 239-65-47, Website: www.fudena.org.ve, E-mail: fudena@fudena.org.ve

# CANAIMA NATIONAL PARK

Canaima National Park in southeast Venezuela, at 11,720 square miles (30,360 km²) one of the world's largest, is a U.N. World Heritage Site set among jungle, savannah, and some of the world's most surreal landscape with high vertical-sided table-topped mesas or tepuis where ecologies have evolved in isolation for millions of years, some with biota found nowhere else. These include purple-red sunflowers and frogs that walk instead of jump, possible remnants, theories go, of prehistoric times when Africa and South America were joined. Some tepuis are still not fully explored. Countless waterfalls include the world's highest, Angel Falls, tumbling 3,230 feet (985 m) from Precambrian rocks 600 million to 2 billion years old on the side of Roraima mesa in the world's longest uninterrupted drop of 2,663 feet (812 m). Wildlife, while not abundant, includes increasingly rare giant and collared anteaters, giant armadillos, giant otters, bush dogs, crab-eating foxes, and little spotted cats, plus some 550 birds including red-billed and red-and-green macaws, fiery-shouldered parakeets, king vultures, paradise tanagers, velvet-browed brilliants, and Guianan cocks-of-the rock, along with 72 reptiles, 55 amphibians. Scheduled flights go to Canaima Lake, where excellent lodging (also camping) is available and tours can be arranged.

# HENRI PITTIER NATIONAL PARK

Henri Pittier National Park is a wildlife treasure-house, especially for birds—some 600 species, one of the highest concentrations in the world, almost as many as in the entire area from Alaska to Mexico. They respond here to the great variety of climate and habitat—something for every kind of bird—from arid Caribbean beaches with lagoons where bright flamingos gather, rising to 6,000 feet (2,000 m) in Cordillera de la Costa Mountains where a v-shaped dip allows passage of migrants from as far away as Argentina and Alaska.

Descending in both directions are cloud and evergreen tropical forest with tumbling mountain streams, semidry deciduous woods and, at the shore, coastal scrub, mangroves, and coconut groves—all in a fairly short distance, a few hours' drive over the two (unconnected) roads winding through.

In trees 200 feet (61 m) tall are helmeted curassows, blood-eared parakeets, bearded blue-bells, and earth's most powerful avian predators, harpy eagles, along with six other eagle species, plus well-named handsome fruiteaters, shining white-tipped quetzals and, in low understory, spectacular golden tanagers and long-tailed sylphs.

Powerful pumas, jaguars, and ocelots prowl the jungle below with giant anteaters and shy 440-pound (200-kg) tapirs. Prehensile-tailed porcupines climb trees where three-toed sloths languidly browse and red howler monkeys make cliffs resound for miles. Marsupial frogs in

moist enclaves advertise for mates with penetrating nocturnal calls issued 250 times an hour, after which females brood young in pouches on their backs.

This spectacular area just two hours west of Caracas was first noticed by dictator Juan Vicente Gomez who started building an elegant hideaway and hotel here; it was left unfinished after his death in 1935. Two years later the area was set aside as Venezuela's 416-square-mile (1,080-km$^2$) first national park, named after the Swiss naturalist who founded the country's park system. In the park is Estacion Biologica de Rancho Grande with zoological museum and trails, reachable

Roseate spoonbills like to be with others of their kind. They fly together in long lines or wedge-shaped formations. They build bulky stick nests together in densely leafed trees and bushes on coastal islands isolated from land predators, often together with herons, ibises and other wading birds. They feed together in tidal ponds and sloughs from the U.S. gulf coast south through northern South America to Argentina.

by road from Maracay, El Limon, or Choroni. Lodging dormitory-style is available at the station; hotels at nearby towns and beaches. Best times are dry season December–March; for bird migration September–October.

## SIERRA NEVADA NATIONAL PARK

Beautiful Sierra Nevada National Park ranges from humid rain forest to Venezuela's highest peaks, northern extensions of the Andes, with wildlife that includes wary pumas, tapirs, jaguars, red howler monkeys, and red brocket deer and, more visibly, birds such as speckled teal, black-and-chestnut buzzard-eagles, Andean snipes, white-capped dippers, several bright hummingbirds. This is one of Venezuela's last refuges for two of its most threatened species, Andean condors and spectacled bears. Lodging and guides are in Merida, reachable by air from Caracas.

## ALSO OF INTEREST

Overlying central Venezuela for roughly a third of the country and extending well into Colombia are **Los Llanos**—the Plains—unearthly expanses of flat, low-lying grass-covered millions-of-years-old riverine deposits of sand, clay, and mud, with ribbons of gallery forest along rivers, dotted with ponds and lakes in the dry season, awash in the wet. Here live some of the greatest wildlife populations—350 bird species including spectacular scarlet ibis flocks, prehistoric hoatzins, high-stepping russet wattled jacanas, maguari and jabiru storks with seven-foot (2+ m) wingspans, clouds of egrets and whistling geese, plus two crocodiles—spectacled and caimans del Orinoco or American crocodiles (poached for their skins)—endangered freshwater dolphins and manatees, and 50 mammals including jaguars, ocelots, tapirs, giant anteaters, dashing little savannah foxes, and omnipresent herds of endearing capybaras, world's largest rodents, which graze underwater as easily as on land.

Two large national parks protect important habitat: **Cinaruco-Capanapareo** (also known as **Santos Luzardo**) and **Aguaro-Guariquito**; but one of the best ways to see Los Llanos is through several hatos or large ranches (notably Hato Pinero, also Hato El Frio, El Cedral, La Trinidad de Arauca and San Leonardo) which have ecotourist facilities with guides.

Wildlife is abundant at all seasons but more visible around watered areas in drier December–April.

**Morrocoy National Park** has significant wading and waterbird populations on beautiful white-sand coastal beaches and islands, also coral reefs, all threatened by heavy tourist pressure. Camping with permits, also hotels in nearby Tucacas.

**Los Roques National Park** with superb marine life is a diver's paradise (and a world's top bone-fishing destination).

**Cueva del Guacharo**—Cave of the Guacharos—is a national monument protecting the area around the country's largest colony of some 15,000 or more nocturnal fruit-eating oilbirds which live in total darkness in the first chamber of this magnificent cave near Caripe.

# SOUTH PACIFIC ISLANDS

KOALA BEARS

# AUSTRALIA

WHEN CAPTAIN COOK RAN HIS HMS
ENDEAVOUR AGROUND OFF AUSTRALIA'S
EASTERN COAST IN 1770, HE KNEW HE'D HIT
SOMETHING UNUSUAL. NOW WE KNOW IT AS THE
GREAT BARRIER REEF, 1,250 MILES (2,000 KM)
LONG, LARGEST STRUCTURE EVER BUILT BY LIVING
CREATURES, AND VISIBLE FROM THE MOON.

AUSTRALIA'S UNIQUE AND DIVERSE WILDLIFE—POUCHED KANGAROOS, EGG-LAYING MAMMALS, FLIGHTLESS BIRDS, CUDDLY KOALA BEARS, AND MORE—BEGAN WHEN IT BROKE OFF FROM THE SUPERCONTINENT GONDWANALAND 55 MILLION YEARS AGO AND DRIFTED FROM ANTARCTICA TO WARMER CLIMES.

Isolated now between Pacific and Indian Oceans with about five percent of the world's land surface—almost three million square miles (7,682,300 km²)—and an undulating coastline 22,831 miles (36,735 km) long, it has plants, animals, and ancient bacteria found nowhere else. They are in more than 500 national parks, including nine U.N. World Heritage Sites, plus some 1,500 other reserves and sanctuaries covering more than 92,200 square miles (240,000 km²). Habitat ranges from humid rain forest and coastal dunes to rugged mountain ranges, vast arid outback which can burst into spectacular bloom, offshore islands and the GREAT BARRIER REEF running parallel to Queensland for 1,250 miles (2,000 km), longest reef on earth.

Until introduction of foreign mammals by Europeans, almost all Australian mammals were marsupials, primitive orders which, lacking placentas, bear young in a pouch, or marsupium. National symbol is the kangaroo—largest being "big reds" up to 200 pounds (91 kg).

Some 120 kinds of marsupials range from "big reds" to tiny mouse-like honey possums that can fit in a human hand. In between are pouched honeygliders, bandicoots, wombats, and spotted quolls along with koala bears and in neighboring Tasmania, doglike Tasmanian devils, known for ferocity, with powerful jaws that can devour entire carcasses, including their bones.

Even more primitive are egg-laying monotremes, the semiaquatic duck-billed platypus which lays eggs in grass-lined nests and suckles young—first reports were discounted in England as a hoax—and echidnas, small mound-like spiny anteaters which carry eggs in pouches where young hatch and stay until their spines get too sharp for their mothers.

# AUSTRALIA

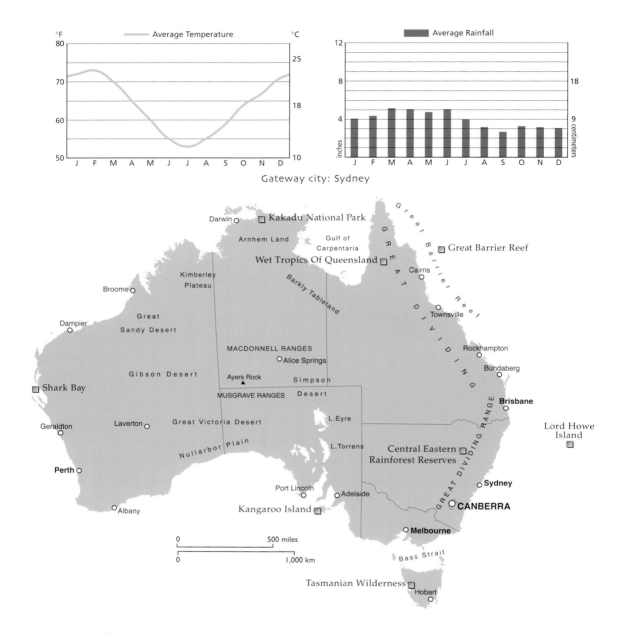

Average Temperature — °F / °C

Average Rainfall — inches / centimeters

Gateway city: Sydney

OPPOSITE: Red kangaroos are largest living marsupials, six feet tall (1.8 m) with heavy four-foot-long (1.2-m) tails on which they rely for balance and self-defense, stabilizing them while they kick out with formidable hind legs. With these legs they jump up to six feet (1.8 m), covering up to 29 feet (8.8 m) in a bound, and run up to 35 miles an hour (56 kph) in short bursts. Their few enemies include introduced dingo dogs and sheep farmers who shoot them on sight to keep them off grazing land (they won't jump over tall fencing but this is regarded as prohibitively costly). Red kangaroos range over scrublands in Australia's central areas, where their coloring camouflages them against red outback soil, but they can vary from red to gray.

## AUSTRALIA

Saltwater or estuarine crocodiles up to 23 feet (7 m) long readily attack humans, sometimes with fatal results, menacing swimmers up to 60 miles (100 km) inland. Freshwater crocs are generally harmless, and distinguished by smaller size and narrow, pointed noses. Both are protected species. Of 140 kinds of snakes, only about 10 percent are poisonous but some are the most venomous in the world. One dose extracted from the most venomous will kill 250,000 mice—but one must watch out as well for taipans, tigers, death adders, and a handful of others which are generally shy but touchy if surprised, as are several poisonous spiders and, in the sea, dangerous box jellyfish (aka sea wasps), blue-ringed octopi, and reef cone shells.

Australia has the world's only wild population of camels, whose ancestors were imported to supply the arid outback and released when their function was usurped by motor vehicles. The other 13 million or so in Africa and the Middle East are all domesticated.

Birds range from fierce wedge-tailed eagles capable of bringing down small kangaroos, with eyesight so keen they can see a rabbit a mile (1.6 km) away, to six-foot-tall (2-m) flightless emus, noisy kookaburras, bowerbirds decorating nuptial rendezvous, and a dazzling array of colorful parrots, cockatoos, finches, honeyeaters. Of more than 750 species, including albatrosses, penguins, and 130 other seabirds—more seabirds than any other country—almost half are found nowhere else.

Threats include habitat loss through logging and agricultural clearing, which destroyed 18,750 square miles (48,600 km²) of native bush late in the 20th century, and which continues. As a result, nearly half the country's passerine birds are in decline and other wildlife has suffered comparably.

Popular as kangaroos are, millions are shot yearly, regarded as competing with sheep and cattle for grazing and waterholes. Ironically, their population increased after attempts to eliminate dingoes, now-native wild dogs originally domesticated by Aborigines, for alleged sheep depredations (actually they largely subsist on rabbits, rats, and mice). The world's longest artificial barrier is a fence 1.5–2.5 yards (1.4–2.4 m) high and some 6,000 miles (9,600 km) long, designed to keep dingoes out of southeastern Australia.

Rental cars are widely available, including 4WD, with good roads, also an internal air network which sometimes offers air passes, and, except in remote areas, a wide range of accommodations is available, also campsites.

---

**FURTHER INFORMATION**

Australian Department of the Environment, Sports and Territories, G.P.O. Box 787, Canberra, ACT 2601, Tel: (+61) 06-274-1111, Fax: (+61) 06-274-1123.

# CENTRAL EASTERN RAINFOREST RESERVES

The Central Eastern Rainforest Reserves (CERRA) is a chain of superb rain forests with plants and animals seldom or never found elsewhere, a U.N. World Heritage Site of more than 50 national parks and reserves stretching more than 500 miles (800 km) along southeastern Australia's Great Escarpment.

Some of the more than 200 rare and threatened species here go back 55 million years or more, before break-up of Australia from Antarctica and the ancient Gondwanaland supercontinent. These remarkable ecosystems, isolated since then in coastal Queensland and New South Wales, cover altogether 1,415 square miles (3,665 km²) with five distinct rain forest types, largely undisturbed by human activity.

Lyrebirds nest here with courtship dances as dramatic as any in the bird world, when males set in motion perhaps the world's most specialized tail feathers in a vibrating dorsal umbrella of lacy plumes and separately scintillating lyre-shaped quills. Meanwhile they disconcert the rest of the forest community by mimicking every species within audible range—rare melodic rufous scrub-birds, marbled and plumed frogmouths, Coxen's fig-parrots, and some 270 other bird species.

Gray goshawks and agile honeygliders maneuver through rain forest canopy where 31 species of bats hang out—literally—some of them visiting and fertilizing 140 species of orchids. A single tree may support a rich mosaic of life with hundreds of orchids, ferns, mosses, and other plant and animal organisms in a myriad ingenious habitat adaptations. Hip-pocket frogs raise tadpoles in skin pouches in males' "hips." Sphagnum frogs care for tadpoles which hatch in holes and emerge only after they grow up. On forest floors, three kinds of bowerbirds build elaborately-festooned nuptial rendezvous, and two orchids live and flower entirely underground.

Lighting up the woodland gloom are butterflies of dozens of species by day and fireflies and luminous fungi by night against a chorus of barking owls, harmonious frogs, and giant three-inch (8-cm) king crickets.

Egg-laying monotremes—aquatic duck-billed platypus and ant-eating spiny short-beaked echidnas—tend secretive nests. Spiny blue crayfish once thought extinct hiss at hikers on the Lamington Track, where Parma wallabies and Hastings river mice were rediscovered recently. New-found botanical "dinosaurs" include Wollemi pines dating back hundreds of millions of years.

Access and special features vary. **Border Ranges National Park** has the spectacular Tweed Range Scenic Drive with trails, campsites, and "Lost World Wilderness." **Lamington** protects the largest remaining tract of undisturbed subtropical rain forest, breathtaking views, dozens of plant and animal species found nowhere else, with nearby lodges and campsites. **Mount Warning**, named by Captain James Cook for dangerous offshore reefs, embraces diverse rain forest biota clothing this rugged peak, relic of an enormous volcano which erupted 23 million years ago.

Eastern gray kangaroos are champion jumpers of the marsupial world, able to leap up to 30 feet (9 m) in a single thrust of powerful Z-shaped hind legs and to go 30 miles an hour (48 kph), both a function of rubber-band-like hind leg tendons. Only a little smaller than "big reds," their tiny one-inch (2.5 cm) babies, or joeys, weigh a half-ounce (15 g) when born, finishing development in the pouch reached only after a laborious climb from the birth canal, there to stay for the next 300 days. Eastern grays are browsers as well as grazers in grasslands and open woodlands throughout Tasmania and most of the eastern Australian provinces.

Lowland rain forests of **Toonumbar National Park** abound in fruit-eating doves, bowerbirds, rare parrots. Coastal **Iluka Reserve** is the largest remaining stand of fragile littoral rain forest. Fossil caves at Riversleigh and Naracoorte have yielded evidence of extinct species not previously known—marsupial lions, pocket-sized koalas, feather-tailed opossums, carnivorous kangaroos.

Unusual forms of subtropical rain forest in **Main Range National Park** shelter ground-dwelling Albert's lyrebirds and eastern bristlebirds. **Dorrigo** is a major CERRA interpretive center with panoramic views of bird-filled forests, especially at nearby Point Lookout. **Springbrook** has untracked wilderness as well as popular trails with breathtaking waterfalls.

Screeching, yellow-tailed, black cockatoos pierce the silence of **Barrington Tops**' mist-shrouded 2,000-year-old glades, along with rufous scrub-birds, satin flycatchers, paradise riflebirds, bell miners, and more quietly below, spotted-tailed quolls, feathertail gliders, and swamp wallabies. **Gilbraltar Range** and **Washpool**, saved after a battle between loggers and conservationists, protect dozens of rare and endangered species—Parma wallabies, long-nosed potoroos, satin and regent bowerbirds, colorful Wompoo fruit doves, king parrots, also koalas, wombats.

---

**FURTHER INFORMATION**

Central Eastern Rainforest Reserves-World Heritage Area, National Park and Wildlife Service, P.O. Box 97, Grafton, New South Wales 2460, Tel: (+61) 02-6640-3516, Fax: (+61) 02-6643-4730; Queensland Department of Environment and Heritage, P.O. Box 155, Albert Street, Brisbane 4002; Department of the Environment, Sports and Territories, G.P.O. Box 787, Canberra, ACT 2601, Tel: (+61) 06-274-1111, Fax: (+61) 06-274-1123.

---

# GREAT BARRIER REEF

When Captain Cook ran his HMS *Endeavour* aground here in 1770 he knew he'd hit something unusual, if inconvenient. Now we know it as the Great Barrier Reef, 1,250 miles (2,000 km) long, largest structure ever built by living creatures, visible from the moon.

More than 1,500 kinds of brilliant tropical fish make their homes in this rich ecosystem regarded as the marine equivalent of terrestrial rain forest and one of the most species-rich on earth.

Armored pinecone fish find prey with cooperation of live-in bacteria that glow green-blue at dusk. Male pipefish become "mothers," incubating embryos in pouches and giving live birth. Amiable groupers 12 feet (3.7 m) long, weighing almost 1,000 pounds (450 kg), strike fear into divers with mock attacks—like barracuda, more curious than aggressive.

Angelfish resembling exquisite undersea butterflies probe coral niches for tiny invertebrates. Orange-white-and-black clown damselfish live painlessly among stinging anemone tentacles, protected by mucus coatings and collecting effortless meals. Bottom-dwelling gobies cohabit burrows with housekeeping shrimp which keep home digs tidy while roommates act as predator "watchdogs."

Even the worms are beautiful—glowing purple flatworms, delicate salmon-pink feather dusters, golden-bedecked Christmas tree worms. Giant clams, one of 4,000 kinds of reef mollusks, gape velvety scarlet and purple mantles 56 inches (140 cm) wide.

Octopi change to any color handy—the blue-ringed flushing iridescent-blue when excited, a warning best heeded as their touch is deadly. Most reef creatures are safer observed than touched. Beautiful cone shells when molested shoot darts with enough venom to kill 300 people. Sea wasps or box jellyfish can cause respiratory arrest. Little sea snakes can bite fatally if provoked.

Homely, endangered dugongs like 13-foot (4-m) undersea blimps munch sea grass in crystalline blue-green waters inside the reef's protection. So do endangered green and loggerhead sea turtles, returned from undersea migrations of hundreds of miles to crawl up white coral sand beaches during summer full moons and lay hundreds of eggs. Raine Island once recorded the greatest known concentration of nesting sea turtles—over 11,000 in a single night.

Overhead, majestic white-bellied sea eagles hover along with stately reef herons, ospreys, pelicans, and frigate birds sailing on 7.5-foot (2+ m) wingspans. Some 242 bird species are supported by and on reef cays and islands, including 40 kinds of seabirds which maintain some of the most significant breeding colonies in the western Pacific—100,000 brown boobies on Heron Island, along with similar numbers of wedge-tailed shearwaters (aka mutton birds) in underground burrows. More than 100 kinds of land birds nest as well.

More than 3,400 reefs ranging in size from under an acre to more than 20 square miles (52 km²) with thousands more smaller reeflets make up this spectacular U.N. World Heritage Site. Some are barely awash at low tide, others form underwater gardens of wondrous color and design in an overall area equal to that of England, Ireland, and Wales combined—some 80,000 square miles (208,000 km²), or twice again as large if one includes surrounding sea.

Charles Darwin, investigating reefs on his famed *Beagle* voyage almost a century after Cook, formed now-accepted theory of how they were formed over millions of years by tiny one-celled animals, each living symbiotically with a tiny plant cell within it. Coral furnish safe havens for plant alga, getting in return food and oxygen released when alga consume corals' nitrogenous wastes and carbon dioxide. When they die, their skeletons support successive generations, enlarging reefs which gradually rise even as their size and weight cause earth around them to subside.

Corals of some 350 species live on the reef in hues and forms as diverse as any in the natural world, from purple sea fans to huge convoluted brain corals, golden and lilac staghorns, pink mushrooms, and crimson sea whips, each home to a profusion of other plant and animal life. Each spring they witness and provide one of the natural world's spectaculars, an explosion of underwater visual fireworks when millions of coral simultaneously spawn one or two nights after a full moon, releasing trillions of pink, red, and orange egg and sperm bundles to find one another and form new generations on their ancestors' ancient homes.

Reef climate is tropical with warm temperatures, high humidity, and variable rainfall, most of it in summer with monsoon (southwest wind) season. Air temperatures range between 75–86°F (24–30°C) in midsummer (January), dropping to 64–73°F (18–23°C) in July. Reef waters' temperatures vary seasonally.

Natural threats range from cyclonic winds with huge waves which destroy fragile reef structures to freshwater runoff after heavy rains, which can reduce salinity to coral-killing levels.

Longer-lasting are human threats—oil drilling and exploration, for which permits were issued but are for the present suspended; unsustainable commercial fishing and bottom trawling; tourist impact from boat discharge of waste, litter, and fuel, plus direct physical damage by anchors, reef-walking, and disturbance of fauna; illegal collecting of coral; and deteriorating water quality in runoff from populated areas. It's thought sporadic outbreaks of coral-eating crown-of-thorns starfish may be due to ecological imbalance caused by human activity.

Coral have delicate temperature requirements. Water below 63.5°F (17.5°C) has adverse effects—but global warming could be even more devastating. Even slightly higher temperatures can cause fatal reef-bleaching due to stress which causes coral to expel their life-giving plant partners; rising water levels would force some below the level where sunlight permits algal photosynthesis.

There are a number of ways to visit the reef. International jets fly to Sydney or Brisbane, from which connecting flights go to various coastal towns—Cairns, Townsville, Mackay, and Rockhampton, among others. Or go by bus, rail, or hire a car and drive along the coast stopping at points which offer pleasant lodging and day trips to the reef, and visit mainland national parks along the way.

Accommodations, both mainland and island, range from adequate to luxurious, or one can camp inexpensively (with permit). See the reef by glass-bottomed boat, snorkel, or scuba. Serious sun protection is a must both in and out of the water. Wear a T-shirt and bring sandals and old tennis shoes for sharp coral sand.

Off Airlie Beach are the Whitsunday Islands and the outer reef. Off Townsville are Hinchinbrook, Magnetic and Orpheus Islands. Off Cairns are Bedarra, Dunk, Fitzroy, Green, Hinchinbrook, Lizard, Thursday, and Orpheus, the Low Isles, many outer reef areas.

One of the best places for breeding seabirds is **Michaelmas Cay**, a day-trip off Cairns. **Lizard** is known for superb diving and snorkeling and fine beaches, with upscale lodging but also camping. **Hinchinbrook** is Australia's largest island national park, mostly untouched wilderness with good

Red-necked wallabies are largest of the wallabies, up to 40 inches (l + m) plus a 30-inch (75 cm) tail, with deep, soft fur, residents of coastal heath communities and eucalypt forests with moderate shrub cover in southeastern Australia and Tasmania, where young may graze along with their mothers while still transported about in her pouch.

lodging, campsites, spectacular rain forests, and granite peaks off long sandy beaches with a glorious coastal walk. **Heron** has good lodging (no camping), outstanding birds, and surrounding waters teeming with life.

The **Whitsundays** are great for sailing with lodging to suit all budgets. **Lady Elliot** has simple lodging, camping, fine diving directly off the beach. **Orpheus** has luxury accommodations with wonderful shells on beach and all the reef attractions.

---

**FURTHER INFORMATION**

Great Barrier Reef Marine Park Authority, P.O. Box 1379, Townsville QLD 4810, Australia, E-mail: Registry@gbrmpa.gov.au

---

## KAKADU NATIONAL PARK

Aboriginals believe huge Kakadu National Park was created in "Dreamtime" when godlike ancestral beings lived here. A look at this dramatically beautiful reserve in the Northern Territory with its ancient land forms (over two billion years old), unearthly solitude, and splendid wildlife makes that entirely understandable.

Kakadu's 8,000 square miles (20,000 km²), one-third owned and leased back by Aboriginal peoples and covering virtually the whole South Alligator River system, was designated a U.N. World Heritage Site for both its wildlife and cultural history. The oldest known human artworks are here, along with wallabies and kangaroos, ferocious and occasionally man-eating saltwater crocodiles up to 33 feet (10 m) long (*Crocodile Dundee* was filmed here), Elizabethan-ruffed frilled lizards speeding along on upright hind legs, and a rainbow of kingfishers and bee-eaters. Some 64 species of mammals include endangered dugongs (like manatees); 280 bird species include rare red goshawks, Gouldian finches, and hooded parrots; 128 kinds of reptiles include endangered loggerhead, green, and hawksbill sea turtles, ten dragons, and four legless lizards; with 77 fish and up to 100,000 kinds of insects.

Habitat ranges from coastal tidal flats with mangrove salt marsh to dry and rain forest, riverine wetlands and near-desert with spectacular waterfalls along a stunning sandstone escarpment 300 miles (500 km) long and 800 feet (250 m) high.

Wedge-tailed eagles—large aggressive raptors able to bring down small kangaroos—circle with whistling hawks and black kites on thermals overhead. Jabiru storks preen seven-foot (2-m) wingspans and forage along watercourses.

Magpie geese gather by tens of thousands around lush billabongs (waterholes) carpeted with white and blue water lilies. With them can be up to two million other waterbirds: green pygmy geese and burdekin ducks—major refuges for these rarities—plus plumed and wandering whistling ducks, pelicans, spoonbills, darters, herons, egrets, ibises.

Sulfur-crested and crimson-tailed black cockatoos squabble in fruiting trees. Brolga cranes with bare scarlet heads reaffirm pair-bonds with high-leaping dances—staid-seeming compared with Australian bustards, which roar and throw their heads back as they inflate feathery throat sacs before they drop, vibrating, to the ground. (Bustards must attract new mates each year.)

Silver barramundi a yard (1 m) long swirl the water's surface. Harmless freshwater crocodiles get a wide berth due to resemblance to dangerous cousins. Shy black wallaroos seldom seen outside Kakadu survive on semidesert by drinking little water, even when available, so their bodies can make the most of scanty nitrogen- and protein-poor vegetation.

Kakadu has over 5,000 sites with Aboriginal rock paintings dating back 25,000 to 40,000 years, continuing up to the 1960s—considered the world's most important rock art and longest unbroken record of any culture. Two of the finest are at **Ubirr** (aka Obiri Rock) and **Nourlangie**, spectacular rock structures of red sandstone dropping off to cliffs, striped orange, white, and black. Paintings on rocks along trails and in cave galleries are in styles evolved over eons, including graphic "x-ray" paintings of internal bone and organ structure depicting wallabies, possums, lizards, tortoises, fish, humans, and long-extinct marsupial tigers. The world's oldest evidence of edge-ground axes was found here.

Threats include government-backed uranium mining on Aboriginal parkland, a continuing controversy, anathema to environmentalists—a U.N. report cited its dangers and polls showed two-thirds of Australians oppose it. Also gold mining is proposed in the ironically-named "conservation zone" at river headwaters with potentially disastrous mercury runoff.

Kakadu has trails, guided walks with rangers, and though it can be rough underfoot and extremely hot, it's fine hiking country for the hardy and well-shod (the Darwin Bushwalking Club, Tel: (+61) 089-85-1484, has walks here and elsewhere). Hats are essential, also water, sunblock, and insect repellent (mosquitoes here are said to wield cutlery).

Jabiru township, built to accommodate mine workers, has lodging, stores, restaurants, and an airport. So does Cooinda near the **Yellow Water** wetlands with large waterbird populations. The park has a number of campsites with varying facilities. Roads, best for 4WD, go to most interesting sites including **Jim Jim** and **Twin Falls**. With permission, tours also go into neighboring **Aboriginal Arnhem Land**.

Some 50 inches (130 mm) of rain fall annually, mostly December–April, deeply flooding lowlands—good for breeding birds and other fauna, as well as vegetation. Grasses then can grow six feet (2 m). Visitors are advised to go in drier May–August, especially toward the latter when wildlife gather around shrinking watercourses and billabongs.

International flights go to Darwin. From there, busses, including tour busses, go to Kakadu (including Jabiru and Cooinda), or rent a vehicle (best 4WD) and drive the 155 miles (250 km) to the park where headquarters just outside Jabiru township can advise on almost any park-related question.

**FURTHER INFORMATION**

Kakadu National Park, Box 71, Jabiru, N.T. 0886, Tel: (+61) 89-79-9101; Department of the Environment, Sports and Territories, G.P.O. Box 787, Canberra, ACT 2601, Tel: (+61) 06-274-1111, Fax: (+61) 06-274-1123; Australian Nature Conservation Agency, G.P.O. Box 636, Canberra, ACT 2501.

# KANGAROO ISLAND

National parks and wilderness conservation lands cover 30 percent of KI's peaceful, rolling 1,737 square miles (4,500 km²) filled with native wildlife and flora—over 850 plant species, which flower spectacularly in the September–October spring, plus goannas—great Australian monitor lizards—wallabies, kangaroos, echidnas, penguins, sea lions, fur seals, offshore migrating whales, and among birds, parrots, flightless emus, ospreys, white-bellied sea eagles, and snowy pelicans. Koalas are so numerous the population has been culled repeatedly for reintroduction elsewhere.

KI has guest houses, camping, and is reachable daily by 30-minute air service from Kingscote and Penneshaw and passenger/car ferry from Adelaide and Cape Jervis. Car, moped, and bike rental.

**FURTHER INFORMATION**

KI Parks, Government Office Building, 37 Dauncey Street, Kingscote 5223, Tel: (+61) 08-8553-2381, Fax: (+61) 08-8553-2531; KI Tourism, P.O. Box 336VG, Penneshaw, Kangaroo Island, South Australia 5222, Tel: (+61) 8-8553-1185, Fax: (+61) 8-8553-1255, E-mail: tourki@kin.on.net

# LORD HOWE ISLAND

Beautiful Lord Howe Island and its surrounding South Pacific islands and islets are a collection of national parks and U.N. World Heritage Sites 375 miles (600 km) east of Australia with huge, important nesting seabird colonies. These include rare providence petrels, half the world population of fleshy-footed shearwaters, gannets, noddies, masked boobies, 100,000 sooty terns, more red-tailed tropic birds than anyplace else, and the world's most southerly coral reefs. Flightless Lord Howe woodhens, one of the world's rarest species, once slaughtered to near-extinction, are now, with protection, here in a small but stable population, among some 130 species.

Lord Howe's dramatic peaks rose as volcanoes from the ocean bottom 7 million years ago and erupted for 500,000 years. Now they are covered with lush green, topped with clouds, filled with life. Of 180 flowering plants, 56 are nowhere else. Of 48 ferns, 19 are only here. Surrounding crystalline waters are filled with more than 490 fish species in an enthralling undersea community of sea stars, urchins, and corals. The 7-by-1.25-mile (11 × 2-km) island has fine snorkeling, diving, trails for hiking, biking, and a range of accommodations, reachable by flights from Sydney and Brisbane. Weather pleasant, humid/subtropical all year.

**FURTHER INFORMATION**

Lord Howe Island Board, Lord Howe Island 2898, Tel: (+61) 065-63-2066, Fax: (+61) 065-63-2127; New South Wales National Parks and Wildlife Service, P.O. Box 1967, 43 Bridge Street, Hurtsville NSW 2220.

OPPOSITE: Tammars are one of the smallest wallabies, hardly larger than big rabbits, with equally small babies, weighing a minuscule 0.01 ounce (0.3 g) when they leave the birth canal and make their way to their mother's pouch. So tightly do they attach themselves to their mother's breasts that the first European who saw these small kangaroos, Dutch sea captain Francisco Pelsaert in 1629, thought the young grew from their mother's mammary glands. Tammars can survive drinking almost no water, thereby conserving nitrogen, making it possible for them to thrive in near-desert conditions with scanty, protein-poor vegetation.

# SHARK BAY

Wild bottlenose dolphins interact with humans here seemingly because they find it interesting and fun—touching, nuzzling, sometimes receiving food but sometimes bringing it to visitors—the best-known natural residents of this U.N. World Heritage Site on Australia's westernmost coast. Covering 8,500 square miles (22,000 km²), it is half on land, half undersea, with lovely islands, inlets, peninsulas, sand and shell beaches, dunes, and over 185 miles (300 km) of magnificent limestone cliffs overlooking underwater marine reserves in a collection of national parks facing on the Indian Ocean.

Here are rare rufous and banded hare-wallabies, marsupial boodies or burrowing bettongs, western barred bandicoots, and over 230 species of birds, including regent parrots and western yellow robins at their northernmost range limit. Delicate fairy terns balance eggs on bare branches. white-bellied sea eagles nest on cliffs and gray-tailed tattlers scout mudflats. **Failure Island** is a key breeding area for handsome Caspian terns.

Shark Bay is migratory staging post for humpback and southern right whales and home to 12.5 percent of the world population of dugongs (aka manatees), more than 10,000 of the gentle, homely, nine-foot (2.7-m) marine beasts, world's only herbivorous marine mammals, believed to have once inspired sailors' thoughts of mermaids.

Great manta rays up to 7.5 yards (7 m) across weighing up to 2 tons heave out of the water and crash down during breeding season. Endangered green and loggerhead sea turtles haul out to nest on sandy beaches. Whale sharks, largest fish in the world—harmless plankton feeders which can be 60 feet (18 m) long—congregate by the hundreds during March and April full moons.

Support for this rich ecosystem is based in what may be the largest and most species-rich sea grass assemblage in the world—1,853 square miles (4,800 km²), thriving here for the past 5,000 years, domain of more than 320 kinds of fish and uncounted millions of smaller marine organisms.

Ashore, nearly 100 kinds of reptiles and amphibians include burrowing sandhill frogs which fulfill all their water needs underground.

Flowering botanicals appear in spectacular carpets during the long blooming season. Of more than 700 species, 25 are rare or threatened and 184 are at either their northern or southern range limit.

OPPOSITE: Leichhardt's grasshoppers are thought by ancient peoples of Arnhem Land in Australia's Northern Territory to be Alyurr, children of a powerful ancestral being, called Lightning Man Namarrgon, due to their appearance in full adult coloring during peak November/December lightning season. Found only in remote parts of Kakadu and Keep River national parks, their extreme rarity is attributed to predation by other insects—wasps and spiders—plus seasonal fires, helpful in controlling brush but not to grasshoppers.

But rarer than all these are ancient inhabitants that are neither plant or animal—odd, dome-shaped living rocks known as the **Stromatolites of Hamelin Pool**, the planet's oldest residents whose families first appeared 3.5 billion years ago and from which all else evolved. They are still being built here by cyanobacteria, more commonly called blue-green algae, in what is regarded as the most significant assembly of phototropic microbial ecosystems in the world and one of the longest known continuing biological lineages.

Dolphins in **Monkey Mia**'s shallow waters have been making and receiving friendly overtures from humans since the 1960s. The interchange is mutually voluntary but visitors need to heed rangers' directives. Studies are under way to determine whether young dolphins raised by mothers fed in the bay do less well than others.

Problems in this western Australian region include pastoral leases which have led to erosion from overgrazing; introduction of feral rabbits, goats, and foxes; commercial fishing, especially bottom trawling which damages marine ecosystems; poaching of rare marine resources; thoughtless tourism and boating which has damaged dugong, turtle, and dolphin populations and habitat; and mining threats.

Shark Bay is some 500 miles (800 km) north of Perth, accessible from there by road or by daily flights through Geraldton. Motel/resort accommodations, also campgrounds, are available at Monkey Mia and Denham. Guided trips set out from both places.

Best times are May–October, but climate is mild and pleasant year-round.

**FURTHER INFORMATION**

Department of Conservation and Land Management (CALM) manages Francois Peron National Park, Hamelin Pool, Shark Bay, and the numerous island nature reserves, reachable at P.O. Box 104, Como, Western Australia 6152; CALM, 67 Knight Street, Denham WA 6537, Tel: (+61) 099-48-1208, Fax: (+61) 099-48-1024; Department of the Environment, Canberra (*See* above).

# TASMANIAN WILDERNESS

This island, which separated from southeastern Australia after the last ice age, has birds and mammals found only rarely on its big northern neighbor due to habitat loss and introduced predator species.

Strange egg-laying mammals like platypus and spiny echidnas are here with elsewhere-unusual marsupials such as spotted-tail quolls, or tiger cats, Tasmanian pademelons, bettongs, potoroos, and fierce Tasmanian devils—world's largest carnivorous marsupials, known for spine-chilling vocalizations and jaws that easily chew and swallow bones. (It's now felt their reputed viciousness may have resulted from cruel, relentless persecution.) There are kangaroos, wallabies, endearing small bearlike wombats, and in surrounding waters, leopard and southern elephant seals, pilot and right whales.

Birds of over 320 species include five kinds of albatross, brown and gray goshawks, white-bellied sea eagles, tawny frogmouths, beautiful firetails, and exceedingly rare orange-bellied parrots with such other endemics as masked owls, dusky robins, green rosellas, 40-spotted pardalotes, brilliant honeyeaters.

Almost 30 percent of Tasmania's 26,405 square miles (68,408 km$^2$) is set aside in dramatically beautiful national parks and reserves in widely diverse habitat—rugged mountains, rivers, bays, sheltered inlets, ancient pines, temperate rain forest, much of it seeming untouched by civilization.

Of special significance is the Tasmanian Wilderness, one of the largest temperate wilderness areas in the southern hemisphere, a U.N. World Heritage Site covering 20 percent of Tasmania, made up of five national parks—CRADLE MOUNTAIN-LAKE ST. CLAIR with its abundant wildlife and superb Overland Track trail, FRANKLIN-GORDON WILD RIVERS, huge, wild SOUTHWEST, HARTZ MOUNTAINS, and WALLS OF JERUSALEM.

In these are most of Tasmania's notable species, plus others—regnans swamp gums growing over 325 feet (100 m) high, world's tallest flowering plants; 3,000-year-old King Billy pines; mountain shrimp unchanged in 250 million years; red-headed velvet worms unchanged in a half-billion years, which fire jets of sticky liquid from head projectiles onto prey.

**Cradle Mountain**, almost 625 square miles (1,610 km$^2$) in the central highlands is known for relatively tame wildlife, gorgeous scenery—rugged mountains, glacial lakes, open alpine moors, deep gorges, and forested valleys—and trails ranging from easy to arduous, including the famous Overland Track. Comfortable lodge and cabins; 53 miles (85 km) south of Davenport. Tel: (+61) 1300-368-550.

**Franklin-Gordon Wild Rivers** is Tasmania's most remote park, more than 1,700 square miles (4,410 km$^2$), 112 miles (180 km) west of Hobart, with high mountains, rivers, challenging bush-walking, rock-climbing, exciting river-rafting. Tel: (+61) 004-717-122 or 004-712-511.

**Southwest** is Tasmania's largest, wildest park, mostly untracked, uninhabited, little visited—scenically dramatic with wild rivers, countless lakes, perhaps the world's last great temperate rain forest, and some 30 animals found nowhere else. Camping. Contact Southwest National Park, P.O. Box 41, Westerway, Tas 7140, Tel: (+61) 002-881-283.

**Hartz Mountains**, 28 square miles (71 km$^2$), 50 miles (80 km) southwest of Hobart, glacier-carved high moorland plateau with magnificent views, picnic facilities, shelter huts, no camping. Tel: (+61) 002-981-577.

OPPOSITE: Tasmanian devils' reputation for ferocity comes from formidable jaws, able to crush all but largest bones so they completely consume carcasses, plus their habit of gaping with every tooth bared, often with growls and high-pitched spine-chilling screams. Usually this reflects fear and uncertainty more than aggression. They are shy, mild-mannered, even affectionate, better at consuming carrion than killing prey. Early stories of savage dispositions resulted, it's now felt, from cruel mistreatment. Small bear-like marsupials, they nurture young in backward-facing pouches. Driven to extinction in Australia, they've been protected in Tasmania since 1941 and are fairly common, especially in Cradle Mountain National Park.

**Walls of Jerusalem**, 200 square miles (518 km²) of spectacular subalpine wilderness, five steep mountain peaks with glacial lakes, ancient pine forests, popular all year with bushwalkers. Bush camping only. South of Liena. Tel: (+61) 003-635-182.

Threats in Tasmania have included logging and dams, especially one on the Gordon River in the 1970s inundating Lake Pedder and its remarkable quartzite beach.

Both Australia and New Zealand have air links to Tasmania. Most popular times are summer December–February. Weather always changeable, with warm, waterproof clothing essential (snow possible in higher elevations anytime).

---

**FURTHER INFORMATION**

Tasmanian Department of Parks and Wildlife, G.P.O. Box 44A. 134 Macquarie Street, Hobart 7001, Tel: (+61) 3-6233-6191, Fax: (+61) 3-6233-2168.

---

# WET TROPICS OF QUEENSLAND

Wet Tropics of Queensland represents only 0.1 percent of the continent's land area but protects 30 percent of its marsupial species, 62 percent of its butterflies, 18 percent of its birds, 30 percent of its frogs, 23 percent of its reptiles. At least 54 of its vertebrates are found no place else, including such rarities as yellow-bellied gliders and brush-tailed bettongs.

Some 1,161 kinds of higher plants have been recorded—many endemic—including 90 kinds of orchids. It is second in the world only to New Caledonia in number of unique species per unit size. It is a U.N. World Heritage Site not only for its scientific importance but for breathtaking natural beauty—dramatic gorges, Australia's highest waterfall, and a combination of virgin tropical rain forest—said to be oldest in the world—with white sandy beaches and fringing reefs between Daintree River and Cedar Bay. Here evolution has been virtually uninterrupted since flowering plants first appeared 130 million years ago. Australia's only recognized Aboriginal rain forest culture is preserved here.

Paralleling the Great Barrier Reef just offshore, Wet Tropics incorporates a patchwork of 19 national parks, 31 state forests, five timber reserves, and Aboriginal and island reserves in a 3,450-square-mile (8,944-km²) protected area stretching from some 125 miles (200 km) north of Cairns to about 185 miles (300 km) south. Mammals include two monotremes—rare egg-laying echidnas and duck-billed platypus—and 37 marsupials, including an isolated population of spotted-tailed quolls (aka tiger cats), engaging-looking but ferocious marsupials, able to pursue and kill small wallabies with a single bite to the neck. Endemics include four kinds of ringtail possums, Australia's only tree-kangaroos, and musky rat-kangaroos, smallest (weighing 17.5 ounces/500 g) and in many respects most primitive of all marsupials (only one with the original mammalian five toes). Here also are tube-nosed insectivorous murina florius bats, considered Australia's rarest living mammal.

Birdlife is the continent's most diverse with more than 370 species, including 23 that are endemic. These include flightless Australian cassowaries—up to six feet (2 m) tall, one of the world's largest birds—striking, with high bony vertical helmets or casques, bright red and blue head skin, and sharp four-inch (12-cm) toe-claws that can disembowel prey. Among others are lovely golden bowerbirds, bridled honeyeaters, Australian fernwrens and chowchillas, which announce their names during the dawn chorus, as well as, more commonly, gorgeous rainbow lorikeets, collared kingfishers, sulfur-crested cockatoos, and emerald doves.

More than 5,000 species of insects and 300 of spiders include barking or bird-eating spiders with six-inch (15-cm) leg-spans; rare and enormous Queensland stag beetles whose closest relatives are in South America, named for antler-like mandibles with which males battle; brilliant *Aenetus monabilis* moths with eight-inch (18-cm) wingspans; Hercules moths, one of the world's largest with up to 10-inch (25-cm) wingspans; and the continent's largest butterflies, Cairns birdwings, sometimes mistaken for birds flying high in the canopy, males bright yellow, green, and blue.

Problems include logging, road-building, mining, and agriculture, both actual and threatened, legal and illegal, in nominally protected as well as adjacent areas which environmentalists think need protection also; land-management conflicts with Aboriginal inhabitants; and a "Skyrail" built for tourism which many feel damages ecosystems of canopy-dwelling species.

Dry season is April–September but as many visitors come in wet as in dry seasons. Dozens of tour companies offer trips, including river cruises, and it's possible to stay at lodges located in mid-rain forest to observe nocturnal wildlife.

---

**FURTHER INFORMATION**

Wet Tropics Management Authority, P.O. Box 2050, Cairns, Queensland, Australia 4002.

# INDONESIA

QUEEN ALEXANDRA'S GIANT BIRDWING
BUTTERFLIES, CHARTREUSE AND BLACK, UP TO
12 INCHES (31 CM) ACROSS, WERE DISCOVERED
WHEN A HUNTER SPOTTED ONE IN THE FOREST
CANOPY, MISTOOK IT FOR A BIRD, AND SHOT IT.

THE INDONESIAN ARCHIPELAGO STRETCHES 3,200 WATERY MILES (5,800 KM) OVER THREE TIME ZONES IN THE PACIFIC AND INDIAN OCEANS AND INCLUDES 17,999 TROPICAL ISLANDS. On them live 206 million people in 300 ethnic groups speaking 583 languages and dialects. Here as well are some of the world's rarest and most interesting and beautiful birds, animals, and plants.

Many of these exist nowhere else. Of Indonesia's 500 mammal species, 210 are endemic. Of more than 1,580 kinds of birds—almost 16 percent of the world's known avifauna—over one-fourth, 430, are endemic. Many survive only on one or two small islands.

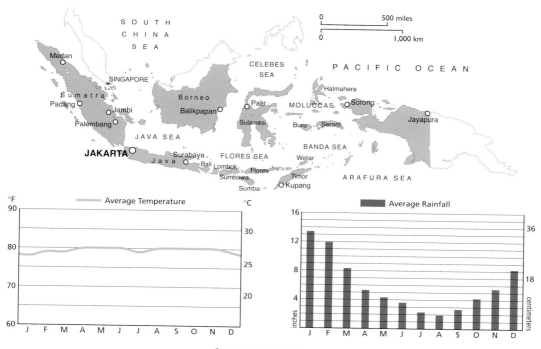

Gateway city: Jakarta

Indonesia covers one percent of the earth's surface but contains 16 percent of its reptiles and amphibians, 12 percent of its mammals, 10 percent of its flowering plant species and, with 8,500 kinds of fish, 25 percent of its piscine species. Landforms range from mangrove swamps with brilliant offshore coral reefs to glaciers and active volcanoes. It has been called the most diverse floral and faunal repository in the world.

Lizards inhabit every corner—tiny geckos on adhesive toe-tips darting after insects on tree-trunk undersides (and house ceilings) and fearsome Komodo dragons up to 13 feet (4+ m) long weighing 165 pounds (75 kg). Toxic saliva of these formidable reptiles causes blood poisoning and death in a buffalo or deer usually within days while the dragon watches and waits for its victim to expire.

Reptiles and amphibians "fly" on side flaps extended so they can glide great distances using tails as steering rudders—bright flaps useful also in attracting mates.

Indonesia extends across the deep oceanic trench marking the "Wallace Line"—historic geographic separation between Oriental and Australasian faunal regions named after early explorer-naturalist Alfred Russel Wallace. (It was in Indonesia that Wallace developed evolutionary theories similar to and contemporary with Darwin's.) Rain forests on one side harbor Asian mainland species such as leaf monkeys and ponderous-beaked hornbills, and on the other Australasian marsupials such as Australian wallabies, spiny anteaters, tree kangaroos, and mouse-like "flying opossums."

Tropical rain forests of Southeast Asia are home to the highest diversity of terrestrial predators in the world, and Indonesia has many of them—Sumatran tigers, common and clouded leopards, wild dogs, ancient hairless wild pigs, and little slow loris, along with irascible, largely vegetarian sun bears. Here also are the world's largest arboreal mammals, shaggy red orangutans which share 94.6 percent of humans' DNA.

Indonesia is home to 15 of the world's 22 species of maleo birds or megapods ("giant-foots") which incubate eggs by burying them in soil warmed by composting action and volcanic steam (their big feet are useful in digging nest holes) from which young emerge fully self-sufficient and able to fly. There are elegantly plumed birds of paradise, turkey-sized pigeons, rare citron-crested cockatoos, fierce hawk-eagles, exquisite fairy-wrens, and a rainbow of colorful sunbirds.

Efforts to save some of the best-known species from disastrous habitat loss have been well-publicized. Among the endangered are orangutans, proboscis monkeys, Javan badaks or rhinos, Sumatran tigers, and Asian elephants.

---

OPPOSITE: Nocturnal flying fox bats may fly 20 miles (32 km) in search of food—fruits of almost any kind, plus flowers, pollen, nectar and sometimes leaves and bark—distance not a problem with wingspans up to four feet (1.2 m). They may eat half their body weight a night. Broad wings wrap tightly around them for protection from rain and cold when roosting, or open to fan back and forth for built-in air conditioning.

Less well-known but equally rare and unique are prehensile-tailed bear-cats or binturongs, Sulawesi's fierce-looking four-tusked babirusa (wild hogs), miniature Anoa buffaloes, Temmink's golden cats, Ajak wild dogs, and massive banteng, nearly one-ton (800-kg) wild cattle.

Dazzling lepidoptera include Queen Alexandra's birdwing butterflies, world's largest at 12 inches (31 cm) across, discovered when a hunter spotted one in the forest canopy, mistook it for a bird and shot it; and Atlas moths, almost as large.

Surrounding seas hold some of the world's rarest and most beautiful shells, including the exquisite glory-of-the-sea, in some of the most beautiful and extensive coral reefs in the world. Great sea turtles nest on beaches. Crabs climb palm trees to clip coconuts which they drop on the ground to open at their leisure. Fish climb trees after insects. Seaweed fronds trail up to 250 feet (75 m).

More than 40,000 flowering plant species include the world's largest blossom, the yard-wide (1-m) rafflesia.

Indonesia's environmental record has been troubled. Logging and widespread forest fires caused by timber and agriculture interests—especially clearing for palm oil—have damaged essential habitat. So have mineral exploration and needs of this world's fifth-largest population, still growing at two percent annually. In recent years government has shown more interest in protecting its unique wildlife by creating national parks and encouraging local projects supportive of conservation efforts. But political unrest has compounded problems, leaving the future uncertain.

Significant areas have been set aside, at least on paper, notably on eight major islands. They cover more than 54,000 square miles (140,000 km²) and include 31 national parks, 62 natural ecotourism parks, 13 game parks, 170 nature reserves, and seven marine parks.

# JAVA

**Ujung Kulon**, regarded as Java's finest national park, not easy to reach but with superb coastal scenery, lush rain forest, coral reefs. The reserve is home to one-horned rhinoceros, banteng, leopards, flying lemurs or culagos, five primate species, violet-tailed sunbirds, glittering green peacocks. Also **Gunung Gede Pangrango National Park**, premier birding site; **Mount Halimun National Park**, with gibbons, leaf monkeys, bird species seldom seen elsewhere; **Karimun Jawa Marine National Park**; **Meru Betiri National Park**, lowland rain forest with leopards, banteng, armored pangolins (Java tigers were last spotted here); **Baluran National Park**, with grasslands reminiscent of Africa or Australia, large herds of grazing mammals, lush birdlife, driving route; **Pulau Dua**, major sanctuary for coastal seabirds, off Banten.

# SUMATRA

**Gunung Leuser National Park**, one of Southeast Asia's most diverse, home to orangutans, Sumatran tigers, Sumatran rhinos, three "flying" animals—squirrels, frogs, and snakes (actually long-distance gliders)—brilliantly plumaged birds, and **Bohorok Orangutan Sanctuary** at Bukit Lawang, all relatively accessible (though large tracts are still termed "unexplored"); beautiful **Kerinci Seblat**, Sumatra's largest national park, home to all but one (orangutans) of its renowned animals (rhinos, tigers, Asian elephants) plus clouded leopards, brilliant birdlife; **Way Kambas**, noted for elephants, best place to see many rare birds; **Bukit Barisan**, difficult to reach but with tigers, Asian elephants, tapirs, and varied flora in habitat from coast to rain forest; and **Lembah Abai Reserve**, known for rafflesia.

# KALIMANTAN (BORNEO)

**Tanjung Puting National Park** with bizarre proboscis monkeys, orangutans, clouded leopards, sun bears, six primate species, walking mudskipper fish, rare and colorful birds including Storm's storks, Bulwer's pheasants, and famous for Birute Galdikas' **Camp Leakey Orangutan Rehabilitation Center**. This center, founded in 1986 and funded by Orangutan Foundation International (www.orangutan.org), is the most important in Indonesia for conservation and rehabilitation of the red apes. Also **Kutai National Park** with Sumatran rhinos, proboscis monkeys, bantengs, 300 bird species; **Kayan Mentarang**, Borneo's largest remaining rain forest, with sun bears, pangolins, clouded leopards, spectacular wild pig migrations; and a new 2,660-square-mile (6,880-km²) area cooperatively reserved since 1994 joining **Bentuang-Karimum** here with Lanjak Entimau in Sarawak (*see* p.615), with important populations of rhinos, leopards, orang-utans, bear-cats, and six entirely new species discovered on the Sarawak side, including a new snake and terrestrial crab but, at least until recently, few visitor facilities.

# SULAWESI

**Lore Lindu National Park**, with endemic miniature buffaloes, gremlin-like spectral tarsiers (world's tiniest primates), ancient hairless babirusas, Sulawesi civet cats, 247 brilliant bird species including several maleos which incubate eggs in compost piles. Also **Bogani Nani Wartabone**, similar wildlife, with woolly-necked storks, eight kingfisher species, Sulawesi serpent-eagles, giant birdwing butterflies; **Tangkoko-Dua Sudara Reserve** with babirusas, Sulawesi hanging-parrots, 47 endemic birds; **Pulau Bunaken Manado Tua**, with superb coral reefs.

# Irian Jaya (Western New Guinea)

**Gunung Lorentz National Park**, with 34 ecosystems including Southeast Asia's only glacial slopes, 123 mammal species, 411 birds, kangaroos, bandicoots, blossom bats, New Guinea harpy eagles, six bird-of-paradise species. Also **Wasur**, about 1,560 square miles (4,050 km²) of lowland forest and white sand beaches with agile wallabies, pied imperial pigeons, large flocks of Brolga cranes.

# Komodo

**Komodo Island National Park** with Komodo dragons, last living dinosaur descendants and world's largest lizards, up to 13 feet (4 m) long; beautiful coral reefs.

# Maluku

**Manusela National Park**, with colorful endemic bird species—salmon-crested cockatoos, metallic pigeons, paradise-kingfishers, eagles, cassowaries—deer, culagos or flying lemurs, orchid-strewn jungles, lovely marine reserve and reefs.

# Bali

**Bali Barat**, savannah with coastal mangroves and southern uplands, prolific birdlife, monkeys, deer, giant banteng cattle, spectacular coral reefs off white sand beaches.

Some of the world's most beautiful and extensive coral reefs (with good snorkeling and scuba diving) are in **Riau archipelago**, at Pular and Pulau Panaitan (at **Ujung Kulon National Park**), Pulau Putri in the **Thousand Islands** (Kepulauan Seribu) off Jakarta, and others, especially in the Moluccas and off Bali.

Of special note among many bird sanctuaries are the small coastal islets of **Dua**, **Rambut**, and **Bokor**, all within easy reach of Jakarta. Also, the island of **Sumba** south of Sulawesi and west of Timor has 10 endemic bird species.

Climate is equatorial—hot and wet in rainy season, other times hot and dry, cooler at higher elevations. Dry seasons are best for viewing, mostly in northern hemisphere summer. Wet seasons start later in southeast but roughly are September–March in Sumatra, October–April in Java, November–May in Bali but April–August in Maluku.

Indonesia's worst storm dropped 31 inches (802 cm) in one day, 3 inches (80 cm) in a half-hour, and humidity anytime can swing from 100 percent at night to 30–55 percent at midday.

Park entry requires permission from forest authority, Direktorat Jenderal Perlindungan dan Konservasi Alam (PKA) or Directorate General of Nature Conservation and Protection, with offices in major towns and branch offices in reserves. Permits necessary also for filming, video, and "related activities." Photo equipment must be declared on entry and exit. Directorate can also provide maps and brochures, advise on plans, and help visitors hire guides.

Tourist facilities can be limited, exceptions being on Java (Ujung Kulon) and Bali. Others have some basic lodges with kitchen use, also guesthouses with varying facilities—check ahead. Insect protection is a MUST against omnipresent stinging ants, scorpions, etc., also sun lotion, hats, long sleeves and pants, boots, and in some places, special socks for leach protection.

Beautiful coral reefs suffer from plundering for aquarium trade, using poison and even explosions to make fishing easier and gather coral for resale. Protected animals are also targets. Ecotourists can help by resisting temptations to buy animal products such as tortoise shells, mounted butterflies, furs, bird-of-paradise feathers, corals, and beautiful seashells and by supporting local conservation efforts.

For impressive overview of country's astounding biodiversity, visit **Ragunan Zoo** in Jakarta with over 4,000 birds and animals and close looks at many of the country's rare and endemic species.

International flights to Jakarta. Inter-island flights available from there.

**FURTHER INFORMATION**

Directorate for National Parks and Tourism, J1, H. Juanda 100, Bogor, Tel: (+62) 0251-21014,
Manggala Wanabakti building block I, 8th floor, J1. Gatot Subroto, Jakarta, Tel: (+62) 0251-572-0227;
Imam Hartadi and Prima, Resource Center WWF, J1. Brenda II, No. 24, Petogogan Blok A,
Jakarta Selatan 121409, Tel: (+62) 021-724-4957; or WWF office, J1 Kramat Pela No. 3, Gandaria Utara,
Jakarta Selatan 12140, Tel: (+62) 021-720-3095/724-5766/725-6501, E-mail: wwf-ip@indo.netet.id

# MALAYSIA

RED-HAIRED, LONG-LIMBED ORANGUTANS—
"MEN OF THE FOREST"—RULE THE JUNGLES,
BUT AIR SPACES ARE RULED NOT ONLY BY BIRDS
BUT NON-WINGED FLIERS, "FLYING" SQUIRRELS, FROGS,
AND SNAKES THAT CAN FLATTEN THEIR BODIES, SPREAD
SKIN FLAPS AND BONE STRUCTURE AND GLIDE SEVERAL
HUNDRED FEET THROUGH THE CANOPY.

S OME OF THE MOST VARIED AND RARE WILDLIFE POPULATIONS ON EARTH FIND HOMES IN ANCIENT RAIN FORESTS OF THIS SMALL SOUTHEAST ASIAN COUNTRY ENCOMPASSING THE MALAYSIAN PENINSULA AND, ACROSS THE WAY IN THE SOUTH CHINA SEA, SABAH AND SARAWAK ON THE NORTH COAST OF BORNEO.

In moist woodlands unchanged for millions of years are giant chartreuse-and-black birdwing butterflies, big as small birds and often mistaken for them as they flutter about the forest canopy, and their night-flying counterparts, Atlas moths 10 inches (25 cm) across.

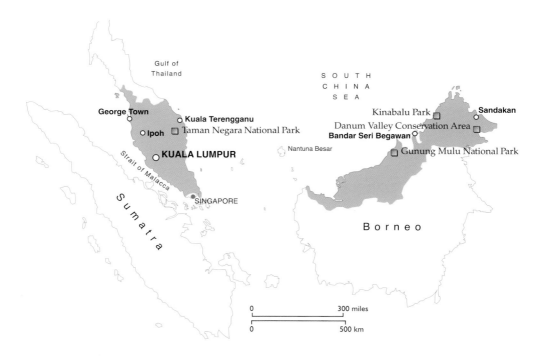

## MALAYSIA

Gentle red-haired orangutans, primate "men of the forest" renowned for their intelligence and endangered by destruction of their tropical woodland homes, hang on in Borneo and Sumatra. Magnificent Asian tigers, their populations decimated by poaching for body parts supposedly useful as aphrodisiacs and in traditional medicine, survive precariously on the Malay Peninsula, where sightings have been reported of individuals almost 10 feet (3 m) long.

Enormous two-horned rhinoceros now known to exist only on peninsular Malaysia and Sabah crash through undergrowth; they are up to eight feet (2.5 m) long, weighing almost a ton (900 kg), once regarded as extinct, still nearly so after surviving almost unchanged for the past 30 million

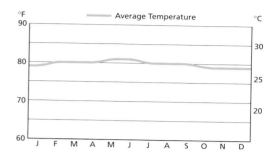

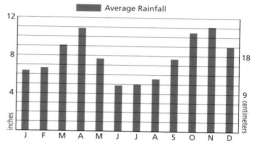

Gateway city: Kuala Lumpur

years. They also are coveted for medicinal body parts. Floppy-nosed proboscis monkeys forage along streams with honey or sun bears (named for sunburst spots on their chests).

Pangolins or scaly anteaters, resembling animated artichokes with large overlapping scales, claw out termite burrows. Tiny big-eyed slow loris are slow until a praying mantis flies by, then lightning-quick in grabbing a meal. Giant flying foxes, world's largest bats with wingspans up to four feet (1.2 m), cluster in hundreds around fruiting trees.

Burly gaur, world's largest wild ox, can stand 6.5 feet (2 m) at the shoulder and weigh up to a ton (900 kg), while at the other end of the size scale, eight-inch-high (20-cm) lesser mouse deer trip about on pencil-sized hooves. These tiny grazers, closer relatives to camels than deer, are storied in Malay folklore for alertness enabling them to outwit such powerful opponents as tigers and elephants.

Some of the world's most beautiful and colorful birds find riverine and forest homes here—more than 700 species, from hornbills with giant multihued bills to hawk-eagles, brilliantly plumaged pheasants, and shimmering, jewel-like orioles, flower-peckers, sunbirds, and bee-eaters.

Others only apparently "fly"—squirrels, frogs, and snakes. Flying squirrels glide up to 330 feet (100 m) on skin-flaps connecting legs fore and aft. Colugos or flying lemurs sail even farther on flaps connecting their tails as well, making them in effect whole-body kites. Frogs spread outsize webs between their toes and snakes flatten their vertebrae, gliding long distances in the canopy, saving the trouble of descending to the ground as they feed in adjoining tall trees.

Botanical features are equally remarkable. Peninsular Malaysia alone has over 8,000 kinds of flowering plants, including 2,000 trees, 800 orchids, and 200 palms. Borneo may have even more in Sarawak and Sabah. The tualang, world's tallest tropical tree, reaches a height of 260 feet (80 m) with a base diameter of almost 10 feet (3 m). Largest leaf ever found was in Sabah as well—one measuring 10 by 6 feet (3 × 1.9 m) on an aroid plant—and the world's largest bloom, the rafflesia, which can span three feet (1 m) and weigh almost 20 pounds (9 kg).

Malaysia is home to some 100 kinds of toads and frogs and more than 100 snake species—mostly inoffensive although black cobras, common in oil palm plantations, often attack workers who unknowingly step on them.

At least four endangered sea turtles nest on sandy beaches. Coral reef inhabitants of stunning beauty and variety reflect connection with both Indian and Pacific Oceans. Equally notable freshwater fish include mudskippers and climbing perch with extra gills enabling them to walk about on mudflats, supported by pectoral fins. Mudskippers actually are able to climb trees. Archer fish squirt pressurized water at overhead insects, getting a meal when their prey fall in the water. There are giant catfish weighing 100 pounds (45 kg).

Much of this diverse wildlife is threatened by hunting and habitat destruction, the result of population and development pressures, some sadly with little or no thought to environmental damage.

National parks and other protected reserves occupy about five percent of Peninsular Malaysia and Sabah and three percent of Sarawak—on the whole, regarded as better run than elsewhere in Southeast Asia. Still, many are small, inadequately protected islands of habitat in a sea of logging and plantations, and more protected land is needed if these natural wonders are to survive.

# PENINSULAR MALAYSIA

## TAMAN NEGARA NATIONAL PARK

Taman Negara is spread over 1,677 wooded square miles (4,343 km²) bisected by mountains, with tigers, elephants, and most of the region's outstanding wildlife which, like its ancient rain forest, has been virtually undisturbed for millions of years. It ranges from dense moist wooded lowlands to cloud and montane habitat with "elfin" trees stunted by life at high altitudes.

Clouded leopards—named for free-form cloud-like markings on their fur—live mostly in trees, crossing from bough to bough, preying on monkeys, squirrels, and birds. Primates swing through the canopy around them—white-handed gibbons whooping loudly and plaintively. Quieter banded and owlish-looking spectacled or dusky leaf monkeys are disclosed most often by long tails drooping through foliage. Pig-tailed macaques forage on the ground along with leopard cats not much bigger than domestic varieties.

Some of the most spectacular forest birds in the world are among 250 avian species—great argus pheasants, males up to 5.5 feet (1.7 m) long including shimmering tails vibrating to bedazzle mates; shy Malaysian peacock pheasants with orange facial patches, blue-green crests, and green eye-spots on wings; crested firebacks with orange bellies and off-white tail plumes; hornbills delicately plucking tiny berries with giant-size bills; brilliant trogons and ground-feeding red, yellow, and blue pittas; green pigeons feeding on fruiting trees; and soaring overhead, changeable hawk eagles and crested serpent eagles.

Not all this is easy to see in forest so dense that up to 240 tree species can be found in a single hectare (2.5 acres)—where visibility is sometimes just a few feet (though most visitors have no trouble seeing and believing there are three million insect species). But the park has a good system of trails with six "hides" or blinds and small huts on stilts with simple sleeping and sanitary facilities near waterholes, salt licks, and grassy clearings. An overnight stay at one of these is not the Ritz but it can be truly memorable—ones farthest from headquarters are best—especially on moonlit nights filled with jungle sounds, luminous fungi and insects, and, aided by strong flashlight or torch, the possibility of glimpsing any of the park's 200 mammal species, including rare Sumatran rhinos (and perhaps a personal visit from a curious palm civet if food isn't securely stashed).

Park maps describe jungle treks of varying lengths, from a few hours to nine days, including one to the summit of Gunung Tahan, at 7,175 feet (2,187 m) Peninsular Malaysia's highest peak. (Visitors must take guides on long treks.) Another, just 50 yards (50 m) north of headquarters-area lodges, visits a beautiful waterfall and rushing stream, often with gray-headed fish-eagles, bright bulbuls and kingfishers and, camouflaged on the rocks, monitor lizards up to 6.5 feet (2 m) long.

A cave shelters fruit and insect-eating bats as well as huge toads, long white racer snakes, and enormous spiders and cockroaches.

Another way to look around is by water, in a small sampan with paddles or quiet engine. Boat transport can be rented or hired with guide.

There is also a swaying 197-foot-long (60-m) aluminum-and-rope canopy walkway from which the jungle can be viewed from 115 feet (35 m) up.

To get to Taman Negara from Kuala Lumpur by bus, go first to Jerantut—where it can be convenient to stay overnight—thence to Tembeling jetty for a river trip to Kuala Tahan park headquarters, a trip which usually brings sightings of kingfishers and crested tree-swifts, blue-bearded bee-eaters, possibly otters and monkeys.

Orangutan mothers nurse their babies up to four years, which means the average female bears only four to five offspring in her life—a disadvantage for this species whose survival is already precarious due to disappearance of rain forest habitat in Borneo and Sumatra. Except for mating, males are more often heard than seen, their "long calls" roaring through trees, produced by over-sized throat sacs that can take in several liters of air. These normally small sacs are found in humans to be enlarged in trumpeters, bass singers and Muslim prayer callers. Photo at Camp Leakey Rehabilitation Project in Indonesia.

Trains also go to Jerantut but at least until recently, schedules were inconvenient. Or by air, thrice-weekly flights go to Sungei Tiang airstrip, 30 minutes from the park by motorized sampan.

The park offers an array of accommodations at and around headquarters, and there's a private lodge just over a mile (2 km) northeast on Sungei Tembeling (for all these, book well ahead).

Headquarters itself can be alive with birds—pied and sometimes rhinoceros hornbills, brown-throated sunbirds, various bright bulbuls and green pigeons, especially if trees are fruiting.

Creation of Taman Negara was largely the work of one man, Theodore Hubback, chief game warden of the then-Federated Malay States, who pressed the colonial government relentlessly for 15 years until it was set aside in 1938. Threats continue, particularly hunting for large animals such as rhinos, tigers, and elephants. Tourism in wet season can erode trails, and dams proposed for hydroelectric projects would drastically alter habitat.

Most comfortable times are drier March–September. Take sun lotion, insect repellent, hats, long-sleeved clothing.

---

**FURTHER INFORMATION**

Wildlife and National Parks Department, Km 10, Jalan Cheras, 56100 Kuala Lumpur, Tel: (+60) 03-905-2872, Fax: (+60) 03-905-2873.

---

Malaysia also includes two states on the northern coast of Borneo—Sabah and Sarawak. (The southern portion of Borneo belongs to Indonesia.)

# SABAH

## DANUM VALLEY CONSERVATION AREA

Many of Sabah's rarest creatures survive here, one of the most important reserves in Southeast Asia, 162 square miles (420 km²) of primary lowland rain forest on the upper reaches of the Segama River, of which the Danum River is a major tributary.

Rare Sumatran rhinos and Asian elephants, orangutans, both greater and lesser mouse deer, bearded pigs (hairier versions of wild boar), clouded leopards and their even rarer small cousins, flat-headed and leopard cats, find homes here, buffered by a surrounding 3,860 square miles (10,000 km²) of forest. This is set aside to be logged selectively by the Sabah Foundation, a group set up for the welfare and education of the Sabah people (also the economy, which environmentalists worry could begin to take priority over habitat preservation).

Among more than 270 bird species are spectacular great argus pheasants, black-and-crimson pittas, Bornean bristleheads, Bornean and black-throated wren-babblers, colorful trogons and kingfishers, and at nightfall, bat hawks and buffy fish owls which visit lights for insects.

Wary creatures can be hard to spot in dense forest, but most—even shy sun bears, orangutans, red leaf monkeys, red giant flying squirrels, and proboscis monkeys—can be glimpsed from time to time from the numerous walking trails around the Danum Valley Field Center. The Center formerly had public accommodations, but these have been supplanted by the Borneo Rain Forest Lodge, which has the same possibilities of seeing wildlife as the Center, with good guides. Night drives along logging roads provide good chances of seeing nocturnal animals, including elephants.

Access is by bus or (costlier) rental car, a rough two-hour drive from the nearest town, Lahad Datu, reachable by air from Sabah's capital, Kota Kinabalu, or Kuching, both jet air destinations.

# KINABALU PARK

Also in Sabah is 291-square-mile (754-km²) Kinabalu Park with the greatest concentration and diversity of unique plants and the highest mountain in Southeast Asia, Mount Kinabalu, still rising at 13,455 feet (4,101 m). Many visitors every year make this beautiful ascent—three hours for the very fit, three days for those wishing to stop en route and savor the natural riches and magnificent scenery. Flora range from virgin tropical forest to alpine. Some 1,000 orchid species have been discovered along with unique rhododendrons, giant crimson rafflesia blooms, the world's largest moss—the *Dawsonia*, up to a yard (1 m) tall—and miniature-to-giant insectivorous pitcher plants, including the world's largest, *Nepenthes rajah*, capable of trapping and consuming small rodents. A (springy) treetop walkway at Poring Hot Springs affords a canopy perspective on squirrels, birds, and many of the spectacular botanicals, with planned orchid, rafflesia, and butterfly gardens (the springs, piped into open-air baths, were developed by Japanese during World War II).

Most numerous among 100 mammals are common tree-shrews, visible along many trails, one of earth's earliest small mammals which evolved and spread worldwide tens of millions of years ago but are now restricted to Southeast Asia. Others among its ecological treasures are unique ferret-badgers, sun bears, and some 300 bird species including mountain bush warblers, Kinabalu friendly warblers, pale-faced bulbuls, and mountain blackeyes. Gray drongos and noisy long-tailed Malaysian tree-pies frequent park headquarters. Hot Springs' visitors see magpie robins and hear melodious white-rumped shamas.

Besides being home of endemic montane species of birds, Kinabalu has many plants, particularly orchids, found nowhere else on earth. Orchids especially have suffered from poaching (and one rich site was converted to a golf course!) but plans are afoot to grow and sell rare species in nurseries to diminish incentive to plunder wild populations.

Park headquarters has well-marked trails both nearby and directions to those higher on the mountain, also restaurants and good hostel and rest-house accommodations, all within walking distance. Accommodations also are available just outside the park and at nearby Ranau, all reachable by bus or, costlier, taxi, rental car, or chartered minibus, or by chartered air to a helipad at park headquarters from Kota Kinabalu 53 miles (85 km) away, or Ranau, 14 miles (22 km). Sunniest, driest weather March–May, wettest October–January, but changeable any time.

---

**FURTHER INFORMATION**

Sabah National Parks, P.O. Box 626, 88806 Kota Kinabalu, Sabah, Tel: (+60) 088-211585, 088-211652, 088-211881.

# SARAWAK

The history of Sarawak, sprawling across northwestern Borneo, reads like Victorian melodrama, ruled from 1838 to the start of World War II by "white rajah" descendants of British adventurer James Brooke who was awarded it by the Brunei Sultanate in gratitude for his quelling tribal rebellions and driving away Bornean pirates.

## GUNUNG MULU NATIONAL PARK

Premier among Sarawak's excellent national parks, this is also the largest, 203 square miles (526 km²) deep in the rain forest. Some 20,000 faunal species include 67 mammals—sun bears, western tarsiers, macaques, leaf monkeys, and Bornean gibbons—262 birds, 281 colorful butterflies, plus 3,500 plants, 170 kinds of orchids, and one of the largest limestone cave systems in the world, dominated by razor-sharp 164-foot-high (50-m) limestone spikes known as the Pinnacles.

Over 150 miles (250 km) of caves have been explored—believed to be only about 30 percent of the total—including the largest cave chamber in the world, Sarawak Chamber, described as equal to 16 football fields, and 32-mile-long (51-km) Clearwater, with marvelous limestone formations and an exquisite clear river with scorpions, giant crickets, frogs, and centipedes. Water-seeps outside it attract superb butterflies, sometimes huge chartreuse-and-black Rajah Brooke's birdwings, usually residents of the high canopy.

Deer Cave is home to nearly a million free-tailed bats which stream out en masse each evening to return at dawn minus a few picked off by waiting bat hawks, their routine duplicated in reverse by daylight-foraging cave swiftlets famous for their saliva-constructed nests, prime ingredient in bird's nest soup. (Similar bat and swift colonies are present in the huge Great Cave in **Niah National Park** near Miri, noted for evidence of human life dating back 40,000 years.)

Eight species of prehistoric-looking hornbills are here, including two of the rarest and largest—helmeted and rhinoceros.

The Pinnacles, an awesome stone forest halfway up Gunung Api, is a three-day trek, only for the fit, rewarded by spectacular scenery. A little longer—perhaps four days—and equally rewarding is the climb up 7,800-foot (2,377-m) Gunung Mulu.

The park, with accommodations (often booked well ahead), is reachable by air daily from Biri and Limbang.

Threats include continued logging, especially along riverbanks, despite international publicity describing vigorous protests by local tribesmen. But loggers have strong political support. Hunting, especially for large animals, also is a major threat. Few remain in areas within a day's walk of park headquarters.

## ALSO OF INTEREST

An exciting new conservation area is **Lanjak-Entimau** adjoining **Batang Ai National Park** and, across the border in Kalimantan, **Bentuang-Karimum National Park** (*see* p.605) in an international joint venture covering altogether some 2.47 million acres (about 1 million ha) of mountainous virgin rain forest, home to more than 1,000 orangutans, more than 20,000 Bornean gibbons, important rhino and clouded leopard populations, and other rare and endangered flora and fauna. More than 1,000 tree species have been found of such value that several sites have been set aside as gene banks and seed sources for the future.

More than 200 bird species include half of all known Bornean endemics, with rare Bulwer's pheasants, gray-headed fish-eagles, Wallace's hawk-eagles and seven kinds of hornbills, including the wrinkled, helmeted, and rhinoceros. Preliminary inventories have found more than a half-dozen new species of fish, crabs, and frogs alone, including a tiny adult frog just 0.4 inch (1 cm) long.

Of some 140 plant species used in traditional native medicine, ecologists are investigating some used for birth control, infertility, and varied disorders, including two found to be AIDS inhibitors.

---

**FURTHER INFORMATION**

National Parks and Wildlife Office, Forest Department (Ibu Pejabat Perhutanan), Wisma Sumber Alam, Jalan Stadium, Petra Jaya, 93660 Kuching, Tel: (+60) 82-442180, Fax: (+60) 82-441377.

---

**Bako National Park** is an accessible reserve in Sarawak, with beautiful scenery and excellent chances to get good views of proboscis monkeys, bearded pigs, silvered leaf monkeys, colugos (aka flying lemurs), and otters. Bako also has spectacular forest formations, including tropical heath forest with many pitcher plants.

Best places to get a good look at orangutans are at three centers where orphaned, injured, or otherwise needy individuals are rehabilitated for release in the wild: **Sepilok Forest Reserve** in Sabah, 45 minutes by bus and minibus from Sandakan which is on the local air network; **Semenggok**, reachable by bus 12 miles (20 km) from Kuching in Sarawak; **Matang Wildlife Center**, 15 miles (25 km) from Kuching. Other species are rehabilitated at these as well, and there are walking trails.

---

**FURTHER INFORMATION ON SARAWAK PARKS**

National Parks and Wildlife Office, Wisma Sumber, Alam, 93050 Kuching, Sarawak, Tel: (+60) 082-442180, Fax: (+60) 082-441377.

---

# NEW ZEALAND

GIANT TREE FERNS TOWER 50 FEET TALL
(15 M) OVER NEW ZEALAND'S FIORDLAND
WHERE GLOWWORMS COVER CAVERN WALLS AND
ROOFS, FLIGHTLESS KIWIS WITH NOSTRILS AT THE
END OF LONG CURVED BILLS SNIFF OUT RAIN FOREST
GRUBS, AND BLUE/GREEN TAKAHES, MOORHENS
LONG THOUGHT EXTINCT, FEED ON TUSSOCK
SHOOTS, ALPINE GRASSES, AND FERN ROOTS.

FURRY, DENSELY-FEATHERED LITTLE KIWIS, NEW ZEALAND'S NATIONAL BIRDS WITH NOSTRILS AT THE END OF THEIR BILLS, LABOR HERE TO LAY MONSTROUS EGGS 20 PERCENT OF THEIR BODY WEIGHT IN SOME OF THE WETTEST RAIN FORESTS IN THE WORLD. They are only one of an array of remarkable species that have been evolving in isolation since this beautiful island country broke off from the supercontinent Gondwanaland more than 100 million years ago.

With no mammal competition except two tiny bats, terrestrial birds could roam in a predator-free environment 1,000 miles (1,600 km) from their nearest neighbor, Australia. Today New Zealand, just twice the size of England (102,347 square miles/265,150 km²), divided into North and South islands, has more flightless birds than anyplace outside Antarctica. Among them are the world's largest parrots, kakapos; world's only alpine parrots, keas; with world's oldest reptiles, dinosaur-like tuataras dating back 250 million years; world's smallest bats; and some of the world's biggest earthworms and oldest trees.

# NEW ZEALAND

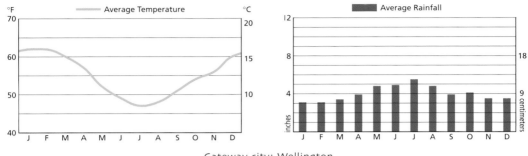

Gateway city: Wellington

When Polynesians, or Maoris, made the first human contact here over 1,000 years ago they found giant moas, birds standing up to 13 feet (4 m) tall, running about unafraid, and huias, birds in which males and females' bills differed uniquely in both form and function. Within a few years both were gone and other species were on their way out. Death sentence for many came with arrival of British Captain James Cook in 1769 bringing not only humans bent on killing everything possible but also destructive mammals such as goats, wild pigs, deer, and rats.

Belatedly awareness came of the value of what has been lost and what remains, and now some 30 percent of New Zealand is set aside in nature reserves. They cover habitat from subtropical to alpine, craggy mountain ranges to beaches, ice and snow-covered glaciers to drenched rain forest, deep fiords, rivers with thunderous waterfalls, and a 9,315-mile (15,000-km) coastline.

New Zealand's marine environment is 15 times larger than the land, ranging from the subtropical north with corals to subantarctic with New Zealand (world's rarest) sea lions, and 13 species of albatross, of which nine are endemic. There are six breeding types of penguins, including four endemics, among them the world's rarest, the yellow-eyed. New Zealand waters contain about half the world's whale species, including some beaked varieties so rare they have never been seen alive, and the world's rarest marine dolphin, the Maui's.

For the visitor there are dolphin, whale, seabird, and seal watching expeditions, the most famous at Kaikoura on the South Island, where one can see sperm whales year round. Off the North Island one can snorkel in warm coastal marine reserves teeming with fish and dolphins.

Some interior reserves are so remote it is unlikely humans have ever set foot there, but most are, at least in part, easily accessible, so that determined birders might see 42 of the 43 remaining endemics on the main islands in a short trip. These include three kiwi species plus keas—cheeky, inquisitive olive-green parrots with vivid crimson underwings; moreporks—endemic owls that announce themselves by name; two penguins and five shorebirds along with unique wrybills with left-pointing beaks (which help trap muddy marine organisms). A rich diversity of seabirds includes visitors from remote Chatham and subantarctic islands supporting a further 18 endemics, including the shore plover.

# Te Wahipounamu World Heritage Site

Outstanding among reserves on the South Island is southwest New Zealand U.N. World Heritage Site, Te Wahipounamu, incorporating four national parks—**Westland**, **Mount Cook**, **Mount Aspiring** and **Fiordland**—plus extensive state land for a total of 10,000 square miles (25,900 km²) in one of the world's largest and most pristine as well as beautiful reserves. Here are New Zealand's highest mountains, longest glaciers, tallest forests, wildest rivers and gorges, most rugged coastline, and largest populations of forest birds. Here is the world's largest buttercup—the Mount Cook "Lily"; one of its tiniest birds—warbler-like riflemen flitting with spiraling flight from tree to tree; and the entire wild population of red-billed takahes, rare flightless rails. Two-thirds of Te Wahipounamu is covered with southern beech-podocarp forest, some trees over 800 years old, descendants of ancient trees of Gondwanaland.

**Fiordland** (anglicized version of the Norwegian "fjord") is 4,850 square miles (12,561 km²), bordered on the east by crystalline lakes fed by some of the world's highest waterfalls and on the west by 14 deeply incised fiords. It is one of the world's largest national parks with endangered species, marine mammals, and some of the wettest places on earth. Southwest winds drop 236 inches

Rockhopper penguins make up in lively looks and disposition for small size, with bright red eyes, orange-red bills, bushy yellow eyebrows which they shake into wild halos during courtship, and loud "ecstatic vocalizations" with which they re-attract mates and re-assert territories of previous years. Both these are vigorously defended against any encroachment, real or imagined, as they hop, pink feet together, over boulder-strewn habitat on rocky coasts of the subantarctic, including Campbell and Auckland Islands. Juveniles occasionally are seen near the New Zealand mainland.

# NEW ZEALAND

(600 cm) of rain on its mountainsides yearly. Giant forest tree ferns grow 50 feet (15 m) tall. Kiwis with vestigial wings sniff out grubs in rain forests with nostrils at tips of long curved bills. Takahes with blue breasts and green backs, believed extinct until rediscovered here, survive in a valley named after them. Glowworms cover cavern walls and roofs. Te Anau and Manapouri have guides and varied accommodations and are ideal starting-places for exploration by sea kayak or by hiking world-renowned trails, especially the Milford Track, which has been called the world's most beautiful walk—or stay overnight on a boat cruising the fiords.

**Westland Park** glaciers are closest to the coast of any in the world, visible from its lush rain forest—scenically incomparable though raining or misty much of the time. **Mount Aspiring** is a remote and spectacular Alpine wilderness with gorgeous and popular walking tracks.

## ALSO OF INTEREST

In addition is **Tongariro** on North Island, a U.N. World Heritage Site and one of the world's oldest national parks, and other smaller set-asides throughout the country, most with visitor centers, pamphlets, and guided walks, many with huts, lodges, and/or campgrounds. A recent plan has been to reestablish as many species as possible on predator-free offshore islands and create "mainland islands" within conservation land, with the goal of reversing species decline by the year 2020.

International flights go to Auckland or Wellington on the North Island or Christchurch on the South Island, at all of which one can rent cars to drive everywhere on good roads, or get InterCity Travel passes which cover trains, ferries, and an extensive bus network. Many places have good hotels, motels, backpackers' hostels, well-equipped campgrounds, and restaurants.

Best times are September–December spring, though warm sunny weather often lasts through March. Mountains can be cool with heavy rains, snow and gales possible year-round, and rain can be almost continuous on the west coast of South Island.

Department of Conservation offices at visitor centers throughout the country offer advice and excellent pamphlets on "Exploring New Zealand Parks." Several good books describe New Zealand's spectacular walks and trails.

---

**FURTHER INFORMATION**

New Zealand Department of Conservation, P.O. Box 10-420, Wellington, New Zealand, Tel: (+64) 4-471-0726, Fax: (+64) 4-471-1082. Also Royal Forest and Bird Society, P.O. Box 631, Wellington.

# PAPUA NEW GUINEA

BIRDS OF PARADISE WERE NAMED NOT FOR
BEAUTY BUT SUPPOSED HEAVENLY CONNECTIONS
AFTER STUFFED SKINS WITHOUT LEGS WERE SENT
BACK TO EUROPEANS, LEADING THEM TO SURMISE THE
BIRDS HAD NO LEGS BUT DESCENDED TO EARTH FROM
HEAVEN AND SPENT THEIR ENTIRE LIVES IN MIDAIR.

P APUA NEW GUINEA REMAINS MUCH AS NATURALIST ALFRED WALLACE FOUND IT IN 1858, ONE OF THE
WILDEST PLACES ON EARTH WITH "MORE STRANGE, NEW AND BEAUTIFUL NATURAL OBJECTS THAN ANY
OTHER PART OF THE GLOBE."

Most of the world's gorgeous birds of paradise are here, enacting acrobatic and often bizarre
mating rituals. Their names derive not from dazzling plumage but once-supposed celestial

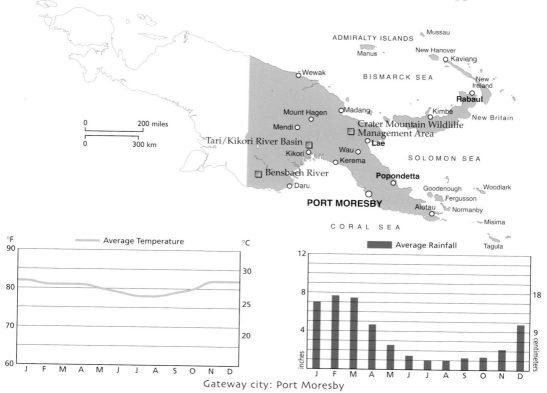

Gateway city: Port Moresby

621

connections—the first brilliantly feathered stuffed skins were sent back to Europe legless, which led to supposition they descended from heaven and soared continually, mating in midair and raising young in nests on males' backs.

Victoria crowned pigeons—world's largest—display ice-lavender, lacy, feather-fan crests several times the size of their heads. Bower birds lure mates with elaborate constructions that are a wonder of the avian world, inventive creations of flowers, grasses, seeds, beetle wings, shells, bits of glass if they can find them, sometimes painted with fruit juice or droppings. Chicken-sized megapods— "big feet"—don't incubate eggs but dig tunnels in volcanic soil where constant geothermal heat incubates them. Flightless six-foot-tall (2-m) cassowaries have a large, daggerlike claw on each foot that can kill and dismember a man. Papua New Guinea has more kinds of parrots, pigeons, and kingfishers than anywhere else in the world.

Orchids grow in every conceivable color, size, and shape—some 3,000 varieties—among some 20,000 kinds of flowering plants, including 1,200 tree species in the lowlands alone.

Giant birdwing butterflies on wingspans nearly a foot (30 cm) across flutter through canopies— the first European hunter who saw one shot it thinking it WAS a bird. Their niche is filled at night by the world's largest moths, the huge Hercules—among 6,000 colorful lepidoptera species.

Tree-climbing kangaroos and spiny, egg-laying echidnas are among some 180 kinds of mammals including some 60 pouched marsupials, evidence of the island's connection until about 6,000 years ago with northern Australia. Large mammal predators are absent—largest are little pouched bronze quolls—one reason for presence of so many unusual birds as well as other small species in this relatively small country of 178,704 square miles (462,843 km²). Only slightly larger than the U.S. state of California, it occupies the eastern half of the island of New Guinea (the western half is Indonesia's Irian Jaya).

About 25,000 kinds of beetles thrive, some so strikingly beautiful they are collected as body ornaments; 160 kinds of frogs; 170 kinds of lizards including both salt and freshwater croco-diles; and 110 kinds of snakes, including sea snakes, tree snakes, and pythons.

Scientists continue to discover new species as they explore this relatively young island. New Guinea was pushed up by collision of two undersea tectonic plates over the past few million years creating rugged, deeply folded terrain which has resulted in separate, isolated develop-ment of a wide variety of human cultures as well as extraordinary biodiversity. People of New Guinea speak over 750 distinctly different indigenous languages.

Habitat ranges from alpine glaciers though forested mountains to flat grasslands, lowland mangrove swamps and golden sand beaches with beautiful offshore coral reefs.

Climate varies over the country. It's hot, humid and wet year-round in the lowlands, wetter December–March and drier May–October, and Port Moresby seasonally is dry, even dusty.

# PAPUA NEW GUINEA

Most visitors arrive by air in Port Moresby, usually from Australia but also Singapore, Manila, and elsewhere. The national airline, Air Niugini, connects larger interior communities. Roads are limited, as are accommodations, but tourist facilities are gradually improving. Water transport is widely available.

Wildlife reserves are few, in large part because of P.N.G.'s traditional land tenure—but the National Parks Board recognizes provincial and local parks as Wildlife Management Areas, and there's growing awareness of the concept of protected species and conservation, spread with help of international conservation organizations such as World Wide Fund for Nature, Wildlife Conservation Society, The Nature Conservancy, and Conservation International. In some cases these groups advise local committees on management of reserve areas.

Echidnas pull off one of nature's most impressive disappearing acts when, as a small spiny mound, they begin to vibrate, gradually subsiding into soft ground until in moments they're gone completely, much as a submarine sinks into water. The vibration is front and back claws digging furiously while side spines do their part, a move to ward off predators. Echidnas are, with platypi, world's only monotremes or egg-laying mammals. They carry their single rubbery egg and young in a pouch, lactating and feeding the puggle or young echidna until it's ejected at two months when its spines, actually modified hairs, become too prickly to tote that way. Echidnas live in New Guinea, Australia, and Tasmania.

OPPOSITE: Green tree pythons look like a bunch of unripe bananas when they coil around a branch in the canopy of a tropical rain forest in New Guinea or Australia. Sensory pits along lips can detect presence of either cold- or warm-blooded prey such as a lizard or small bird. Leathery eggs are incubated 47 days (depending on temperature). Young hatch in brilliant mixed tropical colors, from yellow to brisk-red, all in the same clutch.

Present protected areas are regarded as inadequate in view of P.N.G.'s conservation importance. Traditional landowners have difficulty, however, balancing dangers of environmental destruction with rich rewards offered by multinational logging and mining companies. P.N.G. has vast commercial deposits of gold, copper, and silver, as well as petroleum. Exploitation of reef fisheries is increasingly a problem, as is slash-and-burn agriculture as population grows and traditional village-based farming seems less sustainable.

---

**FURTHER INFORMATION**

National Parks Service, P.O. Box 5749, Boroko.

FOR WILDLIFE MANAGEMENT AREAS—Wildlife Conservation Section,
Department of Environment and Conservation, P.O. Box 6601,
Boroko (Port Moresby), Papua New Guinea.

Research and Conservation Foundation of PNG, P.O. Box 1261,
Goroka, Tel: (+675) 732-3211, Fax: (+675) 732-1121.

---

# BENSBACH RIVER

This vast, wondrous floodplain is alive with birds and animals, many of them fearless because they have had little contact with people in this lightly populated area. Much of the world population of little curlews stage here in migration between Australia and Siberia, among 250 species of migratory and resident waterbirds including rare, stunning Brolga cranes, along with great flocks of waterfowl. During Australian droughts it is a refuge for Australian waterfowl.

Some 60,000 introduced rusa deer graze. Equally at home are agile wallabies and two kinds of crocodiles. Cited by the Ramsar Convention as a Wetland of International Importance, Bensbach is one of several rivers (among others are the Morehead and Mai Russa) that cross this rich plain and drain over tidal mudflats into the Torres Strait. Bensbach is part of the 2,280-square-mile (5,900-km$^2$) Tonda Wildlife Management Area in the Western Province of southwestern P.N.G. on the Indonesian border, managed by a local landowners' committee.

During wet season Bensbach is reachable only by boat or small planes that land at outpost strips. Accommodations are available at the Bensbach Wildlife Lodge—comfortable but on the costly side—and sometimes government guesthouses. Problems include poaching, also active leases for mining and seismic exploration.

> **FURTHER INFORMATION**
>
> P.O. Box 6940, Port Moresby, Tel: (+675) 323-4467.

# CRATER MOUNTAIN WILDLIFE MANAGEMENT AREA

Crater Mountain Wildlife Management Area is one of the best places to see both wildlife and spectacular scenery (plus the culture of friendly villagers who manage it) in P.N.G., covering 1,038 square miles (2,700 km²) ranging from lowland riverine rain forest to forested slopes of Crater Mountain. It's possible to hike with a guide between the various villages or, easier, charter and fly among them. Local accommodation—simple, with local food—is usually available.

> **FURTHER INFORMATION**
>
> PNG Research and Conservation Foundation, P.O. Box 1261, Goroka, Tel: (+675) 732-3211, Fax: (+675) 732-1123.

# TARI/KIKORI RIVER BASIN

Tari/Kikori River Basin in the Gulf Province is in the midst of a region of nearly 8,900 square miles (23,000 km²) of one of the world's densest, most wildlife-rich mountain rain forests, home to tree kangaroos, birds of paradise, hornbills, and cassowaries. It is home also to the renowned Huki wigmen, famous for intricately decorated wigs. The **Kikori Integrated Conservation and Development Project** is the largest conservation area in P.N.G., with lakes, river systems, mountain ranges, marshes and mangroves, and 16 different ethnic peoples, a pilot project in helping local communities integrate conservation with sustainable development. There's an airstrip—also boat access through the maze of waterways—and several guesthouses.

# ALSO OF INTEREST

**Varitata National Park**, 26 miles (42 km) from Port Moresby, with walking trails through upland rain forest and savannah, fine birdlife including birds of paradise visible morning and evening.

# PHILIPPINES

WHEN LORDLY PHILIPPINE MONKEY-EATING
EAGLES ERECT NINE-INCH (23-CM) LANCET
FEATHERS LIKE WILD HALOS AROUND THEIR FIERCELY
PIERCING EYES, DARK FACES, AND AX-SHAPED BILLS, THEY
MAY BE THE MOST SAVAGE-LOOKING RAPTORS ON EARTH.
ABLE TO CAPTURE AND CONSUME MAMMALS LARGER THAN
THEY ARE, NOT ONLY MONKEYS BUT PIGS AND DOGS, THEY ARE
ALSO ONE OF THE WORLD'S MOST ENDANGERED, MAKING
PERHAPS THEIR LAST STAND IN 281-SQUARE-MILE
(729-KM²) MOUNT APO NATIONAL PARK.

"HARDLY ANYWHERE DOES THE NATURE LOVER FIND A
GREATER FILL OF BOUNDLESS TREASURE" THAN THE
PHILIPPINES, GERMAN ETHNOGRAPHER FEDOR JAGOR REPORTED
MORE THAN A CENTURY AGO—"SO LITTLE KNOWN AND
SELDOM VISITED...YET NO LAND IS PLEASANTER."

Much of that remains true despite strains and encroachment of modern life on these 7,107 islands and islets
rimmed with crystalline blue-green water, white sand
beaches, and spectacular coral gardens. Bustling cities
have arisen—but rich forest and coastal
ecosystems have been set aside. Almost a
third of the islands remain uninhabited.
Only about 500 are larger than a half-mile-
square (1 km²), and 2,500 aren't even named.

Birds here include species seldom or never
found elsewhere—great scops owls, Philippine cockatoos,
and superb, highly endangered Philippine monkey-eating
eagles, one of the world's largest and most spectacular
birds of prey. These formidable birds, called by Charles

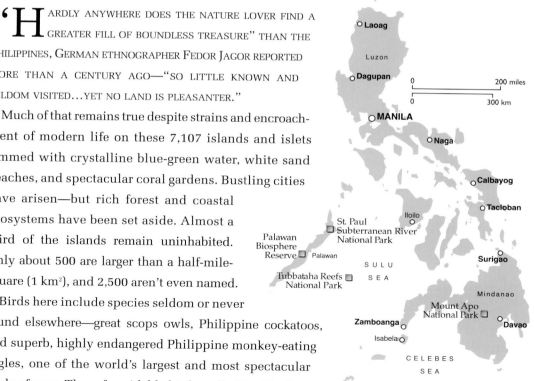

# PHILIPPINES

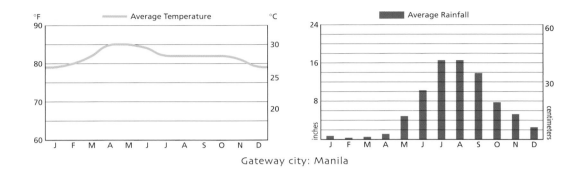

Gateway city: Manila

Lindbergh "air's noblest fliers", with great, fearsome, feathered mantles—perhaps 100 still in existence—easily capture and consume monkeys. They also dine, unfortunately, on rare small mammals such as Philippine flying lemurs, flying fox bats, and fist-sized tabius and tarsiers, world's tiniest primates, all also on the endangered list and likely to remain so while they stay in eagles' range. Fierce small binturongs or bear-cats, rare also, usually can defend themselves.

Many other notable small species are here—red mouse deer of Palawan, world's smallest red deer; sinarapan, less than a half-inch (1 cm) long in Luzon's Lake Buhi, world's smallest edible fish; tamaraw, dwarf short-horned wild buffaloes in the Mindoro Mountains.

Endangered hawksbill and green sea turtles scour out nests on white sand beaches. A rainbow array of tropical fish and crustaceans inhabit magnificent coral reef gardens. Philippines oysters produce pearls coveted for exceptional size, quality, and luster.

Large-scale logging after World War II accompanied by widespread slash-and-burn cultivation caused significant environmental damage to the Philippines as in other Southeast Asian countries. Species previously vulnerable became extinct. Forest cover on larger islands remains only on rugged mountain tops, which have become plant and wildlife havens. Erosion in lower areas led to soil loss, climatic effects, and floods and mudslides that killed thousands and finally aroused public concern, leading to reexamination of environmental policies and a ban on deforestation. A government Department of Environment and Natural Resources was formed, along with citizens' environmental groups. Much remains to be done—river clean-up, a ban on fishing with cyanide and dynamite and taking of endangered species or their parts for food, medicinal trade or pets, and enforcement of existing environmental laws.

Much also remains to be saved—some 580 bird species (including 135 threatened or endangered, third highest, with China, of any country in the world), 100 mammals, 300 kinds of reptiles and amphibians, and uncounted insects that include at least 850 kinds of butterflies and moths, many endemic to just one or two islands. Plants have thrived in the rich volcanic soil, and there are more than 10,000 kinds of trees, flowering shrubs, and gigantic vines and ferns, with more than 900 orchid species in rain forests, mountains, fertile lowlands, and chalky coastal woodlands.

Philippines weather is hot and humid year-round, with seasonal variations over the islands and an average 20 typhoons a year, most (but not all) in August–November. Best times generally are drier December–May.

International jets fly to Manila and Cebu. Inexpensive air passes are available for internal travel (book flights well ahead). Busses and taxis go almost everywhere on major islands. Ferries run between most islands, though they are not regarded as the safest, most comfortable way to travel. Most towns have a range of accommodations.

Terrorist incidents have prompted travel warnings so it is well to inquire about current conditions before finalizing trip plans.

---

**FURTHER INFORMATION**

National Parks Development Committee, Agrifina Circle, T.M. Kalaw Street, Ermita, P.O. Box 4053, Manila, Tel: (+63) 2-302-71-82/2-302-73-81, Fax: (+63) 2-525-33-53; Protected Areas and Wildlife Bureau, Department of Environment and Natural Resources, Visayas Avenue, Diliman, Quezon City, Tel: (+63) 2-978511/15, Fax: (+63) 2-981010, Tlx: 7572000 envinar ph; Haribon Foundation for Conservation of Natural Resources, Suite 901, Richbelt Towers, 17 Annapolis Street, Greenhills, San Juan, Manila, Tel: (+63) 722-7180/722-6357, Fax: (+63) 722-7119.

---

Several dozen national parks and reserves have been set aside, most because of public pressure. Many need to be larger to effectively protect species. All of them together include less than 1.3 percent of land area, far less than most other countries, small or large, around the world. All need support. Visitors can help simply by signing guest books and hiring guides.

# MOUNT APO NATIONAL PARK

Mount Apo National Park was established to protect the Philippines' highest peak, 10,311-foot (3,144-m) "snow-capped" Mount Apo on Mindinao (the "snow" is actually a thick white sulphur crust). Of greater interest to naturalists nowadays are its wild inhabitants—especially the spectacular Philippines monkey-eating eagle, known here also as haribon, one of the world's most redoubtable avian predators and most endangered. More than three feet (1m) tall, with a two-yard (2-m) wingspan, it can capture and consume mammals larger than it is. A single eagle can claim and defend a 25–40-square-mile (70–110-km²) territory. To see one of these magnificent birds in the wild is unforgettable, with its piercing eyes, wild feathered halo, and lordly bearing. Its

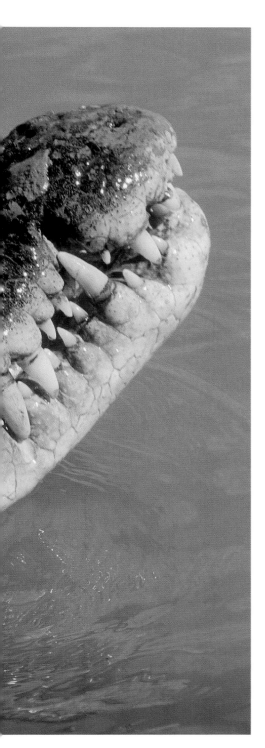

shrieking cry often is issued from a tall treetop near its enormous nest, usually built on a clump of tree-clinging air plants, or while it is circling high overhead.

The park's 281 square miles (728 km²) of wild, lush tropical forest full of orchids, giant pitcher plants, and wildflowers, with hot and cold mineral springs, rushing mountain streams and lakes, hidden water-falls and sulphuric craters, are where this magnificent bird, perhaps 100 still in existence, could make its last stand—though many feel the species is doomed unless the park can be enlarged. The bird also is threatened, as is the park's whole richly diverse ecosystem, by illegal logging, forest fires, agricultural encroachment by settlers, and plans for a massive geothermal energy project with three modular power plants here, opposed by native peoples and environmental groups but still under consideration.

Several walking tracks include three to the top of Mount Apo—a challenging climb requiring a guide and usually several days, best in March–April, with unsurpassed views of some of the most breathtaking scenery anywhere, and splendid vegetation. Climbers may see birds such as Philippine hanging parakeets, white-bellied woodpeckers, amethyst doves, Mindinao scops owls and eagle owls, rufous-bellied hawk eagles, wattled hornbills, celestial blue monarchs,

Estuarine or Australian saltwater crocodiles, world's largest reptiles and most aggressive and dangerous of the crocodiles, are superb swimmers, known to travel 600 miles or more (1,000 km) by sea. Some ocean-going adult males, up to 20 feet (6m) long, weighing up to a ton (1,000 kg), have barnacles on their scales. So despite their name, they've reached and settled throughout Southeast Asia and are equally at home in Papua New Guinea, Indonesia, Sri Lanka, Philippines, Bangladesh, Myanmar, Vietnam, and Thailand.

and Philippine and fire-breasted flowerpeckers. Mammals include sambar deer, wild pigs, and long-tailed macaques.

Park foothills are accessible via good roads 16 miles (25 km) west from Davao City, which has busses, also from Cotabato. Lake Agco has a campsite and cabin (bring your own food). Overnight stays can sometimes be arranged in private homes in nearby Tudaya.

Well worth a visit and support is the **Philippine Eagle Nature Center**, which breeds and cares for the endangered bird a short distance from Davao in Calinan. Jeepney transport to Calinan is available in Davao.

---

**FURTHER INFORMATION**

Department of Environment and Natural Resources (DENR) in Davao. Climbing guides and provisions can be arranged in Kidapawen in North Cotabato.

---

## PALAWAN BIOSPHERE RESERVE

Palawan Biosphere Reserve is an island slash of mountain and tropical rain forest filled with rare and interesting birds and four-footed wildlife, bordered by white sand beaches, ringed by coral reefs some 120 miles (190 km) west of the main Philippines group between the Sulu and China Seas. Isolation has helped maintain its largely pristine state, though with discovery of valuable woods and mineral deposits of chrome, copper, manganese, nickel, as well as oil and gas, it is uncertain how long this will last.

This 5,400-square-mile (14,000 km²) island U.N. Biosphere Reserve, one of the world's largest, is divided into several parts, including two national parks of world renown—ST. PAUL SUB-TERRANEAN RIVER NATIONAL PARK and TUBBATAHA REEFS—plus **Palawan Wildlife Sanctuary**; a **Buffer Zone**; **Core Zone Area**; **Ursula Island Bird Sanctuary**; and **Babumbayan Experimental Forest**.

In the island's forests are rare foot-high (30-cm) Calamian Palawan mouse deer, scaly anteaters, Palawan porcupines, badgers, binturong, and tarsiers. Birds include Palawan peacock-pheasants and close to water, purple herons and threatened Philippine sea eagles. Swallow-like swifts build edible nests on cliffs.

## ST. PAUL'S SUBTERRANEAN RIVER NATIONAL PARK

St. Paul's National Park is named for a subterranean river called one of the world's wonders, at least five navigable miles (8 km), its source still not found, starting with a clear blue coastal lagoon and flowing through caverns of heartstopping beauty. Strange, glittering rock formations of many sizes, shapes, and colors, grow from the cave's ceiling and floor in cathedral-like rooms so profoundly quiet the only audible sounds are boat paddles and twittering of hundreds of thousands (some say millions) of bats. In the silence one hears the echoes that make bats' sonar echolocation systems work. At dusk bats leave and the cave is inhabited in equal numbers by day-flying swifts and swiftlets (white-bellied and pygmy), an unforgettable twilight spectacle when the two groups depart and arrive en masse.

Above ground this small (some say too small) park, set aside with aid arranged by World Wide Fund for Nature through a debt-for-nature swap, is equally remarkable—15 square miles (39 km$^2$) bordered by coral reefs, white sand beaches, mangrove forests, on through mossy and tropical forest to marble mountains. Forests are homes of monkeys, bear-cats, armored pangolins, porcupines, otters, palm civets, lizards (including five-foot [1.5-m] monitors), snakes, and over 80 bird species—rare Palawan peacock-pheasants, Philippine cockatoos, tabon birds, white-bellied sea eagles, stork-billed kingfishers, collared scops owls, and Pacific reef egrets. Over 100 tree species are marked on trails around the ranger station, part of the Palawan Moist Forest noted as one of the WWF Global 2000 Ecoregions with the richest tree flora in Asia.

Ranger headquarters is reachable by boat or short walk from Sabang, which has simple, comfortable accommodations and where guided trips can be arranged, 50 miles (81 km) by (bumpy) jeepney ride north of Puerto Princesa. Camping is sometimes permitted on the beach. Best times to visit are dry December–May.

# TUBBATAHA REEFS MARINE PARK

This U.N. World Heritage Site protects 128 sea square miles (332 km$^2$) and two atolls separated by a five-mile (8-km) channel in the Sulu Sea 100 miles (160 km) east of Palawan, with marine life as rich and diverse as any on earth. Each atoll surrounds a deep blue lagoon bordered by shallow (knee- to waist-high) emerald-green waters and a spectacular drop-off filled with colorful and unusual sea creatures, attracting great numbers of seabirds and renowned for snorkeling and scuba diving. Most tourists use live-in dive boats mid-March–mid-June (other times subject to rough monsoon seas). Tubbataha became a reserve after dynamite, cyanide, and overfishing had taken such a toll that divers and farsighted fishermen reported to the Philippines government that only quick protective measures could prevent complete destruction of this valued nursery for marine species as well as seabirds. Both reefs and species have recovered remarkably, though vigilance and further curtailment of fishing is necessary. Hawksbill and green sea turtles nest, as do sooty, crested, and noddy terns, and brown and red-footed boobies, among 46 bird species. At least 379 fish species of at least 40 families live in and around the brilliant coral in a glorious multispecies nursery for the surrounding sea. Like St. Paul's, a debt-for-nature swap made possible its set-aside, and diving and snorkeling fees now almost support its maintenance and protection. Trips can be arranged in Manila and Cebu City.

**FURTHER INFORMATION**

Tubbataha Foundation, Suite 4E, 227 Salcedo Street, Legaspi Village, Makati, Metro Manila; ALSO 83-A Harvard Street, Cubao, Quezon City; Tel: (+63) 912-42-99, Fax: (+63) 912-42-99.

## OTHER PALAWAN RESERVES

**Ursula Island**, where thousands of birds have traditionally come to roost every evening, though introduced rats have reduced their numbers (boats can be hired for the one-hour crossing at Rio Tuba); **El Nido**, a marine reserve with coral reefs, manta rays, dugongs (manatee-like), mangroves, rain forest; **Caluit Island Sanctuary**, home to introduced African giraffes, zebras, and gazelles, living in harmony with Philippine mouse deer, bear-cats, and crocodiles.

Public transport around 25-by-260-mile (40 × 418-km) Palawan is limited to "tricycles" (motorcycles with sidecars that serve as taxis) and "jeepney" vans or trucks which serve roughly as busses and also hire out with driver-guides. Coastal boats go around the island's perimeter. Hotels are in the capital city, Puerto Princesa, and several resorts on the island's north end. Regular flights come by Philippine Airlines from Manila, and small planes can be chartered on the island. Scuba and snorkel equipment can be rented. Dry season is January–April.

**FURTHER INFORMATION**

Department of Environment and Nature Reserves, Palawan Council for Sustainable Development, P.O. Box 45, Irawan, Puerto Princesa City, 5300 Palawan, Philippines, Tel: (+63) 2-922-24-50/922-45-85.

## ALSO OF INTEREST

Other notable "mainland" Philippine reserves include: **Mount Iglit (Ilig)-Mount Baco Sanctuary** on Mindoro, interesting birds, also last refuge for tamaraw, Philippine dwarf buffaloes; **Mount Kanlaon National Park** centered around Kanlaon volcano, with abundant wildlife, waterfalls, crater lakes, visits arranged from Bacolod; **Quezon National Park**, 112 miles (180 km) southeast of Manila, accessible, beautiful, good wildlife; **Kitanglad National Park** in north-central Bukidnon, mountainous home to a host of rare birds including red harriers, Brahminy kites, Philippine sparrowhawks, and serpent eagles.

# BIBLIOGRAPHY

In addition to the individual titles listed below, we found the Lonely Planet country guides (www.lonelyplanet.com) indispensable, both for research and actual travel. Other series which provided especially useful information were the Bradt Travel Guides (www.bradt-travelguides.com) and the Insight guides (www.insightguides.com).

The reader will note that the sources listed below are alphabetized by title rather than author. While this is unconventional, we chose this approach as being more accessible for a reader interested in a particular country, or a particular subject (e.g. birds). We grouped these listings by continent for the same reason.

## AFRICA

*A Story Like the Wind*, Laurens van der Post, Harcourt Brace Jovanovich, 1986

*Adventuring in East Africa*, Allen Bechky, Sierra Club Books, 1990

*African Elephant*, Roger Di Silvestro, John Wiley & Sons, 1991

*Africa's Top Wildlife Countries*, Mark Nolting, Global Travel Publishers, 1994

*African Wildlife Safaris*, Camerapix, 1989

*Birds of The Gambia and Senegal*, Clive Barlow and Tim Wacher, Pica Press, 1997

*Birds of Kenya and Northern Tanzania*, Zimmerman, Turner, Pearson, Princeton University Press, 1999

*Birds of Western Africa*, Ron Demey, Princeton University Press, 2002

*Botswana Visitors' Guide*, Republic of Botswana, annually

*Collins Field Guide to Birds in East Africa*, W. Serle *et al.*, Harper Collins, 1995

*Cry of the Kalahari*, Mark and Delia Owens, Houghton Mifflin, 1984

*Ecologically Sensitive Sites in Africa*, Vol. I–VI, World Bank, 1993

*Elephant Memories*, Cynthia Moss, William Morrow & Co., 1998

*Etosha National Park*, David Rogers, Struik Publishers, 1994

*Field Guide to Birds of East Africa*, Terry Stevenson and John Fanshawe, T. & A.D. Poyser Ltd, 2002

*Field Guide to the Birds of Gambia and Senegal*, Clive Barlow *et al.*, Yale University Press, 1998

*Field Guide to Birds of West Africa*, W. Serle, G.J. Morel, W. Hartwig, Trafalgar Square Publishing, 1999

*Field Guide to Mammals of Southern Africa*, Chris and Tilde Stuart, Struik Publishers, 1992

*Field Guide to National Parks of East Africa*, John Williams, Houghton Mifflin, 1972

*Gorillas in the Mist*, Dian Fossey, Houghton Mifflin, 1983

*Great Game Parks/Etosha*, David Rogers, Struik Publishers, 1994

*Guide to the Birds of Madagascar*, Olivier Langrand, Yale University Press, 1990

*Guide to Mt Kenya and Kilimanjaro*, Iain Allen, Mountain Club of Kenya, 1991

*Guide to Namibian Game Parks*, Willie and Sandra Olivier, Longman Publishing, 1993

*Guide to Southern African Game and Nature Reserves*, Chris and Tilde Stuart, Struik Publishers, 1994

*Guide to Vegetation of Lope Reserve, Gabon*, Lee White and Kate Abernethy, Wildlife Conservation Society, 1997

*Important Bird Areas in Africa*, Lincoln Fishpool and Michael Evans, Pisces Publishers, 2001

*In the Dust of Kilimanjaro*, David Western, Island Press, 1997

*In the Kingdom of Gorillas*, Bill Weber and Amy Vedder, Simon & Schuster, 2001

*Kruger National Park Visitor's Guide*, Leo Braack, Struik Publishers, 1993

*Lemurs of the Lost World*, J. Wilson, Impact Books, 1990

*Lost World of the Kalahari*, Laurens van der Post, Harcourt Brace Jovanovich, 1986

*Madagascar*, Ken Preston-Mafbaum, Facts on File, 1991

*Madagascar Travels*, Christina Dodwell, Hodder and Stoughton Publishers, 1995

*Madagascar Wildlife*, Hillary Bradt, Globe Pequot Press, 1996

*Mammals of Botswana Field Guide*, Peter Comeley and Salome Meyer, Africa Window, 1994

*Mammals of Madagascar*, Nick Garbutt, Pica Press, 1999

*Mammals of Southern Africa*, John Hanks, McGraw Hill, 1989

*Mauritius*, Royston Ellis, Globe Pequot Press, 1999

*Mountains of the Moon*, Guy Yeoman, Universal Publishers, 1989

*National Audubon Society Field Guide to African Wildlife*, Peter C. Alden *et al.*, Knopf, 1995

*National Parks of East Africa*, John G. Williams, Harper Collins, 1981

*National Parks of South Africa*, Anthony Bannister, Struik Publishers, 1993

*Newman's Birds of South Africa*, Kenneth Newman, Struik Publishers, 2000

*Ngorongoro*, Chris and Tilde Stuart, Struik Publishers, 1995

*Okavango, Sea of Land, Land of Water*, Peter Johnson and Anthony Bannister, Struik Publishers, 1993

*Rain Forests of West Africa*, Claude Martin, Birkhauser Verlag, 1991

*Reunion, Seychelles and Mauritius*, Michelin Travel Publications, 2000

*Roberts' Birds of Southern Africa*, G. Lindsey McLean, New Holland Publishers, 1993

*Rough Guide to West Africa*, Jim Hudgens and Richard Trillo, Rough Guides Publications, 1998

*Safari Companion*, Richard Estes, Chelsea Green Publishers, 1993

*Serengeti*, Mitsuaki Iwago, Chronicle Books, 1986

*Serengeti Shall Not Die*, Bernard Grzimek, Hamish Hamilton Publishers, London, 1960

*Spectrum Guide to Kenya*, Camerapix Publishers, 1993

*Spectrum Guide to Namibia*, Camerapix Publishers, 1993

*Spectrum Guide to Tanzania*, Camerapix Publishers, 1992

*Spectrum Guide to Zimbabwe*, Camerapix Publishers, 1992

*The Giraffe*, Anne Inis Dagg and J. Bristol Foster, Krieger Publishing, 1982

*The Zambezi*, Jan and Fiona Teede, Andre Deutsch Ltd, 1990

*This is Botswana*, Peter Joyce, New Holland Publishers, 1994

*This is Namibia*, Peter Joyce *et al.*, Struik Publishers, 1992

*This is Zimbabwe*, Peter Joyce, Struik Publishers, 1992

*Top Birding Spots in Southern Africa*, Hugh Chittenden, Southern Book Publishers, 1993

*Travellers' Guide to Botswana*, Peter Comley and Salome Meyer, New Holland Publishers, 1994

*Trees of the Okavango Delta/Moremi Game Reserve*, Veronica Roodt, Shell Publishers, 1993

*Waterberg Flora Footpaths*, Patricia Craven and Christine Marrais, Gamsburg Press, 1989

*Where to Watch Birds in Africa*, Nigel Wheatley, Princeton University Press, 1996

*Wild Places of Southern Africa*, Tim O'Hagen, Southern Book Publishers, 1996

*Wildlife Wars*, Richard Leakey and Virginia Morell, St. Martins Press, 2001

*Zaïre*, Christa Mang, Hunter Publishers, 1991

**ANTARCTICA**

*A Field Guide to the Wildlife of the Falkland Islands and South Georgia*, Ian J. Strange, Harper Collins, 1992

*Antarctic Wildlife*, Bryan Sage, Facts on File, 1982

*Antarctica, The Falklands and South Georgia*, Sara Wheeler, Cadogan Guides, 1997

*Natural History of the Antarctic Peninsula*, Sanford Moss, Columbia University Press, 1998

*The Penguins*, Tony Williams, Oxford University Press, 1995

*The Sea and the Ice*, Louis Halle, Houghton Mifflin, 1973

**ASIA**

*A Field Guide to the Birds of China*, J. Mackinnon *et al.*, Oxford University Press, 2000

*A Field Guide to the Birds of Russia and Adjacent Territories*, V.E. Flint *et al.*, Princeton University Press, 1984

*A Field Guide to Birds of Sri Lanka*, John Harrison, Oxford University Press, 1999

*A Handbook of the Birds of China*, Zhenjie Zhao, 1995

*A Pictorial Guide to Birds of the Indian Subcontinent*, Salim Ai and S. Dillon Ripley, Oxford University Press, 1994

*Bharatphur, Bird Paradise*, Martin Ewans, Witherby Publishers, 1989

*Birds in China*, Xu Weishu, Foreign Languages Press, 1989

*Birds of India*, Richard Grimmett *et al.*, Princeton University Press, 1999

*Birds of Nepal*, Richard Grimmett, Princeton University Press, 2000

*Chasing the Monsoon*, Alexander Frater, Viking Press, 1991

*China's Nature Reserves*, Wenhua and Xianying, Foreign Languages Press, 1989

*Collins Handguide to Birds of Indian Subcontinent*, Martin W. Woodcock, Stephen Greene Press, 1980

*Footprint's Myanmar (Burma) Handbook*, Joshua Eliot and Jane Bickersteth, Footprints Publications, 1997

*Guide to Birds in South-East Asia*, Craig Robson, Princeton University Press, 2000

*Guide to Burma*, Nicholas Greenwood, Bradt Publications, 1996

*Living Treasures, an Odyssey Through China's Extraordinary Nature Reserves*, Tang Xiyang, Bantam Books, 1987

*National Parks of Russia*, I.V. Chebakowa, Biodiversity Conservation, 1997

*National Parks of Thailand*, Denis Gray, Communications Resources, 1991

*Natural History of the USSR*, Algirdas Knystautas, McGraw Hill, 1991

*Nature of Russia*, John Massey Stewart, Cross River Press, 1996

*Nature Reserves in U.S.S.R.*, M. Davydova and V. Koshevoi, Progress, 1989

*Nature Reserves of the Himalaya and the Mountains of Central Asia*, Michael Green, IUCN, 1993

*Pandas of Wolong*, George B. Schaller *et al.*, University of Chicago Press, 1985

*Realms of the Russian Bear*, John Sparks, Little Brown & Co., 1992

*Royal Chitwan National Park*, Hemanta R. Mishra and Margaret Jeffries, The Mountaineers, 1991

*Spell of the Tiger*, Sy Montgomery, Houghton Mifflin, 1995

*The Book of Indian Animals*, S.H. Prater, Oxford University Press, 1993

*The Book of Indian Birds*, Salim Ali, Bombay Natural History Society and Oxford University Press, 1996

*Tibet's Hidden Wilderness, Wildlife and Nomads of the Chang Tang Reserve*, Geo. Schaller, Harry N. Abrams Publishers, 1997

*Tiger!*, Simon Barnes, Meridian Boxtree Ltd, 1994

*Tigers and Men*, Richard Ives, Doubleday, 1996

*Tiger's Destiny*, Valmik Thapar, Time Books International, 1992

*Tigers in the Snow*, Peter Matthiessen, North Point Press, 2000

*Tigers: The Secret Life*, Valmik Thapar, Elmtree Books, 1989

*Trekking in Russia and Central Asia*, Frith Maier, The Mountaineers Books, 1994

*Vietnam Handbook*, John Colet and Joshua Eliot, Footprint Handbooks, 1997

*Where to Watch Birds in Asia*, Nigel Wheatley, Princeton University Press, 1996

*Wild China*, John MacKinnon, M.I.T. Press, 1996

*Wildlife of Tibetan Steppe*, George Schaller, University of Chicago Press, 1998

*Wildlife Treasure-Houses, Nature Reserves in Sichuan*, China Forestry Publishing, 1992

*Xishuangbanna, A Nature Reserve of China*, China Forestry Publishing, 1992

*Zapovedniks and National Parks of Russia*, Environmental Education Center, Moscow, 1998

## CARIBBEAN AND CENTRAL AMERICA

*A Guide to the Birds of Panama with Costa Rica, Nicaragua and Honduras*, Robert Ridgely and John A. Gwyne, Princeton University Press, 1989

*A Guide to the Birds of the West Indies*, Herbert Raffaele, Princeton University Press, 1998

*Adventuring in Central America*, Sierra Club Travel Guide, 1995

*Belize Guide*, Paul Glassman, Passport Press, 1989

*Birder's Guide to the Bahama Islands*, Anthony Winter, American Birding Association, 2000

*Birder's Guide to Trinidad and Tobago*, William Murphy, Peregrine Enterprises, 1986

*Birds of Costa Rica*, Aaron D. Sekerak, Lone Pine Publishing, 1996

*Birds of Costa Rica*, G. Gary Stiles and Alexander Skutch, Comstock Publishing, 1989

*Birds of Puerto Rico and the Virgin Islands*, Herbert Raffaele, Princeton University Press, 1989

*Birds of Tikal National Park, Guatemala*, Randell A. Beavers, College Station Publishers, 1992

*Birds of the West Indies*, James Bond, Houghton Mifflin, 1985

*Caribbean Adventures in Nature*, Michael De Freitas, John Muir Publishers, 1999

*Cockscomb Basin Sanctuary*, Katherine Emmons, Angelus Press, 1996

*Costa Rica, A Natural Destination*, Ree Strange Sheck, 1997

*Costa Rica's National Parks and Reserves*, Joseph Frank, Mountaineers Books, 1997

*Exuma Guide*, Stephen Pavlidos, Seaworthy Publications, 1995

*Guide to the Birds of Panama*, Robert Ridgely, Princeton University Press, 1981

*Jaguar: One Man's Struggle to Save Jaguars in the Wild*, Alan Rabinowitz, Harper Collins, 1987

*The Sea Turtle: So Excellent A Fishe*, Archie Carr, University of Texas Press, 1986

*The Windward Road*, Archie Carr, University Press of Florida, 1979

## EUROPE

*Atlas of European Mammals*, A.J. Mitchell-Jones, T. & A.D. Poyser Ltd, 1999

*Biebrza Marshland*, Tomasz Klosowski, Voyager Press, 1994

*Birds of Britain and Europe*, Roger Tory Peterson *et al.*, Houghton Mifflin, 1993

*Bird Guide*, Killian Mullarney *et al.*, Princeton University Press, 1999

*Collins Birds of Britain and Europe*, J. Nicolai *et al.*, Harper Collins, 1994

*England's National Nature Reserves*, Peter Marren, T. & A.D. Poyser Ltd, 2000

*Guide to National Parks of Britain and Europe*, Bob Gibbons, New Holland Publishers, 1994

*Guide to Southern Spain and Gibraltar*, Clive Finlayson, Prion Publishers, 1993

*Handbook of Bird Identification Europe*, Mark Beaman, Princeton University Press, 1998

*Handbook of Birds of the World*, Josep Del Hoyo, Lynx Edicions, 2000

*Important Birds in the U.K.*, Subbuteo Natural History Books, 1996

*Nature Parks of France*, Patrick Delaforce, Windrush Press, 1995

*Provence and The Cote D'Azur*, Dorling Kindersley Travel Guides, 2000

*Seabirds: An Identification Guide*, Peter Harrison, Houghton Mifflin Co., 1991

*Top Birding Spots in Britain and Ireland*, David Tipling, Harper Collins, 1996

*Where to Watch Birds in Britain and Europe*, John Gooders, McGraw Hill, 1988

*Where to Watch Birds in Bulgaria*, Petar Iankov, Pensoft Pulishing, 1996

*Where to Watch Birds in Eastern Europe*, Gerard Gorman, Hamlyn Ltd, 1994

*Where to Watch Birds in Europe and Russia*, Nigel Wheatley, Princeton University Press, 2000

*Wild Scotland*, James McCarthy, Luath Press, 1995

## NORTH AMERICA

*A Birder's Guide to Churchill*, Bonnie Chartier, American Birding Association, 1994

*A Guide to Bird Finding East of the Mississippi*, Olin Sewall Pettingill, Oxford University Press, 1977

*A Guide to North American Bird Clubs*, Jon E. Rickert, Avian Publishing, 1978

*Adventure Guide to the Florida Keys and Everglades National Park*, Joyce and Jon Huber, New World Books, 1997

*Adventuring in Florida*, Allen de Hart, Random House, 1995

*Alberta Wildlife Viewing Guide*, Lone Pine Publishing, 1990

*America's Wildlife Hideaways*, Elaine Furlowe, National Wildlife Federation, 1989

*Aransas National Wildlife Refuge and Birder's Guide*, Barry Jones, Southwest Natural Heritage Association, 1997

*Aransas—A Naturalist's Guide*, Wayne and Martha McAlister, University of Texas Press, 1987

*Arctic National Wildlife Refuge*, Alaska Geographic, 1997

*Audubon Society Encyclopedia of North American Birds*, John K. Terres, Wings Books, 1991

*Big Cypress Swamp and the 10,000 Islands*, Jeff Ripple, University of South Carolina Press, 1997

*Churchill: Polar Bear Capital of the World*, Mark Fleming, Hyperion Press, 1988

*Denali*, Penny Rennick, Alaska Geographic, 1997

*Everglades*, Steven David and John Ogden, St Lucie Press, 1994

*Everglades Handbook*, Thomas W. Lodge, St Lucie Press, 1994

*Everglades; River of Grass*, Marjorie Stoneman Douglas, Pineapple Press, 1997

*Field Guide to Mexico's Birds*, Roger Tory Peterson, Houghton Mifflin, 1997

*Florida Wildlife Viewing Guide*, Susan Cerulean and Ann Morrow, Falcon Press, 1993

*Glacier and Waterton Lakes National Parks*, Vicky Spring, Mountaineers, 1994

*Glacier Country*, John Woods, Douglas & McIntyre, 1987

*Glacier National Park: A Natural History Guide*, David Rockwell, Houghton Mifflin, 1995

*Glacier National Park and Waterton Lakes National Park*, Vicky Spring, Mountaineer Books, 1994

*Glacier Park Wildlife*, Todd Wilkinson, Creative Publishing International, 1993

*Grand Canyon, Zion and Bryce National Parks*, Todd Wilkinson, North Ward Press, 1995

*Guide to the National Parks*, Random House, 1995

*Guide to the National Wildlife Refuges*, Laura and William Riley, Macmillan, 1993

*Guide to the Wilderness Waterway of the Everglades National Park*, William G. Truesdell, University of Miami Press, 1985

*Habitat Guide to Birding East of the Rockies*, Thomas McElroy, Nick Lyons Books, 1974

*Handbook of the Canadian Rockies*, Ben Gadd, Corax Press, 1995

*Hidden Florida Keys and Everglades*, Candace Leslie, Ulysses Press, 1990

*Hoofed Mammals of Jasper and Banff National Parks*, Brad Stelfox et al., Parks and People, 1992

*Katmai Country*, Penny Rennick, Alaska Geographic, 1972

*Katmai National Park and Preserve*, Jean Bodeau, Alaska Natural History Association, 1996

*Kodiak*, Penny Rennick, Alaska Geographic Society, 1972

*Mammals of the National Parks*, Richard Van Gelder, Johns Hopkins University Press, 1982

*Mexican Birds*, Roger Tory Peterson and Edward Chalif, Houghton Mifflin, 1973

*National Geographic's Guide to the National Parks of the U.S.*, 1989

*National Park Guide*, Michael Frome, Simon & Schuster, 1995

*National Parks of Northern Mexico*, R.D. Fisher, Sunracer Publications, 1996

*Natural Wonders of Alaska: Guide to Parks, Preserves and Wild Places*, Kent Sturgis, Country Road, 1994

*Our North American World Heritage*, Mark Swadling, World Heritage Publishing, 1997

*Peterson Field Guides, Eastern Birds*, Roger Tory Peterson, Houghton Mifflin, 1980

*Sierra Club Guide to the National Parks of Pacific Northwest and Alaska*, Sierra Club, 1996

*Sierra Club Guide to the National Parks of the Rocky Mountains and the Great Plains*, Sierra Club, 1996

*Sierra Club Guide to the Natural Areas of Idaho, Montana and Wyoming*, John Perry, Sierra Club, 1988

*Southwest Florida's Wetland Wilderness*, Clyde Butcher, University Press of Florida, 1996

*The Atlantic Shore*, John Hay and Peter Farb, Harper Row, 1966

*The Audubon Ark*, Frank Graham, University of Texas Press, 1992

*The Wild Places*, Milton Rugoff and Ann Guilfoyle, Harper & Row, 1986

*The World of the Polar Bear*, Norbert Rosing, Firefly Books, 1996

*Wild Sanctuaries, Our National Wildlife Refuges—A Heritage Restored*, Robert Murphy, 1968

*Yellowstone Wildlife, A Watcher's Guide*, Todd Wilkinson, North Ward Press, 1992

*Yellowstone Winter Guide*, Jeff Henry, Roberts Rinehart Publishing, 1993

**SOUTH AMERICA**

*Adventurer's Guide to the Brazilian Amazon and The Pantanal*, Pamela Bloom, NTC/Contemporary Publishing, 1997

*Amazon Up Close*, Pamela Bloom, NTC/ Contemporary Publishing, 1997

*Annotated Checklist of Bird and Mammal Species—Manu National Park, Peru*, Field Natural History Museum, 1998

*Argentina Handbook*, Charlie Nurse, Footprint Handbooks, 1998

*Birders' Guide to Explorer's Inn*, Simon Allen, Oxford University Press, 1995

*Birds of Argentina and Uruguay*, Tito Narosky, Vazquez Mazzini Publishers, 1993

*Birds of Colombia*, Steven Hilty and William Brown, Princeton University Press, 1986

*Birds of Venezuela*, Rodolphe Meyer de Schauensse and William Phelps Jr, Princeton University Press, 1978

*Birdwatching in Ecuador and the Galapagos Islands*, Robert Williams et al., Biosphere Publisher, 1996

*Bolivia Handbook*, Alan Murphy, Footprint Handbooks, 1997

*Brazil Handbook*, Ben Box, Footprint Handbooks, 1998

*Chile Handbook*, Charlie Nurse, Footprint Handbooks, 1997

*Ecuador and Galapagos Handbook*, Alan Murphy, Passport Books, 1997

*Ecuador and Its Galapagos Islands*, David Pearson, Ulysses Press, 1999

*Galapagos, A Natural History Guide*, Michael H. Jackson, University of Calgary Press, 1985

*Galapagos Guide*, Alan White and Bruce Epler, Liberi Mundo Publication, 1982

*Guide to Birdwatching in Ecuador and Galapagos*, Tito Narosky, 1997

*Guide to Brazil, Amazon, Pantanal, Coastal Regions*, Alex Bradbury, Hunter Publication, 1991

*Guide to the Birds and Mammals of Patagonia*, Graham Harris, Princeton University Press, 1998

*Guide to the Birds of Colombia*, William H. Brown, Princeton University Press, 1986

*Guide to the Birds of the Galapagos Islands*, Isabel Castro, Princeton University Press, 1996

*Guide to the Birds of Venezuela*, Rodolphe Meyer de Schauensee, Princeton University Press, 1978

*In Patagonia*, Bruce Chatwin, Summit Books, Simon & Schuster, 1977

*Natural Patagonia*, Marcelo Beccaceci, Pangaea Publication, 1998

*Neotropical Companion*, John Kricher, Princeton University Press, 1998

*Neotropical Rainforest Companions*, Louise Emmons, University of Chicago Press, 1997

*Princeton Guide to the Birds and Mammals of Coastal Patagonia*, Graham Harris, Princeton University Press, 1998

*Rough Guide to Peru*, Dilwyn Jenkins, Rough Guides Ltd, 1997

*South American Handbook*, Ben Box, Footprint Handbooks, 1998

*South America's National Parks: A Visitor's Guide*, William C. Leitch, Mountaineers Books, 1990

*Venezuela Handbook*, Alan Murphy, Footprint Handbooks, 1998

*Where to Watch Birds in South America*, Nigel Wheatley, Princeton University Press, 1994

## SOUTH PACIFIC ISLANDS

*A Field Guide to Birds of Borneo, Sumatra and Java*, John MacKinnon and Karen Phillips, Oxford University Press, 1993

*A Field Guide to the Birds of West Malaysia and Singapore*, Allen Jeyerasingam, Oxford University Press, 1999

*A Natural History of Australia*, Tim Berra, Academic Press, 1998

*Adventuring in Australia*, Eric Hoffman, Sierra Club, 1997

*Adventuring in Indonesia*, Holly S. Smith, Sierra Club, 1997

*Australia's World Heritage*, Vincent Serventy, Macmillan, 1996

*Birds of New Guinea*, Bruce Beehler *et al.*, Princeton University Press, 1986

*Complete Guide to the Birds of Australia*, Richard and Sarah Thomas, Frogmouth Publisher, 1999

*Explore Australia*, Robert Hale Ltd Publisher, 1996

*Field Guide to the Birds of Australia*, Graham Pizzey, Princeton University Press, 1996

*Fielding's Birding in Indonesia*, Paul Jebson, Fielding Publications, 1997

*Fielding's Borneo*, Robert Young Pelton, Fielding Publications, 1995

*Globetrotter Guide to Malaysia*, Helen Oon, New Holland Publishers, 1995

*Indo-Pacific Coral Reef Guide*, Gerald Allan and Roger Steene, University of Hawaii Press, 1997

*Kakadu: World of Waterbirds*, Terence Lindsey, 1996

*Key Guide to Australian Mammals*, Leonard Cronin, Reed Books, 1991

*Key Guide to Australia's National Parks*, Leonard Cronin, Reed Books, 1994

*Malaysia, Singapore and Brunei*, C. de Ledesma, M. Lewis and P. Savage, Rough Guides, 1995

*National Parks and Other Wild Places of Indonesia*, J. Cochrane and G. Cubitt, New Holland Publishers, 2000

*New Guinea, An Island Apart*, Neil Nightingale, BBC Books, 1992

*Princeton Field Guides to the Birds of Australia*, Ken Simpson and Nicholas Day, Princeton University Press, 1999

*Reflections of Eden*, Dr Birute Galdikas, Little Brown & Company, 1995

*The Confessions of a Beachcomber*, E.J. Banfield, Dixon-Price Publisher, 2001

*This is Borneo*, Gerald Cubitt *et al.*, New Holland Publishers, 1994

*This is Indonesia*, Christopher Scarlett, Gerald Cubitt, New Holland Publishers, 1995

*This is Malaysia*, Wendy Moore, Gerald Cubitt, New Holland Publishers, 1995

*Throwim Way Leg*, Tim Flannery, Atlantic Monthly Press, 1998

*Where to Watch Birds in Australasia and Oceania*, Nigel Wheatley, Princeton University Press, 1998

*Wild Indonesia*, Tony and Jane Whitten, New Holland Publishers, 1992

*Wild Malaysia*, Junaidi Payne, M.I.T. Press, 1990

*Wildlife of Indonesia*, Kathy MacKinnon, Gramedia Pustaka Utama Publishers, 1992

*Wilson Promontory: Marine and Natural Park, Victoria*, Geoff Wescott, UNSW Press, 1995

## GENERAL

*Animal Kingdoms: Wildlife Sanctuaries of the World*, National Geographic Society, 1995

*Arctic Dreams*, Barry Lopez, Scribners, 1986

*Atlas of Wild Places*, Roger Few, Facts on File, 1994

*Collins Guide to Rare Mammals*, John Burton and Bruce Pearson, Book Sales, 1992

*Collins Pocket Guide of Coral Reef Fishes*, Robert Myers, Trafalgar Square Publisher, 2002

*Encyclopedia of Birds*, edited by Christopher Perrins and Alex Middleton, Facts on File, 1986

*Encyclopedia of Mammals*, David Macdonald, Facts on File, 1985

*Encyclopedia of Reptiles and Amphibians*, edited by Tim Halliday and Kraig Adler, Facts on File, 1986

*Finding Birds Around the World*, Peter Alden, Houghton Mifflin, 1981

# BIBLIOGRAPHY

*Grzimek's Animal Life Encyclopedia*, 13 volumes, edited by Dr Bernhard Grzimek, Van Nostrand Reinhold Co., 1984

*Hidden Worlds of Wildlife*, Christine Eckstrom, National Geographic, Simon & Schuster, 1994

*Hotspots*, Conservation International, 1999

*In the Wild Places*, Janet Trowbridge Bohlen, Island Press, 1993

*Larousse Encyclopedia of Animal Life*, McGraw Hill Book Co., 1967

*Life in the Cold*, Peter Marchand, University Press of New England, 1987

*Life Nature Library*, Time Life Books

*Life of Birds*, Joel Carl Welty, Harcourt Brace, 1996

*Living Planet: Preserving Edens of the World*, Foreword by Walter Cronkite, Crown Publishers, 1999

*National Geographic's Last Wild Places*, National Geographic, 1996

*Natural History of Amphibians*, Robert Stebbins and Nathan Cohen, Princeton University Press, 1997

*Nature's Last Strongholds*, edited by Robert Burton, Oxford University Press, 1991

*Paradise on Earth*, Mark Swadling *et al.*, World Heritage Publishing, 1995

*Protected Areas of the World*, Volumes 1, 2, 3, and 4, International Union for Conservation of Nature, 1992

*Raptor Watch*, Jorje Zalles and Keith Bildstein, Hawk Mountain Sanctuary, 2000

*The Birds of Heaven, Travel With Cranes*, Peter Matthiessen, North Point Press, 2001

*The Life of Birds*, David Attenborough, Princeton University Press, 1998

*The Life of Mammals*, David Attenborough, Princeton University Press, 2002

*Unlocking Secrets of the Unknown*, National Geographic Society, Elizabeth L. Newhouse, Simon & Schuster, 1995

*Wetlands in Danger*, Patrick Dugan, IUCN, 1993

*World of Birds*, David Attenborough, BBC Books, 1998

# INDEX

# ACKNOWLEDGMENTS AND PHOTO CREDITS

## ACKNOWLEDGMENTS

It would have been impossible for us to produce this book without unstinting aid from World Wildlife Fund-U.S. (www.worldwildlife.org) and the Wildlife Conservation Society (www.wcs.org). Their staff members discussed the concept of the book with us, suggested reserves that should be included, and most important of all, read draft entries and corrected many of our errors. Any that remain are our responsibility. We particularly wish to thank Kathryn Fuller and William Eichbaum of WWF and Drs John Robinson and Meade Love Penn of WCS. Others in those organizations who were particularly helpful to us were:

*World Wildlife Fund (www.WWFUS.Org)*
Lucy Aquino Michael C. Baltzer; David Bogardus; Richard Carroll; Hewitt Chizkuya; Monica Chundama; Javier Corcuera; Chopel Dayang; Lou Ann Dietz; Curt Freese; Philipp Goelteboth; C. Gurung; Mary Lou Higgins; Stephanie Hynes; Roger Landivar; Rob Little; Clorinda Maldonado; Robert Mather; Jennifer Montoya; Hermannn Mwageni; Raymond C. Nias; Linda Norgrove; Simon Pepper; Joseph Ramamonjisoa; Mingma Sherpa; Samar Singh; Randall Snodgrass; Jennie Springer; Meg Symington; Martin Tchamba; Adam Tomasek; Chris Weaver; Laura Williams; Margaret Williams; Jean Yamindou.

*Wildlife Conservation Society (www.WCS.org)*
Ana Rita Alves; Felicity Arengo; Jim Barborak; Lorraine Cohen; Peter Coppolillo; Paul Elkan; Charlotte Elton; Joshua Ginsberg; John Goodrich; Melvin Gumal; John Hart; Michael Hedemark; Andrea Heydlauff; J.T. Horbjarnason; Ullas Karanth; Ke Chung Kim; Akoi Koudio; Fiona Maisels; Phil Marshall; Roan McNab; Carolyn Miller; Dale Miquelle; David Moyer; Carolina Murcia; Matt O'Brien; Michael Painter; Megan Parker; Colin Poole; Sylvia Stone; John Thorbjarnarson; Robert B. Wallace; Joe Walston; Lee White; Stuart Williams; Monica Wrobel.

In addition to the help from staff members of these two organizations, we were aided immensely, particularly in fact-checking and criticial comment on draft entries, by the following individuals and organizations:

Bass Abal Abass, Mauritania Embassy, Washington, D.C.; George Archbold, International Crane Foundation (www.savingcranes.org); Deborah Bigio, Fundacion para la Defensa de la Naturaleza; Dr Les Braack, Kruger National Park, South Africa; Joost Brouwer, Ph.D., Wageningen University; Dami Buchori, Wildlife Preservation Trust; Clair Caldes, Bear River NWR, U.S.A.; Annette Carter-Harris, Republic of Ghana, Washington, D.C.; Ravi Corea, private contact for Sri Lanka.

Also, Michele Deakin, Gwai Haanas National Park, Canada; Ron Demey, author, *Birds of Western Africa*; Dr Moussa Sega DIOP, private contact for Senegal; Thomas Edgerton, Arctic NWR, U.S.A.; Dr Wulf Gatter, Cestos River

Survey Team; Shelley Gellatly, Kluane National Park, Canada; Bob Gibbons, private contact for France and Italy; Brent Giezetanner, Aransas NWR, U.S.A.; Judy Glowinski, Banff National Park, Canada; Raphael Guttierez, Sistema Nacional de Areas de Conservacion, Costa Rica; Alvaro Jaramillo, San Francisco Bay Bird Observatory; Björn Jónsson, Valtours; Pim Kremer, Kiboko Safaris.

Also Dr Richard E. Leakey, Kenya Wildlife Service; Jan Lontkowski, Wroclaw University; Isabel Ma. Iturralde, Fundacion Natura; Locke Marshall, Waterton National Park, Canada; David Mihalic, Glacier National Park, U.S.A.; E. B. Mpemba, Tanzania Ministry of Natural Resources and Tourism; Deb Nordeen, Everglades National Park, U.S.A.; Eva Nordvik, Norwegian Polar Institute; Czeslow Okolow, Bialowieza National Park, Poland; Linda Olson, Grand Teton National Park, U.S.A.; Dimi Panitza and Staff, Free and Democratic Bulgaria Foundation; Mary Pearl, Wildlife Preservation Trust (www.WPTI.Org); Daniel Petrescu, private contact for Romania; Daniel Perry, Bosque del Apache NWR, U.S.A.; Cassandra Phillips, Tiscali.co.uk.

Also Iris Ramos, Institute Hondureno de Turismo; Charissa Reid, Yellowstone National Park, U.S.A.; L. Rosenzweig, Fondo Mexicano Para La Conservacion; Peter Ryan, Percy FitzPatrick Institute of Africa Ornithology; Nirmal Jivan Shah, Nature Seychelles; Michael Somerville, Belize Audubon Society; Endre Sos, private contact for Hungary; Andrew Spalton, Omanet; Jane Tranel and Ken Stahlnecker, Denali National Park, U.S.A.; Xun Yan, China Ministry of Forestry; Balzan Zhiombiev, World Conservation Monitoring Center.

Among other organizations that were helpful, and which make important contributions to international conservation, are BirdLife International (www.birdlife.net); CARE International (www.care.org); Conservation International (www.conservation.org); IUCN-World Conservation Union; Peregrine Fund (www.peregrinefund.org).

In preparing the book for publication we had invaluable help from our agent, Richard Parks, our editor, Robert Kirk, David Price-Goodfellow and staff at D & N Publishing, and, in ways too numerous to mention, from Christine Kourian.

## PHOTO CREDITS

Most of the photographs herein were taken in the wild; a few were taken in controlled conditions, such as rehabilitation facilities. All photos, including that on the cover, except for the following, are copyright Laura Riley:

Photos on pp.105, 194–5, 268–9, 274, 280, 363, 402–3, 418–19, © Igor Shpilenok; on pp.310, 370–1, © Nikolai Shpilenok; on p.177, © Colby Loucks/WWF; on p.285, © Bruce Bunting/WWF; on p.510, © Lindsay Chong-Seng; on p.612, © Georgeanne Irvine. Cover back flap photo, © Michael Palmer.

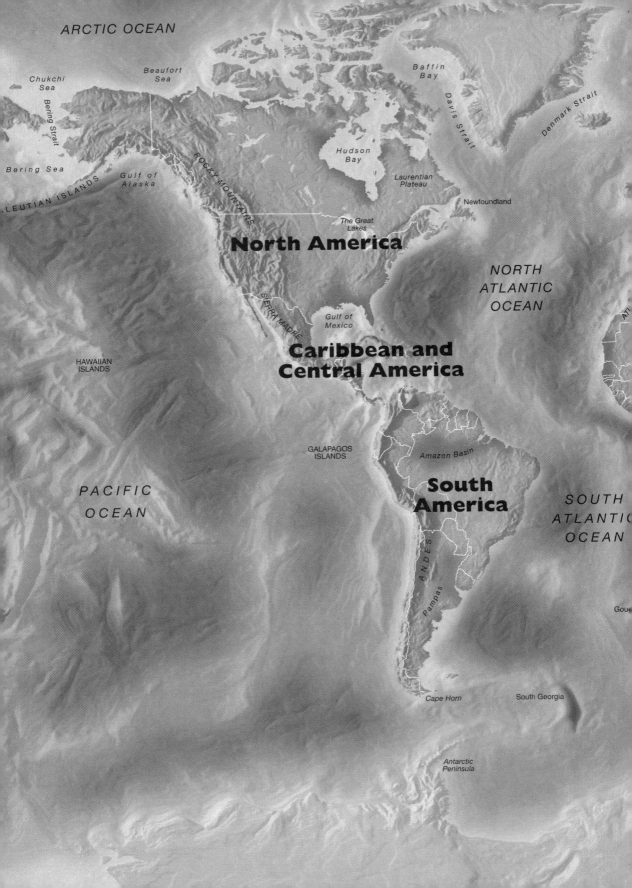